The History of Contra Costa County, California

FREDERICK J. HULANISKI

The History of Contra Costa County, California, F. J. Hulaniski
Jazzybee Verlag Jürgen Beck
86450 Altenmünster, Loschberg 9
Deutschland

ISBN: 9783849671747

www.jazzybee-verlag.de
admin@jazzybee-verlag.de

Printed by Createspace, North Charleston, SC, USA

CONTENTS:

PREFACE 1
INTRODUCTORY BY THE EDITOR 2
CHAPTER I. THE INDIANS... 8
CHAPTER II. EARLY HISTORY OF CALIFORNIA 12
CHAPTER III. MEXICAN LAND GRANTS— PEN-PICTURES OF EARLY DAYS.. 15
CHAPTER IV. PIONEER CITIZENS 21
CHAPTER V. THE BEAR FLAG WAR 28
CHAPTER VI. EXTRACTS FROM GENERAL SUTTER'S DIARY 52
CHAPTER VII. SETTLEMENT AND EARLY HISTORY..................... 61
CHAPTER VIII. CLIMATE—SOIL—AGRICULTURE 67
CHAPTER IX. MINES AND MINERALS 70
CHAPTER X. SAN RAMON VALLEY 73
CHAPTER XI. CENTRAL CONTRA COSTA COUNTY...................... 77
CHAPTER XII. EASTERN CONTRA COSTA COUNTY 87
CHAPTER XIII. DOCTOR JOHN MARSH 99
CHAPTER XIV. MOUNT DIABLO 101
CHAPTER XV. SUMMARY OF THE COUNTY'S RESOURCES.....................105
CHAPTER XVI. EARLY CRIMINAL HISTORY 108
CHAPTER XVII BENCH AND BAR 140
CHAPTER XVIII. EDUCATIONAL 148
CHAPTER XIX. LIBRARY DEVELOPMENT 165
CHAPTER XX. RELIGIOUS 170
CHAPTER XXI. THE MEDICAL PROFESSION...................................178
CHAPTER XXII. BANKING..193
CHAPTER XXIII. TRANSPORTATION 201
CHAPTER XXIV. FRATERNAL SOCIETIES.......................................210

CHAPTER XXV. MARTINEZ 219

CHAPTER XXVI. RICHMOND 231

CHAPTER XXVII. ANTIOCH 250

CHAPTER XXVIII. DANVILLE 268

CHAPTER XXIX. PITTSBURG 270

CHAPTER XXX. BAY POINT 275

CHAPTER XXXI. CROCKETT 277

CHAPTER XXXII. OAKLEY AND SAND LANDS 281

CHAPTER XXXIII. KNIGHTSEN 285

CHAPTER XXXIV. RODEO 287

CHAPTER XXXV. WALNUT CREEK 291

CHAPTER XXXVI. PINOLE 297

CHAPTER XXXVII. PORT COSTA 299

CHAPTER XXXVIII. AVON 300

CHAPTER XXXIX. BYRON 301

Part II BIOGRAPHICAL 303

PREFACE

In presenting this new history of Contra Costa County to the public, we do so in the earnest hope that it will prove to be the most complete compilation of local chronicles that has up to this time been offered to our citizens. The authenticity of the facts contained in the various articles is as absolute as the utmost care could make it. The data have been procured from the best-known authorities, and the biographical sketches, when completed, were subjected to the most searching examination for verification and correction. That no errors will be discovered in this production is too much to hope for; but we do most certainly trust that if any misstatements there be, either in number or by their nature, they will not be found sufficiently important to detract from that character for reliability which it has been our constant aim and endeavor to impart to this history.

In this new work the design has been to make clear the development of ideas and institutions from epoch to epoch. The social and economic conditions of the people have been preserved in the narrative, and much attention has been paid to describing the civil characteristics of the several towns and cities, both in the conduct of their local affairs and in the relation to each other and the county at large. It has been our object in this work to hew straight to the line, simply satisfied to furnish such information as we were able to gather concerning important matters or interesting events, and where the desired materials were lacking we have not attempted to supply the deficiency by filling in the vacant niches with products of the imagination. We have not striven for effect; our object is merely to give an authentic account of facts recent and remote, disposed in a proper and orderly manner, so as to enable our readers to clearly understand the history of their community from its origin down to the present day.

This work is a collection of data by a staff of contributors consisting of the most accurate and capable writers in their respective fields in the county, who here crystallize and preserve the material they have gathered from many sources.

Never, so far as I am aware, has any local history in any county been prepared as this has been. Each writer is in a position to speak with absolute authority upon the subject of which he treats, and it was the intention of the editor that each should present in the most attractive and concise form such material relative to the matter of which he writes as had not appeared in any previous publication. How far that hope has been realized the critical reader may judge. It has also been the aim of the editor to limit the sketches to a statement of such facts as will be of interest to the readers of today and -of importance to those of the years to come.

In sending forth this volume we trust that, in addition to its value as a depository of accurate information and useful knowledge.it will prove an effective instrument in creating a more lively public sentiment regarding historical subjects, and that it will especially foster an interest in the annals of our own county. If my collaborators and myself have helped to perpetuate the memory of the heroism, the fortitude, the suffering, and the achievement of the men and women who placed Contra Costa County, California, in the foremost rank of the counties of this State, we shall be content.

F. J. Hulaniski, Editor.

INTRODUCTORY BY THE EDITOR

I came to California the first time many years ago, before the transcontinental railroads had laid their span across the Great American Desert, coming from New York to San Francisco by way of the Isthmus of Panama. There is as great a difference between the California of today and the California of the days of ox-teams and "prairie schooners" as there is between the aforenamed desert and the Garden of Eden as allegorically described.

Contra Costa County was at that time composed in the main of several large cattle ranches, owned by Spaniards, Mexicans, and Portuguese, with here and there a tiny country crossroads village. It shipped a little wheat and barley to San Francisco in a primitive way, by small sailboats; but agriculture was secondary to the live-stock interests. A cattle ranch in the olden days consisted generally of what might be considered now a fair-sized township, or even a county. There were miles upon miles of as good and fair land as ever lay out of doors then only a barren waste.

People came clear around the Horn in sailing-ships, taking months for the journey, or took a short cut across the Isthmus, as I did, to get here quickly—in about two months. It was at the end of the earth— "No Man's Land," the jumping-off place of creation. Only those who were seeking adventure, or those who joined the gold rush of 1849 and came via ox-team, or those whose health and longevity might be promoted by an exile from civilization and a change of name as well as environment and climate, ventured to where the sun went to bed in effulgent splendor in or apparently near the Golden Gate. I was not actuated, I desire to add by way of parenthesis, by the latter reason.

My second journey to the then famous though still more or less mysterious land of the setting sun, the yellow poppy, the luscious fruits and myriad flowers was six years ago, in search of health, climate, and sea-level, and I found them all here in Contra Costa County, where anybody may find them, with long life, happiness, and comparative riches thrown in for good measure.

Because it was so far west of the center of the country's population, for half a century or more California and Contra Costa County lay basking in sunshine and soft sea-breezes, almost unknown, comparatively speaking, to the outside world. Nearly all the immigrants from over the Atlantic poured through Castle Garden into New York, and from there a few of them gradually drifted westward; but the West of former days was in Illinois, Iowa, and Missouri. Beyond that was a trackless waste ranged by buffalo and peopled by Indians, across which the pony express dashed its perilous way.

When it is considered that two thousand miles of barren mountains, plains, and deserts lay between California and the States east of the Mississippi, not even a railroad crossing them until the rest of the country began to get thickly populated, there should be little wonder that this region was slow in gaining settlers. All that vast domain had to be populated before the restless tide of immigration reached the Pacific Coast. Years passed, new generations grew up, and still this great region, as large as an empire in itself, was sparsely inhabited, its matchless climate and wonderful resources neglected save by the natives and practically unknown to mankind. The rush of the gold-seekers in 1849 started the tide in this direction; then came the railroads, then the people, slowly but surely, when the history of this peerless climate and these heretofore unheard-of natural resources began to leak out to a small extent in the outside world.

Nevertheless, the flow of immigration for a time came at a slow pace.

In recent years, however, a great change has taken place, the result of conditions in the crowded East and the rapid settling of the Middle West. A telegram is now delivered in an hour; a letter in three or four days, instead of a month or longer. New York and San Francisco business men visit one another personally every day in the year and think no more of it than the former did in going out west to Chicago.

In noting the wondrous changes which have taken place even within my own memory, which in matters historical includes comparatively but a fleeting second of time, I feel that it is quite reasonable, and even conservative, to predict that in another such "second of time," during the lives of our children of today, as great changes, or even greater, because this is a more progressive age, are sure to take place, and just as large and important cities as New York and Chicago will be built here in California, at least one of them right here in Contra Costa County—at Richmond, which has grown from nothing a dozen years ago to a city of 23,000 inhabitants as this book is written.

I lived in Chicago before its great fire, and in San Francisco before the railroads crossed the country intervening, and neither of them was very much in the way of a city then. Both these cities had street-cars drawn by horses with bells tinkling on their necks; both had men carrying little ladders which they climbed and lighted with sulphur matches the gas-lamps on the street corners; the telegrapher printed his messages on a long roll of white paper in dots and dashes; of telephones there were none; a bathtub was a luxury of the rich ; and if you had as much as five thousand dollars you were in the plutocratic class. And all that was merely as of yesterday, as time is considered, and yet the onward march of civilization has removed all of these difficulties and many more. Now one can buy a ticket to San Francisco from Chicago or other common points for about fifty dollars and roll in here in a palace car containing bath, barber-shop, dining-car, library-car, and brunette porters with blonde whisk-brooms to brush you off at "twobits" per.

Now the farmers and fruit-growers of Contra Costa County are riding around in two automobiles, one to take the family to the moving-picture show in town and the other for the hired man to honk-honk the butter and eggs and turnips and baled hay and strawberries and several hundred other nice things in and exchange them for bank stock, mortgages on brick blocks, and machines which cut the wheat, thresh it, and sack it ready for market all at the same time—and probably for the next generation they will also grind it into flour, bake it into biscuits, and spread thereon the butter and jam.

In Contra Costa County, California, there is no winter, unless one climbs a high mountain in search of it—just a nice, equitable, refreshing rainy season in the so-called winter months to give old Mother Nature a bath and make the hills and valleys still greener. The only way one can tell it is Christmas-time here is when the merchants make a noise about it in the advertising columns of the newspapers and admonish all to do their Christmas shopping early.

Here one works out of doors every day in the year, if one wants to, in shirt-sleeves, and the markets abound with luscious fruits and vegetables fresh out of the garden 365 days of the year. One can get a big mess of strawberries almost any day, winter or summer, grown in this county and as fine as were ever embellished by cream and sugar, for ten cents a box on an average.

Summer is just the same—bracing breezes from the Pacific come just strong enough to wave the grass and grain and flowers and keep away malaria, the blistering hot winds of the Middle West plains, and the sunstroke and prostration of the Far East. Roses and millions of other beautiful flowers give their beauty to the scene and their fragrance to the breeze. Pick a ripe orange off the tree in your back yard and the blossoms for others are right there at the same time. Times are good, work is plentiful for all who desire work, and good wages are paid.

Surely it is a favored land!

It is a fair land, also, this county of Contra Costa, California. It signifies "Across the Coast," and so it is—across the coast one way from the world-famous cosmopolitan city of San Francisco, and across the coast in another way from a goodly country stretching out toward the north to Oregon, famous also for its apples and umbrellas. I have traveled much and far and for many years, searching always for the country that combined the ideals, and if I have not found it here, then I at least have the satisfaction of knowing that it does not exist on this mundane sphere, but that it is on beyond the clouds, where gold is used for street-paving, where the graphophone is succeeded by harps and horns, where Paris does not set the fashion of crowns and gowns, and where one has to die to get a one-way ticket in Charon's boat thereto.

And after reaching such a land as this golden and glorious California, still I traveled, searching out its most favored spot, and found it, too, right here in the county of Contra Costa, a veritable Western empire in itself, as the reader may judge by a perusal of the succeeding pages of its history. One must travel, even after reaching California, to find the combination of ideals he may have in mind, for this State is approximately four hundred miles wide and seven hundred miles long, and embraces every type of scenery, climate, altitude, and condition imaginable, all within its own boundaries.

In the high Sierras are the snow, the towering mighty mountains, the rocks and altitudes, and the gold, silver, lead, copper, zinc, tungsten, and other precious minerals which pour out their constant stream to enrich the world and all mankind. To the south stretches hundreds of miles of yellow oranges, lemons, and other semi-tropical fruits in orchards laden with a lusciousness known wherever in the world man dwells in civilization. Between are more hundreds of miles of melons, of grapes, of nuts, of vegetables, and of fruitage and flowers such as no other country on the globe produces. And here in Contra Costa they all are combined and rolled into one glorious whole!

Here is gold in the sands of the streams, silver and lead and other metals in the hills, coal beds rich in bitumen, oranges a-plenty for home consumption, grapes that excel the vineyards of Italy, and in such profusion that here is located the largest winery in the world, besides many smaller ones. Here one looks down from the hills at the clouds and mists of the bay below, and then comes down into eternal summer and perennial sunshine and genial warmth. Here the walnut and the almond grow in such profusion that hundreds of carloads of them are shipped to the markets of the world every season, with a growth of almost every known vegetable so plentiful that they go out by trainloads and shiploads far and near. In the Antioch section of this history it will be noted that celery and asparagus are shipped to the Atlantic seaboard, not by the carload but by the trainload, and that the trains are many and long. This county has seventy miles of water-front, on the San Francisco Bay, the San Pablo Bay, the Carquinez Straits, and the Sacramento River, and at Pittsburg and Bay Point the fisheries maintained are so immense in their output and value as to rival the countries of the North or East, the large cities being supplied with fresh fish every day in the year, and the canneries there employing hundreds of men and women.

Richmond is known far and wide as "the Pittsburg of the West," because of its great manufacturing interests, where such industries as the Standard Oil works, with the second largest oil refinery in the world, the Pullman car-shops, the great pipe and steel works, porcelain factories, and dozens of others pour out to ports all over the world a continual stream of manufactured products, have hundreds of millions invested, employ thousands of skilled artisans, and maintain pay-rolls aggregating close to a million a month.

So, it will be seen, this marvelous county not only combines a vast diversity of industries and opportunities, but a diversity of products and vocations, a diversity of hill and dale, of orange groves and mines, of ocean, bay, and river, of agriculture, viniculture, and live-stock, almost anything on earth one may be looking for or desirous of obtaining.

And above all and over all floats serene and ever joyful and salubrious a climate made to order for the enjoyment of mankind by some higher power than we know of save by tradition and intuition.

Now, just a few words about scenery, for scenery is always interesting. There is more scenery here in this county of Contra Costa than in any other one spot of equal area this writer has ever visited, and the great Yosemite, the Grand Canyon, and the Garden of the Gods are all old acquaintances. Here the scenery of mountain, of valley, and of sea are all rolled together in one brain-tangling profusion and immensity like some vast scroll, until one becomes lost in the labyrinth of kaleidoscopic vistas spread out to view from all points of the compass—and it is, like the climate, all free!

And speaking of "The Garden of the Gods," it shall here be asserted and set down as a fact that Contra Costa County, California, is more entitled to that name than any spot in Colorado or elsewhere. For that reason, and because of its entire appropriateness to this favored section, I shall appropriate it here and now, and trust that succeeding generations and other historians who shall come upon the scene when we of today have earned and gone to eternal rest, may hand it down to other generations and historians—The Garden of the Gods!

At Colorado Springs they have a Garden of the Gods, composed of a "cave of the winds," a balancing rock, and several other freaks of nature hewn out of red sandstone by the waters of early ages, and these they capitalized for many thousands, and got the money, and will get more thousands, but the gods have moved away. And no one could blame the gods, after comparing that garden with this one, from the viewpoint of both gods and men, as near as mere man can make such a calculation. You cannot see the gods here in their new abiding-place; but if you are in touch with Nature and Nature's wondrous and beautiful things, you can feel their presence and talk to them, and hear them talk to you, in the same language that the little pink mystery murmurs to you out of the whispering depths of the seashell; the same language as the twang on the harp of godlike inspiration which comes to you out of the panorama of a scenic magnificence and grandeur spread out to view like a leaf torn from one of Milton's great epic poems, or the sighing of the pines and redwoods on the high hilltops in the soft breezes of the sea.

If you would view this Garden of the Gods, go high up on the serpentine boulevard around and on top of the Sobrante hills, overlooking the bays and ocean, high above Oakland, above Berkeley, Piedmont, and Richmond, or on over the Pinole hills to Martinez, or to Mount Diablo in the Concord and Walnut Creek sections of the county, and there eight or nine great California counties lift up their scenic marvels of beauteous splendor for a mixture of awe and admiration — surely a fit habitation for the gods. And there the nodding palms and pines and myriads of sweet-faced poppies and other flowers say that the gods are at home and bid you welcome.

A magnificent boulevard, costing the capitalists who built it something like thirty thousand dollars a mile, winds around, through, and over most of these hills now, from Oakland to and beyond Richmond. The builders of this boulevard have not only opened the most startling vista to the public view; they have caused thousands of trees and millions of shrubs to grow where none grew before, and pink and red and white and yellow flowers, and green bond coupons, to blossom where erstwhile only the sad refrain of the lonely coyote was heard screaming to its mate that it had been three days and a hundred miles between meals.

This boulevard rises to imposing summits and there spreads out to view a scene that would take poets, painters, and musicians, as well as writers, to adequately portray.

This scribe put in years in the Rocky Mountains, and viewed much wondrous scenery, but out here by the placid Pacific, in Contra Costa County, California, I have seen the Royal Gorge, Marshall Pass, the Grand Canon of the Colorado, Eagle Pass, Toltic Gorge, and all the other marvels of the Rockies rolled into one, and then excelled! Why should I not maintain that the name, "The Garden of the Gods," belongs to it?

From the view spread out from any of these Contra Costa hills, over the placid bosom of the bay, lies San Francisco, risen Phoenix-like from its ashes, with its half-million people running a Marathon race of commercial activity. Laving its feet are the waters of the Golden Gate, and far out beyond is the blue sky-line coming down to kiss the bluer ocean somewhere toward Hawaii. Yerba Buena, Alcatraz, Mare Island, San Quentin, the Sonoma hills, college-gowned Berkeley in the foothills below—Oakland, with madding marts of men rife with tremendous traffic, and the white pinnacle of its municipal tower piercing the haze, a monument to man's ambition—Richmond, with two deep-water bays embracing it, belching smoke from a thousand factory furnaces along the water-front and then stretching out in peaceful homelike serenity toward the hills to the east and north! Miles and miles of stately hills and fertile valleys, trees and shrubs and flowers on beyond. If old Satan should take me up there and say, as he is quoted as saying once before, "Fall down and worship me and all you see shall be yours,"

I am afraid there would be a loud bump heard upon the salty, fragrant air, which would be that of my falling down!

The time is near, and already approaching, when much of this startling grandeur will be marred, from a natural standpoint, by the inroads upon it of commercial activity, for the rapid growth of the near-by cities is reaching out to the hills and hill-surrounded vales, and spreading out to still more hills and vales, and the honk of the automobile, the clank of the trolley-car, and the pop and whang of the street-macadamizing machine will soon drive the gods on over into other gardens as yet untrodden by even the moccasin of the aborigine.

But for ages in the past, at present, and for a few years yet into the future, the roads and trails lead up and up and around among Nature's fairest spots on earth, up over cities, villages, hills, valleys, bays, the ocean—up almost to the clouds, where Nature speaks a language of her own, and where is spread out to view hundreds of miles of this fair Contra Costa County, California, a veritable Garden of the Gods.

CHAPTER I. THE INDIANS

IT IS generally conceded by both the early and modern California historians that the Pacific Coast Indians were far inferior as a race to the stalwart Eastern Indians, idealized by Fenimore Cooper. The Indians of the San Francisco Bay region formed no exception to this rule. They lived under the most primitive conditions, with apparently no aspiration for the higher civilization that characterized the Aztecs and Peruvians.

When the white man came upon the scene there were four tribes of Indians in Contra Costa County. These were the Juchiyunes, Acalanes, Bolgones, and Carquinez Indians. They knew practically nothing of the arts of civilization. All the historians of the period describe them as going about in a state of semi-nudity, if not entirely naked. Occasionally the men wore a crude sort of loin-cloth and the women fashioned an apron from tules; these hung from the waist to the knees fore and aft and were open at the sides. In the winter they wore crude garments made from deerskins or feathers of waterfowls.

Little effort was made-toward constructing habitations. In the summer a few boughs interwoven formed their shelter from the sun and occasional showers. In the winter they lived in their wickiups. The latter, as described by Bancroft, "are sometimes erected on the level ground, but more frequently over an excavation three or four feet deep, and varying from ten to thirty feet in diameter. Round the brink of this hole willow poles are sunk upright in the ground and the tops drawn together, forming a conical structure, or the upper ends are bent over and driven into the earth on the opposite side of the pit, thus giving the hut a semi-globular shape. Bushes or strips of bark are then piled up against the poles, and the whole is covered with a thick layer of earth or mud.

In some instances the interstices of the frame are filled with twigs woven crosswise, over and under, between the poles, and the outside covering is of tule reeds, instead of earth. A hole at the top gives egress to the smoke, and a small opening close to the ground admits the occupants. Each hut generally shelters a whole family of relations by blood and marriage, so that the dimensions of the habitation depend on the size of the family."

They were short of stature, sturdily built, with broad shoulders, and were possessed of great strength. Their complexions were swarthy, with less of the copper color of the Eastern Indians. Their features were flat, with none of the aquiline characteristics of the legendary Indian. Their coarse, straight black hair they wore long and unkempt.

They were generally beardless, although Dr. Marsh, in a letter to Lewis Cass in 1846, stated that "they are a hairy race, and some of them have beards that would do honor to a Turk."

Describing the Indians further, in the same letter, Dr. Marsh wrote: "In some individuals the hair grows quite down to the eyebrows, and they may be said to have no foreheads at all. Some few have that peculiar conformation of the eye so remarkable in the Chinese and Tartar races, and entirely different from the common American Indian or the Polynesian, and with this unpromising set of features, some have an animated and agreeable expression of countenance. The general expression of the wild Indian has nothing of the proud and lofty bearing or the haughtiness and ferocity so often seen east of the mountains. It is more commonly indicative of timidity and stupidity."

As to food they were omnivorous, eating anything available, according to the season. They ate various kinds of roots which they dug from the earth. Earthworms and grasshoppers formed a portion of their diet.

They made a primitive sort of bread from the pounded kernel of the buckeye and are said to have used a certain kind of fat worms for shortening.

It is interesting to note that the Indians inhabiting the San Francisco Bay region used no canoes, substituting therefor a rude, makeshift boat fashioned from bundles of tules firmly bound together. These were about ten feet long and pointed at both ends. Until the coming of the Jesuit Fathers the Bay Indians had no other crafts than these tule boats, which were in use as late as 1840. Bancroft offers this explanation: "The probable cause of the absence of boats in Central California, is the scarcity of suitable, favorably located timber. Doubtless if the banks of the Sacramento and the shores of San Francisco Bay had been lined with large, straight fir trees, their waters would have been filled with canoes. Yet, after all, this is but a poor excuse; for not only on the hills and mountains, at a little distance from the water, are forests of fine trees, and quantities of driftwood come floating down every stream during the rainy season, out of which surely sufficient material could be secured for some sort of boats."

The universal remedy prescribed by the Indians for all diseases was the sweat-bath. Every rancheria had its sweat-house or temescal, the latter name having been bestowed by the Franciscan Fathers. The patient after perspiring in the temescal for several hours, to the point of exhaustion, completed the treatment by plunging into the cold waters of a near-by stream. The temescal was always built on the bank of a body of water, preferably a river. The following extract is taken from the account of a pioneer who underwent the ordeal: "A sweat-house is of the shape of an inverted bowl, is generally about forty feet in diameter at the bottom and is built of strong poles and branches of trees, covered with earth to prevent the escape of heat.

There is a small hole near the ground, large enough for the Diggers to creep in one at a time, and another at the top to give out the smoke.

When a dance is given, a large fire is kindled in the center of the edifice, and the crowd assembles, the white spectators crawling in and seating themselves anywhere out of the way. The apertures, above and below, are then closed, and the dancers take their positions.

"Four and twenty squaws, *en dishabille*, on one side of the fire, and as many hombres, *in puris naturalibus*, on the other. Simultaneously with the commencement of the dancing, which is a kind of shuffling hobble-de-hoy, the 'music' bursts forth. Yes, music fit to raise the dead.

A whole legion of devils broke loose. Such screaming, shrieking, yelling, and roaring was never before heard since the foundation of the world. A thousand cross-cut saws filed by steam power—a multitude of tom-cats lashed together and flung over a clothes-line—innumerable pigs under a gate—all combined would produce a heavenly melody compared with it. Yet this uproar, deafening as it is, might possibly be endured, but another sense soon comes to be saluted. Talk of the thousand stinks of the City of Cologne! Here are at least forty thousand combined in one grand overwhelming stench."

He then relates how he was well-nigh overcome in the oppressive atmosphere, from which there was no escape. After being literally "in durance vile" for several hours, the apertures were suddenly thrown open and the Indians rushed out with a whoop and plunged into the icy water, emerging therefrom to sink exhausted on the bank.

The Contra Costa Indians cremated their dead. This practice prevailed among all the Bay Indians. Farther south the Indians buried their dead. The mother or a near relative of the deceased was generally given the distinction of lighting the funeral pyre. All the possessions of the dead were piled around the body and were consumed in the flames. Afterward the ashes were mixed with pitch and smeared on the faces of relatives as a badge of mourning.

They all believed in a continued existence after death, and in all probability, in common with most of the Indians on this continent, had a vague idea of a Great Spirit. They held certain rocks to be sacred and paid veneration to the grizzly bear, whose flesh they would never eat.

The story of these Indians would not be complete without reference to their extreme docility. In the letter previously quoted, Dr. Marsh refers to them as a "race of infants."

"In many instances," he wrote, "when a family of white people have taken a farm in the vicinity of an Indian village, in a short time they would have the whole tribe for willing serfs. They submit to flagellation with more humility than the negroes. Nothing more is necessary for their complete subjugation but kindness in the beginning, and a little well-timed severity when manifestly deserved. It is common for the white man to ask the Indian, when the latter has committed any fault, how many lashes he thinks he deserves. The Indian, with a simplicity and humility almost inconceivable, replies ten or twenty, according to his opinion of the magnitude of the offense. The white man then orders another Indian to inflict the punishment, which is received without the least sign of resentment or discontent."

Dr. Marsh concludes his account with the observation that "throughout all California the Indians are the principal laborers; without them the business of the country could hardly be carried on."

Where are the California Indians today? It is doubtful if one could find a score in all of Contra Costa County, and throughout the State they have been decimated in similar proportion. With the coming of the white man came the plagues of civilization—diseases previously unknown among the Indians. The white man had as a heritage the stamina and resistance of millions of ancestors who had successfully battled with disease; the Indian had not, and Nature remorselessly swept him aside. Measles, smallpox, and cholera, sporadic among the white settlers, assumed the form of a pestilence among the Indians, and took toll of them by thousands.

That the Indians were numerous throughout the State in early times is attested by many explorers, including Kit Carson. He wrote that the valleys of California were full of Indians in 1829, but that when he visited the State in 1859 they had disappeared to a surprising extent. Settlers in localities where Indians were once numerous stated that they knew nothing of the previous history of the Indians. They had undoubtedly been exterminated by a pestilence. Beyond this nothing was known, as the California Indians kept no records. With possibly the sole exception of the Aztecs, the North American Indians were not given to writing memorials for the future historian. Here and there throughout the State, however, are a vast number of piles of stone and circles of earth which mark the sites of once populous rancherias. Nearby are always found the remains of the indispensable sweat-house. These, with their burial-places, about which are always found a large quantity of beads, mortars, and arrow-heads of flint, are all that remain of a once numerous race.

CHAPTER II. EARLY HISTORY OF CALIFORNIA

Before proceeding with the immediate history of Contra Costa County it might be well to give a brief outline of the early history of California—California, whose shores Sir Francis Drake touched and Don Gaspar de Portola explored! California, the land of sunshine and flowers! of romance and gold "in the days of '49"!

Surely it is a promising field; but as this work is to be a history of a locality and not that of the State, the latter will be touched upon only in as far as is necessary to clear the way for what comes afterward—the story of Contra Costa County.

To go back to the very beginning, the discovery and settlement of California was made possible by that intrepid explorer, Vasco Nunez de Balboa. When he gazed out on the Pacific from the summit of a hill in Panama a new world was opened for discovery. He was followed by that ruthless adventurer, Hernando Cortez, who conquered Mexico in 1519, shamelessly butchering its people and devastating its wonderful cities.

The trend was steadily toward the north, but it was not until 1542 that a voyage of discovery was made along the California coast. Captain Juan Rodriguez Cabrillo it was who sailed into what is now known as San Diego Bay on September 28, 1542. In 1602 Don Sebastian Viscaino, who was sent out by Philip III of Spain, discovered Monterey Bay, and a party under him journeyed north as far as the Columbia River.

Then an English explorer and adventurer, Sir Francis Drake, on a marauding expedition, appeared on the scene. It has been a much disputed point with historians ever since as to whether it was in San Francisco Bay that Drake wintered in 1578. It is generally conceded now that it was not San Francisco Bay, but Drake's Bay, a few miles north of the former, and immediately under the lee of Point Reyes.

Drake called the country New Albion, and took possession in the name of his sovereign, Queen Elizabeth. Little if any effort was made by the English to follow in the trail blazed by Drake.

Although the Spanish settled and colonized Lower California early in the sixteenth century, it was not until nearly two hundred years later that any progress was made toward permanently locating in Upper California, as our State was then called. The first permanent settlement in California was made at San Diego in 1769. There, during the same year, the first mission was established.

From Lower California in 1769 an expedition set out under command of Don Gaspar de Portola, first governor of California. This expedition was destined to have a great influence on the later history of California, for it was Don Gaspar who discovered San Francisco Bay, following a journey of innumerable privations and hardships.

Then followed the era of missions in California. The impress of the missions, which formed so important a part in the early history of California, is felt to this day. They stand out as historic monuments to the piety and zeal of their great founder, Father Junipero Serra. Beginning with the mission at San Diego, which he founded in 1769, he established between that year and his death, in 1784, twenty-one missions in California. In founding the mission at Monterey he rediscovered Monterey Bay, the goal of explorers ever since its first discovery by Viscaino, in 1602. Mission San Carlos de Monterey became his headquarters.

Setting out from there, the other missions were established in rapid succession in various parts of the country. He succeeded with the Indians as no one else ever did before or since. He possessed a character of great firmness, balanced by gentleness, kindness, and patience—one best calculated to deal with the Indians, thousands of whom he converted to his faith and who universally mourned his death.

The missions were generally quadrilateral, two stories high, and enclosed a courtyard embellished with fountains and trees. The sides of the quadrangle were usually about six hundred feet long, and the whole enclosed the church, storerooms, workshops, and living quarters.

Young Indian girls inhabited one portion of the mission. They were given careful training and instruction by skilled matrons. Those who showed exceptional talent were given vocal and instrumental training.

None were permitted to leave until of a marriageable age, this with a view of preserving their morality. In the men's quarters the mechanical and agricultural arts were taught.

Let us glance at the daily routine of the missions: All arose at sunrise and proceeded to the church, where they took part in devotional exercises. After partaking of breakfast, they took up their various duties. Following the noonday meal, they enjoyed a siesta, or rest, until two o'clock, after which they resumed work until about an hour before sundown, when the chimes of the evening angelus were heard. From then until supper-time all participated in evening devotions at the church. After supper was the time for recreation, and all took part in dancing, in games, and in all manner of amusements. They did not lack for food, their diet consisting of plenty of the choicest beef and mutton, with vegetables, wheat cakes, and porridge. Such, in brief, was the life of the Indians at the missions.

We will pass rapidly over the next period, during which California belonged to Mexico, which acquired her independence from Spain in 1821, largely through the efforts of one Iturbide, who during the same year caused himself to be declared emperor of Mexico.

This was the time of great land grants. Any citizen of good character, by the payment of a small fee to the Mexican Government, could secure a grant of land of from one to eleven square leagues. These great domains were known as ranchos, and their owners were rancheros. Over their broad acres ranged thousands of cattle, since cattle-raising was the one and only industry. The rancheros, who formed the aristocracy of California prior to American occupation, were extremely hospitable, keeping open house the year round. They were fond of social pleasures, especially of music and dancing, and even their horses were taught to step in time to the guitar. Few, if any, could boast of pure Castilian descent, a varying admixture of Indian blood being the rule, yet many of the women were of notable beauty. Both sexes dressed in a striking and picturesque manner. The men wore wide pantaloons, laced with ribbons through eyelets from the waistband to the hips and fastened with immense silver buttons. For a cloak they wore a gaily colored serape, made from a blanket with a hole cut in the center, through which the head was inserted. The serape hung down to the knees. They were shod with highly polished boots, from which jangled heavy silver spurs, and a broad sombrero tilted back on their heads completed the spectacular costume. The senoritas were no less adept at decking themselves out to advantage, especially on a gala occasion. The favorite ballroom dress was a scarlet petticoat, softened in tone by being covered by a white lawn skirt, while a black velvet waist plentifully decked with spangles heightened the attractive costume. Their only head-dress was the mantilla, or shawl. They were the personification of grace and were famous for their dancing.

The men were skilled equestrians and spent a large part of their time in the saddle. One of their favorite amusements was to pick a silver dollar from the ground while riding by at a gallop. No less skilled were they with the riata, which formed a dangerous weapon in their hands, whether directed against a bull, a bear, or a human enemy.

They were all devout Catholics, their priests belonging to the Franciscan order. Numerous were the saints' days which they kept, in addition to Sundays, which made their working week often much shorter than that observed in this modern age of efficiency.

Their homes were built of adobe, a black clayey loam, which they made into sun-dried bricks, admirably adapted to primitive building conditions. Rough timbers with the bark removed were used for joists and beams, rushes and chaparral sufficing for a thatched roof. When whitewashed within and without the whole was beautiful in its simplicity; nor were they lacking in durability, for many of them are in an excellent state of preservation to this day.

Beef and beans, well-seasoned with chile peppers, formed the most important part of their diet, and these the senoras were capable of preparing in many dishes that were extremely appetizing. Their bread was made from maize ground between two stones, and was baked in the form of thin wafers, known as tortillas.

In 1846 the United States went to war with Mexico, after which, by the treaty of 1848, California became American territory. One year later, a date now famous, the era of the argonauts began. James W. Marshall discovered gold while digging a millrace for Captain Sutter at Coloma, and in 1849 people began flocking to California from the ends of the earth. Round the Horn they came in clipper ships, or across the plains behind ox-teams. The golden halo of romance settled over California, adventurous spirits wooed Fortune at every turn and became wealthy overnight. In 1850 California had sufficient population to admit her to the Union—and here we shall begin the history of Contra Costa County.

CHAPTER III. MEXICAN LAND GRANTS—
PEN-PICTURES OF EARLY DAYS

This chapter deals with the period of great Mexican land grants, those vast dominions of California under the Mexican regime which stretched over thousands of acres of the most fertile lands and laid the foundation for the fortunes of numerous families.

Prior to the cession of California to the United States in 1848, it was possible for any citizen of good character to pay a nominal fee to the Mexican Government and receive a grant of land covering from one to eleven square leagues. Scores of these large grants were distributed over Contra Costa County. Throughout the central and southern part of California the Mexican Government gave away these grants with a lavish hand. When California became American territory the United States sent a representative, William Carey Jones, to California and Mexico to make a special study of land grants. This was done with a view of establishing a perfect title, wherever possible, so that no hardship might be experienced by the then residents of California through the change in governments. In most instances a bona fide title was granted by the United States without inconvenience to the original holders. In later years, however, partition suits were instituted by the heirs of these families, whose descendants were numbered by scores.

These famous suits were carried on through the courts for years, until final decrees in partition were handed down, some of them of very recent date.

The most famous of the partition suits were those affecting the Welch ranch or Rancho las Juntas, the Rancho el Sobrante suit, settled in recent years, and the Marsh grant litigation, known as the suit of T. I. Bergin against Charles B. Sanford, finally partitioned in May, 1912. Much valuable information on early land grants is contained in a historical sketch written by Judge Thomas A. Brown and published in the Contra Costa Gazette in 1876, a portion of which follows:

"During the year 1823 Francisco Castro made application to the Mexican authorities for the San Pablo Rancho, and Ignacio Martinez for the Pinole Rancho, to the extent of four leagues of land each. These men, who were the pioneer white settlers in our county, planted vineyards and pear orchards at their ranchos more than half a century ago. They made little other improvements; each of them built an adobe house and a few corrals. Their neighbors then were the families of Peralta, at San Antonio, and Castro, at San Lorenzo, until about the year 1826, when Jose Maria Amador settled upon the San Ramon Rancho, at Dublin, where he obtained a grant of four leagues of land. During the year 1828 Valencia occupied the Alcalanes Rancho, at Lafayette, Moraga the Lagunas Palos Colorados, or Redwood Rancho, and Felipe Briones the Briones Rancho. Each of these persons made application to the Government for a grant of land; Valencia for three-fourths of a league, and the others for three leagues each. Briones was soon afterward killed by the Indians, near where the town of Clayton now is, while himself and some of his neighbors were attempting to recover some stock which had been stolen by the Indians, and which they were driving toward the San Joaquin plains. During the same year Silvio Pacheco founded the Monte del Diablo Rancho, and settled where the village of Concord is situated, where he has ever since resided, and about the same time Juana Pacheco, a widow, made application for title to the San Miguel Rancho. At that time she resided at San Jose; Ygnacio Sibrian, her nephew, occupied the ranch for her, and built an adobe house near Walnut Creek. These persons afterward obtained grants of land of four square leagues each. During the year 1832 Mariano Castro and Bartolo Pacheco settled upon and made application for the San Ramon Rancho. About the same time William Welch, a Scotchman by birth, petitioned for the tract known as the Welch Rancho, on which a portion of the town of Martinez is situated. Welch resided but a short time on the rancho, and, in consequence of the hostility of the Indians and the entire absence of security, he left the ranch in charge of a few vaqueros and removed his family to San Jose. Welch made his settlement at the place known as the Welch homestead, near Walnut Creek.

Soon after, and about the years 1832 and 1833, the Romero brothers settled at the place known as Tice Valley, and made application for a grant to the sobrante or vacant land lying between the ranchos of San Ramon, Welch Rancho, Alcalanes, and Moraga. They occupied the place for many years, but their application for a grant was finally rejected.

"About the year 1836 two brothers, Jose Miguel and Antonio Mesa, settled upon the New York Rancho, near the place known as Kirker's Pass, and made application to the Government for a grant of the place to the extent of two leagues, which was granted to them under the name of Los Medanos. During the same year Miranda Higuera and Alviso settled upon and made application for a grant for the place called Canada de los Vaqueros, and Jose Noriega made application for the Rancho los Meganos, known as the Marsh Rancho, consisting of three square leagues of land. During the following year, 1837, Noriega sold the rancho to Doctor John Marsh, who settled upon it in the same year, and occupied it afterward until his death, which occurred in 1856. So the Doctor was the first native-born American citizen who ever resided permanently in this county or within its territorial limits as originally defined.

"The Indians, then roaming in bands over the Sacramento and San Joaquin valleys, made a regular business of raiding upon the ranchos in the district north of San Jose and east of the Bay of San Francisco.

The inhabitants of that district were forced to keep constant watch to prevent them from driving away all of their stock, and in their efforts to recover their animals from the Indians it frequently occurred that the latter would give battle to their pursuers, and sometimes were victorious, and in such cases they would get away with the stock.

"Until about 1847, and during the first ten years of his residence on his ranch, Doctor Marsh's neighbors, comprising all the people who then had lands and resided within the present limits of this county, were the Mesas, on the New York Rancho, Miranda and Higuera, on the Canada de los Vaqueros, Salvio Pacheco, on the Monte del Diablo, Ygnacio Sibrian, on the San Miguel, all then considered to be adjoining ranchos, the haciendas, or dwelling-places, on each of them being from twelve to fifteen miles from his. His other neighbors, living from twenty to forty miles from him, were Jose Maria Amador, at the San Ramon Rancho, Pacheco and Castro, on the Rancho San Ramon, Ygnacio Martinez, at Pinole, Moraga, at the Redwoods, Valencia, at the Acalanes, the family of Francisco Castro, at San Pablo, and the vaqueros of Welch, on the Welch Ranch, the widow and family of Felipe Briones, on the Briones Rancho.

"The ranch-owners usually had employed a few vaqueros to herd and care for their stock. These vaqueros were generally mission (or Christianized) Indians. Such was the condition of the country here at the close of the war.

"Very little attention was given to agricultural pursuits further than that nearly every ranch-owner cultivated a few acres of beans and corn and a small potato patch, with a few other vegetables, and a few square rods planted in melons. This was about the extent of farming carried on at the different ranches. Also all of the rancheros, when locating their ranches, planted small vineyards and pear-trees. Many of these vineyards and trees bear fruit to this day.

"At the close of the war about forty-six leagues, embracing about three hundred and twenty square miles of land, was owned or held by persons named in this county. Previous to the settlement in this county by Americans and other foreigners, as they were called by the Californians, but little improvements had been made by any of the Californians, nor did they require much. An adobe house and a few corrals generally comprised all the improvements necessary on a rancho.

"Soon after the close of the war American citizens and citizens of other countries began to settle in the county. During the year 1847 Elam Brown purchased the Acalanes Rancho and settled upon it near the village of Lafayette. In 1848 Colonel William M. Smith purchased from one of the Castros a portion of the place known as the sobrante of the San Pablo, and during the year 1849 quite a number of citizens of the United States and other countries came into the county. They located chiefly in the redwoods between Moraga Valley and San Antonio, for the purpose of manufacturing lumber for market.

"In referring to the names of two of the ranchos, and to the location of the town of Martinez, we have mentioned Monte del Diablo as the name of the rancho of Salvio Pacheco, the Rancho el Pinole as that of Ygnacio Martinez, being located upon the Arroyo del Hambre. Doubtless persons have often inquired how they originated, or why these names were applied to these places. Upon one occasion it was asked of a native Californian, who was quite an old man, and he stated that the names were (as he had learned during his boyhood) given to these places during the beginning of the last century, and he related the facts substantially as follows: The Indians inhabiting the country north of San Jose Valley were very troublesome, so much so that small parties could not travel in the country north of San Jose with safety. The Mexican Government sent a company of troops from Monterey to chastise the Indians, and to correct the leaders of the most troublesome of them. The troops came upon a camp of Indians near the present location of Concord. The Indians retreated into a thicket of willows and undergrowth upon a piece of swamp land near where Fernando Pacheco lived. Night coming on, the troops did not pursue the Indians into the thicket, but divided into squads and partially surrounded the place, intending to make a finish of them in the morning. During the night the troops saw what they believed to be moving lights in different parts of the thicket; the lights appeared to be moving, and they were confident that they had the Indians corralled. In the morning they closed in and charged upon the thicket, but found no Indians, neither had any of them stopped there during the night, as they found upon examination that they had pressed through the place and gone far beyond, and that there was not a human being in the thicket during the night. The troops were bewildered and frightened, being unable to account for the lights which they saw during the night, so they named the place the Devil's Thicket, or Monte del Diablo. The lights were probably produced by phosphorescence, which the troops did not understand and could not comprehend. They immediately left that place, and did not pursue these Indians farther, but immediately moved to the Straits of Carquinez, intending to cross over and go to the Mission of San Rafael. They were unable to cross by reason of high winds and camped at the place near where the town of Martinez now is. Their provisions giving out, and being unable to secure any more, they were forced to abandon the camp. They called the place the Valley of Hunger (Canada del Hambre). They started in the direction of San Francisco, intending to cross the straits, if possible.

On their march they found a village of Indians who had corn from which they manufactured meal (pinole). That camp they named El Pinole. When Salvio Pacheco petitioned for his grant he gave it the name which the Mexican troops had given the thicket which grew there, and the names given the Canada del Hambre and Pinole by that company of Mexican troops have attached to these places ever since. The mountain now called Monte Diablo formerly was called Sierra de los Golgones. Its present name originated with the Americans and other foreign people who came into the county at a comparatively recent date."

EARLY INHABITANTS

The following graphic description of early-day manners and customs was also written by Judge Thomas A. Brown, and was first published in the centennial edition of the Contra Costa Gazette in 1876: "Since its organization, in February, 1850, the population of the county at large has slowly but steadily increased. There was but little increase in the eastern portion of the county until after the discovery of coal, about the year 1860, at Nortonville, since which time that portion of the county has grown rapidly in population, and in increased value of property.

"Many of our people will recollect the carts used in early days by the Californians. They usually traveled from place to place on horseback, but when the family desired to visit a neighbor or go to town the family coach was called into use. That vehicle consisted of two immense wooden wheels, cut or sawed off a log, with holes as near the center as convenient for the axletree, with a tongue lashed to the axle with rawhide thongs. Upon this a frame as wide as the wheels would permit, and from seven to twelve feet in length, was placed, upon which was securely fastened one or two rawhides, with the flesh side down, and a rude frame over the top, upon which to stretch an awning, with rawhide thongs wove around the sides to keep the children from tumbling out.

The female portion of the family, with the small children, would seat themselves in the cart, to which was attached a pair of the best traveling oxen on the ranch. An Indian would drive, or rather lead, the oxen (for he usually walked ahead of them). In this simple, rude contrivance the family would travel twenty or thirty miles a day with as much comfort apparently as people now take in riding in our modern vehicles.

Sometimes several families would ride in a single cart, and visit their friends, go to town for the purpose of shopping, or to attend church."

WILD GAME

The excellent article on wild game which here follows was published in a historical work of 1878:

"There is now, at proper seasons, an abundance of California quail, wild ducks, geese, and other game in this county. In fact, the wild geese along the borders of the rivers are a great nuisance to the farmers. Immense flocks of these light down on the green growing grain and eat it off close to the ground. Farmers sometimes employ hands who do nothing but ride on horseback about the grain-fields, and by use of the shotgun succeed in keeping them off until the time for their departure to another clime arrives. Large flocks of pelicans, both white and gray, are common in the lagoons and tule swamps, as also are cranes and many other water-birds.

"Herds of elk roamed over the San Joaquin plains in early times. Captain Kimball, of Antioch, says on the first morning of his arrival there, in 1849, be saw eighty elk in one drove, feeding a mile south of his house, and shot a fine heifer weighing four hundred pounds. At the same time these plains were covered with wild cattle. These were slaughtered for their hides and tallow, which, at that day, constituted the only currency of the country. Much of the flesh meat in 1850-51 was dried elk. Large herds of them used to feed on the green tule lands and islands opposite Antioch. Their horns were such as to prevent them from running in large bodies. They were frequently lassoed by the vaqueros of California.

"Deer were also thick in this county in early times, in spots not much frequented by horsemen, and were often seen feeding on the bunchgrass about Diablo. There are still a few to be found in the dense timber of the hills.

"Antelope were also numerous. These were fleet, pretty animals, as well as cunning in their habits. One, larger than the rest, by early settlers has often been seen watching while the main body of the kids were at water or on the bottom lands, feeding on green grass. The elk, deer, and antelope are all good swimmers, and frequently visited the islands of the San Joaquin for green food.

"The coyote, or fox, is well known to the Californian—a kind of link between the cat and dog—and is sometimes called prairie-dog but is very different from the animal of that name found on the Western plains. They often followed the immigrant train to pick up the bones and crumbs that fell by the way. They would steal eggs and chickens from the roost, but were great cowards, and a small dog would drive them off.

"The California lion is not a roaring lion, like the African. The head is small, and much like the head of the tiger, being large between the eyes. The neck is without mane. It is said he seldom attacks human beings.

"Grizzly bears were thick in early times, so much so that Dr. Marsh used to say he could have one caught any time by the vaqueros. The bears often took his calves and colts. They would destroy elk, deer, and antelope. A young man was killed by one of them in the dense forest of chamisal, three or four miles from Antioch. This chamisal is a short growth of underbrush, so dense as to be impenetrable by man, and covered about five thousand acres. Wildcats are occasionally seen in parts of Contra Costa County.

"The larger wild animals have probably disappeared forever from this county. It would be interesting to know just when and where the last of these noble animals met their inevitable fate."

Smaller game, however, has by no means disappeared from Contra Costa County. Today, nearly forty years after the above article was written, the sportsman may still find good hunting. At certain times of the year wild geese in abundance are found on the tule front in the eastern section of the county, and ducks and other waterfowls are plentiful along the water-front from Byron to Richmond.

In the valleys of the central section, and especially around the foothills of Mount Diablo, quails are plentiful. The shotgun adept will also find good dove-hunting in the vicinity of Marsh Creek and in Ygnacio Valley.

Deer are scarce now because of the army of hunters that slaughter them as fast as they appear in the foothills of Mount Diablo from the Livermore hills. That the deer increased rapidly when there was a closed season for hunting them is shown by the fact that forty-four fine bucks were brought in on the first day of the open season some years ago, after a long interval of restriction. It is the general opinion that deer would rapidly increase if the ban were again placed on the hunter for a few years.

Excellent fishing rewards the modern Izaak Waltons in the mountain streams and bay waters. Anglers derive great sport from fishing for striped bass, the gameness of which is celebrated. They are most plentiful in the bay waters off Selby and Rodeo but are also to be found along the strip of water from Crockett to Richmond.

CHAPTER IV. PIONEER CITIZENS

Antedating all other pioneers of Contra Costa County were Francisco Castro and Ignacio Martinez. They came in 1823, Castro settling at the present site of San Pablo, and Martinez at Pinole. They each acquired four leagues of land from the Mexican Government, and these ranchos they improved the following year by building adobe residences, planting vineyards and orchards, and building corrals for their live-stock.

The San Pablo rancho contained 19,394.40 acres, and the Pinole rancho extended over 17,786.49 acres. Both reared families whose descendants today rank high in the citizenship of Contra Costa County. Martinez, the county seat, was named for the Martinez family.

DOCTOR JOHN MARSH

The first American settler in Contra Costa was Doctor John Marsh. He achieved much distinction from his letters and descriptive articles, which gave a graphic portrayal of the primitive conditions as he found them. To his facile pen California historians, and Contra Costa County historians especially, are indebted for much of their data relating to the early period.

Doctor Marsh was descended from an old New England family, and was a graduate of Harvard College. Born in Danvers, Massachusetts, in 1799, he came west and conducted a mercantile business in St. Joseph, Missouri, from 1828 until 1835. During the latter year he started on horseback for the Far West, eventually becoming one of an exploring party which visited the Mexican states of Chihuahua and Sonora, thence crossing the Gila River and entering California on the southern border.

Portions of the life history of Doctor Marsh read like a romance, as will be seen from an incident that occurred while on the journey west.

Inadvertently wandering away from his party, he was captured on the plains by the Indians while they were in the midst of exorcising an evil spirit. They were determined to offer him as a sacrifice, and he was saved only by wooing and marrying the chief's pretty daughter, who interceded for him in much the same manner as did Pocahontas for Captain John Smith. Sometime afterward the band crossed the old Santa Fe trail and Doctor Marsh escaped, having the good fortune to fall in with a caravan which finally landed him in California.

For a while he resided in Los Angeles, but in 1837 he obtained from the Mexican Government a grant of land at the foot of Mount Diablo, now the center of Contra Costa County. Here he made his permanent home. He described his tract as being about twelve miles long and about ten miles broad. The Doctor first lived in an adobe building, but later he built the home which afterward became famous as the Stone House. It is situated about four miles from Brentwood. The following description of the Marsh home is taken from the San Francisco Bulletin of July 19, 1856: "The new and beautiful edifice, now nearly completed, is situated in the center of the plain. It is the intention of the proprietor to irrigate this plain by artificial means, using the water of the brook for that purpose. By this process the whole plain in front of the house may be enameled with flowers, or, in process of time, may be dotted with trees, and become a beautiful and extensive park, as the taste of the owner may determine. From a quarry which has been opened upon the estate, an abundant supply of stone for the building has been obtained. It is of the finest quality of freestone, of a beautiful drab or cream color, slightly variegated. The building is quite an architectural gem. The architect, Thomas Boyd, of San Francisco, with a true artistic perception of the beauty of the site, and of what was wanting in the building to make it harmonize with the surrounding scenery, has departed from the stereotyped square box with a piazza running partly or entirely round it, called a house in California, and has adopted the old English domestic style of architecture—a pleasing and appropriate union of manor-house and castle. The arched windows, the peaked roofs and gables, the projecting eaves, the central tower, sixty-five feet in height, boldly springing from the midst and enabling the proprietor to overlook his extensive domain, must be acknowledged by every visitor to be a most felicitous deviation from the prevailing style of rural architecture. The material used is as easily wrought as the Benicia stone in use here, and, like it, hardens by exposure to the air. The corners of the building, as well as the door and window-jambs, sills, and caps, are elaborately wrought, the spaces between the openings being laid with rubble-stone, giving a pleasing variety to the whole exterior. The building has a ground base of sixty by forty feet, and is three stories in height, with three gable windows in the attic looking east, west, and south. On three sides of the building is a piazza, ten feet in width, supported by beautiful octagon pillars; over this is a walk on a level with the second floor, enclosed by an elaborately finished balustrade. The interior arrangements are as carefully planned as possible to subserve the purposes of convenience, comfort, and beautiful finish. The whole cost of the building, it is understood, will not exceed twenty thousand dollars."

The Stone House remained intact until 1868; it was partially destroyed by the great earthquake of that year. It was afterward restored and stands today as one of Contra Costa County's most cherished historic monuments.

Doctor Marsh was eminently successful as a rancher. Great herds of cattle thrived on his broad acres and added to his prosperity. Although for some years he lived a solitary life—his nearest neighbors were from ten to forty miles away—doubtless, with his scholarly attainments he was not lonely. His keen mind and shrewd observation were busily gathering information, which was afterward to enrich the literature of the period. He was a cultivated French and Spanish scholar and is said to have had a deeper insight into French and Spanish manners than any other person of the time. In appearance Doctor Marsh was tall and commanding. He was athletic as a young man, and he remained active and alert throughout his eventful life. Versatile and many-sided, his mind was as young as his body.

Doctor Marsh had passed the half-century mark without finding a mate. Then, in 1851, Romance claimed him for her own. After the briefest of courtships he was married to Miss Abbie Tuck, of Chelmsford, Massachusetts. She had left her home in 1850, braving the dangers of a voyage to California, and came to Santa Clara. During the following year, while visiting Contra Costa County, she met the Doctor, and they were married two weeks later.

On September 24, 1856, Doctor Marsh was foully and brutally murdered and robbed while driving in his buggy on the road from his ranch to Martinez, thirty miles distant. The next morning his horse and empty buggy were found in Martinez, and a few hours later his body was discovered in a ditch by the roadside. He had been stabbed in the left side, about the face and hands, and, as a crowning act of viciousness, his throat had been cut. Three Mexicans committed the crime, according to the confession of Jose Olivas, who admitted being one of the trio. The other two were Juan Garcia and Felipe Moreno, the latter a youth of only nineteen. Olivas maintained that the actual crime was committed by Moreno, and that he himself and Garcia were only accessories. Olivas was captured the next day, and, after making a confession, escaped on the following day. It was ten years before he was recaptured. Moreno was equally successful in eluding the law but was finally taken near Sacramento about the same time that Olivas was caught. He was sentenced to life imprisonment in 1867. Because of his staunch assertion that he had taken no part in the actual commission of the crime, Olivas received a lighter sentence. Juan Garcia was never found.

The following article, written by Doctor Marsh and published in the New Orleans Picayune in 1846, is so fine an example of his graphic style and is so replete with information of the period that it is well worth reproducing here in full: "Messrs. Editors: Certain willful, malicious and ill-disposed neighbors of mine have entered into a conspiracy against me. They have, for some time past, instigated no doubt by their indolence and evil dispositions, been teasing me to write articles for newspapers in the United States. They represented to me that the people there are very desirous to have correct information relative to California, and that they cannot easily obtain it. That although several works on this country have recently been published they are not entitled to implicit confidence, either because the writers were hasty travelers, unacquainted with the language of the inhabitants, and not possessed of the requisite information, or that these works were published to answer a particular purpose, which was not exactly that of the naked truth. As I have heretofore thought it better to attend to my own business rather than undertake to enlighten the people of the United States about California, these same ill-disposed neighbors of mine have undertaken to place me under an interdict. They declare that unless I will write articles for the American newspapers none of the said newspapers shall reach me. Now, as these enemies of mine live in Monterey, where foreign intelligence first arrives, they have actually stopped my newspapers, and I am thus compelled to write, or not have the privilege of reading the news. You will perceive, therefore, that if my effusions are worthless the fault is not mine, but of those who have forced me to write against my will. I have hesitated to what journal to address my precious communications, but have finally selected the Picayune, because we consider it the best for Mexican and Texan news, in which we feel a deep interest, and partly because we have a sort of fellow-feeling for Mr. Kendall, on account of his romantic pilgrimage to New and Old Mexico.

"The European who first saw California was Grijalva, who commanded a naval expedition fitted out by Cortez the Conqueror, in the year 1534. He discovered the southern part of Lower California, which he supposed to be an island, and this opinion was for a long time entertained by the Spaniards. Lower, or Old California, is for the most part an uninhabited and uninhabitable desert, as remarkable for its extent and sterility as Upper California is for its fertility and beauty. The country now known as Upper California was discovered by Juan Rodriguez Cabrillo, in the year 1542. The first settlement of the Spaniards in the territory was begun at the port of San Diego, on the first of May, 1769. The first governor of Upper California was Don Gaspar de Portola, a captain of dragoons in the Spanish army. The first attempts at settlements were made by founding missions, which were gradually extended along the coast toward the north, wherever suitable situations could be found. The last of these missions that was attempted was at Sonoma, which was begun about twenty-five years ago. It was nipped in the bud by the revolutions that severed Mexico from the crown of Spain. These missions, as long as the Spanish power lasted, were in a most flourishing condition, possessed nearly all the good lands in the country, and were occupied by upward of twenty thousand converted Indians. Since the revolution these missions, like everything else in the Mexican territory, have gone rapidly to decay. At present most of them are entirely abolished, their immense wealth dissipated, and the lands apportioned out among private individuals. It has been usual to state the population of Upper California at five thousand persons of Spanish descent and twenty thousand Indians. This estimate may have been near the truth twenty years ago. At present the population may be stated in round numbers at seven thousand Spaniards and ten thousand civilized, or rather domesticated, Indians. To this may be added about seven hundred Americans, one hundred English, Irish, and Scotch, and about one hundred French, Germans, and Italians. Within the territorial limits of Upper California, taking the parallel of forty-two degrees for the northern and the Colorado for the southeastern boundaries, are an immense number of wild, naked brute Indians. Their number, of course, can only be conjectured. They probably exceed a million, and may possibly amount to double that number.

"The climate of California is remarkably different from that of the United States. This difference consists mainly in its regularity and uniformity. From May to October the wind is invariably from the northwest, and during this time it never rains and the sky is brilliant, clear, and serene. The weather during this time is temperate, and rarely oppressively warm. The nights are agreeably cool, and many of the inhabitants sleep in the open air the year round. From October to May the wind blows frequently from the southeast and is always followed by rain. Snow never falls except on the mountains, and frost is rare except in December and January. A proof of the mildness of the climate this moment presents itself in the shape of a humming-bird, which I just saw from the open window, and this on the first day of February, in latitude thirty-eight degrees. Wheat is sown from October until March, and maize from March to July. As regards human health and comfort, the climate is incomparably better than that of any part of the United States. It is much the most healthy country I have ever seen or have any knowledge of. There is absolutely no disease whatever that can be attributed to the influence of the climate. The whole territory is traversed by ranges of mountains, which run parallel to each other and to the coast. The highest points may be about four thousand feet above the level of the sea; in most places much lower, and in many parts they dwindle to low hills. They are everywhere covered with grass and vegetation, and many of the valleys and northern declivities abound with finest timber trees. Between these ranges of mountains are level valleys, or rather plains, of every width, from five miles to fifty. The magnificent valley through which flow the San Joaquin and Sacramento rivers, is five hundred miles long, with an average width of forty or fifty. It is intersected laterally by many smaller rivers abounding with salmon.

The whole region abounds with vast herds of wild horses, elk, and antelope. The only inhabitants of this vast valley (which is capable of supporting a nation) are about one hundred and fifty Americans and a few miserable Indians. The Bay of San Francisco, into which all these rivers flow, and which is the natural outlet of all this region, is considered by nautical men as one of the finest harbors in the world. It consists of two principal arms, diverging from the entrance in nearly opposite directions, and each about fifty miles long, with an average width of eight or ten miles. It is perfectly sheltered from every wind, has great depth of water, is easily accessible at all times, and has space enough to contain half the ships in the world. The entrance is less than a mile wide and could easily be fortified so as to make it entirely impregnable.

The vicinity abounds in the finest timber for ship-building and in fact everything necessary to make it a great naval and commercial depot. Near the entrance of this magnificent harbor, within the last seven years, has grown up the flourishing town of Yerba Buena, built and inhabited entirely by Americans and Englishmen.

"The agricultural capabilities of California are as yet imperfectly developed. It is well adapted to the productions of Spain, Portugal, and Italy, and the region lying in similar latitudes on the western coast of Europe. The whole of it is remarkably adapted to the culture of the vine. Brandy and wine of excellent quality are already made in considerable quantities; olives, figs, and almonds grow well; apples, pears, and peaches produce abundantly, and, in the southern part, oranges. Cotton is beginning to be cultivated and promises to succeed well. It is the finest country for wheat I have ever seen. Fifty for one is about the average crop, with very imperfect cultivation. One hundred-fold is not uncommon, and even one hundred and fifty has been produced. Maize grows tolerably well, but not equal to that in some parts of the United States. Hemp, flax, and tobacco have been cultivated on a small scale and succeed well. The rearing of cattle is at present the principal pursuit of the inhabitants, and the most profitable. As a pastoral country California is unsurpassed, and perhaps unequaled, in the world. The pasturage is most abundant and of very excellent quality. No less than seven kinds of clover are indigenous here, and four of them are unknown in the United States. Oats grow spontaneously all over the coast, throughout its whole extent. In one place, near the river Merced, a little barley was accidentally scattered by a traveler, and it has continued to reproduce itself for fifteen years. I have known five successive crops of wheat in as many years from one sowing. All kinds of grasses, as well as the cereal gramma, produce an uncommon quantity of seed, and this is probably the reason why cattle do not reach their greatest degree of fatness until about a month after the grass is dry.

"If these desultory remarks on some of the topics relative to this country should be found to contain interest for your readers, at some future time you may expect to hear something of the commerce of the country, its great mineral wealth, its political history (a most fruitful theme), and of the manners and customs of its inhabitants, from one of your fellow-citizens who has been here more than ten years and has taken some pains to become acquainted with the country he has selected for his home."

The above communication was signed "Essex," and was dated February, 1846. To those who are familiar with present-day conditions in California the statements of Doctor Marsh, written over seventy years ago, seem most prophetic.

ELAM BROWN

Second among the American trail-blazers of Contra Costa County was Elam Brown. He had a varied and adventurous life, no small portion of which was spent in Contra Costa County, in whose affairs he played an important part.

He was born in Herkimer County, New York, June 10, 1797. The hardy traits of the pioneer were his birthright. As a child twelve months old he experienced his first migration when his parents moved to Berkshire, Massachusetts. When he was seven they came west to Ohio, where they braved numerous hardships in true pioneer style.

To the north of their little settlement, which they named Berkshire, for the home they had left in Massachusetts, the nearest settlement was one hundred miles away, on the shore of Lake Erie. To the south the nearest settlement was fifteen miles distant. In Berkshire the lad first dipped into books, and, although his opportunities were few, he developed a taste for literature that remained with him through life.

In 1818, at the age of twenty-one, he set out on foot for the French trading-post of St. Louis, Missouri, five hundred miles away. During the following winter he rafted unsuccessfully on the Missouri River.

Then he went to Illinois, where he farmed on shares for the next three years, during which time he married the daughter of Thomas Allen.

His next venture was in moving west to what was known as the Platte Purchase, a tract of land bordering on the Missouri River, acquired by the Government from the Indians in 1836. There he cleared one hundred and eighty acres of land, on which he resided for ten years. It was there that his first wife died. He then determined to emigrate to the Pacific Coast, and in 1846 he headed a company and started on the long journey westward across the plains. He was appointed captain of the fourteen families that left the Missouri on May 14. They had innumerable adventures, and Captain Elam Brown was equal to every emergency. More than once his diplomatic treatment of the Indians averted disaster. On one occasion a large force of hostile braves menaced their path, but Elam Brown came forward and smoked the pipe of peace with their chieftains. Then he signaled for the Indians to open their lines. They did so and the wagon-train passed through unmolested. The party forded all the rivers, as there was not one ferry or bridge on their entire journey. The stout-hearted little band entered California October 10, 1846, and toward the end of the same month they arrived at the present site of Sacramento, continuing thence to Santa Clara, where most of the party settled.

Scarcely rested from the long trek across the continent, Elam Brown sought for fresh fields of adventure. He joined the forces under General John C. Fremont which were fighting General Castro, in an echo of the Mexican war in central California. He also took an active part in suppressing the Mexican freebooter, Sanchez. The winter of 1847 ne spent in the San Antonio redwoods, whipsawing lumber and boating his product across the bay to San Francisco.

It was difficult at this time to buy land in California. The Mexican residents were solemnly pledged not to sell a foot of ground or give any information regarding land. But in the fall Elam Brown finally learned that William A. Leidesdorff, a San Francisco trader, had a ranch for sale. This was the Rancho Alcalanes, where the present town of Lafayette is situated. The ranch was stocked with three hundred head of cattle. This tract became the permanent home of Elam Brown in Contra Costa County. He soon became enthusiastic over its possibilities. He was especially pleased with the mild California winters, in marked contrast with the severe snow-storms of the East. It was his first experience in a land where it was not necessary to feed cattle through the winter months.

Up to this time there was no government in California, except the military rule of Colonel Mason. On account of dissension over the slavery question, Congress had taken no steps toward the formation of a State. In 1848 General Riley superseded Mason. He straightway issued a proclamation authorizing the people to elect delegates to a constitutional convention.

The convention met in Monterey September 1, 1849. Elam Brown was one of the thirty-seven delegates who framed the constitution. These delegates had come from nearly every State in the Union. They were the virile immigrants who had the courage to seek their fortunes in a new land. With but few statute-books to guide them, they framed a constitution that admirably stood the test of time for nearly thirty years.

California had become a State, but, because of the slavery agitation, Congress refused to recognize her as such. It was not until 1850 that California was admitted to the Union, enjoying the distinction of never having had a territorial government. Throughout this period Elam Brown served the State ably and unceasingly. He was a member of the first two sessions of the legislature and was urged to run for the United States Senate. But he felt that the destinies of his State by adoption had been safely guided past the critical point and he retired to pastoral scenes. There on the Rancho Alcalanes the stalwart pioneer rounded out his days to a venerable age.

FELIX COATS

As the years go by the pioneers of Contra Costa County are one by one answering the last roll-call, and few of the early trail-blazers now remain. The latest summons by death was on June 10, 1916, when Felix Grundy Coats, of Tassajara, was called. The end came to the pioneer at his home after an illness extending over a period of several weeks and was directly due to the infirmities of old age.

Felix Grundy Coats was a native of Callaway County, Missouri, where he was born on August 9, 1828, being at his death nearly eighty-eight years old. In May, 1849, with a number of emigrants, he left Missouri for California, and in September of the same year the party arrived at Grass Valley. Felix Coats then began mining on the American River, and later operated a pack-train between Sacramento and Stony Bar. In the fall of 1852 he came to Contra Costa County and remained a short time, returning to the mines. In the following year he returned to Contra Costa County, purchasing the ranch of three hundred and ninety acres in Tassajara, where he resided the remainder of his days.

On February 23, 1860, Felix Coats married Miss Lavina Doggett, of Tassajara. Three sons and three daughters survive their father. They are W. Nolan Coats, of St. Helena; James L. Coats, internal revenue inspector, of Stockton; Bethel S. Coats, of San Jose; Mrs. Ella Seiler and Mrs. Jennie White, of San Francisco; and Mrs. Mary Horton, of Tassajara.

CHAPTER V. THE BEAR FLAG WAR

In the early part of the last century California would appear to have found extreme favor in the jealous eyes of three great powers. We have elsewhere shown what the Russians did on the coast, and how they actually gained a foothold at Bodega and Fort Ross, Sonoma County.

In the year 1818 Governor Sola received a communication from Friar Marquinez, of Guadalajara, Spain, wherein he informed his excellency of the rumors of war between the United States and Spain, while in February of the following year Father Jose Sanchez wrote to the same official that there is a report abroad of the fitting out of an American expedition into New Mexico. Both of these epistles remark that California is the coveted prize. Great Britain wanted it, it is said, for several reasons, the chief of which was that in the possession of so extended a coast-line she would have the finest harbors in the world for her fleets. This desire would appear to have been still manifested in 1840, for we find in February of that year, in the New York Express, the following: "The rumor has reached New Orleans from Mexico of the cession to England of the Californias. The cession of the two provinces would give to Great Britain an extensive and valuable territory in a part of the world where she has long been anxious to gain a foothold, besides securing an object still more desirable—a spacious range of seacoast on the Pacific, stretching more than eight thousand miles from the forty-second degree of latitude south, sweeping the peninsula of California, and embracing the harbors of that gulf, the finest in North America."

These rumors, so rife between the years of 1842 and 1846, necessitated the maintenance of a large and powerful fleet by both Americans and British on the Pacific Ocean, each closely observing the other. The first move in the deep game on the part of the United States was in September, 1842, by Commodore Ap Catesby Jones. He became possessed of two newspapers which appear to have caused him to take immediate action. One of these, published in New Orleans, stated that California had been ceded by Mexico to Great Britain in consideration of the sum of seven millions of dollars; the other, a Mexican publication, caused him to believe that war had been declared between the two countries. The sudden departure of two of the British vessels strengthened him in this belief, and that they were en route for Panama to embark soldiers from the West Indies for the occupation of California.

To forestall this move of "perfidious Albion," Commodore Jones left Callao, Peru, on September 7, 1842, crowding all sail, ostensibly for the port of Monterey, but when two days out his squadron hove to, a council of the captains of the flag-ship "Cyane" and the "Dale" was held, when the decision was come to that possession should be taken of California at all hazards, and abide by the consequences, whatever they might be. The accompanying letter from an officer of the "Dale," dated at Panama September 23, 1842, tells its own story: "We sailed from Callao on the 7th of September, in company with the 'United States' and 'Cyane' sloop, but on the tenth day out, the 17th, separated, and bore up for this port. Just previous to our departure, two British ships-of-war, the razee 'Dublin,' fifty guns, and the sloopof-war 'Champion,' eighteen guns, sailed thence on secret service. This mysterious movement of Admiral Thomas elicited a hundred comments and conjectures as to his destination, the most probable of which seemed to be that he was bound for the northwest coast of Mexico, where it is surmised that a British settlement (station) is to be located in accordance with a secret convention between the Mexican and English governments, and it is among the on dits in the squadron that the frigate 'United States,' 'Cyane,' and 'Dale' are to rendezvous as soon as possible at Monterey, to keep an eye on John Bull's movements in that quarter."

These rumors were all strengthened by the fact that eight hundred troops had been embarked at Mazatlan in February, 1842, by General Micheltorena, to assist the English, it was apprehended, to carry out the secret treaty whereby California was to be handed over to Great Britain. Of these troops, who were mostly convicts, Micheltorena lost a great number by desertion, and, after much delay and vexation, marched out of Mazatlan on July 25, 1842, with only four hundred and fifty men, arriving at San Diego on August 25th. Between Los Angeles and Santa Barbara, with his army reduced from desertion to but three hundred men, at 11 o'clock on the night of October 24th, he received the astounding intelligence that Commodore Jones had entered the port of Monterey, with the frigate "United States" and the corvette "Cyane," landed an armed force, hauled down the Mexican flag, hoisted the American in its place, and issued a proclamation declaring California to be henceforth belonging to the United States. These startling occurrences took place on October 19, 1842. On the 28th the Commodore reflected on his latest achievement, and becoming convinced that an error had been committed, he lowered the American ensign, replaced it with that of Mexico, and on the following day saluted it, sailed for Mazatlan, and reported his proceedings to Washington.

On hearing of the capture of Monterey the Mexican general withdrew to the mission of San Fernando, and there remained for some time, where he finally, on the horizon being cleared, transferred his staff to Los Angeles, and there entertained Commodore Jones on January 19,1843.

The recall of Jones was demanded by the Mexican minister at Washington, which was complied with, and Captain Alexander J. Dallas instructed to relieve him of the command of the Pacific squadron. Dallas at once proceeded to Callao via Panama, to assume his new functions, and on arrival took the "Erie," an old store-ship, and proceeded in search of the Commodore, who had in the meantime received intelligence of the turn affairs had taken, kept steering from port to port, and finally, after touching at Valparaiso, Chile, he sailed for home around Cape Horn. The reign of Captain Dallas was short; he died on board the frigate "Savannah," at Callao, June 3, 1844, and was succeeded by Commodore John Drake Sloat.

Between the years 1844 and 1846 the American and British fleets keenly watched each other and anxiously awaited the declaration of war between Mexico and the United States. During this time the revolution which drove General Micheltorena and his army from California had broken out and been quelled, while the Oregon boundary and the annexation of Texas were questions which kept the naval authorities at fever heat.

Let us now leave these American and British sailors with their mighty ships jealously watching the movements of each other, to consider the doings of one who before long was to take a prominent part in the affairs of California.

In the month of March, 1845, Brevet-Captain John Charles Fremont departed from Washington for the purpose of organizing a third expedition for the topographical survey of Oregon and California, having finished which, he left Bent's Fort on or about the 16th of April, his command consisting of sixty-two men, six of whom were Delaware Indians. It is not our wish here, nor indeed have we the space, to tell of the hardships endured and the perilous journeys made by Fremont, Kit Carson, Theodore Talbot, and others of that band, whose wanderings have formed the theme of many a ravishing tale; our duty will permit only of defining the part taken by them in regard to our special subject.

About June 1, 1846, General Jose Castro, with Lieutenant Francisco de Arci, his secretary, left the Santa Clara Mission, where they had ensconced themselves after pursuing Fremont from that district, and, passing through Yerba Buena (San Francisco), crossed the bay to the mission of San Rafael, and there collected a number of horses, which he directed Arci to take to Sonoma, with as many more as he could capture on the way, and from there proceed with all haste to the Santa Clara Mission by way of Knight's Landing and Sutter's Fort. These horses were intended to be used against Fremont and Governor Pio Pico by Castro, both of whom had defied his authority. On June 5th Castro moved from Santa Clara to Monterey, and on the 12th, while on his return, was met by a courier bearing the intelligence that Lieutenant Arci had been surprised and taken prisoner on the 10th by a band of adventurers, who had seized a large number of the horses which he had in charge for the headquarters at Santa Clara. Here was a dilemma. Castro's education in writing had been sadly neglected—it is said he could only paint his signature—and being without his amanuensis, he at once returned to Monterey, and on June 12th dictated a letter through ex-Governor Juan B. Alvarado to the prefect, Manuel Castro, saying that the time had come when their differences should be laid aside and conjoint action taken for the defense and protection of their common country, at the same time asking that he should collect all the men and horses possible and send them to Santa Clara. He then returned to his headquarters, and on the 17th promulgated a soul-stirring proclamation to the settlers.

When Lieutenant Arci left Sonoma with the caballada of horses and mares, crossing the dividing ridge, he passed up the Sacramento Valley to Knight's Landing, on the left bank of the Sacramento River, about fifteen miles north of the present city of Sacramento. When Lieutenant Arci reached the ferry, or crossing, he met Mrs. Knight, to whom, on account of her being a New Mexican by birth, and therefore thought to be trustworthy, he confided the secret of the expedition. Such knowledge was too much for an ordinary feminine bosom to contain. She told her husband, and he, in assisting the officer to cross with his horses, gave him fair words, so that suspicion might be lulled, and then, striding his fleetest horse, made direct for Captain Fremont's camp at the confluence of the Feather and Yuba rivers, where he arrived early in the morning of June 9th. Here Knight, who found some twenty settlers that had arrived earlier than he discussing matters, communicated to Captain Fremont and the settlers that Lieutenant Arci had the evening before crossed at his landing, bound to Santa Clara via the Cosumne River; that Arci had told Mrs. Knight in confidence that the animals were intended to be used by Castro in expelling the American settlers from the country; and that it was also the intention to fortify the Bear River Pass above the rancho of William Johnson, thereby putting a stop to all immigration, a move of Castro's that was strengthened by the return to Sutter's Fort on June 7th of a force that had gone out to chastise the Mokelumne Indians, who had been threatening to burn the settlers' crops, incited thereto, presumably, by Castro.

Fremont, while encamped at The Buttes, was visited by nearly all the settlers, and from them gleaned vast stores of fresh information hitherto unknown to him. This information was to the effect that the greater proportion of foreigners in the country had become Mexican citizens, and married native women for the sake of procuring land, and through them had become possessed of deep secrets supposed to be known only to the prominent Californians. It was also reported that a convention had been held at the San Juan Mission to decide which of the two nations, America or Great Britain, should guarantee protection to California against all others for certain privileges and considerations.

Lieutenant Revere says: "I have been favored by an intelligent member of the Junta with the following authentic report of the substance of Pico's speech to that illustrious body of statesmen: "'Excellent Sirs: To what a deplorable condition is our country reduced! Mexico, professing to be our mother and our protectress, has given us neither arms nor money, nor the material of war for our defense. She is not likely to do anything in our behalf, although she is quite willing to afflict us with her extortionate minions, who come hither in the guise of soldiers and civil officers, to harass and oppress our people. We possess a glorious country, capable of attaining a physical and moral greatness corresponding with the grandeur and beauty which an Almighty hand has stamped on the face of our beloved California. But, although nature has been prodigal, it cannot be denied that we are not in a position to avail ourselves of her bounties. Our population is not large, and it is sparsely scattered over valley and mountain, covering an immense area of virgin soil, destitute of roads, and traversed with difficulty; hence it is hardly possible to collect an army of any considerable force. Our people are poor, as well as few, and cannot well govern themselves and maintain a decent show of sovereign power. Although we live in the midst of plenty, we lay up nothing, but tilling the earth in an imperfect manner, all our time is required to provide subsistence for ourselves and our families. Thus circumstanced, we find ourselves suddenly threatened by hordes of Yankee emigrants, who have already begun to flock into our country, and whose progress we cannot arrest. Already have the wagons of that perfidious people scaled the almost inaccessible summits of the Sierra Nevada, crossed the entire continent and penetrated the fruitful valley of the Sacramento. What that astounding people will next undertake I cannot say, but in whatever enterprise they will be sure to prove successful. Already are these adventurous land voyagers spreading themselves far and wide over a country which seems suited to their tastes.

They are cultivating farms, establishing vineyards, erecting mills, sawing up lumber, building workshops, and doing a thousand other things which seem natural to them, but which Californians despise. What, then, are we to do? Shall we remain supine while these daring strangers are overrunning our fertile plains and gradually outnumbering and displacing us? Shall these incursions go on unchecked, until we shall become strangers in our own land? We cannot successfully oppose them by our own unaided power, and the swelling tide of immigration renders the odds against us more formidable every day. We cannot stand alone against them, nor can we creditably maintain our independence even against Mexico; but there is something we can do which will elevate our country, strengthen her at all points, and yet enable us to preserve our identity and remain masters of our own soil. Perhaps what I am about to suggest may seem to some faint-hearted and dishonorable, but to me it does not seem so. It is the last hope of a feeble people, struggling against a tyrannical government which claims their submission at home, and threatened by bands of avaricious strangers from without, voluntarily to connect themselves with a power able and willing to defend and preserve them. It is the right and the duty of the weak to demand support from the strong, provided the demand be made upon terms just to both parties. I see no dishonor in this last refuge of the oppressed and powerless, and I boldly avow that such is the step that I would have California take. There are two great powers in Europe which seem destined to divide between them the unappropriated countries of the world. They have large fleets and armies not unpracticed in the art of war. Is it not better to connect ourselves with one of those powerful nations than to struggle on without hope, as we are doing now? Is it not better that one of them should be invited to send a fleet and an army, to defend and protect California, rather than we should fall an easy prey to the lawless adventurers who are overrunning our beautiful country? I pronounce for annexation to France or England, and the people of California will never regret having taken my advice. They will no longer be subjected to the trouble and grievous expense of governing themselves; and their beef and their grain, which they produce in such abundance, would find a ready market among the newcomers. But, I hear someone say: "No monarchy"! But is not monarchy better than anarchy? Is not existence in some shape better than annihilation. No monarch! And what is there so terrible in a monarchy? Have we not all lived under a monarchy far more despotic than that of France or England, and were not our people happy under it? Have not the leading men among our agriculturists been bred beneath the royal rule of Spain, and have they been happier since the mock Republic of Mexico has supplied its place? Nay, does not every man abhor the miserable abortion christened the Republic of Mexico, and look back with regret to the golden days of the Spanish monarchy? Let us restore that glorious era. Then may our people go quietly to their ranchos, and live there as of yore, leading a thoughtless and merry life, untroubled by politics or cares of state, sure of what is their own, and safe from the incursions of the Yankees, who would soon be forced to retreat to their own country.'"

It was a happy thing for California, and, as the sequel proved, for the views of the Government of the United States, that a man was found at this juncture whose ideals were more enlightened and consonant with the times than those of the rulers of his country, both civil and military. Patriotism was half his soul; he therefore could not silently witness the land of his birth sold to any monarchy, however old; and he rightly judged that, although foreign protection might postpone, it could not avert that assumption of power which was beginning to make itself felt. Possessed at the time of no political power, and having had few early advantages, still his position was so exalted and his character so highly respected by both the foreign and native population, that he had been invited to participate in the deliberations of the Junta. This man was Don Mariano Guadalupe Vallejo. Born in California, he commenced his career in the army as an *alferez*, or ensign, and in this humble grade he volunteered, at the suggestion of the Mexican Government, with a command of fifty soldiers, to establish a colony on the north side of the Bay of San Francisco, for the protection of the frontier. He effectually subdued the hostile Indians inhabiting that then remote region, and laid the foundation of a reputation for integrity, judgment, and ability unequaled by any of his countrymen. Although quite a young man, he had already filled the highest offices in the province and had at this time retired to private life near his estate in the vicinity of the town of Sonoma. He did not hesitate to oppose with all his strength the views advanced by Pico and Castro.

He spoke nearly as follows: "I cannot, gentlemen, coincide in opinion with the military and civil functionaries who have advocated the cession of our country to France or England. It is most true that to rely any longer on Mexico to govern and defend us would be idle and absurd. To this extent I fully agree with my distinguished colleagues. It is also true that we possess a noble country, every way calculated from position and resources to become great and powerful. For that very reason I would not have her a mere dependency upon a foreign monarchy, naturally alien, or at least indifferent, to our interests and our welfare. It is not to be denied that feeble nations have in former times thrown themselves upon the protection of their powerful neighbors. The Britons invoked the aid of the warlike Saxons, and fell an easy prey to their protectors, who seized their lands and treated them like slaves. Long before that time feeble and distracted provinces had appealed for aid to the all-conquering arms of imperial Rome, and they were at the same time protected and subjugated by their grasping ally. Even could we tolerate the idea of dependence, ought we to go to distant Europe for a master? What possible sympathy could exist between us and a nation separated from us by two vast oceans? But waiving this insuperable objection, how could we endure to come under the domination of a monarchy? For, although others speak lightly of a form of government, as a freeman I cannot do so. We are republicans—badly governed and badly situated as we are, still we are all, in sentiment, republicans. So far as we are governed at all, we at least profess to be self-governed. Who, then, that possesses true patriotism will consent to subject himself and his children to the caprices of a foreign king and his official minions? But, it is asked, if we do not throw ourselves upon the protection of France or England, what shall we do? I do not come here to support the existing order of things, but I come prepared to propose instant and effective action to extricate our country from her present forlorn condition. My opinion is made up that we must persevere in throwing off the galling yoke of Mexico and proclaim our independence of her forever. We have endured her official cormorants arid her villainous soldiery until we can endure no longer. All will probably agree with me that we ought at once to rid ourselves of what remains of Mexican domination. But some profess to doubt our ability to maintain our position. To my mind there comes no doubt. Look at Texas and see how long she withstood the power of united Mexico. The resources of Texas are not to be compared with ours, and she was so much nearer to her enemy than we are. Our position is so remote, either by land or sea, that we are in no danger from Mexican invasion. Why, then, should we hesitate still to assert our independence? We have indeed taken the first step, by electing our own governor, but another remains to be taken. I will mention it plainly and distinctly—it is annexation to the United States. In contemplating this consummation of our destiny, I feel nothing but pleasure, and I ask you to share it. Discard old prejudices, disregard old customs, and prepare for the glorious change which awaits our country. Why should we shrink from incorporating ourselves with the happiest, freest nation in the world, destined soon to be the most wealthy and powerful? Why should we go abroad for protection when this great nation is our adjoining neighbor? When we join our fortunes to hers, we shall not become subjects but fellow-citizens, possessing all the rights of the people of the United States, and choosing our own federal and local rulers. We shall have a stable government and just laws. California will grow strong and flourish, and her people will be prosperous, happy, and free. Look not therefore with jealousy upon the hardy pioneers who scale our mountains and cultivate our unoccupied plains, but rather welcome them as brothers who come to share with us a common destiny."

Such was the extent of General Vallejo's observations. Those who listened to him, however, were far behind in general knowledge and intelligence. His arguments failed to carry conviction to the greater number of his auditors. But the bold position taken by him was the cause of an immediate adjournment of the Junta, no result having been arrived at concerning the weighty affairs on which they had met to deliberate. On his retiring from the Junta he embodied the views he had expressed in a letter to Don Pio Pico and reiterated his refusal to participate in any action having for its end the adoption of any protection other than that of the United States. In this communication he also declared that he would never serve under any government which was prepared to surrender California to a European power. He then returned to his estates, there to await the issue of events.

We left William Knight at Fremont's camp, where he had arrived on the morning of June 9, 1846, imparting to that officer and the twenty settlers who had there assembled information of Castro's intended attack. At ten o'clock that morning a party of eleven men, under the oldest member, Ezekiel Merritt, started in pursuit of Lieutenant Arci and his horses. On their arrival at Hock farm they were joined by two more, and toward evening, having crossed the American River at Sinclair's, reached the rancho of Allen Montgomery, sixty miles from Fremont's camp at the Buttes, and there supped. Here they received intelligence that Lieutenant Arci had reached Sutter's Fort on the 8th, and had that morning resumed his march, intending to camp that night at the rancho of Martin Murphy, twenty miles south of the Cosumne River. Supper finished and a short rest indulged in, the party were once more in the saddle, being strengthened by the addition of Montgomery and another man, making the total force fifteen. They proceeded to within about five miles of Murphy's, and there lay concealed until daylight, when they were again on the move, and continued to within half a mile of the camp. Unperceived, they cautiously advanced to within a short distance, and then suddenly charging, secured the lieutenant and his party, as well as the horses. Lieutenant Arci was permitted to retain his sword, each of his party was given a horse wherewith to reach Santa Clara, and a person traveling with him was permitted to take six of the animals which he claimed as private property.

The lieutenant was then instructed to depart and say to his chief, General Castro, that the remainder of the horses were at his disposal whenever he should wish to come and take them. The Americans at once returned to Montgomery's with the horses, and there breakfasted; that night, the 10th, they encamped twenty-seven miles above Sutter's Fort on the rancho of Nicholas Allgier, a German, not far from the mouth of Bear River, and in the morning, ascertaining that Fremont had moved his camp hither from the Buttes, they joined him in the morning of the 11th, having traveled about one hundred and fifty miles in forty-eight hours.

On arriving at Fremont's camp it was found that the garrison had been considerably augmented by the arrival of more settlers, who were all ardently discussing the events of the last two days and its probable results. After a full hearing it was determined by them that, having gone so far, their only chance of safety was in a rapid march to the town of Sonoma to effect its capture, and to accomplish this before the news of the stoppage of Lieutenant Arci and his horses could have time to reach that garrison. It was felt that should this design prove successful all further obstacles to the eventual capture of the country would have vanished. The daring band then reorganized, still retaining, in his position of captain, Ezekiel Merritt. At three o'clock in the afternoon of June 12th, under their leader, they left Fremont's camp for Sonoma, one hundred and twenty miles distant, and, traveling all night, passed the rancho of William Gordon, about ten miles from the present town of Woodland, Yolo County, who they desired to inform all Americans that could be trusted of their intention. At nine o'clock in the morning of the 13th they reached Captain John Grigsby's, at the head of Napa Valley, and were joined by William L. Todd, William Scott, and others. Here the company, which now mustered thirty-three men, was reorganized and addressed by Dr. Robert Semple. Not desiring, however, to reach Sonoma until daylight, they halted here till midnight, when they once more resumed their march, and before it was yet the dawn of June 14th, surprised and captured the garrison of Sonoma, consisting of six soldiers, nine pieces of artillery, and some small arms, etc., "all private property being religiously respected; and in generations to come their children's children may look back with pride and pleasure upon the commencement of a revolution which was carried on by their fathers' fathers upon principles as high and holy as the laws of eternal justice."

Their distinguished prisoners were General Mariano Guadalupe Vallejo, Lieutenant-Colonel Victor Prudon, Captain Don Salvador Mundo Vallejo, brother to General Vallejo, and Mr. Jacob Primer Leese, brother-in-law to General Vallejo.

We now lay before the reader the account of this episode, as described by General Vallejo at the centennial exercises held at Santa Rosa, Sonoma County, July 4, 1876: "I have now to say something of the epoch which inaugurated a new era for this country. A little before dawn on June 14, 1846, a party of hunters and trappers, with some foreign settlers, under command of Captain Merritt, Doctor Semple, and William B. Ide, surrounded my residence at Sonoma, and without firing a shot made prisoners of myself, then commander of the northern frontier, of Lieutenant-Colonel Victor Prudon, Captain Salvador Vallejo, and Jacob P. Leese. I should here state that down to October, 1845, I had maintained at my own expense a respectable garrison at Sonoma, which often, in union with the settlers, did good service in campaigns against the Indians; but at last, tired of spending money which the Mexican Government never refunded, I disbanded the force, and most of the soldiers who had constituted it left Sonoma. Thus in June, 1846, the plaza was entirely unprotected, although there were ten pieces of artillery, with other arms and munitions of war. The parties who unfurled the Bear Flag were well aware that Sonoma was without defense and lost no time in taking advantage of this fact and carrying out their plans. Years before, I had urgently represented to the government of Mexico the necessity of stationing a sufficient force on the frontier, else Sonoma would be lost, which would be equivalent to leaving the rest of the country an easy prey to the invader. What think you, my friends, were the instructions sent me in reply to my repeated demands for means to fortify the country?

These instructions were that I should at once force the immigrants to recross the Sierra Nevada and depart from the territory of the republic. To say nothing of the inhumanity of these orders, their execution was physically impossible—first, because the immigrants came in autumn, when snow covered the Sierra so quickly as to make a return impracticable. Under the circumstances, not only 1, but Comandante General Castro, resolved to provide the immigrants with letters of security, that they might remain temporarily in the country. We always made a show of authority, but well convinced all the time that we had no power to resist the invasion which was coming upon us. With the frankness of a soldier, I can assure you that the American immigrants never had cause to complain of the treatment they received at the hands of either authorities or citizens. They carried us as prisoners to Sacramento and kept us in a calaboose for sixty days or more, until the authority of the United States made itself respected, and the honorable and humane Commodore Stockton returned us to our hearths."

On the seizure of their prisoners the revolutionists at once took steps to appoint a captain, who was found in the person of John Grigsby, for Ezekiel Merritt did not wish to retain the permanent command. A meeting was then called at the barracks, situated at the northeast corner of the plaza, under the presidency of William B. Ide, Doctor Semple being secretary. At this conference Semple urged the independence of the country, stating that having once commenced they must proceed, for to turn back was certain death. Before the dissolution of the convention, however, rumors were rife that secret emissaries were being dispatched to the Mexican rancheros to inform them of the recent occurrences; therefore, to prevent any attempt at a rescue, it was deemed best to transfer their prisoners to Sutter's Fort, where the danger of such would be less.

Before transferring their prisoners, however, a treaty, or agreement, was entered into between the captives and the captors, which will appear in the annexed documents kindly furnished to us by General Vallejo, and which have never before been given to the public. The first is in English, signed by the principal actors in the revolution, and reads: "We, the undersigned, having resolved to establish a government upon republican principles, in connection with others of our fellow-citizens, and having taken up arms to support it, we have taken three Mexican officers as prisoners, M. G. Vallejo, Lieut. Col. Victor Prudon, and Captain D. Salvador Vallejo; having formed and published to the world no regular plan of government, feel it our duty to say that it is not our intention to take or injure any person who is not found in opposition to the cause, nor will we take or destroy the property of private individuals further than is necessary for our immediate support.

"EZEKIEL MERRITT,
"R. Semple,
"William Fallon,
"Samuel Kelsey."

The second, in the Spanish language, reads as follows: "Conste pr. la preste. qe. habiendo sido sorprendido pr. una numeros a fuerza armada qe. me tomo prisionero y a los gefes y oficiales qe. estaban de guarnicion en esta plaza de la qe. se apodero la espresada fuerza, habiendola encontrado absolutamte. indefensa, tanto yo. como los S. S. oficiales qe. suscribero comprometemos nuestra palabra de honor de qe. estando bajo las garantias de prisionero de guerra, no tomaremos las armas ni a favor ni contra repetida fuerza armada de quien hemos recibiro la intimacion del momto. y un escrito firmado qe. garantiza nuestras vidas, familias de intereses, y los de todo el vecindario de esta jurisdn. mientras no hagamos oposicion. Sonoma, Junio 14 de 1846.

"VcR Prudon   M G Vallejo,
"Salvador Vallejo."

But let us proceed with our narrative of the removal of General Vallejo, his brother, and Prudon to Sutter's Fort. A guard, consisting of William B. Ide, as captain, Captain Grigsby, Captain Merritt, Kit Carson, William Hargrave, and five others left Sonoma for Sutter's Fort with their prisoners upon horses actually supplied by General Vallejo himself. We are told that on the first night after leaving Sonoma with their prisoners the revolutionists, with singular inconsistency, encamped and went to sleep without setting sentinel or guard; that during the night they were surrounded by a party under command of Juan de Padilla, who crept up stealthily and awoke one of the prisoners, telling him that there was with him close at hand a strong, well-armed force of rancheros, who, if need be, could surprise and slay the Americans before there was time for them to fly to arms, but that he (Padilla) before giving such instructions, awaited the orders of General Vallejo, whose rank entitled him to the command of any such demonstration.

The general was cautiously aroused and the scheme divulged to him, but with a self-sacrifice which cannot be too highly commended answered that he should go voluntarily with his guardians, that he anticipated a speedy and satisfactory settlement of the whole matter, advised Padilla to return to his rancho and disperse his band, and positively refused to permit any violence to the guard, as he was convinced that such would lead to disastrous consequences, and probably involve the rancheros and their families in ruin without accomplishing any good result. Lieutenant Revere says of this episode: "This was not told to me by Vallejo, but by a person who was present, and it tallies well with the account given by the revolutionists themselves, several of whom informed me that no guard was kept by them that night, and that the prisoners might have easily escaped had they felt so inclined. The same person also told me that when Vallejo was called out of bed and made a prisoner in his own house, he requested to be informed as to the plans and objects of the revolutionists, signifying his readiness to collect and take command of a force of his countrymen in the cause of independence."

Having traveled about two-thirds of the way from Sutter's Fort, Captain Merritt and Kit Carson rode on ahead with the news of the capture of Sonoma, desiring that arrangements be made for the reception of the prisoners. They entered the fort early in the morning of June 16th. That evening the rest of the party, with their prisoners, came and were handed over to the safe-keeping of Captain Sutter, who, it is said, was severely censured by Captain Fremont for his indulgence to them.

Mr. Thomas C. Lancey, the author of several interesting letters on this subject that appeared in The Pioneer during the year 1878, remarks: "There have been so many questions raised during this year (1878) in relation to the date of the hoisting of the 'Bear Flag,' who made it, and what material it was manufactured from, as well as the date of the capture of Sonoma and the number of men who marched that morning, that I shall give the statements of several who are entitled to a hearing, as they were actors in that drama.

"The writer of this (Mr. Lancey) was here in 1846, and served during the war, and has never left the country since, but was not one of those who were found to be able to form a correct opinion as to the correctness of these dates. Doctor Robert Semple, who was one of that party from the first, says in his diary that they entered Sonoma at early dawn on the 14th of June, 1846, thirty-three men, rank and file. William B. Ide, who was chosen their commander, says in his diary the same. Captain Henry L. Ford, another of this number, says, or rather his historian, S. H. W., of Santa Cruz, whom I take to be the Rev. S.

H. Willey, makes him say, that they captured Sonoma on the 12th of June, with thirty-three men. Lieutenant William Baldridge, one of the party, makes the date the 14th of June, and the number of men twenty-three. Lieutenant Joseph Warren Revere, of the United States ship 'Portsmouth,' who hauled down the 'Bear Flag' and hoisted the American flag on the 9th of July, and at a later date commanded the garrison, says the place was captured on the 14th of June."

To this list is now added the documentary evidence produced above, fixing the date of capture of General Vallejo and his officers, and therefore the taking of Sonoma, as June 14, 1846.

On the seizure of the citadel of Sonoma, the Independents found floating from the flagstaff-head the flag of Mexico, a fact which had escaped notice during the bustle of the morning. It was at once lowered, and they set to work to devise a banner which they should claim as their own. They were as one on the subject of there being a star on the groundwork, but they taxed their ingenuity to have some other device, for the "lone star" had been already appropriated by Texas.

So many accounts of the manufacture of this insignia have been published that we give the reader those quoted by the writer in The Pioneer: "A piece of cotton cloth," says Mr. Lancy, "was obtained, and a man by the name of Todd proceeded to paint from a pot of red paint a star in the corner. Before he was finished, Henry L. Ford, one of the party, proposes to paint on the center, facing the star, a grizzly bear.

This was unanimously agreed to, and the grizzly bear was painted accordingly. When it was done, the flag was taken to the flagstaff, and hoisted amid the hurrahs of the little party, who swore to defend it with their lives."

Of this matter Lieutenant Revere says: "A flag was also hoisted bearing a grizzly bear rampant, with one stripe below, and the words 'Republic of California' above the bear, and a single star in the Union."

This is the evidence of the officer who hauled down the Bear Flag and replaced it with the Stars and Stripes on July 9, 1846.

The Western Shore Gazetteer has the following version: "On the 14th of June, 1846, this little handful of men proclaimed California a free and independent republic, and on that day hoisted their flag, known as the 'Bear Flag'; this consisted of a strip of worn-out cotton domestic, furnished by Mrs. Kelley, bordered with red flannel, furnished by Mrs.

John Sears, who had fled from some distant part to Sonoma for safety upon hearing that war had been thus commenced. In the center of the flag was a representation of a bear en passant, painted with Venetian red, and in one corner was painted a star of the same color. Under the bear were inscribed the words 'Republic of California,' put on with common writing-ink. This flag is preserved by the

California Pioneer Association, and may be seen at their rooms in San Francisco. It was designed and executed by W. L. Todd."

The Sonoma Democrat, under the caption "A true history of the Bear Flag," tells its story: "The rest of the revolutionary party remained in possession of the town. Among them were three young men, Todd, Benjamin Duell, and Thomas Cowie. A few days after the capture, in a casual conversation between these young men, the matter of a flag came up. They had no authority to raise the American flag, and they determined to make one. Their general idea was to imitate, without following too closely, their national ensign. Mrs. W. B. Elliott had been brought to the town of Sonoma by her husband from his ranch on the Mark West Creek, for safety. The old Elliott cabin may be seen to this day on Mark West Creek, about a mile above the springs. From Mrs. Elliott, Ben Duell got a piece of new red flannel, some white domestic, needles and thread. A piece of blue drilling was obtained elsewhere.

From this material, without consulting with anyone else, these three young men made the Bear Flag. Cowie had been a saddler. Duell had also served a short time at the same trade. To form the flag Duell and Cowie sewed together alternate strips of red, white, and blue. Todd drew in the upper corner a star and painted on the lower a rude picture of a grizzly bear, which was not standing, as has been sometimes represented, but was drawn with head down. The bear was afterward adopted as the design of the great seal of the State of California. On the original flag it was so rudely executed that two of those who saw it raised have told us that it looked more like a hog than a bear. Be that as it may, its meaning was plain—that the revolutionary party would, if necessary, fight their way through at all hazards. In the language of our informant, it meant that there was no back out; they intended to fight it out. There were no halyards on the flagstaff which stood in front of the barracks. It was again reared, and the flag, which was soon to be replaced by that of the republic, for the first time floated on the breeze."

Besides the above-quoted authorities, John S. Hittell, historian of the Society of California Pioneers, San Francisco, and H. H. Bancroft, the Pacific Coast historian, affixed the dates of the raising of the Bear Flag as June 12th and June 15th, respectively. William Winter, secretary of the Association of Territorial Pioneers of California, and Mr. Lancey questioned the correctness of these dates and entered into correspondence with all the men known to be alive who were of that party and others who were likely to throw any light on the subject.

Among many answers received, we quote the following portion of a letter from James G. Bleak:

"St. George, Utah, 16th of April, 1878.

"To William Winter, Esq.,

"Secretary Association of Territorial Pioneers of California.

"Dear Sir: Your communication of 3rd instant is placed in my hands by the widow of a departed friend, James M. Ide, son of William B., as I have at present in my charge some of his papers. In reply to your question asking for the 'correct date' of raising the 'Bear Flag' at Sonoma, in 1846, I will quote from the writing of William B. Ide, deceased: 'The said Bear Flag [was] made of plane [plain] cotton cloth, and ornamented with the red flannel of a shirt from the back of one of the men, and christened by the 'California Republic' in red paint letters on both sides; [it] was raised upon the standard where had floated on the breeze the Mexican flag aforetime; it was the 14th of June, '46.

Our whole number was twenty-four all told. The mechanism of the flag was performed by William L. Todd, of Illinois. The Grizzly Bear was chosen as an emblem of strength and unyielding resistance.'"

The following testimony, conveyed to the Los Angeles Express from the artist of the flag, we now produce as possibly the best that can be found: "Los Angeles, January 11, 1878.

"Your letter of the 9th inst. came duly to hand, and in answer I have to say in regard to the making of the original bear flag of California, at Sonoma, in 1846, that when the Americans, who had taken up arms against the Spanish regime, had determined what kind of a flag should be adopted, the following persons performed the work: Granville P. Swift, Peter Storm, Henry L. Ford, and myself; we procured, in the house where we made our headquarters, a piece of new unbleached cotton domestic, not quite a yard wide, with stripes of red flannel about four inches wide, furnished by Mrs. John Sears, on the lower side of the canvas. On the upper left-hand corner was a star, and in the center was the image made to represent a grizzly bear passant, so common in this country at the time. The bear and star were painted with paint made of linseed oil and Venetian red or Spanish brown. Underneath the bear were the words 'California Republic.' The other persons engaged with me got the materials together, while I acted as artist. The forms of the bear and star and the letters were first outlined with pen and ink by myself, and the two forms were filled in with the red paint, but the letters with ink. The flag mentioned by Mr. Hittell, with the bear rampant, was made, as I always understood, at Santa Barbara, and was painted black. Allow me to say, that at that time there was not a wheelwright shop in California. The flag I painted I saw in the rooms of the California Pioneers in San Francisco, in 1870, and the Secretary will show it to any person who will call on him at any time. If it is the one I painted, it will be known by a mistake in tinting out the words 'California Republic.' The letters were first lined out with a pen, and I left out the letter T and lined out the letter 'C in its place. But afterwards I lined out the letter T over the 'C, so that the last syllable of 'Republic' looks as if the two last letters were blended.

"Yours respectfully, "Wm. L. Todd."

The San Francisco Evening Post of April 20, 1874, has the following: "General Sherman has just forwarded to the Society of California Pioneers the guidon which the Bear Company bore at the time of the conquest of California. The relic is of white silk, with a two-inch-wide red stripe at the bottom, and a bear in the center, over which is the inscription: 'Republic of California.' It is accompanied by the following letter from the donor: "'Society of California Pioneers, San Francisco, California,— "'Gentlemen: At the suggestion of General Sherman, I beg leave to send to your society herewith a guidon, formerly belonging to the Sonoma troop of the California battalion of 1846, for preservation. This guidon I found among the effects of that troop when I hauled down the bear flag and substituted the flag of the United States at Sonoma, on the 9th of July, 1846, and have preserved it ever since.

"'Very respectfully, etc.,

"'Jos. W. Revere, Brigadier-General.

" 'Morristown, N. J., February 20, 1874.'"

The garrison being now in possession, it was necessary to elect officers; therefore, Henry L. Ford was elected first lieutenant, Granville P. Swift first sergeant, and Samuel Gibson second sergeant. Sentries were posted, and a system of military routine inaugurated. In the forenoon, while on parade, Lieutenant Ford addressed the company in these words: "My countrymen: We have taken upon ourselves a very responsible duty. We have entered into a war with the Mexican nation.

We are bound to defend each other or be shot. There is no halfway place about it. To defend ourselves we must have discipline. Each of you has had a voice in choosing your officers. Now they are chosen, they must be obeyed." To which the entire band responded that the authority of the officers should be supported. The words of William B. Ide, in continuation of the letter quoted above, throw further light upon the machinery of the civil-military force: "The men were divided into two companies of ten each. The First Artillery were busily engaged in putting the cannons in order, which were charged doubly with grape and canister. The First Rifle Company were busied in cleaning, repairing, and loading the small arms. The commander, after setting a guard and posting a sentinel on one of the highest buildings, to watch the approach of any persons who might feel a curiosity to inspect our operations, directed his leisure to the establishment of some system of finance, whereby all the defenders' families might be brought within the lines of our garrison and supported. Ten thousand pounds of flour were purchased on the credit of the Government, and deposited with the garrison; and an account was opened, on terms agreed upon, for a supply of beef and a few barrels of salt constituted our main supplies.

Whisky was contrabanded altogether. After the first round of duties was performed, as many as could be spared off guard were called together, and our situation fully explained to the men by the commanders of the garrison.

"It was fully represented that our success—nay, our very life—depended on the magnanimity and justice of our course of conduct, coupled with sleepless vigilance and care. (But ere this we had gathered as many of the surrounding citizens as possible and placed them out of harm's way between four strong walls. They were more than twice our number.) The commander chose from these strangers the most intelligent, and by the use of an interpreter went on to explain the cause of our coming together; our determination to offer equal protection and equal justice to all good and virtuous citizens; and we had not called them there to rob them of any portion of their property or to disturb them in their social relations with one another; nor yet to desecrate their religion."

As will be learned from the foregoing, the number of those who were under the protection of the Bear Flag within Sonoma had been considerably increased. A messenger had been dispatched to San Francisco to inform Captain Montgomery, of the United States ship "Portsmouth," of the action taken by the little garrison, with the further statement that it was the intention of the insurgents never to lay down their arms until the independence of their adopted country had been established. Another message was dispatched about this time, but in a different direction. Lieutenant Ford, finding that the magazine was short of powder, sent two men named Cowie and Fowler, to the Sotoyome Rancho, owned by H. D. Fitch, for a bag of gun-powder. The messenger to San Francisco returned, the latter two never. Before starting they were cautioned against proceeding by traveled ways—good advice, which, however, they followed for only the first ten miles of their journey, when they struck into the main thoroughfare into Santa Rosa. At about two miles from that place they were attacked and slaughtered by a party of Californians. Two others were dispatched on special duties; they too were captured but were better treated. Receiving no intelligence from either of the parties, foul play was suspected; therefore, on the morning of the 20th of June Sergeant Gibson, with four men, was ordered to proceed to the Sotoyome Rancho, learn, if possible, the whereabouts of the missing men, and procure the powder. They went as directed, secured the ammunition, but got no news of the missing men. As they were passing Santa Rosa on their return, they were attacked at daylight by a few Californians, and, turning upon their assailants, captured two of them, Blas Angelina and Bernardino Garcia, alias Three-Fingered Jack, and took them to Sonoma. They told of the taking and slaying of Cowie and Fowler, and that their captors were Ramon Mesa Domingo, Mesa Juan Padilla, Ramon Carrillo, Bernardino Garcia, Bias Angelina, Francisco Tibran, Ygnacio Balensuella, Juan Peralta, Juan Soleto, Inaguan Carrillo, Mariano Merando, Francisco Garcia, and Ygnacio Stigger. The story of their death is a sad one. After Cowie and Fowler had been seized by the Californians, they encamped for the night, and the following morning determined in council what should be the fate of their captives. A swarthy New Mexican, named Mesa Juan Padilla, and Three-Fingered Jack, the Californian, were loudest in their denunciation of the prisoners as deserving of death, and unhappily their counsels prevailed. The unfortunate young men were then led out, stripped naked, bound to a tree with a lariat, while for a time the inhuman monsters practiced knife-throwing at their naked bodies, the victims praying to be shot. They then began throwing stones at them, one of which broke the jaw of Fowler. The fiend Three-Fingered Jack, then advancing, thrust the end of his riata (a rawhide rope) through Fowler's mouth, cut an incision in his throat, and then made a tie by which the jaw was dragged out. They next proceeded to kill them slowly with their knives. Cowie, who had fainted, had the flesh stripped from his arms and shoulders, and pieces of flesh were cut from their bodies and crammed into their mouths, they being finally disemboweled. Their mutilated remains were afterward found and buried where they fell, upon the farm now owned by George Moore, two miles north of Santa Rosa. No stone marks the grave of these pioneers, one of whom took so conspicuous a part in the events which gave to the Union the great State of California. Three-Fingered Jack was killed by Captain Harry Love's rangers July 27, 1853, at Pinola Pass, near the Merced River, with the bandit Joaquin Murietta, while Ramon Carrillo met his death at the hands of the Vigilantes between Los Angeles and San Diego May 21, 1864. At the time of his death, the above murder, in which it was said he was implicated, became the subject of newspaper comment; indeed, so bitter was the tone of the press that on June 4, 1864, the Sonoma Democrat published a letter from Julio Carrillo, a respected citizen of Santa Rosa, an extract from which we reproduce: "But I wish more particularly to call attention to an old charge, which I presume owes its revival to the same source: That my brother, Ramon Carrillo, was connected with the murder of two Americans, who had been taken prisoners by a company commanded by one Padilla in 1846. I presume this charge first originated from the fact that my brother had been active in raising the company which was commanded by Padilla, and from the further fact that the murder occurred near the Santa Rosa farm then occupied by my mother's family.

Notwithstanding these appearances, I have proof which is incontestable that my brother was not connected with this affair and was not even aware that these men had been taken prisoners until after they had been killed.

The act was disapproved by all the native Californians at the time, excepting those implicated in the killing, and caused a difference which was never entirely healed. There are, as I believe, many Americans now living in this vicinity, who were here at the time, and who know the facts I have mentioned. I am ready to furnish proof of what I have said to any who may desire it."

The messenger dispatched to the United States ship "Portsmouth" returned on the 17th in company with First Lieutenant John Storny Missroom and John E. Montgomery, son and clerk of Captain Montgomery, who dispatched by express letters from that officer to Fremont and Sutter. These arrived the following day, the 18th, and on the 19th Fremont came to Sutter's with twenty-two men, bringing Jose Noriega, of San Jose, and Vicente Peralta, as prisoners.

At Sonoma, on June 18th, Captain William B. Ide, with the consent of the garrison, issued the following: "A proclamation to all persons and citizens of the district of Sonoma, requesting them to remain at peace and follow their rightful occupations without fear of molestation.

"The commander-in-chief of the troops assembled at the fortress of Sonoma gives his inviolable pledge to all persons in California not found under arms, that they shall not be disturbed in their persons, their property, or social relations with one another by men under his command.

"He also solemnly declares his object to be: first, to defend himself and companions in arms, who were invited to this country by a promise of lands on which to settle themselves and families; who were also promised a republican government; when, having arrived in California, they were denied the privilege of buying or renting lands of their friends, who, instead of being allowed to participate in or being protected by a republican government, were oppressed by a military despotism; who were even threatened by proclamation by the chief officers of the aforesaid despotism with extermination if they should not depart out of the country, leaving all their property, arms and beasts of burden; and thus deprived of their means of flight or defense, were to be driven through deserts inhabited by hostile Indians to certain destruction.

"To overthrow a government which has seized upon the property of the missions for its individual aggrandizement; which has ruined and shamefully oppressed the laboring people of California by enormous exactions on goods imported into the country, is the determined purpose of the brave men who are associated under my command.

"I also solemnly declare my object, in the second place, to be to invite all peaceable and good citizens of California who are friendly to the maintenance of good order and equal rights, and I do hereby invite them to repair to my camp at Sonoma, without delay, to assist us in establishing and perpetuating a republican government which shall secure to all civil and religious liberty; which shall encourage virtue and literature; which shall leave unshackled by fetters, agriculture, commerce, and manufactures.

"I further declare that I rely upon the rectitude of our intentions, to the favor of heaven and the bravery of those who are bound and associated with me by the principles of self-preservation, by the love of truth and the hatred of tyranny, for my hope of success.

"I furthermore declare that I believe that a government, to be prosperous and happy, must originate with the people who are friendly to its existence; that the citizens are its guardians, the officers its servants, its glory its reward.

William B. Ide.

"Headquarters, Sonoma, June 18,1846."

The Pioneer says that William B. Ide was born in Ohio, came overland to California, reaching Sutter's Fort in October, 1845. On June 7, 1847, Governor Mason appointed him land surveyor for the Northern District of California, and in the same month he was appointed justice of the peace at Cache Creek. At an early day he got a grant of land called the Rancho Barranca Colorado, just below Red Creek, in Colusa County, as it was then organized. In 1851 he was elected county treasurer, with an assessment-roll of $373,260, and moved with the county seat to Monroeville, at the mouth of Stoney Creek. On September 3, 1851, he was elected county judge of Colusa County and practiced law, having a license. Judge Ide died of smallpox at Monroeville on December 18, 1852, aged fifty years.

Let us for a moment turn to the doings of Castro. On June 17th he issued two proclamations, one to the new, the other to the old citizens and foreigners. Appended are translations:

"The citizen, Jose Castro, Lieutenant-Colonel of Cavalry in the Mexican Army, and acting General Commandant of the Department of California.

"Fellow Citizens: The contemptible policy of the agents of the United States of North America in this department has induced a number of adventurers, who, regardless of the rights of men, have designedly commenced an invasion, possessing themselves of the town of Sonoma, taking by surprise all the place, the military commander of that border, Col. Don Mariano Guadalupe Vallejo, Lieutenant-Colonel Don Victor Prudon, Captain Don Salvador Vallejo, and Mr. Jacob P. Leese.

"Fellow-countrymen, the defense of our liberty, the true religion which our fathers possessed, and our independence, call upon us to sacrifice ourselves rather than lose those inestimable blessings. Banish from your hearts all petty resentments; turn you, and behold yourselves, these families, these innocent little ones, which have unfortunately fallen into the hands of our enemies, dragged from the bosoms of their fathers, who are prisoners among foreigners and are calling upon us to succor them. There is still time for us to rise en masse, as irresistible as retribution. You need not doubt but that Divine Providence will direct us in the way to glory. You should not vacillate because of the smallness of the garrison of the general headquarters, for he who will first sacrifice himself, will be your friend and fellow-citizen,

"Jose Castro.

"Headquarters, Santa Clara, June 17, 1846."

"The citizen, Jose Castro, Lieutenant-Colonel of Cavalry in the Mexican Army, and Acting Commandant of the Department of California.

"All foreigners residing among us, occupied with their business, may rest assured of the protection of all the authorities of the department while they refrain entirely from all revolutionary movements.

"The General Comandancia under my charge will never proceed with vigor against any persons, neither will its authority result in mere words, wanting proof to support it; declarations shall be taken, proofs executed, and the liberty and rights of the laborious, which is ever commendable, shall be protected.

"Let the fortunes of war take its chance with those ungrateful men who, with arms in their hands, have attacked the country, without recollecting that they were treated by the undersigned with all the indulgence of which he is so characteristic. The imperative inhabitants of the department are witness to the truth of this. I have nothing to fear; my duty leads me to death or victory. I am a Mexican soldier, and I will be free and independent, or I will gladly die for those inestimable blessings. "Jose Castro.

"Headquarters, Santa Clara, June 17, 1846."

On June 20th a body of about seventy Californians, under Captain Jose Joaquin de la Torre, crossed the Bay of San Francisco, and having joined Correo and Padilla, marched to the vicinity of San Rafael, while General Castro had, by the utmost pressure, raised his forces to two hundred and fifty men, most of them being forced volunteers. Of this system of recruiting Lieutenant Revere says: "I heard that on a feast day, when the rancheros came to the mission in their 'go-to-meeting' clothes, with their wives and children, Castro seized their horses and forced the men to volunteer in defense of their homes, against los salvajes Americanos. Castro, at the head of his army, on the evening of the 27th of June, marched out of Santa Clara, and proceeding around the head of the Bay of San Francisco as far as the San Leandro Creek, halted on the rancho of Estudillo, where we shall leave them for the present.

Captain J. C. Fremont, having concluded that it had become his duty to take a personal part in the revolution which he had fostered, on June 21st transferred his impedimenta to the safe-keeping of Captain Sutter at the fort, and recrossing the American River encamped on the Sinclair Rancho, where he was joined by Pearson B. Redding and all the trappers about Sutter's Fort, and there awaited orders. On the afternoon of the 23rd Harrison Pierce, who had settled in Napa Valley in 1843, came into their camp, having ridden the eighty miles with but one change of horses, which he procured from John R. Wolfskill, on Putah Creek, now Solano County, and conveyed to Fremont the intelligence that the little garrison at Sonoma was greatly excited consequent on news received that General Castro, with a considerable force, was advancing on the town and hurling threats of recapture and hanging of the rebels. On receiving the promise of Fremont to come to their rescue as soon as he could, putting ninety men into the saddle, Pierce obtained a fresh mount and returned without drawing rein to the anxious garrison, who received him and his message with every demonstration of joy. Fremont, having found horses for his ninety mounted rifles, left the Sinclair Rancho on June 23rd—a curious looking cavalcade, truly.

One of the party writes of them: "There were Americans, French, English, Swiss, Poles, Russians, Prussians, Chileans, Germans, Greeks, Austrians, Pawnees, native Indians, etc., all riding side by side, and talking a polyglot lingual hash never exceeded in diversibility since the confusion of tongues at the Tower of Babel. Some wore the relics of their homespun garments, some relied upon the antelope and the bear for their wardrobe, some lightly habited in buckskin leggings and a coat of war-paint, and their weapons were equally various. There was the grim old hunter, with his long heavy rifle, the farmer with his double-barreled shot-gun, the Indian with his bow and arrows, and others with horse-pistols, revolvers, sabers, ships' cutlasses, bowie-knives and 'pepper-boxes' (Allen's revolvers)."

Though the Bear Flag army was incongruous in personnel, as a body it was composed of the best fighting material. Each of them was inured to hardship and privation, self-reliant, fertile in resources, versed in woodcraft and Indian fighting, accustomed to handling fire-arms, and full of energy and daring. It was a band of hardy adventurers, such as in an earlier age wrested this land from the feebler aborigines. With this band Fremont arrived at Sonoma at two o'clock in the morning of June 25, 1846, having made forced marches.

The reader may not have forgotten the capture and horrible butchery of Cowie and Fowler by the Padilla party. A few days thereafter, while William L. Todd (the artist of the Bear Flag) was trying to catch a horse a little distance from the barracks at Sonoma, he was captured by the same gang, and afterward, falling in with another man, he too was taken prisoner. The party several times signified their intention of slaying Todd, but he, fortunately knowing something of the Spanish tongue, was able to make them understand that his death would seal General Vallejo's doom, and this saved his life. He and his companion in misfortune, with whom he had no opportunity to converse, and who appeared to be an Englishman—a half fool and common loafer—were conveyed to the Indian rancheria called Olompoli, some eight miles from Petaluma.

For the purpose of liberating the prisoners and keeping the enemy in check until the arrival of Captain Fremont, Lieutenant Ford mustered a squad, variously stated at from twenty to twenty-three men, among whom were Granville P. Swift, Samuel Kelsey, William Baldridge, and Frank Bedwell, and on June 23rd, taking with them from Sonoma the two prisoners, Blas Angelina and Three-Fingered Jack, marched for where it was thought the Californians had established their headquarters. Here they learned from some Indians, under considerable military pressure, that the California troops had left three hours before. They now partook of a hasty meal, and with one of the Indians as guide proceeded toward the Laguna de San Antonio, and that night halted within half a mile of the enemy's camp. At dawn they charged the place and took the only men they found there prisoners; their number was four, the remainder having left for San Rafael.

Four men were left here to guard their prisoners and horses, and Ford, with fourteen others, started in pursuit of the enemy. Leaving the lagoon of San Antonio and striking into the road leading to San Rafael, after a quick ride of four miles, they came in sight of the house where the Californians had passed the night with their two prisoners, Todd and his companion, and were then enjoying themselves within its walls. Ford's men were as ignorant of their proximity as were the Californians of theirs. However, when the advance guard arrived in sight of the corral, and perceiving it to be full of horses, with a number of Indian vaqueros around it, they made a brilliant dash to prevent the animals from being turned loose. While exulting over their good fortune at this unlooked-for addition to their cavalry arm, they were surprised to see the Californians rush out of the house and mount their already saddled quadrupeds.

It should be said that the house was situated on the edge of a plain, some sixty yards from a grove of brushwood. In a moment Ford formed his men into two half companies and charged the enemy, who, perceiving the movement, retreated behind the grove of trees. From his position Ford counted them and found that there were eighty-five.

Notwithstanding he had but fourteen in his ranks, nothing daunted, he dismounted his men, and. taking advantage of the protection offered by the brushwood, prepared for action. The Californians, observing this evolution, became emboldened and prepared for a charge. On this Ford calmly awaited the attack, giving stringent orders that his rear rank should hold their fire until the enemy were well up. On they came with shouts, the brandishing of swords, and the flash of pistols, until within thirty yards of the Americans, whose front rank then opened a withering fire and emptied the saddles of eight of the Mexican soldiery. On receiving this volley the enemy wheeled to the right-about and made a break for the hills, while Ford's rear rank played upon them at long range, causing three more to bite the earth and wounding two others. The remainder retreated helter-skelter to a hill in the direction of San Rafael, leaving the two prisoners in the house. Ford's little force, having now attained the object of their expedition, secured their prisoners of war, and going to the corral where the enemy had a large drove of horses changed their jaded nags for fresh ones, took the remaining animals, some four hundred, and retraced their victorious steps to Sonoma, where they were heartily welcomed by their anxious countrymen, who had feared for their safety.

We last left Captain Fremont at Sonoma, where he had arrived at two o'clock in the morning of the 25th of June. After giving his men and horses a short rest and receiving a small addition to his force, he was once more in the saddle and started for San Rafael, where it was said Castro had joined De la Torre with two hundred and fifty men.

At four o'clock in the afternoon they came in sight of the position thought to be occupied by the enemy. They approached cautiously until quite close, then charged, the first three to enter being Fremont, Kit Carson, and J. W. Marshall (the future discoverer of gold), but they found the lines occupied by only four men, Captain Torre having left some three hours previously. Fremont camped on the ground that night, and on the following morning dispatched scouting parties, while the main body remained at San Rafael for three days. Captain Torre had departed, no one knew whither; he left not a trace; but General Castro was seen from the commanding hills behind approaching on the other side of the bay. One evening a scout brought in an Indian, on whom was found a letter from Torre to Castro, purporting to inform the latter that he would that night concentrate his forces and march upon Sonoma and attack it in the morning.

Captain Gillespie and Lieutenant Ford held that the letter was a ruse designed for the purpose of drawing the American forces back to Sonoma, and thus leave an avenue of escape open for the Californians.

Opinions on the subject were divided; however, by midnight every man of them was in Sonoma. It was afterward known that they had passed the night within a mile of Captain de la Torre's camp, who, on ascertaining the departure of the revolutionists, effected his escape to Santa Clara via. Sausalito.

On or about the 26th of June, Lieutenant Joseph W. Revere, of the sloop-of-war "Portsmouth," in company with Doctor Andrew A. Henderson and a boatload of supplies, arrived at Sutter's Fort; there arriving also on the same day a party of men from Oregon, who at once cast their lot with the Bear Flag band, while on the 28th another boat, with Lieutenants Washington and Bartlett, put in an appearance. Of this visit of Lieutenant Revere to what afterward became Sacramento City, he says: "On arriving at the 'Embarcadero' (landing) were were not surprised to find a mounted guard of 'patriots,' who had long been apprised by the Indians that a boat was ascending the river. These Indians were indeed important auxiliaries to the revolutionists during the short period of strife between the parties contending for the sovereignty of California. Having been most cruelly treated by the Spanish race, murdered even on slight provocation, when their oppressors made marauding expeditions for servants, and when captured compelled to labor for their unsparing task-masters, the Indians throughout the country hailed the day when the hardy strangers from beyond the Sierra Nevada rose up in arms against the hijos del pais (sons of the country).

Entertaining an exalted opinion of the skill and prowess of the Americans and knowing from experience that they were of a milder and less sanguinary character than the rancheros, they anticipated a complete deliverance from their burdens, and assisted the revolutionists to the full extent of their humble abilities.

"Emerging from the woods lining the river, we stood upon a plain of immense extent, bounded on the west by the heavy timber which marks the course of the Sacramento, the dim outline of the Sierra Nevada appearing in the distance. We now came to some extensive fields of wheat in full bearing, waving gracefully in the gentle breeze like the billows of the sea, and saw the whitewashed walls of the fort, situated on a small eminence commanding the approaches on all sides.

"We were met and welcomed by Captain Sutter and the officer in command of the garrison, but the appearance of things indicated that our reception would have been very different had we come on a hostile errand.

"The appearance of the fort, with its cremated walls, fortified gateway and bastioned angles; the heavily bearded, fierce-looking hunters and trappers, armed with rifles, bowie-knives, and pistols; their ornamented hunting-shirts and gartered leggings; their long hair, turbaned with colored handkerchiefs; their wild and almost savage looks and dauntless and independent bearing; the wagons filled with golden grain; the arid, and yet fertile plains; the caballadas driven across it by wild, shouting Indians, enveloped in clouds of dust, and the dashing horsemen scouring the fields in every direction; all these accessories conspired to carry me back to the romantic East, and I could almost fancy again that I was once more the guest of some powerful Arab chieftain in his desert stronghold. Everything bore the impress of vigilance and preparation for defense, and not without reason, for Castro, then at the Pueblo de San Jose with a force of several hundred men, well provided with horses and artillery, had threatened to march upon the valley of the Sacramento.

"The fort consists of a parallelogram, enclosed by adobe walls fifteen feet high and two thick, with bastions or towers at the angles, the walls of which are four feet thick, and their embrasures so arranged as to flank the curtain on all sides. A good house occupies the center of the interior area, serving for officers' quarters, armories, guard and state rooms, and also for a kind of citadel. There is a second wall on the inner face, the space between it and the outer wall being roofed and divided into workshops, quarters, etc., and the usual offices are provided, and also a well of good water. Corrals for the cattle and horses of the garrison are conveniently placed where they can be under the eye of the guard. Cannon frown from the various embrasures, and the ensemble presents the very ideal of a border fortress. It must have astonished the natives when this monument of the white man's skill arose from the plain and showed its dreadful teeth in the midst of those peaceful solitudes.

"I found during this visit that General Vallejo and his companions were rigorously guarded by the 'patriots,' but I saw him and had some conversation with him, which it was easy to see excited a very ridiculous amount of suspicion on the part of his vigilant jailers, whose position, however, as revolutionists was a little ticklish and incited in them that distrust which in dangerous times is inseparable from low and ignorant minds. Indeed they carried their doubts so far as to threaten to shoot Sutter for being polite to his captives."

Fremont, with his men having partaken of the early meal, on the morning of the 27th of June returned to San Rafael, being absent only twenty-four hours.

Castro, who had been for three days watching the movements of Fremont from the other side of the bay, sent three men, Don Jose Reyes Berryessa (a retired sergeant of the Presidio company of San Francisco) and Ramon and Francisco de Haro (twin sons of Don Francisco de Haro, alcalde of San Francisco in 1838-39), to reconnoiter, and these three landed on what is now known as Point San Quentin. Here they were seized, with their arms, and on them were found written orders from Castro to Captain de la Torre (who it was not known had made his escape to Santa Clara) to kill every foreign man, woman, and -child. These men were shot on the spot—first, as spies, and, second, in retaliation for the Americans so cruelly butchered by the Californians. General Castro, fearing that he might, if caught, share the fate of his spies, left the rancho of the Estudillos, and after a hasty march arrived at the Santa Clara Mission on June 29, 1846.

Captain William D. Phelps, of Lexington, Mass., who was lying at Sausalito with his bark, the "Moscow," remarks (according to Mr. Lancey): "When Fremont passed San Rafael in pursuit of Captain de la Torre's party I had just left them, and he sent me word that he would drive them to Sausalito that night, when they could not escape unless they got my boats. I hastened back to the ship and made all safe. There was a large launch lying near the beach; this was anchored farther off, and I put provisions on board to be ready for Fremont should he need her. At night there was a boat on the shore. Torre's party must shortly arrive, and show fight or surrender. Toward morning we heard them arrive, and to our surprise they were seen passing with a small boat from the shore to the launch; a small boat had arrived from Yerba Buena during the night, which had proved their salvation. I dispatched a note to the commander of the 'Portsmouth' sloop-of-war, then lying at Yerba Buena, a cove (now San Francisco), informing him of their movements, and intimating that a couple of his boats could easily intercept and capture them. Captain Montgomery replied that not having received any official notice of war existing he could not act in the matter.

"It was thus the poor scamps escaped. They pulled clear of the ship, and thus escaped supping on grape and canister, which we had prepared for them.

"Fremont arrived and camped opposite my vessel, the bark 'Moscow,' the following night. They were early astir the next morning, when I landed to visit Captain Fremont, and were all variously employed in taking care of their horses, mending saddles, cleaning their arms, etc.

I had not up to this time seen Fremont, but from reports of his character and exploits my imagination had painted him as a large-sized, martial-looking man or personage, towering above his companions, whiskered, and ferocious-looking.

"I took a survey of the party but could not discover anyone who looked as I thought the captain to look. Seeing a tall, lank, Kentucky-looking chap (Doctor R. Semple), dressed in a greasy deerskin hunting-shirt, with trousers to match, and which terminated just below the knees, his head surmounted by a coonskin cap, tail in front, who, I supposed, was an officer, as he was giving orders to the men, I approached and asked if the captain was in camp. He looked, and pointed to a slender-made, well-proportioned man sitting in front of the tent. His dress was a. blue woolen shirt of somewhat novel style, open at the neck, trimmed with white and with a star on each point of the collar (a man-of-war-'s-man's shirt), over this a deerskin hunting-shirt, trimmed and fringed, which had evidently seen hard times or service, his head unencumbered by hat or cap, but had a light cotton handkerchief bound around it, and deerskin moccasins completed the suit, which if not fashionable for Broadway, or for a presentation dress at court, struck me as being an excellent rig to scud under or fight in. A few minutes' conversation convinced me that I stood in the presence of the king of the Rocky Mountains."

Captain Fremont and his men remained at Sausalito until July 2nd, when they left for Sonoma, and there prepared for a more perfect organization, their plan being to keep the Californians to the southern part of the State until the immigrants then on their way had time to cross the Sierra Nevada into California. On the 4th the national holiday was celebrated with due pomp; while on the 5th the California battalion of mounted riflemen, two hundred and fifty strong, was organized.

Brevet Captain John C. Fremont, Second Lieutenant of Topographical Engineers, was chosen commandant; First Lieutenant of Marines Archibald H. Gillespie, adjutant and inspector, with the rank of captain. Says Fremont: "In concert and in co-operation with the American settlers, and in the brief space of thirty days, all was accomplished north of the Bay of San Francisco, and independence declared on the 5th of July. This was done at Sonoma, where the American settlers had assembled. I was called to my position and by the general voice to the chief direction of affairs, and on the 6th of July, at the head of the mounted riflemen, set out to find Castro.

"We had to make the circuit of the head of the bay, crossing the Sacramento River (at Knight's Landing). On the 10th of July, when within ten miles of Sutter's Fort, we received (by the hands of William Scott) the joyful intelligence that Commodore John Drake Sloat was at Monterey and had taken it on the 7th of July, and that war existed between the United States and Mexico. Instantly we pulled down the Flag of Independence (Bear Flag) and ran up that of the United States, amid general rejoicing and a national salute of twenty-one guns on the morning of the 11th from Sutter's Fort, with a brass four-pounder called 'Sutter'."

We find that at two o'clock on the morning of July 9th Lieutenant Joseph Warren Revere of the "Portsmouth" left that ship in one of her boats, and reaching the garrison at Sonoma at noon of that day, hauled down the Bear Flag and raised in its place the Stars and Stripes, and at the same time forwarded a United States flag to Sutter's Fort by the hands of William Scott, and another to Captain Stephen Smith at Bodega. Thus ended what was called the Bear Flag war.

The following is the Mexican account of the Bear Flag war: "About a year before the commencement of the war a band of adventurers, proceeding from the United States, and scattering over the vast territory of California, awaited only the signal of their Government to take the first step in the contest for usurpation. Various acts committed by these adventurers in violation of the laws of the country indicated their intentions. But, unfortunately, the authorities then existing, divided among themselves, neither desired nor knew how to arrest the tempest. In the month of July, 1846, Captain Fremont, an engineer of the U. S. A., entered the Mexican territory with a few mounted riflemen, under the pretext of a scientific commission, and solicited and obtained from the commandant-general, Don Jose Castro, permission to traverse the country. Three months afterwards, on the 19th of May (June 14th), that same force and their commander took possession by armed force and surprised the important town of Sonoma, seizing all the artillery, ammunition, armaments, etc., which it contained.

"The adventurers, scattered along the Sacramento River, amounted to about four hundred, one hundred and sixty men having joined their force. They proclaimed for themselves and on their own authority the independence of California, raising a rose-colored flag with a bear and a star. The result of this scandalous proceeding was the plundering of the property of some Mexicans and the assassination of others— three men shot as spies by Fremont, who, faithful to their duty to the country, wished to make resistance. The commandant-general demanded explanations on the subject of the commander of an American ship-of-war, the 'Portsmouth,' anchored in the Bay of San Francisco; and although it was positively known that munitions of war, arms, and clothing were sent on shore to the adventurers, the commander, J. B. Montgomery, replied that 'neither the Government of the United States nor the subalterns had any part in the insurrection, and that the American authorities ought, therefore, to punish its authors in conformity with the laws.'"

CHAPTER VI. EXTRACTS FROM GENERAL JOHN A. SUTTER'S DIARY

I left the State of Missouri, where I had resided for many years, on the first of April, 1838, and traveled with a party of men under Capt. Tripps, of the American Fur Company, to their rendezvous in the Rocky Mountains (Wind River Valley). From there I traveled with six brave men to Oregon, as I considered myself not strong enough to cross the Sierra Nevada and go direct to California, (which was my intention from my start, having got some information from a gentleman from Mexico, who had been in California).

Under a good many dangers and other troubles I passed the different forts or trading posts of the Hudson Bay Company, and arrived at the Mission at The Dalles on the Columbia River. From this place I crossed straight, through thick and thin, and arrived to the great astonishment of the inhabitants. I arrived after seven days in the Valley of the Williamette, while others with good guides, arrived in seventeen days previous my crossing. At Fort Vancouver I was very hospitably received and invited to pass the winter with the gentlemen of the company, but as a vessel of the company was ready to sail for the Sandwich Islands, I took passage in her in the hopes of soon getting passage from there to California. But five long months I had to wait for an opportunity to leave, but not direct to California, except far out of my way to the Russian American colonies on the northwest coast, to Sitka, the residence of the Governor, (Latitude 57).

I remained there one month and delivered the cargo of the Brig Clementine, as I had charge of the vessel, and then sailed down the coast in heavy gales, and entered in distress in the Port of San Francisco, on the second of July 1839. An officer and fifteen soldiers came on board and ordered me out, saying that Monterey was the port of entry. At last, I was allowed 48 hours to get provisions (as we were starving) and did some repairing on the brig.

In Monterey I arranged my affairs with the Custom House and presented myself to Governor Alvarado and told my intention to settle here in this country, and that I have brought with me five white men and eight Kanacas (two of them married). Three of the white men were mechanics; he was very glad to hear that, and particularly when I told him I intended to settle in the interior, on the banks of the River Sacramento, because the Indians at this time would not allow white men, and particularly of Spanish origin, to come near them; they were very hostile, and stole the horses from the inhabitants near San Jose.

I got a general passport for my small colony, and permission to select a territory wherever I would find it convenient, and to come in one year's time again to Monterey to get my citizenship and the title to the land, which I have done so, and not only this, I received a high civil office.

When I left Yerba Buena, (now San Francisco)', after having leaved the brig and dispatched her back to the S. J., I bought several small boats (launches) and chartered the Schooner "Isabella" for my exploring journey to the inland rivers, and particularly to find the mouth of the River Sacramento, as I could find nobody who could give me information, only that they knew there were some very large rivers in the interior.

It took me eight days before I could find the entrance to the Sacramento, as it is very deceiving and very easy to pass by; how it happened to several officers of the Navy afterwards, which refused to take a pilot.

About ten miles below Sacramento City I fell in with the first Indians, which were all armed and painted and looked very hostile. They was about 200 men, as some of them understood a little Spanish I could make a kind of treaty with them, and the two which understood Spanish came with me and made me a little better acquainted with the country. All other Indians on the Up River hided themselves in the bushes, and on the mouth of the Feather River they runned all away so soon they discovered us. I was examining the country a little further up with a boat, while the larger crafts let go their Ankers, on my return all the white men came to me and asked me how much longer I intended to travel with them in such a Wilderness.

The following morning I gave orders to return, and entered in the American River, landed at the Farmer tannery on the 12th Augt. 1839.

Gave orders to get everything on shore, pitch the tents and mount the three cannons, called the White men and told them that all those which are not contented could leave on board the Isabella next morning and that I would settle with them immediately and remain alone with the canecas, of 6 men 3 remained, and 3 of them I gave passage to Yerbabuena.

The Indians was first troublesome, and came frequently, and would it not have been for the cannons, they would have killed us for sake of my property, which they like very much, and this intention they had very often, how they have confessed to me afterwards, when on good terms. I had a large Bull Dog, which saved my life 3 times, when they came slyly near the house in the night, he got hold of them and barked most severely.

In a short time moved my camps on the very spot where now the ruins of Sutter's fort stands, made acquaintance with a few Indians which came to work for a short time making Adobes, and the Canacas was building 3 grass houses, like it is customary on the Sandwich Islands. Before I came here, I purchased Cattle and Horses on the Rancho of Senor Martinez and had great difficulties and trouble to get them up and received them at least on the 22nd. of October 1839. Not less than 8 men wanted to be in the party, as they was afraid of the Indians, and had good reason to be so.

Before I got the cattle, we was hunting Deer & Elk etc. and so afterwards to safe the Cattle, as I had then only about 500 head, 50 horses and a mandana of 25 mares. One year that is in the fall of 1840, I bought 1000 head of Cattle of Don Antonio Sunol and a many horses more of Don Joaquin Gomez, and others. In the fall 1839 I have built an adobe house, covered with tule, and two other small buildings, which in the middle of the fort, they were afterwards destroyed by fire. At the same time we cut a road through the woods where the City of Sacramento stand, then we made the new Embarcadero, where the old Zinkhouse stands now. After this it was time to make a garden and to sow some Wheat &c we broke up the soil with poor Californian plows, I had a few Californians employed as Baqueros, and 2 of them making Cal. Carts & stocking the plougs etc.

In the spring 1840, the Indians began to be troublesome all around me, Killing and Wounding Cattle, stealing horses, and threatening to attack us en Mass, I was obliged to make campaigns against them and punished them severely, a little later about 2 a 300 was approaching and got United on Consumne River, but I was not waiting for them. Left a small Garrison at home, Canons & other Arms loaded, and left with 6 brave men and 2 Boqueros in the night, and took them by surprise at Day light. The fighting was a little hard, but after having lost about 30 men, they was willing to make a treaty with me, and after this lecon they behalved very well and became my best friends and Soldiers, with which I had been assisted to conquer the whole Sacramento and a part of the San Joaquin Valley.

At that time the communication with the Bay was very long and dangerous, particularly in open Boats, it is a very great wonder that we got not Swamped a many times, all time with an Indian Crew and a Canaca at the helm. Once it took me (in December 1839) 16 days to go down to Yerba buena and return, I went down again on the 22d Xber 39, to Yerba buena and on account of the inclemency of the Weather and the strong current in the River I need a whole month (17 days coming up) and nearly all the provisions spoiled.

On the 23d Augt. 1841, Capt. Ringold of Comadore Wilkes Exploring Squadron, arrived on the Embarcasero, piloted by one of the launches Indian crew, without this they would not have found so easy the entrance of the Sacramento. They had 6 whaleboats & 1 launch 7 Officers and about 50 men in all, I was very glad indeed to see them, sent immediately saddled horses for the Officers, and my Clerk with an invitation to come and see me, at their arrival I fired a salute, and furnished them with what they needed. They was right surprised to find me up here in this Wilderness, it made a good impression upon the Indians to see so many whites are coming to see me, they surveyed the river as far as the Butes.

September 4th 1841. Arrived the Russian Govr Mr. Alexander Rottiheff on board the Schooner Sacramento, and offered me their whole Establishment at Bodega & Ross for sale, and invited me to come right with him, as there is a Russian Vessel at Bodega, and some Officers with plien power, to transact this business with me, and particularly they would give me the preference, as they became all acquainted with me, during a month's stay at Sitka. I left and went with him down to the Bay in company with Capt. Ringold's Expedition, what for a fleet, we thought then, is on the River. Arriving at Bodega, we came very soon to terms, from there we went to Fort Ross where they showed me everything and returned to Bodega again, and before the vessel sailed we dined on board the Helena, and closed the bargain for $30,000, which has been paid. And other property, was a separate account which had been first paid.

On the 28th of September I dispatched a number of men and my Clerk by land to Bodega, to receive the Cattle, Horses, Mules & Sheep, to bring them up to Sutter's Fort, called then New Helvetia, by crossing the Sacramento they lost me from about 2000 head about a 100, which drowned in the river, but of most of them we could safe the hides, our Cal. Banknotes at the time.

March 6th, 1842, Capt. Fremont arrived at the port with Kit Carson, told me he was an officer of the U. S. and left a party behind in Distress and on foot, the few surviving Mules was packed only with the most necessary, I received him politely and his company likewise as an old acquaintance. The next morning I furnished them with fresh horses & a Vaquero, with a pack loaded with necessary supplies for his men. Capt.

Fremont found in my establishment every morning what he needed, that he could travell without Delay, he could not have found it so by a Spaniard, perhaps by a great Many and with loosing a great deal of time.

I sold him about 60 Mules & about 25 horses, and fat young steers or Beef Cattle, all the Mules & horses got shoed, on the 23d March, all was ready and on the 24th he left with his party for the U. States.

As an Officer of the Govt it was my duty to report to the Govt that Capt. Fremont arrived, Genl. Micheltorena dispatched Lieut. Col. Teles (afterwards Gov. of Sinalo) with Capt., Lieut. & 25 Dragoons to inquire what Captain Fremont's business was here; but he was en route as the arrive only on the 27th, from this time on Exploring, Hunting and Trapping parties has been started, at the same time Agricultural and Mechanical business was progressing from year to year, and more notice has been taken, of my Establishment, it became even a fame, and some Early Distinguished Travvelers, like Doctor Sandells, Wasnesensky & others, Captains of Trading Vessels and Supercargoes & even Californians (after the Indians was subdued) came and paid me a visit and was astonished to see what For Work of all kinds has been done. Small Emigrant parties arrived, and brought me some Very valuable Men, with one of those was Major Bidwell (he was about 4 years in my employ). Major Redding and Major Hensley with 11 other brave men arrived alone, both of these gentlemen has been 2 years in my employ, with these parties excellent mechanics arrived, which all was employed by me, likewise good farmers. We made immediately Amer. ploughs was made in my Shops and all kind of work done, every year the Russians was bound to furnish me with good Iron and Steel and Files, articles which could not be got here, likewise Indian Beeds and the most important of all was 100 lb of fine Rifle & 100 lb of Canon powder, and several 100 lb of lead (every year) with these I was careful like with Gold.

June 3d 1846. I left in company with Major Reading and most all of the men in my employ, for a Campaign with the Mukelemney Indians, which has been engaged by Castro and his officers to revolutionize all the Indians against me, to Kill all the foreigners, burn their houses, Wheat fields, etc. These Mukelemney Indians had great promesses and some of them was finely dressed and equiped, and those came apparently on a friendly visit to the fort and vicinity and had long Conversation with the Influential Men of the Indians, and one night a number of them entered in my Potrero (a kind of closed pasture) and was Ketching horses to drive the whole Cavalada away with them the sentinel at the fort heard the distant Noise of these Horses, and gave due notice, & immediately I left with about 6 well armed Men and attacked them, but they could make their escape in the woods (where Sac. City now stands) and so I left a guard with the horses. As we had to cross the Mukelemney River on rafts, one of those rafts capsized with 10 Rifles, and six prs of pistols, a good supply of Ammunition, and the Clothing of about 24 Men, and Major Reading and another man nearly drowned.

June 16th 1846. Merritt and Kit Carson arrived with news of Sonoma beeing occupied by the Americans, and the same evening arrived as prissoners, Genl. Vallejo, Don Salvador Vallejo, Lt. Col. Prudon & M. Leese, and given under my charge and Care, I have treated them with Irindness and so good as I could, which was reported to Fremont, and he then told me that prissoners ought not to be treated so, than I told him, if it is not right how I treat them, to give them in charge of somebody else.

Capt. Montgomery did send an Amer. flag by Lieut. Revere than in command of Sonoma, and some dispatches to Fremont, I received the Order to hiss the flag by Sunrise from Lt. Revere, long time before daybreak, I got ready with loading the Cannons and when it was day the roaring of the Canons got the people all stirring. Some them made long faces, as they thought if the Bear flag would remain there would be a better chance to rob and plunder. Capt. Fremont received orders to proceed to Monterey with his forces, Capt. Montgomery provided for the upper Country, established Garrisons in all important places, Yerba buena, Sonoma, San Jose, and fort Sacramento. Lieut Missroon came to organize our Garrison better and more Numbers of White men and Indians of my former Soldiers and gave me the Command of this fort.

The Indians have not yet received their pay yet for their services, only each one a shirt and a pre. of pants, & abt. 12 men got Coats. So went the war on in California. Capt. Fremont was nearly all time engaged in the lower Country and made himself Governor, until Genl. Kearney arrived, when an other revolution took place. And Fremont for disobeying orders was made prisoner by Genl. Kearney, who took him afterwards with him to the U. States by Land across the Mountains. After the war I was anxious that business should go on like before, and on the 28th. May 1847, Marshall & Gingery, Two Millwrights, I employed to survey the large millraise for the Flour Mill at Brighton.

May 13th, 1847. Mr. Marshall commenced the great work of the large Millraise, with ploughs and scrapers.

July 20th 1847. Got all the necessary timber and frame of the millbuilding.

Augt. 25th. Capt. Hart of the Mormon Battailon arrived, with a good many of his Men on their way to Great Salt Lake, they had orders for Govt. horses, which I delivered to them (war horses) not paid for yet.

They bought provisions and got Blacksmith work done. I employed about 80 Men of them, some as Mechanics, some as laborers, on the Mill and Millraise at Brighton, some as laborers at the Sawmill at Columa.

Augt. 28th 1847. Marshall moved, with P. Wisners family and the working hands to Columa, and began to work briskly on the sawmill.

Septr. 10th. Mr. Saml. Brannan returned from the great Salt Lake, and announced a large Emigration by Land. On the 19th. the Garrison was removed, Lieut't Per Lee took her down to San Francisco.

Novr. 1th. Getting with a great deal of trouble and with breaking wagons the four runs of Millstones, to the Mill Sit (Brighton) from the Mountains.

December 22. Received about 2000 fruit trees with great expenses from fort Ross, Napa Valley and other places, which was given in care of men who called themselves Gardeners, and nearly all of the trees was neglected by them and died.

January 28th. 1848. Marshall arrived in the evening, it was raining very heavy, but he told me that he came on important business, after we was alone in a private Room he showed me the first specimens of Gold, that is he was not certain if it was Gold or not, but he thought it might be; immediately I made the proof and found that it was Gold; I told him even that most of all is 23 Carat Gold; he wished that I should come up with him immediately, but I told him that I have to give first my orders to the people in all my factories and shops.

February 1th. Left for the sawmill attended by a Baquero (Olimpio), was absent 2nd, 3rd, 4th & 5th. I examined myself every thing and picked up a few Specimens of Gold myself in the tail race of the Sawmill, this Gold and others which Marshall and some of the other laborers gave to me (it was found while in my employ and wages), I told him that I would a ring got made of it as soon as a Goldsmith would be here.

I had a talk with my employed people all at the Sawmill, I told them that as they do know now that this Metal is Gold, I wished they would do me the great favor and keep it secret only 6 weeks, because my large flour mill at Brighton would have been in Operation in such a time, which undertaking would have been a fortune for me, and unfortunately the people would not keep it secret, and so I lost on this Mill at the lowest calculation about $25,000.

March 7th. The first party of Marmons, employed by me left for washing and digging gold, and very soon all followed, and left me only the sick and the lame behind. And at this time I could say that everybody left me from the Clerk to the Cook. What for great damages I had to suffer in my tannery which was just doing a profitable and extensive business, and the vatts was left filled and a quantity of half finished leather was spoiled, likewise a large quantity of raw hides collected by the farmers and of my own killing. The same thing was in every branch of business which I carried on at the time. I began to harvest my wheat, while others was digging and washing Gold, but even the Indians could not be keeped longer at work, they was impatient to run to the mines, and other Indians had informed them of the Gold and its value; and so I had to leave more than two-thirds of my harvest in the fields.

April 18, 1848, more curious people arrived, bound for the Mountains. I left for Columa, in company with Major P. B. Reading and Mr. Kenbel (Editor of the Alta-California) we were absent 4 days. We was prospecting and found silver and iron in abundance.

April 28th. A great many people more went up to the Mountains. This day the Saw Mill was in operation and the first lumber has been sawed in the whole upper Country.

May 11th. Saml. Brannan was building a store at Natoma, Marmon Islands, and have done a very large and heavy business.

May 15th. Paid of all the mormons which has been employed by me, in building these Mills and other mechanical trades, all of them made their pile, and some of them became rich and wealthy, but all of them was bound to the great Salt Lake and spent there their fortunes to the honor and glory of the Lord!

May 19th. The great rush from San Francisco arrived at the fort, all my friends and acquaintances filled up the houses and the whole fort, I had only a little Indian boy, to make them roasted Ripps etc. as my Cooks left me like everybody else, the Merchants, Doctors, Lawyers, Sea Captains, all came up and did not know what to do, all was in confusion, all left their wives and families in San Francisco, and those which had none locked their doors, abandoned their houses, offered them for sale cheap, (a few hundred dollars, house and lot, lots which are worth now $100,000 and more) some of these men were just greaszy.

Some of the Merchants has been the most prudentest of the Whole, visited the mines, and returned immediately and began to do a very profitable business, and soon Vessels came from everywhere with all kind of Merchandise, the whole old thrash which was laying for years unsold, on the coasts of South and Central America, Mexici, Sandwich Islands, etc. all found a good market here.

Mr. Brannan was erecting a very large Warehouse and have done an immense business, connected with Howard & Green, S. Francisco.

May 21th. Saml. Kyberg errected or established the first Hotel in the fort, in the larger building, and made a great deal of Money. A great many traders deposited a great deal of goods in my Store (an Indian was the Key Keeper and performed very well) afterwards every little Shanty became a Warehouse and Store, the fort was then a veritable Bazzar. As white people would not be employed at the Time, I had a few good Indians attending to the Ferry Boat, and every night came up, and delivered the Received Ferryage to me, after deducting for a few bottles of brandy, for the whole of them, perhaps some white people at the time would not have acted as honestly.

May 25th. The travelling to the mines was increasing from day to day and no more Notice was taken, as the people arrived from South America, Mexico, Sandwich Islands, Oregon, etc. All the Ships Crews, and Soldiers deserted. In the beginning of July, Col. Mason our military Governor, with Capt. Sherman (Secretary of State) Capt. Folsom Quartrmstr, and an Escort of which some deserted, and some other gentlemen, travelled in company with the Governor.

As we wanted to celebrate the 4th of July, we invited the Governor and his suite to remain with us, and he accepted. Kyberg gave us a good diner, everything was pretty well arranged. Pinkett was the Orator. It was well done enough for such a new Country and in such an excitement and confusion. And from this time on you know how everything was going on here. One thing is certain that the people looked on my property as their own, and in the winter of 1849 to 1850. A great number of Horses has been stolen from me, whole Manadas of Mares driven away and taken to Oregon, etc. Nearly my whole stock of cattle has been killed, several Thousand, and left me a very small Quantity. The same has been done with my large stock of Hogs, which was running like ever under nobodies care and so it was easy to steal them. I had no idea that people could be so Mean, and that they would do a wholesale business in Stealing.

On the Upper Sacramento, that is from the Buttes downward to the point or mouth of Feather River, there was most of all my stock running, and during the Overflow the Cattle was in a many bands on high spots like Islands, there was a fine chance to approach them in small Boats and shoot them, this business has been very successfully done by one party of 5 men (partners)! which had besides hired people, and Boat's Crews, which transported the Beef to the Market at Sacramento City and furnished that city with my own beef, and because these Men was nearly alone, on account of the Overflow, and Monopolized the Market.

In the spring of 1850, these 5 men divided their spoil of $60,000 clear profits made of Cattle, all of them left for the Atlantic State; one of them returned again the Winter from 1850 to 51, hired a new Band of Robers to follow the same business and kill of the balance of the few that was left. My Baqueros found out this Nest of thiefs in their camp butchering just some heads of my Cattle. on their return they informed me what they have seen, in the neighborhood of the same camp they saw some more cows shot dead, which the rascals then butchered. Imediately I did send to Nicolaus for the Sheriff (Jas Hopkins) as then at the time we had laws in force ?!? after all was stolen and destroyed the Sheriff arrived at Hock Farm, I furnished him a posse of my employed Men. they proceeded over on the Sacramento to where the thiefs were encamped, as the Sheriff wanted to arrest them, they just jumped in their Boats and off they went; the Sheriff threatened them to fire at them, but they was all laughing they went at large.

One day my son was riding after Stock a few miles below Hock Farm, he found a man, (his name was Owens) butchering one of our finest milch Cows (of Durham stock of Chile, which cost $300). He told the man that he could not take the Meat, that he would go home and get people, and so he has done, and he got People and a Wagon and returned to the Spot, but Owens found it good to clear out. 2 Brothers of this man, was respectable Merchants in Lexington, Mo. and afterwards in Westport well acquainted with me, he came one day in my house and brought me their compliments, I received him well, and afterwards turned out to be a thief. How many of this kind came to California which loosed their little honor by crossing the Isthmus or the plains. I had nothing at all to do with speculation, but stuck by the plough, but by paying such high Wages, and particularly under Kyburg management, I have done this business with a heavy loss as the produce had no more the Value like before, and from the time on Kyburg left I curtailed my business considerable, and so far that I do all at present with my family and a few Indian Servants. I did not speculate, only occupied my land, in the hope that would be before long decided and in my favor by the U. S. Land Commission; but now already have 2 years and 3 months elapsed, and I am waiting now very anxiously for the decision, which will revive or bring me to the untimely grave.

All the other circumstances you know all yourself, perhaps I have repeated many things which I wrote in the first 3 sheets, because I had them not to see what I wrote, and as it is now several months, I must have forgotten. Well, it is only a kind of memorandum, and not a History at all, only to remember you on the different periods when such and such things happened.

I need not mention again, that all the visitors has always been hospitably received and treated. That all the sick and wounded found always Medical assistance, Gratis, as I had nearly all the time a physician in my employ. The assistance to the Emigrants, that is all well known. I don't need to write anything about this.

I think now from all this you can form some facts, and that you can mention how thousands and thousands made their fortunes from this Gold Discovery produced through my industry and energy, (some wise Merchants and others in San Francisco called the building of this Sawmill another of Sutter's folly) and this folly saved not only the Mercantile world from bankruptcy, but even our Genl. Govt., but for me it has turned out a folly, then without having discovered the Gold, I would have become the richest wealthiest man on the Pacific Shore.

(Signed) J. A. Sutter.

James C. Ward, who visited General Sutter in 1848, says of him: "A Swiss by birth, he held during the reign of Charles X. the rank of Captain in the French Army. He purchased the buildings at Fort Ross, just north of Bodega, of the Russians, and as he proposed to settle the wilderness to the north of the Bay of San Francisco with European immigrants, the Mexican Government made him a grant of eleven leagues of land on the Sacramento River. After landing, he camped, surrounded by hostile savages, in the open plain where the fort was afterward built, and the next morning, after dressing in full uniform, he went, accompanied by his Indian servant, both well-armed, to the Indian village nearby. The savages were informed through an interpreter that he came to them as a friend, and if he would help them a little with their labor, he would make them presents.

"The Indians were set to work to make adobes, of which the fort was built. It is a parallelogram in form, with two bastions. In the middle of the square is a building two stories high, containing four rooms, and a counting-room upstairs. A blacksmith shop, mill for grinding corn, serape manufactory and dwelling are around it, built against the walls of the fort. At one time he had a well-drilled force of thirty Indians within its walls, with guards posted night and day for its defense. No one reached it without being fed and lodged.

"I passed the evening of my arrival, after supper, in his company. His manners are polished, and the impression he makes on everyone is very favorable. In figure he is of medium height, rather stout, but well made.

His head is round, features regular, with smiling and agreeable expression; complexion healthy and roseate. He wears his hair cut close, and his moustache trimmed short, *a la militaire*. He dressed very neatly in frock coat, pantaloons and cap of blue, and with his gold-headed malacca in hand, you would rather suppose him prepared for a saunter on the Boulevards than a consultation with Simplon, his Indian alcalde, about hands required for the day's work, or ox teams to be dispatched here and there."

CHAPTER VII. SETTLEMENT AND EARLY HISTORY

Contra Costa County became a definite locality in 1850, created by the California legislature that opened its initial session at San Jose on December 15, 1849. At that time twenty-seven counties were established. In later years, by subdivision, they were increased to fifty-eight.

General M. G. Vallejo, who was probably better informed on early California history than any other man of his period, in a report to the legislature on the derivation of the names of the several counties, paid this tribute to Contra Costa County: "The name signifies 'Opposite Coast,' and the country is so called from its situation opposite San Francisco, in an easterly direction. It is undoubtedly one of the most fertile counties in the State, possessing rich agricultural lands, which embrace an interior coast of thirty leagues, extending along the bays of Santa Clara, San Francisco, San Pablo, the Straits of Carquinez, the Bay of Suisun, and the San Joaquin River; a circumstance which, united to its mild climate, will render it very important.

"The pueblo of Martinez is its chief town, and the 'New York of the Pacific,' as well as other towns on the shores of San Pablo and the San Joaquin, will soon effectually contribute to its importance." So spake General Vallejo half a century ago.

When the treaty of peace was signed with Mexico in 1848 there was but one American citizen living permanently in the region that we now know as Contra Costa County. This solitary representative of the United States was Doctor John Marsh. He lived at the base of Mount Diablo, and later came into considerable prominence. Elam Brown, the founder of Lafayette, was also among the early illustrious citizens of Contra Costa County. He was a member of the Constitutional Convention which met at Monterey in September 1849. The constitution was completed after six weeks of deliberation and was adopted by the people at an election on the 13th of the following November.

Another citizen mentioned in the chronicles of the times was Captain Seth M. Swain, of Martinez. To him belonged the distinction of carrying the first mail up the Sacramento River, in the schooner "John Dunlap." All the mail was in one bag, and Captain Swain received six hundred dollars for the voyage, although the total amount of postage on the mail amounted to less than sixty dollars.

LEGISLATIVE HISTORY

Contra Costa County originally comprised 1500 square miles of territory, but in 1853 it was reduced nearly one-half, the portion which Contra Costa County lost helping to form the newly created Alameda County. The ceded territory constituted the southern and western half of Contra Costa County. After this change she retained, as at present, 877 square miles.

The act to form Alameda County was passed by the legislature in session at Benicia. The county of Santa Clara was represented in the assembly by Henry C. Smith and W. S. Letcher. Contra Costa County was represented by H. W. Carpentier. Then, as now, San Jose was the county seat of Santa Clara County, and Martinez occupied a similar position in Contra Costa County. The desire for a new county arose out of the fact that the inhabitants of Santa Clara County residing near where Oakland is today were compelled to cross a range of mountains to reach their county seat, San Jose, thirty miles away. A petition, signed by citizens of both counties, asking that a new county be formed, was presented to the legislature by H. C. Smith. It was in response to this petition that the legislative act of 1853 was passed which made Contra Costa and Santa Clara counties the parents of Alameda.

Commenting on this topic in a "Centennial Paper," published in the Contra Costa Gazette in 1876, Doctor J. R. Howard wrote: "By the creation of Alameda County we lost more than half of our shore-line on the San Francisco Bay, and a valuable territory of land, with not less than three prosperous and handsome trade centers now clustering and growing on the opposite coast.

"Still, Contra Costa County has a most enviable natural position on the map of the State, with advantages possessed by few other counties.

"It is now bounded by the San Joaquin River, Suisun Bay, Straits of Carquinez, and San Pablo Bay on the north; by San Francisco Bay and Alameda County on the west; by Alameda County on the south, and San Joaquin County on the east. The map shows our geographical position to be about midway of the coast-line of the State, immediately in front and contiguous to the great heart of the State, with a shoreline of seventy miles or more on our northern border, along the magnificently linked system of bays, strait, and main rivers of the interior."

A comparison of the original boundary with the present boundary, as taken from the records, will make apparent to the reader the amount of territory lost by Contra Costa County. At the risk of being tedious, both are here given in full.

The original boundary as established by the legislature in 1849, was as follows: "Beginning at the mouth of Alameda Creek and running thence in a southwesterly direction to the middle of the Bay of San Francisco; thence in a northerly or northwesterly direction, following as near as may be the middle of the bay to the Straits of San Pablo; thence up the middle of the Bay of San Pablo to the Straits of Carquinez; thence running up the middle of said straits to the Suisun Bay, and up the middle of said bay to the mouth of the San Joaquin River; thence following up the middle of said river to the place known as Pescadero, or Lower Crossing; thence in a direct line to the northwest corner of Santa Clara County, which is on the summit of the Coast Range, near the source of Alameda Creek; thence down the middle of said creek to its mouth, which was the place of beginning, including the islands of San Pablo, Coreacas, and Tesoro. The seat of justice shall be at the town of Martinez."

The present boundary, as established by the legislature on March 25, 1853, when Alameda County was formed from the southern part of Contra Costa County and a slice of Santa Clara County, is as follows: "Beginning in the Bay of San Francisco, at the northwest point of Red Rock, being the common corner of Marin, Contra Costa, and San Francisco [counties]; thence up the Straits and Bay of San Pablo, on the eastern boundary of Marin, to the point of intersection with the line bearing south twenty-six and one-half degrees east, and about six and one-quarter miles distant from the southwest corner of Napa County, forming the common corner of Marin, Solano, Sonoma, and Contra Costa [counties]; thence to the Straits of Carquinez; thence up said straits and Suisun Bay, to the mouth of the San Joaquin River; thence up said river to the confluence of the west and main channels thereof, as laid down in Gibbe's map; thence up said west channel to a point about ten miles below Moore and Rhode's ranch, at a bend where the said west channel, running downward, takes a general course north, the point being on the westerly line of San Joaquin County, and forming the northeast corner of Alameda and southeast corner of Contra Costa [counties] ; thence on the northern line of Alameda, as laid down on Horace A. Higley's map, to the easterly line of San Francisco City and County; thence due northwest along said easterly line of San Francisco, four and one-half miles, more or less, to the place of beginning, the county seat, Martinez."

SENATORIAL DISTRICTS

In the first division of the State into counties Contra Costa County elected a State senator jointly with Santa Clara County; and this method of procedure remained in force until 1854, when it elected a joint senator with San Joaquin County. A change was again made in 1862, whereby one senator served Contra Costa and Marin counties, which situation still remains in effect.

JUDICIAL DISTRICTS

When California was divided into judicial districts, on March 29, 1850, John M. Watson became judge of the Third District, which comprised the counties of Contra Costa, Santa Clara, Santa Cruz, and Monterey. In 1853 Contra Costa was attached to the Seventh Judicial District, which included Solano, Napa, Sonoma, and Marin counties.

Change followed change, and in March, 1862, the county was placed in the Fourth Judicial District, being in the following year annexed to the Third District. It became a part of the Fifteenth District in 1864, and remained so until the adoption of the new constitution, establishing the various superior courts.

THE COURT OF SESSIONS

In the early days of Contra Costa County all the county business was transacted by the Court of Sessions. These courts were authorized by the legislative act of April 11, 1850. The court comprised the county judge, who presided at the sessions, assisted by two justices of the peace. The latter, who sat as associate justices, were chosen by their brother justices from the entire number elected in the county. All the intricate civil machinery of the county was administered by this court, and, according to reports of the period, it succeeded admirably. The numerous duties of the court included the examination and settling of all accounts charged against the county; the auditing of the books of all officers who handled county funds; the directing and raising of funds through taxation on real and personal property; the management of public roads, turnpikes, canals, and bridges; and the division of the county into townships and the establishment of election precincts. The preceding list, which covers only a few of the most important duties of the court, would indicate that the positions held by these officials were no sinecures.

The first county judge of Contra Costa County after its creation was F. M. Warmcastle, who took office on April 17, 1850. The associate justices were Absolom Peak and Edward G. Guest. Thomas A. Brown, a son of Elam Brown, was county clerk. The first sheriff of Contra Costa County was Nathaniel Jones.

One of the first acts performed by the Court of Sessions, on April 17, 1850, was the partitioning of the county into three townships, comprising Martinez, San Antonio, and New York (now Pittsburg). A further peep into the records of the period reveals the fact that on May 13, 1850, the court convened and ordered that all real and personal property of the county be assessed and fixed the amount of tax thereon for county expenses at twenty-five cents on the hundred dollars. A like sum for the construction of public buildings was ordered collected. The county clerk was directed to secure a suitable building for temporary use as a courthouse. On June 3, 1850, the county clerk was directed to receive sealed bids for the erection of a county jail.

On August 19th of the same year the court fixed the license to be collected on certain occupations. To vend goods, wares, and merchandise, with a capital of five thousand dollars or less, a license of twenty dollars per annum was collected. The vender of spirituous, vinous, malt, and fermented liquors had first to pay a license of fifty dollars per annum.

On the same date a license was granted to Oliver C. Coffin (ominous name!) to establish a ferry between Martinez and Benicia, after he had filed a bond in the amount of two thousand dollars. The court permitted him to charge the following fares: For each foot man, $1; man and horse, $2.50; single horse, mule or ox, $2; wagon, $5; carriage, $4; each head of sheep or hogs, 50 cents.

In early times the roads of Contra Costa County were few and far between. Here and there they wound about over the country, following the lines of least resistance, in many instances only enlarged trails.

Naturally, one of the first acts performed by the Court of Sessions was the establishment of road districts and the creation of new highways.

This step was taken on July 20, 1850, when seven road districts were established. Two districts were defined between Martinez and Pueblo de San Jose, the overseers appointed being N. B. Smith and Joseph Rothenhostler. The streets of Martinez comprised district three, and A. Van Heme Ellis was placed in charge of them, as supervisor. District four was the road traveled from Martinez, by way of the home of Silvio Pacheco, to New York of the Pacific (now Pittsburg). Henry F. Joye was appointed overseer. The road from the Moraga Redwoods to its intersection with the Martinez and San Jose highway was designated as district five, its overseer being E. Miller. Elam Brown was appointed overseer of district six, the road that connected his rancho with that of Vicente Castro, and which intersected the road from the Moraga Redwoods to Martinez. District seven extended from the crossing of the San Joaquin River to the Pueblo de San Jose and was placed in charge of Greene Patterson. At the same meeting of the court an order was established requiring all able-bodied men between the ages of eighteen and forty-five to perform their share of road work during five days of each year.

From this time forward rapid strides were made in the building and improvement of roads. On July 15, 1852, orders were issued for the laying out of the road between Oakland and San Pablo. By 1860 there were seventeen road districts within the county limits. Today no better roads are found elsewhere in the State of California than in Contra Costa, for which condition the citizens of the present age are vastly indebted to the zeal of the pioneer road-builders. The modern phases of Contra Costa roads will be discussed in another chapter.

BOARD OF SUPERVISORS

The first Board of Supervisors for Contra Costa County was elected June 14, 1852, comprising the following five members: William Patten, Samuel H. Robinson, Victor Castro, Robert Farrelly, and T. J. Keefer.

Upon the board devolved all the duties of administering county affairs, previously performed by the Court of Sessions.

A glance at the assessment report made by Supervisor Samuel H. Robinson, on July 23, 1852, throws considerable light on the large landholdings of the period, these being whole or in part of the old Mexican land grants. The largest individual holdings were those of W. Castro, who was assessed $82,704 on 27,568 acres, at the rate of three dollars an acre. Silvio Pacheco paid taxes on an assessment of $141,696, covering his rancho of 17,712 acres, at eight dollars an acre. The land holdings of Doctor John Marsh, which also comprised 17,712 acres, was assessed at one dollar an acre. The farm of Jose Jesus Vallejo, which covered 19,926 acres, was assessed at $99,630. These are but a few of the largest holdings. The assessment-roll shows scores of others ranging from one thousand to ten thousand acres.

The Board of Supervisors continued in existence until replaced by the Court of Sessions, on March 25, 1854. Following an act of the legislature, passed March 20, 1855, the Board of Supervisors again came into being, and since then has remained permanent in county affairs.

Passing on to the year 1856, it is found that on the 17th of November the Union Hotel, of Martinez, was destroyed by fire, and with it most of the records of the county treasurer, Robert E. Borden, who was also proprietor of the hotel. He made a report to the Board of Supervisors, showing that a thousand dollars was saved, but that nineteen hundred dollars was lost. Concurring in the belief that the loss was unavoidable, the board succeeded in having Borden relieved of the obligation of making good the loss.

An act of unusual magnanimity on the part of a county official was recorded on the 5th of February, 1861. On that date Judge Thomas A. Brown released the county from paying him six thousand dollars, this sum being a portion of his salary for four years as county judge. The salary provided by law was twenty-five hundred dollars a year, but Judge Brown declared in favor of a salary of one thousand dollars a year, which sum he drew, and at the end of his term refunded to the county the accrued six thousand dollars.

No unusual events are recorded during the intervening years until June 20, 1868, when an election was held, submitting to a vote of the people the proposition for the county to make a donation to the Martinez & Danville Railroad Company. This was to aid in the construction of a railroad from Martinez to Danville. The proposition was defeated by a vote of 391 in favor to 522 against.

Further records for the year 1868 show that the courthouse sustained grave damages from the great earthquake of October 21st, and that the District Court was compelled to meet in the carpenter shop of E. W. Hiller, the former office being considered insecure. On October 23rd extensive repairs were begun on the courthouse. The record for 1868 ends with the authorization of R. B. Hard to build a calaboose at Antioch. For the benefit of the uninitiated, it is here explained that the word calaboose is derived from the Spanish phrase el calabozo (the jail). The granting of permission to build calabooses forms no small part of the records of those days.

That coyotes were still numerous in 1876 is evidenced by the action of the Board of Supervisors, on February 9th of that year, in offering a bounty on the scalps and ears of these canny pests.

The trend of the times is eloquently set forth in the brief record of the vote on Chinese immigration, at the election of September 7, 1879.

For Chinese immigration 16 votes; against Chinese immigration, 2039 votes; majority against Chinese immigration, 2023 votes. Such was the laconic but decisive verdict.

Early in 1880 a number of franchises for the erection of wharves were granted to Port Costa, a hamlet then fast coming into prominence as a shipping point and also because it was there that the steamer "Solano" landed its western-bound trains from the Atlantic. The records of that year show also that the Northern Railroad Company had over twenty-three miles of railroad in the county, while the San Pablo & Tulare Railroad Company had more than thirty-four. The former was valued at $13,060 a mile, and the latter at $11,200. An official seal for the Board of Supervisors was ordered on July 7, 1880. The design chosen was a sheaf of grain, a horn of plenty, with grapes and melons, all surrounded by the words, "Board of Supervisors of Contra Costa County, California."

During 1880 the public debt of the county, amounting to $94,100, was funded, and bonds bearing interest at six per cent and payable semiannually, were directed to be issued on August 4th. One month later another debt of $38,000 was ordered funded by the issuance of bonds bearing interest at the above rate.

Contra Costa County was rapidly emerging from pioneer conditions. Small but thriving towns were springing up all along her water-front; shipping was receiving a great impetus from her numerous products, including millions of bushels of grain, which were marketed all over the world; orchards and vegetable gardens were thriving in her fertile valleys; roads and schools were rapidly improved and railroad communication was steadily increasing.

Turning from the pioneer days, the commercial growth of the county and its cities will be taken up in the succeeding chapters.

CHAPTER VIII. CLIMATE—SOIL—HORTICULTURE—AGRICULTURE

The climate of Contra Costa County is ideal; it is the golden mean between the extremes of heat and cold. Sheltered on the western border by a wall of hills, this district knows no cold winds or heavy fogs. No matter how raw and cold the winds may blow through the Golden Gate, they do not reach past this barrier. Even during the winter months there is an abundance of sunshine between showers, and the climate may be said to be balmy the year around. The annual rainfall is twelve to eighteen inches, or enough to insure good crops without irrigation.

However, of late years it has been possible to secure much larger returns by augmenting nature, and large irrigation projects have sprung up. These will be treated under another heading.

In the present chapter we will take up the products of the soil under three classifications—horticultural, agricultural, and viticultural. Horticultural embraces the various fruit-and nut-bearing trees, agricultural applies to the general field of farming, and the term viticultural is confined solely to the raising of grapes.

Contra Costa County's principal horticultural products are pears, walnuts, almonds, prunes, peaches, apricots, cherries, apples, and olives.

Pears form one of the most remunerative crops in the county. Formerly it was difficult to combat the numerous insects that preyed upon this fruit, but through the aid of the State experimental institutions it has been found possible to eliminate the pests by spraying the trees, at a cost of about twenty dollars an acre. Pears do best on heavy, loamy soil, and Bartlett pears are preferred by the cannery men. First-class pear land can be bought at from $200 to $400 an acre. Approximately ten years is required for pears to mature, but after that they will bring in, under average conditions, about $300 to the acre in gross returns, or about $150 profit. The best results are obtained by grafting on to quince roots. But as Bartletts do not join well with the quince, the difficulty has to be overcome by a clever system of intermediate grafting. The Duchess or Hardy pear is first grafted to the quince, and the Bartlett will then unite with either of these.

Thanks to the best of transportation facilities, the raising of prunes is now a very profitable industry. Ten years ago the local prune market was undeveloped, and prunes were considered a risky crop. Today the grower averages four cents a pound, which will bring in from $200 to $400 to the acre, one half of which will be profit. No better prunes are raised elsewhere in the State than in Contra Costa County. The fruit is of a large size, and the conditions for drying are ideal, there being no heavy fogs to wet or mold the drying products. The French prune is the most satisfactory, as it ripens earliest.

The western end of the county is the home of the peach and apricot. Here the individual growers have set out orchards of various sizes, and the large canning companies have planted vast tracts. Both fruits are raised at a handsome profit.

The eastern section of the county is best adapted to almond-raising. Nor is there any likelihood at present of this field being overcrowded.

The supply does not keep pace with the demand, and it is necessary to import large quantities of almonds every year. Almonds should be planted in light sandy loam, and different varieties should be set out, as cross-pollination is an important factor in successful almond-growing.

Who has not longed to visit Japan in cherry-blossom time? Perhaps the nearest approach to realizing that desire is to be in Contra Costa County during the same period. Cherries are the tenderest of trees and demand the best care, including tillage, drainage, and the highest quality of soil. They will reward the painstaking horticulturist with big returns—sometimes as high as twenty dollars' worth of fruit from a single tree. The Royal Ann and the Bing are best adapted to Contra Costa County.

During late years olives have been very successfully grown in this region. Once it was the general opinion that olives would do well on poor soil, but this has been found to be a fallacy. Those who get the best results are careful to select the right kind of land and give the trees plenty of attention.

The walnuts of Contra Costa County vie with those of any other section of the State. Although a fairly recent industry, walnut-growing bids fair to become a very important factor in the horticultural activities of the county.

Contra Costa County possesses some wonderfully fertile farming lands, especially those which lie along the deltas of the Sacramento and San Joaquin rivers. Here the prize potatoes are grown by the hundreds of thousands of sacks. A large trade has been built up with the Eastern and Central States, which receive potatoes from this section by the trainload.

The small islands lying adjacent to the mainland are phenomenally rich in soil, and the finest vegetables are raised thereon. Contra Costa County is famed for its celery, the white variety, which thrives on the delta lands; likewise its asparagus, which is grown by the hundreds of acres. The green corn from this region is the first to reach the San Francisco market. One might continue the list endlessly, for every kind of garden truck is at home in Contra Costa.

A large amount of alfalfa is grown in the eastern part of the county, and each year shows an increase over the acreage of the previous year.

Alfalfa requires an abundance of water and good soil, both of which are to be had in this region. Plenty of good alfalfa land can still be bought at reasonable prices. Alfalfa is one of the most profitable of agricultural products, as from three to five crops can be mowed yearly, and it has a number of by-products that also bring good returns. It is an ideal stock food and manifests itself in a great improvement in the appearance of the live-stock wherever it is grown.

Wheat, barley, and oats comprise the grain products of the county. The average yield is about twelve centals to the acre, but among the islands of the deltas, where the heaviest crops are garnered, the reward is sometimes as high as twenty-five centals. Contra Costa County has completed a cycle in grain-raising. Fifty or sixty years ago enormous crops of grain were raised. Local seaports were famous for their shipments of grain, which was carried to the ends of the earth by vessels from all nations.

The one difficulty was that the farmers at that time neglected to put back into the soil the valuable elements which they removed, and in time their lands yielded no more than half a crop. But the modern farmer, who must be a scientific farmer if he would succeed, has repaired the omissions of his predecessors. He has given back to the grain-lands the nitrates and fertilizers they require, and the grain yield is again well to the front. The cycle has been completed.

The vineyards of Contra Costa County have become famous the world over. The soil and climatic conditions are peculiarly favorable to the successful growing of dry-wine grapes, out of which has emerged a great industry. Vineyards have quadrupled in twenty years, the acreage increasing from 1500 to over 6000. Wineries have grown from fifteen to fifty in the same length of time. The well-known Italian-Swiss Colony, where a vast amount of California champagne is made, owns 1200 acres of grape land in the county. The success of this industry is largely due to the expert knowledge that has been brought to bear upon it. The choicest cuttings obtainable have been brought from all over the world—from Europe, Asia Minor, Persia, and Egypt—and care has been taken to transplant them in the right kind of soil. The importance of the vine in Contra Costa is evidenced by the fact that the largest wine-cellar in the world is situated at Winehaven, near Richmond.

In concluding this chapter, a word of gratuitous warning is extended to the neophyte farmer whose enthusiasm outruns his judgment. No one should undertake to make his livelihood out of the soil, "in the sweat of his brow," without first giving the matter careful thought. He should consult some of the men who have succeeded and find out how they did it. He should ascertain whether soil and climate are adapted to the things he intends to raise. Also, he should not begin on a scale beyond the limits of his capital. Successful farming is a science, and he who follows it as such will succeed, while he who does not is doomed to certain failure.

CHAPTER IX. MINES AND MINERALS

In 1863 a great excitement was created by the discovery of copper in the county, and one really worthy of the "good times" in mining districts. All at once, nobody could tell why, a grand copper excitement arose, which permeated the whole community. It was reported by various parties that the mountains were full of the ores of copper of untold, because of unknown, richness. Simultaneously with this grand discovery every unemployed man turned prospector. Blankets and bacon, beans and hard bread rose to a premium, and the hills were lighted up at night with hundreds of camp-fires. Hammers and picks were in great demand, and there is ocular evidence even to this day that not a boulder or projecting rock escaped the notice of the prospectors. It was a question of probabilities that were bound soon to harden into certainties. Indeed, it was only a short time before copper prospects were possessed of a definite value. Claims were opened, companies formed, and stock issued on the most liberal scale. Everything wore the couleur de rose.

As usual upon similar occasions, there was great strife about claims. Some were "jumped" on the ground of some informality twice in twenty-four hours. Heavy prices were paid for "choice" ground, and it is quite safe to say that old Mount Diablo's sides and summit have never since borne such an enormous valuation. It seemed as though the whole community had been bitten by the mining tarantula. The excitement lasted for several weeks, growing fiercer from day to day. Scores of men, laden with specimens, thronged the hotels and saloons, and nothing was talked of but "big strikes" and "astounding developments."

Clayton was the center of these mining operations, and town lots were sold at high prices. The ruling price for shares in the Pioneer was $4; in the Eureka, $3.50 and up. Hundreds of companies were formed, and each had hosts of advocates. Shafts were sunk and some ore obtained, and, according to one assay, "there was $48.33 in gold and $243 in silver to the ton"! The first shipment of ore to San Francisco was in September, 1863, of one ton, from the Pioneer claim. Smelting works were erected at Antioch, and the following prices offered: For copper of eight-per-cent quality, $15 per ton; for twelve-per-cent quality, $25 per ton.

Men of experience and practical skill partook of the illusion. All at once the bubble burst. The millionaires of the day left their rude camps in the mountains, and, with ragged breeches and boots out at the toes, subsided at once into despondency and less exciting employment. The hotel- and saloon-keepers, to say nothing of the editors, proceeded to disencumber their premises of accumulated tons of specimens of all kinds of "shiny rocks" to be found within an area of thirty miles square, making quite a contribution to the paving material of the streets.

Silver mines were staked out and partially worked in 1860. The first discovery of silver was made by L. H. Hastings and was taken from the east side of the mountain.

Paint deposits were discovered in 1862 by Doctor Hough, of Martinez, on the banks of the El Hambre Creek. Specimens showed a large number of distinct tints, or colors.

Petroleum wells were sunk near Antioch in 1865, and much land covered with claims. In 1868 oil was also found on the ranch of Dr. Carothers, about three miles from San Pablo, and not less than $25,000 was spent in experiments, fixtures, oil-tanks, retorts, distilleries, etc., but from all these discoveries oil in paying quantities has never been obtained.

Salt was found at a spring near the Marsh ranch, and a company was formed to conduct its operation, but we do not learn that any success followed.

Lime quarries were opened, and in 1862 large quantities of lime were manufactured in the neighborhood of Pacheco from stone found about six miles from Mount Diablo. These quarries, opened in 1850, were the first discovered in the State, and were very profitable.

CEMENT

The cement industry of California is showing a rapid increase. The works of the Cowell Cement Company, one of the greatest plants in the world, are located in Contra Costa County, between Concord and Clayton. Several hundred men are constantly employed at these works, the average annual pay-roll amounting to upward of a quarter of a million dollars.

A railroad was built by the company for the purpose of connecting its great works with the outside world. The road is a standard-gauge line and connects with the Southern Pacific, the Santa Fe, and the Oakland, Antioch & Eastern lines at Bay Point, serving the needs of the rich and fertile Clayton Valley.

COAL

In 1859, at Horse Haven Valley, six miles south of Antioch, William C. Israel, in cleaning out a spring on his land, discovered a vein of coal.

In connection with his father and brother George, he opened the vein for a short distance; but not having capital to work it, they disposed of their interest to James T. Watkins, and one Noyes, who, either from want of knowledge or resources, failed to open the vein so as to make its operation successful. They abandoned the mine in 1861.

On December 22, 1859, at a distance of three and a half miles west of Horse Haven Valley, Francis Somers and James T. Cruikshank discovered the vein of coal which since became known as the Black Diamond vein. Somers and Cruikshank and their associates, W. S. Hawxhurst and Samuel Adams, located the lands afterward known as the Manhattan and Eureka coal mines. George Hawxhurst and George H. P. and William Henderson, in company with Francis Somers, opened the outcropping of the same vein, where were afterward developed the Black Diamond and Cumberland mines; but, believing that the expense of making roads was beyond their means, they made no attempt to secure title. The Black Diamond Mine was subsequently located by Noah Norton, and the Cumberland mine went into the hands of Francis Such and others. These coal lands, with others adjoining, became noted as the Black Diamond Coal Mines.

Frank Such disposed of his interest in the Cumberland Mine to C. T. Cutter, Asher Tyler, Josiah Sturgis, and L. C. Wittenmeyer, all of Martinez. It was from their efforts and capital that the Cumberland Mine was successfully opened and worked, and roads were constructed from it to Clayton and New York Landing (now Pittsburg). They also assisted Noah Norton to open the Black Diamond Mine.

The Pittsburg Mine, east of the Eureka, was located by George H. P. Henderson, who entered into a contract with Ezra Clark to open the mine, in the developing of which the vein of coal known as the Clark vein was discovered.

The Central Coal Mine, east of Pittsburg, was located by John E. Wright. The year following William B. Stewart became connected with it. The Union Mine, north of the Manhattan, was located by George Hawxhurst. The Independence Mine, north of the Eureka, was purchased from Major Richard Charnoch, by Greenhood & Neubauer. The Manhattan Union, Eureka, and Independent comprise the mines forming the basin in which the town of Somersville was situated, and from which there was a railroad for the transportation of coal to Pittsburg Landing on the San Joaquin River. The Cumberland, Black Diamond, Mount Hope, and other lands comprised the basin of the town of Nortonville. From there ran a railroad for the transportation of coal to New York Landing, at the head of Suisun Bay. From the mines enumerated there were about two hundred thousand tons of coal per annum shipped. What is known as the old Central Mine, originally located by William B. Stewart, was operated by Shattuck & Hillegas, of Oakland, and was later sold to the Empire Coal Mine & Railroad Company and was operated by that corporation in conjunction with the Empire Mine.

The Empire Company opened in 1876. It has a magnificent vein of coal, with a railroad to the mine. The mine is six miles from Antioch, within three-fourths of a mile of the first opening made on the coal veins of the county by the Israels. It was owned by George Hawxhurst and John C. Rouse, who, after operating several years, hauling coal by team from the mines to tide-water at Antioch, sold a half-interest in the Empire and Central mines to M. W. Belshaw and Egbert Judson, and formed a co-partnership under the name of Empire Coal Mine & Railroad Company. With the funds supplied by Belshaw and Judson, a narrow-gauge railroad was constructed from the mine to Antioch, and thereafter all coal was transported by rail to this water shipping-point.

After the discovery of the Oregon and Washington coal mines, the Mount Diablo coal being of an inferior quality, was unable to compete, and eventually oil, the steam fuel of today, finished the coal mining in this county. At the present time all the mines are closed and filled with water, the rails were taken up, and probably the mines will never again be operated, unless for the purpose of generating electric power at the several mines, which probably could be done at a profit. Such a project has been carefully considered by owners of the several properties, who figure that the short transmission lines to the industrial centers would counterbalance the additional cost of generating the juice as compared with the electric companies now generating electric power hundreds of miles away in the mountains.

The coal-mining interest rapidly became one of the most important ones of the county. It built up four towns, viz., Somersville, Nortonville, New York Landing (now Pittsburg), and Pittsburg Landing, and added greatly toward the town of Antioch. These mines produced in 1877 108,678 tons of coal, valued at $650,000, as given by the assessor for that year, and 3000 acres of coal lands, valued at $163,300. The tunnels of these mines were high enough for an ordinary-size man to stand erect and about five feet in width. They generally run on an incline to the gangway, and the loaded cars were drawn by mules to the foot of the incline and hoisted to the surface, where they were dumped into bunkers, and from these bunkers emptied into railroad cars and transported by rail to the different landings. The coal was then taken to San Francisco and other cities by river steamers.

CHAPTER X. SAN RAMON VALLEY

It was on such a perfect day in June, 1847, that a canvas-covered wagon drawn by oxen slowly wound its way through a beautiful valley.

This "prairie schooner" carried a little family of home-seekers, and as the oxen moved laboriously along, the scene which greeted the eye at every turn of the winding path called forth exclamations of admiration from the occupants of the wagon. At length the travelers halted the oxen, that they might better gaze and admire the picture of beauty and serenity that was spread before them. On every side, the valley and surrounding hills were covered with thick, velvety clover, and with wild oats standing waist high, waving and rippling in the summer breeze, like the bosom of a lake. The western hills were clumped with oaks, maples, and shrubs; willows and mottled-trunked sycamores fringed the little stream at their left; while the mountains which formed the eastern wall of the valley seemed ever at their side as they journeyed southward. Cattle grazing on the luxuriant grasses, the chirp and twitter of birds, and the drowsy hum of insects completed a picture of beauty, peace, and contentment. Save for the bridle path which was the only guide of our travelers, and for a tule-thatched hut near the stream, used as a rude shelter by Spanish vaqueros when night overtook them in this region, there was nothing to show the hand of man.

This was San Ramon Valley as it looked when first viewed by Americans, when they stopped their ox-team on that June day so long ago, just north of the spot where the village of Alamo now stands. No wonder that the head of that little family bared his brow, as he stood amid the wild oats and exclaimed half in prophecy, half in determination, "Some time we will have a home in this valley." This was before the discovery of gold in California, and this little family were homeseekers, not gold-hunters. But because of the Mexican war which was raging at that time, they sought a settlement for protection, and Pueblo (now San Jose) was their destination.

Four years later, the year 1851, found our home-makers back in the San Ramon Valley, accompanied by another family. These two families, with two others, who joined them later, purchased four leagues of land in the Romero grant, paying for it four thousand dollars.

Is not our pride in our valley justifiable, when one considers that these people who had journeyed by wagon and ox-team over half a continent, and who had the whole State of California to choose from, chose for their home the heart of the San Ramon?

Some changes marked the valley during the four years that had passed, notably the building of adobe houses, which were homes of Spanish families. Viewed through the lapse of years, we associate the adobe with the romantic and the picturesque. Built of adobe bricks dried in the sun, their thick walls and deeply framed doorways and windows afforded warmth in winter and coolness in summer. Every adobe house was surrounded by a portico, about whose rude pillars clambered vines of the mission grape, and in every dooryard bloomed the fragrant Castilian rose of old Spain. The adobes call to mind tales of the gay, care-free life of the Spanish days in California. We think of the fandango, the soft music of the guitar, and the horsemen with their wide sombreros, their bright-colored serapes, their jingling spurs, and their horses no less gaily bedecked in silver-mounted bridles, and saddles with monstrous tapaderas.

But one may ask why in our valley today we find no descendants of these gay, pleasure-loving people. That question may be answered in two words—the "manana" of the ease-loving Spaniard, and the "today" of the hustling, progressive American.

Soon after the coming of the first American home-makers in 1851, others followed, and the fifties saw the arrival of many settlers in the valley. There followed a season of prosperity. Farms were improved with houses, barns, and granaries, a few fruit trees were set out, and gardens planted. The fertile land, little of which had ever known a plowshare, under American thrift was cultivated and made to produce abundantly.

In the midst of this prosperity, a heavy blow fell upon the residents. The Spanish grants under which title the people had bought their land, became the cause of years of litigation, and many residents were forced to pay for their land a second time.

In those days all were neighbors in the fullest sense of the word, helping one another by an exchange of work, all joining together in their few social affairs, and ready to aid when sickness or death entered a home. Doctors were far away, and trained nurses were unknown, but it was nothing unusual for a pioneer mother to ride miles on horseback, often with a baby in her arms, to care for a sick neighbor.

The first post-office in San Ramon Valley was established in 1853 and named "Alamo"—a Spanish word meaning poplar tree. The post office was given quarters at the home of John M. Jones, who lived in an adobe house that crowned the knoll of the O. J. Reis home-site just north of Alamo. Mr. Jones was the first postmaster, and his wife, Mrs. Mary A. Jones, was his deputy. For many years Alamo was the only post-office between Martinez and Mission San Jose. The mail was carried between these two points by a man with a horse and cart, who made a round trip twice each week.

Alamo is the second oldest town in the county, Martinez being the oldest. The first house in the town of Alamo was built by a man named George Engelmeyer. He at first had a shoe-shop, but soon enlarged his shop to a general merchandise store and did such a thriving business that in a short time he had to employ a clerk. Other shops soon followed—blacksmith, harness, and butcher shops, and a hotel. In 1858 the frame building still standing under the maples and walnuts on the west side of the street was built. The lower floor of this building was used as the general merchandise store of Lomax & Smart, while the upper floor was the Masonic lodge-room. Alamo Lodge No. 122, F. & A. M., which now holds its meetings at Walnut Creek, was organized at Alamo in 1858, and this old building was its first home. In 1860 a two-story brick structure was erected on the west side of the street, on the property now owned by Mrs. George Smith. Wolfe & Cohen were the owners of the general merchandise store which occupied the lower story, while the Masonic lodge moved from its first location into the more commodious quarters of the upper story of the new brick building. The bricks of which this building was constructed, were made by G. W. Webster, who lived on what is now the Van Gorden place. The brick-kiln was situated on the Rancho el Rio, just across the creek from the Van Gorden pear orchard. In the great earthquake of 1868 the building mentioned was badly damaged and was soon afterward torn down.

The ruin known as the Foster House is of historic interest. It was erected in 1857 by James Foster, of Maine, and the staunch timbers of which it is constructed were made from trees which grew in the Maine woods. The lumber for the house was sawed, shaped, and fitted, all ready to put together, then shipped around the Horn to its destined home. Mr. Foster was a wheelwright, and wagons, carriages, furniture, and even coffins, when occasion required, were turned out from his shop with a neatness and finish that would do credit to the present day.

In 1854 the first school in San Ramon Valley opened its doors in a little house which stood in the northern part of what is now the Kendall property, near the cemetery. Richard Webster was the first teacher.

Soon after, a church (Cumberland Presbyterian) was built near the schoolhouse, on the lot which is now a driveway leading to the cemetery. For a while a school was conducted in a little house that stood on a bedrock knoll a short distance north of the point where the Southern Pacific Railroad crosses the county road between Alamo and Walnut Creek. This was known as the "Wall" schoolhouse, being near the home of Captain Wall, at that time the owner of the Foulds ranch.

In 1859 leading residents organized the Contra Costa Educational Association, and erected the Union Academy, a boarding and day school. The academy opened for instruction in June, 1860, with Rev. David McClure as its first principal, while Silas Stone, John M. Jones, and Robert Love comprised its first board of trustees. The Union Academy was a large three-story structure, centrally located between Alamo and Danville, on the west side of the county road, on land that is now a prune orchard belonging to Mr. E. B. Anderson. The fine locusts which grace the roadway at that spot were planted in the days of the academy, to adorn the entrance to its grounds. John H. Braly, in later years principal of the San Jose Normal School, succeeded Dr. McClure as principal. Mr. Braly's successor was Rev. Robert King, and in 1868, during his principalship, the academy was destroyed by fire, and was never rebuilt. The church building almost directly opposite the academy site afforded temporary school accommodations. In the meantime other towns had sprung up—Danville, Limerick (now San Ramon), and Walnut Creek, situated at the junction of Walnut and San Ramon creeks. District schools were established at Alamo and at these younger towns.

In 1910, by popular vote of Danville, San Ramon, Alamo, Green Valley, and Sycamore districts, a high school was established at Danville, and named the San Ramon Valley Union High School. Although still in its infancy, it gives promise of becoming a power in the land.

In nothing does history show progress in greater degree than in modes of transportation. Beginning with that ox-team which "geehawed" its way through our valley in 1847, we may trace the means of travel next by the saddle-horse, then by carriages drawn by horses.

Next came the steam railroad with the advent of the Southern Pacific in 1891; in more recent years scores of automobiles, and now since 1914 the Oakland, Antioch & Eastern Railway, land us in the metropolis in less than two hours.

Since the coming of our first American settlers in 1851, the years have brought many changes besides those of transportation. Many of the big ranches have been divided into smaller holdings. With the increase of population and more intensive farming, land has steadily increased in value, and, instead of being sold by the "league," it is measured to the hundredth of an acre. Instead of the scattering farmhouses of the fifties, the valley and foothills are dotted with comfortable and attractive homes.

Better facilities for handling perishable products, have changed many grain-fields into orchards, and fruit from San Ramon Valley now commands the highest prices in the markets of Eastern cities.

CHAPTER XI. CENTRAL CONTRA COSTA COUNTY

No phrases of speech can fitly portray the panorama of changes that have passed before this one narrow field of vision during the comparatively brief period of time 'twixt then and now. An appreciable representation of these should be pictured by the genius of a Michael Angelo upon a furlong canvas. It is only by this means that the contrasting of then and now can be presented to the quick glance of comprehension.

The very face of the landscape has been changed; the names and customs and the very elements of society have changed. If real improvements and real progress are to be tested or measured by the comparative happiness of men and women, then there have been no improvements, no progress. It is only change. The old picture has been rudely effaced by social vandalism, and the canvas bedaubed with a new representation.

The features and the life of the landscape have been changed. Standing upon the mountain-tops sixty years ago, in the beginning of the month of May, one there and then beheld the broad-spreading plains and the gracefully undulating hills all clothed in verdure and beautified, as if by special ornamentation, with scattered groves of evergreen oaks, and here and there the tortuous fringes and dense clusters of the willows, marking the course of the rivulets and the locations of the living springs. This was simple inanimate nature, but the life of the landscape were the cattle upon a thousand hills. Myriads of cattle, bovine cattle, all spotted cattle, were feeding and roaming without limit over all the land, over all the sides and summits of the green hills, and over all the green-covered valleys and plains—these valleys and hills around us here. And there note also the dashing, picturesque vaquero, with his swinging lariat, making his oft-repeated charges among those wild flocks, arousing headlong stampedes among them. No prim, prudish artificial fencing of unsightly posts and boards then disfigured the landscape. Property boundaries of territory were marked only by natural monuments. The mountain's crest, the meandering creek, the isolated boulder, the venerable oak, the living spring, the shore of the sea—these were the landmarks of the ranchero's wide domains. Nor was this pueblo of ours (Concord) thought worthy of artificial protection; whole bands of these wild cattle together would come charging down from the hills, and careering through the streets, would escape the fierce pursuit of a dozen vaqueros. No foolish artificial fencing then.

Over all the land no vandal plow had ever scarred and mutilated the face of nature, over all the land no square miles of nature's green had been discolored to the dirty brown of tillage; but the whole earth, from the Sierras to the Pacific sea, was one limitless, universal pasture-land, resting beautiful and grand under the glorious brightness of a California sunshine.

The elements of society have changed. Sixty years ago the Spanish population was the elemental rule—all others were only the exception.

There were the Alvarados, the Castros, the Martinez, the Sepulvedas, the Estudillos, the Moragas, the Briones, the Sunols, the Sotos, the Peraltas, the Altemeranos, the Amadors, the Mirandas, the Berryessas, the Pachecos, the Bacas, the Higueras, the Alvisos, the Naviagas—all these proud, grand old families, each under the benignant rule of its kind old patriarch. It was most delightful to be among them at their homes — these rich, extravagant, hospitable, confiding, simple-minded, old-fashioned people. There was no shoddyism discovered there; all their surroundings were old-fashioned, neat, and comfortable. Just think of that sumptuous dinner of Spanish cookery and those luxurious feather beds after the fatiguing hard day's ride on horseback. The young men of each household, although sometimes reckless and wild like other boys, were polite, sprightly, and handsome. The young women were beautiful and graceful, with manners most charming. One never will forget those social fandangos. Now the Spanish noun fandango is often used by stupid Americanos as an expression of contempt. But this comprehensive Spanish word has the same purport as the two English words "social party." Their beautiful dances were the very poetry of motion, and they were tastefully adopted by well-bred American society.

There was another seemingly barbarous amusement which had been adopted hundreds of years before from the Moorish customs. We refer to the renowned Spanish bull-fight, which at one time was as popular as it was dangerous.

We have said the Spanish ranchero was extravagant in his mode of living. Well, why not? He could well afford to be extravagant, for he was rich, very rich. There were those dozen solid silver candlesticks; there were those solid silver salvers three feet long; there were those quaint old Mexican table sets of solid silver. The ladies of the household were provided with sumptuous and most costly apparel. He had gold in abundance, the proceeds from the ready sale of his thousands of beef cattle. And what could he do with all this gold? He said, "Let us have sport with it," and so he and his neighboring rancheros had their regular gambling set-to every Sunday evening after church. His wide domain of square leagues more than equaled any German principality.

That earthquake proof adobe cottage, that vineyard, that bubbling spring of purest water, that sparkling living brook, that cool shade of waving willows, the soft breeze of a peculiar climate, that quiet seclusion from the striving world, made up his beautiful garden of paradise. Conscious of his independence and wealth, of his thousands for him and for his for all coming time, he never dreamt of a reverse of fortune.

But a change came over the spirit of his dream. The unscrupulous Yankee finds his resting-place. A few thousand dollars in gold coin is temptingly exhibited; the wine circulates freely, with the oft-repeated "Buena salud"; conversation becomes interesting and animated, and the patriarch and his household are charmed with their new-found acquaintance, the artful and polished visitor. A loan of this money is most graciously tendered by this most liberal stranger; a little more wine is taken for the stomach's sake, with another "Buena salud" all around, and the proffered loan is as graciously accepted, more to oblige the accomplished guest than for any possible need or use for the ready cash; a promissory note, prepared beforehand, written in English, and made payable one day after date, bearing interest at the rate of seven per cent a month, to be compounded monthly, is accepted, and the usual accompanying death-pledge upon that principality of square leagues, is mirthfully executed by the confiding, simple-minded, illiterate Spaniard as if it were a passing jest. So much droll ceremony with reference to that mere trifle of money was light comedy to him, in the amusing program of the day's entertainment. Time rolls on— months, years pass away. Where does that elegant gentleman keep himself? Why does he not come and get his money? Surely he is a most indulgent creditor. The illiterate Spaniard has no conception of the cumulative effect of interest compounded. In the lapse of time the insignificant financial comedy is scarcely remembered. Eventually, a polite note is received, as coming from the court, with reference to that almost forgotten subject. Of course, there is nothing to be said by way of objection; it is all right. Why, then, should he trouble himself with giving any heed to it? That little affair of a few thousand dollars can be refunded any day. Why does not the gentleman come and pay us a visit? That little matter of money is ready for him any day. He promised to come and see us again.

More years have glided into the past, and that paltry item of interest has regularly and steadily compounded over a hundred times; the principal and interest have gradually rolled up to the immense amount of two hundred and fifty thousand dollars—a full quarter of a million!

In time the mortgage is foreclosed. Then comes the auction sale; and there the prowling agent of the relentless creditor, without competition, bids in those many square miles of land for only a half of the enormous debt. It is then only that the credulous dreaming Spanish family is startled and awakened as by an earthquake shock! The business was complicated and needed the deft handling of financial ability. Redemption is impossible. The final judicial process is the closing act of the drama, and that splendid estate comes under the dominion of the stranger. The patriarch and his numerous household are exiled from their home forever, while indigence and wretched want attend them as they scatter and wander away.

EARLY SETTLEMENT

During the year 1828 the Rancho Monte del Diablo, comprising four leagues of land, was granted to Don Salvio Pacheco, a gentleman who was widely known throughout the department of California, and held many high offices in the gift of the Mexican Government. At that time he was a resident of the Pueblo de San Jose, and it was not until the year 1834 that he took actual possession and commenced stocking his vast property with cattle—for be it remembered that the early Californian was a stock-raiser rather than a farmer. Don Salvio died at his residence near Concord. This gentleman came to the rancho during a portion of each year. In 1845 he brought his family to the county and made his permanent home in Contra Costa. In the early days the Pachecos owned fully five thousand head of cattle, while it may be stated, as showing that the rancho life was not always one of indolence, that it was usual to shut up for the night as many as one thousand calves.

Up until 1852 there was no accession to the foreign population of the township under consideration. In that year we learn that Asa Bowen settled on the place later occupied by Silverio Soto and William C. Prince. In the same year Benjamin Shreve resided a short time in Ygnacio Valley, but afterward moved to Lafayette.

It should be mentioned that in 1850 valuable lime quarries were discovered at the foot of Mount Diablo by Frank Such, who at once commenced the task of developing them. In company with W. E. Whitney, Such supplied vast quantities of the lime for the mortar that was first used in San Francisco, the material being shipped from the landing six miles from the mouth of Mount Diablo Creek. Excellent kilns, capable of burning four hundred and fifty barrels at a time, and yielding three thousand barrels per month, were there erected.

In November, 1852, Randolph H. Wight, for many years one of the Board of Supervisors of Contra Costa County, settled in the New York Valley, where he resided with his brother until 1857, when he moved to his own residence. On his arrival Mr. Wight found the Olmstead and Strode families settled here, the former living in a house built in 1850—the first dwelling in that portion of the township—where later stood the Stone House, first occupied by Joseph Anderson, and afterward by Daniel Cunningham. In that year the first orchards were planted in New York Valley section of Township Number Three.

Our readers are all familiar with the stretch of territory forming the high land between Mount Diablo and Walnut Creek, then embraced in English and Kapp's property, comprising some three thousand acres in all, and usually called the Government Ranch. This name, however, is misleading. We are informed by reliable authority that the ranch was never the property of the Government, nor was it leased by them.

It was purchased by two officers of the Quartermaster's Department of the United States Army, Majors Allen and Loring, in or about 1851. From the fact of the army mules being pastured there at one time, the public gave the tract the name of the Government Ranch. It was one league of the Pacheco grant, and was sold to Majors Allen and L-oring for $12,500. There the two officers shortly after erected several buildings, but these have not been used for residence for years. These buildings, ready to be set up, were imported from Norway. They were constructed without nails, and, as all the parts were numbered, they were easily put together. Major Allen never lived on the ranch. On Loring's death, however, he acquired that gentleman's share and afterward sold out to Doctor L. C. Frisbie, of Solano County, who disposed of it to Judge S. C. Hastings. One-half of it was bought by G. W. Colby from Judge Hastings, who gave the remaining moiety to his son, C. F. D. Hastings, who sold it to Barry Baldwin, and from him it passed to the hands of other owners.

We now come to that epoch when every available acre of the township was taken up by squatters—not a quarter-section but had been taken possession of by those dispirited men from the mines.

Prominent among those to settle in Ygnacio Valley in 1851 was James T. Walker, the nephew of the renowned Captain Joe Walker.

He built himself a beautiful home and owned a large estate of hill and valley lands. His house commanded one of the most magnificent prospects conceivable, as it took in the fertile valley, dotted with umbrageous oaks, and blended in the blue distance with Suisun Bay and the hills beyond. In the same year Mr. Walker's companion, Frank McClellan, settled on the place where Lawrence Geary resided. Of the others who came in the year 1853 were "Jerry" Morgan, George Petwin, Penniman, Seymour, Myron Gibson, Robert McPherson, Alonzo Plumley, the Smiths, Ben Hockabout, "Hank," Henry, and John Davis, and Vandermark. Seymour settled near the section where W. C. Prince was located; Barnheisel occupied a point near Major's farm; Ed. Legrand had a forty-acre tract above the Lohse place, and known afterward as the Shannon tract; Morgan was located where J. F. S. Smith resided, his cabin being on the hill once occupied by the barn; Myron and John Gibson and James Toomey occupied a portion of the splendid ranch later owned by Munson Gregory, and as far as Bray's residence in Pine Canon. In October, 1853, Doctor E. F. Hough, then of Martinez, located in Ygnacio Valley, entered upon the practice of his profession, and after some obstructiveness on the part of native Californians, established a lasting popularity. He also opened a store and house of entertainment, which he conducted until 1855, when, disposing of his interest, he removed to the county seat. This was the first store in the township. In 1853 Prince bargained with Asa Bowen for his farm; he found on the place a full crop of sweet potatoes of some fifteen to twenty acres in extent. It was in 1852 or 1853 that the first crop of wheat in this section was sown. On May 3, 1853, Samuel S. Bacon came to the Government Ranch, and in the fall built a stable for fourteen mules, for Majors Allen and Loring of the United States Army.

Of the very few names remembered, those of Bishop and Van Ryder may be mentioned; they resided on the place now owned by Charles S. Lohse, where they cultivated a small patch of wheat in partnership. At that period there was not a semblance of a town in the county save at Martinez. F. L. Such was foreman for a San Francisco firm, and had the limekiln mentioned elsewhere; it was situated on the right bank of the branch of Mount Diablo Creek, where he established a landing.

The creek was then sufficiently large for craft of nearly one hundred tons; today it is almost filled up. The lime enterprise was continued until 1862; then it lay dormant for a time, and under the supervision of another firm was revived and worked until about the year 1870. In later years it was again taken up, and has continued to the present time a large and profitable industry.

In the New York Valley district in 1853 Charles L. Bird located on the land then owned by the Colby estate, C. J. Pramberg, and Hilshin and Johnson. Toward the end of the year Knight settled on what was later the Cunningham estate. In the spring of that year Charles N. Wight joined his brother in that section. Here, in 1853, the first land was plowed, and about seven acres sowed in wheat. An excellent crop was the out-turn, but, owing to the want of proper threshing facilities, not much good resulted.

The parents of S. P. Davis, of Brentwood, located in the Pacheco Valley, near Clayton, October 17, 1853, and with their son resided for many years in that region.

In the spring of 1854, William C. Prince, who came to his uncle, Elam Brown, in 1849, removed from Lafayette to his farm in Ygnacio Valley, which he purchased the year previous. In 1854, including squatters, there were fully twenty-five families settled in Ygnacio Valley, the produce of which was shipped from the embarcadero at Pacheco to San Francisco. Cultivation had become general and immense crops were raised. In that year came to Bay Point district, Newton Woodruff, accompanied by his brothers Asa, Philo, and Simeon, the last of whom remained some five or six years. The first school in the township was established in that year in Ygnacio Valley.

Among the settlers of the township in 1855 was C. B. Porter, who served in both the upper and lower house in the State legislature and was well known as the editor and proprietor of the Contra Costa Gazette.

In 1855 Ignacio Soto joined his brothers, who had preceded him to Contra Costa County, on the thousand-acre tract in the Ygnacio Valley. Here he resided until his death, which occurred June 15, 1882. In 1857 Munson Gregory acquired, and in 1858 settled on, his Ygnacio Valley ranch. In 1857 E. R. McPherson settled in the Ygnacio Valley, and on December 4th George P. Loucks took up his residence in the township. Mr. Loucks, besides having filled the office of county clerk, also held a seat on the Board of Supervisors of Contra Costa County.

In 1858 David S. Woodruff settled at Bay Point and Syranus Standish in Pacheco. In 1859 J. A. Littlefield and Theodore Downing became residents of the township, and in 1860 Ludwig Anderson and D. G. Barnett each located in the town of Pacheco.

The reader will naturally remark that the foregoing gentlemen are not all of those that settled in the township, still they are the only names that are remembered by many of the oldest residents. We will now turn to a few remarks upon the villages in Township Number Three.

In 1845 the first abode of any kind to be erected in this vast country was made of skins of cattle, elk, bear, and deer, and was erected upon the bank of the lake in the vicinity of the Galindo homestead.

In the late forties and early fifties the present old adobe building, later the property of Mrs. Holler, was erected, and during the old days of Spanish grandeur was the scene of many notable weddings, as well as many state affairs and social functions. Today it remains intact, except that the tile roof has been replaced with shingles and weatherboards have been placed upon the outside to protect the sturdy walls from the ravages of time.

There is a long porch on either side of the building, giving a commanding view of the country for miles in every direction, a popular feature in the days when the roving herds of wild deer, elk, bear, and prowling Indians made life exciting for the early settler. It is hardly conceivable by the present generation that deer and elk were so thick in this section that they were lassoed. There are today choice specimens of horns preserved in many homes as relics of that bygone time.

CONCORD

In the year 1869, owing to the continued yearly flooding of the town of Pacheco, whereby the inhabitants were put to great expense for raising buildings, etc., Salvio Pacheco, Fernando Pacheco, and Francisco Galindo, to whom belonged the land, offered to lay out a town some two miles east of Pacheco. The plot was surveyed by Lewis Castro and laid off into lots and streets. It contained twenty acres, divided into nineteen blocks and a plaza.

In the naming of the new town there was much variety of disputation. At first the Spanish population and donors of the land wanted it to be named Todos Santos (All Saints), by which name it is recorded.

The Americans had dubbed it Drunken Indian, with that genius that the early pioneers displayed for the science of nomenclature. But it was finally left to the public to give it the name of Concord, by which it is now officially known.

In 1870 a school was started in its precincts, first taught by Mrs. Henry Polley, nee Carpenter. In 1873 a handsome Catholic church was erected and was duly dedicated November 5, 1876.

Don Salvio Pacheco died at his residence at Concord, August 9, 1876, at the age of eighty-five years. He was born near San Diego, and his entire life was spent in California. For a number of years he was alcalde of the Pueblo de San Jose and also several times a member of the Departmental Assembly, earning an honorable reputation in the discharge of public duties. The grant of Monte del Diablo, embracing four leagues of land, was made to him by Governor Micheltorena in 1834, but it was some ten or twelve years later when he established his residence on the property, where he continued to reside till the time of his death.

In the laying out and the opening up of the town of Concord it was decided by the donors to give those of the residents and business men of Pacheco who would locate in the new town a certain number of lots free. Among the first to take advantage of this new scheme was Samuel Bacon. He had suffered from the floods of Pacheco, where he had a store. He therefore came to the new town, and in June, 1869, completed his store, which will be remembered by many of our citizens as standing on the location of the present First National Bank building.

Later he erected a residence next his store, and here Samuel Bacon and his wife continued to reside until his death, which occurred about twenty years ago. This dwelling was also removed to make room for the bank building.

In the summer of 1869 Charles Lohse erected a machine-shop opposite Bacon's store, and Henry Loring (now deceased) erected what was first known as Klein's Hotel, now called the Concord Hotel. During that summer several buildings were erected and there sprang up a number of business establishments.

John Brawand and George Gavin, both deceased, were among the first settlers in Concord, and their children and grandchildren are now prominently identified with the business and social welfare of the community. Charles Lohse is perhaps the only one now living (1916) of those who came to the town in its infancy. He resides on his fine farm in Ygnacio Valley and is hale and hearty in spite of the fact that he is over ninety years old.

Where the Bank of Concord building now stands was located a frame building occupied by Foskett & Elsworthy as a butcher shop, which they occupied until the January block was completed, when they moved to the store formerly occupied by Levinson.

Where the cafe of the Concord Inn now stands was located the Mount Diablo Hotel, now on Mount Diablo Street, corner of Lincoln.

The old Mount Diablo Hotel continued for years under the management of John Wichers until his death, after which many managers controlled its destinies, until some years ago, when it was sold to make way for a more important structure, and the Salvio-Street portion of the Concord Inn was erected thereon.

In 1898 Joe F. Rosa took charge of the Concord Hotel. Although enlarged and modernized, it still retains some of its old-time features.

Concord's first bakery was opened by John Lambert in a small frame building on the site of Manuel Nunes' property. In 1889 he built the frame building which has served since then as his bakery. In later years he erected two brick buildings upon his adjoining property.

In 1892 the present grammar school was built, and in 1906 the present high-school building was erected.

Concord continued upon the even tenor of its way until, on February 5, 1905, it became an incorporated city, and then and there Concord awoke. The first step in the march of progress was electric lights for both streets and buildings. Next came the inaugurating of a water system for both fire and commercial purposes, to be closely followed by a modern sewer system, and last of all of the great improvements, that of street-work. Concord has completed its streets, having every thoroughfare within its incorporated borders paved, and it is doubtful if there is another city of its size in the State of California that can make such a statement.

With the advent of the Oakland, Antioch & Eastern Railway, in 1912, Concord experienced quite a boom, during which time many old landmarks gave way to large modern buildings.

Concord is a city well worth seeing, with its paved streets, its fine business buildings and pretty residences, its nice park, and, above all, its mild and agreeable climate.

During the last few years poultrymen have realized the advantages of the climate for the rearing of poultry, and its easy access to the large bay cities makes it an ideal country. They are fast locating in central Contra Costa adjacent to Concord, and already many poultry ranches are located within these confines.

For the last thirty-five years Concord has been served with a weekly newspaper, the first issue of the Concord Sun having come out about that time under the editorship of S. Fargeon, now deceased. The Sun had its setting a few years later but was immediately revived and renamed the Concord Transcript by Hart A. Downer. Succeeding Downer J. S. Taylor assumed control and for a number of years held sway, selling out to H. E. Griffith, who after a few years disposed of the paper to Mrs. N. K. Cushing. This was in 1905, and Mrs. Cushing continued at the helm for five years. In April, 1910, a number of prominent citizens of Concord purchased the paper and formed a corporation known as the Transcript Publishing Company, employing J. R. Boothe as editor. In the period from the formation of the corporation until the summer of 1913 a number of different editors endeavored to steer the craft, but for the company the paper was not a paying venture, and at the time stated T. G. Elbury and S. W. Holcomb bought up the stock. They remained in control less than a year, disposing of the business to the present management on March 1, 1914. The paper has been under Miss Catherine Burke's control ever since, and is counted one of the most successful newspapers, both financially and otherwise, in Contra Costa County. The Transcript is published every Thursday afternoon, and is a seven-column eight-page paper.

Concord today is well equipped with business of all kinds—two banks, several general merchandise stores, hardware-stores, good hotels, drug-stores, garages, machine-shops and blacksmith-shops, three churches, a good fire department, and in fact every convenience that goes to make up a city where people enjoy living.

Salvio Pacheco, in July, 1852, was assessed for 17,712 acres of land, valued at 8141,696, or eight dollars an acre.

The present board of trustees of Concord are E. J. Randall (chairman), Clark Jaquith, Charles Dunn, Joseph Rosa, and Henry Bott.

PACHECO

In 1860 Hale & Fassett, with Doctor Carothers, purchased the site of Pacheco and laid it out in town lots. With a keen perception of the natural advantages of the situation, its proximity to an embarcadero, and its lying on the main line of travel, these enterprising gentlemen at once commenced building. Hale & Fassett erected a store and a large warehouse at the bayside, and in a short time were doing a large profitable business. Others came in, lots were bought, and the place soon had the elements of prosperity.

Long before Pacheco came into existence, however, G. L. Walrath had in 1853 erected the residence later occupied by George P. Loucks.

As far back as 1853 there was a warehouse owned by Lathrop, Fish, and Walrath, that later was possessed by Bray Brothers, of San Francisco, while in 1857 Mr. Loucks built another 150 feet in length, and in 1858 there was 125 feet added to it. This stood on the bank of Walnut Creek, about one mile east of the town. In the fall of 1862, owing to the rapid filling in of the stream, it was moved down the creek about three-quarters of a mile. In 1857 W. K. Hendricks acquired land from Mr. Loucks, and on it built the mill. These two enterprises were the primary causes of the starting of Pacheco.

At an early date the creek had its course to the rear of the store of John Gambs, while the county road ran along the line of the creek. The earliest sailing-craft to ply to the locality were those trading to the lime-kiln of F. L. Such. The first to come to Louck's wharf were the "C. E. Long," Captain Gus. Henderson, and the "Ida," Captain Ludwig Anderson.

The land on which the town stands was surveyed by J. B. Abbott, and on it Hale & Fassett built the first house, it being the long store later occupied by John Gambs. About the same time Ludwig Anderson erected his residence, while the first brick house was put up by Elijah Hook. The first hotel was opened by Woodford, and thus the town had its start. In 1860 J. H. Troy's first fire-proof building was completed.

Almost in the year of its birth Pacheco was visited by a devastating fire. On August 11, 1860, a fire broke out in the village, when the store of Elijah Hook, known as the "Farmers' Block," the concrete block of Doctor J. H. Carothers, and several other buildings were consumed, with a loss of about $26,400. A little more than seven years later another disastrous conflagration took place; on August 15, 1867, the Pacheco flour mills were totally destroyed. This loss was a public as well as a private calamity. The loss, amounting to no less than from $14,000 to $16,000, on which there was no insurance, was a very severe one to the proprietor, W. J. Ireland, and swept away the earnings of a life of industry. Besides the loss of the mills, about $2000 worth of wheat and flour was consumed, the property of various farmers in the vicinity.

The next fire that occurred was the burning of Judge Warmcastle's farmhouse on April 1, 1870. The building was rented by Mr. Minaker.

The last of all these conflagrations and the most destructive took place on the morning of Tuesday, September 5, 1871, when the village was once more visited by the fire fiend and damage done to the amount of $30,000 and more. The principal losers were E. Hook, three buildings and stock—loss, $18,000; L. F. Mareno, building, harness stock, and household goods—loss, $2500; Bunker & Porter, Contra Costa Gazette —loss, $2000; Odd Fellows Hall—loss, $2000; L. Anderson—loss, $500; J. H. Troy—loss, $500.

When Pacheco Fire Engine Company No. 1 was organized we have been unable to gather, nor do we know who its first officers were, but that there was such an organization is certain, for we find Don Salvio Pacheco, on February 16, 1861, presenting them with a handsome banner, trimmed with gold lace, and surmounted with a golden eagle.

On September 12, 1863, Pacheco Lodge No. 117, I. O. O. F., was organized in Pacheco, with the following officers: Paul Shirley, N. G.; W. T. Hendrick, T. G.; L. B. Farish, secretary; John Gambs, treasurer; J. H. Carothers, warden. It was removed a few years later to Concord. In 1914 the building was remodeled throughout and is now one of the finest fraternal halls in Contra Costa County.

The great earthquake which occurred at eight o'clock on the morning of October 21, 1868, did considerable damage in Pacheco among the brick and concrete buildings, though a number of the frame buildings also suffered.

On May 29, 1869, the Western Union Telegraph Company completed their line to Pacheco, en route to Antioch. On June 19 in that year Mohawk Tribe No. 20, I. O. R. M., was instituted in Pacheco.

On December 29, 1870, the certificate of incorporation of the Contra Costa Savings & Loan Bank was filed. The following were the directors: Barry Baldwin, G. M. Bryant, Walter K. Dell, John Gambs, W.

M. Hale. The capital stock was laid at $50,000, and the existence of the corporation was limited to fifty years.

On February 6, 1871, the Pacheco Tobacco Company was incorporated, with a capital stock of $10,000, for the purpose of curing and manufacturing tobacco.

The first church built in Pacheco was the Presbyterian, in 1862, and later a Roman Catholic church, and at a still later date the meetinghouse of the Congregational church.

In the year 1859 a schoolhouse was constructed, and D. S. Woodruff was the first instructor. This continued until 1872, when it was deemed advisable to acquire a new school site, adjacent to the Catholic church, where it would be less likely to be flooded than in its former position.

The Pacheco flour-mill was erected in 1857, by W. T. Hendrick, who afterward disposed of it to W. J. Ireland.

L. Anderson's lumber yard was established by Capt. Ludwig Anderson in 1860.

CHAPTER XII. EASTERN CONTRA COSTA COUNTY

That portion of Contra Costa County lying east of the Mount Diablo Range—which includes a fringe of the great delta—has long been known and referred to as "Eastern Contra Costa," its boundaries being well defined by the Diablo Range on the west and the western branch of the San Joaquin, known as Old River, following it to its intersection with the main river, thence to Suisun Bay.

The history of this particular section is not of absorbing interest in its occupation and settlement—rather commonplace in its historical importance as an integral part of the State—but in the compilation of the history of Contra Costa County is worthy of a conspicuous place, inasmuch as it has long been recognized as one of the garden-spots of the State and as the early home of one of California's most noted pioneers.

Therefore, you who scan these pages will not expect a thrilling or tragic story of frontier life, nor yet a recital of dramatic scenes traced with the graphic pen of a Gibbon or in the elegant diction of a Macaulay.

but rather in the plain, unvarnished tongue of one who came early upon the scene, will the simple story of conditions and of incidents and men who were the first to drift into this primitive and unpeopled land be told—men who had courageously braved the dangers of land and sea to reach it, and who came bringing their household gods, their traditions and civilization with them, to establish here on the Pacific Coast their homes and altars, to assist in building a new State, and to build into its foundations the principles of justice and freedom. So surely as they have done this, so surely have they made history, and so surely is the record worthy of transmission to posterity that the yet unborn may read in gratification of their pride in their ancestors who laid the foundations of this great commonwealth, perpetuating therein the rich and inestimable legacy they had received as a heritage from their American ancestry.

Imagine yourself standing in the basket of a tethered balloon 3849 feet above the earth, with an unobstructed view of the world below. You would gaze with inspirations of delight upon the picture thus presented.

Standing on the summit of Mount Diablo, that cone-like pinnacle that rises to the above elevation in the central part of Contra Costa County, a panoramic view is obtained that, however gifted, no artist's brush could paint or pen faithfully portray. It is simply a wonderful and interesting picture of valleys "cradled in the hills," of farms, orchards, hamlets, towns, cities—long stretches of watercourses, silvery in the sunlight—great bays and far-reaching inlets, with sail and steam craft crawling on their surface like flies on a gigantic mirror—vast areas of plains—the islands of the great delta of the Sacramento and San Joaquin rivers; and beyond, dim in the distance, the Sierras lift their lofty and luminous summits, snow-crested, into the imperial blue of unclouded skies.

Westward the busy mart of San Francisco with its peopled streets and moving car-lines, its domes and steepled churches, the long lines of drifting smoke from furnace fires—the Golden Gate and the Farallon Islands, and, far beyond the shore line of the continent, the gray waste of the ocean even to the horizon's verge—in all directions, far as the eye can reach, tinted with light and shadow and rifts of color, extends this scenic picture.

It is from this viewpoint that I invite you to look down upon the eastern portion of Contra Costa County. The narrow rim of rounded and rapidly descending foothills that adjoin the mountains on the east, and which remind one of bubbles on the surface of a boiling cauldron, soon disappear, merged into a slightly descending plain that stretches away eastward to the great tule delta that from this height appears like a great splash of green on the landscape, separated into islands by glinting and tortuous watercourses.

Here, in a conspicuous locality on this plain, near the foothills, on the line of the Southern Pacific Railroad, stands the village of Brentwood.

Its environment is the twenty-five or thirty sections of free alluvial soil created by the joint action and wash of Marsh and Kellogg creeks, that drain the eastern watershed of Mount Diablo and the Black Hills. It is a neat country village with broad smooth streets and cement sidewalks.

It excusedly boasts of a beautiful hotel built of fortified concrete, in the Mission style of architecture, regardless of cost in construction or appointment, an ornamental bank building, and, owing to the central location, a high school has been established that is modestly hidden in the heart of the village. This is supplemented by a manual-training school and all the accessories that go to constitute it an up-to-date institution of learning, duly accredited to the University of California. It has, also, a fine grammar school, two churches, stores, shops, and business houses incidental to a modern village, a large grain warehouse that handles thousands of tons of wheat and barley, the products of its fertile acres.

It would be pleasant to dilate on the future of this favored section, to speak of the splendid system of irrigation constructed and completed, to picture these broad acres, that once were waving grain-fields, painted with the living green of alfalfa and orchard, dotted with the homes of the small farmer living upon and cultivating his crops in conscious security against the fickle seasons with their insufficient rainfalls, with every advantage of transportation by rail and water, with a climate free from sea fogs or chilling summer winds, and canopied for eight months in the year by cloudless skies, distant only sixty-two and a half miles from the civic center of San Francisco.

But this is not history, and it is of the past rather than of the present or future that we propose to speak. The writer drifted into this section in the summer of 1853. At that date there was no habitation between the lower crossing of the San Joaquin, near where the railroad now crosses, and Marsh Landing, except that of Doctor John Marsh, whose home was on the edge of the foothills several miles from the usually traveled road that skirted the tules. A belt of fine old oaks that grew on the delta of Kellogg Creek was a conspicuous landmark, for the reason that it was the first bunch of timber found north of the four creeks on the west side, a distance of two hundred miles, and received the appellation of "The Point of Timber," a designation that still applies to that locality.

A luxuriant growth of alfilaria and wild oats covered the plains and foothills—too rank in many places to cut for hay; and on the wash of Sand Creek, when the soil had been flooded, the oats were so tall that the antelope and cattle made trails through and underneath them, and it was possible for a horseman to lap the heads of the oats together over his shoulders while sitting on his horse.

Doctor Marsh asserted ownership to the whole country, claiming under the title of a Spanish grant. His boundaries were from a round-topped hill standing in the range southwest of Byron, known as Brushy Peak, to the river, thence following the river to Antioch, thence to the place of beginning, embracing some thirty-two or more leagues of land.

His cattle ran wild and in scattered bunches over this splendid domain, unbroken even to the rodeo. Not until 1852 were they handled, beyond branding and ear-marking the calves, when he let the contract to a party to gentle them. The rodeo ground was on the tule front, on what is now known as the Portman ranch, near Knightsen, and when the job was completed one man could round up the entire herd—and Doctor Marsh was out of pocket $3000. The Doctor had built a story-and-a-half cottage and extended a narrow wharf into the river at the eastern end of the sand bluff above Antioch. This was known as Marsh Landing but was occupied in 1853 by a Creole Frenchman by the name of Leonard.

Leonard had "jumped" the place, and a suit was then pending against him, instituted by the Doctor, for forcible entry and detainer.

The Stockton steamboats were calling there, and Leonard had made some arrangement for the exchange of mail. Antioch had two or three houses; Captain Kimball, Parson Smith, and, if I remember, J. C. McMaster, were the principal residents. Fowler had established a ranch over on the point and occupied it with his family. There was the hull of a dismantled ship lying in the mud at New York Landing below Antioch, now Pittsburg. City sites in the early days were as eagerly sought after as the glittering gold of the mines. Every available point was located where it was thought a trade center could be established and city lots were staked for sale. Thus eastern Contra Costa came in for its share.

The New York of the Pacific, Antioch, and Marsh Landing were located, and sixty-five years thereafter the hopeful anticipations of their founders are in process of realization, particularly as to the former.

The smoke from her many furnace fires attest the wisdom of the location of Pittsburg as a center of industry, and the more conspicuous site of Antioch that is fast assuming city proportions, with the advantages of deep water at her piers, the custom of the isles, and her railroad facilities, will insure her steady and permanent growth.

Possibly the dreams of Doctor Marsh would have materialized also if the coal-croppings on his ranch had developed as anticipated—but alas! "the best laid plans of mice and men gang aft aglee."

During the year settlers began to drop in along the tule front; John Dobbinspeck, with his family, took up a claim just east of Marsh Landing and built a little domicile out of split material hauled from the redwoods. His wife had brought with her several quarts of peach pits; these were planted in the moist tule edge and made trees suitable for transplanting the ensuing spring. Perkins, a Yankee sailor with a Kanaka wife, located on the front at a point between Oakley and the landing. He was elected justice of the peace, and I remember his first case.

A little Irishman had contracted to dig a certain number of rods of fence ditch, at fifty cents a rod,' for John Osborne, who had made a location in the live oaks. Osborne thought the sturdy little fellow could dig about eight rods a day, and thus make fair wages; but "Johnny"

turned himself loose in the sand and made it fly. At night he had nearly twenty rods! Osborne refused to pay, and Johnny sued. "Perk" opened court in his living-room. There was a table and four chairs. Just before seating himself he reached into a cupboard and pulled out a half-gallon demijohn of whiskey. "Now, boys, let's all have a snootful"—and we all joined him. Then he called the case. Johnny stated his side—told what the agreement was and how much he made. "Perk," without further testimony, said, "He ought to be paid."

"D—n it," replied Osborne, "I'm ready to pay for what he has done, but I won't stand for the balance of it at fifty cents a rod."

"Be jabers, ye will, or I'll knock the face off ye." interlarded Johnny.

"Here, here!" shouted Perkins, as he jumped from his chair and threw off his coat; "you can't knock anybody's face off in this court.

Sit down, both of you." And they meekly complied. "Now, see here," he continued; "you must compromise. Don't be a hog, Johnny. You can dig that ditch for thirty cents a rod, can't you? And, Osborne, you are willing to pay that, ain't you?" They nodded approval. "Well, let it go at that. And now let's take a drink on it." This they did also, and went their way, no costs assessed, pleased with "Perk's" manner of dispensing justice.

During the summer and fall other settlers dropped in. Richardson, on the Dellwood place, Fred Babbe, on the Sellers quarter, and Fulton Sanders, at the old Iron House, Drake and Dean as neighbors. Later the Dobbinspecks sold their place and went to Napa. Dean left his location with Drake and went up on the creek and located, taking the peach-trees and planting them there, for Marsh's cattle at a later time to destroy.

There had been attempts made to settle on other parts of the big ranch, but the discouragements were many. No fence laws to protect the crops from the cattle, the variable seasons, and the lack of building material were the handicaps that protected the Doctor in the peaceful possession of his ranges; and this continued until the commissioners reduced his claim to three instead of thirty leagues, and its boundaries were finally determined by the surveyor-general of the State. The ensuing years up to 1868 brought their annual influx of settlers, eager to avail themselves of the low-priced lands obtainable either at the double minimum price or to purchase the railroad land—the alternate sections—for five dollars an acre.

Successful experiments had been made in raising wheat, and in 1868 there was a bountiful crop; but the ensuing year the rainfall was lighter, and in 1870 there was less—in fact, crops were a failure, with a single exception: Matt Burling had a piece of land plowed ready for the seed in the spring of 1869. Fearful of losing his high-priced seed, he held it back until the ensuing fall; then he took his chances and put it in the dry fallow soil. The few inches of rain of the season of 1870 were sufficient to start it, and it matured a generous crop without further moisture. But the secret of successful wheat-growing in eastern Contra Costa was solved—by thus concentrating the two seasons' rainfall in one crop the subsequent failures were eliminated.

The drought of 1871, following the short rainfall of 1870, was disastrous, particularly to those who were making their start in farming.

Seed-wheat was selling at two and a half to three cents, hay was unobtainable, and the stock were dying by thousands, sheep were unsaleable at seventy-five cents a head, and Sherman Island straw, coarse, woody, and laden with ashes, was readily saleable at twenty to twenty-five dollars a ton! But on Christmas day, 1871, the Lord opened his pluvial blessing, nor ceased until miniature cataracts were chasing each other down the sides of Mount Diablo, the rivers torrents, and the country flooded.

This resulted in a luxuriant harvest, and from that on wheat became the great staple. Landings were constructed—one at Point of Timber, connecting by canal with Italian Slough, owned and controlled by farmers; another at the Iron House, by Fassett & McCauley—this landing was later abandoned because of a canal dug by Starr & Company for Fred Babbe that connects with Dutch Slough, and is known as Babbe's Landing. Large shipments of wheat were made over the Marsh Landing, and Antioch became a veritable entrepot. The Grangers partially loaded one of their sea-going vessels there. The Tulare & San Pablo Railroad was completed in 1879, and stations were established at Antioch, Brentwood, and Byron. Warehouses were built to accommodate the rapidly increasing production, Dean & Company building at Brentwood in 1880, and also at Byron in 1882.

The towns above named became flourishing villages, schools were established, and accommodations extended by the construction of beautiful buildings; and finally a high-school district was organized and a building erected in Brentwood that in its location will ever be accepted as the monumental mistake of the trustees.

It was not without a struggle that the wheat-growers of eastern Contra Costa attained to this degree of prosperity. In the earlier stages of the industry they were not only handicapped by the dry years, but by their lack of credit—their inability to obtain loans from the city banks, even at exorbitant rates of interest—and not until the organization of the Grange and the establishment of their own bank could they obtain a dollar from Moneybags. Sometimes a friendly broker would extend the grower some accommodation, but then it usually carried with it the privilege of handling his crop in the fall at a round commission. Not only this—he was also beset by conscienceless wheat-buyers and market manipulators working in combination to beat him, and with no trifling success. These efforts became so pronounced that the wheat-growers of the State were called to meet in convention in San Francisco for the purpose of forming a State Farmers' Union. While we were discussing the pros and cons of the situation, a man knocked for admission and asked to be heard. He was invited to the platform and introduced as Mr. Baxter. He stated that he was the representative of the National Grange, and that his mission was to establish the organization on this coast. He explained its workings and object so satisfactorily that we gave willing ear, and when he advised us to go home and organize granges, and thus work together, and harmoniously, in our business and social affairs, we consented, and went to work enthusiastically. In a short time Baxter came up and instituted the Point of Timber Grange No. 14, with the following officers: R. G. Dean, master; M. A. Walton, overseer; J. H. Baldwin, lecturer; J. B. Henderson, steward; A. Richardson, assistant steward; A. Plumley, chaplain; Thomas McCabe, treasurer; J. E. W. Casey, secretary; Mrs. J. H. Baldwin, Ceres; Mrs. C. M. Casey, Pomona; Mrs. J. B. Henderson, Flora; Mrs. J. E. W. Casey, stewardess.

The specific object of the organization of the grange was to buy and sell direct—sell to the consumer and buy from the manufacturer and eliminate the middleman. This we were anxious to do, as we were conscious of being robbed, by being obliged to sell our wheat for $28 to $30 a ton, when it was worth from $60 to $65 in Liverpool. On investigation, we found that Isaac Friedlander, of San Francisco, was handling all the tonnage, chartering every wheat-carrier that entered the harbor, and that we could get no ships to transport our grain unless we outbid him. His plan was simple: engage the ship for about 24 shillings ($6) a ton, pay brokers $38 to $40 a ton f. o. b. ship, the wheat thus costing him $2.25, or not to exceed $2.30, a cental. "Now, Mr. Broker, you go into the country and buy the wheat as cheap as you can, and I will take all you can get at the above figures." The brokers districted the State, assigning a certain area to each, on an agreement not to compete against each other in buying. The growers were helpless, they could get but the one bid—that of their local buyer; he offered according to his whim—Monday, $1.40; Tuesday, $1.42 ½ ; Wednesday, $1.45 —and Thursday he was "out of the market." Saturday he was in again with an offer of $1.42 ½ ! The following week, finding that he was getting only the small lots that could not be held, owing to the necessities of the owner, he put the price to $1.47 ½ and $1.50, moving the bulk of the crop at that figure. Later, to persistent holders, he advanced the price until the last lots passed into his hands at $1.60. He could have paid this price for the whole crop and still have made a handsome profit, as he was receiving from Friedlander $2.25 or $2.30, and realizing a profit of from $5.00 to $15.00 per ton, while Friedlander himself was disposing of his cargoes afloat at a profit of equal amount. A revolt on the part of the wheat-growers from this condition of affairs was inevitable. Is it any wonder that the wheat-growers and farmers flocked to the grange? It was their only avenue of escape from the clutch of the shipper and broker.

The State Grange was organized, a bank was instituted, a business association established, and Mr. Wolcott, a highly connected broker from New York, was invited by the State Grange to establish himself in San Francisco in the grain trade and act as agent through whom the members would ship their wheat. He received the backing of the London & San Francisco Bank, which made the requisite advances on Grangers' cargoes, and we began to load his chartered ships. Of course, Friedlander and his friends resented this opposition and began to force up the price of tonnage. We authorized Wolcott to outbid him, and.

standing on either side of a table in the Merchants Exchange, they bid a ship to 80 shillings ($20) a ton freight! —and the growers loaded it, receiving their advance of $25 a ton—and that's all they got. To the writer's knowledge, there was some eastern Contra Costa wheat on board of that vessel, but he had the satisfaction of assisting in breaking Friedlander's monopoly and in forcing him to compromise with his creditors on the basis of twenty cents on the dollar; and. owing to the fact that vessels came competing for cargo and dropped their rates to 16 shillings ($4) a ton, the writer was enabled to sell his wheat the ensuing season for $2.25 a cental in Babbe's Landing. After the Friedlander episode growers received better prices for their wheat, although there were several attempts made to corner the market, but only with disastrous results, wherein some of them dropped their twenty-dollar pieces like rain in a spring shower.

Irrigation at this era was beginning to receive public attention, but the riparian laws that had grown musty on our statute-books, and the vested rights under them that had become as fixtures in the public mind, interfered with the free appropriation of water, and so much opposition was manifested that it required political action and reconstruction on the part of the law-making power of the State to remove them.

Hence, taking advantage of the drift of public opinion when the conventions of the two leading political parties met, resolutions were adopted "favoring irrigation," thus modestly but surely opening the way for the introduction of a plank. "Wherein we favor the amendment to the riparian law and indorse a general and comprehensive system of irrigation" was inserted. Thus committing the party to the proposition, any plausible scheme that might be introduced would be sure to meet with favor and be enacted into law. It was under these favorable conditions that a scheme was promoted to construct a canal from Tulare Lake to Antioch and irrigate the whole west side of the San Joaquin—and herein lies the historical reference to the project as significant of the influence of the Point of Timber Grange in defeating it. The proposition originated at Greysonville. It was honestly conceived and honorably intended—simply for the land-owners along the route to associate themselves, assess their property, build the ditch, and own it themselves.

Antioch and Point of Timber granges were notified and invited to participate. They responded by each sending delegates to attend the convention to be held at Greysonville, Captain Kimball from Antioch, and R. G. Dean et al. from the Point of Timber. The plan was freely discussed, estimates submitted, and much enthusiasm manifested when a committee was appointed to formulate a law under which the ditch could be constructed and which would be submitted to a subsequent convention for ratification. The delegates reported to their home granges but Point of Timber treated the project with much indifference—wheat-growing had become profitable through the system of summer-fallowing, and irrigation was not especially favored. With Antioch it was different. It was proposed to make the canal navigable for the transportation of freight on flat-bottomed barges, and Antioch was to be the outlet. J. P. Abbot, editor of the Antioch Ledger, Tom Carter, a contractor, and Frank Williams, a saloon-keeper, were especially enthusiastic for its construction. At a subsequent convention the formulated law was considered, adopted, and a committee appointed to present it to the legislature. Its provisions were carefully considered and all interests guarded, and it permitted a vote of the districts (there being five) to adopt or reject. So we as land-owners felt safe, and quite regardless of its provisions returned to our plows.

The measure was introduced as the West Side Land Owners' Irrigation Canal bill. From reading the legislative reports we noticed the bill was dragging, but that another—"The Scrivner Supplemental Bill"— had been introduced and was well on its way to its final passage. Chancing to meet Carter in San Francisco, the writer inquired: "Tom, how is the West Side scheme getting along?" Tom smiled as he replied: "Oh, there's nothing in that bill; but the other one is all right. We can make some money out of that; and, by the way, you are slated for one of the trustees." I was frightened, for the scheme of the supplemental bill flashed through my mind. Hurrying to the telegraph office I wired to a friend in Sacramento for a copy of the supplemental bill. It was in Antioch on my return, and, startled at its provisions, I hastened to call the grange in session to consider it. Promptly they appointed a committee to visit Sacramento to defeat it.

The committee found the bill had passed the lower house and had been sent to the senate, and by them referred to its judiciary committee. An appeal was made to Senator Paul Shirley, but he would do nothing, as the "party was committed by its platform to assist irrigation, and this was the only bill that would pass." Assemblyman Charles Wood was surprised at our opposition; he "supposed we all favored the measure." He had procured some slight amendment and then voted for it. He must be "consistent," and could do nothing to help us. "Get us a hearing before the judiciary committee," we pleaded; but he was obdurate. Finally, through Senator Shirley, the committee gave us a hearing, and we argued strenuously against the iniquity, but to no purpose. Our last resort was the ear of Governor Irwin. He would not veto the measure, but he kindly consented to return it with the request that it be amended to provide for a survey and estimate of cost, also that the law be submitted to a vote of the people for confirmation or rejection. That was sufficient; the bill was amended, the survey was made, and the estimate of cost, which exceeded $3,500,000, submitted. The expense of the survey was put up by Williams, and the State authorities would not reimburse him; and when the vote was taken the law was voted down all along the line. This was a very narrow and fortunate escape from serious consequences, for had the bill become a law we would have been assessed out of all proportion for our share of the expense of construction, as our land was more valuable than that up the valley, and the probability is that no water would have reached here, owing to the insufficient supply.

Long prior to the transition from the pastoral to the agricultural era —long before Doctor Marsh had the opportunity to see thousands of acres of his big ranch a shimmering wheat-field, or to hear the drone of the leviathan-like threshing machine crawling over the fields, feeding into its insatiable maw the ripened grain, only to be thrown out in filled bags ready for delivery to the stations—ere he had seen this, other than in his optimistic dreams of the future, the Doctor had built for himself a massive stone dwelling, a fitting residence for the princely proprietor of his 13,316 acres. The site is an ideal one—in the portal of a pretty valley extending back into the hills. Facing the east, it possesses a commanding view of the plain, even as far as the eye can reach across the tule delta, fringed by century-old oaks and skirted by a willow-fringed creek with a living stream of water. But ere he had an opportunity to occupy this palatial structure, so like in its style of architecture and in its manorial proportions some old English residence, the Doctor was murdered—assassinated by the ruthless hand of a drunken Mexican vaquero.

The inherited ranch remained in the family for several years, the stock was gradually disposed of, and finally it was purchased by a promotor, one Jack Williams, backed principally by the Sanford family of New York. Williams' plan was to open up the coal vein that was known to exist on the ranch, build a railroad to Marsh Landing, where there was deep water-frontage on the river, and establish a shipping point and a manufacturing center. The scheme was an ambitious one, and practical, provided the coal mine developed. Williams organized the Brentwood Coal Company; he secured two sections of land adjacent to the landing, erected a substantial wharf extending to deep water, opened the coal measure with a double-compartment working shaft, supplied expensive hoisting machinery, built boarding- and tenement-houses for the miners, employed an expensive expert engineer, and spent money lavishly. Things were booming for a while—but alas for the result! The coal vein was found to be narrow, it lay deep under the surface, was of inferior quality, and the water flowed into the shaft in great volume. The bubble burst. Jack dropped out of sight. Sanford came out and took over the Brentwood Coal Company's effects and assumed the debt due to the Clay Street Bank, from which a heavy loan had been obtained. Taxes were unpaid, interest defaulted, and some other claims pressing, and finally the ranch was sold for taxes and bought in by the Clay

Street Bank and ownership asserted. M. B. Ivory was placed in possession as superintendent and agent, San ford instituted suit, and years of expensive litigation followed.

In the meantime, the big ranch was let to tenant farmers on the basis of one-third and one-quarter of the crop delivered in sack at the warehouse as rent, and the proceeds went into the coffers of the bank. One by one the litigants and lawyers died, until there was but one of the claimants left. To her, Miss Josephine Sanford, the property was finally awarded. The bank was ousted under the plea of having held the property in trust; hence it was compelled to give an accounting. The bank's original claim was for a loan of $150,000, to which was added some $50,000 more, paid to quiet title. The rentals had been paid to the bank for sixteen years, averaging not less than $30,000, aggregating $480,000. And still the bank asserted a claim of over $600,000 against the estate! This was finally adjusted, and a claim of $220,000 allowed.

Balfour, Guthrie & Company advanced this sum to Miss Sanford, and R. G. Dean was placed in charge of the ranch as superintendent and manager; but within a short period Miss Sanford passed away, and then another eleven years of litigation ensued. But it was eventually settled by partition, and finally the Los Meganos, or Marsh ranch, passed by purchase to its present owners, Balfour, Guthrie & Company, who have inaugurated the extensive system of concrete-lined canals, electric pumping-stations, and distributing ditches, covering the entire area of the irrigable section of the ranch, and capable of watering twenty thousand acres. This is the key that will unlock the Aladdin-like riches imprisoned in its generous soil and enable the historians to write a new and interesting page on the agricultural resources of eastern Contra Costa County, covering the wealth and variety of its products.

Already the fiat of change has gone forth—2000 acres of alfalfa, 1500 acres of sugar beets, and orchards of walnuts—and this is only a beginning for this favored section.

Where no sea-fogs come to linger,
Where no blizzards dare intrude,
Where no ghastly icy finger
Touches bloom, or plant, or frond.
Where with water, soil and sun
Kindly Nature will respond
In multiples for everyone.

The foregoing is but an epitome of the past. There are many interesting details of personal experience of the first settlers—their discouragements, their strenuous efforts to make headway against adverse conditions, the inroads of the cattle by which they were surrounded, the dry and rainless years that sometimes came in pairs, like 1870 and 1871, the deluge of 1862 and 1872, necessitating loans and mortgages at exorbitant rates of interest, usually two per cent per month and difficult to obtain at that rate, frequently followed by the sheriff and a change of ownership. But eventually the day of the mortgage and the fear of the sheriff passed, thanks to Mathias Burlingen, who discovered and exemplified the system of cultivation of the cereals by "summer fallow," or more widely known as "dry farming."

That portion of the delta region within the limits of Contra Costa County is not without its history of experimental farming and reclamation that resulted in alternate failure and success of the various owners during its half-century of occupancy. The Jersey Island, the Sand Mound District, the Byron Tract, Clifton Court, and the margin on our northern front extending from Babbe's Landing to Marsh Landing, each has a distinctive record that in the story of their reclamation would be interesting reading; and perhaps when the history of the great delta —composed of many thousands of acres, once a pestilential and mosquito-breeding swamp, now reclaimed by massive levees, surrounded by deep-channeled waterways, crossed by railroads and cemented highways, dotted with packing-houses and manufacturing plants, beautiful homes and villages, its wealth of products poured by trainloads into hungry Eastern markets—is written it will be perused with absorbing interest as a story of achievement, of failures and disappointments, of disaster by fire and flood, conquered and controlled by indefatigable and persistent effort, a story of man's mastery over the forces of Nature never excelled even in the fabled achievements of the gods. Many abortive attempts were made at farming "the rules," and one, not without its amusing side, was that of a party of Kentuckians in the early seventies. A wealthy and enthusiastic resident of that State returned home after a successful money-making career in California, poured into willing ears the story of the wonderful richness of the tule islands.

He had invested largely in them under the Swamp and Overflowed Land Act, which in its favorable conditions enabled a party to acquire title simply by reclaiming them. He induced a company of young men— clerks, bank employees, and visionaries, who had never soiled their hands at hard labor—to come out here and get rich by farming the tules. Their plan was to employ Chinamen to build a peat levee along the river-bank, burn the tules and meadow-grass, and sow wheat in the ashes. There was little work for them to do—principally to oversee the Chinamen, and this they did by sitting on the levee smoking their pipes, in great glee. "How is it possible, Mr. D., that you, an old resident here, allowed this opportunity to escape you?" they asked the writer when visiting them while engaged in their fortune-building enterprise.

My reply was not a boost to their enthusiasm, and they smilingly regretted my ignorance of the conditions.

But wheat does not mature here until July, and June is the month when "Old Sol" sends down his rays in melting temperatures. The snow usually lies deep on the Sierras at this season of the year, and melts freely, pouring its ever-increasing volume of water into the rivers, raising them to flooding heights, originally inundating the entire tule delta. That promising wheat-field had to run the gauntlet of the June freshets. They came in full proportion, floating their dried and sponge-like levees away bodily, and a few days later the beautiful wheat-field that was to be an object lesson to illustrate to the California farmer not only the fertility of the peat land, but how easily it could be reclaimed and cultivated, was the rich feeding-ground for a million, more or less, of mallard ducks. The sadly disappointed Kentuckians did not stay to repeat their folly, but "folded their tents like the Arabs, and as silently stole away." The object lesson was not lost, however. It was found that a heavier material than peat must be used and larger and higher levees constructed than was possible to build by hand labor. Hence the clamshell dredge, with its hundred-foot boom, was brought into requisition and the problem of permanent reclamation of the delta was solved.

In the early fifties the great tule swamp was a terra incognita, exposed only along the watercourses and the front, where it joined the upland. The rank growth of tules, higher in places than horse and rider, and its floating meadows were a barrier to its occupancy for any practical purpose. Sand mounds, many acres in extent, above the highest water-levels, were the home and breeding ground for a band of elk, found and exterminated by market hunters. They pursued a profitable industry in trapping otter and beaver, to a final extermination of these also.

There is another section of the eastern slope that has not been especially referred to, but which is worthy of mention, as its historical antecedents date back eons of time, perhaps to that period when the pillared ruins of Karnak lay unchiseled in their quarries and the Pyramids were an undeveloped dream in the minds of the Pharaohs. Reference is made to the sand belt commonly known as the "Sand and Live Oak District." The writer has a theory that this district was once a great sand bar covering many sections. Its western apex near Antioch and its eastern near Brentwood, created by the rotary action of water that covered it to a great depth—in fact, an island lake whose waters washed the foothills of the parallel ranges, and extended for three hundred miles in a northerly and southerly direction. That there was a rotary current in this lake, caused by the prevailing trade winds that sweep southward along the eastern foothills of the Mount Diablo range, creating a current strongly accelerated by the inflow of a thousand streams, from the Sierra watershed, extending from Mount Whitney to Mount Shasta, thus forcing a current to flow northward on the east side and southward on the west side. These currents running in opposite directions on each side by the lake received an increasing momentum from the Sacramento and its tributaries, and in its ceaseless rotary action created a great central eddy that deposited its sand and silt and built up a huge middle ground, or sand-bar, which the receding water left bare after cutting its way through the barrier of hills at Port Costa, admitting the ocean tides that in their ebb and flow ultimately wore deep the waterway of the Straits of Carquinez.

We allege that the sand plains of Stanislaus, Tuolumne, Merced, Madera, and Fresno counties, are evidence of the existence of the great body of fresh water whose waves rolled over them in slowly shoaling depth as the lake gradually receded, spreading the sandy deposits of the streams that were carried far out into the lake, leaving it to be smoothed into level areas miles and miles in extent by the action of the water.

Of course, this valley occupied by the lake was created by the upheaval of the Diablo Range long subsequent to the upheaval of the Sierras, as evidenced by the system of dead rivers that came down from the northwest, cross-cutting the Sierras, the broken and distorted channels of which the miner's pick developed, and sections of which are found thousands of feet above the present sea-level. It was the water-worn, smooth gold found in the ravines and gulches, and covered deep in the gravel beds of the hydraulic claims that was spilled from the old channels of these torrential streams when they were broken up and destroyed by the later upheaval. The great sand bar in Contra Costa County was finally left exposed by the gradually receding lake, its smooth and drifting surface to be eroded by summer winds into mounds and depressions until kindly Nature stopped the process by covering it with a dense growth of unyielding chamisal brush and a fringe of live-oaks.

In this condition it was found by the early settlers—the hiding-place of wild animals.

In 1854 Fred Babbe and a party killed a grizzly bear in the chamisal and secured one of its cubs, which the writer saw chained to the tent-stake of Fulton Sanders; and he himself surprised a couple of half-grown California lions near the edge of the brush, and, being on horseback, drove them into a tree. Having no rifle, he spread his saddle blanket under the tree, supposing that would hold them, but on his return with his gun they were gone; the mother lion, probably being nearby, had called them down. And even at this date there was a band of thirty or forty head of cattle, wilder than deer, that found refuge in the brush, venturing out only at night for food and water, returning to their shelter with the first break of dawn. It was exciting sport for a couple of horsemen to conceal themselves in the edge of the brush near the O'Brien place and await the cattle coming in, and, when sufficiently close, rush out and lasso or shoot down a fat two- or three-year-old.

Sixty-two years have wrought a wonderful change in the old sandbar. There is little evidence remaining of former primitive conditions.

In the spring it is an immense bouquet of particolored bloom of fruit trees and almonds. It is seamed with thoroughfares. A transcontinental railroad furnishes transportation for its many carloads of products, and its industries support the flourishing village of Oakley—one of the most pretentious of all the growing trade centers of Contra Costa County.

CHAPTER XIII. DOCTOR JOHN MARSH

Contra Costa County's history would not be complete unless it gave prominence to the man around whose name clusters so much of historical interest—to one of its earlier and most intelligent pioneers—to the man who paved the "way for future empires" and whose acts and utterances appear to us to have been inspirational and prophetic. It is to Doctor John Marsh the country, and particularly Contra Costa County, owes a debt of gratitude which it can never repay, even though it inscribe his name high on the roll of honor and write its acknowledgment in letters of gold into the tomes of history. When the destiny of our Golden State was hanging in the balance, when the question of its remaining a Mexican province or becoming a part of United States territory was being debated, when Daniel Webster from his seat in the Senate was thundering his stentorian invectives against the confirmation of its purchase, asserting that the "whole country west of the Rocky Mountains was an arid waste that a crow could starve to death to fly over," it was the historical letters of Doctor Marsh addressed to the Honorable Lewis Cass, then Secretary of State, that largely influenced him to close the deal and take over California with its eight hundred miles of coast line. Had he done no more than this, the great service was monumental and deserving of our highest consideration.

Quoting from one of the Doctor's letters, under date of 1846, wherein he referred to the productive capabilities of the wonderful land, he said: "The agricultural resources of California are but imperfectly developed, the whole is remarkably adapted to the cultivation of the vine, olive, and figs, and almonds grow well. It is the finest country for wheat I have ever seen; fifty for one is an average crop with very imperfect cultivation, a hundred-fold is not uncommon, and even one hundred and fifty has been produced." When we reflect that these words were written nearly seventy years ago, when California was an unbroken wilder ness; when these broad plains were the undisturbed stamping-ground of vast herds of elk, antelope, wild cattle, and wilder mustangs; when the only homes were the scattered missions and the haciendas of the cattle barons, and the only commerce a limited traffic in hides and tallow, we are impressed with the inspirational and prophetic character of the statement, and at once credit the Doctor with being a far-sighted and practical observer.

He had drifted into this summerland of the Pacific imbued, no doubt, with a wanderlust, a love of primitive conditions, and the unrestrained freedom of the frontier, although he had tasted of Boston estheticism and culture, having graduated from Harvard. He knew the country from Yuma to the Oregon line, but, ignoring the opportunity of selecting a location in other parts of the country, had with excellent judgment chosen the eastern portion of Contra Costa for his future home.

He had with truly prophetic instinct looked forward to the day when this broad domain would be under the protection of his native flag, when the great watercourses of the State would beat as throbbing arteries with life and commerce, when great and growing cities would be planted along their margins, or seated by the Golden Gate, watching the full-freighted argosies of the world riding in imperial splendor upon the bosom of the magnificent bay, represented by every national emblem. Undoubtedly, he had pictured to himself the incoming tide of humanity, rising higher and higher in the great West, flowing with steady and irresistible sweep across the great plains, until, stopped by the Western ocean, it would eddy and flow back into the valleys, over these "arid wastes," and along the sunny slopes, until California would become a great, populous, and wealthy state.

Hides and tallow, as articles of export, he saw would be relegated to the past and other enterprises and industries engross the attention of the coming multitude. Then the vision of limitless wheat-fields with their "hundred-fold" waving a ripening luxuriance in these fertile valleys, the vine-clad hills and olive orchards, and caught in the summer wind the fragrance of almond-blossoms. It was no Utopian dream—his prophecy has long since passed to its fulfillment, and its verification justifies the judgment of the Doctor in the selection of his home.

Here, under the shadow of Mount Diablo, in a sequestered spot, shaded by grand old oaks that stand like sentinels, at the very portal of one of the most romantic and picturesque canadas of the State, he located and built his home. The building itself is a prototype of the man—grand in its outlines, massive in its manorial proportions, solid as the enduring hills by which it was surrounded. Here he was content to sit down and bide his time when the surging tide of immigration that was eddying around him, turned by natural barriers from its path, returned to seek beside himself the advantage that he had considered so fully years before. It came ere he was aware, clamorous for his acres, restricting him to the lines of his original concession.

Then some careless or designing hand scattered wheat upon the soil, and lo! the scene changed as by the touch of an enchanter's wand.

Wheat-fields pressing upon and overspreading the limits of his grant were spoken into existence and their yield was indeed "fifty and an hundred-fold." No vision or prophecy was ever more truthfully fulfilled, and at this writing, if the Doctor were alive, he could see the sunlight reflected from the sheen of emerald fields and glinting cottages through clumps of shade-trees that mark the habitations of prosperous cultivators of the single cereal.

More than this, he could see the thriving town of Brentwood on his ranch, with all its concomitants of hotels, stores, business houses, churches, and schools—a smart, enterprising, and progressive people, who have built in the fullest confidence of the future prosperity of this locality. And, if the Doctor so desired, he could see from his own door the passing trains that haul their unbroken cargoes from ocean to ocean or bear their passengers in hurrying cars to and fro from all parts of the world, and read his daily paper three hours from the press. Probably his greatest surprise would be to see the elaborate system of canals created and completed for irrigating the beautiful valley and the hundreds of acres of alfalfa to which it has been seeded, and to note the spirit of change that is weaving its silken web over the destinies of the ranch, of which, notwithstanding his remarkable foresight, he could scarcely have dreamed, or its possibilities, as developed by the modern system of scientific farming by the application of water to the soil, to intensify production and render its happy possessor independent of the variable seasons and the drought, thus yielding in multiples beyond the visionary estimates.

CHAPTER XIV. MOUNT DIABLO

Mount Diablo deserves and shall have a special chapter all to itself. Occupying almost the exact center of Contra Costa County, this mountain is one of the most conspicuous landmarks of the State. Its prominence arises not from its size—for it is but 3896 feet in height—but from its isolation. It is the only peak of any prominence in Contra Costa County, rearing its head above all the surrounding hills.

Whence arose the name Mount Diablo? The following version was given in a report to the legislature in 1850, by General Vallejo, that excellent authority on Californiana, quoted in a previous chapter: "In 1806 a military expedition from San Francisco marched against the tribe 'Bolgones,' who were encamped at the foot of the mount; the Indians were prepared to receive the expedition, and a hot engagement ensued in the large hollow fronting the western side of the mount; as the victory was about to be decided in favor of the Indians, an unknown personage, decorated with the most extraordinary plumage, and making divers movements, suddenly appeared near the combatants. The Indians were victorious, and the incognito (puy) departed toward the mount. The defeated soldiers, on ascertaining that the spirit went through the same ceremony daily and at all hours, named the mount 'Diablo,' in allusion to its mysterious inhabitant, that continued thus to make his appearance until the tribe was subdued by the troops in command of Lieutenant Gabriel Moraga, in a second campaign of the same year. In the aboriginal tongue 'puy' signifies 'evil spirit'; in Spanish it means 'diablo,' and doubtless it signifies 'devil' in the Anglo-American language."

Referring to Mount Diablo, in the same report General Vallejo said: "It was intended so to call the county, but both branches of the legislature, after warm debates on the subject (the representatives of the county opposing the said name), resolved on the less profane one of 'Contra Costa'."

There are at least half a dozen other legends woven around Mount Diablo. A tale which is said to have been culled from the archives of one of the old missions is about as follows: When, in 1769, the Spanish padres came to found missions among the aborigines, the Indians brought them gifts of gold nuggets from a high mountain not far from San Francisco Bay. This peak, according to their traditions, had once belched forth fire and smoke. The padres, fearing that gold might prove "the root of all evil" to these primitive people, determined to forestall further search for the precious metal. Secretly poisoning all the gold in their possession, the padres placed it in a tub of water, from which they bade the Indians make their dogs drink. When all the dogs died the superstitious fear of the Indians was aroused and they were diverted from using gold as a medium of exchange and never again sought it in the mountains. Thenceforth the mountain from which the gold was obtained became known as Monte Diablo, or Devil's Mountain.

Still another story comes from the pen of Bret Harte. He relates that the worthy padre from the old mission San Pablo climbed the now historic promontory, seeking new converts, or striving in some similar manner to extend the dominion of the church. On reaching the summit he encountered no less a personage than the Evil One himself in the corporeal form of a gigantic bear. Changing from bear to human form in a most disconcerting manner, the demon attacked the padre and all but slew him. When the padre escaped and related his unusual experience, the mountain was named El Monte Diablo.

With one more tale we will leave the domain of legend and take up the later aspects of Mount Diablo. The following account is quoted in full from an early historical work: "The mountain is also said to take its name from a marvelous phenomenon witnessed amongst its wild and precipitous gorges, at a time when, in the language of an old trapper, 'Injuns war plenty and white women war not.' It is related that once, in an expedition against the horse-thief tribes who inhabited the valley of the San Joaquin, as far down as the base of the mountain, the native Californians came up with a party of the freebooters, laden with the spoils of a hunt, and immediately gave chase, driving them up the steep defiles which form the ascent of the mountain on one side. Elated with the prospect of securing and meting out punishment to the robbers, they were pressing hard after them, when lo! from a cavernous opening in their path there issued forth such fierce flames, accompanied by so terrible a roaring that, thinking themselves within a data's throw of the principal entrance to his Infernal Majesty's summer palace, the astonished rancheros, with many 'Carajos!' and 'Carambas!' and like profane ejaculations, forgot their hostile errand and, turning tail, scampered down the mountain faster than they had gone up. Reciting the adventure to their fellow-rancheros on their return, it was unanimously agreed that the Devil and his chief steward had fixed their abode in the mountain and, in compliment to the great original dealer in hoof and horns, they gave the present name of Mount Diablo to the scene of their late terrific exploit and discomfiture. As for the Indians, who, as they declared, all mysteriously disappeared as the flames rose in view, of course the Dons afterwards insisted that they were the favored children of the Devil!"

Mount Diablo was once a volcano. The outline of part of the crater can still be traced, and bits of lava and igneous rock can be found in the canons from the top of this picturesque peak to the bottom.

The central mass of Mount Diablo is composed of metamorphic sandstone and is about six miles long and one and a half miles wide. Large quantities of jasper rock filled with fine quartz are found near the summit. Throughout are found a considerable amount of other minerals, including serpentine and siliceous slate.

In reality Mount Diablo comprises two peaks, which can be viewed to best advantage from the northwest or southeast. The two peaks are about three miles apart, the southwestern peak comprising Mount Diablo proper. The other mount is known as the North Peak and is about two hundred and sixty feet lower than Mount Diablo.

Innumerable oyster-shells and petrified shell-fish, resembling those now found on the shores of the Atlantic, are scattered about its summit, all of which indicate that long ago Mount Diablo occupied the floor of the ocean instead of its present eminence.

The summit of Mount Diablo was selected in 1876 as the initial point for a continental triangulation survey. A station was established by Professor Davidson, of the Coast Survey party, after taking careful measurements to establish a base-line of eleven miles on the plains of Yolo County. The transcontinental survey established an absolutely accurate basis for future surveys by the United States.

The view from the top of the mountain is awe-inspiring. A grand panorama, covering not less than forty thousand square miles, or an area nearly equal to the State of New York, is spread out before the beholder. A scope of country four hundred miles from north to south is plainly visible on a clear day. Away to the west is the broad Pacific.

To the east the view extends to the very crest of the Sierras. It is an excellent point from which to study the topography of a large portion of California, from twelve to fifteen counties often being visible. The vast interior valley of the State appears like a relief map. The most northern point visible is Lassen's Buttes, two hundred miles distant, and Mount Hamilton, upon which is located the Lick observatory, is discernible in the south. Each time the eye encircles the horizon new scenes and added grandeur are discovered. Turning again to the east, one beholds the Sacramento and San Joaquin valleys, with their magnificent rivers. On the south the broad expanse of San Francisco Bay comes into view.

Across the bay to the west lies San Francisco, enthroned, like Rome, among her hills, her streets plainly visible. A nearer view discloses Yerba Buena Island, Alcatraz, and the Golden Gate. Close at hand is San Pablo Bay and all its inlets. Out upon the Pacific the eye rests upon the Farallones de las Grayles, twenty miles beyond the Golden Gate.

Reverting to the north, Martinez, the Straits of Carquinez, Benicia, Vallejo, and Mare Island swing into view. One might multiply this description indefinitely, but the foregoing will suffice as a partial delineation of the magnitude of the view from this summit. Those who care to gain first-hand information will find a journey to the top of Mount Diablo distinctly worthwhile.

Due largely to the energy of one man, R. N. Burgess, a Contra Costa product, the Mount Diablo Scenic Boulevard, now winds to the top by easy stages, and it is not a difficult matter to climb this historic peak.

Mr. Burgess saw the wonderful possibilities for home-building in the picturesque vales that nestle about Mount Diablo. He interested New York capitalists, and they invested $1,095,000, founding the Mount Diablo Villa Homes Association, which controls the Mount Diablo estate of ten thousand acres. These men say that the next few years will see ten thousand people living in magnificent villas among the sheltering crags of old Mount Diablo. Their plans also include an appropriately designed tavern, in which cloisters and stairways will be the dominant note, clinging to the very top of the mountain. Closely following the contour of the peak, from a distance the buildings will appear to be a part of the mountain itself. Towering over all will be an observatory with a large telescope. To those who gaze through the giant lens the beautiful surrounding country will seem to be close at hand.

And now we will leave Mount Diablo with an observation that possibly should have been made earlier in the chapter—that the grizzled old sentinel was first seen by white men in the remote days of 1772.

Father Juan Crespi, friend and associate of Father Junipero Serra, the mission builder, first glimpsed its peak while exploring San Francisco Bay, after that great harbor was discovered from the land side by Don Gaspar de Portola. Father Crespi was accompanied by Captain Don Pedro Fagis, of the Presidio of Monterey.

The late S. J. Bennett, of Martinez, in the late '70s drove the first stage that ever reached the top of this mountain. The road at that time was kept in good condition, the expenses of its up-keep being defrayed with the toll exacted from passengers and teams. Up the mountain slopes on either side were groves of oak and pine, and at times they were green with chaparral. As one continued to ascend, the declivities became more bold and broken. Making up the sides were many wild glens, dark with vines and shrubbery. At an elevation of twenty-five hundred feet was a neat, well-kept hotel, open the year around, with good accommodations for travelers. Parties could leave their teams here, and, if they desired to do so, could make the remainder of the way to the top on foot. However, in the early days there was no difficulty in reaching the summit with a good team. At about five hundred feet from the top was a never-failing spring of pure soft water.

Besides grand old Mount Diablo, there are other peaks of considerable elevation: Rocky Mound, 1921 feet, and Redwood Peak, 1635 feet high, both in the range of Contra Costa Hills; Bushy Knob, 1742 feet, and Gray's Peak, 1921 feet.

CHAPTER XV. SUMMARY OF THE COUNTY'S RESOURCES

As the tourist or globe-trotter stands on the deck of the ocean liner passing through the famous portals of the Golden Gate from the broad and trackless Pacific and enters the harbor of San Francisco, his gaze rests upon a high range of hills on the eastern shore of the bay—hills at whose feet cities teeming with the life of commerce and trade have been built. Huge oil-tanks give notice of the location nearby of the greatest oil refineries in the West; and the smoke boiling upward from hundreds of tall chimneys tells its own story of the prosperity and commercial advantages which this region possesses.

The eye of the traveler has fallen on Contra Costa County, bordered along its entire seventy miles of water-front with busy factories almost surrounding a prosperous interior region of fertile valleys, vine-clad hills, and well-kept orchards. Dotted here and there are the thriving interior towns, connected by rapid-transit steam and electric railway lines. Along the northern and eastern boundary tranquilly flow the waters of the mighty San Joaquin. Standing guard over all, and towering high above the plain, is historic, romantic Mount Diablo.

Second in industrial wealth and importance in the State, foremost in the production of structural materials, and supplying the finest wines and fruits on the market, Contra Costa County stands preeminent among her fifty-seven sister counties. Rapidly overhauling San Francisco, her only rival for manufacturing supremacy, it is only a question of time until Contra Costa shall occupy first place in this field. The manufacturing interests of Richmond alone exceed those of most of the big cities of the coast; Martinez will soon be in the same position, and Pittsburg leads many of the other cities of the State.

As the new manufacturing era begins to dawn for the Pacific Coast, and especially for the San Francisco Bay region, Contra Costa County will develop faster than ever industrially, to this region will come the greatest plants to be found in the West. That this is no idle prophecy is shown by the immense factories already located in Contra Costa County.

Among the peculiar and distinctive advantages that Contra Costa County possesses for manufacturing and commercial enterprises, is the deep water-frontage along its shore line, where the largest oceangoing ships can be accommodated at all times. Paralleling the shore are two great transcontinental railroads, the Southern Pacific and the Santa Fe, with a maximum of sixty-three trains daily. Thus Contra Costa County is assured of the best transportation facilities by both land and water. Surrounded on three sides by water, which insures a temperate climate, this section also enjoys cheap river transportation.

The eastern shores bathe in the fresh waters of the San Joaquin, while on the north and west are the salt waters of San Francisco Bay.

For two dollars a ton fruit is carried from Martinez to San Francisco, a distance of thirty-five miles, the rivers steamers giving practically an express service. Fruit picked at five o'clock in the evening is delivered in San Francisco early the following morning.

The eastern section of the county is rapidly responding to two vast improvement projects—irrigation and reclamation. The irrigation activities have been described at length in another portion of this work.

A large part of the reclaimed land of the delta of the San Joaquin is in Contra Costa County. These delta lands repeat in California the story of productivity of the deltas of the Nile, the Euphrates, and the Mississippi. Reclamation is effected by levees built by clam-shell dredgers, immense machines operated by steam-engines and equipped with electric plants and powerful search-lights, enabling the work to go forward night and day. The levees average a height of fourteen feet and a width of a hundred and twenty-five feet at the base. The crops are irrigated by water carried over the levee by siphons. When the irrigation is completed the surplus water is thrown back into the stream by immense pumps worked by electric power. In the process of levee construction navigable channels are cut around every island. The crops are marketed by river boats and barges at low transportation cost. On these lands are grown two-thirds of the potatoes, beans, onions, celery, and asparagus produced in the State. As grass-lands, for hay and forage, they have no equal. At many points dairying is an established industry of long standing, and the reputation of the delta butter is wide-spread. It is safe to say that reclamation activities of the future will far exceed those of the past, bringing under cultivation large tracts of hitherto unproductive lands.

In the interior section of the county are a dozen or more fertile and picturesque valleys, in which are grown the choicest orchard fruits and the finest variety of grapes. The famous San Ramon Valley and the Alhambra, Pacheco, Ygnacio, and Clayton valleys in reality comprise one large valley, continuous for about thirty miles, and varying in width from one-half to fifteen miles. It is supposed that a broad arm of the bay once penetrated this section, as the lands are sedimentary and very rich, with a fine depth of soil. Here are found the large orchards of pears, prunes, peaches, almonds, apricots, and walnuts. The valley region also includes the smaller and separate Stone, San Pablo, Pinole, Rodeo, Franklin, and Briones valleys. These valleys are also quite rich and are all well-watered by running streams. A portion of the great San Joaquin Valley is in eastern Contra Costa County, where its average width is about twenty miles. Sloping gently from Mount Diablo to the San Joaquin River, it adds sixty thousand acres to the alluvial soil of that region. Some of the best farming lands of the county are found there. Some of the choicest and coziest home spots in the entire county are in the valley region.

Exceptional school advantages are to be found in Contra Costa County. The county now maintains seven union high schools, as follows: The Liberty Union High School, at Brentwood; the Riverview High School, at Antioch; the Mount Diablo High School, at Concord; the San Ramon Valley High School, at Danville; the Alhambra High School, at Martinez; the John Swett High School, at Crockett; and the Richmond High School, at Richmond. Provision is made for the cost of educating children who do not live in any high-school district.

It is now possible for a child in any part of the county to obtain a high-school education without cost or unusual hardship.

Keeping pace with all other sections of the country, the active exponents of the good-roads movement are working with enthusiasm to bring the roads of the county to the highest state of perfection.

Their success is attested by numerous scenic boulevards in the various sections of the county. While much remains to be done, the movement received a great impetus from the location of the State highway through the county. The activity of the various towns in street improvements has also contributed largely toward the making of better roads.

Each year sees more and more automobile travel, which has been so great a factor in bringing good roads throughout the land.

In taking leave of Contra Costa County the writer craves the indulgence of the reader if he has at times appeared to resort to a large extent in superlatives. Nothing short of superlatives will serve in describing many of the fields in which this section excels. Emerging from a romantic background, beginning in the days of the old Spanish Dons, her commercial rise has largely been achieved in the past dozen years. Who shall say what the next decade shall bring?

CHAPTER XVI. EARLY CRIMINAL HISTORY

The People vs. Wempett and Wampett. —On September 28, 1850, two Indians named Wempett and Wampett were found guilty of manslaughter by a jury and sentenced to pay a fine of one dollar and two weeks' imprisonment, but who their victim was, or what were the circumstances of the case, the records do not divulge.

Murder of Aparicio Morales. —On May 29, 1852, Jose Antonio, an Indian, stabbed Aparicio Morales at or near the residence of Doctor Tennent in Pinole, from the effects of which Morales died. Antonio was duly tried before C. P. Hester, district judge, found guilty July 9, 1852, and sentenced to be hanged. He was executed August 20, 1852. He was hanged from the limb of a sycamore tree in the suburbs of the village of Martinez. A barrel was placed in an old cart, and the condemned man required to stand on that ticklish foundation while the rope was adjusted. The cart was finally driven away, and the poor fellow tumbled off the barrel and into eternity.

Killing of Ignacio Flores, alias Figaro. —The victim in this case was killed at a place known as the "Chicken Ranch," on October 30, 1853. He came to his death by severe wounds from knife and pistol at the hands of Miguel Nabaro, his wife Antonia and Rafael Soto being apprehended as accessories to the act. On trial the accessory Antonia was discharged, but there is no record of what became of the others.

Murder of James M. Gordon. —The particulars of this deed were communicated to a Stockton newspaper by Doctor Marsh at the time of its occurrence. About seven o'clock in the evening of October 2, 1854, three men came to the house of J. M. Gordon, near Doctor Marsh's, and desired him to give them directions about the road, saying that they had lost their way. As soon as Gordon went to his door, he was shot by one of the party; another of them fired at him also, but missed him. One of the balls struck Gordon, inflicting a mortal wound. Gordon fled in the darkness, and with difficulty reached Doctor Marsh's house, about two miles distant. The object of the ruffians was undoubtedly robbery, as the house was found to be ransacked. The men were traced and ultimately arrested in San Francisco. They were Henry H. Monroe, Andrew Hollenstein, and Thomas Addison. Monroe was duly tried for murder, convicted, and hanged November 24, 1854. While awaiting his execution Addison attempted his rescue, for which he was indicted by the Grand Jury, and imprisoned, but on January 20, 1855, made his escape from jail and has never been captured. The other accomplice, Hollenstein, was handed over to the custody of the sheriff of Solano County in the same month.

Killing of Terrence H. McDonald. —It appears that on June 11, 1856, Rafael, an Indian, and Isabel, an Indian squaw, stabbed Terrence H. McDonald on the right side of the neck, from which he died instantly, the deed being committed in his own dwelling. September 5, 1856, they were convicted of manslaughter, the man sentenced to ten years and the woman to eighteen months imprisonment in the State prison. There was also an accomplice, who was discharged.

Murder of Doctor John Marsh. —Perhaps no more horrible crime than the murder of this pioneer can be found in the pages of any history, and certainly no better example of justice following the guilty than that which tracked one of the murderers to punishment eleven years after the commission of his foul deed. Doctor Marsh had been for many years—long before the American occupation of California— the owner of the Los Meganos Rancho, of which he became possessed, as we have elsewhere stated, by purchase, in the year 1837. Here he dwelt, surrounded by his people, flocks, and herds, for full two decades.

On or about the 24th of September, 1856, business called him from his farm to Martinez, some thirty miles distant. In the gray dawn of the following morning his horse and buggy were found in the town of Martinez, but without an occupant. Then followed the search, which led to the discovery of his body in a roadside ditch, immediately upon which the pursuit of the murderers was undertaken. On the day following Jose Antonio Olivas was captured; after making confession as to certain money found in his possession, taken from the body of the murdered victim, and implicating Felipe Moreno as principal in the deed, he was tried and convicted, but, escaping from jail, he eluded justice for more than ten years. In September, 1866, he was recaptured in Santa Barbara County, and brought to Contra Costa to await his trial.

About the same time Felipe Moreno was taken in Sacramento, where he was going under the alias of Don Castro. When arrested he made desperate efforts to escape but being mastered was quickly handcuffed and incarcerated. The third party implicated in the terrible murder, Juan Garcia, has up to the present time eluded justice. The trial of Felipe Moreno for the murder of Doctor Marsh was commenced on Saturday, September 23, 1867, and on the following Thursday the jury brought a verdict of murder in the second degree against the prisoner. The principal and only positive witness for the prosecution on this trial was Jose Antonio Olivas, one of the three persons indicted for the murder. Separate trials for the prisoners had been procured by District Attorney Mills, with the purpose of using the testimony of Olivas for the State and corroborating it, as to material points, by that of unimpeachable and disinterested witnesses. The defense relied mainly upon being able to prove an alibi; but notwithstanding the very able efforts of the counsel for the prisoner, M. S. Chase, of Martinez, the testimony failed to convince the jury, as the verdict shows, although it was not as severe as might have been expected, possibly because of the youth of the prisoner, and the doubt remaining as to whether he may have been the principal actor in the perpetration of the murder, or merely an accessory. The story of the Doctor's death, as told by Olivas, is as follows: On the morning of September 24, 1856, the date of the murder, Jose Antonio Olivas and Felipe Moreno, aged twenty-five and nineteen years respectively, in company with some females, came into the village of Martinez, where, having attended church, they proceeded to Pinole, returning from there between four and five o'clock that same evening. They almost immediately continued their journey to Pacheco alone, and when reaching the hill about a mile from Martinez paused a while to await the arrival of one Garcia, who was expected to meet them. Olivas then went on ahead for about two hundred yards, when he was overtaken by his comrades, and the three urged their horses into a gallop. While so proceeding they met a man named Swanson. Not long after this circumstance Doctor Marsh was observed to be coming in his buggy. Hereupon he was accosted by Olivas, who asked him for certain money due him for services as a vaquero, to which the Doctor replied that he would be paid on his return from San Francisco, but that he had no money with him then. The deceased now rode away, while the party remained behind and concocted a scheme to kill him, but finally arranged that he should only be robbed. They then followed in pursuit, and on overtaking their victim, Olivas, by Moreno's orders, seized the Doctor's horse by the head, while Moreno jumped into the buggy and Garcia stood guard alongside. The deceased at once faced his enemy and said, "Do you want to kill me?" to which he received the reply, "No," from Olivas, and "Yes" from Moreno, and, notwithstanding the dissuasions of his companions, this youthful fiend slashed the unfortunate man in the face with a knife. He was then dragged out of the vehicle and fell to the ground, being before, however, wounded in the hand; Olivas having then dismounted, as he says, for the purpose of assisting the Doctor, who came toward and struck at him, a scuffle ensued, Olivas crying to Moreno to free him. Thereupon Moreno observed, "Why should I let go this old cabron?" and forthwith stabbed his prostrate victim in the side. Upon receiving this wound the Doctor cried aloud, when Moreno was prepared to repeat the operation, but was pushed away by Olivas, who parried a cut made at him. The Doctor now attempted to rise but was only able to stagger a short distance and fell into a ditch dead. His pockets were then rifled by Garcia and Moreno, who afterward cut his throat, the deed being witnessed by Olivas from his saddle. This terrible crime being perpetrated, the triumvirate repaired to the top of a convenient hill and there divided the booty, whence they repaired to some houses for the night and afterward fled, and for ten years and upward escaped the iron hand of the law. Moreno was sentenced to imprisonment for life in the State prison on November 29, 1867.

Murder of Nicholas Brenzel. —A most atrocious murder was committed near the San Domingo Rancho on May 21, 1859. A man named John Mohr was accused of killing Nicholas Brenzel by striking him with a scythe and was duly arrested in Martinez. From the testimony of the wife of the deceased, it would appear that Brenzel and Mohr, who were both Germans, were engaged during the year in cultivating a ranch together. Mohr owed Brenzel several hundred dollars borrowed money, and Brenzel asked him if he would not pay a portion of it, as he wished to purchase some grain-sacks. On Mohr's refusal to let his partner have any money, Brenzel replied that he would go to San Francisco, borrow the money there, and purchase the sacks on his own account. This conversation took place in the house on the morning of the crime. A few minutes afterward the wife of Brenzel heard a cry of distress, and on going to the door saw Mohr with a scythe-blade in his hand, and nearby was the prostrate and bleeding form of her husband. She asked Mohr why he had killed her husband. He replied, "I did it because I wanted to," and then threw down the scythe, seized a spade, and endeavored to strike the dying man again.

Killing of an Unknown Man.—At an early hour on the morning of October 13, 1859, several citizens living in the vicinity of Lafayette missed their saddles, and it was at once conjectured that horse-thieves had visited the neighborhood, several horses having been stolen from that district a week previously. The alarm was given, and in a very short time a party of six or eight citizens started out and soon got on the trail of the supposed plunderers, those in pursuit being guided by fresh tracks of horses. The trail led across the hills in the direction of San Ramon Valley, crossing it about a mile on the west side of Alamo, and thence toward Mount Diablo. They proved to the Mexicans who had picketed their horses and encamped on the ground close by, having with them saddles belonging to David Carrick and Homer Shuey. They were suddenly surprised by their pursuers and ordered to surrender, a command to which they paid no attention, but endeavored to make their escape.

They were fired upon by the citizens, when one of their number fell mortally wounded, having been shot through the head. The other two took to the chaparral, but as soon as they became aware that the pursuing party was endeavoring to capture them at all hazards the rascals came out of the bush and gave themselves up. The wounded man was conveyed to the Walnut Creek House, where he died the same night.

He was a Mexican, apparently about twenty-five years of age, and on his body was found a letter from the noted desperado, Tiburcio Vasquez, dated from the State prison at San Quentin, and bearing the superscription, "Sra. Dona Guadalupe Cantua—by the hand of S. T. Bsa," who the victim doubtless was.

Killing of Edward Norris. —This tragedy took place at Conkling's Hotel, on the road between Lafayette and Oakland, on the evening of December 11, 1859. The particulars, as gleaned from the Contra Costa Gazette, are as follows: A. H. Houston, of San Francisco, was the owner of some five hundred acres of the Sobrante claim, on the San Pablo Creek. The property had been squatted on by settlers, with all of whom, save one, Mr. Houston had compromised, so as to obtain full possession. This one, a man named Edward Norris, had fenced in some seventy acres of Houston's land and refused to give up possession. On December 10th Houston went over to his ranch for the purpose of making some arrangement toward a peaceable settlement of the dispute. He visited the house of Mr. Norris on Sunday, the 11th, but not finding the latter at home, left a request that he would on his return call at his (Houston's) farm-house and have a talk with him before the hour necessary to start to take the last boat that was to leave Oakland. Houston then returned to his house, and, after waiting as long as possible, he left word with his father-in-law, W. C. Pease, who was in charge of the property, to settle the matter peaceably, by paying Norris a reasonable sum to leave quietly. Norris, however, did not come to the house, and in the evening Pease went over to the hotel nearby, kept by Conkling, for the purpose of getting supper. While eating, a crowd of men arrived at the hotel, among whom was Norris. They were in the bar-room while Pease was in the dining-room. The conversation of Norris and his friends was upon the matter in dispute between the former and Houston. Pease, hearing his name mentioned in not very complimentary terms, stepped to the door of the apartment in which Norris and the others were conversing, and, drawing a pistol, demanded to know who had anything to say against "Old Pease," at the same time raising his pistol, cocking it, and threatening to shoot the first man who raised a finger. Norris, who was in the act of drinking as Pease entered, put down his glass on the table; some harsh words then passed between Pease and Norris; the latter, who was unarmed, reached forward to seize the pistol, when Pease instantly fired, and Norris fell dead, having been shot through the heart. Pease was tried for manslaughter and on January 26, 1861, was acquitted.

Killing of Sadello Catiyo. —During a drunken brawl at the house of Jose Silva, in Rodeo Valley, on the night of May 10, 1860, a Chileno named Sadello Catiyo, was killed by his countryman, Assesso Gayarado.

Murder of Guadalupe Tapia. —Guadalupe Tapia, a Mexican, was mortally wounded with a knife on July 4, 1860, by Ramon Ruiz. They were seen together near Alamo, each having a horse, though dismounted, and just previous to the attack deceased was observed to be reclining on the ground holding his animal by his bridle.

Ruiz now suddenly rushed upon him with a knife, inflicting a terrible wound in the abdomen, from the effects of which he died in a few hours. The murderer was arrested, but at his trial, which took place January 16, 1861, he was discharged, the jury disagreeing, there being eleven in favor of conviction of murder in the first degree and one for manslaughter.

Killing of N. Nathan. —The Gazette of February 15, 1862, says: "The body of N. Nathan was found near Pinole a few days since, much decayed." The verdict of the inquest was that he had been robbed and murdered. His license as a peddler bore date about the middle of December, 1861. He was aged about twenty-one years and had no relatives in California.

Killing of Patrick Finnegan. —On the evening of November 30, 1862, Patrick Finnegan was shot at Clayton, under the following circumstances: It would appear that a troupe of minstrels gave a performance at the Clayton House in the evening to a rather noisy audience. At its conclusion one of the company was somewhat roughly handled by certain parties present, and R. L. Bradley handed him a pistol, telling him to protect himself. He did not use it but returned it soon after.

One account of the affair was that in passing the pistol back it was accidentally discharged; while another eye-witness stated positively that on receiving it Bradley willfully shot Finnegan. The ball struck deceased on the left side of his nose, passing into the head and killing him instantly. Bradley mounted a horse and made his escape.

Killing of James Magee. —On December 1, 1862, James Magee was shot and killed by James Tice. There had been a difficulty between the parties, and in the afternoon in question Tice, who had been drinking, went to the ranch of the deceased, and some hard words passed between them. Tice at length wished to shake hands, to which Magee objected, telling him he was drunk, and ordering him off the premises.

Magee had a shot-gun in his hand at the time, which he had gone into the house for. He turned as if to leave the spot, when Tice presented his pistol and shot him in the left side. He exclaimed, "Oh, I'm a dead man sure!" and almost immediately expired. Tice mounted his horse, rode to Martinez, and put himself in the custody of the sheriff. Deceased owned a valuable ranch in the Moraga Valley, and had accumulated a handsome property. Tice was duly tried before Hon. S. F. Reynolds, district judge, May 30, 1863, when a jury returned a verdict of not guilty.

Murder of Louis d'Alencon. —On the night of Thursday, or the morning of Friday, March 12-13, 1863, Louis d'Alencon, the keeper of the Valley House near Martinez, was murdered by some person or persons unknown. The last that was seen of the deceased alive was on Thursday night by the hired man, an old friend and fellow countryman who lodged with him, when, having shut up the house, they partook of a drink together before retiring for the night, the man then going to bed leaving D'Alencon in the bar-room, where he was in the frequent habit of sitting up all night engaged in writing, he being a regular correspondent of the French newspapers in San Francisco. The companion soon fell asleep and was not disturbed by any unusual noise but thought that had there been such he would have noticed it, as he was used to D'Alencon's habit of being up and moving about all night. At a very early hour on Friday morning, Pancho Flores, passing the Valley House on the way to a rodeo, noted the door ajar, and saw the body of D'Alencon lying on the floor between it and the bar. Pancho tried to enter but was unable to open the door wide enough on account of the position in which the inanimate form lay. He therefore went around to the back of the house, awoke the hired man, and asked him what drunken man was asleep in the bar. The two then went to ascertain and were horrified to find D'Alencon stretched on his back on the floor, dead, and weltering in his blood.

Murder of an Unknown Man.—A stranger, dressed in working clothes, arrived at San Pablo on the night of August 4, 1863, and, after eating supper at the hotel, took his blanket and proceeded a short distance up the road, when he turned off into a wheat-field, spread his bedding, and lay down. The following morning he was found there quite dead, with a wound in the temple, apparently caused by a blow from a heavy instrument. The body was yet warm when discovered.

Killing of John Pete. —On January 11, 1864, one Frank McCann killed John Pete in a quarrel over a game of cards at San Pablo, but what the particulars of the outrage were we have been unable to gather.

Murder of Martine Berryessa. —On February 8, 1864, at the town of Old Pinole, Martine Berryessa was stabbed with a knife by a man who was known by the solitary name of Francisco. Death was almost instantaneous. The facts of the case are these: Some two or three weeks before hard words had passed between the parties, and a charge of horse-stealing was bandied from one to the other. Thereupon a scuffle ensued, in which a cut was received in the leg by Francisco. They then separated, after threats were made by Francisco, and they did not cross each other again until the day of the fatal meeting, when Francisco and two men with him were for some hours at Pinole. Just as they were about leaving, they saw Berryessa, and, going up to him, Francisco observed that somebody wanted him at a place nearby. Berryessa refused to go with them, whereupon he was told he should be made to go, and Francisco drew a pistol upon him. He held up his hands as if to ward off the shot or to seize the weapon, and then, instead of firing the pistol, Francisco unsheathed a knife and stabbed him under the arm. It entered his back immediately below the shoulder, penetrating the lungs, and causing him to fall dead. The murderer and his two companions then fled. Francisco being caught by the bystanders, after a short chase, was lodged in the jail at Martinez.

Murder of Aravena. —On June 17, 1864, a Chileno named Aravena was killed under the following circumstances: It seems for some unexplained reason, he attacked a man named Humboldt, a resident of Oakland, Alameda County, who, in self-defense, turned on the deceased and slew him.

Murder of a Man Named "Jo."—In the month of June, 1874, but on what day we cannot ascertain, a man called "Jo" was stabbed by one Alvarez at Pinole. The cause was liquor and jealousy. Alvarez delivered himself up to the authorities but was discharged.

Murder of Jesus Diana. —The following murder was committed November 12, 1864, under the most vengeful and brutal circumstances.

It appears that a Mexican by the name of Luis Romero had been living in a family of the same nationality a few miles from Pinole. In that household was included a young woman about sixteen years old, the sister of the mistress of the house. This young girl's name was Jesus Diana. Romero was courting her and was very anxious to marry her. She, however, refused all his solicitations, whereat he was very much incensed. Immediately after breakfast on the morning of the fatal day he took his gun and started off, as he said, on a hunting trip. Only a few moments passed, however, before he came back to the house and found the married sister outside at a well nearby. The murdered girl was within, washing dishes. He then went in and stabbed her in the back with a common butcher knife. Her screams quickly brought the absent sister to the door. Upon the latter crying out to Romero to desist, he turned upon her too, with the same knife, when she ran away. He called to her not to be afraid, for he should kill himself also. He then went back, took the gun, put it to his own throat, holding it under the chin so that the charge would pass into his brain, and thus killed himself. Before doing so, however, he stabbed the girl in several places, one of the wounds going entirely through the body.

Murder of Valencia. —On August 25, 1866, a Mexican, or native Californian, named Valencia, died at Martinez from the effects of a wound received at the hands of Jesus Garcia, on the previous Tuesday.

It is said there was no provocation for the assault, although some quarrel had occurred between the parties. The attack was made with a stick or club of oak wood, with which the deceased was severely beaten upon the head and other parts of the body. Garcia was arrested, tried, and on December 27th sentenced by District Judge Dwindle to imprisonment for two years in the State prison.

Murder of Mrs. Elizabeth Robinson. —The following most brutal murder was committed on the night of December 26, 1866, on the person of Mrs. Elizabeth Robinson, an aged woman who dwelt in the vicinity of the Roman Catholic church. The facts of the case as alleged are these: The body of the deceased was discovered lying upon the floor by the child of a neighbor sometime during the forenoon of Thursday, the 27th, and upon this information a number of persons immediately repaired to the premises and found the body in a night-dress upon the floor of the rear room, with the head, face, arms, and hands fearfully cut and gashed and several stabs in the breasts and throat, one of the latter being entirely through the neck, from front to back. Near the body was a piece of candle and a candlestick. The appearances led to the belief that the deceased, aroused by the noise made in entering the house, had risen from her bed, lighted the candle, and on entering the rear room from which the noise proceeded received a severe blow upon the forehead, followed by assaults with the knife, against which the gashes upon the arms and hands showed that she made a protracted but unavailing struggle. The floor of the house displayed bloody tracks, and upon one of the partitions was the full print of a bloody hand, made by the murderer probably on groping his way through the dark. There were also the marks of bloody fingers on the sliding window, showing that he had carefully closed it on his retreat from the premises. The object of the murder was undoubtedly plunder, as the deceased, who was about seventy-five years of age, by a long life of toil, had accumulated some property, and may have been supposed to have money with her in the house, which had all the appearances of having been searched after the life of the woman had been taken. Two days later a mixed-blood Mexican and Indian, called Manuel Jaurez, was arrested under circumstances that tended strongly to identify him with the murder, several of the articles belonging to Mrs. Robinson having been found in his house in Martinez. He was duly incarcerated, and, after a trial lasting an entire week, was found guilty of murder, the testimony against him being entirely circumstantial, but most conclusive. On May 10, 1867, he was sentenced to be hanged on June 28th, on which day he was executed at the jail at

Martinez. Before the carrying out of the sentence, in response to a notice that he was at liberty to say anything he might desire to communicate before execution, in substance he remarked: "In a few minutes I shall be in the presence of my God, and I now declare that I am innocent of the crime for which I am to die; and what I have previously confessed I did in the hope of escaping punishment."

Killing of Sacramento Leibas. —On the evening of January 7, 1867, Sacramento Leibas was shot and fatally wounded by Antonio Figueroa in the Pastor House, a saloon and boarding-house in Pacheco, and principally patronized by native Californians. A difficulty had existed between the parties for some time, and several weeks before deceased complained of Figueroa for threats against his life, but the evidence submitted to Justice of the Peace Sayles, before whom the case was brought, did not warrant placing him under bonds. On the evening of the killing three men came into the saloon together, Bonifacio Pacheco, Espirito Almosan, and Antonio Figueroa, all somewhat under the influence of liquor. Figueroa commenced to abuse Leibas, who replied, "It's all right; I don't want any words." He then directed his conversation to Antonio Leibas, brother of the deceased, in the same strain, and finally the remainder of those present came in for a share of his vituperation. After a while he went out, but soon returned, followed by Pacheco, who was apparently endeavoring to hold his arm. Figueroa raised a pistol, pointed it at Sacramento Leibas, who was standing behind the counter, and fired, the ball taking effect near the heart of the unfortunate man, who died in about an hour and a half. Notwithstanding being pursued, Figueroa escaped. Pacheco and Almosan were arrested as accessories, and after examination were discharged for want of evidence. They were subsequently rearrested and lodged in jail at Martinez. Figueroa was traced to a point on the San Joaquin, near Firebaugh's Ferry, where it is supposed he obtained a crossing in a boat kept there by a party of Sonorans. The accessories were found not guilty May 18th and discharged.

Killing of Peter Lynch. —It appears from the records that sometime previous to the committing of this deed a Portuguese named Antonio Corquillo had been in the employ of Peter Lynch, who resided on San Pablo Creek. On a certain Saturday evening in the month of March, 1867, a bottle of liquor was taken to the cabin where both men lived, and both becoming intoxicated a quarrel ensued. The Portuguese finally went to his bed but was soon after assailed by Lynch. A struggle ensued, and in self-defense Corquillo seized a monkey-wrench from a tool-chest nearby and dealt Lynch a fatal blow. He made a full confession, surrendered himself to the authorities, and on May 11, 1867, was tried and acquitted.

Killing of Enoch J. Davis. —One of the proprietors of the Cumberland house, at the Black Diamond Coal Mines, named Enoch J. Davis, died March 1, 1867, from the effects of a knife wound inflicted by William Bowen some ten days prior to the decease. From the testimony given at the inquest it appears that Bowen and another party got into a quarrel over a game of cards and were ordered by Davis to go out of the house and settle their difficulty; they accordingly went out, and after a scuffle returned, still disputing, when Davis again ordered them away to fight the matter out, at the same time applying some derogatory epithets to Bowen, upon which he ran to his room and returned with a knife, asking Davis if he had called him a "son of ," and upon Davis replying that he did, plunged the knife into his breast; then going back to the room, in which there were several other lodgers, threw the bloody weapon on the table and declared he would take the life of any man who called him such a name. Davis's wound was not at first thought to be mortal, and Bowen remained at the place until within a few days of his victim's death, when he left.

Killing of William Nesbit. —The circumstances of this case are from the dying deposition of the victim. The murder was committed near Somersville on the night of December 21, 1866. On that night, a difficulty having originally occurred between Nesbit and George Vernon, he (Nesbit) went to the house of Vernon for the purpose of settling the difficulty without further trouble. Stopping at Vernon's door, he told him that he wished to talk with him peaceably and settle their difficulty without further words. Vernon said, "All right; wait until I get my boots and I will come and talk with you." Vernon went into the house and returned instantly with a pistol, and while Nesbit was sitting on the porch fired at him, the ball striking him in the breast. As he jumped to run he again shot him in the back. He also fired other shots which did not strike him. On April 24, 1867, Vernon was found guilty of manslaughter and sentenced to ten years' imprisonment in the State prison. In 1871 he was pardoned, the grounds given by Governor Haight for so doing being: "There are serious doubts of his guilt, and it is the opinion of many of the citizens of said [Contra Costa] county that he should not have been convicted, and these doubts seem well founded."

Killing of S. A. Carpenter. —On September 30, 1868, S. A. Carpenter, an old and well-known resident of Alamo, was found dead in a trail leading over a ridge to his residence, about two hundred yards from where the body was discovered. His horse, all saddled, had been previously found roaming about, the circumstance which led to the search. The deceased was in his shirt-sleeves, as if only a temporary absence was intended. He had been shot through the body, the ball entering the right side just below and behind the arm and coming out of the right side a short distance below the nipple. There was no apparent deflection in its course, and, passing about an inch below the heart, produced death almost instantaneously. From its evident force, the ball was thought to have been discharged from a rifle or heavy revolver.

His pantaloons were also cut in the folds on the left side, apparently by a ball that had passed clear of the body. Carpenter is described as a man of very eccentric disposition. He was unmarried and lived alone in a little spot that he had surrounded with a wealth of floral beauty.

Shrubs of various kinds were artistically trained in the most attractive style, and flowers of countless hues unfolded in beauty and mingled their fragrance around his humble dwelling. His house was a model of neatness and order that would have won encomiums from the most thrifty housewife, and the general aspect of the place gave evidence of the esthetic traits of its possessor. Some little time before, Carpenter gave unmistakable proof of insanity, and was for a time removed to Stockton; after his return he had not been generally regarded as of sound mind. He was very irritable and disposed to be quarrelsome toward his neighbors and all others with whom he came in contact. He had made threats to poison stock, and in many ways made enemies. Possibly someone unaware of, or unwilling to allow for his infirmity, may have compassed his death in revenge for injuries received at his hands. Be that as it may—the murderer made his escape.

Killing of Mrs. Laura Walker. —A man named Walker, who lived on the farm of Mr. Sellers, near the Kirker Pass, on the Nortonville side, was arrested on September 5, 1869, for causing the death of his wife by beating her. Both the accused and deceased are reported to have been indulging excessively in drink at the house of a neighbor, and the beating occurred on the way home. On November 30, 1870, Walker was convicted of manslaughter, when a motion was made for a new trial, which was denied, and the prisoner sentenced to ten years' imprisonment in the State prison.

Killing of Jose Vaca. —In an affray at the village of Concord on May 2, 1869, a California Indian named Jose Vaca was killed by another called Fernando Feliz. The deceased had been well known in the vicinity for a long time as a drunken, brawling, besotted fellow, the other being also well known as a quiet, inoffensive person, past the meridian of life, and afflicted from early age with an infirmity that made him a cripple. It appears that the deceased, who had been drinking to inebriation. approached the hut of Feliz with a bottle and wanted him to drink, an invitation he declined, saying that "much whiskey is no good," but told the other he would make a fire and give him something to eat. While making the fire Jose seized hold of him, saying, "Now, I've got you where I want you, and mean to kill you," thereupon striking him a heavy blow with the bottle and breaking it. Fernando, struggled to defend himself, Jose meanwhile slashing and punching his face with the fragments of the bottle, still held in his hand by the neck. In the scuffle that ensued, they got outside of the shanty, where Fernando found an opportunity to seize a large knife with which he gave his antagonist two or three lunges, one of which, as was found on the postmortem examination, passed entirely through the heart, severed the fourth rib, and killed him instantly. A judgment of justifiable homicide was returned.

Killing of George Minchell. —George Minchell, who, with his family, had been living in Ygnacio Valley, about two miles from Pacheco, and farming on the lands of Charles S. Lohse, was shot at his own door on the morning of September 8, 1870, by a man named William Donovan, who had been in his employ and claimed an unpaid balance of wages, while, it was asserted on the other hand, that he had been overpaid eight dollars. It is said that Donovan visited the house of the deceased on the previous evening, demanding payment of the claimed dues in abusive and threatening language. Minchell directed him to leave the house and followed him out. A moment afterward the discharge of a pistol was heard, and Minchell re-entered the door, saying to his wife, "Mary, I am shot." "You are not going to die, George, are you?" "Yes, Mary," and he immediately dropped dead upon the floor.

Donovan was arrested, and when the sheriff approached him with the manacles, he exclaimed, fully realizing his situation, "Oh, God, this is what drink has brought me!" He was duly tried and convicted, and on December 8th, sentenced to be hanged on February 3, 1871. Judgment was stayed, however, and on April 15th Donovan was granted a new trial on the ground that a continuance asked for the defendant on the former trial was improperly denied. The continuance was demanded for the procuring of witnesses to prove that the prisoner had been an inmate of an insane asylum, and it was denied on the admission of the prosecution that the fact alleged would be proved by the required witnesses if they were present. The Supreme Court decided that this admission was not sufficient, and that the defendant was entitled to an opportunity of proving the fact. The case was moved to the San Francisco courts, and on December 12, 1871, Donovan was again convicted of murder in the first degree. Afterward, in February, 1872, a motion for a new trial was sent on appeal to the Supreme Court, which issued a writ to stay execution of sentence until the "pending motion is heard and decided," and on June 27th directed that an order be entered affirming the judgment of the court below and directing the lower court to fix a day to carry the sentence into execution. He was again sentenced to be hanged on December 13th. In the meantime a petition to pardon the murderer had been sent to the governor, who declined to interfere, but ultimately execution was stayed by Governor Booth, who was moved thereto by an immense petition for a commutation of sentence.

Killing of Herman Heyder. —From November 18 to 25, 1870, the Fifteenth District Court was occupied with the trial of Mathew Caspar, indicted for the murder of Herman Heyder, by poison, put into the food served to him by the accused, when the deceased was a visitor at his house some ten or twelve miles southeast of Antioch. The general facts and features of the case may be briefly summarized as follows: On the 6th or 7th of September, 1870, Heyder and Caspar were brought into Antioch, at one o'clock in the morning, Heyder lying in the bottom of the wagon and Caspar sitting upon the seat beside the driver. Both were represented to Doctor Howard to be suffering from the effects of strychnine taken with the food they had eaten for supper at the house of Caspar some five or six hours before. Heyder died soon after reaching Antioch. Caspar recovered, and, from the medical testimony and other facts subsequently developed or considered, it appeared doubtful if he had exhibited any symptoms of having been poisoned at all. A jury was summoned to make investigations in the case. After a patient, thorough, and protracted investigation Caspar was held on their finding to answer before the grand jury on a charge of poisoning Heyder.

The finding of this jury, and, presumably, of the grand jury, was based wholly upon strong circumstantial evidence of the guilt of the accused.

It was, in the first place, almost inconceivable that so atrocious and diabolical a crime could have been committed without some motive of envy or cupidity; but the most diligent inquiry failed to develop a fact or suggestion which warranted suspicion that anyone had been prompted by such motives to enter Caspar's house in his absence and mingle strychnine with the various condiments and articles of food which would be eaten by him on his return, for the purpose of killing him.

Large quantities of strychnine were found in the sugar-bowl, in the pepper-box, in the salt upon the table, in the syrup, in the butter, in the batter-pan, and in the flap-jacks, eaten at least by Heyder for supper— for he was unquestionably poisoned, exhibited all the most painful symptoms, and died within a few hours after the fatal meal. Strychnine was found in his stomach, on chemical analysis of the contents, and in the undigested portions of the cakes he had eaten. The question then arose with the jury of inquest, Had Caspar any motive which would possibly have prompted him to such an attempt to destroy the life of his visitor and guest? It was shown that Caspar and Heyder had been acquainted for some time; had worked together in herding sheep; that Heyder had money, and that Caspar had been trying for some time to borrow several hundred dollars from him. His statements in relation to the preparation of the supper when Heyder came with him to the house, after having been with him when he had been working during the afternoon, and many other circumstances developed in the investigation, produced a conviction of Caspar's guilt in the minds of the jury of inquest; and the testimony before the grand jury doubtless produced such conviction there as to warrant his indictment for the murder. With the strong circumstantial evidence of guilt which had warranted the findings of the two juries, the prosecution at the trial brought in the testimony of the two prisoners confined in the jail, to prove an admission to them in prison on the part of Caspar that he did the poisoning.

This was the only testimony purporting to be of a positive character against the prisoner, and it probably had not the weight with the jury that the testimony of persons unaccused of crime would have had, though these prisoners had no apparent motive for testifying falsely against the life of another. It is therefore not surprising that, under their solemn responsibilities, with no alternative but condemnation to death or acquittal, the jury should have failed to find a verdict according with the general conviction of the prisoner's guilt.

Killing of James Fergusson. —A stranger named James Fergusson, on his way from Gilroy, where he had been employed in the redwoods, to his home at Windsor, Sonoma County, arrived at Martinez too late to cross the ferry on the evening of June 4, 1871, and met a violent death between midnight and Monday morning, under circumstances of a peculiarly painful nature. The deceased was accompanied by his three sons, aged respectively eighteen, thirteen, and ten years, and being obliged to remain overnight at Martinez put up their horses in the stable of the Alhambra Hotel, where he and the two younger lads at a later hour made camp beds, the eldest boy at a still later hour going to his bed in their wagon, which stood in the stable yard. During the evening Fergusson had been drinking pretty freely, and obtained from George Gordon Moor, Sr., the sum of $175, which deceased had given him to take charge of. This money was not found on his body. At about eight o'clock p. m. he went to the saloon of Francisco Saurez and there remained until one o'clock on Monday morning, leaving at the same time as did Alexander Naghel, William Higgins, and K. W. Taylor. The first of these, whose testimony is the most important relative to material facts, stated at the inquest that while there, Taylor playing on a guitar and Saurez on an accordion, deceased jumped up and began talking about soldiering, saying that he had command of fifteen hundred men.

Not much attention was paid to what he said, and after a little they all drank together. The deceased then began showing the sword and fist exercises with his cane and fists, most of them joining in the play. Deceased then asked Taylor to take the stick (for attack) and he would defend himself with his fists. After one or two passes Fergusson said to Taylor, "I could have hit you, so and so." Taylor replied, "I could have knocked the knuckles off of you," etc. After a general "skylarking,"

Taylor handed the stick back to deceased, who, in flourishing it, dropped it on the floor, then giving it a kick that sent it over the screen. Saurez picked the stick up and told the deceased he would keep it until he went away. After this Taylor and Saurez played the guitar and accordion, and deceased wanted them to play "Dixie." They complied, playing and singing, Fergusson joining in the chorus. Negro and Irish songs were then sung. Then Higgins asked for a Union song. The deceased said, "Anyone that will sing a Union song is a d—d son of a —." No reply was made to this remark by anyone. Taylor sang one or two more songs, and afterward a Union patriotic song. After more singing, Saurez said, "Let's all go to bed." Taylor said, "Let's all take a drink." All drank except the deceased, who got up and said he "had a boy twelve years old in his wagon over there, and that he had made that boy fetch his man." Taylor said there was no use talking about that now; the war was over.

Deceased then began talking about one Southerner being equal to five Yankees. Taylor and Saurez were at this time looking over the accounts of the latter, and while thus employed, and while the deceased was bragging about being able to whip five Yankees, Higgins, who was sitting on the billiard-table, came forward and proposed that all should go home. Taylor said, "We will all go home if Saurez will treat." Saurez treated, and all drank, including deceased. Taylor, Higgins, and Naghel then went out of the saloon and started toward the bridge. The deceased started at the same time, but turned back to enter the saloon, when Saurez ejected him, telling him to go home and go to bed, as he wanted to shut up. Naghel further stated that he left Taylor in order to go down the street; that the deceased walked up against Taylor, who then turned aside and tried to avoid him. Naghel then walked back to where they were. Deceased again walked up against Taylor, who said, "Go away from me. I don't know who you are, and don't want you to follow me. Go about your business." At this Taylor gave him a shove and he fell backward. After he got up Naghel told him he had better go away, but he would not, and persistently thrust his society upon them. Naghel then asked him where his wagon was. He pointed to where it stood, and he was told to go to it. He started in that direction, Taylor, Higgins, and Naghel walking after him toward the residence of the first named, deceased walking on the sidewalk and they in the middle of the street. When deceased reached Wittenmyer's corner he halted and turned back, still walking on the sidewalk, and went around the corner towards Sturges' Hotel. The three then remained talking for a short time in the middle of the street and opposite the thoroughfare leading to Brent's warehouse. While standing there, Fergusson came back from the direction of the Alhambra Hotel, and approached in the middle of the street to within about fifteen steps, when he dropped on one knee, with a gun pointed in the direction in which they stood. Naghel remarked to his companions, "He has a gun; look out!" They all thereupon concealed themselves in separate places of safety, and the deceased got up to follow. Naghel ran again in the direction of Brent's warehouse, but did not notice where the other two went. He saw, however, deceased drop on one knee as before and saw the flash of a gun. A few seconds later he heard Taylor call for Brown. Naghel then went back to Brown's porch. He (Sheriff Warren Brown) brought out a carbine and gave it to Taylor, cautioning him to be "very careful, for it would go off easy," and, "not to shoot if he could help it" or words to that effect. In the meantime Naghel was dispatched for Gift, to arrest the man. Taylor then took up his position by the railing near the end of the bridge. He now saw deceased approaching, holding his gun as if ready to fire, and searching about him for someone. Seeing Higgins, he pointed the weapon toward him. At this moment Taylor stepped to the end of the bridge and ordered him to hold up his gun. He immediately wheeled around and pointed it at Taylor, when he (Taylor) fired and killed him. Taylor then handed himself over to the sheriff, who had now come up. The jury found a verdict that deceased was killed by K. W. Taylor, the shot being in self-defense.

Killing of Silverio Monjas. —Of this affair the Contra Costa Gazette of July 8, 1871, has the following: "During the past week the people of the central portion of the county have been intensely excited by occurrences growing out of the disputed ownership and possession of a certain portion of the Moraga grant, about which there has been much litigation and contention for several years. The land in question is claimed on one side by Isaac Yoakum and on the other by members of the Moraga family. Some two months or more ago the sheriff, by writ of the District Court, was directed to put Yoakum in possession of the lands, then occupied by a portion of the Moraga family, but he had, as is claimed, no authority in executing the writ to remove and dispossess such of the Moraga children as were not named in the instrument, and he refused to do so, Yoakum, or his agent, as is said, refusing at the time to accept possession unless all the Moragas and their personal effects were removed. Yoakum subsequently, however, went into occupancy of the portion of the premises to which the writ entitled him, and the Moragas remained in possession, as the sheriff had left them, of a portion of the land claimed by Yoakum, and to which, as we understand, he would have been entitled under the judgment of the court but for an error of omission in the complaint in action, upon which the judgment was rendered in his favor. From this situation of affairs, both parties claiming and believing they had legal and equitable rights which they were justified in asserting and defending, much heat and bitterness has arisen, and several serious collisions have occurred to the imminent peril of life on both sides. Sometime early in May several rifle-shots were fired at one of the Moragas, and the horse he was riding was killed by a man in the employ of Yoakum named William Steele, who was at that time, together with one of the Yoakum boys, under one thousand-dollar bonds to answer before the grand jury of the county.

Since that time the temper of the hostile parties has not improved, and threatening demonstrations and preparations have been made on both sides, with no very serious results, however, until last Sunday (July 1st), when Silverio Monjas, one of the Moraga party, was shot by William Steele, as he affirms, in self-defense. On the previous day there had been a collision between the parties and a good deal of shooting. In the melee one of the Moraga girls was struck with a gun and severely hurt by Yoakum, and the horse he was riding was fatally shot. Reports of these occurrences spread rapidly about the county and created a degree of excitement and manifestations of indignation seldom produced in our usually quiet and moderate community; and the excitement and indignation reached a higher pitch on Saturday, after the shooting of Monjas, threatening to culminate in a vengeful outbreak against the Yoakum party. In the heat of the excitement many intemperate and improper charges and threats were made, which a cooler judgment and fuller knowledge of facts would not justify. Sheriff Brown was on the ground shortly after the shooting of Monjas on Saturday, and, on the information of Yoakum, found and arrested Steele. Yoakum voluntarily offered to surrender himself to the sheriff for examination before any competent magistrate upon any charge that might be preferred against him, and accompanied the sheriff to Walnut Creek, where, on finding Justice Slitz was absent, they proceeded to Pacheco, and on reaching that place found that Justice Ashbrook was also from home. Yoakum here declined to accompany the officer further, though he offered to give his word or bond for appearance whenever and for whatever purpose required. As the sheriff had no warrant or authority whatever for detaining him, he was allowed to go; and the sheriff has been highly censured therefor, but, so far as we can see, without the slightest reason."

Monjas, who was shot by Steele, died about three o'clock on Saturday morning, and a jury of inquest, summoned and sworn on Sunday by Justice Allen, continued their inquiries until Monday evening, when the inquest was adjourned to ten o'clock

Saturday morning at Walnut Creek. Steele was brought before Justice Ashbrook for examination on Thursday; the people in the conduct of the case were represented by District Attorney Mills, and the defendant by Judge Blake, of Oakland.

The examination was concluded on Friday afternoon, and Steele was held to answer for murder without admission to bail. The jury of inquest found Isaac Yoakum to be accessory to the killing of said Silverio Monjas. He was brought before Justice Ashbrook, of Pacheco, on July 10th, to answer to the charge of assault with a deadly weapon, with intent to commit bodily injury upon the person of Gunecinda Moraga, in Moraga Valley, on June 30, 1871. On motion of Judge Warmcastle, acting for District Attorney Mills, the charge was modified to one of assault and battery. The defendant, contrary to the express desire of the court, and the prosecution, objected to trial of the charge by jury, and in deference to his objection the case was tried without a jury. The trial occupied the greater part of the 10th and 11th of July. The defendant conducted the case in his own behalf, assisted by a young lady, his daughter, who wrote out the testimony as given in by the witnesses.

The evidence produced clearly sustained the charge and established that the defendant had proved an aggravated assault upon the Moraga girl, striking her twice with his gun and inflicting severe hurts upon her person, while, at the request of his herder, she and her sister were assisting him to drive the defendant's sheep away from the enclosure held by the Moraga family. Yoakum was found guilty and fined five hundred dollars but gave notice of appeal. On the charge of being accessory with William Steele in the killing of Silverio Monjas, Isaac Yoakum was brought before Justice Wood, of Danville, on July 24th, examination being continued till the 27th, and at its conclusion he was held upon bail of three thousand dollars to answer to the charge.

The case of George Steele was tried in Alameda County, before the Third District Court, whose term commenced February 19, 1872. The case was transferred for trial on the motion and affidavits of the prisoner's counsel to the effect that existing prejudice would prevent an impartial trial in Contra Costa County. The case was set for March 4, 1872, and on that date he was acquitted. He was then held on the charge of an assault to murder, with bail bonds fixed at two thousand dollars.

Killing of Patrick Sullivan. —On the afternoon of October 28, 1871, Justice Ashbrook, of Pacheco, was notified of the death of Patrick Sullivan at the residence of James Sullivan, his brother, near Bay Point, from a gun discharged at his head by Mrs. Catherine Sullivan, the wife of James. Of the untoward affair we find from the testimony adduced that James Sullivan was absent from home for several days, and had returned only on the 24th of October, but heard nothing from his wife that anything unpleasant had transpired, but observed that she did not speak to his brother, nor he to her, and on the 27th his brother told him that he must look out for another man, as he was going to leave. On the day of the killing they had been sowing wheat in the forenoon and all were at the dinner-table as usual, but his wife did not eat, a circumstance that Sullivan attributed to her being unwell. After eating he (the husband)' moved back his chair and was reading a newspaper, when he was startled by the discharge of a gun in the room, and, on looking up, saw Mrs. Sullivan standing in the pantry door with a gun, and saw his brother fall forward on the table. Shocked and alarmed, he sprang up and rushed out of the door, his wife following with the gun in her hands, and the children clinging to her skirts. In his excitement and agony of mind, he exclaimed, "My God, what have you done? Was it an accident?" To which his wife replied: "No; I shot him. He deserved it. He was a villain. He attempted a vile outrage on me!" She then told him that the deceased, on the night of the 23rd had forced open the window, entered her bedroom, and attempted to outrage her, but she had fought him off, and on her declaring that she would take the children and go to Cunningham's (one of the neighbors) for protection, he threatened if she did so, or if she reported a word of the matter to her husband, he would kill her. On the following morning, after she had passed a sleepless night, while she was preparing kindling wood to light a fire, he came in, threw his arms around her and attempted to force her into his room, but she fought him off with the butcher knife she was using to split the kindling, and her little boy, who had been awakened by the noise, coming into the kitchen, he retired; but during the morning, and before the return of her husband, the deceased found an opportunity to renew his threat to kill her if she reported a word of what had occurred. All the testimony and collateral circumstances seemed to sustain Mrs. Sullivan's statement of the matter to her husband, and the statement she made upon the inquest and the examination is the same. She was apprehended and held on five thousand dollars bail to answer to the charge before the grand jury. Mrs. Sullivan was duly arraigned and the case set for November 24, 1871, when she was very properly acquitted.

Killing of Peter Peters. —On March 14, 1872, a Welshman named Peter Peters was shot and mortally wounded by a fellow-countryman named Job Heycock. From the testimony given before the coroner's jury, it appears that Heycock was aroused from his sleep on Thursday morning between the hours of four and five o'clock by a great noise in the room adjoining his bedroom. He got up, went into the next room, taking with him a loaded double-barrelled shot-gun. It was quite dark there, but he thought he noticed somebody going upstairs. He called out to him to stop but receiving no answer he fired. The deceased fell down to the bottom of the stairs. Heycock approached him, found him to be Peter Peters, a very particular friend of his. It also appeared from the testimony that William Rees, a person living with Heycock, was about lighting a fire in the kitchen when the deceased approached the window from the outside, broke a pane of glass, raised the window and came in. Rees did not know who the person was, his light having gone out, and was frightened so that he ran upstairs, causing thereby a great noise, which woke everybody in the house. The jury of inquest returned a verdict of justifiable homicide.

In regard to the principal of this affair, the following "strange story" appeared above the signature "W" in the Alameda Advocate of May 11, 1872: "In 1837, on the 26th of November, the cosmopolitan community of Crumlin, a small village in Monmouthshire, in the western part of England, were aroused and somewhat bewildered by the commission of a foul crime, the perpetrators of which did not only escape, but so skillfully covered their tracks that discovery seemed impossible.

A recent disclosure made under very singular circumstances, as will be seen from this brief narrative, has brought to light this once-thought impenetrable mystery. The circumstances may not be unfamiliar to many of the old residents of Monmouthshire. The victim was a young man by the name of Mason, who was found dead on the old Crumlin bridge with his body mangled in a fearful manner. A few weeks after this foul crime had been committed, three men disappeared from the village very mysteriously to parts unknown. There has been strong suspicion that these were the guilty parties. One of the three was named Peter Peters, better known in this country as 'Welsh Pete.' For fifteen years he had been rambling through the different mining districts of California; the last few years he has been laboring in the Mount Diablo coal mines. His voyage through life had been anything but pleasant.

Given very much to dissipation, under the effects of which he was laboring on the morning of the 12th of February last, when he, at about five o'clock leaped from his bed, imagining that he was surrounded by a host of enemies with various kinds of weapons in their hands, with the intention of taking his life. He ran into an adjoining house for protection and jumped through the window of a back kitchen. Heycock, the proprietor, heard the noise and went to the kitchen door with his gun in his hand, and, as he says, called three times. Hearing no reply, he discharged the contents of his gun into Welsh Pete's body, when he fell to the floor. In a few moments he seemed quite conscious, and Heycock promptly dispatched a messenger for medical assistance, acknowledging that he had made a mistake. The utmost attention was paid to the wounded man, yet he gradually became more feeble; but his strength and voice were spared to make a clear confession of being accessory to the murder of Mason on the old Crumlin bridge thirty-five years before. At ten o'clock the same day his symptoms became worse and in a few moments after he breathed his last."

Murder of Valentine Eischler. —On November 16, 1872, one Valentine Eischler, a German, was killed on Marsh Creek, about eight miles southeast of Antioch, near what is called the "Chamisal." He was living with his wife upon a small farm and had in his employ one Marshal Martin. During the stay of Martin, Mrs. Eischler formed a determination to get rid of her husband, and several plans were formed by her and Martin for carrying into effect her deadly purpose. In pursuance of the plan, Martin went to Antioch one day and purchased a quantity of arsenic, and when he came home she mixed some of it with stewed pumpkin and put it on the table for supper. But it so happened that Eischler did not partake of any of it. The next morning it was thrown down the privy vault. A few days after she repeated the dish, but Martin claimed that he persuaded her to throw it away. She then wanted Martin to tell Eischler that there were some pigs for sale at Point of Timber, and to go along with him in the wagon, get him to drinking, and then buy a bottle of whiskey and put arsenic into it. Martin went along with Eischler, but for some reason the plan did not succeed. Another plan was then formed by which Martin was to knock Eischler off the wagon on the way home from Antioch and run the wagon over his head.

A neighbor riding home with them prevented this plan. Then she suggested that Martin should shoot him. Martin had a revolver which he had purchased from a man who got it in Vallejo, and it would be necessary to go there to get cartridges to fit it. She gave him the money to go there, and he got the cartridges and returned. The day upon which the murder was committed, Eischler went to Antioch for a load of flour; Martin accompanied him, according to instructions. Before starting Mrs. Eischler placed an old blanket in the wagon so that Martin, after killing Eischler, could wrap the body in it, and when he returned she would go with him to an old well nearby, throw the body down the well, pour coal oil upon it and burn it up. Martin's heart failed him, and he did not shoot Eischler. When they returned she was very angry with Martin for not carrying out her plan, and told him that he did not love her, or he would do as she wished him to. After unloading the flour and putting the horses in the stable (it being about 4 p. m.), as Martin testified, he went about doing the chores, and Eischler commenced making a doubletree. He had a piece of coupling, an axe, saw, hatchet, and jack-knife, and was using the wagon-tongue as a workbench. Martin says that while he was watering a cow, which had to be led to water by a rope, Mrs. Eischler came out and commenced talking to her husband. They had some very high words. He heard Eischler say to his wife, "Woman, take your clothes and go back to the w house where you came from." Then Mrs. Eischler stepped back and, picking up the axe, said, "I'll give you w house," and struck her husband on the back of the head, knocking him over the wagon-tongue so that his body doubled over it; then she straddled the tongue and struck him two more blows on the front part of the head. Then she called Martin to come and help her drag the body into the stable. After placing it in the stable Martin went to saddle his horse for the purpose of going to the Good Templar's lodge at Eden Plains schoolhouse, about two miles away. While fixing his horse, he said that she went into the stable and struck the victim two more blows with the axe, and that when she came out she said that she had found him sitting up, but that she had fixed him now. When Martin returned from the lodge she told him to go and arouse the neighbors and tell them that Eischler was dead in the stable, and that the horses had kicked him to death. He obeyed her instructions. When the neighbors came some of them suspected that he had been murdered. The next day, when they went to examine the body, they found a great many horehound burrs on the woolen shirt of the deceased, and by this means they found where the body had been dragged to the stable. Afterward they noticed the flies gathering upon Martin's shoes and pants, and this fact, together with the burrs upon the woolen shirt, led them to make search for the place where the murder had been committed. During this search Martin was very active in leading them off in different directions, but finally they came to the wagon and examined the sandy soil around it. They soon found a damp place and putting some of the sand in a basin of water it exhibited a bloody color, and a greasy scum arose to the surface. Martin and the woman were then arrested and taken to Antioch, where they both made confession, each charging the other, however, with having directly done the murder. Martin's testimony under cross-examination on the trial substantially agreed with this summary of the facts of the case. Martin was duly executed January 23, 1874, having previously made a full confession of his share in the dreadful crime. On the scaffold he said, "Gentlemen, I am here on this platform to die an innocent man. That woman deserves ten times as much to die." It is not meet that we should here note the details of his execution; these will remain in the minds of many of our readers. The wife of the victim of the barbarous drama has been ever since an inmate of the lunatic asylum at Stockton.

Killing of Jamiens. —What is known as "Sidney Flat," about half a mile below Somersville, was the scene of a most wanton murder, committed about one o'clock in the morning of January 27, 1873. Two wretched and disorderly brothels, to the annoyance and mortification of the respectable residents of Somersville, had been for some time shamelessly maintained on Sidney Flat. At the hour named, as is gathered from the evidence, a drunken inmate of one of the establishments, named Hattie Davis, in company with an American, was on the way from one of these houses to the other, which are separated by a distance of two or three hundred yards, followed by a Mexican named Jamiens and a Mexican boy about seventeen years of age. Jamiens was playing upon a toy musical instrument, and the boy was carrying a bottle of whiskey. The woman's drunken brawling attracted the attention of some of the visitors at the brothel she was approaching, and several of the men, among whom was James Carroll, started from the house toward them. On meeting, one of the number named Green said the woman asked him to take her home but on his attempting to do so the man who was with her tried to detain her, and he knocked him down.

At this moment the two Mexicans joined the group, Jamiens playing upon his harmonica, the toy instrument before mentioned. Carroll asked the Mexican boy what he had in his hand, and upon being answered that it was whisky he snatched the bottle from the boy and knocked him down, either with the bottle or his pistol, and turning on Jamiens, fired.

Jamiens fell, exclaiming, "I am shot through the head," which were his last words, though he did not cease to breathe for some three or four hours afterward. The deceased had been employed for some time at the Somersville mines, where he bore a good character and was generally known by the name of "Frank." On April 18th Carroll was convicted of murder in the second degree and was sentenced to twenty years' imprisonment in the State prison.

Killing of Michael Duffy. —Thomas Redfern was arrested on the afternoon of June 21, 1873, at his residence, about a mile south of Martinez, for having shot and dangerously wounded Michael Duffy. The wounded man was removed from Redfern's place, where the shooting occurred, to the county hospital, and his right arm from the elbow to the shoulder was found shockingly shattered and mangled by the shot, which had entered the side of the neck, shattering the bones about the head of the spinal column and the base of the skull. He died July 4th.

Redfern, it seems, had taken Duffy out to his house some days before and had been spending most of the time there in convivial indulgences, until a quarrel arose between them which culminated in the shooting. May 14, 1874, Redfern was declared by a jury not guilty.

Murder of Martin Gersbach. —The locality known as the Hertsel place, on San Pablo Creek, some three miles below what is called Telegraph Road crossing, was the scene of a murder on the evening of August 1, 1873, almost precisely parallel in cause and circumstances with the Eischler murder mentioned above. If there be any difference at all, it is that in the last deed both the implicated parties were apparently persons of competent mental capacity and responsibility, while in the other case neither of them, perhaps, were up to the common measure of mental competency and sense of responsibility. In both cases the wife and the paramour plotted the death of the husband, attempted it repeatedly by means of poison, and finally compassed it by a direct assault with murderous weapons—in the former case with an axe, and in the latter with pistol-shot, hammer, and axe.

Martin Gersbach was a German by birth, some thirty years of age, who, by industry and frugality, had accumulated a little money, some three or four thousand dollars, it was said, and had been a lessee of the place where he had lived with his family, and where he was murdered, for something more than a year. His wife was a woman of about the same age, of German parentage and American birth. The paramour murderer, Nash, alias William Osterhaus, was a man about the same age, also of German parentage and American birth. By the woman's statement, Nash was engaged by her husband about Christmas, 1872, to work on the place, and he soon began to pay her some improper attentions, which she slightly resented at first, but soon began to accept and encourage. When the character of the subsisting intimacy became apparent to her husband, he became enraged, and threatened to procure a divorce; but as he did not move in the matter further, they plotted to kill him, first dosing him with croton oil, given one day when he complained of being sick, then trying to have him take arsenic to counteract the effects of the oil, and then by putting laudanum in his coffee, which he would not drink after the first taste. They then tried to dispose of him by saturating his pillow with chloroform, but without avail. Nash then determined to pick a quarrel with Gersbach for the opportunity it might offer of killing him but was unable to arouse his resentment.

Finally, on the night of the murder, as she stated, after the woman and her husband had retired to bed, Nash, who occupied a room upstairs, called for Gersbach to come up there. Gersbach, instead of complying, rose from the bed on which he was lying, with his clothes on, and hurried out of the house. As he did so, Nash came downstairs with a pistol in each hand. He ran out after Gersbach, and she heard six shots fired in quick succession. She then heard a low groan, and, on going to the door, met Nash, who said Martin was shot. Just then he groaned. Nash at once took a hammer from the kitchen, went out to where Gersbach lay, and she heard several blows of the hammer on his head. Nash then returned and said he had finished him. He told her he would go over and tell Roland, a neighbor, he had killed Martin in self-defense, but just as he was about to go Martin groaned again. Nash went out to where he lay, and she heard heavy dull blows given; then Nash returned to her and said he had finished him with an axe. Then Nash went off to carry his report of the death of Gersbach, and when he returned, before morning, said he would have to leave. He changed his bloody clothes, took about thirty or forty dollars that belonged to his victim, and went away. Such was the woman's statement. The officers found the bloodstained cast-off clothing of the murderer, his pistol with six empty chambers, and the blood and hair-clotted hammer in the room he had occupied, and spots of blood about the floor. Near the spot where the body of his victim fell they found the other pistol, fully charged.

After the murder Nash went to the house of a neighbor named Muir, a few hundred yards distant from that of the murdered man and called him up. Muir's dogs made such threatening demonstrations that he remained some little distance off. The barking of the dogs was so furious that Muir could not distinctly hear what he said, further than that Gersbach had been killed, and he therefore went over with Nash, or following him, and found the wounded man still alive. Muir requested Nash to help him carry the wounded man into the house, but he refused to do so, and while Muir was gone for other help, as we understood, Nash changed his clothes, and left the place. The murdered man lingered until August 4th and was sufficiently conscious during a portion of the time to give intelligent directions for the care of his boy and his property affairs by a friend, and to clearly designate Nash as his murderer.

After more than a week's hunt night and day among the hills, following up the scent of every reported straggler, and in almost every instance finding they had been on the trail of the wrong man, and while Sheriff Ivory and his staff of officers were still scouring the hills and valleys for Nash, a telegram was received from Governor Booth with the information that he had been captured at Battle Mountain, Nevada.

Under-Sheriff Hunsaker immediately dispatched a courier to find Sheriff Ivory and telegraphed to the Battle Mountain justice that he would start for the prisoner immediately, inquiring at the same time if he had a description of Nash and was sure he had him. A reply was received from the justice later in the evening that he had the description and the prisoner acknowledged himself the man. The courier sent for Ivory found him above Danville, shaping his course toward Tassajara. He at once returned homeward, and with all speed made his way to Battle Mountain. Nash was duly tried, found guilty May 1, 1874, and sentenced to imprisonment for life.

In the case of Mary Gersbach, the jury, after three days' and nights' deliberation, failed to agree. She was again tried, with a like result in December. 1874. The case dragged its slow length along up until November 9, 1875, when District Attorney Mills applied to the Supreme Court for peremptory writ of mandate and review in the case of Mary Gersbach, which was denied. On Wednesday, November 17th, she was discharged from custody on her own bond of five thousand dollars.

Homicide of George Muth. —The village of San Pablo was the scene of another bloody murder; the date was August 10, 1873. The victim in this case was George Muth, a young German, who had lived some years in the vicinity, and was generally liked and respected. He was killed by Henry Ploeger, also a German, who lived usually in San Francisco, but for some years during part of each season had been engaged in hay pressing and had been so employed in San Pablo at the time of the slaying. He had, some time back, it is said, sold a hay-press to Muth, and was displeased with him because he had engaged in business rivalry with him. On August 10, 1873, both parties were at the village, and both had been drinking, though it was a very unusual thing for Muth to do so. Ploeger had made threats against Muth, and the latter, just as Ploeger was about to mount his horse, crossed from the opposite side of the road and laid his hand on his (Ploeger's) shoulder, asking him what he was threatening him for or what had he against him, or some question of such purport. Ploeger instantly drew his pistol and shot him through the heart, killing him instantly. Ploeger claimed that he anticipated an attack with a pistol when he drew his, and that the shooting was unintentional. The bystanders, however, did not seem to have been impressed with such belief, and were inclined to execute summary justice on the spot, regarding it as an act of unprovoked and wanton murder. The prisoner was held by the officers and safely taken to the jail at Martinez, November 27, 1873. He was convicted of manslaughter and sentenced to six years imprisonment in the State prison.

Killing of Ramon Chavis. —A native Californian half-breed named Ramon Chavis was shot by Constable John Wilcox on August 23, 1874, at San Pablo. It appears that the deceased had been at the house of Wilcox, drinking and quarreling during the evening, and Wilcox had several times been obliged to intervene to stop fights in which he had engaged. Before the shooting Wilcox had retired to bed, but was called up by someone who said that deceased and someone else were killing somebody. Wilcox got up and partially dressed himself, took his pistol and went out, to find Chavis and another partially drunken man charging their horses and riding over a man they had thrown down in the road, who was a half-demented person residing in the place. Wilcox commanded them to desist, when Chavis rode off a few yards, wheeled his horse and charged on him. When within a few feet Wilcox fired, and Chavis fell with a shot under the eye-socket. The coroner's jury found that the homicide was justifiable.

Murder of Ah Hung.—The salient facts in this case are as follows: The deceased, Ah Hung, some two months previously opened a new laundry at Pacheco, and subsequently took Ah Sing into partnership relations. There was also a Chinese boy, Ung Gow, employed in the establishment. They all retired as usual on the night of January 16, 1876, Ah Hung sleeping in an inner apartment, Ah Sing in an outer room, on a table, and the boy, Ung Gow, on the floor under the table. About daylight the boy was awakened by a noise and heard Ah Hung exclaiming that he was killed. He ran into the room and saw Ah Sing attempting to haul him off the bed and chopping him with a hatchet. The boy attempted to pull Ah Sing away, but he turned and struck at him with the hatchet, inflicting one or two cuts, saying that he would kill him too.

Ung Gow ran out to escape him, and went directly to the other washhouse, up the street, to give the alarm and find protection, but was refused admittance and driven away. He then went to Tiedeman's place and reported what had occurred. Constable Henry Wells was the first to visit the scene of the homicide and there found the deceased in the front apartment, still with life enough remaining to make some moans of suffering, and most horribly hacked. He survived but a few moments.

From the appearance of the place it was evident that the dead man had made a fearful struggle for life after being mortally wounded, the floor and walls were marked with bloody hand-prints, showing where he had endeavored to regain his feet, while blood-clots, and even pieces of bone from his skull, lay about the floor and on the walls. The murderer was captured and had on his person clothing and money, together with a purse, all identified as the property of the deceased. April 19, 1876, Ah Sing was tried, convicted of murder in the second degree, and was sentenced to forty-five years imprisonment in the State prison.

Killing of Jose Arrayo. —A bloody affray occurred on March 2, 1877, about three-quarters of a mile from Walnut Creek, when Jose Arrayo was stabbed by Ramon Romero, who was at once arrested. Arrayo died on the 10th of March, and Romero was committed on the charge of murder, for which he was tried, found guilty November 23, 1877, and imprisoned for life in the State prison.

Killing of James Mills. —On June 18, 1877, a young man named Mills was fatally stabbed in an affray with P. B. Martin. It would appear that ill-feeling had existed for some time between the parties, which culminated in a fight on the day named. Mills died on June 24th, and Martin was arrested, tried, and on April 20, 1878, found not guilty.

Killing of George Mitchell. —At an early hour on February 1, 1878, it was rumored about Antioch that George Mitchell, an old resident of that town, was not to be found, and there was a strong suspicion that he had been murdered. About half-past ten o'clock on Thursday night he accompanied William Brunkhorst to his residence on Front Street with a lantern, the night being dark and stormy. Mitchell was duly sober and told Brunkhorst on parting that he was going to Dahnken's saloon on the wharf, where he slept, and retire for the night. Carson Dahnken had closed the saloon. In about fifteen minutes after Mitchell left Brunkhorst a pistol-shot was heard on the wharf by several parties, but it seems no one went out to ascertain the occasion of the shooting. Dahnken, who slept in the rear of the saloon-building, said he also heard the breaking of a lantern, the broken glass of which, together with several spots of clotted blood, was plainly to be seen upon the wharf. It was believed from the circumstances that Mitchell had been murdered and thrown into the river from off the wharf. Poles were brought and a moment's search proved that such was the case.

The dead body of Mitchell was brought from the water and a bullet hole or knife-wound found on his left side over the heart. Suspicion at once fastened upon William Hank, a German, in charge of the schooner "A. P. Jordan," which had been lying at anchor a few miles down the river. Hank had been in town on Thursday, drinking freely, exhibited a pistol, and was once during the day prevented from shooting at a man in Martin's saloon. Shortly after the shooting Hank went into Gordon's saloon and told the bar-keeper that he had just killed a man on the wharf, his (Hank's) clothes being at the time quite bloody, with his nose, face, and lips scratched and bleeding. Going out of the saloon he fired at some dogs, and finally went to Dahnken's hotel and entered the room of Joseph Parker, a boarder. Parker awoke and finding a strange man in the room inquired what he wanted; Hank said he was a stranger in the house and wanted a room. He finally slept upon a lounge in the sitting-room, where his pistol was found in the morning by Dahnken.

While search was being made for Mitchell on Friday morning, Hank left the wharf in his sailboat for his schooner. As soon as the body of Mitchell was found, Constable Pitts, with two Italian fishermen, started in pursuit with a boat and overtook him. Pitts got into his (Hank's) boat, and on being told that he (Pitts) was an officer come to arrest him Hank leaped overboard. He was handcuffed by the constable while in the water, taken into the boat, tied, and brought, shivering with cold from his voluntary bath, to Antioch. George Mitchell was an Englishman, forty-seven years of age, and had lived in Antioch and its vicinity since 1859. On April 24, 1878, Hank was tried and acquitted. Immediately after trial, and ere he had left the court-room, he was joined in matrimony to Mary Augusta Raymond, who was present during the proceedings and watched the case with eager interest.

Killing of Jose Reyes Berryessa. —On Monday evening, May 20, 1878, near the crossing of West Main and Castro streets, in the town of Martinez, Jose Reyes Berryessa, a native of California, made an assault upon Louis Kamp, in resisting which he shot and killed his assailant. It appears that Kamp was passing along the street toward the bridge carrying a pail of water, when Berryessa approached and addressed him angrily in Spanish, Kamp answering him in the same language. Berryessa then assaulted him with violent blows of his fists, causing him to drop his water-bucket, then grappled and threw him repeatedly and violently, either with his fist or with a stone cutting his face and causing a copious flow of blood. Just then Constable Gift's attention being attracted to the affray, he ran up, pulled Berryessa off, and commanding the peace, told them they were both under arrest and must go with him before the justice. Kamp said he would go, but Berryessa defied the officer insultingly, and immediately renewed the assault upon Kamp, striking and again throwing and falling upon him and hitting him with a stone while down. Gift again pulled him off, but he struggled free, making threatening demonstrations toward Kamp, who was then upon his feet, according to the testimony, backing away while drawing a pistol from his right hip pocket, which he presented and fired just as

Berryessa, in breaking from Gift's hold to reach him, was turned partially sidewise, some ten or twelve feet from him, and shot into his right side just below the nipple. Berryessa stooped, placed both hands on the wounded part, walked to the sidewalk from near the middle of the street, sat down, and in a few seconds expired. The verdict of the coroner's jury was that the killing was justifiable.

Death of an Unknown Man.—The Contra Costa Gazette of March 22, 1879, has the following: "We mentioned last week that the body of a man, sometime dead, was found on the afternoon of the 13th inst, on Hyde's ranch, about four miles south of Cornwall station, and that Coroner Hiller had gone up to hold an inquest. Following is the verdict of the inquest: 'We, the jury summoned to inquire into the cause of the death of a man found on the 13th day of March, 1879, lying on the ranch of F. A. Hyde, caught in the fence dividing the lands of said Hyde and W. E. Whitney, having viewed the body and heard the testimony presented, on our oaths do say, that from the evidence we suppose his name to be Levy Gish, aged about thirty years, nativity unknown, and that he came to his death sometime in the first part of March, 1879, the exact date being unknown and that his death was caused by violence, but by whose act is to the jury unknown. Hyde's Ranch, March 14, 1879. Signed: A. A. Hadley, B. K. Walker, Thomas Prichard, Wm. Fahy, Lewis H. Abbott, John Tepe, W. J. Whitney, Joseph McCloskey. The body was that of a man apparently between thirty and thirty-five years of age, about five feet seven or eight inches in height, with fine brown hair, curling in small curls all over his head, and reddish mustache, no beard, dressed in light-colored cassimere pants, dark-brown striped calico shirt, with undershirt made of flour sacks having the brand of the Kern River Mills, hickory outside shirt, old boots with tops cut off, and no coat on body. The body, with a bullet or bludgeon wound on the back of the head, was found lying on the west of the fence dividing the land of Hyde from the land of W. E. Whitney. Both feet were through between the pickets, apparently caught while he was endeavoring to get over the fence. The body was lying partially on the left side, with the left arm bent up under it and the right arm extending upward and in front of the face, the sleeve of the shirt drawn up over the hand. About twenty-five feet from the body, along near the fence, there were signs of a struggle, the ground being torn up and a great deal of blood on it and some hair from the head of the deceased on the pickets. Some four or five feet from the fence lay a pair of new gray blankets with a great deal of blood on them, and near them an old coat very much wrinkled and a great deal of blood on it and curls of hair similar to that on the man's head and on the blanket.

Near the head of the body lay a pair of blankets similar to the others, but clean, rolled up and not tied, a black felt hat, and a letter from Abram S. Gish addressed to Levy Gish, Ellis Station, dated October, 1870. Over the fence about twenty feet from the body was an account of sales of wheat and a letter dated March 6, 1871, from Bryant & Cook, Commission Merchants, San Francisco, addressed 'Levy Gish, Ellis Station.' The body had evidently been lying there six or eight days.

"Constable Erwin, of Point of Timber, has since been at Martinez, where Mr. Hiller has the effects found with the body, and has identified the pants, and from the description is satisfied that the man is one whom he arrested February 25th, with two others, for burglarizing Peter Swift's house near Point of Timber, and found in his possession five letters directed to Levy Gish, Ellis, and Moore's Landing. The men were taken by Erwin to Antioch and lodged in jail there, and the same night broke out and decamped. Erwin also identifies the coat as one that was worn by one of the companions of the deceased when arrested, but the coat then worn by him was of a better style and quality. The probability is strong, therefore, that the dead man was one of the three fugitive burglars, who received his death wound at the hands of his companions, or some other unknown person or persons, within a short time after their escape from the Antioch lock-up. It could hardly have occurred immediately after, as the ground where the body was found had been marked when wet, in the death struggles of the deceased, and it did not rain until several days after their breaking out on the morning of February 26th. It may therefore be inferred that they remained somewhere concealed in the neighborhood for possibly a week or more, there being no way of determining when the supposed murder was committed further than that, from the condition of the body, it could not have been less than eight or ten days before the remains were discovered, and it must have been after the rains of the first week in the month had softened the hard dry ground.

"It will be remembered by our readers that we mentioned the arrest last week of four tramps by Constable Gift, at the Granger's hay-barn, on suspicion that they may have had something to do with the burglary of Blum's store and safe, but as nothing was disclosed that would warrant their being held in custody they were turned loose. Now, from the description and other circumstances, Erwin is confident that two of these persons were the same that he arrested for the Point of Timber burglary and placed in the Antioch lock-up with the man since found dead. The coat worn by one of the men arrested here Erwin is confident was the one worn by the deceased when he made the arrest at the Point of Timber, and the coat found near the body, which is now in the keeping of Coroner Hiller, Erwin identified as one worn by one of the other persons he arrested and lodged in the Antioch lock-up, allowing them, after search, and taking from them a dirk and pocket knife, to retain a bag containing clothing, and among other articles a blouse similar to one which these tramps, while held in jail here, gave to one of the prisoners confined there awaiting trial. On these circumstances and other facts, which it may not be judicious to mention here, the inference is justified that two, if not all four, of this tramp party, are implicated in the murder, and warrants have been issued for their arrest."

The Antioch Ledger of March 1st had the following report of the arrest and escape of the burglars: "Three tramps, who gave their names as John Sullivan, Charles Williams, and William Dency, broke into Peter Swift's house, situated near the Salt Pond, Point of Timber, about nine o'clock Tuesday morning, and appropriated to their own use a suit of clothes, a quantity of food, and sundry other articles. Swift was absent at work in the field. Missing the property shortly after, he procured a warrant from Justice Cary, and Constable Erwin overtook and arrested the parties near the Point of Timber schoolhouse. They were brought to Antioch Tuesday evening and confined in the town jail, to await trial the following morning. Erwin visited the jail premises at midnight and finding his captives secure, retired, but in the morning discovered that the trio had departed. Though thoroughly searched when placed in confinement, they had cut off a two-inch plank about a foot above the floor, pried it off and were free. It is evident the cutting was not done with a knife but was evidently the work of a chisel or small hatchet. It is also apparent that they were furnished the necessary implements by outside parties. A knot-hole in one of the planks had been enlarged from the outside so as to admit of an instrument two inches in diameter. In answer to letters addressed to them for information relating to Levy Gish, presumed to have been a resident of that vicinity, Coroner Hiller has learned from the postmaster and constable at Ellis that the person is now living in San Diego County, from whence a letter written by him on the 5th inst. has been received at Ellis. They informed Hiller that the cabin Gish formerly occupied was recently broken into and rifled by tramps, who are presumed to have taken away the letters addressed to Gish which were found by Constable Erwin when he made the arrest at Point of Timber and those found near the dead body on Hyde's ranch, and which led the jury to presume that the name of the deceased was Levy Gish, who, as now appears, is doubtless alive and well in San Diego County, while some other name belonged to the dead and probably murdered man."

Murder of Langbhen. —The following particulars relating to this tragedy, which occurred near Marsh Landing on May 16, 1879, are an excerpt from the San Francisco Bulletin: "The tules in the vicinity of Antioch were the scene of a horrible tragedy last Friday morning, consisting of the murder of two children, aged respectively six years and four years, by their father, and the latter's suicide. Some six weeks ago he took up his quarters on a vegetable ranch owned by his nephew near Marsh Landing, a place about five miles from Antioch. Langbhen and his family were fresh from Faderland. They were quite industrious people, the most affectionate relations existing between husband and wife and between parents and children. For the want of anything better to do, Langbhen worked on his nephew's farm, cultivating small fruits and vegetables, which the nephew took to Antioch and sold. The nephew boarded with the family. While working in the fields Langbhen was usually accompanied by his two children, who whiled the time away in playing and weeding. At half-past four on Friday morning Langbhen got up and prepared breakfast for his nephew, as was his wont, and after the latter left for Antioch with a load of strawberries he went to the field to work; soon after his children followed him. At about eight o'clock Langbhen was seen by Max Klein, a neighbor, who was at the time cutting potatoes in his barn, a few rods from the Langbhen residence, to tie the shoe-lace of the little girl. He was then seen to take the two children to the adjacent tules; soon after he was observed coming out of the tules without the children and walking rapidly toward his house. Immediately after he reached it, Mrs. Langbhen rushed out in an excited state, throwing up her hands in despair, and talking excitedly in German. This was followed quickly by the discharge of a gun. The neighbors naturally enough rushed to the scene. Fleckaman, a next-door neighbor to the Langbhens, reached the house first, and entering it he beheld a horrible sight. Langbhen was leaning against the wall, almost doubled up, and dead, with a double-barreled shotgun grasped firmly in his hands and the muzzle in his mouth, with his toe against the trigger.

The charge had passed into the unfortunate man's head and spattered his brains all over the room. After partly recovering from the shock a search was begun for the children, who were missing. About an hour later the two were found by a Portuguese gardener, lying dead side by side in the tules, not far from where Langbhen had been seen to emerge.

The little girl's skull had been smashed with a heavy blunt instrument and her throat cut from ear to ear, severing the jugular vein, and a piece of flesh had been cut out of one of her hands. The boy's body bore no marks of violence, excepting that his head was nearly severed from the trunk. Near the bodies were found the apron worn by Langbhen at the time he slaughtered his children, and the heavy bludgeon with which it is supposed he beat in the skull of his little daughter. Both articles were covered with blood. The throats of the little ones are supposed to have been cut with a scythe blade or some similar instrument, as in each case the frightful wound had been inflicted with one blow.

But no such weapon, or any other corresponding to it, could be found, although a most careful search was made in the neighborhood."

Murder of a China woman. —A China woman was stabbed and killed by a Chinaman named Ah Yen on September 27, 1879, at Antioch. On examination it appeared that the man who killed her, and another Chinaman, who claimed to own the woman, having bought her for one hundred and eighty dollars, came to Antioch together three or four weeks previously from one of the mountain mining districts. What the relationship of the parties was, or what the provocation for the murderous assault, whether hatred, jealousy, revenge, or suddenly aroused anger, was not made clear by the evidence adduced at the examination. Ah Yen was tried, convicted of murder in the second degree, and sentenced to twenty-eight years in the State prison.

Killing of Thomas Sheridan. —A serious affray occurred on June 12, 1880, in Moraga Valley, which resulted in the death of Thomas Sheridan, a young man of eighteen or nineteen years of age. The difficulty occurred on land lying south or southeast of the Moraga Rancho, claimed as being in the Sobrante grant, but supposed to be public land, and occupied as such for ten years past. Upon a quarter-section of this land, with consent, or upon bargain with the original squatter claimant, S. S. Kendall, an old resident of the Moraga Valley, had cut a quantity of wood. Whether the original claimant had technically lost his right or not is a matter of dispute, but the land for the last year or two had been claimed and occupied by John Sheridan and his family. Kendall being a cripple, having a few years before suffered the loss of a leg, and anticipating some opposition in removing the wood, engaged a neighbor, T. B. Fulton, and a negro named Charles Mingo, to load and haul it away.

These men went out for the purpose armed with a breech-loading rifle and a revolver. On undertaking to load the wood Mrs. Sheridan came out and forbade them doing so. She was followed by Sheridan, armed with a hatchet, Thomas Sheridan, with a double-barreled gun, and a man named Gleeson, with a single-barreled gun. As the statements go, Sheridan attacked Fulton with the hatchet, striking him several times upon the head and inflicting some severe cuts. Gleeson also struck him once or twice with his gun. Mingo, holding his rifle in one hand, seized Sheridan with the other, and endeavored to drag him off Fulton.

Thomas Sheridan, at a distance of a few yards, leveled his gun at Mingo, and walked around, approaching nearer, to get in range to shoot him without danger of shooting his father, Mingo meanwhile endeavoring to keep the father as a shield between himself and the son. The latter, however, gained a position of advantage where Mingo saw that he would have a clear shot at him. Mingo then hastily dropped the barrel of his own rifle to range with the breech at his hip and fired, the ball entering the abdomen of young Sheridan and causing his death within half or three-quarters of an hour.

Killing of Manuel Sibrian. —Manuel Sibrian was shot and killed with a pistol by Narciso Miranda on July 1, 1880, at the place of the latter's residence in the San

Ramon hills, about a mile southwest of Alamo. Both men were native Californians of Mexican descent, Miranda living in the hills on adjoining claims of supposed Government land, though also claimed by Carpentier as part of the Sobrante grant. It is said that there had been bad feeling for a long time between Miranda and the deceased, arising from disputes as to the rightful claim of the latter to the land he had been occupying. As we are informed, the land was taken up on pre-emption claim some years ago by Miranda's father, who had since died, and who permitted Sibrian to temporarily occupy it when he had nowhere to put his family, after having been obliged to leave a residence property he had previously occupied. On the part of the Miranda family, it is asserted that Sibrian, since their father's death, has wrongfully claimed and insisted on retaining possession of the land as his own. On the day mentioned, at the meeting that resulted in his death, he went to Miranda's house in anger and made an attack upon him with a club, to which Miranda responded by shooting him several times in the abdomen with a revolving derringer pistol. Miranda was duly tried, convicted of manslaughter, and sentenced to one year and one month's imprisonment in the State prison.

Killing of Louis Farreri. —A series of affrays occurred on the night of March 19, 1881, at Nortonville, between Italians and persons of other nationalities employed about the coal mines there, in one of which an Italian named Louis Farreri received a blow upon the head from a slung-shot, club, or stone that resulted in his death a few hours after the occurrence. From what we learn in relation to the matter, it appears that a considerable number of Italian laborers had been employed in the mine, cutting out coal, at less than the usual rates of compensation, thus creating an unfriendly feeling between them and the regular miners of other nationalities there employed, but which had not prior to this occurrence led to any personal collisions. Recently, however, a number of miners of rough habits had arrived at Nortonville from the north coast mines and had shown a disposition to engage in personal affrays with the Italians, and, from such evidence as had been elicited, they are presumed to have been the assailants in Saturday night's encounters, of which there were several prior to that in which Farreri received the fatal injury. This occurred about midnight, when, as testified by another Italian who was with the deceased, they were assailed by half a dozen or more persons and Farreri knocked down, while the witness took flight. Farreri was found shortly afterward by a countryman lying in a partial stupor upon the ground where he had fallen. On being aroused, he complained of violent pain in the head, but was able to walk, and his countryman attended him to the gate of his residence, after seeing him enter which he left him. A little later another countryman passing noticed him lying upon the stoop of the house moaning. He assisted him into the kitchen and urged him to go to bed; but Farreri said his head hurt him very much, and he would rest where he was. Thinking he was only affected by drink, and would soon sleep off its effects, the man left him there, without awakening the wife or children of the sufferer. Still later, another Italian passing the house and hearing the groans, entered the kitchen and found Farreri upon the floor complaining that his head hurt him. Mrs. Farreri was called up, and she thought he was affected by drinking. After her countryman left, Mrs. Farreri remained in the kitchen with her husband until he fell into a doze, and appeared to be sleeping without suffering much pain, when she returned to her bed, about three o'clock, but on awakening about daylight and going to him she found him dead. In the absence of Coroner Guy, a jury was summoned, an inquest held on Sunday by Justice Wall, and a verdict found of death from natural causes and "the visitation of God." District Attorney Chase went up on Monday, and at his instance a jury was summoned and inquest held by Coroner Guy.

The testimony of Doctors Leffler and Wemple, given upon a post-mortem examination, went to show that the skull of the deceased had been fractured by a club, stone, slung-shot, or some other heavy, dull weapon, and that death was caused thereby. Many other witnesses were examined, but no testimony found by which the act could be fixed upon any particular person or persons, although some six or eight had been arrested on presumption of implication in the assault, all of them recent comers to the place from the north coast, and a verdict was found that the deceased came to his death from a skull fracture, caused by the blow of some instrument in the hands of some unknown person.

The deceased is said to have been a generally quiet and well-disposed man, who left a widow and four children unprovided for.

Killing of Patrick Sullivan. —Patrick Sullivan, who lived with his family on the Wildcat branch of the San Pablo Creek, left Oakland on Monday evening, March 28, 1881, in his wagon, and never reached his home. Alarmed by his protracted absence, his family and friends instituted search for him Tuesday morning, and his dead body was found riddled with buckshot, and one arm around the axletree of the wagon, several hundred yards below the road near the creek. From appearances it was concluded that after being shot he fell forward over the front of the wagon and grasped the axletree in an unconscious dying effort, the horses breaking from the road and running (dragging the body) to the place near the creek where the wagon was found. The firing had been heard by some of the people living in the vicinity the previous evening, and foot-tracks were found about the place in the road where it was evident the fatal shot was delivered, and from the direction of these tracks and the fact that there had been a long existing feud between himself and the deceased, suspicion led to the arrest of a neighbor named Robert Lyle, in whose house was found a double-barreled shotgun. An inquest was held on the body by Deputy Coroner Livingston, and a verdict found on Thursday that the deceased came to his death from a gun-shot wound inflicted by some person unknown to the jury.

Lyle was taken down from the jail on Friday, April 1st, for examination at San Pablo, on accusation of the murder. Sullivan left a wife and seven or eight children. Lyle was held to answer and trial set for April 11, 1881, when he was discharged.

Killing of Sheridan. —The circumstances of the case as related are: That the Sheridan boys, sons of John Sheridan, living in Grizzly Canon, found that one of their goats had been killed by a coyote, which had partaken of the flesh to the satisfaction of its hunger, but probably would return to feast upon the carcass, when they hoped by lying in ambush to shoot the plunderer of their flock. Accordingly, on the evening of May 11, 1881, they invited a neighbor, Michael Hennessy, to join them, and went out about dusk, taking a position behind a bush some thirty yards more or less from the carcass of the goat, John Sheridan, the elder of the brothers, having a rifle, and Daniel C, the younger, a boy of fourteen years, having no weapon. They were soon afterward joined by Hennessy, with a double-barreled shot-gun. Hennessy selected an ambush position for himself some little distance from that occupied by the boys, and directed the younger one, who had no weapon, to go to a tree on the top of the ridge behind and above his position, where he could have a good outlook over the ground, and if he saw the coyote to make a signal. Hennessy then took the position he had chosen, and, after lying quietly in wait for nearly half an hour, heard a rustling in the grass or brush on his left, and looking in that direction, at a distance of some twenty or thirty yards, saw a moving object that he took to be the head of a coyote peering warily about, as if suspicious that danger might be lurking near for him. In the belief that it was a coyote, Hennessy raised his gun, but lowered it to assure himself of the position of the supposed animal, and, without the most distant thought that the boy was anywhere in that direction, raised his gun again and fired.

The poor lad instantly cried, "It's me you've shot! I'm killed!" Hennessy exclaimed, "My God, John, I've shot Connie! Run for help!" and ran immediately to the wounded boy, took him in his arms, and held him until some neighbors called by the brother came, when they carried the lifeless body to the house. The boy survived only ten or fifteen minutes after Hennessy reached him, but never spoke again after exclaiming that he had been shot and killed. The jury of inquest found in accordance with the facts, that the killing was purely accidental.

Killing of Christian Smith.—The following article is from the Contra Costa Gazette of July 9, 1881: "Last Monday morning, July 4, 1881, about 8 o'clock, when the jail cells were unlocked to let the prisoners out into the corridor for breakfast, Henry Grosser, awaiting trial on charge of murder for the killing of Christian Smith on Marsh Creek in May, did not come out with the others, and one of them looking into the cell, discovered his body hanging from the center ventilating grating in the ceiling, or crown sheet. All warmth had left the body, and from facts afterward learned it is supposed to have been hanging there from about midnight. A jury of inquest was immediately organized by Deputy Coroner Livingston, and inquiries as to circumstances of the suicide proceeded with. It was ascertained by examination that the deceased had knotted a flour sack of the fifty-pound size tightly around his neck, and, the ends being short after first crossing, to complete the knot, had been laid back and wound with twine to fasten them. Through the collar thus formed the leg of a pair of drawers had been inserted, the ends passed up between and brought down over the grating bars and tightly knotted, the deceased standing upon an empty candle-box to do this, then pushing the candle-box away with his feet, and leaving himself suspended to die by suffocation, as there was no fall sufficient to break the spinal column, and although the hands being free, had there not been great determination to effect the purpose, he could have reached up and unloosed the knot, as there might have been an inclination to do for relief from the choking sensation. But it is not probable that such attempt was made, or some sound of it would have been heard by the occupant of the adjoining cell, who was awake and heard the noise made by the box when, as is supposed, it was pushed from under him upon the iron floor. On hearing this noise the prisoner called to Grosser and inquired if he was awake but got no response and heard no further sound. When found in the morning, the arms were hanging close to the body and the feet within two or three inches of the floor.

"Grosser was a German by birth, about fifty years of age, but in appearance ten years or more older. After having been for some years in this country he returned to Germany, where he married and came back with his wife about twelve years ago.

They have since had four children, three girls and one boy. The eldest child is about twelve, and the youngest one year of age. They have been living upon Marsh Creek for some three years and have been well thought of by their neighbors as people of good character and of hard-working, industrious habits.

Before moving to that neighborhood they had, either as share partners or employees, business relations with Smith, for the killing of whom Grosser was to have been tried on charge of murder. The land upon which they lived was purchased by Smith, and a deed for one half of it was afterward made to Mrs. Grosser, in consideration, as the Grossers claimed, of a lot of sheep sold or transferred in exchange to him.

The business of farming and stock-keeping on the place at Marsh Creek appears to have been engaged in upon some partnership basis or understanding between the Grossers and Smith, and there has within the past year grown up difficulties about settlement of the business between them. Smith's family lived at Oakland, but he was frequently at Marsh Creek, and spent considerable of his time at Grosser's. A short time before Smith was shot, Grosser said his wife had informed him that he had made grossly improper proposals and approaches to her, which greatly shocked and enraged him. He then resolved to resent a repetition of such insults should they be offered, and on Smith's next visit to the ranch he armed himself with a pistol, procured for the purpose, and seeing him enter the milk-cellar, he followed to find that he had seized and thrown Mrs. Grosser upon the ground. He thereupon fired; the shot missed and Smith ran out, but as he passed he fired again, shooting him in the arm. Smith continued running until he fell on receiving another shot in the body, from the effects of which he died two days afterward.

Grosser, after calling to a man nearby and telling what he had done, ran to a neighboring house, which he entered in a frenzy of excitement and said he had killed Smith. Neighbors were quickly gathered, who removed Smith to the house and found Mrs. Grosser upon the milk-cellar floor in a swoon, with her lower limbs exposed below the knees. It was half an hour before she became conscious and was able to relate the circumstances of the assault until the moment of being thrown upon the ground, when she swooned and became unconscious. The statements of the circumstances made by Grosser and his wife were accepted as the truth by the neighbors generally. But rumors soon gained currency that an improper intimacy known to Grosser had subsisted for some time between his wife and Smith, and that the story of the assault upon her had been invented to furnish a reason for killing him in the hope of thus being able to avoid payment of what they owed him. It was upon such testimony as was offered in support of the charge or theory of such a design that Grosser was held for trial on the charge of murder, the case having been set for Tuesday next. All day Friday, Saturday, and Sunday were spent by Mrs. Grosser in company with her husband, and she seemed deeply distressed by the reports reflecting upon her character and the charges of plotting the murder of Smith. About ten o'clock Sunday night Grosser called to Robert Lyle, in an adjoining cell on one side of his, and asked if he could lend him a pencil. Lyle replied that he could and threw his pencil up through the ventilating grating in such a way that it fell through the grating of Grosser's cell. With this pencil he is supposed to have concluded a writing covering four or five sheets of note-paper, commencing with the date of July 1st. This writing was found between the pages of a magazine or pamphlet in the cell. It is somewhat disconnectedly written and is without signature. In substance, it is as follows: "'I herewith make a statement. From what I hear, they are making numerous charges about me and my wife. About the larceny of sheep, when under attachment, I had no reason to suppose I was doing wrong in moving them over the county line. Mr. White and others knew all about the matter. I was attending to the sheep for Smith, and always thought he was a respectable man until of late. The horses and stock were assessed to me and my wife by Smith's request, as he said it would be better to have the taxes all paid together. A year ago last fall Smith requested me to sell the cattle if I could get twenty-five dollars per head for them all around. I told him it would be impossible, they were too poor, and then he told me to do the best I could with them. When he came back from Europe, he was well satisfied with what I had done.

I told him about the crop and everything. He thought it best not to sell the grain until it would bring a better price. I gave him an order on Charles Clayton to sell, and understood him to say that he had sold, but don't know as yet what he got, but told me he had the account. When we undertook to settle I knew I owed him. I proposed to let him have the growing crop. He said he would rather not take it, as there was no telling what it would be. I know he has paid out money for lumber and other things. I would have settled with him, but he would not pay half the store bill, as he had agreed. He had boarded with us most of the time last winter, and I had kept no account of it. I had also boarded all the men chopping wood and had hauled it for him to Brentwood. When we commenced farming together I was to have half his horses, two of them valued at $150 and three others at $60. I had two cows; one died and the other was with calf. I let him have that one for another, from which I raised a calf until it was a cow. I let them run with his. He had a great many, and I was to have the pick of two from the lot, but he took away all the calves and said he would make it right. When we first started with sheep, I had $700 coming to me for which I and my wife had worked, and which I took in lambs at $2 a head. I then turned them over to him and went to work for him at $30 per month. My wife was cooking for herders and shearers when the sheep were sheared at the place where we lived, and sometimes at other places. I worked for him until I moved over to Marsh Creek. In regard to this affair, most any other man would have done the same. I am satisfied my wife never had any improper intercourse with Smith or any other man. I was never inside a jail until now. I never spent money unnecessarily. All I had I got honestly. I hear they are trying to make out that my wife is a prostitute, which I can't listen to no more—that hurts my feelings so much that I am tired of living.' "Then follows a statement of small sums due from Smith and himself together to various individuals, and the writing concludes as follows: 'I never, never thought of getting in this trouble a day or two before it happened. I often walked from place to place. I did not know what I was looking for. I am indebted to Mr. Welch $12 for that pistol. I think I am going to a better world. I forgive everybody the same I would take myself. I was too easy (or accommodating) for my own good.'"

CHAPTER XVII BENCH AND BAR

The history of the bench of Contra Costa County may be divided into two periods—first, the period from the time of the organization of the State under the constitution of 1849 to the adoption of the constitution of 1879, and, second, the period from the adoption of the constitution of 1879 to the present time.

The county of Contra Costa was organized by an act of the first legislature, in 1850, at its first session. This act also established the county seat at the town of Martinez, where it has ever since remained.

The constitution of 1849 vested the judicial powers of the State of California in a supreme court, a district court, county courts, and justices of the peace. The California legislature, in its first session in 1850, vested the judicial powers in accordance with the constitution of 1849, as follows: The State was divided into nine judicial districts, which districts were composed of the several counties, and the county of Contra Costa was placed in the Third Judicial District, then composed of the counties of Branceforte, Santa Clara, Contra Costa, and Monterey.

The constitution of 1849 also provided that the judges of the district courts should be appointed by the joint vote of the legislature at its first meeting, and such judges to hold office for two years from the first day of January next after their election, after which said judges should be elected by the qualified electors of their respective districts at the general election and hold office for the term of six years.

By the act of the legislature of 1853 the county of Contra Costa was transferred from the Third Judicial District to the Seventh Judicial District, which district embraced the counties of Solano, Napa, Sonoma, and Marin, and said county continued to be in the Seventh Judicial District until 1862, when it was again transferred from the Seventh Judicial District to the Fourth Judicial District, which district embraced this county and a portion of the city and county of San Francisco lying north and east of Clay and Kearny streets. Contra Costa County continued to be a part of the Fourth Judicial District until, by an act of the legislature of 1863, it was annexed to the Third Judicial District, composed of the counties of Monterey, Santa Cruz, Santa Clara, Alameda, and Contra Costa, and continued to be annexed to the said district until, by an act of the legislature of 1864, it was annexed to the Fifteenth Judicial District, composed of that portion of the city and county of San Francisco included in the Twelfth Judicial District and the Fourth Judicial District and Contra Costa County, and continued annexed to said district until the adoption of the constitution of 1879.

The judges of the District Court were as follows: At its first session in 1850 said legislature by joint vote elected John Watson, and he held the office of the judge of the Third Judicial District until 1851, when he resigned, and C. P. Hester was appointed by the governor and filled the office until the next election, and at the next election, in 1853, Hester was elected and continued to preside as judge of said district until Contra Costa County was attached to the Seventh Judicial District, when E. W. McKinstry was elected judge of said district and continued to preside until March, 1862, when the county was annexed to the Fourth Judicial District, with Samuel F. Reynolds then presiding, who continued to act as such judge until April 25, 1863. At that date Contra Costa County was annexed to the Third Judicial District, of which Samuel B. McKee was the judge presiding, who continued to act as such judge until April 4, 1864. Contra Costa County was then annexed to the Fifteenth Judicial

District, wherein Samuel H. Dwindle was judge, and who through subsequent re-elections continued to act in that capacity until January, 1880, when the constitution of 1879 changed the judicial system.

By an act of the first session of the legislature of 1850 a county court was established in Contra Costa County, over which from that time up to the adoption of the constitution of 1879, the following judges presided: F. M. Warmcastle, 1850-53; J. F. Williams, 1853; R. N. Wood, 1853-55; George F. Worth, 1855-56; Thomas A. Brown, 1857-63; Mark Shepard, 1864-70; C. W. Lander, 1871-73; Thomas A. Brown, 1874-78.

SECOND PERIOD T

he constitution of 1879 vested the judicial powers of the State in a supreme court, a superior court, justices of the peace, and such inferior courts as the legislature may establish in any incorporated city or town or city and county, and also provided there shall be in each of the organized counties or cities and counties of the State a superior court, for each of which at least one judge shall be elected by the qualified electors at the general State election to be held in 1879. Contra Costa County was assigned one judge. At the election of 1879 Thomas A. Brown was elected to that office, and presided until his death in 1886, when Judge F. M. Warmcastle was appointed by the governor as his successor. Judge Warmcastle held the office only until after the election of 1886, when Joseph P. Jones was elected and continued to act as such judge until his death, in early part of 1900. William S. Wells was then appointed by the governor to succeed Judge Jones and occupied the bench until January, 1909. Judge R. H. Latimer was elected at the general election of 1908 to succeed Judge Wells and has continued to act as judge of said court ever since that date. By an act of the legislature of 1913 the county of Contra Costa was assigned two judges, and at the general election of 1914 A. B. McKenzie was elected to preside over the second department of the court, and at present fills that position.

MEMBERS OF THE BAR OF CONTRA COSTA

Thomas A. Brown was born on October 16, 1823, in Greene County, State of Illinois, and is the eldest of four children of Elam and Sarah Brown. During his infancy the family moved to Morgan County, Illinois, where they settled on a farm about ten miles west of Jacksonville.

The family resided there until 1837, when they moved to Platte County, Missouri, where they again settled on a farm near the town of Weston.

During 1842 and 1843 the settlement of the country about the mouth of the Columbia River, in Oregon, and emigration to California and other places west of the Rocky Mountains were beginning to be agitated, and in May, 1843, Brown joined a party of emigrants and crossed the mountains to Oregon. He arrived at Willamette Falls late in the fall of that year. On that journey the party suffered many annoyances and privations not common to travelers who now cross the plains from the Missouri River to the Pacific Ocean. This little band left Westport, near the western line of Missouri. After crossing the west boundary of Missouri the country until Fort Laramie was reached was entirely uninhabited by white people. At that place there were a few traders. Thence they proceeded to Fort Bridger, from there to Fort Hall, and thence to Fort Boise near the Granderonde Valley on Snake River, which was an unbroken wilderness. There were a few trappers at Fort Bridger, others at Fort Hall and Fort Boise, and Doctor Whitman and some others at Walla Walla. These were the only white people found on the route from the Missouri line to Fort Vancouver. There were plenty of Indians, but not generally troublesome. At that time Oregon was considered to be about as far away from other civilized society as it was possible to get.

There were then a few hundred white people, generally very good people, in what is now the State of Oregon. To illustrate the condition of things then, the only regular communication with the United States was by sailing vessels or by the annual immigration. Messengers bearing news required about six months to make the trip in one direction, or twelve months to get word in return. The people who went across the mountains in 1843 left Missouri in May of that year. The nominations of candidates for President and Vice-President were not made until afterward. It was not known by them who was nominated or elected President until late in the fall of 1844, six or seven months after Polk had been inaugurated.

While in Oregon Brown resided the greater portion of the time at Oregon City, and was engaged chiefly in the business of surveying and as civil engineer. He surveyed a great number of claims for settlers in different parts of the Territory, and also several town-sites, among others that of Portland, now the principal city of the State. The survey of Portland was made about 1844, and while there engaged the surveyors were compelled to live in a tent on the bank of the river, there being up to that time no house at that place.

During the early part of the year 1847, Brown came to California on a visit to his father and family, who had crossed the plains during the summer of 1846, and then resided at the mission of Santa Clara. He remained in California a few weeks, and then went back to Oregon for the purpose of closing up his business, intending to return to California. While making preparations to return to this State, news of the discovery of gold at Sutter's Mill reached Oregon and resulted in a general rush from that country to this. Brown returned to California by sea, and by reason of bad weather did not arrive at San Francisco until late in the fall of 1848. He remained during the winter at the mission of San Jose.

In the spring of 1849, with a party, he went into the mines, where he remained but a few months, returning and settling at Martinez, where he has ever since resided. During 1849 he, his brother Warren, and his brother-in-law, N. B. Smith, engaged in mercantile business, which they soon abandoned. During the same year Brown was appointed alcalde of the district by the then governor of California. He held that office until the organization of the county government in April, 1850, when he was elected county clerk and recorder, and held that office until 1855, when he retired from that position and was elected supervisor, holding that office for one year.

During his term of office as county clerk he commenced the study of law and was admitted to practice in the District Court in the year 1855.

Soon after this he entered into active practice. In 1860 he was licensed to practice in the Supreme Court and the several courts of the State, as well as in the United States District and Circuit courts in this State.

He continued in active practice until January, 1880, when he was elected and qualified as judge of the Superior Court, when he gave up private practice entirely. He was elected county judge in 1856 and continued in that office until January, 1864.

At a meeting of the members of the Contra Costa bar in open court at the courthouse in Martinez, on Thursday, December 10, 1863, the following preamble and resolutions were unanimously adopted, and on motion were entered in the minutes: "In County Court, State of California, Contra Costa County, Hon. Thomas A. Brown presiding, December 10, 1863.

"Whereas, Hon. Thomas A. Brown being about to retire from the bench, we, the members of the bar, deem it just and respectful to express and record our appreciation of the integrity and ability with which, during the last eight years, he has discharged the various duties which have devolved upon him as the judge of this court; therefore— "Resolved, That it is the unanimous sentiment of the members of this bar that Hon. Thomas A. Brown, during a continuous term of eight years in the official capacity of judge of this court, has earned for himself the reputation of an urbane, able, and upright judge.

"Resolved, That it is the unanimous request of the members of this bar that the foregoing proceeding, preamble, and resolutions be entered in the minutes of this court."

In 1865 he was elected to the assembly and served during the sessions of the legislature for 1865-66 and for the years 1867-68. In the session of 1865-66, Judge Brown was chairman of the judiciary committee in the assembly, and at the next session had the Republican nomination for the United States Senate when Eugene Casserly was elected.

In January, 1874, he was appointed county judge, to fill the vacancy caused by the death of Judge Lander. On the expiration of the term he was elected to that office, and held it until January, 1880, when he became judge of the Superior Court. While he held the office of county judge his practice as attorney was confined to business in the District Courts, the Supreme Court, and the Federal Courts.

Joseph P. Jones was born in Owen County, Indiana, January 27, 1844. In 1853, when he was nine years old, his parents moved to Marion County, Oregon, where he attended the common schools, and afterward entering the Willamette University, at Salem, there received a thorough scholastic training, and finally graduated, Artium Baccoloureus, in 1864.

In 1865, he returned to Indiana, matriculated at the State University, in Bloomington, where he entered upon the study of law, and graduated therefrom in 1867. His legal curriculum finished, he returned to Oregon, but shortly after located at the mines in the northern portion of California, where he resided until December, 1869. In that year he came to Martinez, Contra Costa County, and entered upon the practice of his profession, in which he has achieved considerable success. Upon the election of Hiram Mills to the post of district attorney, Jones was appointed deputy to the office and continued as such until the fall of 1875, when he was nominated and elected on the Republican ticket to the office of district attorney, the functions of which he held until March, 1878. After a lapse of two years, he again entered the political arena, and in the fall of 1880 was elected to the assembly, and served at the general and extra sessions of the legislature, being a member of the judiciary committee, as well as chairman of the committee on federal relations. He is now practicing his profession in partnership with Hiram Mills, a lawyer long associated with Contra Costa, under the style of Mills & Jones. He married in Martinez, February 2, 1870, Jennie Frazer, a native of Oregon, and has three surviving children—Madison R., Thomas Rodney, and Carl Richard.

F. M. Warmcastle, born November 16, 1815, at the town of Butler, Butler County, Pennsylvania, went to Pittsburg at the age of seventeen, remaining there some three years. He then went to Maysville, Kentucky, and remained there until 1839, spending the winters in the Southwest flat-boating and distributing agricultural implements. On leaving Kentucky, he went to Liberty, Clay County, Missouri, early in 1840, remaining there until 1841, engaged in manufacturing wagons, plows, etc. After this he located in Platte City, the county seat of Platte County, Missouri, read law, and in the year 1842 emigrated to Nott County, Missouri, and was admitted to the bar at the spring session of the Circuit Court of Savannah, the county seat of Andrew County, Missouri, Judge D. R. Atchison presiding, Peter H. Burnett, circuit attorney. He located that year in that portion of Nott County afterward (1844)' organized as the county of Atchison, practiced law at Linden, the county seat, and represented the county in the Missouri legislature, as its first representative, in 1846. He joined the volunteer service, as first lieutenant of Captain Creig's company of Missouri mounted volunteers, in the spring of 1847, was mustered into the service of the United States at Fort Leavenworth and was appointed acting assistant commissary of subsistence. The command was ordered to the Indian country to overawe the Indian tribes, there being no military force in the direction of Oregon, the rifle regiment raised a few years before for that purpose having been ordered to Mexico.

He remained in the Indian country until the winter of 1848, was mustered out of service at Fort Leavenworth, leaving for California in 1849, overland, and was among the first immigrants to arrive at Sacramento, about the middle of August of that year. He went to the mines on the Yuba River, stayed there until the early rains, and, returning to Sacramento, remained there a short time. About that time the election to ratify the constitution of the new State came off, and the election immediately followed for State officers and members of the legislature.

Warmcastle then went to Benicia, crossing the Straits of Carquinez at Martinez, and from there through what is now Contra Costa and Alameda counties, via the mission of San Jose, proceeded to the city of San Jose, remaining there a spectator of the daily sessions of the legislature, and becoming somewhat acquainted with many of the men who afterward occupied official positions in the State, returning to Martinez in February of 1850. In the spring the several counties of the State having been organized by the legislature at its first session, he was elected county judge of Contra Costa County, and held the position until December, 1853, when he resigned, having been elected to the assembly. At the close of the legislative session he resumed the practice of the law in Martinez.

He was married at San Francisco in February, 1855 and resided in Martinez until the fall of that year, when he located some six miles from Martinez, on a farm that he bought in 1852 and improved. This farm is situated one mile south of the town of Pacheco, not then in existence. He was elected to the assembly in 1857, and in 1860 was elected to the State senate in the district composed of the counties of Contra Costa and San Joaquin.

Between the years 1870 and 1874, he visited the Eastern States twice, being absent about one and a half years. He resided on his farm until 1877, when he was elected district attorney for Contra Costa County, holding the office for two years, since which time he has been engaged in the practice of the law. At present he is living in Martinez.

Among the many attorneys who have belonged to the bar of Contra Costa County since the organization of the county, besides those who have held judicial positions as hereinbefore stated, are the following: J. F. Williams, the first district attorney of this county; L. B. Mizner, who removed to Solano County and practiced law there for a number of years before his death; Hiram Mills, who was district attorney of the county for fourteen years, between 1855 and 1875, afterward practicing law until his death; Mark Shepard, who was district attorney for one term, and then practiced law until his death; George W. Bailey for a number of years prior to his death was a prominent member of this bar; C. W. Lander from 1869 to the time of his death, in 1874, was one of the prominent members of this bar; L. M. Brown, a brother of the late Judge Thomas A. Brown, practiced here from 1870 to the time of his death, in 1874; A. P. Needles, who for a short time before moving to San Francisco was a member of this bar; Eli R. Chase practiced here from 1865 up to the time of his death, a few years ago, and was district attorney for two terms; W. S. Tinning, who has been the leader of the bar for a number of years, commenced the practice of law here 1880 and has continued ever since. We also have had G. W. Bowie, A. H. Griffith, W. B. Wallace, Jr., and C. Y. Brown, all of whom have passed away. C. Y. Brown held the office of district attorney here for a number of years prior to his death.

The bar has grown rapidly and has now among its members in Martinez, M. R. Jones, son of the late Judge J. P. Jones, Ralph Wight, Rex Boyer, E. B. Taylor, Leo F. Tormey, Archie Tinning, son of W. S. Tinning, J. E. Rodgers, A. F. Bray and John O. Wyatt; in Richmond, T. H. DeLap, H. V. Alvarado, J. G. Gerlach, D. J. Hall, C. S. Hannum, C. D. Horner, H. E. Jacobs, J. M. Opsahl, Wilber S. Pierce, W. S. Robenson, H. J. Wildgrube, Lee D. Windrem; in Antioch, A. C. Hartley and Matthew Ward; in Pittsburg, R. N. Wolf; in Concord, A. S. Sherlock.

Judge John H. Watson was appointed the first district judge of the Third Judicial District, which included the counties of Contra Costa, Santa Clara, Santa Cruz, and Monterey. He died at Elko, Nevada. He was a pioneer of California and Nevada and the founder of Watsonville, California. He was also a State senator.

Hon. Craven P. Hester was born May 17, 1796. Studied law at Charleston under Judge Scott, one of the judges of the Supreme Court of Indiana. In 1821 he removed to Bloomington, Indiana, where he continued to practice until 1849, when he crossed the plains with his family to California. He was elected district attorney of the Third Judicial District in October, 1850. In May, 1851, he resigned that office and was forthwith appointed by the governor judge of the district, to fill the vacancy occasioned by the resignation of Judge Watson. In September following he was elected to the same office until the next general election in 1852, when he was re-elected for the full term of six years.

Judge E. W. McKinstry was born in Detroit, Michigan, in 1826. He came to California in June, 1849, and engaged in law practice at Sacramento in 1850, was in the first legislature, and was elected adjutant general at the age of twenty-four years.

In 1851 he opened a law office in Napa, and in the fall of 1852 he was elected district judge for the district comprising Napa and contiguous counties, being re-elected in September, 1858, but resigned in November, 1862. In 1863 he was the Democratic candidate for lieutenant-governor and was defeated with his ticket. He went to Washoe, Nevada, in the flush times, and in 1864 he and John R. McConnell and W. C. Wallace were the Democratic nominees for supreme justices of the State of Nevada.

Returning to California, and locating in San Francisco, he was, in October, 1867, elected county judge on the Democratic ticket for a term of four years from January 1, 1868. In October, 1869, he was elected judge of the Twelfth District Court as an independent candidate over the regular Democratic nominee, R. R. Provines. In 1873, again as an independent candidate, he was elected a justice of the Supreme Court over Samuel H. Dwindle, Republican.

Judge McKinstry resigned from the Supreme Bench on October 1, 1888, to become professor of municipal law in the Hastings Law College, San Francisco, but in 1890 again took up the practice of the law. He died in San Jose, California, November 1, 1901.

Judge Samuel F. Reynolds was a native of New York State, and died February 12, 1877, of apoplexy, at the age of sixty-eight years. He came to California in the early days and filled the office of district judge of the Fourth Judicial District for a term of six years, after which he resumed active practice in the profession. He was a prominent Odd Fellow, in which order he filled several important offices.

Samuel H. Dwindle was born in 1822 in Cazenovia, Madison County, New York, and came to this State in 1850, locating in Sonora, Tuolumne County. He soon removed to San Francisco and continued to practice law. In 1858-59 Judge Dwindle was a law partner of E. D. Baker. In 1865, when the Fifteenth Judicial District was created, comprising a part of San Francisco and all of Contra Costa County, Governor Low appointed him to the bench of that court, and at the next general election he was chosen by the people for a full term of six years.

Judge Dwindle presided at the first trial of Laura D. Fair, who was convicted before him of the murder of A. P. Crittenden, and he sentenced her to death in 1870. Judge Dwindle died January 12, 1886, of apoplexy, at his home in San Francisco.

Hon. William S. Wells, at present presiding in department four of the Superior Court of Alameda County, enjoys the distinction of being the first superior judge in the county to receive the Republican nomination for that office direct from the people. Judge Wells was born in Fairfield, Solano County, June 24, 1861. His father practiced law in Solano County, and later in San Francisco. He resided in Oakland at the time of his death, which occurred on Christmas day, 1878.

Judge Wells attended the public schools, and later entered St. Augustine College, Benicia, and completed his studies at the University of California. He was admitted to the bar in 1884 and began the practice of his profession in Contra Costa County. In 1886 he received the appointment of assistant district attorney of this county. He was appointed judge of the Superior Court of this county January 26, 1899, in place of Joseph P. Jones, deceased. Judge Wells was afterward elected to fill the unexpired term and again for a full term, which expired in January, 1909. In April of the same year he was appointed to the Superior Court of Alameda County.

Judge Wells is prominently known in fraternal circles, being past grand master of Masons of California, and a member of Oakland Lodge, No. 191. He is also a member of the B. P. O. E. and the Woodmen of the World.

Alfred Bailey McKenzie, judge of the Superior Court of Contra Costa County, department two, was born at Goderich, Ontario, in 1861. He came to the United States in 1880 and followed mercantile pursuits in New York until 1891, when he came to California, and in 1892 entered Hastings College of the Law and graduated with the class of 1895, receiving the degree of Bachelor of Laws from the University of California. In June, 1895, he commenced the practice of law at Martinez, and has resided there ever since. In November, 1914, he was elected judge of the Superior Court of the State of California, in and for the county of Contra Costa, for a new department of the court, which office was created by the legislature in 1912, to take effect at the general election of 1914. At the time of his election to the bench he was district attorney of Contra Costa County, to which office he was elected in 1910.

In 1897 Judge McKenzie married Melvina I. Durham, a school teacher and a graduate of the San Jose State Normal School. Mrs. McKenzie is a daughter of J. E. Durham, who is one of the early settlers in Contra Costa County.

Judge McKenzie is a Republican and was chairman of the Republican County Central Committee during the campaign of 1908.

CHAPTER XVIII. EDUCATIONAL

EARLY MARTINEZ SCHOOLS

The first school in Martinez, in the early part of 1850, was taught by Beverly R. Holliday. Holliday had his first experience in school-teaching in Illinois, at the early age of fifteen years. After coming to Martinez, he passed an examination and was declared qualified to teach.

His school at first consisted of five or six pupils from two or three families. These pupils gathered in the Blossom house, later known as the Gift house, near Thomas Hill, at the entrance of Bay View Park. During the two terms that Holliday taught the number of pupils increased from six to twenty-six.

In the fall of 1850 Holliday was succeeded by M. Laughlin. In 1851 Mrs. Rice was the teacher in an old house, and there were about thirteen pupils. Hinckley was the next teacher; he taught a three-month term in 1852, in a house which stood on Mills Street near Main, used in after years for a Chinese laundry. Six or seven pupils attended this school. In 1853 Moore taught in a small brick building near the corner of Main and Ferry streets. He had only a few pupils and did not teach long. Later in 1853 Mrs. Phoebe R. Alley taught in a house owned by C. C. Swain. She lived upstairs and used her kitchen as a school-room. Rough seats were made and a curtain drawn to hide the kitchen stove.

The sessions lasted from 9 to 12 and from 1 to 4. Between sessions the school-room was again used for a kitchen. It was during Mrs. Alley's term as teacher that the school first received aid from the State. Before beginning to teach she was examined by the board of trustees. The scholars studied whatever they liked best. School-books were of varied assortments, each pupil bringing a different book, as there was no law providing for the uniformity of text-books. Hiram Mills was the next teacher. He taught a six-month term in 1854, in a brick building on Ferry Street. The pupils varied their exercises with recitations, original essays, and songs.

In 1854 the Rev. Mr. Sanbourne had a school in a small house that was a part of Mrs. Henry Hale's dwelling, but afterward in a building situated on Main Street, near the site of the Blum block. This school was an ambitious one, and its friends offered prizes to those who had the highest standing. The girls received most of the prizes, and sometimes two and three prizes each. A debating society and spelling-school frequently held forth in the evening. These "spelling downs" were attended by old and young alike, and doctors and lawyers would try their skill against the others. J. Vandermark, the first superintendent of schools in this county, held office during this year.

In 1856, Doctor Holmes taught in a double house; besides doing service as a schoolhouse, it was used as church, courthouse, and Masonic lodge hall. Later in 1856 Miss Gregory, a graduate of Oberlin College, taught in this building. This was considered a fine school of thirty-three pupils. Miss Charlotte Worth was assistant. In 1857 Miss Gregory was succeeded by Miss Jane Lyon. Twenty pupils were taking high school work, and there were twelve primary scholars, besides the intermediate grades. The building was too small for such a school, and Miss Lyon had to teach the primary classes at noon while eating her lunch.

Her time was fully occupied from eight in the morning till late in the evening. She labored under difficulties through lack of books and apparatus, supplying much of the equipment herself. During the winter a stove was borrowed and fuel was furnished by the pupils. The stovepipe consisted of three lengths of different sizes, which teacher and pupils put together with mortar and wire. Just as two visitors entered the school, down came the stove-pipe. Miss Lyon stated to her guests that the school was not in order just then, but if they would kindly step out and take a view of the hills she would soon be ready to receive them. In the early part of 1858 Miss Lyon accepted a position in the Sacramento schools, and Miss Eliza May filled the vacancy caused by Miss Lyon resigning. Miss May remained during two terms, and also took an active part in the social life of Martinez. S. H. Bushnell was next employed, coming in September, 1858. One of his pupils relates an incident that was typical of that time: Two boys were to be punished and were sent out to cut a switch. They went to the creek, cut a fine green poison-oak switch, and brought it in to the teacher. The boys had a vacation lasting two weeks, while the teacher nursed a bad case of poison-oak. The pupils numbered forty-eight, too large an attendance for so small a building. In 1860 the school was removed to the lower floor of the Masonic Hall. Bushnell continued teaching for two years in this building. In May, 1873, a two-story schoolhouse of four rooms was erected. D. T. Fowler was the last teacher in the Masonic Hall and the first in the new building. He was assisted in the new building by his wife and Miss Conners. As the public funds permitted only an eight-month school, the ladies formed an Educational Aid Society, of which Mrs. Alley was president. Money was raised by entertainments and private subscription to pay the teachers for two months more, so that a ten-month school could be maintained. The society also purchased school-desks, bought a piano, and laid a two-plank sidewalk from Main Street to the schoolhouse.

About 1888 a law was passed which provided for a two-year high school course in the public schools. Miss Clara K. Wittenmyer was then principal of the Martinez grammar school. Under this law she established a class, at first teaching both grammar and high-school classes herself. Later Miss Bertola taught the graduating class of the grammar school and Miss Wittenmyer taught the high school.

Some members of the class who were preparing to teach carried twenty-two subjects. Two classes were graduated, and the work was praised by University of California examiners. This was the beginning of high-school work in Contra Costa County. As the law proved defective, the work was discontinued. A few years later a private high school was maintained under the direction of E. Stoddard and continued until a law providing for a union high school was passed.

With the addition of two rooms in 1890, this building provided for the educational needs of the community until 1907, when a building of modern type, containing nine class-rooms and a large auditorium, was erected on the same site.

The growth of the school was gradual until 1915, then, by converting assembly hall and play-room into class-rooms, besides erecting temporary buildings, the increase in attendance was taken care of. In July, 1916, a $52,000 bond was voted for the erection of a new building to face the present structure but separated from it by a town park which had been turned over by the authorities to the school trustees for the use of the children.

The growth of the school is shown by an increase in attendance of two hundred in 1906 to six hundred in 1916.

In 1901 the Alhambra Union High School, composed of Martinez, Vine Hill, Franklin, Alhambra, and Briones districts, was established in Martinez.

PITTSBURG SCHOOL

The growth of the school system of Pittsburg is one of the most remarkable and interesting bits of history in the annals of our county. The splendid schools now existing in this thriving industrial center had their beginning when a small dwelling-house was moved bodily from Nortonville on a flat-car and deposited upon a lot which had been secured only by the pardonable subterfuge of representing that a livery stable was to be erected upon it.

The little dwelling soon proved inadequate and was sold to Charles Wilson, and, with additions, is still used by him as a residence. The electors erected what was considered at that time a large schoolhouse, the old brick school that still stands and renders service as a schoolroom. This also was outgrown and was supplemented by two wooden one-room buildings, which served until 1905, when the people erected a $20,000 modern building.

It was only a short time, however, that children overflowed from this new building into the "old brick school," and it was necessary to rent several buildings from private owners and to construct temporary quarters. To relieve this situation, the people erected a building which, when completed, will cost from $85,000 to $90,000, and from present indications the growth will be such as to necessitate further equipment within a very few years.

EASTERN CONTRA COSTA COUNTY

It is a noteworthy and highly creditable fact that the early settlers of eastern Contra Costa County generally considered the school as an institution of primary importance. The foundations of their schoolhouses were laid contemporaneous with, and in some instances before, their places of worship.

Usually the start was made by voluntary contributions of materials —labor or money for their construction—and the buildings were cheap or of a temporary nature that later were found inadequate, and gave place to the larger, more commodious, and ornamental structures that now adorn every considerable center of population.

It will be recalled that the first settlements were made along the water-front, skirting the margin of the delta, scattering and not contiguous, and a trudge of two or three miles by the pupil to reach the schoolhouse was not unusual; but as the population increased the distance lessened, until there are few localities left where the distance is more than a pleasant morning stroll from home to the schoolhouse door.

Antioch being the oldest community was the first to erect a schoolhouse and lay the foundation of a schooling with all the best traditions of its State of Maine progenitors. Captain Kimball and Parson Smith brought with them from their New England homes to the new and unpeopled land the spirit and exalted hopes that characterized their Pilgrim ancestry—the little red schoolhouse and the church spire were the symbols of their faith in the progress of humanity, and they made haste to build them deep into the superstructure of the social fabric of the new empire that they came here to aid in constructing; hence the schoolhouse came early to the front, continuing thus until it culminated in the splendid high-school edifice that graces a conspicuous prominence.

The gathering population in the vicinity of the Iron House (that derives its name from the odd conceit of one of its early settlers, who, for the lack of other material, weather-boarded his cabin with scraps of sheet iron and tin cut from discarded oil-cans) created the necessity for a school-building, and in 1868 one was erected. The site chosen was on the north side of the road just east of Marsh Creek, near the Santa Fe Railroad crossing. Later the building was removed to its present site, and in 1896 it was replaced with a new and artistically designed structure. The area of the Iron House district formerly embraced all of the territory between Antioch district and Eden Plain, including the Jersey Island and Sand Mound tracts of the delta. In 1885 or 1886 these tracts were segregated from it and the Sand Mound district organized. A small schoolhouse was erected on the north side of Taylor Slough and a school maintained there for several years, but later abandoned.

The first movement to establish a school in the Eden Plain country was made in the summer of 1868. This school building was erected by voluntary subscription of labor and material on the premises of John Pierce, and a school maintained there for months before the district was permanently organized. Here it remained for some thirty-eight years, when a new site was purchased on the northeast corner of section 5 and the present structure erected. The building is large and ornamental, monumental of the progressive spirit of Knightsen and vicinity.

As a historical item, we note in passing that it was at Eden Plain the first Methodist Episcopal church was erected. It was a small steepleless building and stood on the southeast quarter of section 5. It was nearly opposite the schoolhouse and was built in 1868. Later it was removed to the town of Brentwood, occupied for service there for a while, then sold and used for a lodge-room, later as a private residence, and finally destroyed by fire in the conflagration of 1915.

The influx of settlers into the Point of Timber section in the latter '60s resulted in the organization of the Excelsior School District and the location of the school building on the southeast corner of the Netherton quarter. The style of construction and the lack of facilities ultimately resulted in its demolition and the construction of a unique and pleasing structure in the Mission style of architecture, in keeping with the rich agricultural surroundings.

The completion of the railroad in 1878, and the establishment of a station at that point, brought the town of Byron into existence and a cluster of population that was soon followed by the building of a schoolhouse and church that seemingly go hand in hand. But several years ago that enterprising town outgrew the primitive schoolhouse and built a beautiful and creditable building that is representative of the progressive spirit of its citizens.

As the county settled and the population grew, a school became a necessity not long to be ignored in the country south of Byron; willing hands came readily to assist, and a small, though convenient, building was erected that accommodates that sparsely settled locality. The Hot Springs District, reaching to the county line, will not be long content with the miniature pattern of "the little red schoolhouse" of our boyhood days, but in the larger future that is opening up in the construction of its irrigation system there will come a demand for the accommodation of a rapidly growing population, whose interests, following in the line of its pioneers, will be centered in its schools.

The organization of the Vasco Grant District and the building of a school in that sparsely settled region is an apt illustration of the desires of all classes to avail themselves of the advantages afforded by our primary schools. As early as 1869 the Deer Valley people organized a school district and erected a schoolhouse on the farm of W. C. Haney, which was later removed to the Stockton ranch, a mile and a half to the northeast, to accommodate the near-by children of the coal miners. Here after a time the old building was disposed of and a new building erected on its present site, just behind the hill from its original location.

The writer is not in possession of the date of the organization of the Lone Tree District (named from and presumably in honor of the lone oak-tree that stands near—a solitary sentinel of the valley that seems strangely out of place in treeless and shrubless surroundings). A new and handsome school building occupies the site of the original structure, indicative of the intelligent interest that the patrons manifest in school matters.

The last of thirteen districts, but by no means the least in growing importance, is the Live Oak District, established to accommodate the population of what is known as the "sand country" and comprising the thriving and growing village of Oakley. The schoolhouse is located on the south side of the main thoroughfare leading from the town of Antioch and is a large up-to-date structure and destined to become one of the most populous schools of the whole number. It is new, the latest addition to our educational institutions. There are no memories of the past, no venerated associations clustering around it, no participants in the active affairs of life who can look back reverently and say, "Within its storied walls I studied out the confusing problems of algebra, or learned the rudiments of the three Rs, that carried me successfully through life," for it is yet new and without its traditions.

The last of our references is to the organization of Brentwood School District, the thirteenth in the order named, though older than some others. The year 1878 seems to have been the fortuitous epoch, as the advent of the railroad and the opening up of the Brentwood Coal Mines induced the laying out of the town by the owners of the Los Meganos Rancho. Ample room was set apart for schools and churches, and the gathering inhabitants were not slow to avail themselves of the bequest.

Under the active leadership of A. Duffenbach, a district was organized and a large single-room building erected—principally by donation. This served to accommodate the community until the latter '80s, when a contract was let for the construction of a large two-room addition, at a cost of $4300, built in the Eastlake style of architecture, with ample covered porches all around the structure. It was also provided with a bell, the first "these valleys and rocks ever heard," and two teachers were employed.

It would have been in accordance with the writer's desire to hand down to posterity through these historical pages the honored names of the trustees and founders of these public schools; but in many instances no record is extant to refer to, and only a few are still remembered, and the record would therefore be only partial, and apparently discriminative. In their public-spirited endeavors to promote the welfare of the rising generation in the establishment and promotion of the free school system—often done at an unusual and unselfish sacrifice of their time and money—they earned the gratitude of succeeding generations. Also, would it have been a pleasure to have recorded herein a list of all the teachers employed in the various schools, but, as only a partial list could be obtained, it was deemed best not to mention any.

HIGH SCHOOLS

The establishment of the high school as an intermediate between the grammar school and the university was intended to complete the chain in our State educational system from the kindergarten to the university.

The necessity was long felt, and communities were not slow to avail themselves of the opportunity to organize high-school districts. Antioch was the first to move in this respect, and some of her leading citizens, with Charles Montgomery, then editor of the Antioch Ledger, took an active part in the circulation of a petition to the county superintendent to call an election in the various districts for the purpose of uniting with Antioch in the foundation of a high-school district, with the view of locating the school at that point. The signatures of the trustees of several of the districts were obtained with the intention of securing the majority of the thirteen districts; but the Brentwood trustees absolutely refused to sign the petition, on the ground that Brentwood was centrally located, that it was surrounded by districts contiguous in territory, and that it was the logical and proper place for the location of a high school. The position taken by the Brentwood board was very bitterly resented by the editor of the Ledger in a three-column article reflecting on the motives of Mr. Dean, especially in refusing to call an election, and thus preventing his constituents from voting on the proposition.

The stand taken by the board of trustees finally resulted in the retention of the territory, and when the proposition was afterward made to establish a high school at Brentwood the surrounding districts of Excelsior, Byron, Liberty, Deer Valley, Lone Tree, Live Oak, and Eden Plain readily assented, and the district was organized under the title of Liberty Union High School. Antioch organized under the name of Riverview.

The first sessions of the Liberty Union High School were held for two or more seasons in the rear room of the grammar-school building. In 1906 a high-school building was erected at a cost of $8500, and at this date (March, 1917) a corps of six teachers are employed.

Riverview has also erected a fine new building, and both institutions are fully equipped and accredited to the University of California.

SYCAMORE DISTRICT SCHOOL

This school was organized in 1865, in a little plain redwood building. The ground upon which it stood was donated to the cause by Wade Hays. Rude benches without backs were the only seats, and, as there were no desks, the pupils placed their books beside them on the floor.

In 1868 money was raised by subscription among the residents of the district, and the old building was replaced by one more in keeping with the times. The new schoolhouse was constructed by Mr. Dole, who also made the seats and the teacher's desk.

The first teacher in 1865 was Miss Mary Hall, now Mrs. Moore, of Los Angeles. Next came Mr. Clark, then Mr. Fletcher, and Miss Simpson, now Mrs. Brite. A. J. Young, of Danville, taught from 1869 to 1873, and has seen many of the children of those days grow to manhood and womanhood, for he and his good wife (later a teacher in the same school) have lived in their Danville home all the years since.

From 1873 until 1890 the following teachers presided over the Sycamore school: Mrs. Rice, Miss Hoag, Miss Hammond, Miss Lewis, Miss Alison, Miss Mower, Mrs. Young, Mr. Burrel, Mr. Root, Mr. Mantz, Mr. Sheats, Mr. Sears, Miss Herrington, Miss Asmus, Miss Ida Hall (now of Danville school), Miss Kate Howard (now Mrs. Charles J. Wood), and from 1890 until the present Miss Charlotte Wood has held sway. Of these all are living, so far as I know, excepting Mr. Burrel and Mr. Root. Mr. and Mrs. Young, Mrs. Brite, Miss Hall, Miss Howard, and Miss Wood have resided continuously in this vicinity since serving their terms as teachers.

A few years ago a caving of the creek bank necessitated moving the schoolhouse several feet nearer the road than the original location, and a little later the interior was remodeled.

The Sycamore schoolhouse, in its earlier years particularly, was the social center of the neighborhood, and has been the scene of many a happy gathering in its fifty years' existence.

The first trustees were Wade Hays and Charles Wood, who held the office many years. The present board are Mrs. J. L. Coats and Charles J. Wood.

DANVILLE PUBLIC SCHOOL

The Danville district was cut off from the San Ramon district in 1865. The land for the first schoolhouse was donated by two old settlers, Mr. Ramsey and Mr. Nicholson. As a village was beginning to grow where the town of Danville now is, the schoolhouse was moved to its present location in 1871. The first trustees were R. O. Baldwin, J. O. Boone, and Jonathan Hoag. R. O. Baldwin remained trustee as long as he lived.

Many teachers have done good work in the Danville school; but tribute must be paid to the veteran teacher still living near Danville, A. J. Young, whose influence for good has molded the characters of many of the best citizens of the San Ramon Valley. After teaching eight years in San Ramon, four years in Sycamore, and four years in Tassajara, he devoted more than seventeen years of his busy life to teaching in the Danville school. During that time he spent a number of years as a member of the county board of education.

Danville has grown to such an extent that, whereas a few years ago but one teacher was employed, there are now two teachers who are preparing pupils to enter the excellent San Ramon Valley High School.

The trustees at the present time are C. W. Close, whose father was formerly a trustee, A. J. Abrott, and S. Johnson.

EDEN PLAIN SCHOOL

In the spring of 1868 the community of Eden Plains held a meeting for the purpose of forming a school district. The question arose as to where the school should be located. After some discussion, John Pierce was chosen to select the spot, and he located it in his own premises. Next in order was the getting of the lumber onto the grounds, for transportation was a difficult problem in those days.

This was accomplished, however, and in a short time the schoolhouse was completed. This building served its purpose for thirty-eight years. Miss Mary Lockhart was the first teacher, she remaining three months until the district was legally formed and was paid by the patrons of the school. The next teacher was Mark Sickle.

In 1905 it was found necessary to build a new schoolhouse, to be located nearer to the town of Knightsen. Four acres was purchased for a school site. The new structure was completed in June, 1906, at a cost of $7000 for building and grounds. It was occupied during the fall term of that year.

In 1914 the number of pupils had increased so much that it was necessary to employ two teachers. The present teachers are Miss Edna Heidorn, principal, and Miss Pearl Gandrup, assistant. The number of pupils now enrolled is thirty-seven.

IRON HOUSE SCHOOL

Late in the sixties the pioneers of the tule country in eastern Contra Costa County established the Iron House School District, naming it from a house lined with sheet-iron in that vicinity, and electing Mesdames Sellers, Babbe, and Walton as their first trustees. The first building was a mile west of the present site. School was opened with fifteen pupils.

In 1883 Mr. Emerson donated a portion of his fine ranche for school-grounds, to revert to his estate should they ever cease to use it for that purpose and the schoolhouse was moved to its present site, a quarter of a mile south of the old Babbe landing. Miss Angie Wakeman was the first teacher. She later became an actress under the name of Keith Wakeman. She is now a successful photo-play writer in New York.

In 1896, under the leadership of F. Morton, Thomas Rooney, and Frank Nugent, the present substantial building was erected.

In years gone by as many as sixty-five pupils have attended the school. At the present time thirty are pursuing their studies under Mrs. Alice Collis, a teacher of experience and ability, with the splendid co-operation of E. B. Sellers, H. Tretheway, and J. Minta, as trustees.

DEER VALLEY SCHOOL

The Deer Valley School was established and built in 1869. The land was donated by W. C. Haney. The first trustees' meeting was held at the home of W. C. Haney, and W. C. Haney, W. J. Smith, and J. R. Filkins were elected to fill the duties of trustees until June, 1870; later J. R. Filkins moved away and the vacancy was filled by J. O. Diffin. The schoolhouse has been in three different locations.

It was moved to within a short distance of its first location on the northwest corner of the Haney place, now occupied by the Bettencourts, then a mile and a half northeast on the Stockton ranch (now occupied by J. Van Buren). This was done to secure the children from the near-by mines. Then, as the house was old, it was abandoned, and a new building was erected where it now stands.

The first teacher was Miss Emma McElroy, who was succeeded by Miss Susan Robinson (later Mrs. R. G. Houston, of Byron). Other teachers were Miss Anzette Taylor, of Byron (later Mrs. Richardson), and Miss Helana Calson. Later Mr. J. G. Parker taught for some years.

The first pupils who attended were Mellisa Haney (now Mrs. Smith, of San Francisco), Sarah Haney (now Mrs. S. Hobson, of Antioch), T. C. Haney, of Antioch, Rosa Diffin (now Mrs. W. P. Howard, of Marsh Creek), William Juett, John Haney (dead some years), Eugene Filkins, and George and Mary Smith.

LONE TREE SCHOOL

The Lone Tree School was established in 1869. The first trustees were James Talbot, James Hornback, and Woodhull Smith. Others were C. L. Donaldson, Thomas Shannon, and Robert Love; still later, John Fitzpatrick, H. B. Juett, Michael Campion, and C. A. Maylott; and again, Henry Heidorn, Patrick O'Brien, and Frank McFarland. The first teachers were Miss Fancher, Miss Dickson, and Susie Robinson; then Miss Jackson, Miss Eva Wilk, Miss Avyette Taylor, Ella B. Shaw, and Carrie C. Clifford. Among the first pupils were William and Fannie Hornback, Abraham and Emma Harris, William and Laura Donaldson, Fannie Newton, James Talbot, Caroline Levaria, John and Philo Fancher, Joe and Mary Laws, Sarah, Mary, and Annie Smith, Joseph and Alex. Miller, James and John Carey, Sylvester Wristen, Dan Carey, Valentine Blair, George and Elijah Wills, Agnes and Mary Lewis, Eli Plater, Frank, Antoinette, Caroline, and Anna Rasette, Patrick and Edward O'Brien, William and Frank Robinson, Janet and Archibald Love; afterward the younger members of these families, including the Fitzpatricks, Shannons, Campions, Grennens, Juetts, Sullengers, Wealches, Heidorns, Lynches, Ganns, Haneys, and Maylotts.

The second building was erected in 1883. The deed for the lot was secured from Chas. McLaughlin the day before he was killed, in 1883. The third building was erected in 1908. The location has never been changed.

CONCORD GRAMMAR SCHOOL

In 1870, just one year after the laying out of the town of Concord, the grammar school was started. The first teacher was Miss Annie Carpenter, who afterward became Mrs. Henry Polley. A good two- story building was erected at the corner of Grant and Bonifacio streets. It consisted of only two class-rooms and library, but in the course of a few years this was inadequate for the growing attendance. Several buildings about town were used as extra class-rooms, even after a new building for primary classes was put up across the street from the old one. An old building near the corner of Mount Diablo and Colfax streets and the upper room in the Fireman's Hall were used for a time, but both proved very unsatisfactory. It was finally decided to build a schoolhouse of sufficient size to accommodate the growing attendance for many years, and in 1892 a modern six class-room building was completed. It stands several blocks from the center of town on the Willow Pass road. Since its erection a one-bungalow has been added, and some of the class-rooms divided, indicating at the present time a very crowded condition. The old schoolhouse stands today at the corner of Grant and Salvio streets, two blocks from its original location, a landmark in the town.

Today the Concord Grammar School ranks among the best in the country, with an attendance of nearly three hundred and a corps of eight teachers. E. A. Palmer, the Misses Helen Morehouse, of San Francisco, Eleanor Bertola, of Alameda, Agnes Hoey, of Martinez, Grace Smith, Charlotte Boyd, Ellen Thurber, and Mary McKenzie, of Concord. Among former teachers are several well-known people in the county—W. S. Tinning, a prominent attorney of Martinez; Miss Ida Hall, of Alamo; Mrs. Susie Dunn DeSoto, now of Rio Vista; Dr. Mariana Bertola, a physician of note in San Francisco; A. A. Bailey, for many years superintendent of schools in Contra Costa County; Mrs. Jasper H. Wells, wife of the present county clerk; Mrs. S. W. Cunningham, of Bay Point; Mrs. Thomas G. Smith and Mrs. F. F. Neff, of Concord.

VINE HILL SCHOOL

Twenty-five years ago (1892) October first our school building was completed. The teacher, Mrs. Matson, opened school with an attendance of twenty pupils, earning a salary of forty dollars per month.

The schoolhouse is a structure of the old frame type. The district was bonded for sixteen hundred dollars to build it. In 1916 improvements costing five hundred dollars were made in the building. The lot on which the building stands contains an acre of land, and was purchased for the sum of three hundred dollars. The first trustees were Captain J. F. Thoroe, James Kelly, and H. S. Ivey.

Our school today has a daily attendance of thirty-five pupils, from first grade to eighth grade. The present teacher, Ethel B. Bernier, is paid ninety dollars a month, having taught here six years.

The board of trustees at present are George H. Wright (clerk), Mrs. Julia Chandler Hill, and John Simonds.

THE RICHMOND SCHOOLS

When in the year 1900, as the Santa Fe was completing its railway lines and terminals, the people began to settle in that territory that was soon to become the city of Richmond, it was part of the San Pablo School District. Consequently, when it became necessary to establish a school to provide for the children of these families the demand had to be met by the trustees of the San Pablo School District, who at that time were J. R. Nystrom, Harry Ells, and John Peres.

The first school was opened in March, 1901, in Richards' Hall, with fifteen pupils and A. Odell as teacher. The school was under the supervision of Mrs. L. E. Benedict, who at that time was principal of the San Pablo school. Mr. Odell taught for some time, when he was taken with typhoid fever and Miss Clesta Rumrill took his place.

The school was moved from Richards' Hall to the basement of the Methodist church, to remain there until a building could be erected to accommodate it. There was considerable discussion as to a proper location for the school site; but it was finally located on Standard Avenue, near the Standard Oil Refinery, the site having been given for school purposes by the Tewksbury estate.

In 1901 a two-room building was completed and the school moved into it, with Miss Emily Boorman as teacher and an attendance that had increased to eighty-seven pupils. In July of the same year W. T. Helms had been placed in charge of the schools in the San Pablo District, which then included this school at Point Richmond, with one teacher, three teachers at San Pablo, and two at Stege, making six teachers in all. Today, just fifteen years later, this same territory requires a force of over eighty-five teachers. What was then a small rural school system has in this short space of time developed into a modern city school system.

The building erected at the Standard Avenue school site had only two rooms, and it soon became necessary to add an additional teacher.

People also began to settle at the east side of town, and the first school there was opened in the loft of a small barn at the corner of Ohio and Sixth streets, with Miss Elizabeth S. Carpenter as teacher.

The San Pablo School District was very large and the means of communication and travel very difficult. It was soon apparent that the schools could not be covered with San Pablo school as the center of administration. Consequently, in 1903 the district was divided into three districts, made up of the San Pablo School District, the Richmond School District, and the Stege School District. For the balance of the year Mr. Helms remained with the San Pablo school as principal, but in 1904 was chosen to head the Richmond School District, which at that time was in a very poor condition, owing to the lack of funds, accommodations, and general organization. It soon became apparent that Richmond was to become a city of considerable size, and that buildings, sites, etc., should be provided with a view to future growth and development.

The school at Standard Avenue soon outgrew the two-room building, and a six-room building was erected at that site. To accommodate the rapidly growing east side a four-room building was erected at a site on Tenth Street, donated by the Richmond Land Company. A few years later it was necessary to increase this four-room building to double its size and to provide schools for the Santa Fe section and the North Richmond section. A site was secured in the Turpin tract, and a four-room building erected and named the Peres School, after John Peres, who had been a trustee since the beginning of the city. In the Santa Fe section a four-room building was erected and named the Nystrom School, after John R. Nystrom, who had been president of the board for a number of years, and who gave much of his time to the demands of the growing district.

The district grew very rapidly and it was soon felt that a high school was needed. In 1907, due to the efforts of the Rev. D. W. Calfee, John Roth, and others, an election was called, and it was unanimously voted to establish a union high school, to be composed of Richmond, San Pablo, and Stege districts. L. D. Dimm, of Richmond, W. F. Belding, of San Pablo, and B. B. McClellan, of Stege, were chosen as trustees to establish the school. With a desire to secure perfect cooperation between the high school and the grade schools, they selected Mr. Helms to act as supervising principal of the high school as well as that of the grade schools.

The high school was opened and organized in August, 1907, at the old two-room school building at Standard Avenue, with B. X. Tucker, Miss Ruth Peterson, and

Miss Alberta Bell as faculty, and an enrollment of about forty-five pupils. Plans were at once started for the erection of a permanent building. Eighty-five thousand dollars in bonds were voted, and in January, 1909, the school was moved to the present "Cass A" building, which had been erected at the site chosen at Twenty-third Street near Macdonald Avenue.

In 1909 a very important thing happened in the school history of Richmond. The citizens decided to adopt a charter form of government. In that year a modern charter was approved by the legislature, and Richmond became a charter city. In so far as the school department was concerned, this charter contained many provisions far in advance of their time, and which are now considered highly desirable for any modern school department. The underlying principles kept the schools from all possible political contagion, based the selection and tenure of teachers on efficiency, and made the city superintendent of schools head of the school system and responsible for its success. The directors were given long terms of office (six years) and the elections arranged to take place in the even-numbered years, while the election for councilmen was held in the odd-numbered years. In this way there is very little possibility for the issues at a council election becoming involved in a school election, and in consequence school elections have been quiet, free from politics, and have attracted the highest class of citizenship to seek office. Excellent teachers have been secured, because they are assured that as long as they give excellent services their positions are secure. The department has been free from all sorts of strife, wrangling, and discord. The policy has been to provide the best schools possible for the money expended, without ostentation or advertising of any kind.

In 1912 the citizens of Point Richmond had outgrown the second building, and it was decided to erect a larger and permanent building at a more suitable site. By a vote of the citizens of the district a site on Richmond Avenue was chosen and the Washington School erected.

In 1913 the residents of the Stege School District, feeling that they could secure better advantages by becoming a part of the Richmond School District, were annexed to the Richmond District by the board of supervisors, thus bringing back the Richmond District to almost the same size as the original San Pablo School District from which it started. San Pablo District still remains a distinct district.

At the present time the Richmond School District has nine graded schools— Washington, Lincoln, Peres, Nystrom, Stege, Fairmont, Grant, Pullman, Winehaven, and the high school.

In place of the enrollment of thirty-six pupils in 1900, we have an enrollment of over twenty-five hundred pupils. These are housed in modern, sanitary buildings containing all the latest devices for ventilation and heating and other equipment necessary to provide everything modern in the course of study, such as manual training, cooking, sewing, etc.

In addition to the so-called regular subjects, excellent instruction is furnished along modern lines, as special teachers are employed in music, sewing, cooking, manual training, penmanship, and drawing.

In order to interest the pupils of the upper grades, their work has been further broadened along the lines of study such as is incorporated in what are known as intermediate schools, by the introduction of algebra, German, and Spanish. In order that children may progress rapidly, and to reduce the number of laggards as much as possible, promotions are semi-annual, or as often as occasion may require. All the newer buildings are fitted with windows that can be thrown open to make each room an open-air school, and every attention is given to the health of the children. Adjustable desks are provided, so that the seating may be as correct as it is possible to make it. With a view to further promoting the health of the children, a trained nurse is employed, and careful investigation is made of all absences. She consults with parents and uses every means to improve the physical condition of the children. In this way, and with the close co-operation of the health department, the Richmond schools have never been closed on account of an epidemic.

In the high school, in addition to the regular courses required in order that students who desire may enter the University of California, other courses are offered, enabling a student to secure a good practical education should he not continue in school after graduating from high school. Special attention is given to courses in music, art, manual training, and domestic science. The high school has a very strong commercial department, which enables young men or young women to prepare for a business career.

The school department of Richmond has always been fortunate in the loyal support of a loyal public. It has never been disturbed by factions among its patrons. It has been indeed fortunate in the class of men who have been chosen from time to time to conduct its affairs. In the grammar schools such prominent and capable men as John R. Nystrom, John Peres, Harry Ells, James Cruickshank, E. O. Gowe, Dr. J. L. Bedwell, Otto Poulsen, and E. L. Jones are recalled, while the high school shall always cherish the names of W. F. Belding, B. B. McClellan, and L. D. Dimm.

At the present time the board of education of the elementary school department is composed of J. N. Long (president), J. O. Ford, and R. E. Slattery. The high school board is composed of E. H. Harlow (president), W. S. McRacken, J. F. Brooks, H. W. M. Mergenthal, and Edward Hoffman.

ANTIOCH GRAMMAR SCHOOL

In 1890 the trustees, H. F. Bude, J. Rio Baker, and D. P. Mahan, noticed the crowded condition and promoted the erection of a new schoolhouse. They were entirely successful, and as a result of their efforts a building, one of the finest in the county, was erected. So far did they look into the future that the building is still occupied, although it is also fast becoming too small. At first only the lower floor was occupied, but upon the founding of the Riverview Union High School the upper floor was used by that institution. It was only for a few years, however, as the increasing attendance in the grammar school made it necessary for the high school to seek new quarters.

The work so well started has been continued by the boards that followed. M. D. Field, Mrs. Paulo Donlon, and Doctor W. S. George, the present trustees, deserve great credit for the manner in which they have kept the school abreast of the times during the past few years.

Special courses in manual training, domestic science, and music have been introduced, and in the yard steel playground apparatus has been built. Antioch is justly proud of her school, which is among the foremost in the county.

MOUNT DIABLO UNION HIGH SCHOOL

This school was organized in the spring of 1901. The board that was chosen that year, and was in office from the first of July, consisted of E. J. Randall, president; M. T. Sickal, secretary, and Messrs. Kirkwood, Putnam, Parkinson, Sutton, and Miss Loucks. Two rooms were secured in the grammar-school building and school opened in August, with G. W. Wright (principal) and Miss Maud Grover as the teachers.

Miss Grover later married Mr. Chandler, now a member of the State Water Commission, and resides in Berkeley. There were thirty or forty pupils the first year, six of them from other high schools and the others in the first-year class.

The next year Miss Gulielma R. Crocker was added to the teaching force, and a small room in the grammar-school building was secured for a recitation room and was also used for such laboratory work as could be done under such conditions. There were three graduates this year—Misses Elinor Godfrey, Helen Godfrey, and Lucille Busey.

For the third year of the school, 1903-04, Miss Sara Lunny was secured to take the place of Miss Grover, who resigned to be married.

There were three graduates this year also—Miss Grace Crawford, Miss Agnes Williams, and Leonard Martin. In the meantime Mr. Sickal had moved to Concord, and George Whitman succeeded him as a member of the board of trustees. Mr. Parkinson also gave way to Mr. Tormey, and Mr. Gehringer took the place of Mr. Sutton.

As soon as it had a graduating class the school was examined and accredited by the State University. The course of study was the regular academic course, but even with this the school had now outgrown its accommodations, and the board began to discuss the question of a new schoolhouse. A room was now secured in Odd Fellows Hall and equipped for laboratory work for both chemistry and physics. A bond election was called to secure money to build a new house. The bonds received a majority but failed to obtain the necessary two-thirds vote.

After some time a second bond election was called, the bonds failing to carry this time by a few votes. If the writer remembers correctly, six votes were needed to make the two-thirds majority. In the meantime the question of the legality of the organization of the district was raised, and the matter was taken to the Superior Court for decision.

The court decided that the organization was legal. The board now decided to erect the building by direct tax. Through the generosity of Mr. Maltby, a site was donated and the building was constructed in the summer of 1905.

At the election of trustees Mrs. Bancroft was chosen to succeed Mr. Whitman and Mr. Douglas was chosen to take the place of Mr. Kirkwood, who had moved out of the district. Herbert Kitridge was chosen principal for the year 1905-06. After four years' occupancy of the grammar-school quarters, school was opened in the new building.

In the last six years vast changes have taken place in the Mount Diablo region, and these changes have been reflected in the Mount Diablo Union High School. This section of the county has been electrified by being brought into closer communication with the cities about San Francisco Bay. And the school responding, as schools always do, to conditions in the community about it, has itself developed into a new life.

In 1910 the school occupied a six-room building on a lot of three and a half acres and offered a course which was strictly academic and preparatory to the normal schools and the State University. Today it is crowding eleven rooms on a ten-acre lot and has broadened its curriculum to include some of those vocational subjects for which there is so wide-spread a demand.

This growth has been gradual, as all healthful growth must be. It is interesting to note the steps by which it has come about. In the summer of 1911, the trustees purchased something over six acres of land immediately adjoining the old triangular lot, thus making a rectangular piece of property approximately six hundred feet to a side. At the same time, they connected the building with the newly installed sewer system and made the sanitary equipment of the building thoroughly up to date. The following winter the board laid a concrete sidewalk along the front of the school property, anticipating the work which the town soon after took up.

In the spring of 1912, the trustees and student body, working together, laid out a quarter-mile track and erected a grand stand. The annual track meets of the Contra Costa Athletic League have been held on this ground since that time, and it is probable that the league will continue to hold its field meets in Concord for some years to come, since Mount Diablo is the only school in the county which owns athletic grounds large enough for this purpose.

During the summer and early fall of 1912, the high-school building was materially enlarged by the addition of an assembly-room. The farsighted policy of the trustees in laying a hardwood floor in this room has been a source of pleasure to the students ever since. It is the best dancing floor in Concord. For the more prosaic every-day use of a study-room, the hall will seat one hundred or more pupils. And when seated as an auditorium, it will accommodate three hundred. The stage at the east end is large enough for concerts and for commencement exercises, but it has proved too small for the plays which the students give every fall.

The lower story of this annex was finished in the summer of 1913 to form two rooms, one of which is now used as a sewing-room and the other as a kitchen.

The manual-training shop was originally located in the basement but work soon outgrew these quarters. In the fall of 1914 it became necessary to erect a separate building to accommodate the students in this highly useful and practical subject.

Early in 1916 it became evident that the number of regular classrooms available would not be sufficient for the size of the school, and later in the year the trustees evolved a plan by which the building can be gradually enlarged, each addition forming, when completed, a part of what will be a unified whole. In accordance with this plan, two new recitation-rooms have been added.

The growth in numbers of the school has been perhaps its most impressive development. In 1910 it had five teachers; now it has ten. In 1910 the total enrollment of students was fifty-eight; now it is 155, and there are fifty-seven students in the entering class alone.

The graduates of the school have made a highly creditable showing in whatever line of work they have undertaken, the record of those who have gone to the State University being especially commendable.

A remarkable feature of the school is the permanence of its governing bodies. There has been but one change in the board of trustees since 1910. The principal and three assistants have also held their positions during the same period. This permanence has made possible the maintenance of a consistent policy of development and the attainment of a high degree of efficiency.

RIVERVIEW UNION HIGH SCHOOL

This school was organized in 1903 through the efforts of W. S. Moore, principal of the grammar school at Antioch. A union of the districts of Live Oak, Summersville, Black Diamond (now Pittsburg), and Antioch formed the Riverview High School District. The upper floor in the grammar-school building was used for the class-rooms. There were thirty-two pupils, all freshmen, and two teachers, Mr. Moore and Miss Hagemayer. H. F. Beede, president of the board of trustees for seven years, was the main factor in the maintenance of the school. Six of the first thirty-two pupils graduated in 1907 and the inspector from the State University decided that their work was of such a quality that they could be recommended to that institution.

The high school remained in the quarters of the grammar school until 1911, when the present building was completed, Mr. Kitridge being the first principal. In 1913 a domestic science department was installed and a manual-training room was completed. Next year a chemistry laboratory was added and a few class rooms finished. In 1915 the manual-training classes were so large that a new building was necessary, so, under the directions of Mr. Cater, the manual-training teacher, a new building was constructed by his pupils.

In 1914-15 some work was done on the grounds, but they are not yet completed. Many trees were put out and the driveway finished, but there is still a great deal of work to be done.

The number of pupils in attendance has increased each year until at present (1916) there are one hundred and thirty enrolled in the school.

LIVE OAK SCHOOL

In 1885, on a lot about a mile and a half from Oakley, the former dwelling-house of Mr. Ruckstuhl was remodeled for a school, which was named Live Oak, as trees of that species abound in the vicinity.

There was one teacher in charge, and about twenty-five children, who had been attending surrounding district schools, came to the new school. The members of the first board of trustees were William Fleckhammer, J. Ruckstuhl, and J. T. Wheelhan.

In 1903, at a cost of four thousand dollars, the present building was constructed. Somewhat later, when another teacher was added, the one large recitation-room was divided into two rooms. At present there are forty-three promising future citizens in the Live Oak school. All the regular subjects are studied, but with few extras, as each teacher has four grades.

HOT SPRINGS SCHOOL

Hot Springs schoolhouse was erected in 1911, at a cost of about $3600.

The original board of trustees were John Armstrong, Jr. (clerk), Henry Mehrtens, and George Stone. Miss Grace Brennaman was chosen as teacher. Twelve pupils constituted the school attendance.

The school has now (1916) an attendance of eighteen. Henry Mehrtens, Herman Krumland, and John Armstrong, Jr., clerk, are the present members of the board.

At present there is a good playground equipment, being bought with money raised by entertainments given by the children.

CHAPTER XIX. LIBRARY DEVELOPMENT

The library history of Contra Costa County previous to 1913, when the county library was established, is that of the attempts of small communities to supply themselves with a reading-room for the circulation of books and magazines. These pioneer efforts met with many obstacles, but the earnest and unflagging zeal of a few enthusiastic workers held the clubs and associations together until subscription libraries had been started.

The struggle of each is a story in itself, the recording of which brings back the names of many early residents now held in memory and of many more who still hold the same interest in the larger library that they did in the one of small beginnings.

MARTINEZ LIBRARY

The Martinez library goes back to October 24, 1883, when a little club was formed with five charter members, the Misses Julia Fish, Jane Grey Frazer, Marion Taylor, Carrie Cutler, and Louise Corbert, for the purpose of working for a free reading-room. They called themselves the E. Q. V. Society but kept steadily before them the idea of a reading room whenever they might be able to accomplish it. In 1885 a book social was given, netting one hundred and fifty books. Immediately the Martinez Free Reading-Room and Library Association was organized, officers elected, and the public invited to become members by paying dues of twenty-five cents a month. This membership grew and great interest was shown. The use of a room had been given by Doctor John Strenzel in a building owned by him on Main Street and was prepared for use by the young people of the town. Generous contributions of time, money, and talent were given freely in the many entertainments and benefits that were devised for this purpose. In 1893 a lot on a prominent corner on Main Street was donated by Mrs. John Strenzel and her daughter, Mrs. John Muir. The lot was thirty-two feet frontage by ninety-six in depth and deeded with the provision that the building placed thereon must be always devoted to library purposes.

The association now filed articles of incorporation, and a deed was shortly afterward executed, which contained a provision that a two-story brick building covering the entire lot be placed there within two years, or the property would revert to the Strenzel estate. A canvassing committee was immediately appointed, and by May reported more than $1700 pledged.

Byron Brown offered free of charge his services as architect and supervisor of the building, a generous gift, since it left all funds to go to actual work of construction. Everybody was interested, and the town trustees agreed to lease the rear portion of the lower floor—a room for town meetings and offices and a large room for the fire apparatus. The upper floor was to be leased for a term of years by the I. O. O. F., thus insuring an income with which to meet interest and reduce the debt that must be incurred to erect the building. When the bids came in the lowest, $6371, was found to be that of C. H. Ludden, who thus become the builder. In the latter part of February, 1896, the building was completed, furnished, and occupied, with a debt of $3800 to be paid by the efforts of the association, represented by a board of seven trustees, elected annually. This debt was reduced in ten years by entertainments of all kinds to a little over $800. When the earthquake caused damages to the amount of $1400, again the people in their interest for the welfare of the library collected $900, so the whole debt then stood at $1300. This was paid off in the next five years; on its twenty-fifth anniversary its fifteen-year note of indebtedness was burned.

With the establishment of the county library it was not possible to keep up the subscriptions. The town trustees came to the aid of the institution, and with the books borrowed from the county library, numbering 1076 volumes for the year 1915-16, the growth and use has been steady. The circulation of books from the county collection alone amounted to 7870 volumes for the year.

ANTIOCH LIBRARY

The first efforts in Antioch toward providing reading for the public were made by a library club, each member of which contributed five dollars as the purchase price of two books. The books were exchanged at house-to-house meetings. About 1904 Mr. Williams, with the idea of helping the boys of the town, started a small reading-room in a store on Main Street, but later built a gymnasium and library-room on the corner of Third and F streets. A small fee was charged for the use of the books, and, with his mother, he kept this reading-room open for five or six years. In 1911 a part of the membership of the Woman's Club started a library association, each contributing one dollar a year and as many books as she could spare from her shelves. The books were kept in the clubhouse and were distributed each week by one of the members. Later Miss Carrie Williamson was appointed librarian, and she has had charge continuously. When the county library was established in 1913, Antioch co-operated at once and gave the use of its clubhouse for the county library books, which, together with those accumulated, were circulated freely. Miss Williamson continued in charge and has been unflagging in furthering the interests of the library.

Through the efforts of Mrs. Mary L. Fulton, Mrs. Keeney, and Mrs. Frederika J. West, funds were raised to buy a corner lot for the building that the Carnegie Corporation donated to the county. This building, costing $2550, was planned by Frances Reid, and is now in process of building. Though small, the building will be very convenient and a great pleasure to the people. The circulation for the year from the Antioch branch was 8838 volumes.

CONCORD LIBRARY

On October 29, 1906, a mass meeting was called and met in Odd Fellows Hall for the purpose of organizing a public library and reading room. Doctor George McKenzie was elected chairman and Miss G. R. Crocker secretary, with the additional names on the committee of Joseph Boyd, W. A. Kirkwood, and Mrs. F. F. Neff. At the next meeting the following permanent officers were elected: President, W. A. Kirkwood; vice-president, Mrs. H. H. Elworthy; secretary, Miss G. R. Crocker; treasurer, Joseph Boyd; directors, Mr. Pingree, Mr. Gehringer, Mr. Spencer, Mr. Randall, and Miss Skinner.

The first location was in the Fire Hall and books received by donation, others borrowed from the State Library and Oakland Club, were circulated. Miss Skinner was the first librarian and Mr. Martin first assistant, the latter receiving ten dollars a month. Dues were twenty-five cents a month. Frequent entertainments were given to provide for the new books and maintenance. A strong interest has always been felt by the library association in the welfare of its reading-room, and when the county library was formed it was among the first to grasp at the idea of enlarging its usefulness and joined immediately. Mrs. Ballenger, who had been a most interested and faithful librarian for a number of years, was forced to give up the work from ill-health, and Mrs.

H. Elise Williams was appointed and has held the position for the past two years. A pleasant room in the Foskett building was rented by a continuation of this same library association and the books and magazines are supplied by the county library. The circulation for the past year was 7903 volumes. The Carnegie Corporation also donated the sum of $2500 for a branch building, which will be erected in the near future.

CROCKETT LIBRARY

In 1908 the Crolona Men's Club was formed in Crockett, the membership composed largely of men from the California & Hawaiian Sugar Refining Company. The company and a number of men interested donated about six hundred volumes and provided the clubhouse. In 1910 the Y. M. C. A. assumed control of the Crolona Club. When the county library was established the collection at the Y. M. C. A., becoming a part of the county library, was accessioned and a charging system installed.

Ever since that time the collection has been added to by the county library and frequent exchanges have been made. After it became apparent that the clubhouse was too small for its purposes a new Y. M. C. A. building was started in 1914 and was completely furnished and equipped by the sugar company. In this commodious building a large reading room was provided. The old building was remodeled and fitted up for the Crockett Girls' Club and another collection of books started for them. Every effort has been made by the company to stimulate and meet the intellectual demands of the community.

RICHMOND LIBRARY

The Richmond Library Club was formed August 16, 1907, with Mrs. W. W. Felch as chairman of the library committee. The club rented a small room on the corner of Sixth Street and Macdonald Avenue, and the library was kept open by a committee of women, among whom were Mrs. W. W. Felch, Mrs. E. B. Smallwood, Mrs. C. Smith, Mrs. Clarence Jenkins, and Mrs. C. B. Evans. Books were donated and entertainments given to meet the expenses. In 1908 a request was made to the Carnegie Corporation for a library building, the Woman's Improvement Club having given five lots in a central location on Nevin Avenue for a site. A gift of $17,500 was granted upon the usual conditions, and in June, 1909, the first meeting of the board of trustees was held. Mrs. E. B. Smallwood was elected president, Harry Adkison secretary, and as directors Mrs. George W. Topping, L. D. Dimm, and J. C. Bedwell.

Mrs. Alice G. Whitbeck, of Berkeley, was appointed the first librarian, May 2, 1910. The library was dedicated with appropriate exercises August 17, 1910. Great interest was shown in its development, generous and adequate support was given by the city trustees, and after three successful years, in which the library became a vital part of the community, Mrs. Whitbeck resigned to take charge of the county library, and Miss Della M. Wilsey, of Pomona, was appointed librarian. Several changes at that time were made in the library staff. At the time of the resignation of Mrs. Whitbeck plans were made and partially carried out to install a children's room in the basement, the three years' growth proving the inadequacy of the room originally planned as such. This room, very pretty and complete in all its appointments, was finished, but another two years' growth showed the necessity of using the still larger assembly room for the children and turning their room into a cataloging and workroom. The present children's room, in charge of Miss Ruth Epperson, is one of the most attractive in the State. The library has made wonderful strides during Miss Wilsey's administration and is now one of the best-appointed libraries of its size in the State.

At the time of the establishment of the county library, and for three years thereafter, the Richmond Public Library was a part of the county library system, but in January, 1916, withdrew, and is now the only part of the county not affiliated with the county library.

WALNUT CREEK LIBRARY

At the time of the establishment of the county library the members of the Woman's Club of the town were contemplating a reading-room in their clubhouse and had gathered a number of books together. Realizing the great help that the county library would be for them, they put off opening their reading-room until that institution could help them in preparing and adding to their collection. For the first year a committee of ladies kept the library open and distributed the books. Later Mrs. Hempstead was appointed librarian and has continued in office ever since.

The library moved its quarters twice before the new Carnegie county branch building was ready for occupancy, August, 1916. The gift of the Carnegie building brought great delight to the town, and when the question of a site was talked of the Burgess Company donated a lot upon which a very delightful little bungalow library has-been designed and built by Randolph Hook.

PITTSBURG LIBRARY

There had been no move in Pittsburg to circulate books until a gift of several hundred volumes was made to the town by the Honorable Sumner Crosby. In January these were cataloged by the county librarian and installed in locked bookcases in the town hall. Mrs. George Minaker was appointed librarian and has kept the library open and the interest sustained. Mr. Crosby made an additional gift of several hundred books, which lack of space has prevented shelving. Pittsburg needs a building with special attention to the work with the children. This will undoubtedly be brought about in the near future. Its juvenile circulation is larger than that of any other branch in the county.

THE COUNTY LIBRARY

The accounts already given of the efforts and the accomplishments of those efforts in the small towns of the county bring us to the establishment of the county library in July, 1913. Actual work commenced in October with Mrs. Whitbeck as librarian and Miss Anne Weyand (now Mrs. Dennis Dehan) as assistant. A room was rented from the Martinez Library Association and immediate steps were taken to form branches around the county and to get the schools interested in co-operating. As a result of rapid and well-organized work, books were sent to twenty-eight places the first year. Some of these were the reading rooms already mentioned; others were merely deposits in stores, post offices, private homes, and in isolated schools. At the end of the second year there were fifty-two depositories for the books, and the circulation from all the branches increased from 21,942 volumes the first year to 61,569 volumes the second year. At the end of the third year, sixty-two depositories were recorded, thirty-three of which were schools. A total of 900 shipments were made from the office, and a circulation of 73,054 volumes recorded from all branches. The growth of the office work called for an exact system of card files and records. The great demand for special books from all parts of the county and the pressure of the work with the schools necessitated renting another room at the end of the second year. Even now the quarters are very much cramped.

Mrs. Whitbeck and one assistant did the work the first year, but in order to carry on the library, with its rapid growth and popularity, a trained cataloger and apprentice help were necessary. A heavy part of the work has been that of the schools. There were sent out from the office last year 8100 books and 6184 were returned for exchange. Magazines have been taken for all the schools, as well as a generous number for the branches. This work with the schools has been at all times a pleasure, both on account of the hearty and full approbation and assistance of the county superintendent of schools, W. H. Hanlon, and of the full measure of appreciation shown by the teachers served. There are a number of smaller schools that have not yet joined, but the growth has been steady, and we hope before another year to enroll all the schools in the county.

There are at present thirty-four counties operating county libraries, and Contra Costa County is next to the smallest county and was the eighteenth to start. It was, however, at the last reckoning of statistics, ninth in the number of volumes, eighth in number of branches, seventh in number of schools, eleventh in circulation, and seventh in income raised by tax levy. Although a comparison of the counties is hardly fair because of such vastly different conditions under which each county librarian works, it at least shows that Contra Costa County is well to the fore in its library work and development.

CHAPTER XX. RELIGIOUS

EARLY CHURCHES OF MARTINEZ

The good people of early Martinez took thought as to their churches without delay. The Roman Catholics were the first to hold services.

Father Schimel was the first priest to officiate and the services were held in the old building which stood on Smith Street and was afterward used as a barn. This building was erected in 1849 by Judge Brown, Warren Brown, and N. B. Smith as a store, and in it the first mercantile establishment of Martinez was opened. After its sale to the Catholics, from far and near the Spanish rancheros on Sunday gathered with their wives and children to attend mass and afterward hold a merry reunion. From 1850 to 1851 the Catholics used this structure as a place of worship; then they began the construction of an adobe building, which was not completed. In 1855 a church was built on Estudillo Street, which was blown down by a gale in 1866. Among the early priests were Fathers Vincent, Vallarassa, and Dominick.

The New England pioneers of Martinez were largely members of the Protestant Episcopal church, which seems somewhat strange, when we remember that the Congregational is the leading church of New England. For some years these pioneer Episcopalians were obliged to attend church in Benicia, where services of the Church of England had been held since 1854. In 1855 the Rev. Orange Clarke held services in Martinez, and in 1858 the Rev. Elijah Hager, chaplain U. S. N., at that date rector of St. Paul's Church, Benicia, officiated in Martinez from time to time. From 1860 to 1866 the Rev. James Cameron, of Benicia, held Episcopal services in the Methodist church. The Rev. Henry G. Perry followed in 1866 and established a Sunday-school and library.

Plans and specifications for a church building were prepared, but the Martinez Episcopalians still remained members of the Benicia church, and it was not until 1869 that, through the exertions of certain ladies of the church, money was raised and the present building was begun and completed. Grace Church was consecrated by the Rt. Rev. William Ingraham Kip, D. D., on Sunday, July 10, 1870. He was assisted by the Revs. Doctor Breck and E. C. Cowan. Previous to this date the Missionary College of St. Augustine, at Benicia, had had charge of the work in Martinez, but in 1870 the associate mission of the college came to an end. Doctor J. A. Merrick, formerly connected with the mission, became pastor of the Martinez church. Other early pastors of Grace Church were the Rev. William Benet, the Rev. William Tucker, the Rev. Henry Monges, and the Rev. James Abercrombie, D. D. The beautiful memorial chancel window which ornaments Grace Church was made by Edward Colgate, of New York, and was placed New Year's day, 1882, in memory of the founder of the church, the Rev. James Breck, D. D. The stone font was a gift by the youth of the parish on Easter Sunday of the same year. The altar, prayer-desk, and seat were given to the church on Thanksgiving and Christmas days, 1881, by the Rev. Mr. Abercrombie and Elam Brown.

The Congregational church of Martinez was organized June 18, 1874. It is a much younger church society, therefore, than its sisters of the Catholic and Episcopal faith. The first pastor was the Rev. W. S. Clark, who was succeeded in 1875 by the Rev. E. B. Tuttle. During the four years of Turtle's ministry the membership increased. The

Methodist church, for years the only Protestant church structure in the town, was purchased and services were held in it until 1886, when, under the pastorate of Rev. Mr. Baille, a new edifice was built. One of the pastors, Rev. A. Drachms, has served as chaplain in San Quentin prison for a number of years.

About 1854 S. Swain gave lots on which to build a church. The property was deeded to the Methodist society, with the understanding that, when not occupied by them, other denominations could use it. The church was built by donations from the residents of the town. The women agreed to finish the interior of the church. They gave a supper in the building. The price of the tickets for supper, admitting two persons, was five dollars. A party was given the same evening in Union Hall. Holders of tickets for supper were admitted to the dance free.

Those pioneer women had an eye to business, and they raised a round sum of money. The following are names of the clergymen who officiated until the property was sold to the Congregational society, about the year 1873: Willmot, Methodist; Yager, Presbyterian; May, Methodist; McClure, Congregational; Urmy, Methodist; McDonald, Episcopalian; Cameron, Episcopalian; Breck, Episcopalian; Woodbridge, Presbyterian; Warren, Congregational.

Back in 1879, on the 27th and 28th of March, for the benefit of the Congregational church fund, one of the most elaborate and successful entertainments ever given in Martinez took place. It was in charge of Mrs. James Weeks, who, as Miss Jane Lyons, one of the early Martinez teachers, arranged the first school exhibition ever presented in this town. She gave much time and thought to the production of the program and made many of the costumes herself.

In a reminiscence of this entertainment, Mrs. Weeks says that the large rude building in which it was given was admirably fitted to her requirements. The mechanism of the stage was arranged by a young man then connected with the church, and it worked perfectly. The peacocks which drew Juno's chariot were made of pasteboard and paper, painted to imitate the plumage of the real birds. They were drawn by invisible wires across the stage. Iris flew through the air in advance of the chariot, and so perfectly did the sliding apparatus work that the delusion of flight was excellent. The first scene was the fairy scene, which showed a forest with two fountains playing. The edge of the stage was turfed and dotted over with pansies. The rocks were made of fruit boxes, painted to simulate stones. Fairies were perched everywhere.

During the scene the music of "A Midsummer Night's Dream" was played on a piano in the gallery. The playing was fine, but the spectators did not listen to it, for they became so excited at the beauty of the tableaus that they rose to their feet and shouted with pleasure, drowning the sweet strains. A beautiful rainbow, made of wire and tarleton, was exhibited during the Norse scenes, and was an excellent imitation of the heavenly arch.

Several prominent Martinez people took characters in the different scenes, among them being George Sherman, who represented Jupiter; Mrs. Sherman, Juno; Mr. Wittenmyer, Mars; Mr. Bailhache, Pluto; Mrs. Davenport, Persephone; Mrs. Mathews, Roman Liberty.

These two entertainments netted two hundred dollars for the church fund.

CONGREGATIONALIST

The Congregationalists instituted their first societies in this county in 1863, in which year they organized two churches, one at Crockett and the other at Clayton. These churches have continued their existence all these years and have served the communities in which they exist with faithfulness. The oldest Congregational church building in the county is that at Clayton, erected in 1868. Crockett has had two church buildings, the first being built in 1883. In 1913 it was so completely remodeled and enlarged as to become practically a new building. The present pastor of this church, the Rev. E. O. Chapel, was the pastor at that time.

In 1865 the society at Antioch was organized and soon thereafter erected a building, which was succeeded in 1891 by the present large and beautiful church. In 1910 a handsome and commodious parsonage was added. The Antioch church is one of the most beautiful and well-kept church properties in the entire county. The Rev. A. B. Roberts has been the pastor since 1912.

Nine years elapsed before another Congregational church was started in the county. In 1874 a society was organized at Martinez. From that time this organization has worked uninterruptedly, and today they have a very attractive church and an uncommonly convenient and commodious manse, centrally and beautifully situated at the county seat. This society numbers among its members now, as it has in the years gone by, many of the substantial and influential men and women of the community. To meet the needs of this rapidly growing center, the church has just called the Rev. George E. Atkinson to become its pastor. He entered upon his work at the beginning of September, 1916. This church is facing a great opportunity and facing it with courage.

In 1882 a church was started at New York Landing, called the Black Diamond Congregational Church. This organization worshiped in the brick schoolhouse for some time, until the church building, at Nortonville was moved to Black Diamond; then later, with the change of the name of the town to Pittsburg, the church's name was changed accordingly. This organization in the years just passed has done much good in the community. It is fully abreast the times. The adequate and artistic parsonage, built a little over a year since, is the home of their energetic and pushing pastor, the Rev. C. C. Champlin. It is just announced that two splendid lots, one on either side of the church property, have been given to the church, looking forward in the near future to the erection of a building adequate to their growing community needs. This church aspires to meet the needs of the Protestant community for all sorts of church and social life.

The Port Costa church was organized and built in 1891. Here a Sunday-school has been maintained faithfully for these years, and the congregation has depended for the most part for its preaching either upon a student from the seminary or a pastor of one of the neighboring churches at Crockett or Benicia.

The Bay Point church was built in 1909 by the co-operation of the community, the lumber company, and the Congregational Conference. A society was organized in 1910. A parsonage was erected two years later. This church has therefore just begun a service that is much needed. '" 3 The last society to be organized in this county by the Congregationalists was at Richmond, in 1915. Its activities are confined to the district across the railroad tracks toward the hills, entirely away from the existing churches, and in response to a demand by the people in that vicinity.

At its organization the pastors of several churches in other parts of the city of Richmond were present, and the council decided to start this church in response to the people's statement of its need in the community. The Rev. J. B. Orr is its pastor at the present time. The rapid growth in membership and in the number of Sunday-school pupils testifies to a good future in store for it.

Perhaps the best page of Congregational history in this county consists in the church deaths it has had. In 1877 a church was started at Pacheco and continued to exist as long as it seemed that a center of any considerable size would exist there. Thus the denomination manifested its desire to be of service to communities that might need it. In 1903, to meet the needs of the newly organized community, a church was started at Oakley. Later the Methodist church at Neroly moved into town; still later a Baptist church was organized. There seemed to be no room for so many Protestant societies in so small a community. The Congregationalists therefore sold the church to the improvement club, and their members work with the Methodist church, thus doing in this county what needs to be done in many places, consolidate little churches into larger ones.

BAPTIST

Baptist history in Contra Costa County is of quality rather than quantity. There are only four Baptist churches now at work in this county, the oldest of which is the San Pablo church. Our Gospel Boat colporteur is visiting a number of towns with a view of organizing missions and churches in destitute religious fields, but this is of the future rather than the present.

The San Pablo church was first organized in the old town of San Pablo, and later was moved to the new town. It is the only Protestant church in the community, and the only Baptist church in the State, so far as we know, that has its own cemetery.

The next oldest is the church at Oakley, which was organized August 10, 1911, with a charter membership of seventeen. This church gave liberally to missions during that year, as they averaged over three dollars a member.

The Point Richmond church was organized in 1911, with a membership of eighteen. Their growth has been steady, and they now have a membership of forty-four.

Calvary Church, Richmond, was organized as a branch of the Point Richmond church January 8, 1912, with a charter membership of thirty-two. They also have had a steady influx of members, now having 108. This church since its organization has always taken a keen interest in missions, having met its budget and sometimes exceeding it every year.

At the present time the Point Richmond church is the only church that has a pastor, although the others will probably call one soon. The Rev. C. W. Howd, a student at the Berkeley Divinity School, is supplying the Point Richmond church as pastor very acceptably.

CHRISTIAN SCIENTIST

The inauguration of the Christian Science movement in Contra Costa County dates from the early part of January, 1909, when seven women who had felt the healing touch of divine love, and whose gratitude could only find expression in giving to the field that which had been of such inestimable value to themselves, met in a private residence and perfected plans for the holding of Christian Science services. Accordingly, two second-floor rooms were rented in the building occupying the southeast corner of Macdonald Avenue and Seventh Street, and the first service was held there on January 17th. Soon, however, these rooms proved inadequate, and it was decided to erect a small building, to be used as a Christian Science reading-room, on a lot in Sixteenth Street owned by one of their number, and in it all the activities of the movement were conducted.

With the removal into their new building in April the attendance increased. The interest manifested seemed to justify an organization, and on May 5, 1909, the Christian Science society of Richmond was organized with eighteen members. In the spring of 1910 the society purchased a lot in Nevin Avenue near Fifteenth Street and moved their building thereon.

While these activities were being conducted the Christian Scientists in the county seat were not unmindful of the good to be accomplished in their field by united action, so only about one year after the Richmond society was organized a similar organization was formed in Martinez, which is still being maintained and is making a steady and stable growth.

The organization of a society which followed close upon that of Martinez was that of Stege, it being formed in the latter part of the year 1910.

Meanwhile Christian Scientists in Antioch were holding meetings in a private residence, but early in the year 1911, as more and more interest was manifested in the work, the hall of the Odd Fellows and Masons was secured, where their services are still being held. In July of the same year the Christian Science society of Antioch was formed, and later purchased a desirable lot and is now contemplating building.

In June, 1912, the society at Richmond disbanded and reorganized as the First Church of Christ, Scientist, in Richmond, and since that time they have twice found it necessary to seek larger quarters; the first time in Pythian Castle, and about one year later in the auditorium of the new building of the Richmond Club, 1125 Nevin Avenue, near Twelfth Street, where their services are now being held.

In July, 1912, the society at Stege reorganized, and Stege having been in the meantime annexed to Richmond, this organization became known as the Second Church of Christ, Scientist, in Richmond. A lot was purchased on Bay Avenue and a small building erected, and there services are still being conducted.

In February, 1913, two women at Walnut Creek began reading the lesson-sermons together, and as this became known others joined them, and very soon the room was outgrown. In April a temporary organization was formed and later Masonic Hall was secured for their regular services. A permanent organization was effected in January, 1914, and a growing interest is being continually manifested in the work there.

The experience at Walnut Creek was not at all unusual and was repeated in Pinole in the summer of 1914, when three persons began reading the lesson-sermons in a private residence and were soon compelled to seek larger quarters. Great interest in Christian Science is being manifested there, and it is only a matter of a little time when the work will be organized.

All the Christian Science organizations have Sunday-schools which are being largely attended, the children being particularly receptive to the truth and verifying the saying of our Master: "Whosoever shall not receive the kingdom of God as a little child shall in no wise enter therein."

The Churches of Christ, Scientist, as well as some of the societies, maintain free reading-rooms and circulating libraries, thus affording the public an opportunity to read or purchase authorized Christian Science literature.

The reader will have noticed that the growth of Christian Science in Contra Costa County has not been phenomenal, but steady and stable; the foundational work being thoroughly well done, the future growth of the movement is assured.

Mary Baker Eddy, the discoverer and founder of Christian Science, denned the church as "The structure of Truth and Love," "That institution which affords proof of its utility," and Christian Scientists everywhere are proving that it does "elevate the race" and is "casting out errors and healing the sick."

EPISCOPAL

The first services of this church within the present boundaries of Contra Costa County, so far as there is any record, was held by the Rt.

Rev. William Ingraham Kip, D. D., Bishop of California, at Martinez, in 1855 or 1856. These were followed in the next few years by occasional service as lay-readers by one or another of the United States Army officers from the arsenal at Benicia. In 1869 a missionary parish was formed and a small church building erected under the direction of the Rev. E. C. Cowan, of Doctor Lloyd Breck's associate mission at Benicia, and named Grace Church.

Under the ministrations of a succession of earnest clergy the parish had a healthy growth, and on the excellent site originally chosen there have since been erected a suitable church building and rectory with other improvements, and a considerable extension of these buildings is now being planned. The present resident priest in charge is the Rev. E. G. Davies.

The next church, called St. Paul's, was built at Walnut Creek in 1891, where a most devoted little band of people have faithfully sustained services under the direction of the Rev. Hamilton Lee, the Rev. Hale Townsend, and others.

At Richmond services were begun and Trinity Church was organized in 1901, by the Rev. D. O. Kelly. A good parsonage on a fine site well up on the hill looking out over the bay toward the Marin County hills, was soon afterward built, and later a church near the business center of the city. The original plan of the beginners of the church here contemplated an institutional work, as best suited to the prospective industrial character of the place. It is hoped such a plan may yet be realized. At present, as in fact it has been from the beginning, nominally at least, the administration of the mission here is under the Venerable John A. Emery, archdeacon of the diocese, through the Cathedral Staff for Missions.

A branch of the Seamen's Institute of the diocese, at Port Costa, with its reading-rooms and chapel nestled upon the hillside overlooking the wharves, should be mentioned as an interesting and valuable work for seafaring men.

Occasional services are held at several other points, as Concord and Lafayette, in the interior of the county.

METHODIST EPISCOPAL

The original Methodist church of Martinez was built on lot 1, block 32, of the original survey of the town. On December 13, 1853, the lot was donated by Seth M. Swain to the following trustees: Isaac P. Van Hagew, William S. Bryant, and Stephen B. Cook. Lots 1 and 2, block 32, and the buildings thereon, were sold to the Congregational church for one thousand dollars on February 8, 1878, by the following trustees: Orris Falls, H. M. Stanage, and W. C. Pratt.

On April 23, 1888, the Rev. M. D. Buck, presiding elder of the Napa district, purchased lots 7 and 8, block 23, for $350, which money was part of sale of original property. On August 2, 1889, the Rev. J. M. Van Every, the pastor, secured a quitclaim deed for them, and the lots were conveyed to the following trustees: James M. Stowe, Samuel Kelly, and D. R. Thomas. On May 30, 1889, a church was organized, but, after consultation with an attorney, it was thought illegal, since the day was a legal holiday. Because of needed time to secure a proper title, the organization was delayed until August 12, 1889, when it took place at Masonic Hall, with the Rev. J. M. Van Every as president and Fanny Van Every as secretary. Brother Van Every brought his family to Martinez, March 22, 1889, and preached his first sermon in Martinez, March 24, 1889, in Bennett's Hall, to a congregation of nine people.

Within a week or two a Sunday-school was formed, and after a month of services in Bennett's Hall the congregation moved to Masonic Hall.

On May 9, 1889, a ladies' aid society was formed. During May and June a course of lectures was given by the following pastors: The Rev. W. W. Case, D. D., pastor of Central Methodist Church, San Francisco; the Rev. Robert Bentley, D. D., presiding elder of Oakland district; and the Rev. E. R. Dille, D. D., pastor of First Methodist Church, Oakland.

On September 16, 1889, Rev. Jas. Blackledge was appointed to Martinez. In March, 1890, Antioch was joined to the charge, and there the pastor preached every Sunday evening. About the same time he also organized a Sunday-school at Pinole and preached there Sunday afternoons.

At the fourth quarterly conference the following trustees were approved: C. F. Diehl, Samuel Kelly, and Hart A. Downer. It was decided to purchase a more central location for the church property, so lots 1 and 2, block 39, were bought from Byron Brown for one thousand dollars, Doctor J. Strentzel lending the money to the trustees for one year without interest. Building on the new church, which was to cost about twenty-five hundred dollars, was begun August 16, 1890. The Rev. D. Brill was appointed to Martinez September 20, 1890.

The new pastor found the frame of the church up and partly enclosed and no money in sight to complete the enterprise.

During the year Doctor Strenzel died, but Mrs. Strenzel and her daughter, Mrs. John Muir, continued to be of great financial help to the church, as Doctor Strenzel had been.

The lots purchased during Brother Van Every's pastorate were sold for six hundred dollars, and shortly after a contract was let to build a parsonage adjoining the church for six hundred and fifty dollars.

On February 15, 1891, the church was opened for dedication, but because of a severe rain-storm was postponed until March.

The Rev. G. M. Meese was pastor in 1893 and 1894. On Christmas day, 1894, Mrs. Strenzel presented to the board of trustees the canceled note for one thousand dollars. This left the church with an indebtedness of two hundred and eighty dollars. During the year Mrs.

Strenzel and Mrs. Muir spent two hundred dollars in improvements on the church. A new organ was secured, and Mrs. Muir paid the bill.

March 2, 1895, Martinez was made a circuit with Pinole.

The pastors of the Martinez church, with time of their pastorate, are as follows: John M. Van Every, March 22, 1889, to September, 1889; James Blackledge, September 16, 1889, to September, 1890; D. Brill, September 20, 1890, to September, 1893; G. M. Meese, September 11, 1893, to September, 1895; E. B. Winning, September 16, 1895, to September, 1896; S. Kinsey, September 15, 1896, to September, 1899; Thomas Leak, September 12, 1899, to September, 1901; J. R. Wolfe, September, 1901, to September, 1902; T. C. Gale, September, 1902; Leon E. Bell, September 19, 1903, to December 27, 1903; George F. Samwell, September, 1904, to September, 1905; M. J. Gough, September, 1905, to September, 1907; E. H. Mackay, September, 1907, to September, 1908; E. J. Bristow, September, 1908, to September, 1910; L. C. Carroll, December, 1915, to date.

Antioch became a charge by itself in 1890, and has continued since, with pastors in charge as follows, in the order named: F. A. Morrow, 1901-1902; J. M. Barnhart, 1902-1906; C. B. Sylvester, January 14, 1907, to September, 1908; T. A. Towner, 1908-1909; Earnest Grigg, 1909-1911; D. O. Colgrove, 1911-1912; L. P. Walker, 1912-1914; W. C. Howard, 1914-1915; and the present pastor, Charles Swithenbank, appointed by Bishop Edwin H. Hughes at the Annual Conference held in San Francisco, in September, 1915.

SEVENTH-DAY ADVENTIST

The Byron Seventh-Day Adventist church was organized in 1913, with a membership of fourteen. A handsome new church was erected in that year costing one thousand dollars. Religious worship is held each Sabbath at three p. m., and Sabbath-school is held at two p. m. on Sabbath day. Doctor J. VV. Hammond, of Byron, is elder, and his wife is treasurer.

CHAPTER XXI. THE MEDICAL PROFESSION

According to early Indian traditions of the San Francisco Bay section of California, there were both medicine-men and medicine-women. The superstitions of these primitive people attributed to them supernatural powers, in virtue of which they were held equal to the chiefs of their tribe. All honor to the medicine-man when he could bring back to his tribesmen strength and endurance for conquests, but should he fail he was apt to be physically punished for his shortcomings.

The great cure-all was the sweat-bath in the sweat-house, or temescal, which, quoting from Bancroft's "Native Races of the Pacific States," "was built in the shape of an inverted bowl, generally about forty feet in diameter at the bottom, built of strong poles and branches of trees, covered with earth to prevent the escape of heat. There was a small hole near the ground, large enough for Diggers to creep in, one at a time, and another at the top to give out the smoke. When a dance is given, a large fire is kindled in the center of the edifice, and the crowd assembles. The apertures, both above and below, are then closed, and the dancers take their positions. Simultaneously with the commencement of the dancing, which is a kind of shuffling hobble-de-hoy, the 'music' bursts forth. Yes, music fit to raise the dead. A whole legion of devils broke loose. Such screaming, shrieking, yelling and roaring was never before heard since the foundation of the world. A thousand cross-cut saws filed by steam power—a multitude of tom-cats lashed together and flung over a clothes-line—innumerable pigs under a gate—all combined would produce a heavenly melody compared to this; yet this uproar, deafening as it is, might possibly be endured, but another sense soon comes to be saluted. Talk of the thousand stinks of the City of Cologne. Here are at least forty thousand combined in one grand overwhelming stench.

Round about the roaring fire the Indians go capering, jumping, and screaming, with the perspiration streaming from every pore. They rush frantically around the walls in hope to discover some weak point through which they may find egress, but the house seems to have been constructed purposely to frustrate such attempts. More furious than caged lions, they rush bodily against the sides, but the stout poles resist every onset." The medicine-man of the rancheria would then open the door and, followed by all the inmates, rush wildly to the river, into which they would plunge, and those who survived the awful shock would gather on the bank to sleep off their exhaustion, and the fandango was over.

In 1833 cholera killed thousands of Indians, destroying whole settlements, and even tribes, often not leaving enough of the living to dispose of the dead.

The dead were held sacred. The burying-ground was a place of religious worship and prayer, although the majority of Indian dead of this section were burned. The funeral bier was a weird scene of wild orgies and cantations of friends and relatives of the deceased.

Mount Diablo, practically centrally situated and rising to a height of nearly four thousand feet, causes a climatography which is peculiar only to Contra Costa County. The ocean winds of the summer and the southeast winds of the winter, blowing against its ragged rocks, antagonize and yet harmonize the seasons most perfectly. The western half of the county, cool and temperate, with a daily ocean breeze, has always been practically free from epidemics of contagious diseases, yet the frail and anemic are here subject to the catarrhal congestions of mucous-membrane diseases.

The great central valley, with its coast windbreak of western hills sheltering it from the fog and the force of heavy winds and giving a modified temperature under the fog-bank without its disagreeable features, forms a recreating and recuperating spot second to none in the United States.

The eastern half, as it dips into the San Joaquin Valley from which the winds are shifted by the great Mount Diablo, has a temperature of fifteen to twenty degrees higher, which, while giving health to the frail and anemic, is somewhat endemic to typhoid and malaria infections.

The mountains of mineral deposits, with the winter rainfall percolating through their crevices, send forth many and various mineral springs. Throughout the county there are many springs of good clear, healthful water, and others with various degrees of saturation with the compounds of sodium, calcium, magnesia, and iron.

The Grand Canon Springs, near Richmond, under the management of I. N. Gates; the Alhambra Springs, under the management of L. M. Lasell; and the Ferndale Springs, in the valleys back of Martinez, are exceptionally good table waters. They are being bottled and shipped by the thousands of gallons and serve to advertise in many homes one of the wonders of Contra Costa County.

September 7, 1847, in Saline, Mich., Lewis Risdon Mead was born. He came to California in 1863, by the way of the Isthmus of Panama, and became identified with his uncle, Orange Risdon, the founder of the Risdon Iron Works, of San Francisco. Orange Risdon located and bought from the Government two hundred acres of land in what is now eastern Contra Costa County, believing that the mineral springs that were located upon the same were of considerable financial value. Under his direction, his nephew, Lewis Risdon Mead, with a party of surveyors, surveyed the tract to ascertain definitely whether or not these springs were located upon the property. Mr. Risdon intended the erection of a large salt-evaporating plant and had the iron pans made at his works in San Francisco, to be sent to what is now Byron, for the purpose of evaporating this water and collecting the salt. Mr. Mead, on going to the place for his survey, found many campers that told him stories of people who had been cured of rheumatism and allied conditions by bathing and drinking these natural waters. In 1868 Mr. Mead built a bath-tub and a small house on what was known as "the sulphur spring," and it received a liberal patronage. In 1872 its popularity had grown so that a ten-room house was built to accommodate the bathers. In 1877 it was rented by H. C. Gallagher, now of Denver, Colorado, who built several bath-houses at the different springs and established a stage-line thence to Byron. In 1880 Mr. Mead again took possession of the springs, and their wonderful development and popularity throughout California, the United States, and abroad were due entirely to his personal management. He caused the salt-beds to be filled with ten or twelve feet of good earth, in order to grow the beautiful trees and shrubbery which now surround the hotel. In 1901 the first hotel, erected at a cost of $50,000, was destroyed by fire. In 1902 this was supplanted by a $150,000 Moorish building, built by Reid Brothers, of San Francisco, after which Byron Hot Springs became one of the best-known resorts in California. Unfortunately, this hotel was burned in 1912. It was, however, replaced in 1914 by another fire-proof building, costing $100,000. A few days after Mr. Mead furnished the writer this data he died from acute bronchial pneumonia, June 13, 1916. There has been no man who has been more active and helpful in the development and the growth and welfare of Contra Costa County than

Lewis Risdon Mead. He has left his handiwork written as an enduring monument in the large industry which he developed, in the cordial friendship with the men of affairs of central California, and in the health and affection portrayed in the countenances of thousands of people who were relieved of suffering to become useful and happy men and women, owing to his organization and work. He was an active Mason, one of the founders of Brooklyn Lodge No. 225, of Oakland, and a member of the Knights Templars and of the Mystic Shrine. He was also a regent of the University of California and president of the Mechanics Institute of San Francisco for many years. He was an active Republican, and at all times a constructive builder.

The early history of Contra Costa County is largely a record of the work of physicians who were lured to the Golden West by the spirit of adventure. In each section of the county is the name of some physician who was a determining factor in its material development.

The most striking character in the early drama of Contra Costa County is that of Doctor John Marsh, who was born in Danvers, Massachusetts, June 5, 1799. His academic work was taken at Harvard University, from which he graduated. His medical course was taken at Fort Snelling (now St. Paul), Minnesota, after which his love of adventure started him on his course. He traveled through practically the whole United States, engaging in the Indian wars of the West from 1828 to 1835. He drifted through the southern portions of the United States and northern Mexico, reaching what is now Los Angeles, and coming north to the base of the great Mount Diablo about 1836 or 1837. Doctor Marsh's personal appearance was commanding, his adroitness as a manager great. He had seen much of life, was a keen observer of men and things, was a thorough French and Spanish scholar, and had a very versatile mind. Many articles from his pen, descriptive of the country and dealing with the romance of the early Spanish-Indian days of California, appeared in Eastern publications. He obtained a grant of several thousand acres of land from the Mexican Government on the east base of Mount Diablo, which title was later confirmed by the United States. This he stocked with cattle. When the gold excitement came his land and cattle greatly advanced in value, until he became a very wealthy man. Doctor Marsh was not actively engaged in his professional calling, practicing only among the many people he employed, and who were settled upon his large estate, and those of his neighbors and friends. On September 24, 1856, he was foully murdered by three discharged employees near Concord, while on his way to Martinez.

Doctor S. J. Tennent was born in Liverpool, England, January 5, 1818, and graduated in medicine from London University. Being enthused with a spirit of romance and adventure, he shipped on board a whaling vessel for the Sandwich Islands, where for a few years he practiced medicine, becoming physician to the king of the islands. His roving disposition caused him to drift to San Francisco, where he landed a short time prior to the period of the discovery of gold in California. On September 8, 1849, he married Rafaela Martinez, daughter of the commandant of the Presidio of San Francisco. On account of this marriage he inherited a large tract of land between Pinole and Martinez and gave his attention principally to farming and stock-raising.

On April 11, 1854, he was appointed county physician, which position he held until February 8, 1872. He established the first drug-store in Martinez, in 1858.

Doctor E. F. Hough was born in New York October 23, 1823, graduating from Berea College, Ohio, in 1839, and studying medicine in Cleveland, Ohio. He came to California with the first rush for gold.

After spending a short time at various parts of the State, he came to Contra Costa County in October, 1853, and settled in the Ygnacio Valley, where he was one of the earliest settlers. There being very few white citizens, and the practice of medicine not being at all lucrative, he opened a store, which he abandoned in 1855 and came to Martinez, where he established the Hough Hotel, which he conducted for a quarter of a century. It is said he was the first discoverer of mineral paints in California. While a man of affairs and influence in the social development of the county, he was never actively engaged in the practice of medicine.

The grand old patriarch of Contra Costa County was without question Doctor James H. Carothers. He was born in Beaver County, Pennsylvania, September 5, 1823. His academic work was taken at Ohio Wesleyan University, Delaware, Ohio, and he graduated in medicine from Miami Medical University. He came to California in 1852, visited many different sections of the State, and finally decided upon Contra Costa County as his home. He went back to Ohio to bring his family to his new home, and in 1854 returned to California for permanent residence in Contra Costa County, where he actively established himself in the practice of medicine. About 1860 he bought sixty acres of land from Don Salvador Pacheco and laid out the town of Pacheco. Here he built stores, houses, and his own residence, and this town was for a long time the active business center of central Contra Costa County. In 1869 he was elected to the State legislature upon the Republican ticket.

On August 5, 1874, he was appointed county physician, which position he held for many years. In 1874 he moved back to Martinez, and this place remained his home until his death. His practice extended the full length of Contra Costa County, and he will always stand out as the most noted man in the medical history of Contra Costa County. He assisted in organizing the California State Medical Society, and in June, 1877, organized and became president of the first Contra Costa Medical Society, and in this society he always maintained an active membership.

Among those who had the good fortune to know Doctor Carothers he will be remembered as one of the brightest and most successful characters it was ever their lot to meet.

ANTIOCH.—In Antioch it appears that the first physician was Doctor Samuel Adams, who located about 1853, and confined his work to the treating of ulcers and tumors, which he invariably diagnosed as cancers. He died in 1880. About 1860 Doctor John R. Howard located in Antioch, and actively practiced medicine until 1874, when he moved to Oakland. About 1864 Doctor Van Black and Doctor Mayberry located.

Doctor Ruggles came in 1866. Doctor Emmett L. Wemple located in Nortonville in 1873, and in a short time moved to Antioch, from which place he extensively practiced medicine in eastern Contra Costa County until 1888, when he moved to San Francisco. Doctor M. C. Parkison located in Antioch in 1875, where he continued to practice medicine until his death in 1910. Doctor Frank Rattan bought the practice of Doctor E. L. Wemple in 1888, and continued to practice in Antioch until 1901, when he moved to Martinez. Doctor T. B. De Witt came in 1891, and practiced a short time, and then moved to San Francisco. Doctor W. S. George came to Antioch a few months after Doctor Rattan and has been in continuous practice since that time. Besides being a very busy physician, he has always been very active in the social and political affairs of his town and county. Doctor J. W. De Witt located in Antioch in 1894, after his uncle moved to San Francisco. He has been in continuous active practice throughout eastern Contra Costa County since that time. He is one of the most active men in this county at the present time. Doctor Chas. B. Fisher located in Antioch in 1906 and remained about one year. Doctor Edward A. Diggins came to Antioch in 1911 from San Francisco, since which time he has continued to practice in Antioch. Shortly after his arrival in Antioch he established a private hospital, which he conducted for a short time. Doctor Carlotta R. Deckelman located in Antioch in 1915, and has built up a good practice.

The following is an early fee schedule from the office of Doctor M. C. Parkison, adopted by the physicians of Contra Costa County early in 1870: The following rates of charges have been agreed upon by the undersigned physicians of Contra Costa County:

For each prescription or advice at office $2.00
For special office examination 5.00
For each visit in town during day time 2.50
For each visit in town during night time, 10 p. m. to 7 a. m. 5.00
For visits one mile from residence and under five miles $3.00 to 5.00
For visits over five miles from residence, per mile ... 1.00
For visits in consultation with usual mileage fee 5.00
For ordinary midwifery with usual mileage fee 20.00
For midwifery when instruments are required. $40.00 to 100.00

M. C. Parkison, M. D.
O. B. Adams, M. D.
E. L. Wemple, M. D.
G. E. Alexander, M. D.
John Leffler, M.D.
D. Walker, M. D.
J. H. Carothers, M. D.
H. V. Mott, M. D.

EXTRACT FROM CODE OF ETHICS

"A physician ought not to take charge of, or prescribe for, a patient who has recently been under the care of another member of the faculty in the same illness, except in cases of sudden emergency, or in consultation with the physician previously in attendance, or when the latter has relinquished the case, or been regularly notified that his services are no longer desired."

BAY POINT. —At the time of the establishment of the C. A. Smith Lumber Company at Bay Point in 1911, Doctor George McKenzie, of Concord, established an emergency hospital for the care of the sick and injured of the company. He has been continuously in charge of it since that time. In 1911 Doctor Orlando Pearson located in Bay Point, where he remained six months.

BRENTWOOD. —A great deal can be written concerning the early doctors of the vicinity of Brentwood and Byron. The earliest and most conspicuous is that of Doctor John Marsh, whose history has been briefly given. Doctor Patterson located near Bethany in the eastern end of the county in the late '60s. His practice reached as far as the neighborhood of Antioch. He remained a good many years. Doctor C. A. E. Hertell practiced in the district about 1869 or 1870. He was a Methodist minister and located at what was known as Point of Timber. He was of the old school and believed that calomel was the Hercules of Materia Medica. Doctor Meyers located in the vicinity in the '70s, and was known as the French doctor who performed miracles. Doctor Charles Connors came to Brentwood in 1886 or 1887 from Los Angeles and remained about two years. Doctor H. V. Mott located in Marsh Creek about 1880, later removing to Brentwood, where he practiced until he died. Doctor J. E. Marsh came to Brentwood about 1898, practicing a short time. Doctor William B. Marsh located in Brentwood in 1893 and practiced a short time. He was followed by his brother-in-law, Doctor C. A. Bell, who remained two years. Doctor J. W. Ellis located on a farm near Oakley in 1896 and practiced until 1904. At present he is retired from active work. Doctor H. Rozsas located in Brentwood in 1900 and practiced one year. He was followed by Doctor J. T. Gardner, who practiced for a short time. Doctor A. C. Bowerman then located in Brentwood, where he remained one year. Doctor George F. Wise followed Doctor Gardner. After remaining eighteen months, he was compelled to leave on account of poor health. Doctor Frank S. Cook came to Brentwood immediately following the earthquake and fire in San Francisco, and he is still actively practicing his profession. He is widely known, particularly on account of his genial personality, in eastern Contra Costa County, and is a prominent factor in its present development. Doctor L. B. Weatherbee located in Oakley in 1914 and has a very good practice.

BYRON. —The first man to locate in Byron was Doctor W. K. Doherty. His custom was to scatter handbills in the street, drifting them from the porches and windows, announcing himself as "the great venereal doctor." Doctor J. W. Hammond was next to locate in Byron, about 1898, where he has been continuously in active practice. He has deservedly enjoyed the utmost confidence of the people of this vicinity.

Doctor Louis Mead, whose father was the founder and able manager of the Byron Hot Springs for many years, was resident physician at the springs about 1906. After remaining there for a few years, he moved to San Francisco.

CONCORD. —In 1853 Doctor E. F. Hough located in the Ygnacio Valley, conducting a store and practicing medicine. He moved to Martinez in 1855. There was no physician located in this vicinity until Doctor J. H. Carothers located the town of Pacheco, where he resided until 1876. When Doctor Carothers moved to Martinez to assume the position of county health officer, Doctor Leffler moved to Pacheco, and practiced in Pacheco and Concord until 1891, when he returned to Martinez.

About 1880 Doctor Edmund Bragdon moved from Martinez to Concord, and remained until about 1888, when he returned to Martinez.

Doctor F. Bass practiced for a short time in 1886. Doctor Hayward G. Thomas came to Concord in 1887, when, after three years in general practice, he removed to Oakland, where he now lives, and limits his practice to eye, ear, nose, and throat work. In 1890 Doctor F. F. Neff, a graduate of Jefferson Medical College, located in Concord. He is one of the very finest types of men, has been continuously closely connected with the development of Concord, has an exceptionally large practice, and possesses a host of loyal friends. The people of Concord have been particularly fortunate in their medical care. As a colleague of Doctor Neff's, Doctor George McKenzie, of Toronto University, located here in 1891. He is a very efficient, attentive, and busy physician, has continuously been in charge of the emergency hospital at Bay Point, and has taken a particular interest in the development of the Concord school system. Doctor McKenzie is a brother of Superior Judge A. B. McKenzie. Doctor Hamlin was located in Concord for a short time in the early '90s. During the smallpox epidemic of 1900 and 1901, Doctor E. A. Ormsby, brother of Assistant District Attorney A. S. Ormsby, was located in Concord. Doctor W. N. Finney located in Concord in 1912 and has a very good practice. Doctor E. E. Johnson came in 1914. He is a man of ability and will build up a very good practice.

COWELL. —Doctor W. E. Bixby was the first physician for the Cowell-Portland Cement Company. He practiced from 1909 to 1913, and in 1913 Doctor F. B. Cone succeeded him. Doctor C. C. Fitzgibbon succeeded Doctor Cone in 1914 and is now resident physician. Besides the company work he has a very good general practice.

CROCKETT. —Doctor J. S. Riley moved from Port Costa to Crockett in 1893 and established a very extensive practice. He always had a great interest in all civic affairs, and during his long practice in this vicinity aided greatly in its development. After a very useful life, he died from cancer of the tongue in 1909. Doctor H. N. Yates located in Valona in 1897, established a very extensive practice, and remained about six years. Doctor F. S. Cook came to Crockett in 1898 and remained about eighteen months. Doctor William C. Yates became associated with his brother, Doctor H. N. Yates, about 1901, and remained in Crockett about two years. Doctor Otto M. Schultz came to Crockett in 1901, but only remained a short time. Doctor J. W. Key moved from Pinole to Crockett in 1902, remained there several years, and built up an extensive practice. Doctor A. H. White located in Crockett in 1906 and remained about eighteen months. He established a hospital in Valona, which he conducted for a short time. Doctor George W. Sweetser came to Crockett in 1907 and remained until 1914. Doctor William F. Booth and his brother, Edwin F. Booth, after conducting a general merchandise store in Valona for several years, studied naturopathy, and registered to practice in Valona in 1907 and 1909 respectively. Doctor F. A. McManus located in Crockett in 1912, and after a few months of busy practice, while returning from making a call upon a patient, was accidentally killed by a Southern Pacific train at Vallejo Junction. Doctor J. G. Harrington located for a few months in 1914. Doctor J. H. Adams came to Crockett in 1914 and has built up a very extensive practice along this section of the water-front. Doctor G. M. O'Malley came in 1915 and has made many friends during the short time he has been here.

DANVILLE. —The first physician to locate in Danville was Doctor J. S. Labaree, who came in 1854 and remained until his death, in 1860.

Doctor George E. Alexander located here in 1870 and remained several years. Doctor E. R. Layne practiced for a short time in 1894. Doctor George W. Desrosier located in 1896 and remained a short time. Doctor H. C. Reamer located in 1901 and built up an extensive practice. He retired in 1915 on account of poor health. In 1916 Doctor Love came from Pasadena to Danville and has a good practice.

MARTINEZ. —In 1849 Doctor William B. Bolton located in what is now Martinez. In the list of names of voters of 1850 appears the name of Doctor George Lawrence. Doctor John Strentzel came in 1853 and was one of the most active of the early men of central Contra Costa County. He helped organize and was the first master of the Alhambra Grange, and was active in the building and management of the Grangers' warehouse. Doctor J. H. Carothers came to Martinez in 1852, but only remained a short time, and moved to Pacheco. He later relocated in Martinez in 1874. Doctor E. F. Hough moved from the Ygnacio Valley to Martinez in 1855. He spent most of his time conducting a hotel, although he did some active practice. Doctor C. A. Ruggles located in 1858. Doctor Charles E. Holbrook located late in the '60s, and succeeding in 1872 Doctor S. J. Tennent, of Pinole Valley, as county physician.

Doctor Edmund Bragdon located in 1872, remained a few years, and then moved to Concord. He later returned to Martinez, where he died.

Doctor John Leffler located in 1874, moved to Pacheco in 1876, and returned to Martinez again in 1891, where he died. About 1875 Doctor J. R. Howard located in Martinez. He was a man of considerable literary ability. Several of his articles appeared in the early periodicals, being mostly descriptive of central California. Doctor H. V. Bernett located in Martinez in 1877. Doctor E. E. Brown, who was a resident of Martinez, and whose family were to a great extent the molders of the early political and social affairs of central Contra Costa County, graduated at the Kentucky School of Medicine in 1882, and immediately located in Martinez. He built up a very extensive practice and held many positions of honor and trust in the community, being county physician for many years. He died in Martinez in 1913. The first woman physician, Mrs. M. A. Howard, located in 1885, remaining only a few months. Doctor Charles G. Merrell came to Martinez in 1886, remained two years, and moved to San Francisco in 1888. Doctor John B. Tennent, the son of Doctor S. J. Tennent, one of the first settlers of Contra Costa County, was the first county physician—from 1895 to 1897.

He graduated at the Cooper Medical College in 1888 and returned to the county of his birth, soon becoming one of the busiest and best-known men in Contra Costa County. After a few short years of active work, he died in October, 1897. Doctor Joseph T. Breneman located in Martinez in 1892 and soon established a very large practice. He served as county health officer for many years, having charge during the smallpox epidemic in the years 1900 to 1901, and at one time had one hundred and fifty-three cases in quarantine. It is stated that no case gave a history of previous vaccination. In 1908 he established a private hospital in Martinez, which he conducted for some time. He moved to Rust in 1911. Doctor Mary Leonard Murphy located in 1897 and remained until 1901. In 1899, at the time of the building of the San Joaquin Valley Railroad, now part of the Santa Fe system, Doctor A. P. Mulligan was the railroad company's surgeon, and remained in Martinez and vicinity during the period of construction. Doctor John E. Fleming located in Martinez in 1893 and remained only a short time. Doctor Frank Rattan moved from Antioch to Martinez in 1901 and built up an extensive practice. He established a drug-store, which he personally conducted. After a few years of very hard work, Doctor Rattan was compelled to retire on account of ill-health. He has been practically confined to his home for several years, but in defiance of his painful malady he has at all times preserved his cheerful and cordial friendships.

His retirement from active practice has been deeply regretted, both by his colleagues and his many loyal friends. Doctor George W. Sweetser first came to Martinez in 1903. He remained four years, then moved to Crockett, returning again to Martinez in 1914. Doctor Sweetser has a legion of friends and has a very extensive practice. Doctor George P. Wintermute came to Martinez in 1897 and remained one year. In 1905 Doctor Edwin Merrithew moved from Geyserville to Martinez. His cheerful personality and attention to his work has made him one of the busiest men of Contra Costa County. He has been county physician since 1910. Doctor William S. Lavy came to Martinez in 1910 and remained for eighteen months. Doctor E. B. Fitzpatrick became associated with Doctor Frank Rattan in 1911, and two years later, when Doctor Rattan was forced to retire on account of ill-health, succeeded him.

He has been secretary of the County Medical Society for many years and is a very busy man. He was married in September, 1916. Doctor J. H. Hawkins located in Martinez in 1915 and for the short time which he has been here, is building up a very good practice.

NORTONVILLE.—Dr. Emmett L. Wemple located in 1873 and remained a short time. Doctor Joseph L. Woolford practiced in the late '70s. Doctor R. D. Spedding succeeded Doctor Woolford. Doctor Hugo Rozsas had an extensive practice in Nortonville until the mines closed down in 1884.

PINOLE.—Doctor S. J. Tennent came to what is now Pinole in 1849, but did not devote his entire time to the practice of medicine, although he served as county physician for a number of years. Doctor J. McI. Morrison located in Pinole in 1896, and was the first actual active practitioner in the town. Doctor Morrison remained in Pinole for about four years, and in 1905 relocated there for a few months. Doctor R. B. Stanley Smith located in Pinole in 1901 and remained about one year.

Doctor J. W. Key came in 1901 and stayed one year. Doctor Herbert Watt practiced in Pinole from 1902 to 1905. Doctor Devore followed Doctor Key, and Doctor H. Y. Baldwin came in 1906 and remained for a few months. Doctor M. L. Fernandez came from San Francisco to Pinole in 1906 and has been in continuous practice here since that time.

Pinole was the birthplace of Doctor Fernandez and his boyhood home. His father had very extensive business interests here. The Doctor has established a very extensive practice and is undoubtedly one of the busiest men in Contra Costa County. He also has extensive business interests. Doctor F. P. McManus came as an assistant to Doctor Fernandez in 1916 and is resident physician at the Hercules Powder Company.

PITTSBURG. —The history of a considerable part of the growth and development of Pittsburg can be written around the name of Doctor Frank S. Gregory. He graduated from the Cooper Medical College in 1900, and soon after located in Pittsburg. He had the confidence and patronage of the entire population of this city and was very active in its economic and social development, serving for many years as chairman of the city council and as a member of its school board. He was perhaps the most active man in Pittsburg in its civic development. In 1914 he made an extended visit in the East while engaged in postgraduate studies, and after returning to California located in Redwood City. In 1913 Doctor Lucian A. Bauter located in Pittsburg and has built up a good practice. Doctor W. A. Nicolson succeeded Doctor F. S. Gregory and remained for about a year and a half, and later removed to Oakland. Doctor S. H. Marks succeeded Doctor Nicolson, and has made many friends, building up an extensive practice. Doctor H. E. Peters located in Pittsburg early in 1915. He is a man with a very genial personality and of good medical training and is a very busy practitioner.

PORT COSTA. —The first physician to locate along the Port Costa Crockett water-front was Doctor J. S. Riley, who came to Port Costa in 1882, and was physician for the Southern Pacific Company until 1893. Doctor A. W. Rickey came to Port Costa in 1892 and was appointed the Southern Pacific Company's physician, to succeed Doctor Riley, and remained in Port Costa until 1912. He served as county physician from 1905 to 1911.

RICHMOND. —The first physician to locate in Richmond was Doctor L. T. Gorsuch, who came to Richmond in the early part of 1901. He was the first surgeon of the Santa Fe Railroad Company, had a good practice, and built a fine home. He unfortunately contracted pulmonary tuberculosis and was forced to leave Richmond in May, 1903, going to the mountains for his health. He died that fall. Doctor George W. Stockwell came to Richmond from San Pablo in the summer of 1901, practiced for about two years, when he succumbed to an attack of acute appendicitis. Doctor P. C. Campbell came to Richmond in the fall of 1901 and has been in continuous practice since that time. He has always been a very popular man. He was a member of Governor Pardee's staff and had charge of the State medical aid during the earthquake and fire in San Francisco. He served as assemblyman in this district in 1908 and was president of the County Medical Society in 1916.

Doctor J. McI. Morrison came from Pinole to Richmond late in the fall of 1903 and enjoyed a good practice. He served as city health officer, remaining in Richmond until 1911, when he went to Portola. He died of cancer of the stomach in 1913. Doctor L. Goldschmidt located in Richmond for a few months in 1902, then moved to Los Angeles, where he now lives. Doctor U. S. Abbott and Doctor H. N. Barney came to Richmond on the same Santa Fe ferry-boat early in 1902. Doctor Abbott assisted Doctor Gorsuch in his practice for a few months, when he became ship surgeon on a German steamer and went to Germany.

After spending a short time in German cities he returned to New York for short postgraduate work, and located in Grand Junction, Colorado, where he lived until 1908. He came to Richmond in 1908 and became associated with Doctor C. L. Abbott in establishing the Abbott Hospital. He has many friends and a good practice. Doctor Barney served as city health officer and has always had an extensive practice. On account of his cheerful personality, he is prominent in fraternal circles.

Ill-health forced him to retire in 1916, a fact that is deeply regretted by his colleagues and many loyal friends. Doctor H. F. Worley assisted Doctor Gorsuch in his practice for a few months during his illness.

Doctor C. L. Abbott moved from San Pablo to Richmond in the summer of 1902, succeeding Doctor Gorsuch. He has served as surgeon for the Santa Fe Railroad Company since 1903, was a member of the committee which secured the incorporation of the city of Richmond, has served as county coroner since 1907, and was a member of the board of freeholders which drafted the first city charter. Doctor C. R. Blake came in 1903, and at all times has had an extensive practice. He reorganized the city health department and has given to the city of Richmond undoubtedly one of the best health departments of any city of its size. Doctor Blake since 1914 has been limiting his practice to eye, ear, nose, and throat work, being the first of Richmond's medical men to take up a specialty. Doctor L. K. Riley came to Richmond in 1903, has always had a good practice, and has found time to assist in the civic affairs of the city. Doctor W. B. Brown came to Richmond early in 1903 and published the Richmond Terminal newspaper. He has always been a good booster for the town. Dr. William S. Lucas arrived in Richmond in the fall of 1903. He has always been attentive and an efficient man in his work, has lived continuously in Richmond, and has an extensive practice. Doctor W. E. Cunningham came to Richmond in 1905. He has a splendid personality, is attentive and capable in his work, and is now one of the best-known men in Contra Costa County. He built a fine business building on Macdonald Avenue in 1916.

Doctor J. W. O'Brien located in Richmond in 1906, remained about one year, then moved to Sacramento, where he now lives. Doctor Marguerite Deininger-Keser came to Richmond as an assistant to Doctor C. L. Abbott in 1907, and after two years of associated practice with the latter, established her own office. She has always had a good practice and many loyal friends. Doctor A. E. Byron came to Richmond in 1907 as a representative of the North American Hospital Association.

He remained about eighteen months, and was succeeded by Doctor Thornburg, who remained about nine months. Doctor H. V. Prouty succeeded Dr. Thornburg in the Hospital Association, and established a private hospital on Twelfth Street, which he conducted for a short time. Doctor Prouty lived in Richmond about three years. Doctor L. A. Martin moved from San Pablo to Richmond in 1911 and was house physician to the Abbott Hospital until 1914, when he assumed a similar position with the Roosevelt Hospital and moved to Berkeley. Doctor Hall Vestal came to Richmond in the fall of 1910. He has an extensive practice and has taken a considerable interest in the social and civic affairs of the city. Doctor R. Del Mas located in Richmond for a few months in the winter of 1911 and 1912. Doctor W. E. Caesar came to Richmond in 1912 and soon built up a very good practice. He established the Barrett Sanitarium in 1916, which he now conducts. Doctor H. T. Risdon in 1912 located in Richmond for a few months. Doctor S. M. Benner came in 1912 and remained one year. Doctor C. H. Woodruff, osteopath, located in 1913, and remained until 1916, when he moved to Napa. Doctor H. L. Carpenter came in 1913, and for the short time he has been here has a very big practice. He is well liked by his colleagues and has many loyal friends. Doctor W. W. Frazer came to Richmond in 1913 and has a good practice. Doctor J. B. Taylor located in Richmond for a few months in 1914. Doctor I. B. March came to Richmond in 1914 and established a good practice. He entered the U. S. Army Medical Reserve staff in 1916 and is now stationed at Monterey. Doctor C. H. Gibbons registered to practice in Richmond in 1914.

Doctor H. N. Belgum established the Belgum Sanitarium in 1914 for the care of nervous diseases and is medical superintendent of the same. In 1915 Doctor M. F. Underwood was located here for a few months.

RUST. —In 1911 Dr. Joseph T. Breneman located at Rust.

SAN PABLO. —About 1855 Doctor David Goodale came to San Pablo, settled on a ranch, and engaged in farming and stock-raising. His practice of medicine was limited to that of his employees and neighbors. He died about 1885 in San Francisco. Doctor Jacob M. Tewksbury came from South America to San Pablo and bought a large tract of land, which he leased to tenants. He did not actively engage in the practice of medicine, and part of the time lived in San Francisco. He died in the early '70s. Doctor Kingsbury was the first man to devote his entire time to the practice of medicine. He located in 1868 and remained about four years. Doctor Dunbar came in 1870 and remained five years. Doctor O. B. Adams came from Oakland in 1876 and built up an extensive practice, later returning to Oakland, but continued to have a large practice through the San Pablo country. Doctor Hatch also located in 1876 but remained only a short time. Doctor C. C. Kelley practiced for a few months in 1877. Doctor L. Wallendorff located here in 1878. He continued his study of medicine at the California Medical College at Oakland and had his original certificate canceled in April, 1880, registering as a graduate from the California Medical College. He remained in San Pablo about four years. Doctor Harwood came in 1880 and remained about one year. Doctor Bramman located in what is now Rust and practiced in the vicinity of San Pablo. Doctor Larkin came to San Pablo in 1884 and remained about two years. Doctor Smith practiced for a few months in 1885. Doctor John Gardner located in 1887 and remained about three years. Doctor C. E. Camp first came to San Pablo about 1891, where he continued to practice until 1899, when he moved to Honolulu. He returned to San Pablo again in 1908, where he has since resided. Doctor Camp has at all times had a very extensive practice throughout the San Pablo Valley and is undoubtedly the best-known practitioner in this vicinity. Doctor J. McI. Morrison located in 1894, remained two years, and moved to Pinole. Doctor E. G. Bennett located in 1898, practiced two years, then moved to Petaluma. Doctor George W. Stockwell succeeded Doctor Camp in 1899, remained about eighteen months, then moved to Richmond. Doctor C. L. Abbott succeeded Dr. Bennett in August, 1900, remained eighteen months, then moved to Richmond. Doctor L. A. Martin succeeded Doctor Abbott in 1902, remained in San Pablo until 1911, when he moved to Richmond.

WALNUT CREEK. —The first physician reported to have been located in what is now Walnut Creek was Doctor Smith, about 1859. In 1868 Doctor Rowan was located at Bareges Springs and practiced in the vicinity of Walnut Creek for about ten years. Doctor C. C. Kelley located here in 1877 for a short time. Doctor J. E. Pearson came in 1878. Doctor W. E. Hook, a brother of Supervisor Vincent Hook, after graduating at the University of California, returned to Walnut Creek, where he practiced a short time. Unfortunately, Doctor Hook died at a very early age. Doctor E. E. Brown practiced here for a short time about 1880. Doctor W. F. Lynch came in 1885. Doctor Joseph T. Breneman was here from 1895 to 1897. Doctor C. R. Leech practiced here from 1897 to 1902. Doctor Fred Watt came in 1902 and remained until 1904.

Doctor C. R. Leech returned to Walnut Creek in 1904 and has since that time made it his home. To think of Walnut Creek is to think of Doctor Leech, a man of excellent personality and exceptional ability. He has a very extensive practice throughout the San Ramon Valley.

Doctor Charles Allen Stevens, osteopath, practiced for a short time in 1907. Doctor Carolyn C. Cole came in 1910 and devoted part of her time to the practice of medicine. Doctor Louise A. Oldenbourg, who is specializing in anesthetics, has made Walnut Creek her home since 1915.

HOSPITALS. —Prior to 1880 the Board of Supervisors awarded contracts to private persons for the board and care of indigent sick, the price of clothing and medicine and physician's bills not to be taken into consideration. These contracts were awarded for one year. On June 16, 1880, the board purchased lots 163-165 of the original survey of the town of Martinez, for the sum of $825, to be used as the site for the county infirmary. In 1881 the contract was let for the erection of three one-story buildings for hospital purposes, upon the county hospital grounds, according to plans and specifications prepared by E. W. Hiller.

The contract was let to Lamb & Ferrie for $3225. In 1910, according to plans and specifications furnished by Architect Weeks, R. H. Ingraham, contractor, built the first wing of the present hospital, at a cost 1 of about $40,000, and in 1914 the second wing was built, at a cost of $36,000. The hospital grounds contain seven acres. In 1910-11 there were 298 patients admitted to the hospital; in 1915-16 there were 666 patients admitted. The hospital staff consists of a superintendent, a surgeon-in-chief, an assistant surgeon, a matron, and five graduate nurses. Statistics for the year ending June 30, 1916, are as follows: The average daily number of patients, 97.22; the average daily per capita cost, seventy-eight cents; average daily number of employees, fifteen.

Patients are admitted to the county hospital by permits from their supervisor. All classes of cases are admitted. Paid patients are charged for at the rate of fifteen dollars a week for room and board, including general nursing. The ward rates are ten dollars a week. Special nurse's board is fifty cents a day. The county hospital has juvenile detention and insane detention departments. W. H. Hough has been superintendent practically ever since the completion of the new building, in 1910, during which time he has been an efficient, capable manager, and established the first organized and regular system of accounting. The Hercules Powder Company established an emergency hospital at Hercules in 1902, which has been continuously conducted. Doctor A. H. White established a private hospital at Valona in 1906, which he conducted for about two months. Doctor Joseph T. Breneman established a private hospital in Martinez in 1907, which he conducted for about six months.

Doctor C. L. Abbott and Doctor U. S. Abbott established the Abbott Hospital in Point Richmond in 1908. This hospital had a capacity of twenty-five beds. Doctor L. A. Martin was medical superintendent. It was a general hospital until 1913, since which time it has been conducted only as an emergency hospital. Doctor George McKenzie established an emergency hospital at Bay Point in 1909, of which he still has charge. Doctor Edward A. Diggins established the Valley Hospital at Antioch in 1911, which he conducted about one year. Miss Jeanie Craven established the Craven Hospital at Richmond in 1913, which she has continuously conducted. It is the largest general hospital besides the county hospital in the county. Doctor Blumenburg established the "A-B-C" Hospital at Walnut Creek in 1914. The Standard Oil Company has a beautiful and complete emergency hospital at its refinery in Richmond, established in 1915. During the first year there were over four thousand patients treated at this hospital. Doctor Charles A. Dukes is surgeon-in-chief; Doctor C. L. Abbott, Doctor U. S. Abbott, Doctor W. S. Lucas, and Doctor W. E. Cunningham are associate surgeons. Miss N. Y. Frazer is nurse in charge, and Miss Lydiksen assistant nurse. Doctor W. E. Caesar established the Barrett Sanitarium in Richmond in 1916.

COUNTY PHYSICIANS. —The first county physician was Doctor S. J. Tennent, appointed April 11, 1854. He served until February 8, 1872, when he was succeeded by Doctor Charles E. Holbrook. Doctor Holbrook resigned August 5, 1874 and was succeeded by Doctor J. H. Carothers. Doctor H. Bernett succeeded Doctor Carothers August 4, 1880 and served until February 4, 1895. Doctor J. B.

Tennent was then appointed and served until January 18, 1897. Doctor E. E. Brown was then appointed and held the position until February 1, 1897. He was then succeeded by Doctor J. B. Tennent, who served until November 1, 1897, when he died. Doctor E. E. Brown was then appointed and served until January 3, 1903. Doctor A. W. Rickey succeeded Doctor Brown until March 6, 1911, when Doctor Edwin Merrithew was appointed, and has served continuously since that time.

COUNTY HEALTH OFFICERS. —When Dr. J. H. Carothers was appointed county physician in 1874 he also assumed the position of county health officer, which he held until 1882. Dr. H. Bernett, who was then county physician, was appointed health officer and served until 1895. From 1895 until June, 1897, there was a health officer appointed in each supervisor district. On June 1, 1897, Doctor Joseph T. Breneman was appointed and served until July 8, 1904, when he was succeeded by Doctor George McKenzie. Doctor W. S. George, of Antioch, was appointed September 5, 1905, and served until September 7, 1906, when his successor, Doctor J. W. De Witt, was appointed. Doctor Frank S. Gregory was appointed September 5, 1908, and served until September 5, 1911, when Doctor W. S. George was appointed to the position, which he has held continuously since that time.

HEALTH DEPARTMENT OF RICHMOND. —The first health officer appointed in the city of Richmond was Doctor H. N. Barney, having been appointed November 27, 1905. He served until April 28, 1908, when he was succeeded by Doctor J. McI. Morrison, who served until July 6, 1909, when Doctor H. N. Barney was again appointed to the position of commissioner of health under the new charter. On March 6, 1910, he was succeeded by Doctor C. R. Blake, who has served continuously up to the present time. The sanitary requirements of the growing city have caused the health department to grow from one man, a single health officer without a city office, to the present force, which consists of a commissioner of health, a sanitary inspector, two assistant sanitary inspectors, a chemist, a market and meat inspector, and a stenographer.

The department is active in every line that will benefit the health of its citizens. Vacant lots are kept clean of all rubbish, official fly-traps and rat-traps are in operation all over the city. Meat markets, vegetable markets, hotels, stores, stables, and back yards are regularly inspected.

Milk is regularly tested in the city laboratory. All milk sold in the city is required to be pasteurized. Before this regulation was adopted there was an average every month of from one to five cases of typhoid fever in the city, but since the pasteurizing law went into effect, nine months ago, only one case of typhoid fever has been reported, and there has not been a single death from intestinal disease of any infant under one year of age. In 1908 several cases of bubonic plague were reported in Contra Costa County, and an investigation was conducted by the United States Public Health Service under Doctor Blue, surgeon in charge for the Pacific Coast District. Doctor Long had direct charge of the investigation in Contra Costa County. Upon examination of squirrels and rats it was found that the plague infection was prevalent in both. A campaign to make a free plague zone surrounding Contra Costa County and Alameda County was inaugurated, and thousands of squirrels and rats were destroyed. There have been found 1629 infected ground squirrels. Six cases of plague have been reported in Contra Costa County, four of whom died.

COUNTY MEDICAL SOCIETY. —The Contra Costa County Medical Society was first organized in June, 1877, with Doctor J. H. Carothers, president, and Doctor E. L. Wemple, secretary. Other members were Doctors H. V. Mott, John McFayden, John Leffler, Walter Hook, O. B. Adams, W. B. Bolton, and Edmund Bragdon, Jr. This society had meetings in the different towns of the county for six years, and finally went out of existence in 1884. The presidents were: J. H. Carothers, 1877; Edmund Bragdon, Jr., 1878; John Leffler, 1879; W. B. Bolton, 1880; O. B. Adams, 1881; Walter Hook, 1882; H. V. Mott, 1883. Doctor E. L. Wemple remained secretary during this entire period. In 1889 a reorganization took place in Martinez. Doctor Edmund Bragdon, Jr., was made president, and John B. Tennent became secretary. Other members were Doctors Frank Rattan, J. H. Carothers, H. G. Thomas, F. F. Neff, A. W. Rickey, F. S. Cook and W. S. George. This society lasted for only three years. The presidents were Doctor Edmund Bragdon, Jr., 1889; Doctor Frank Rattan, 1900; Doctor J. H. Carothers, 1901. Doctor John B. Tennent remained secretary. In 1902 the society was again brought into existence. Doctor Joseph T. Breneman, as president, and Doctor F. F. Neff, as secretary, were the officers for the first year. Other members were Doctors Frank Rattan, E. E. Brown, C. L. Abbott, A. W. Rickey, J. H. Carothers, F. S. Cook, Geo. McKenzie, and W. S. George. This society died during the third year. Presidents were Joseph T. Breneman, 1902; E. E. Brown, 1903; Geo. McKenzie, 1904. Dr. F. F. Neff remained secretary. The present society was formed in 1906. Doctor C. L. Abbott was elected president and J. W. Key secretary. Other members were Doctors Frank Rattan, Geo. McKenzie, F. F. Neff, F. S. Cook, E. E. Brown, Joseph T. Breneman, W. S. George, A. W. Rickey, and J. H. Carothers. The presidents were C. L. Abbott, 1906; Joseph T. Breneman, 1907; Frank Rattan, 1908; F. F. Neff, 1909; C. R. Leech, 1910; C. R. Blake, 1911; H. N. Barney, 1912; W. S. George, 1913; U. S. Abbott, 1914 and 1915; P. C. Campbell, 1916. The secretaries were J. W. Key, 1906 to 1908; Frank Rattan, 1908 to 1912; E. B. Fitzpatrick, 1912 to 1916. Members at present (1916) are F. F. Neff, F. S. Cook, C. R. Leech, E. B. Fitzpatrick, J. H. Hammond, H. L. Carpenter, M. L. Fernandez, H. N. Barney, W. J. Caesar, C. R. Blake, Frank Rattan, Louise A. Oldenbourg, G. W. Sweetser, E. W. Merrithew, G. M. O'Malley, C. E. Camp, P. C. Campbell, W. S. Lucas, A. W. Rickey, C. L. Abbott, U. S. Abbott, C. C. Fitz-Gibbon, and F. P. McManus.

CHAPTER XXII. BANKING

In the early history of Contra Costa County, before the organization of any regular bank, banking was more or less informally carried on by merchants and other private parties. This form of banking varied; in some cases the merchant having a safe was requested to keep a sack containing funds belonging to customers, and out of these funds he paid out money for the owner upon written order or otherwise.

In other cases he accepted the money and mingled it with his own, making use of it if needed in his business, being ready to meet orders drawn on him when presented. In some cases he allowed the owner a small amount of interest, and in some cases the care of the money was considered proper compensation.

Hale & Brother, general merchants in the town of Pacheco, was one of the firms doing this business. Wheat was very high and the fanners had large crops. They soon had plenty of money, and made a practice of asking William Hale, senior member of the firm, to loan their surplus funds on good mortgages. This business grew to such proportions that to avoid discrimination he began taking the money, allowing the owner a certain per cent, and loaning it out on his own account. With this beginning a bank was organized and incorporated on December 29, 1870, with a capital stock of $50,000, and under the incorporate name of the Contra Costa Savings & Loan Bank. The principal place of business was in the town of Pacheco, and the following men were named as directors: W. K. Dell, G. M. Bryant, John Gambs, Barry Baldwin, and W. M. Hale.

The business was limited to savings and loan only, and on March 27, 1872, the Contra Costa Bank was incorporated to do a general banking business, the capital stock, principal place of business, and directors being the same as those of the bank previously mentioned.

This enterprise was so successful and seemed to meet the growing needs of the country to such an extent, that Hale & Brother sold out their store in Pacheco and came to the county seat, Martinez, where they became associated with L. I. Fish, Charles Fish, and others in the organization of the Bank of Martinez. The bank in Pacheco went out of business, and the Bank of Martinez is now the oldest incorporated bank in the county. It was incorporated on October 7, 1873. The board of directors chosen at the time of incorporation was made up of the following: L. I. Fish, William W. Cameron, Simon Blum, Henry M. Hale, and William M. Hale. Among the original stockholders the following names appear in addition to the above-named directors: Charles Fish, B. Baldwin, and Isaac Ayer.

L. I. Fish was the first president and William M. Hale the first cashier, his brother, Henry M. Hale, acting as bookkeeper and general assistant. The Hales constituted the active force behind the counter for the first ten years of the existence of the bank.

It was originally incorporated with a capital stock of $50,000, but it was soon evident that this was not sufficient, and on May 26, 1875, the capital was increased to $100,000.

William M. Hale's health failing, in July, 1883, he finally resigned his position as cashier. He lived only a few weeks longer, passing away on August 20, 1883. Henry M. Hale was then elected cashier, and W. A. Hale, son of William M. Hale, was appointed bookkeeper and general assistant in July, 1883.

L. I. Fish continued as president of the bank until July, 1890, when he retired from active business, sold his interest in the bank, thereby ceasing to be its president. L. C. Wittenmyer was chosen to succeed him.

The affairs of the bank continued under the management of L. C. Wittenmyer as president and H. M. Hale as cashier until January 9, 1899, when, owing to the death of H. M. Hale, which occurred on January 6, 1899, and to the fact that Wittenmyer had disposed of his stock in the bank, James Rankin was elected president and W. A. Hale cashier.

In May, 1900, it became necessary to have a vice-president, and that office being created, W. S. Tinning was elected the first vice-president of the bank.

On October 15, 1901, James Rankin died, having acted as president of the bank for less than three years. While his tenure of office was short, he had nevertheless served at a time and in a manner which contributed much to the rapid growth of the bank, which began about that time.

On January 13, 1902, W. S. Tinning was elected president, and J. M. Stow vice-president, W. A. Hale continuing as cashier. The only other changes in the officers of the bank since that date occurred when A. E. Dunkel succeeded J. M. Stow as vice-president in January, 1909. The position of assistant cashier was created in January, 1906, and Lee Durham was appointed to that position.

In June, 1913, Durham left the bank to become cashier of a new bank that was about to be started in Brentwood, and Frank R. Jones was made assistant cashier. At the same time a second assistant cashier was needed, and Miss Janet Rankin was appointed, both these officers having served on the clerical force for over ten years.

In addition to the above record of the officials of the bank, there have been many prominent men who have served as directors; the list is too long to be fully set forth here. However, in addition to the various presidents, vice-presidents, and cashiers already named, there might be mentioned Bernardo Fernandez, Simon Blum, Charles Fish, John Tormey, Patrick Tormey, J. H. Carothers, and A. B. Coleman, who each served on the board of directors. Of these Bernardo Fernandez has the distinction of having served the longest in that capacity. He was appointed to fill a vacancy on the board on August 13, 1877, and served thereafter continuously until his death on May 12, 1912, a period of nearly thirty-five years.

The present board of directors is composed of W. S. Tinning, A. E. Dunkel, James E. Rodgers, Thomas B. Fernandez, and W. A. Hale. Since it was founded in 1873 the Bank of Martinez has consistently grown. In 1880 the total resources amounted to $310,000; in 1890, $496,000; in 1897, $528,500; in 1903, $623,700; in 1910, $949,000; and in 1916, $1,300,000. The uniformity of its growth indicates that its structure is sound, with no weak spots occasioned by too rapid growth at any one time. Yet the older it has grown the greater has been the percentage of increase, thus evincing no signs of decay, and there is no reason to doubt that when the half-century mark is reached it will have two million dollars in resources.

BANK OF ANTIOCH. —Under wise and able management, the Bank of Antioch has grown to its present proportions and importance. It is due to progressive policies that this bank has become what it is today in the commercial and financial life of Antioch.

The Bank of Antioch was organized September 12, 1891, with the following board of directors: S. G. Little (president)', J. C. Rouse, H. F. Beede, J. Rio Baker (vice-president), R. Harkinson (secretary).

The capital stock was $100,000, with $70,000 paid up. The present board consists of C. M. Belshaw, president; J. Rio Baker, vice-president; R. Harkinson, secretary and cashier; Seth Davison, and H. F. Beede.

At present the bank has a paid-up capital of $100,000 and a surplus of $25,000, owns its building, which, together with fixtures, cost about $7500. The total resources are now $725,000.

The safe-deposit department and storage vaults are constructed in accordance with the latest and most modern ideas. There is a large and commodious directors room, and the advice of the officers of the bank is ever at the disposal of its clients.

CONTRA COSTA COUNTY BANK. —The growth of the Contra Costa County Bank, of Pittsburg, California, has been a most remarkable one.

Under the wise and able management it has grown steadily, and is considered one of the most substantial banking institutions in Contra Costa County. Guido Todaro, the present cashier, has had much to do with its progressive policies. The bank is devoted to all branches of modern banking.

The Contra Costa County Bank was organized in 1903 and started business on January 1, 1914. The organizers were C. A. Hooper, Andrew Sbarbaro, M. Cody, D. H. Henny, Geo. W. Hooper, and D. A. Bender. The first officers elected were as follows: D. A. Bender, president; M. Cody, vice-president; Guido Todaro, cashier. Following are the names of present officers of the bank: W. E. Creed, president; W. J. Buchanan, vice-president; G. Todaro, cashier; Miss N. Canevaro, assistant cashier.

The bank started with a capital stock of $50,000. It now owns its own building, which was erected at a cost of $8600, and is unexcelled for its equipment and banking facilities. The safe-deposit department and storage vaults of this institution deserve special attention, as they are constructed in accordance with the latest ideas.

The directors of the bank are: W. E. Creed, C. J. Wood, A. Sbarbaro, W. J. Buchanan, Otis Loveridge, N. Canevaro, and G. Todaro.

BANK OF PINOLE. —The Bank of Pinole was organized in the town of Pinole on October 25, 1905, under the direction of E. M. Downer, with a capital stock of $25,000. A consistent and steady growth has been maintained until at the present time it ranks amongst the foremost of the financial institutions of the county. In 1908 the Crockett branch of the institution was founded, and it has also enjoyed the same advancement as the home office. In 1910, as a result of the progress made, it was necessary to increase the capital stock from $25,000 to $50,000.

The bank has cared for the financial needs of that section of Contra Costa County situated along the water-front from Pinole to Port Costa, which takes in a very busy manufacturing district. The bank's business has been conducted in a very creditable and up-to-date manner, all modern methods and appliances being used, and it has given patrons the service that is now looked for by the progressive business man.

In 1915 the home office at Pinole was housed in a magnificent stone building of Gothic architecture, equipped with every modern convenience for the use of its patrons. Italian marble counters with heavy old brass railing, together with a rich finish in mahogany in the way of furniture, give the interior an effect seldom seen outside the large cities.

The steel and concrete vault is fitted with a massive steel screw door, with modern time-locks, and inside the vault are located the coin-safes and safe-deposit boxes. A feature of the building is the beautiful directors' room, which is also finished in mahogany. This is a very restful and spacious apartment and is at the disposal of patrons when not used by the directors.

In 1916 the Crockett branch entered its new home, a stately brick structure of the Georgian style, and, as in the home office, every appliance and convenience known to modern banking for the purpose of safeguarding the valuables of the bank and its patrons have been installed.

Conservativeness consistent with the progress of the territory in which the bank is located and the times in general has been the policy of the board of directors, and the result has been very gratifying both to its patrons and management. The present officers are E. M. Downer, president; J. P. Connors, vice-president; S. S. MacKinlay, second vice president; L. E. Hart, cashier; T. W. Hutchinson, assistant cashier.

Directors: E. M. Downer, J. P. Connors, S. S. MacKinlay, Dr. M. L. Fernandez, E. D. Armstrong, J. A. Fraser, W. A. Davis, J. P. Tormey, and L. E. Hart. The present capital of the bank is $50,000, and the surplus $54,000.

FIRST NATIONAL BANK OF CONTRA COSTA COUNTY. —This bank was organized and charter granted May 16, 1907, and opened for business July 7, 1907, with the following officers and directors: President, E. A. Majors; vice-president, A. E. Blum; cashier, M. E. Glucksman. Directors: E. A. Majors, A. E. Blum, E. J. Randall, M. E. Glucksman, and W. K. Cole. Its capital stock was $25,000. In April, 1908, the capital stock was increased from $25,000 to $50,000. In June, 1909, the directors were E. A. Majors, A. E. Blum, E. J. Randall, F. A. Hodapp, W. L. Cole, M. E. Glucksman, and L. W. Brubeck. The bank building occupies a lot at the corner of Maine and Las Juntas streets and was started in April and completed in August, 1908.

In November, 1909, M. E. Glucksman resigned as cashier and E. J. Randall was elected. In January, 1910, M. E. Jones was added to the directors. On March 9, 1910, L. W. Brubeck resigned as director. From January, 1911, to January, 1917, the directors of the First National Bank of Contra Costa County are as follows: E. A. Majors, A. E. Blum, E. J. Randall, W. K. Cole, F. A. Hodapp, M. R. Jones, L. M. La Selle. Up to the year of 1915, deposits gradually grew to $350,000, and in 1916 increased to over $600,000.

The safe-deposit vault is constructed of armor-plate steel and is the best and strongest protection yet devised by science. The bank maintains a separate compartment so arranged that one may meet his friends and transact private business or attend to personal correspondence. The officers and directors have made this bank one of the leading banks of this county.

SAN RAMON VALLEY BANK. —This is one of the leading banks of Contra Costa County. Since its organization, June 28, 1907, it has had a steady growth. It transacts a general commercial and savings banking business, in all respects in accordance with the laws governing commercial and savings banks in this State. The capital stock is $75,000.

The first officers of the bank were John Hackett, president; A. H. Cope, vice-president; Arthur Burton, second vice-president; Joseph Silveria, cashier and secretary.

Temporary quarters were occupied while the new bank building was under construction. The bank occupies a fireproof building of steel and concrete, fronting the business street in Walnut Creek. The cost of the building was $8000, and the fixtures $4000. The interior is arranged so as to secure the best working conditions, being roomy and well ventilated. The fireproof vault, which is of the most modern type, is equipped with safe-deposit boxes.

The present officers are N. S. Boone, president; Arthur Burton, vice president; Norman H. Bennett, cashier and secretary. The Danville branch of the San Ramon Valley Bank was established in May, 1911, and a new bank building costing $15,000 was erected. The same officers and board of directors control both banks. Commercial and savings business are transacted in the Danville bank, and a healthy financial growth has been enjoyed by this branch since it started. The present board of directors are N. H. Bennett, Arthur Burton, N. S. Boone, A. P. Borges, W. S. Burpee, John F. Baldwin, Ely I. Hutchison. On November 1, 1916, the combined deposits of both banks were $476,000.

THE MECHANICS BANK OF RICHMOND.—The Mechanics Bank has had a steady growth coincident with the growth and development of Richmond. This bank transacts a commercial and savings business in all respects in accordance with the laws governing such banks.

The Mechanics Bank was organized August 15, 1907, with a capital stock of $25,000. The directors and stockholders at time of organization were L. I. Cowgill, Charles Nelson, Joseph Iverson, H. C. Morris, S. C. Denson, L. N. McDonald, and F. W. Judson. The capital stock was increased to $50,000 on October 5, 1912, and on July 27, 1916, the bank again increased its stock to $100,000.

L. J. Cowgill served as president from 1907 to 1909. B. H. Griffins acted in this capacity from 1909 to 1915. The other officers during 1909 to 1915 were Joseph Iverson, vice-president, and W. L. Ballenger, cashier. The present officers of the Mechanics Bank are as follows: President, John H. Nicholl; first vice-president, J. F. Carlston; second vice president and manager, E. M. Downer; cashier, W. L. Ballenger; assistant cashiers, Chris. Escobar and George Lee. The directors are John H. Nicholl, J. F. Carlston, E. M. Tilden, J. F. Brooks, H. A. Johnston, C. M. Brewer, and E. M. Downer. These are all men of ability, and by their intelligence and progressive management have made the Mechanics Bank of Richmond one of the strongest and safest business institutions in Contra Costa County.

The bank's resources are over $1,000,000. The safe-deposit department is amply equipped with the most modern features known to banking for safety.

FIRST NATIONAL BANK OF RICHMOND. —The First National Bank of Richmond opened for business May 24, 1910, in the Florin Building, and in December of the same year it moved to its own building at the corner of Sixth Street and Macdonald Avenue. Its capital at organization was $100,000, and the original board of directors and officers were as follows: Clinton E. Worden (director First National Bank, San Francisco, president First National Bank, Bakersfield, vice-president First Federal Trust Co., San Francisco), president; E. A. Gowe (assistant cashier Standard Oil Company, secretary East Shore & Suburban Ry. Co.), vice-president; Charles J. Crary, cashier; L. D. Dimm, manager Standard Oil Company; V. A. Fenner, hardware merchant; James K. Lynch, president American Bankers Association, vice-president First National Bank, San Francisco, president Clearing House, San Francisco, president Citizens National Bank, Alameda, director Federal Reserve Bank, San Francisco; J. M. Quay, vice-president Pacific Telephone & Telegraph Co., director Spring Valley Water Company.

On May 26th, a few days after the opening of the bank, E. A. Gowe died, and L. D. Dimm was elected his successor as vice-president, and his vacancy on the board was taken by J. C. Black, chief engineer of the Standard Oil Company. Since then Charles H. Robertson, at that time superintendent of the East Shore & Suburban Railway Company, F. E. Beck, manager of the Pullman Company, H. W. Pulse, of Pulse Bros., and C. J. Sheperd, cashier, have been added to the board of directors. W. P. Clarke and L. G. Bonzagni served temporarily as assistant cashiers of the bank, and C. L. LeMasters and L. C. Pontious as cashiers.

In 1911 Charles J. Crary was elected vice-president and manager of the bank and in 1912 C. J. Shepherd came to the bank as cashier, remaining in that position until January, 1915, when he became affiliated with the Federal Reserve Bank of San Francisco.

In November, 1915, T. H. DeLap, who had efficiently served the bank as attorney for many years, was elected a director, vice J. C. Black, who resigned on account of moving to Los Angeles, and in January, 1916, Warren H. McBryde, assistant superintendent of the Hercules Powder Company, at Hercules, was elected a director to succeed C. J. Shepherd.

During the years 1910 and 1911 and part of 1912 Charles J. Crary also occupied the office of city treasurer of Richmond. The bank today has over 1700 active customers on its books. The motto of the First National Bank and its affiliated savings institution, the Richmond Savings Bank, is "Strength and Service." It has been very progressive from the start, keenly interested in the upbuilding of the city of Richmond, yet withal it is conservative in the point of proceeding safely, realizing that strength is the first requisite of a good bank.

As the two banks have grown their service has extended, and their equipment in the way of necessary banking fixtures and machinery is of the most complete order. In addition to its capital of $100,000, it has built up surplus and undivided profits amounting to approximately $23,000, and its deposits average close to $400,000.

RICHMOND SAVINGS BANK. —The Richmond Savings Bank opened for business July 1, 1911, with the same officers and directors as the First National Bank of Richmond, and almost the same stockholders.

Their directors have continued identical. It is located with the First National Bank. The growth of the Richmond Savings Bank has been constant and very satisfactory, as shown by deposit totals given below. In 1913, on account of increased deposits, the capital was increased from $25,000 to $50,000. Its earned surplus and undivided profits amount to approximately $10,000. Though the youngest bank in the city, in point of deposits it is the largest. Both the First National Bank and the Richmond Savings Bank have been constant advertisers, using the newspapers and many other means, not only to advertise their business, but in an effort to encourage thrift and savings among the people of the city. Clinton E. Worden, president of the First National Bank and the Richmond Savings Bank, has been an earnest worker in pushing the banks to the front, assisted by Charles J. Crary, who has been the active manager of both banks since their organization, and with them there has been an efficient corps of assistants and a strong board of directors, having amongst their number men interested in the largest enterprises in the city.

Deposit growth is shown herewith: December 30, 1911, $73,249.11; December 31, 1912, $190,679.70; December 31, 1913, $313,171.94; December 31, 1914, $407,903.12; December 31, 1915, $486,600.80. Total number of accounts March 1, 1916, over 2400.

The combined assets of the First National Bank and the Richmond Savings Bank at the last published report on March 7, 1916, were $1,194,478.13.

FIRST NATIONAL BANK OF CONCORD. —Among the solid, conservative, and most thoroughly reliable moneyed institutions of Contra Costa County is numbered the First National Bank of Concord. The charter was received March 9, 1911, and the following were the officers: F. W. Foskett, president; H. H. Elworthy, vice-president; W. L. Brown, cashier. The board of directors was composed of the following gentlemen: P. Roche, John Sutton, E. H. Shibley, A. C. Gehringer, C. R. Devereaux, J. M. Lavazzola, J. V. Enloe, and William Ford. The capital stock was $25,000.

In 1912 Brown resigned as cashier and L. A. Stevenson was elected to the position. The bank actually started business March 20, 1911 and occupied temporary quarters for eight months while the new Foskett & Elworthy building was being erected.

The present officers of the bank are F. W. Foskett, president; H. H. Elworthy, vice-president; L. A. Stevenson, cashier. The new building cost $35,000, and the interior furnishing $3500. The capital stock was increased to $50,000 on January 1, 1917.

THE BANK OF BYRON. —The Bank of Byron is one of the reliable and conservative banks of Contra Costa County. It was organized May 1, 1911 and is a branch of the Bank of Tracy. The Bank of Tracy is one of the older banking situations of San Joaquin County, and has been a great influence in community development. The Byron bank has the following officers: John C. Drodge, president; William Schmidt, vice president; O. H. Root, secretary; Alfred L. Bovo, manager.

All of these men have proved their capabilities in representative times of endeavor and are recognized as far-sighted, keen, and discriminating business men. Under the efficient management of Alfred L. Bovo, the Byron Bank has enjoyed a steady and rapid growth, and this bank is known today as being among the leading financial institutions of Contra Costa County. The bank owns its own building and has one of the most modern safe-deposit equipments in the county. The building was erected at a cost of $6000, and the fixtures are of the latest design and were installed at a cost of $2500. The resident directors are Mott Preston and J. Saxoner.

FIRST NATIONAL BANK OF WALNUT CREEK. —This bank was organized September, 1912, with a capital stock of $25,000. Officers: A. H. Cope, president; James Stow, vice-president; H. G. Flint, cashier. Directors: A. H. Cope, James Stow, H. G. Flint, Peter Thompson, and R. N. Burgess. The present officers of the bank are R. N. Burgess, president; C. G. Gould, vice-president; W. L. White, second vice-president; Armond Stow, cashier. The present directors are G. C. Squires, R. N. Burgess, C. G. Gould, W. L. White, and Armond Stow.

The safe-deposit vaults are of the most modern type and the furniture and fixtures cost about $8000.

BANK OF BRENTWOOD. —For many years Brentwood has been an important grain center, and much inconvenience was experienced by the lack of facilities for exchange, but not until the Los Meganos Rancho, with its 13,000 acres, upon which the town of Brentwood is located, fell into the hands of Balfour, Guthrie & Co. was the necessity for a bank fully recognized. The rapid development of this magnificent property forced the issue, and the bank was established.

An ornate concrete building that looks every inch a bank was constructed at a cost for furniture and equipment of $15,000. The interior is handsomely finished and supplied with a steel-lined vault and Tisco manganese safe and is in every particular up to date.

Starting with a capital of $50,000, with $25,000 paid up, it opened its doors for business on July 15, 1913, and at this date, three and a half years later, is handling assets of nearly $200,000. The officers of the bank are as follows: President, R. G. Dean; vice president, Robert Wallace, Jr.; cashier, Lee Durham. The directors are R. G. Dean, Alexander Burness, Robert Wallace, Jr., R. F. MacLeod, and Frank H. Ludinghouse.

THE FIRST NATIONAL BANK OF ANTIOCH. —On Tuesday, January 3, 1911, the First National Bank of Antioch and the Antioch Bank of Savings opened their doors to the public. The First National Bank of Antioch has a capital stock of $25,000, while the Antioch Bank of Savings has an authorized capital of $50,000, with $25,000 paid up.

The officers of both banks are the same, namely: J. L. Harding, president; J. A. West, vice-president and manager; Herbert A. West, cashier. The directors are as follows: J. L. Harding, J. A. West, E. C. Werrell, J. Arata, W. C. Williamson, J. G. Prewett, and Manuel Baeta. The board of directors are made up of prominent merchants, farmers, and capitalists. The bank has about fifty stockholders. The bank is a handsome structure of the Mission style of architecture, two stories high, and is built of reinforced concrete. The main floor is 25 by 52 feet, and the second floor is fitted up for up-to-date offices. The safe-deposit vaults are modern in every regard. The bank has installed an electric burglar-alarm system, also a convenient and attractive vault with manganese steel safe (latest pattern and burglar proof).

The institution was organized through the efforts of John A. and Herbert A. West. The present officers of the bank are J. A. West, president; J. G. Prewett, vice-president; H. A. West, cashier.

CHAPTER XXIII. TRANSPORTATION

THE FIRST CARQUINEZ STRAITS FERRY

For many years the only ferry on the waters flowing from the Sacramento River out through the Golden Gate was maintained at Martinez.

This was the point at which all travelers crossed the Straits of Carquinez when journeying north or south, and it was here, about 1849, that the first ferry was established. In that year Doctor Semple, of Benicia, established a ferry running from Benicia to a point near the spot now occupied by Alhambra Cemetery. This boat was at first propelled by oars, but later a wheel was put on the boat and it was run by horse-power. This was continued until 1851, when Captain Oliver C. Coffin purchased the flat-bottomed ferry-boat "Ione," which commenced carrying passengers across the San Joaquin River between Antioch and Collinsville about the year 1850. Captain Coffin brought the boat to Martinez and remodeled it to suit his needs here. At Antioch the craft had been propelled across the river by horse-power, but that primitive mode of ferrying would not do at Martinez, so an engine was put into the "Ione," and the craft was propelled by steam.

The "Ione" plied regularly between Martinez and Benicia until July, 1854, carrying passengers and freight. The boat landing was at the foot of Ferry Street. There was no wharf or ferry slip at that time, but the boat ran close to the bank and an apron was used to connect it with the shore.

After being relieved from ferry duty in 1854, the "Ione" was used for a time as a float for a pile-driver, but for many years the hull has been rotting in the tules near the Ferry Street wharf, where it was grounded and abandoned when its days of usefulness were past.

Before the "Ione" was taken from the route, a short wharf was built, as the straits commenced to fill with earth washed down from the country above, and it was found impossible to effect a landing. The filling continued, and it became necessary to extend the wharf from time to time until it reached two thousand feet beyond the point where the steamer landed when her first trips were made.

In 1853 a steam ferry-boat was framed in New York and brought around Cape Horn to Martinez, where it arrived in the spring of 1854.

The craft was put together here, and was launched in April, 1854, but did not commence to run regularly until July of that year. It was called the "Carquinez," and was the property of Captain Oliver C, Charles G.f and Henry Coffin. Seth M. Swain was also at one-time captain of this boat.

Great numbers of cattle, sheep, and hogs were conveyed across the straits in the early days, it being not an uncommon thing for a thousand head of stock to be carried over in one day. Many of the animals were wild and unruly, and momentary excitement was sometimes caused on the trip by a frightened steer leaping over the rail into the water.

A large corral was built on the ground now occupied by the Southern Pacific Company, and into this enclosure the stock were driven while awaiting transportation. This corral was not a flimsy affair by any means but was composed of a double tier of cordwood four feet long and piled about six feet high. This wood was used for making steam on the ferry, but enough was always kept on hand to form a substantial corral.

The business of ferrying was very profitable, as stock was constantly on the move between the north and the south, it being the custom to drive the animals back and forth to obtain the benefit of the best pasturage. A charge was made of one dollar a head to ferry cattle across the straits during the time the "Ione" and the "Carquinez" were on the route. The ferry-boat also carried the mails, and, in addition to the other passenger traffic, many Martinez children attending school at Benicia were daily passengers. People going to and from San Francisco were also frequent patrons of the ferry, as it was necessary for the residents of the country south of the straits to go to Benicia to take the steamer that plied between Sacramento and the city by the Golden Gate.

The "Carquinez" was finally condemned as unsafe, and a new boat, called the "Benicia," was constructed under the direction of Charles Henry, of Danville. The engine used on the "Carquinez" was transferred to the "Benicia," and the old craft was broken up about the year 1877. It was sometime after the railroad was built that the ferry between Martinez and Benicia was discontinued, owing to the competition of the railroad company's mammoth ferry-boat "Solano," which commenced to ply between Benicia and Port Costa. The subsequent history of the "Benicia" is not known, but for some time she was engaged in traffic in the vicinity of Coronado.

RIVER COMMUNICATION

The Sacramento River is navigable from the bay northward to Sacramento, 120 miles, for large, commodious steamers, as fine as any upon the rivers in the Eastern States. They ply daily to Sacramento, stopping at Martinez, New York, and Antioch; smaller light-craft steamers ply regularly to Red Bluff, 250 miles farther, and on the Feather River, sixty miles, to Marysville. The San Joaquin River is also navigable for large steamers, which ply daily to Stockton, 120 miles. Above Stockton, light-draft vessels ascend toward Visalia, 200 miles, and also for some distance up its branches, the Stanislaus and Tuolumne rivers, and also the Mokelumne River. The light-draft steamers on all these rivers carry with them large barges, in which the crops of the farmers, firewood, and other products are cheaply and rapidly transported to a market at San Francisco at very low rates. A number of the creeks and sloughs emptying into the Bay of Suisun are also navigable, and are ascended by numerous steamers and sailing craft, which carry freight and passengers at reasonable prices. Thus a large portion of the county is to a great extent independent of the railroad, while the competition between land and water carriage insures low rates of freights and fares on both.

The San Joaquin River is divided into three branches, known, respectively, as the west, middle, and east channels—the last-named being not only the main stream, but the one used by the steamboats and sailing vessels bound to and from Stockton—or, at least within four miles of that city, from which point the Stockton Slough is used. The east (or main) channel is navigable for small stern-wheel steamboats as far as Fresno City.

The first mail ever carried up the Sacramento River was on July 24, 1849, by Captain Seth M. Swain, of Martinez, in the schooner "John Dunlap." The mail matter was all contained in one bag, and the captain received six hundred dollars for the service, while the entire postage on the contents of the mail was less than sixty dollars.

SUISUN BAY

This is one of the chief bays that border the Contra Costa coast. Many of the gold-seekers here found a watery grave or foundered upon the middle grounds of the bay. In the fall of 1850 a schooner struck on the lower end of the middle ground. The wind and waves soon broke her up, and the flour with which she was laden was cast upon the bay. Those coming up the bay could pick up a barrel or two for use, and one boat was engaged a long time in salvaging the flour, which was sold to the baker at New York of the Pacific for five dollars a barrel. Supposing the flour to be worthless, some refused to give any price. However, it was but little damaged; even after a week's soaking in the waters of the bay—wetting the barrel and flour half an inch deep, making the whole mass impervious to water.

Another schooner struck on a less dangerous ground three miles from New York Landing. As she was strong and staunchly built, she sat upon the sand of the middle ground, and the sailors could walk around her at low tide. The captain and crew found a near cut to the channel, and, by the use of miners' spades and with the help of the passengers, they dug a way for the schooner to the nearest point of the channel. The wind and tide serving right, a kedge anchor was put out, and the schooner and cargo were saved. They all went up the bay rejoicing at their good luck and their escape from the dangers of Suisun Bay.

Before a perfect chart of the bay was made, a number of boats, filled with the hurrying crowds compelled to navigate these waters on their trips to Stockton and Sacramento, were stove in and swamped upon the middle sand-bars. On one occasion, when a boat was foundered, the passengers, after swimming to the south shore across the channel, were compelled to swim a slough a hundred feet wide before they could reach New York Landing. Whale-boats have tied up at this place for a week at a time, awaiting favorable winds before venturing on Suisun Bay.

In 1850 the ship "Henry Lee" was cast ashore near the landing and lay there for about a year before she was finally floated and sent to sea again.

From a mile below Antioch to Marsh's Landing, three miles above the town, there are neither rocks nor shoals, making a clear channel, with an average depth of forty feet, where four or five vessels may swing at anchor side by side.

SOUTHERN PACIFIC RAILWAY

In 1877, after a number of surveys had been made, it was decided by the owners of the Central Pacific line to build through Contra Costa County, on account of its natural advantages and scenic beauty, thus filling in the last link of one of the most central routes across the country, and the road was completed in 1878.

After the completion of the line, and settlers began to arrive, there was a steady growth of population throughout the entire county. The stage-coaches that had been running to the various points in the county disappeared one by one, and the old sailboats, such as were operated in the early days by one of Richmond's first settlers, John R. Nystrom, were found to be too slow to take care of the freight traffic. The older villages likewise soon became scenes of activity, having a steady growth, so that we now have a number of cities and towns, and rank in the State as the leading county in manufacturing. The principal industries are located at Antioch, Pittsburg, Nichols, Bay Point, Avon, Peyton, Mococo, Martinez, Port Costa, Crockett, Selby, Oleum, Rodeo, Hercules, Giant, Richmond and Stege. Of these the two principal cities leading in manufacturing are Richmond and Pittsburg. Other cities and towns in the county located along this portion of the line, and which owe their origin or upbuilding to the Southern Pacific Company, are Byron, Brentwood, Neroly, Newlove, Prince, Los Medanos, McAvoy, Amorce, Nevada Dock, Martinez, Eckley, Vallejo Junction, Tormey, Pinole, Krieger, Sobrante, and San Pablo.

Byron, shortly after the line was completed, became greatly noted for its mineral springs, these being rated as among the best of their kind in the United States, and since the advent of the railroad have been visited by thousands of people from all parts of the world, not only by those who are in search of health, but by all who desire to benefit from their invigorating and healthful properties.

Antioch is the emporium of an agricultural section that produces more food supplies than any other part of the county. It sends out annually a large tonnage of hay, grain, celery, asparagus, onions, potatoes, grapes, peaches, apricots, almonds, wine, lumber, and live-stock. The largest paper-mill in the State is located at Antioch, and the city also boasts of one of the largest asparagus plants.

Pittsburg, formerly known as Cornwall and Black Diamond, has a population of over five thousand people. It is situated not only on the Southern Pacific line, but also on deep water where California's two greatest rivers, the San Joaquin and the Sacramento, join to form Suisun Bay. These rivers furnish an unlimited supply of good water for boiler and manufacturing purposes, and factories having their own water-frontage can install pumping plants, giving an independent supply.

A great many industries have located in this city on account of its excellent railroad and water facilities. Among the enterprises shipping millions of pounds of freight from Pittsburg annually are the Columbia Steel Company, Redwood Manufacturing Company, Diamond Brick Company, Bowers Rubber Works, Johnson & Lanteri Shipyards, American Fish & Oyster Company, Lindenburger & Company, California Fruit Canners Association, and the Sacramento River Packers Association.

Bay Point is the location of some large industries, among which is the C. A. Smith Lumber Company, famous for its great wholesale plant, shipping during the year thousands of carloads of its products to various parts of the country.

Nichols, Peyton and Mococo have their chemical plants.

Port Costa is noted for its large grain elevators, located near water as well as rail, and handles during the summer seasons immense quantities of cereals.

Selby's great smelters, controlled by the Selby Smelting & Lead Company, make heavy shipments of gold, silver, and lead by freight and express.

Oleum is the location of the Union Oil Company's great refinery.

Hercules and Giant have the extensive manufacturing plants of the Hercules Powder Company and the Giant Powder Company.

At Stege is located the California Cap Works.

Richmond is the largest city in the county and has had the most rapid growth. About 1900 it had a small station at Barrett Avenue, but later a depot was erected by the Southern Pacific Company at Macdonald Avenue. In 1905 at this depot there was handled 107,332 tons of freight; in 1910, 535,492 tons; in 1914, 738,304 tons. The largest refinery west of Whiting, Indiana, being located here, and owned by the Standard Oil Company, has had much to do with the growth of the town. Other large plants, such as the California Wine Association, Western Pipe & Steel Company, The Pullman Company, Pacific Sanitary Manufacturing Company, Richmond Feed & Grain Company, Schreck Furniture Company, Pacific Porcelain Ware Company, Berkeley Steel Company, and others, doing a large business, have added much to the growth and prosperity of this growing center.

The people of the San Ramon Valley, seeing the prosperous condition of the cities along the main line, and the advantages to be gained by having rail transportation, petitioned the Southern Pacific Company to build a road through that valley, and the San Ramon branch was built in the year 1890, opening up one of the most fertile fruit and agricultural valleys in the State. Yearly numerous carload shipments of green and dried fruits, nuts, and agricultural products are moving from Walnut Creek, Danville, Concord, and the smaller towns located on this branch, such as San Ramon, Osage, Alamo, Widboro, Oxlay, Las Junitas, Hookston, Nacio, and Galindo.

The passenger service of the Southern Pacific Company in Contra Costa County is unexcelled, both as to the number of trains and equipment, there being forty-four trains daily between Richmond and Port Costa, fifteen between Port Costa and Byron, and four trains daily on the San Ramon branch. Commutation tickets for individuals or families with various limits enable the citizens to travel cheaply to various parts of the county. Since its inception, the line has been double-tracked between most of the principal points and has four main-line tracks leading into Richmond. It is equipped with block signals, and no expense is spared by the management in making it the safe line to travel on. The Southern Pacific has the "Safety Medal" awarded by the American Museum of Safety, so that Contra Costa County can boast of having not only the best but the safest of railroad facilities.

THE ATCHISON, TOPEKA & SANTA FE

In the early part of 1895 the general feeling that central California and San Francisco needed the competition of another transcontinental railway crystallized in the subscription, mainly from San Francisco residents and merchants, of approximately two and a half millions of dollars, to be applied to the construction of a railway from San Francisco through Stockton to Bakersfield. As a result of this subscription, on February 25, 1895, the articles of incorporation of the San Francisco & San Joaquin Valley Railroad Company were filed, the first directors being as follows: Claus Spreckels, John D. Spreckels, W. F. Whittier, J. B. Stetson, Robert Watt, A. H. Payson, Charles Holbrook, Lewis Gerstle, Alvinza Hayward, Isaac Upham, Thomas Magee.

In order to insure against the possibility of the new company's being absorbed by its predecessor, the voting power of all of its stock was placed in the hands of a board of trustees composed as follows: Thomas Brown, Daniel Meyer, Lovell White, James Cross, A. B. Spreckels, James D. Phelan, O. D. Baldwin, F. W. Van Sicklen, Christian de Guigne.

In February, 1896, the trustees and the directors joined in executing a mortgage on the entire property as security for an issue of six million dollars in bonds, the proceeds of which were to be used in the completion and equipment of the line.

It was decided at the outset to begin construction at Stockton, building south to Bakersfield, the reason being that a water connection could be had with Stockton, and in this way the new property might be made to earn an income from the start and before undertaking the comparatively costly work between Stockton and San Francisco.

The survey for the new road began at Stockton on April 18, 1895, and actual construction on July 22 of the same year. The track reached Merced on Thanksgiving day, 1895, and Fresno on October 5, 1896, from which town a regular passenger and freight service was inaugurated with Stockton, with a San Francisco connection maintained by traffic arrangement with the boats between Stockton and that point.

During the year 1899, as a result of negotiations to that end, which had been conducted during the preceding year, and after a full discussion between the public, the trustees, and the stockholders, the property was sold to the Atchison, Topeka & Santa Fe Railway Company, the price paid being the assumption of the outstanding bonded indebtedness and par for the stock. By this arrangement the stockholders lost the interest on their money during the period of construction but believed themselves fully justified in this by the advantage which would result— and which was their main object in inaugurating the enterprise—in the competitive service of another transcontinental road for San Francisco and central California.

During 1899 and 1900 the line between Stockton and San Francisco, with the Point Richmond terminal, was completed. This work practically exhausted the funds derived from the stock subscription and bonded issue, and the Point Richmond and San Francisco terminals and the boats, barges, and tugs used for freight and passenger connection between Point Richmond and San Francisco were provided for by funds advanced by the Santa Fe Company.

Shortly after the acquisition of the property by the Santa Fe Company, it secured through negotiations with the Southern Pacific Company what amounts to half-ownership in the latter's line between Bakersfield and Mohave, where a junction was had with the existing Santa Fe lines, thus completing a transcontinental railway from San Francisco to Chicago under one ownership.

The Santa Fe shops were located at Richmond in 1900, during which time trains, engines, and cars were taken care of in the open on temporary tracks. The machine-shops were completed sufficiently to move the headquarters from Stockton to Richmond January 26, 1901, on which date the headquarters were abandoned at Stockton and established at Richmond. The choice of Richmond for headquarter machine shops was principally on account of climatic conditions, making it better for shop artisans, particularly during the summer months, getting away from the heat of the San Joaquin Valley.

The investment at Richmond consists approximately of the following items: Right of way, $473,737.26; grading, $14,375-36; tracks, $79,09048; buildings, shop machinery and tools, water and oil facilities, $423,568.53. Total, $990,771.63.

There are employed at present in all departments, including engine and train employees, about seven hundred men. About three hundred locomotives, twenty-five thousand freight cars, and sixteen thousand passenger cars are repaired yearly. The pay-roll amounts to approximately $45,000 a month.

THE OAKLAND, ANTIOCH & EASTERN RAILWAY

A twelve-hundred-volt electric line between San Francisco, Oakland, Danville, Pittsburg, and Sacramento, while young in history, is furnishing the patrons along its way with every necessary railway service known to the present day.

The road-bed, of first importance, is rock-ballasted from the company's own rock quarry and crusher at Valle Vista. Many of the passenger-coaches are of steel, and all of the new equipment to be purchased in the future will be of steel construction. The coaches have roomy and comfortable seats. Parlor observation-cars are run on three of the fast-express trains each way, "The Comet," "The Meteor," and "The Sacramento Valley Limited." The observation-cars on the two latter trains run through to Chico via the Northern Electric Railway and make the round trip daily. The entire line is protected by automatic block signals and traverses a section of country noted for its scenery and beautiful fertile valleys.

Passengers leave San Francisco via the Key Route ferry, Market Street, crossing the bay to the Key Route mole, Oakland, where the Oakland, Antioch & Eastern Railway train is boarded. The train passes through the heart of the city of Oakland over Fortieth Street to the Oakland depot at Fortieth Street and Shafter Avenue, then along Shatter Avenue to the Berkeley Hills, where the train climbs along the sides of these picturesque ridges. Near the top, at Cape Horn, a rift in the mountainous hills shows a grand panoramic view of Oakland, Alameda, and the waters beyond. After this parting view of the city of Oakland, the train passes through steep wooded hills of green foliage until the highest point is reached, where the train enters a tunnel, the eastern end of which opens into Redwood Canon, a natural picnic park about three miles long. Here may be seen almost every kind of California tree and wild plant from the redwoods, standing straight and tall, to the numerous varieties of ferns and wild roses which grow in rank profusion everywhere.

Emerging from Redwood Canon you see the Moraga Valley spread out like a map below. Presently the train is on the floor of this fertile and beautiful valley at Moraga Station, the center of a settlement of commuters.

After leaving Moraga, Country Club, Burton, and Lafayette in their turn, the train enters the San Ramon Valley at Saranap, where a branch line extends to the prettily situated towns of Alamo, Danville, and Diablo Station at the foot of Mount Diablo, where an auto stage can be taken to the summit, from which point a wonderful view is had of the surrounding country. By reason of the continuous clear weather around Mount Diablo, one is almost always assured of a good clear view.

Walnut Creek, the center of commercial activity of San Ramon Valley, is surrounded by orchards and gardens. Large oaks, characteristic of this section, mark the unusual depth and fertility of the soil. Farther on is Meinert Station, on the edge of Pacheco Valley. The center of the business activity of this valley is Concord, situated at the foot of Mount Diablo, at the junction of Pacheco, San Ramon, and Ygnacio valleys. It is a pretty little town of historical interest in connection with early California. It has paved streets, sewer and water systems, as well as gas and electric light.

Next comes Bay Point, on the shores of Suisun Bay. The train then follows along the bay, passing West Pittsburg, where a branch line connects the thriving industrial city of Pittsburg with the main line, until Mallard Island is reached. Here the Suisun Bay is only 2200 feet wide, and the entire train is ferried across on the steel boat "Ramon," propelled by gasoline engines of unusual power. The "Ramon" is fitted with comforts and conveniences for passengers who wish to get off the train and stretch themselves while crossing the bay. A lunch-room is maintained on the lower deck.

After leaving Chipps Island, on the opposite shore, the train presently crosses Montezuma Slough at Dutton Station, then, passing Molena Station, at the foot of the Montezuma Hills, traverses an extensive territory of large ranches.

After leaving Dixon Junction, where a branch line runs to Dixon, an important town of Solano County, the train proceeds through Maine Prairie, Bunker, Millar, and Saxon, and then crosses the Yolo Basin to Glide Landing. On the bank of the Sacramento River, following this river through the fertile and productive lands of West Sacramento and crossing over the M-Street bridge enters Sacramento at Front and M streets. Passengers may alight from the train at Third and K streets or the terminal depot at Third and I streets.

The beginning of the railroad grew out of the minds of a few enterprising men of Contra Costa County and vicinity. The principal founders were A. W. Maltby, of Concord; Walter Arnstein, of Alamo, now president; Samuel L. Napthaly, of San Francisco, now vice-president; and Harry A. Mitchell, of San Francisco, now secretary and general manager. The gentlemen were familiar with all the fertile valleys of Moraga, San Ramon, Ygnacio, and Pacheco, but deplored the roundabout routes that connected these valleys with the bay cities. Hiring expert engineers to make a report of the feasibility of a direct line between San Francisco and the above-mentioned valleys, the present route of the railroad was decided upon after checking up the report of the engineers. As soon as this decision was made the Oakland & Antioch Railway was organized and incorporated in January, 1909. Building was started February 1909, at Bay Point, and the line was put into operation between Bay Point and Walnut Creek in May, 1911. Still building toward Oakland, and extending the service as the track was built, the Oakland & Antioch Railway was completed and service installed between Bay Point and Oakland in April, 1913.

On April 1, 1911, the Oakland, Antioch & Eastern Railway was incorporated to build a line from Bay Point to Sacramento, with a branch line about two miles long from West Pittsburg to Pittsburg. Building commenced in July, 1912, and the line from Bay Point to Pittsburg was completed and put into operation in August, 1913. In the meantime, the Oakland, Antioch & Eastern Railway leased the Oakland & Antioch Railway and also the San Ramon Valley Railroad, running from Saranap on the main line to Danville. Finally, in September, 1913, the Oakland, Antioch & Eastern Railway was completed to Sacramento and put into service the same month.

Since then the railway has been broadening out in its field of service to its patrons. Trains at convenient hours were put on between San Francisco and Concord for the commuters who live in the pretty towns in Contra Costa County and work in Oakland and San Francisco. Low commutation rates and excursion fares were arranged for. Freight service was looked after closely to develop it to the needs of the communities along the line. This led to putting on a fast fruit and vegetable train during the season to make delivery at Oakland at 4 o'clock in the morning. Through freight connections were secured with the Southern Pacific, Western Pacific, and Santa Fe railroads, which resulted in reducing the freight rate to eastern points. This encouraged fruit shippers to erect packing-houses adjacent to the large acreages of heavily producing orchards. At the present time a rice experiment farm at Millar Station is the result of the efforts of this company to get the farmers interested in more profitable crops.

The distance from San Francisco to Sacramento is 92.9 miles, with branch lines as follows: Saranap to Diablo, nine miles; Meinert to Walwood, three miles; West Pittsburg to Pittsburg, two miles.

CHAPTER XXIV. FRATERNAL SOCIETIES

MASONIC

Martinez Lodge No. 41, F. &A. M., was granted dispensation for a lodge July 26, 1852. It was continued upon application on August 3, 1853, and a charter ordered to be issued on May 3, 1854. Its first returns appear in the proceedings of the Grand Lodge of California in May, 1854, with the following officers and members: Officers—Robert N. Wood, W. M.; J. Mitchell, S. W.; H. Mills, J. W.; D. Small, treasurer; J. S. Days, secretary; J. Tucker, S. D.; E. T. Weld, J. D.; S. Russell, tyler. Master Masons—S. G. Briggs, A. Hooper, J. T. Trippin, J. S. Walls. No. 41 has been honored by having two of its members elected to office in the Grand Lodge. In 1854 Robert N. Wood was elected and installed Junior Grand Warden, and William S. Wells was elected and installed Grand Master of the Grand Lodge of California. The oldest member on the roll is Barry Baldwin Osborn, raised July 21, 1866. Martinez Lodge owns its hall, built in 1859 by subscription from its members. The hall was remodeled and refurnished in 1908. In the early '60s the lower hall was used as a school-room. There are ten Past Masters on the roll of members: Ed. McLeod, William S. Wells, Henry V. Alvarado, Reuben L. Ulsh, Alvin B. Wilson, William A. Hale, Otto K. Smith, Brooke L. Moore, Ernest H. Shibley, Fred J. Stewart. The present officers are William R. Sharkey, W. M.; Thomas B. Swift, S. W.; Conrad O. Nelson, J. W.; William A. Hale, treasurer; Orville E. Hayward, secretary (13th year); Evan Glandon Davies, chaplain; Rex L. Boyer, S. D.; Absalom F. Bray, J. D.; Fred J. Stewart, marshal; Ernest O. Talbott and Earl B. Fitzpatrick, stewards; George H. Lyford, tyler. Number of members on the roll, 88. Carquinez Lodge No. 337 and Mount Diablo Lodge No. 448 were organized by members from Martinez Lodge.

Alamo Lodge No. 122, F. & A. M., was granted a charter by the Grand Lodge at the city of Sacramento on the 13th of May A. L. 5858 (1858), to assemble and work as a regular lodge of Free and Accepted Masons at the town of Alamo, Contra Costa County, California. On the 4th of January, A. L. 5873, permission was granted by the Grand Lodge to remove its place of meeting from Alamo to the town of Walnut Creek, in the same county, which is the place of meeting at the present time. On the 13th of May, A. L. 5908, Alamo Lodge celebrated its fiftieth anniversary. The brethren and their invited brethren of different lodges of the county gathered at a fine banquet and speeches were made by Past Grand Master W. S. Wells, District Inspector Louis N. Buttner, Brother Fred V. Wood, and others present. While Alamo Lodge has past a half-century mark, it has made a steady and regular growth, although its membership at present is not remarkably large. It has experienced a condition of harmony within its jurisdiction as well as with its sister jurisdictions, and also stands high as a good worker. With the able assistance of Almona Chapter No. 214, O. E. S., the Masonic Hall Association has been organized, stock has been sold, and plans are now under way to build a temple costing in the neighborhood of $6000 or $7000. This temple will not only be an honor to our fraternity but to the public as well.

Antioch Lodge No. 175, F. & A. M., was granted dispensation June 15, 1865, and was constituted October 12th of the same year. Officers: Francis Williams, W. M.; Emory T. Mills, S. W.; John C. O'Brien, J. W.; John E. Wright, treasurer; James J. McNulty, secretary. Charter members: Francis Williams, Seth W. Bradford, John C.

O'Brien, James J. McNulty, Thomas Cryan, John P. Walton, Stephen Jessup, Daniel H. Cleaves, Jackson W. Ong, Norman Adams, Richard Charnock, John E. Wright, Mark Kline, Emory T. Mills, Raswell B. Hard.

On the evening of December 20, 1898, the following brethren residing in or near the town of Crockett, Contra Costa County, met and prepared a petition for a dispensation to form a lodge under the name of Carquinez Lodge: Edmund Freund, John Sinnot Rowan, Theodore Despard Moiles, Edward Curran, Alvin Augustine Paul, Daniel McTaggart, William Simpson Garwood, Herbert George Powers, Arthur Wellesley Beam. The following brethren also signed the petition: Philip Richard Moignard, Paul Beda, Erastus Perkins Lasell, Thomas Allen Harris, Charles Louis Hedemark, Henry Louis Webber, Homer A. Billings. The dispensation was granted April 26, 1899, by Grand Master Frank Marion Angellotti, and the first meeting was held April 29, 1899, with the following officers: H. G. Powers, W. M.; J. S. Rowan, S. W.; E. Freund, J. W.; T. D. Moiles, treasurer; P. R. Moignard, secretary; W .S. Garwood, S. D.; A. W. Beam, J. D.; A. A. Paul, marshal; C. L. Hedemark and E. P. Lasell, stewards; T. A. Harris, tyler. A charter was granted on October 12, 1899, and Carquinez Lodge No. 337 was constituted October 28, 1899, by Grand Master Charles L. Patton, the following officers being installed by him: H. G. Powers, W. M.; E. Freund, S. W.; A. W. Beam, J. W.; C. L. Hedemark, treasurer; P. R. Moignard, secretary; W. S. Garwood, S. D.; A. A. Paul, J. D.; Homer A. Billings, marshal; G. M. Hodgkins and S. T. Johnson, stewards; James Thompson, tyler. H. G. Powers, the first master, was appointed secretary of the lodge February 2, 1901, and was continued in that office until his death, which occurred January 4, 1915. A notable occasion in the history of Carquinez Lodge was the past masters' night, June 20, 1914, when every past master of the lodge was present and occupied the stations and places in the order of their seniority and conferred the third degree of Masonry upon Brother James Rollett. The following past masters were present and took part in the conferring of the degree: H. G. Powers, 1900; Ed. Freund, 1901; W. S. Garwood, 1902; A. W. Beam, 1903-1905; Geo. Jones, 1906; J. L. Gabbs, 1907; A. A. Paul 1908; J. H. Dorman, 1909; J. E. Hughes, 1910-1914; W. M. Laidlaw, 1911; C. P. Thomas, 1912; T. M. Bolton, 1913. The following is an excerpt from the minutes of this meeting: "The occasion was a memorable one, as every one of the past masters of the lodge was present, also every officer. It is doubtful if at the expiration of another fifteen years the secretary at that time will be able to make a like statement." This remark of Brother Powers seems almost prophetic, as it was only a few short months until he himself passed to the Great Beyond, making it impossible ever again to hold such a reunion. The following are the officers for the current year (1917): Peter Miller, Jr., W. M.; Francis Paschal Doughty, S. W.; Joseph Junior Burdon, J. W.; George Jones, treasurer; Jacob Erratt Hughes, secretary; George Herbert Whiteman, chaplain; Roy Austin Nelson, S. D.; William Marten Adams, J. D.; Chandlar Holten Smith, marshal; Yargen Nelson and Clair B. Payson, stewards; James King, tyler.

Brentwood Lodge No. 345, F. & A. M., was organized in February, 1902, and received its charter from the Grand Lodge on October 15, 1902. There were thirteen charter members, and the lodge now has a membership of eighty-six. The present officers for the Masonic year are P. F. Bucholtz, W. M.; J. F. Bruns, S. W.; Alexander Burness, J. W.; H. Bruns, treasurer; Bruce Grove, secretary; O. C. Prewett, marshal;

Robert Wallace, Jr., chaplain; R. H. Wallace, S. D.; H. Logan, J. D.; Alan Monroe and Thomas Steward, stewards; J. Kindergen, tyler. A new hall will be built in the near future.

Hardly had the little village which was in so short a time to develop into the city of Richmond gotten under way when the dozen or so Masons among the first settlers began to have meetings and to talk of organizing a lodge. There were many discouraging features. There were no streets—only cow-trails, which became impassable in the rainy weather. Those living at a distance had to travel by horse and buggy. It was hard to secure a building that would pass the requirements of a meeting-place. But what was lacking in other things was made up in enthusiasm, and the first meeting of McKinley Lodge No. 347, was held on August 18, 1902, at what was then known as Richard's Hall. Brother Harry Ells was selected to be master of the new lodge, and much credit for the success of the organization is due to his untiring efforts, which have not in the slightest degree lessened to the present time. The brethren of Durant Lodge No. 268, of Berkeley, gave much assistance in instructing the officers, and finally recommended the newly organized body to the Grand Lodge. The petition to the Grand Lodge was signed by sixteen master masons, and they were granted a dispensation by Grand Master William S. Wells on April 5, 1902, and on November 8, 1902, the lodge was constituted by the Grand Lodge under Grand Master Orrin Staples Henderson, who has always manifested an interest in the lodge, as evidenced by occasional visits. The growth of the lodge has been healthy and steady. In 1912 the population of Richmond had increased so rapidly that it was felt that there was room for a second lodge, and, upon recommendation of the lodge, the grand master constituted Alpha Lodge No. 431, which, like its parent, is enjoying a healthy growth, and the two lodges are now carrying on the work of Masonry side by side in peace and harmony. The following is a list of those who have served the lodge as master: Harry L. Ells, 1902-1904; Doctor H. M. Barney, 1905; Doctor J. McMorrison, 1906; Palen Church, 1907; W. H. Johnston, 1908; A. H. Campbell, 1909; Frank M. Palmer, 1910; J. H. Runirell, 1911; W. B. Richmond, 1912; W. E. Rose, 1913; C. J. Peterson, 1914; E. L. Jones, 1915. The officers of the lodge for the current year (1917) are: H. E. Jacobs, W. M.; M. H. Carey, S. W.; C. H. Foote, J. W.; W. S. McRacken, treasurer; W. T. Helms, secretary; R. C. Fernold, S. D.; F. G. Blackhart, J. D.; T. H. Summers and W. M. Parks, stewards; F. L. Jones, chaplain; C. J. Peterson, marshal; R. L. Adams, tyler. The membership roll is now nearing the two hundred mark.

Pinole Lodge No. 353 held its preliminary meeting November 11, 1902, at which John Bermingham was elected chairman, and the charter was granted by Grand Master Orin S. Henderson on February 17, 1903, when J. C. F. Hall was elected master, A. Greenfield, senior warden. The lodge was organized with eighteen members, since which time it has added ninety-eight, and has lost five by death and twenty-three by dimit and other causes, having at present eighty-eight members.

Our finances are in good shape, the lodge is prosperous, and there will be added many good members during the next few months. A. Greenfield is filling the station of master for the second term, he having been the second master. S. V. Sharp, a young man and an active and zealous member, is senior warden, and A. D. Hinton, a hard-working and energetic brother, is junior warden. The last two are residents of Rodeo, whence the lodge has obtained some of its best members.

For many years the Masons of Pittsburg, California, plied back and forth faithfully attending their lodge at Antioch, a distance of seven miles, and this at a time when roads were not State highways and automobiles were unknown. Oftentimes it was noticeable that the majority at lodge were the Pittsburg members, notwithstanding the difficulties in getting there. When the town began to grow and the number of Masons increased, there began to rank in the breast of one of the members who had served the offices and for two years as master of Antioch Lodge No. 175, a cherished hope that a lodge might be instituted in his home town, Pittsburg. When at last it was brought before the other members at the home of A. V. McFaul on November 25, 1911, a great deal of enthusiasm was manifested and by January 20, 1912, the arrangements of details incident to the organization of Pittsburg Lodge No. 429 were completed. Twenty-two Master Masons, mostly dimitting from Antioch Lodge No. 175, comprised the new lodge, whose first meeting under dispensation was held February 20, 1912. The officers chosen were: Archie Valentine McFaul, W. M.; Ernest Herman Ward, S. W.; Harry W. Reinhart, J. W.; Bernard P. Lanteri, treasurer; Warren George Hubbard Croxon, secretary; Albert Hendricks Jongeneel, chaplain; James Shirley Hornsby, S. D.; John Lowes, J. D.; William James Buchanan, marshal; Weaver McPherson Bailey and David Israel, stewards; George Minaker, tyler. Charter was granted October 10,1912, and on November 9, 1912, the lodge was instituted and officers installed.

Grand Master W. P. Filmer officiated and Grand Secretary John Whicher, Grand Junior Deacon Fred B. Ward, with L. N. Buttner, Inspector of the Twenty-eighth Masonic District, attended the ceremonies. At the present time the membership has increased to double the original number, and on February 26, 1916, this event was celebrated by entertaining some of the neighbor lodges in an elaborate manner.

In 1912 a number of Masons, seeing the needs of an additional lodge at Richmond, on account of the rapid growth and the large territory that Richmond covers, petitioned the Grand Lodge for a special dispensation to form a new lodge. Under date of June 4, 1912, the lodge was organized with twenty-five charter members, under a special dispensation, dated May 24, 1912, issued by Past Grand Master Alonzo J. Monroe. The lodge under this special dispensation conferred the several degrees on a number of candidates and received a number of brothers by affiliation. October 10, 1912, a charter was issued by Grand Master Alonzo J. Monroe, and on November 12,1912, the lodge was constituted by Grand Master William P. Filmer and other officers of the Grand Lodge. The first officers of the lodge were: Hershey Annin Stiver, W. M.; James Edward Maxfield, S. W.; Thomas Thayer, J. W.; Leonard Little, treasurer; Albert Hamilton Poage, secretary; Edward Howe Harlow, chaplain; Luke Joseph Glavinovich, S. D.; Richard Edmond Slattery, J. D.; Ross Lewis Calfee, marshal; Clyde Everett Hopping and Walter Alexander Maier, stewards; Max Michaels, tyler. Since 19121913, Thomas Thayer and Luke Joseph Glavinovich have served as master. Richard Edmond Slattery is at present master. The lodge has had a steady growth and has a membership of over two hundred.

The history of Mount Diablo Lodge No. 448 is short on account of its recent founding, but if a detailed account of its early days was to be given it would show an unlimited amount of enthusiasm on the part of the handful of faithful members of the craft who felt that it was their duty and pleasure to promote the interests of the order in this part of Contra Costa County. The Grand Lodge of California granted a dispensation to the Masons in this locality on May 21, 1916, authorizing them to form, open, and conduct a Masonic lodge according to the ancient custom of the order. The first meeting was held May 30,1915. The lodge continued to work under this dispensation until October 17th of the same year, when the grand lodge granted this present charter. On that date the lodge was constituted and its officers installed by the grand lodge in the Masonic Temple in Oakland, Benjamin F. Bledsoe, Grand Master. L. L. Martin was the first master; Michaelis Neusteadter the senior warden and Charles W. Thissell, junior warden. Twenty-three members signed the by-laws. At the present writing the membership has reached forty, and, with the increasing enthusiasm on the part of all, the future of Mount Diablo Lodge No. 448, F. & A. M., will be at least an honor and pleasure to all members of the craft in Concord and the adjoining towns.

Dispensation to organize Antioch Chapter No. 65, R. A. M., was granted June 3, 1884; charter was issued April 29, 1885; and the chapter was constituted May 13, 1885. Officers: C. H. Frink, high priest; D. D. Wills, king; J. C. O'Brien, scribe; D. G. Darby, treasurer; W. H. Dobyns secretary; James Carter, captain of host; G. C. Wright, principal sojourner; S. H. McKellips, royal arch captain; Geo. Holliday, master of third vail; J. P. Abbott, master of second vail; N. W. Smith, master of first vail, and Geo. A. Minaker, guard.

Ariel Chapter No. 42, Order of the Eastern Star, was instituted in Antioch on March 30, 1880, with the following as charter members and officers: George Rice, worthy patron; Elizabeth Williams, worthy matron; Alice Rouse, associate matron; Clarence Frink, secretary; Mary Frink, treasurer; A. R. Jessup, conductress; Bertha Jacobs, associate conductress; Annie McKellips, Adah; Kate Forman, Ruth; Mary E. Smith, Esther; Nellie G. Abbott, Martha; Alice Harkinson, Electa. Beginning with meager numbers, the chapter has grown into one of the leading institutions of the city, and now has a membership of more than 140. Its roster contains the names of many of the leading people of Antioch, and the social functions for which the chapter stands sponsor are among the principal events in the community.

Crockett Chapter No. 184, O. E. S., was organized September 7, 1900. The officers at that time were: Emily Olletha Walker, worthy matron; Edmund Freund, worthy patron; Libbie Emma Reid, associate matron; Charles Philip Thomas, secretary; Edmund Robert Reid, treasurer; Emma Mary Hedemark, conductress; Nancy Calwell Moiles, associate conductress; Henrietta Maria Enos, Adah; Kate Emily Edwards, Ruth; Minnie Perrin Freund, Esther; Harriet Delila Weyman, Martha; Marie Schneider, Electa; Marie Thompson, warder; James Thompson, sentinel. Present officers: Maud Alice Gay, worthy matron; Jacob Erratt Hughes, worthy patron; Amelia Kleinkopf, associate matron; Helena C. Paul, secretary; Annie Edwards, treasurer; Grayce Anna Laidlaw, conductress; Annie J. Edwards, associate conductress; Enid Elizabeth Staples, Adah; Elizabeth Colinina Helen Burdon, Ruth; Louise Antonia Adams, Esther; Margaret Hughes, Martha; Daisy Stemmle, Electa; Sarah Davies Jones, warder; John Henry Dorman, sentinel; George Jones, chaplain; Louise Smith, marshal; Lurah Lennon Madden, organist; District Deputy Grand Matron of the Twenty-fifth District, Ethel I. Sweetser. Membership at the present time, 83.

Pinole Chapter No. 220, O. E. S., was instituted on February 23, 1904, by Grand Patron McNoble, assisted by Grand Secretary Kate J. Willats. Miss Susie Willats was also present and assisted. Following is a list of the fifteen charter members: Abraham Greenfield, Belle Greenfield, Jennie Paterson, Bertha Evans, Ellen E. Barrett, Emma Holliday, C. H. Holliday, Lillie E. Lehmkuhl, Chas. F. Lehmkuhl, May Enloe, Joseph V. Enloe, Lottie Pfeiffer, George W. Pfeiffer, Emily McKenzie (affiliation), William McKenzie (affiliation). Officers at that time: Lillie E. Lehmkuhl, worthy matron; William McKenzie, worthy patron; Jennie Paterson, associate matron; Joseph V. Enloe, secretary; Abraham Greenfield, treasurer; Emily McKenzie, conductress; Bertha Evans, associate conductress; Belle Greenfield, Adah; Emma Holliday, Ruth; May Enloe, Esther; Ellen Barrett, Martha; Lottie Pfeiffer, Electa; Charles F. Lehmkuhl, warder; George W. Pfeiffer, sentinel. Present officers (1916): Mary C. Woy, worthy matron; Henry McCullough, worthy patron; Isabell Fraser, associate matron; Ella Gerrish, secretary ; George Pfeiffer, treasurer; Goldie Sill, conductress; Nellie Graham, associate conductress; Minnie Higuera, Adah; Lillie Lehmkuhl, Ruth; Grace Piquett, Esther; Emily McKenzie, Martha; Lucia Robison, Electa; Lillie Catlett, chaplain; Lottie Pfeiffer, marshal; Gara Hughes, organist; William McKenzie, warder; Stephen Johnston, sentinel. Total membership, 47. Finance account, good. Masonic support, good. Harmony and sociability prevail.

Almona Chapter No. 214, O. E. S., was organized at Walnut Creek, September 5, 1903, with the following officers: Edith Clark, worthy matron; William Meese, worthy patron; Xarrissa Hill, associate matron; Lena C. Anderson, secretary; Mary Walker, treasurer; Ethel Flournoy, conductress; Ruby Harlan, associate conductress; Lizzie Lawrence, Adah; Mary Burpee, Ruth; Laura Hood, Esther; Lucy Hull, Electa; Lillian Close, chaplain; Nellie Fulton, organizer; Elizabeth Ramage, warder; James M. Stow, sentinel. The officers at present are as follows: May Elizabeth Stuchs, Lafayette, worthy matron; Harry Thurman Silver, Walnut Creek, worthy patron; Lizzie Adelaide Duncan, Walnut Creek, associate matron; May Spencer, Walnut Creek, secretary; Mary Burpee, Walnut Creek, treasurer; Eva Berry Leech, Walnut Creek, conductress; Adele Hook, Hookston, associate conductress; Maude Jones Silver, Walnut Creek, Adah; Ruby Burpee-Harlan, Walnut Creek, Ruth; Irene Bodva, Danville, Esther; Cora Billings Weister, Danville, Martha; Josephine Hook, Hookston, Electa; Lillian Grass, Danville, chaplain; Leona B. Abiott, Danville, marshal; Ida Hall, Alamo, organist; Louise Hook, Hookston, warder; Louis Irwin Stuchs, Lafayette, sentinel. The chapter lost by death, April 13, Belle Fiddis Brooks, associate conductress, and June 16, 1916, Anna Journal, conductress, so have had to substitute those two offices. Present membership, 117. Have $950 worth of stock in Masonic Hall Association. The Masonic Temple is in course of construction.

Los Ceritos Chapter No. 234, 0. E. S., was organized at Martinez July 22, 1905, with the following officers: Margaret V. Borland, worthy matron; William A. Hale, worthy patron; Mary E. Hayward, associate matron; Vesta E. Wilson, secretary; George A. Wiley, treasurer; Rebecca Pasch, conductress; Jennie I. Hale, associate conductreess; Grace S. Morrow, Adah; Linny Wiley, Ruth; Elizabeth S. Stewart, Esther; Beulah C. Hodapp, Martha; Ednette M. Ingraham, Electa; Margaret Crilley, warder; R. H. Latimer, sentinel. Present officers: Geneva H. Gleese, worthy matron; Joseph A. Royster, worthy patron; Rachel H. Elliott, associate matron; Mary E. Hayward, secretary; Don O. Brillhart, treasurer; Clara W. Van Prooyen, conductress;

Margaret L. Peck, associate conductress; Nannie E. Sharkey, Adah; Jennie A. Brillhart, Ruth; Olive W. Reed, Esther; Viola R. Coleman, Martha; Alta B. Hoadley, Electa; Sarah J. Davies, chaplain; Vesta E. Wilson, organist; Agnes S. Royster, warder; Orville E. Hayward, sentinel. Emma L. McClellan, marshal, died September 1, 1916. Present membership, 81.

Acantha Chapter No. 249, O. E. S., was organized at Richmond, September 7, 1906. Instituted by Grand Patron Florin Jones, assisted by Grand Treasurer Helen M. Seaman, acting as grand marshal, and Grand Secretary Kate J. Willats. The following were the officers for the first year: Margaret J. Schoen, worthy matron; Frederick M. Neville, worthy patron; Winifred Stockwell, associate matron; Anna Neville, conductress; Lola Jean McWay, associate conductress; Palmerton C. Campbell, secretary; Nathan J. Pritchard, treasurer; Mary E. Campbell, Adah; Kate McVicker, Ruth; Bessie Pritchard, Esther; Julia Odell, Martha; Amy McRacken, Electa; Eleanor Gregory, warder; Samuel Smith, sentinel; Alfeus Odell, chaplain. The present officers are as follows: Caroline Kinney, worthy matron; Clyde C. Olney, worthy patron; Fannie I. Rowland, associate matron; Bernice McCormick, secretary; Marietta Duncan, treasurer; Cora C. Thayer, conductress; Martha A. Chandler, associate conductress; Edna Christie, Adah Ethel Swearingen, Ruth; Sadie V. Osler, Esther; Della A. Long, Martha; Mary A. McDonough, Electa; John E. Breese, chaplain; Myrtle A. Stiver, marshal; Anna B. Miller, organist; Anna M. Radcliffe, warden; Jesse A. Osler, sentinel. Present membership, 199, with two more elected to affiliate, and two petitions for initiations received September 8, 1916, which was tenth anniversary of the chapter. From July 1, 1915, to July 1, 1916, received thirty-one into membership. The chapter is prosperous in every way, the members taking great interest, as is manifested by the attendance at the meetings.

RICHMOND LODGE NO. 1251, B. P. O. E.

On May 2, 1911, twenty-nine Elks signed a petition expressing their willingness and desire to organize an Elks Lodge in Richmond, and from that date begins the history of Elkdom in Richmond and Contra Costa County. Then came the meetings, where were discussed many things looking toward the advent of the fraternity and of obtaining the consent of Berkeley Lodge No. 1002, our mother-lodge. A committee was formed, and on the floor of the Berkeley lodge the request was made, and simultaneously the officers and brothers of that lodge arose and responded as being in favor of instituting such lodge and gave the committee guarantees of their heartiest assistance and support. From the request of Berkeley followed the request to the D. D. G. E. R., F. G. S. Conlon, of San Francisco. With Berkeley lodge, he was invited to Richmond on Sunday, at which time he was driven through the city to the Standard Oil Company's plant and that of the California Wine Association at Winehaven, to impress upon him the permanency of our institutions and resources. On returning we repaired to Brother Wylie's restaurant where a feed was spread. From there we went into session at Brother Abbott's office, and after laying our propositions before the D. D. G. E. R. he replied that from the spirit and enthusiasm shown he would sanction the project with his indorsement. A dispensation was asked and granted August 1,1911.

Eighteen of the twenty-nine petitioners met in Brother C. J. Rihn's office and selected the officers for the term, as follows: C. L. Abbott, exalted ruler; A. C. Lang, esteemed leading knight; C. J. Rihn, loyal knight; H. G. Biggs, lecturing knight; F. W. Smith, secretary; F. C. Schram, treasurer; W. V. Keltz, A. H. Burnett, and E. W. O'Brien, trustees; H. E. French, tyler; J. A. Bell, esquire; R. Bankhead, chaplain; D. H. Carpenter, inner guard.

After the officers had been selected came the question of institution, whom to invite, and how to care for them. A motion was made and approved to limit the expenditure to $150 and invite the mother-lodge with certain representatives of the neighboring lodges. Soon thereafter we concluded to invite all the Elks about the bay and let the expense take care of itself. On the night of September 19, 1911, twenty-five hundred visitors were in Richmond, and there was an institution unexampled and a spread of viands and vintage fit for the gods. Immediately succeeding meetings gave an impetus toward purchasing suitable property, so that when the time to build should arrive we would at least have our site. The Hall Association was incorporated January 26, 1912. The directors were as follows: C. L. Abbott, president; A. C. Lang, vice-president; W. T. Helms, secretary; E. M. Downer, treasurer; A. H. Burnett, F. C. Schram, H. W. Tuller, E. M. Tilden, M. L. Fernandez. The first meeting of directors was on February 3, 1912.

Two lots on Tenth and Macdonald Avenue being available, Brother E., M. Tilden, in behalf of the lodge, February 14, 1912, purchased the same at a cost of $12,000. Only a short time elapsed before we decided to sell more stock and issue bonds toward the building of a home. The contract for the basement was let on October 31, 1912. The contract for the building was let on April 25, 1913. The building, costing $78,000, was accepted January 26, 1914. The furnishings cost $22,000. The present structure with its beauty of architecture and many accommodations is the result. It stands out as the best and most modern building in Richmond, and is acknowledged the greatest private asset of our fast-growing city. It is a home for Elks, come from where they may. All are invited, all are welcome.

The Past Exalted Rulers are: Doctor C. L. Abbott, A. C. Lang, and Harcourt G. Biggs. The present officers are as follows: J. A. Bell, exalted ruler; Howard French, esteemed leading knight; Herman W. Tuller, esteemed loyal knight; Clare Horner, esteemed lecturing knight; J. P. Arnold, secretary; J. O. Ford, treasurer; W. S. Pierce, esquire; Rev. Thomas A. Boyer, chaplain; Joe Dietrich, inner guard; Peter Brown, tyler. Trustees: A. H. Burnett, D. H. Carpenter, and J. A. McVittie. Presley Neville, organist. Charter Members: C. L. Abbott, R. Bankhead, J. A. Bell, H. G. Biggs, A. H. Burnett, D. H. Carpenter, Charles Dalton, B. E. Fariss, H. E. French, J. E. Lowney, W. A. LaSalle, J. R. Froberg, J. J. Grant, W. E. Hanson, N. R. Jackson, W. V. Keltz, C. F. Kings, A. C. Lang, J. W. Melbourne, E .W. O'Brien, John Purnhagen, Chas. J. Rihn, H. L. Rutley, F. C. Schram, O. E. Smedley, Frank W. Smith, J. W. Switzer, E. H. Truax, Oliver Wylie.

NATIVE SONS OF THE GOLDEN WEST

General Winn Parlor No. 32, Antioch.—Instituted Saturday, July 26, 1884, by Grand President Steinbach, with a membership of 25. C. F. Montgomery, president, and C. M. Belshaw, secretary.

Mount Diablo Parlor No. 101, Martinez.—Instituted February 7, 1887, by Grand President Decker and D. D. G. P., C. M. Belshaw, with a membership of seventeen. T. A. McMahon, president, and F. L. Glass, secretary.

Central Parlor No. 140, Walnut Creek.—Instituted June 19, 1889, by Grand President Frank D. Ryan, with a membership of 39. E. B. Anderson, president, and James A. Black, secretary. Dissolved April 25, 1896.

Byron Parlor No. 170, Byron. — Instituted February 7, 1891, by Grand President Miller, with a membership of 20. W. H Johnston, president, and W. H. Lewis, secretary.

Sunrise Parlor No. 204, Pinole.—Instituted Agust 4, 1899, by Grand President Frank Mattison, with a membership of 33. J. W. Wilson, president, and John Wunderlich, secretary. Dissolved April 27, 1906.

Carquinez Parlor No. 205, Crockett.—Instituted August 5, 1899, by Grand President Frank Mattison, with a membership of 44. W. H. McDonald, president, and H. T. Smith, secretary.

Richmond Parlor No. 217, Richmond.—Instituted January 6, 1903, by Grand President Byington, with a membership of 21. C. F. Grant, president, and J. D. Grant, secretary.

Concord Parlor No. 245, Concord.—Instituted November 2, 1908, by Grand Organizer Andrew Mocker, with a membership of 30. A. C. Gehringer, president, and C. Hook, secretary.

Diamond Parlor No. 246, Pittsburg.—Instituted February 4, 1909, by Grand Organizer Mocker, with a membership of 27. W. G. H. Croxon, president, and L. H. Schmalholz, secretary.

San Ramon Valley Parlor No. 249, Danville.—Instituted April 10, 1909, by Grand Organizer Mocker, with a membership of 23. C. G. Goold, president, and S. H. Flournoy, secretary.

CHAPTER XXV. MARTINEZ

The first settlement of the region contingent to the city of Martinez, the county seat of Contra Costa County, was made nearly a century ago.

In the year 1823, over twenty years before gold was discovered in California, and before the eyes of the East, and in fact the entire world, turned toward the Golden West, Ignacio Martinez and Francisco Castro applied for and received grants to vast tracts of land, the latter receiving what was known as the San Pablo Rancho, and Martinez receiving the Pinole grant. Their nearest neighbors were the Peraltas and the Castros, of San Antonio and San Lorenzo. Martinez and Castro erected adobe residences, pretentious ones for that period, built barns, and planted trees and vines, becoming the first fruit- and grape-growers in Contra Costa County. Other families followed, but the haciendas of these two grandees were the hub of the life and the activity of this section.

There were no roads in those days. Trails led here and there across the valleys of waving corn and over the hills where the virgin oak flourished. Fences were unknown; these early settlers did not fence off one piece of their land from another but allowed their cattle to roam at will.

The first of the two above-named ranchos was named for Saint Paul (San Pablo), who was one of the most enthusiastic as well as favorite disciples of the Savior. The other, and the one with which we are concerned in this article, derives its name from pinole (meal), the story being told that a band of hungry Mexicans, who had been in pursuit of a band of Indians in the foothills of Mount Diablo, had their hunger appeased at a small settlement on San Pablo Bay en route to the Mission San Rafael. The small and nearly famished band passed through the valley of El Hambre (the vale of hunger), and their first food was a mess of meal obtained at this point, which they thereupon designated Pinole, and when Ignacio Martinez was granted these leagues of land he perpetuated the name given the region by the famished troopers.

In 1832 William Welch, a Scotchman, secured title to the tract of land known as the Welch (or Las Juntas) Rancho, on which a portion of the city of Martinez now stands.

From that time up to the discovery of gold at Sutter's mill there was little development of this region. In 1849 Colonel William M. Smith, acting as agent for the Martinez family, from whom the city derives its name, decided upon founding a town. In furtherance of this project he employed Thomas A. Brown, who later became superior judge, to survey and lay out one hundred and twenty acres on the westerly side of El Hambre Creek. This was promptly done, and the tract being subdivided, the lots and blocks were quickly sold and the building of houses and stores commenced. The first building erected in the town was the home of Doctor Leffler, built by Nicholas Hunsaker, and the second by Judge Brown, in which he, with his brother Warren and Napoleon B. Smith, opened the first trading-post in the county. The house later occupied by E. W. Miller was built for a store for Boorham & Dana in 1849. About the same time a store was erected for Howard & Wells. It was managed by Howard Havens, who later became the cashier of the Donohoe-Kelly Bank of San Francisco.

In 1850-51 the first addition to the town was surveyed by Judge Brown, under instructions from the owners of the Welch Rancho, El Hambre Creek being the line which divides the original survey (Pinole) from the additional survey (Welch, or Las

Juntas). This tract consisted of between five hundred and six hundred acres and was also laid out in blocks and lots. The first buildings erected were the houses of Wise, Douglas, Lawless, McMahon, Doctor Bolton, and the Contra Costa News office. The Douglas house, it might be noted in passing, was used as the first office of the county clerk.

In 1850 a negro named Jones opened a hotel on the site where the Alhambra Hotel was opened in later years and for a long period conducted by Josiah Sturges. At this time the adobe residence of Vicente Martinez stood on what later became known as the Doctor John Strentzel property, but other adobes were built soon after, closer to the heart of the town.

In 1851 the first school was opened in the house which Judge Brown and his family occupied later, the school-room being used for a meeting-house on Sundays, and the court, during its session, and the Masonic lodge holding their meetings upstairs. R. B. McNair was the first teacher, although it has been stated that B. R. Holliday taught the first school in the town.

Even in those early times Martinez had efficient teachers, but the lack of a suitable school-building was felt. Although complaint was made in 1858 that the school was not kept open for a sufficient period during the year, it was not until 1872 that the difficulty was solved by the erection of an adequate building. This was accomplished by the levying of a special school-district tax, by which over six thousand dollars was raised for the first permanent schoolhouse in Martinez. Today the schools of this town will compare favorably with any others in the State.

In 1852 the Union Hotel was built on the site of the James Hoey residence, and was for years conducted by Captain R. E. Borden, then county treasurer.

On January 25, 1851, a petition signed by the citizens of Martinez was presented to the Court of Sessions, through District Attorney J. F. Williams, praying for the incorporation of the town of Martinez. The petition reads as follows: "To the Honorable F. M. Warmcastle, County Judge: Your petitioners, citizens of Martinez, pray your honor to incorporate the following metes and bounds to be known as the town of Martinez and to establish therein a police for their local government and regulation of any commons pertaining to such town to wit: Commencing at a point opposite the old ferry-house in the Straits of Carquinez, one fourth of a mile from high-water mark; thence up the Straits of Carquinez in a straight line one mile to a one one-fourth of a mile from high-water mark; thence running in a southeasterly direction at right angles with the first line, one mile; thence running in a northwesterly direction at right angles with the last line, one mile; thence in a northeasterly direction at right angles with the last line to the place of beginning, so as to include one mile square."

The court thereupon ordered that the town of Martinez be duly incorporated, and the order provided that the election of the first trustees be held on February 8, 1851. After a brief period, the Supreme Court declared the act under which the incorporation had been effected void.

Incorporation anew under the general law was objected to as involving too much expense and machinery, and for over a quarter century, until 1876, Martinez continued as a village, without corporate being or authority.

From the year 1852 on the town began to assert itself and became known far and wide. Many new buildings were erected and a general era of prosperity ensued.

The Contra Costa Gazette, one of the oldest newspapers in the State of California, was established in Martinez on Saturday, September 18, 1858, by W. B. Soule & Company. For nearly three-score years, without missing an issue, this publication has recorded each week the events which have contributed to the history of Contra Costa County. The files at many times have been used as reference by the archivists of the University of California in the compilation of California history.

Throughout its entire existence the politics of the paper have remained Republican. On the seventh publication the management was changed and C. R. K. Bonnard and B. E. Hillsman became the owners. From its first issue the paper appeared in four pages of seven columns, well edited and printed, at a subscription price of five dollars a year. The Bonnard Company controlled the Gazette until February 26, 1859, when it was purchased by W. Bradford, who became the sole owner. Bradford conducted the paper alone until April 28, 1860, when he sold an undivided half interest to R. R. Bunker. Under this management it was published until March 23, 1861, when Bradford disposed of his interest to W. W. Theobalds. With the development of the grain-shipping industry and agricultural activity at Pacheco, situated five miles from Martinez, that community became the leading commercial center of the county.

In September, 1861, the Gazette was moved to Pacheco. In that town it was published for twelve years. The brick building, of which the plant occupied the second floor, was badly damaged by an earthquake on October 21, 1868. A near-by barn was secured, and, after many difficulties in moving the machinery and type from the shattered structure, the paper was published at its usual time. On July 8, 1865, another change occurred in the management, when C. B. Porter purchased the interest of Theobalds. The life of the Gazette has not been without its misfortunes, the second of which occurred in September, 1871. One morning a fire broke out in the building, and before it could be extinguished every scrap of material and machinery had been destroyed. Within forty-eight hours an entire new plant had been secured and the paper appeared on its usual day of issue. Subsequent to the gradual decline of Pacheco as a shipping center, the Gazette was moved back to Martinez in November, 1873. A new frame structure was erected for the use of the paper in Main Street, on the present site of the Gazette building. On March 3, 1882, F. K. Foster, a newspaperman well known throughout the State, purchased a third interest in the publication, which he held until November 3, 1883, when Porter severed his connection with the concern and a co-partnership was formed between Bunker and Foster.

This firm conducted the paper until August 27, 1887, when Thomas S. Davenport purchased the interest of Foster. On January 4, 1888, appeared the first publication of the Gazette as a semi-weekly. The size of the paper was decreased from seven to six columns, four pages. After being published at this size until April 11, 1888, the increase of business necessitated its enlargement to eight columns. James Foster, on October 3, 1888, purchased from Davenport a half interest, which he held, with Bunker as a partner, until his death, on July 17, 1893. After being published for five years as a semi-weekly, the paper was restored on January 7, 1893 to a weekly publication. Following the death of Foster, his interest was sold to Wallace Clarence Brown, who edited the paper in conjunction with Bunker. After thirty-six years as a part owner of the Gazette, Bunker disposed of his interest to Brown on December 7,1895.

After conducting the paper for three years, Brown sold the entire business in 1898 to G. E. Milnes. On March 1, 1900, the Daily Press, the first successful daily paper in Contra Costa County, was established in Martinez by W. A. Rugg. After publishing the Press for four years, Rugg disposed of the paper to the Gazette Publishing Company, which changed the name to the Daily Gazette. In 1907 Rugg, the former editor of the Daily Press, purchased from G. E. Milnes the controlling interest in the Gazette Publishing Company, and from that time on the management of the two publications has remained the same.

The California Express was published at Martinez about 1867 by Alexander Montgomery, who had in 1861 commenced the publication of the Napa Echo, which violently opposed the administration of President Lincoln, and every measure taken to subdue the Southern Rebellion. Its circulation and patronage were limited, and in a pecuniary point of view it was never successful. Still it kept on until April, 1865, when it suspended publication on the morning of the announcement of Lincoln's assassination. After its removal to Martinez it continued regularly for about two years.

The Enterprise was started in Martinez in 1871 by J. W. Collier as a democratic paper. It was, however, printed in San Francisco, the publication office being at Martinez. It lived but a short time.

The Contra Costa Standard was established at Pacheco in 1873. In October, 1877, it was removed to Martinez. It has been one of the influential weekly publications in the central section of the State in that it has always advocated and worked for those principles that make for progress and the development of the county's interests. The Martinez Daily Standard is published in conjunction with the weekly Contra Costa Standard. Both are owned by the Contra Costa Publishing Company, a joint stock company. The daily was established in 1911 and has become an influential factor in the county's affairs. In politics these two publications are of Republican affiliation and strong advocates of Republican policies, though of the more progressive or independent type.

The weekly consists of eight pages and is published on Saturday. The daily is a four-page publication and is issued every evening except Sunday. Will R. Sharkey is the editor and manager of both publications.

On November 6, 1858, W. K. Leavitt was given the contract for the building of the Roman Catholic church, which was blown down about 1866, whereupon the present edifice was erected.

On April 8, 1859, Martinez and Benicia were first joined by telegraph and on June 6th of the same year Mette & Co. established the first stage line between Martinez and Oakland.

On September 17, 1860, Martinez Engine Company No. 1 was organized. On February 15, 1862, the ladies of Martinez raised a fund of one hundred dollars in a few hours for the fencing of the Alhambra Cemetery. In May, 1867, Coffin & Standish erected a flour-mill which was later occupied by Black's cannery.

The Martinez Water Company was incorporated on September 5,1871.

Martinez Hook and Ladder Company was organized on February 4, 1871.

In February, 1876, the citizens of Martinez, mindful of the fact that the corporate existence of the town had lapsed many years before, reincorporated the municipality, the boundaries being defined as follows:

"Beginning at a point where the fence dividing the lands of J. P. Jones and L. I. Fish touches the Straits of Carquinez; thence southwardly along the said fence and continuing the same course to the line of the homestead tract of H. Bush; thence westwardly along the north line of Bush's homestead tract to the Arroyo del Hambre; thence southerly along said arroyo to the center of G Street; thence westwardly along G Street to the western boundary of the town of Martinez as originally surveyed; thence northwardly, following the western boundary of the town plat to the Straits of Carquinez; thence eastwardly along the shores of the Straits of Carquinez to the place of beginning." On May 23, 1876, Thomas McMahon and L. C. Wittenmyer were elected two of the three trustees and J. R. L. Smith assessor and tax-collector.

In the year 1879 the Bush homestead property was purchased for the site of a Roman Catholic college, which was later erected by the Christian Brothers Society of St. Mary's College and given the name of the De La Salle Institute.

Ten years previous to this time, Grace Church (Protestant-Episcopal) was built, although the many communicants who resided here had attended worship since 1854 at St. Paul's Church, Benicia, at times having services here in the Methodist church. The Rev. E. P. Gray was the first pastor, and the parish is now in charge of the Rev. E. Glandon Davies. The Congregational church was organized in Martinez on June 18, 1874, and the first resident pastor was the Rev. W. S. Clark. A few years later the Methodist church building was purchased. The work of the church is now under the direction of the Rev. Clarence A. Stone.

In the spring of 1874 the Contra Costa News was established in the town of Pacheco, but was later removed to Martinez, where it existed under various managements and under numerous names until it has become the Contra Costa Standard.

The Alhambra Cemetery (Protestant) was originally a portion of the Pinole grant included within the boundaries of the town of Martinez by the original survey. The area is five acres and is now the property of the association organized for the purpose of managing its affairs. Contiguous to Alhambra Cemetery is St. Catherine's Cemetery (Roman Catholic)' where many of the early settlers in this county and town have been laid to rest.

For several years Shirley & Mizner operated the ferry between Martinez and Benicia, continuing in that business, with a landing at the foot of Ferry Street, until the late '70s, when they sold out to the Northern Railway Company, which, together with the San Pablo & Tulare Railway Company, built the first railroad through Martinez. The original line from Oakland east—the "golden spike" line—was built through Martinez, via Tracy, Lathrop, and Lodi, to Sacramento, the Benicia-Sacramento line—the "Calpe"—being constructed several years later.

The old Morgan House, erected in 1885 at the corner of Main and Ferry streets, was destroyed by fire in 1887, and Bernardo Fernandez, who had acquired the property, immediately started the erection of the Martinez Hotel, which stands today on the property, a three-story structure, lately remodeled, but which at the time was the most pretentious building in the county. In the same year the Congregational church as it stands today was erected and two years later the Martinez Electric Light & Gas Company was started.

It is no exaggeration to state that Martinez is one of the most picturesque towns in the State. It has a sylvan beauty all its own; shade-trees abound on every street and hedges and flowering plants surround most of the residences. Climate and soil are such that some of the finest fruits and flowers of Contra Costa County are grown in its vicinity. In the near-by valleys are situated some of the finest vineyards and orchards in the State. They are made possible largely by the mountain range which shelters this region from sea-winds. Through this range the Straits of Carquinez have forced their way.

Situated on the Straits of Carquinez, all the commerce of the Sacramento and San Joaquin rivers is brought in touch with Martinez, a goodly share of which she receives. Suisun Bay, about three miles wide at this point, lies directly in front of the town. Across the channel lies Benicia, with its army barracks, and its big railroad ferry, and beyond which may be seen the purple and gently rolling contour of the Coast Range mountains. On the southern side of the straits, Martinez nestles in a crescent-shaped cove, sheltered on the west by a wall of hills which rise abruptly from the water, affording an effective barrier against the trade-winds of the Pacific and forming a picturesque background.

Like all other communities, Martinez has suffered the usual loss from devastating fires. The first serious conflagration occurred in September, 1856, when the Union Hotel and Blum's, Lazar's, and Hook's stores were destroyed. No serious fire occurred again until July 18, 1867; on this date the mansion on the Gift place was destroyed. Then followed another interval of almost the same duration, but on December 12, 1876, a group of five fine buildings on the southwest corner of Main and Ferry streets was obliterated. A sixth building, belonging to John McCann, also suffered heavy damage, but he made sufficient repairs to again occupy it by the 30th of December. Fire again visited Martinez on March 16, 1877, on this occasion the home of Mrs. Jane E. Chase being destroyed, and on January 6, 1878, the Granger's Restaurant, owned by F. D. Briare, met a similar fate. A loss that was severely felt occurred on March 8, 1880, when the Alhambra schoolhouse was burned to the ground. Doubtless there have been occasional conflagrations since this last date, but they are here omitted as lacking in the historical interest of the earlier disasters. Today Martinez has a thoroughly modern and efficient fire equipment, of which its citizens are justly proud, and the town is thus effectually insured against serious disaster from fire.

The first serious earthquake to be felt by Martinez was on Wednesday, October 21, 1868, considerable damage being caused by a temblor that simultaneously visited various other parts of the State. The new stone building of the Alhambra Hotel was damaged to the extent of having two of its walls thrown down. The walls of the brick buildings belonging to Blum, Lazar, Colman, and the Fish Brothers were considerably cracked. The heaviest toll was levied on the courthouse, a part of the top and rear walls of which was thrown down.

In common with cities of other sections of the State, Martinez felt the severe earthquake of April 18, 1906, but the damage sustained was slight and such as could be speedily repaired. It may be mentioned at this point that no lives were lost on either occasion. The observation is often made in California that earthquakes in this region are far less to be feared than the devastating cyclones and thunder-storms in the East.

In the old days, when the town was under the spell of the Spanish influence, along with the other sections of central and southern California, there was no great haste about doing things. Her population, in which the Latin races predominated, basked in the wonderful California climate, devoid of ambition to enter the lists of commercialism with its attendant hurry and rush. A living could be made with comparatively little toil, and why disturb oneself beyond procuring the necessaries of life? There was always manana, and today one might enjoy a siesta.

The old-time afternoon siesta lengthened into years instead of hours. Its sway persisted for six decades, and then it passed out as completely as once had been its dominion. Martinez is living today. Gone are manana and the siesta, for Martinez, keeping pace with the other thriving cities of Contra Costa County, has awakened to the keen throb of commercial activity and civic pride.

The population of Martinez has grown so rapidly in the past two years (1915-16) that hotels and restaurants have been hard pressed to keep pace with the demand for accommodations, although many new buildings have been erected and old ones have been remodeled and enlarged. This was all brought about by the Royal Dutch Shell Company.

Selecting Martinez, with its splendid transportation facilities, both by water and rail, as being in every way desirable for the location of its oil refineries, this great concern purchased four hundred acres of land in and adjacent to the town, embracing the Arnstein, Cutler, and Potter holdings, began active building operations toward the end of 1914, and erected a $5,000,000 refinery to employ over two thousand men. The California branch of the immense Dutch-English syndicate is known as the Shell Oil Company of California and is capitalized at $55,000,000.

The parent corporation has extensive oil holdings in the Dutch East Indies, Romania, Russia, and Egypt, and is a large manufacturer of gasoline, kerosene, and lubricating oils and greases. The California operations began with the purchase of some of the finest holdings in the Coalinga oil-fields. A pipe-line eight inches in diameter now extends from the Coalinga oil holdings to the refinery at Martinez, a distance of 176 miles. It is capable of supplying about 15,000 barrels of crude oil per day. In less than two years this company has accomplished a vast amount of work. The first view of the Shell properties is met over the hill and just east of the main refinery. Here are seen twenty mammoth steel tanks, capable of holding in the aggregate over a million barrels of crude oil. These tanks cost a total of over $300,000. Counting all, big and little, the company will have about 175 tanks, with a total capacity of over three million barrels.

At the central refinery one's attention is first arrested by the Trumble plant. Here are found an immense maze and network of pipes that carry in the crude oil, to go through the various stages of refinement, at the rate of ten thousand barrels a day. It all looks like Greek to the visitor, although the guide seems to have a mass of information at the end of his tongue. He talks glibly of superheaters, dephlegmators, and condensers, and we have to take his word for it and pass on. Soon we find' ourselves in the big boiler-house, where eight Heine water-tube boilers supply all the steam for the refinery. Although they develop two thousand horse-power, only two men are required to watch over them. The place is scrupulously clean throughout.

Just in front of the boiler-house the pumping plant is situated. Twenty great pumps are kept busy pumping the distilled product, in its various stages, to the storage-tanks, where the finished product is kept. A little farther along we come to the two colossal cooling towers, which help to economize on the water consumption, which is a large item in a plant of this size. Passing around to the north, we view the kerosene agitators, with a capacity of treating four thousand barrels. Then we find ourselves at the bleaching-house, where the celebrated Shell lubricants are made. Our time grows short, so we rapidly pass on to the machine shops and main storehouse, both marvels of efficiency.

Along the water-front all the varied activities of filling and shipping barreled and canned light oils are carried on. Here a wharf thirty-three hundred feet long stretches out to deep water, where there is a depth of thirty-two feet at low tide, enabling the largest ocean-going vessels to load at all times of the year. Extending from the product tanks to the docks are seven pipe-lines, enabling vessels to load with five thousand barrels of any one product in an hour. All parts of the refinery are connected with the wharf by a narrow-gauge railway.

Some idea of the vast amount of work that has been done is gained from the fact that over four hundred thousand cubic feet of earth has been excavated for the erection of tanks, buildings, and the construction of roads. About seven thousand cubic feet of concrete has been laid down for the foundations of buildings. Upward of four miles of macadamized roads extend to all parts of the large tract, and over forty miles of pipe-line has been laid to date.

Starting with a pay-roll of three thousand dollars a month in December, 1914, the Shell Oil Company was paying forty-three thousand dollars a month in December, 1915. The pay-roll is doubtless much larger now, with the addition of many skilled men to operate the plant.

Just east of the city, at the terminus of a 275-mile pipe-line from the Kern-Midway field near Bakersfield, the refinery of the Associated Oil Company is situated. Work is now (in the summer of 1916) being pushed forward to double the capacity of the refinery, to take care of its rapidly increasing business. The capacity of the new plant will be twenty-five thousand barrels a day, the refined products including gasoline, distillate, kerosene, and benzine. The annual output will be worth about three million dollars, and the annual pay-roll will approach $150,000.

The Associated Oil Company has also leased and operates, in connection with its own plant, the refinery of the American Oriental Oil Company at Martinez.

Another industry of which Martinez is proud is the Mountain Copper Company, situated about a mile and a half northeast, just beyond the city limits, occupying Bullshead Point, on the shore of Suisun Bay.

Here one beholds an immense chimney, surrounded by factory buildings. An immense sign, large enough to be read miles away, bears the name "Mococo," by which the community is known. The title was derived from the first two letters of each of the words Mountain Copper Company. This institution, which is largely controlled by English capital and which operates entirely in California, has been in existence since 1894. Since that year it has operated four copper mines in Shasta County, including the famous Iron Mountain mine, from which twenty million dollars' worth of copper was taken before it showed signs of being exhausted, when other mines were developed to take its place. The company now smelts all its ores at the Mococo plant, established in 1905.

A smelter at Keswick, in Shasta County, was abandoned in 1907, and a similar plant in New Jersey was closed down in 1906, it being found more economical and satisfactory in every way to perform all the work at the local plant. To accomplish this the establishment runs day and night the year round.

The product from the mines is divided into two classes, known as siliceous ore and sulphide ore. The former carries about three per cent of copper and the latter is rich in sulphuric acid. The siliceous ore 1s melted, and from it is extracted blister copper, which is molded into "pigs" weighing two hundred and forty pounds each. The sulphide ore is shipped to the various manufacturers of sulphuric acid on the Pacific Coast, including the Standard Oil Company, the General Chemical Company, and the Du Pont Powder Company. After roasting out the sulphur, the residue, containing about one per cent of copper and a small amount of gold and silver, is returned to the Mountain Copper Company. The company also has its own sulphuric-acid plant, utilizing the sulphur from the Iron Mountain ore.

Of growing interest to California agriculturists is the superior quality of fertilizer which Mococo plant turns out from its by-products. It is commercially known as superphosphate and is the basis of all mixed fertilizers. The plant is capable of manufacturing about thirty thousand tons of fertilizer a year. Owing to the fertility of California's soil, agriculturists in the past have used very little fertilizer, but it is coming more and more into use, especially by the far-sighted and scientific farmers. According to T. B. Smith, the superintendent of the company, "the State of California at present uses only from forty thousand to fifty thousand tons of fertilizer a year, while some smaller States back East use from seven hundred thousand to eight hundred thousand tons; but they'll all have to come to it." The company's holdings cover fifty-five acres of highland and twenty-five acres of marsh. The smelter has a capacity of four hundred tons of ore a day, or a monthly output of five hundred tons of blister copper. The heat is contributed by three immense reverberating furnaces, the largest of which consumes ninety-three hundred gallons of fuel-oil a day, the other two requiring seven thousand gallons each. Copper smelting takes place at a temperature of thirteen hundred degrees centigrade, and the process requires the highest degree of accuracy. An error of five minutes over or under would spoil an entire batch, but such a mistake has not occurred in six years.

A foreman, who is a master in his line, is always on the watch. The various products are valued at two and a quarter million dollars annually, and the yearly pay-roll is nearly half a million dollars, four hundred men being employed.

The operations are conducted in such a manner that no injurious odors are released, and this condition permits the most luxurious plant life to flourish about the grounds. Here are found a variety of fruits, banks of poppies and lupine, and even a field of hay. It is asserted that a similar sight will not be found at any other smelter in the world.

Martinez has numerous other commercial and industrial interests, of which time and space forbid more than a brief mention. These include one distinctly home product, the Stephenson patent cooler, manufactured by the L. Anderson Lumber Company. The device is an iceless cooler, a great boon to housewives, enabling them to keep vegetables, meats, and cooked foods from one meal to another with none of the inconveniences of a refrigerator. There is also a great demand for it among dairymen. The secret of the cooler, which resembles an ordinary cupboard, is in its burlap side-walls, a water-pan beneath, and tubes for the circulation of air. In a room at a temperature of ninety degrees, the thermometer in the cooler stands at sixty degrees. E. J. Randall, a resident of Concord, is the manager of the company. He gives the sales his personal attention, and states that the cooler now sells in many States of the Union, and even as far away as Cuba. It has never been necessary to employ a road salesman, as the demand has kept the plant running to full capacity. About fifteen hundred were manufactured last year. The Anderson Company also operates a complete lumber yard and is one of the oldest lumber and building-material concerns in the section.

Another long-established business institution is the J. E. Colton Winery on West Howard Street. Colton has been engaged in viticulture for over twenty years, and has a fine fifty-acre vineyard, half of which is devoted to table grapes and half to wine grapes. Aged wines are his specialty. Each year over 125,000 gallons of the best quality of dry wines is produced, and this finds a ready sale throughout the State.

The Colton Winery, the largest independent winery in the county, is operated under the most sanitary conditions possible. Colton, who is serving his first term as city trustee and mayor, is a strong exponent of the City Beautiful idea.

MARTINEZ DEVELOPMENT BOARD

All the functions of a chamber of commerce are performed by the recently organized Martinez Development Board, whose membership comprises some of the most wide-awake citizens of Martinez. The new organization is backed by the business men of the community and is making every effort to enhance the growth of the town and further its commercial interests. Judge C. H. Hayden, member of the city council, is president of the board; O. K. Smith, a prominent official of the Mountain Copper Company, is vice-president; Don C. Ray, district manager for the Pacific Gas & Electric Company, is secretary; A. E. Dunkel, former county recorder, now head of a large abstract and title business, is treasurer. The board of governors consists of the following prominent citizens: J. E. Rodgers, R. R. Veale, Hardin Morrow, A. E. Blum, E. A. Majors, A. E. Dunkel, B. Schapiro, and C. M. Wooster.

Although organized late in 1915, the Martinez Development Board carried to a successful conclusion a number of large projects before the end of the year. A very important matter which is being ably conducted by the Board is that of settling all litigation over landholdings along the city water-front, so that there will be no obstruction in the way of manufacturing and other interests using this acreage for the future welfare of Martinez. During the past year (1916) the activities of the board have been largely directed toward obtaining a new charter for Martinez, in keeping with the larger growth and activities of the municipality. The organization is also working diligently in favor of a city-owned water supply, improvements in paved streets, and for bond issues to make these projects possible.

PUBLIC BUILDINGS

Among the newer public buildings that reflect great credit on Martinez is the county hospital, recently erected at a cost of seventy thousand dollars. It is picturesquely situated on a promontory overlooking the city proper. Constructed of brick and concrete, the handsome structure comprises three stories, made up of two main wings, with a connecting bridge, or corridor. The surrounding grounds are maintained in a manner quite in keeping with the dignity and beauty of the edifice. Here a skilled staff of physicians and surgeons ministers to the unfortunate and suffering in a most competent and efficient manner.

The new city hall is located in the heart of town. In this building are conducted all the municipal affairs which are now administered at the courthouse.

Most impressive of all the public buildings of Martinez is the courthouse, which was erected in 1901, at a cost of six hundred thousand dollars. It comprises two full stories and a basement, granite and concrete being used in its construction. The whole is topped by a magnificent dome that lends the appearance of a capital building. One is equally impressed with the interior, all of the offices being handsomely equipped with Oriental rugs and mission furniture, the equal of which is seldom found in a building of this kind.

Martinez became the county seat in 1851, and such it has remained ever since. The present county officials are as follows: Superior judges, R. H. Latimer and A. B. McKenzie, both of Martinez; supervisors, Zeb Knott, of Richmond, J. P. Casey, of Port Costa, Vincent Hook, of Concord, W. J. Buchanan, of Pittsburg, and J. H. Trythall, of Antioch; county clerk, J. H. Wells, of Martinez; district attorney, T. D. Johnston, of Martinez; sheriff, R. R. Veale, of Martinez; auditor, A. N. Sullenger, of Martinez; recorder, M. H. Hurley, of Martinez; assessor, George O. Meese, of Martinez; tax collector, M. W. Joost, of Martinez; treasurer, J. Rio Baker, of Martinez; superintendent of schools, W. H. Hanlon, of Martinez; coroner, Doctor C. L. Abbott, of Richmond ; public administrator, C. E. Daley, of Martinez; surveyor, Ralph R. Arnold, of Martinez; superintendent of county hospital, W. H. Hough, of Martinez; county physician, E. W. Merrithew, of Martinez; probation officer, A. J. McMahon, of Martinez; health officer, W. S. George, of Antioch.

The following miscellaneous items form a part of the history of the town of Martinez: Commercial Hotel, Main Street, built in 1892; destroyed by fire in 1904. County Hospital established in the '90s, new brick building built in 1910, and new addition in 1915. Atchison, Topeka & Santa Fe line built through in 1891. Courthouse erected in 1901, at cost of over $600,000; Hall of Records proposed directly across street, in property acquired several years ago. Fire started August 19, 1904, in Stephenson patent cooler factory, wiping out two blocks, including the Curry livery stable, the opera-house, the Bank of Martinez, the McNamara-Winkelman block, Rankin building, and Commercial Hotel. Mountain Copper smelter erected in 1892, employing nearly 300 men. Bullshead Oil Works, now American Oriental Company, built refinery in 1905. Martinez Electric Light & Gas Works inaugurated in 1887. Pacific Coast Steel & Iron Manufacturing Company built steel works in 1884. Northern Railway Company (Southern Pacific) and San Pablo & Tulare Railroad Company built through here in late '70s.

Shirley & Mizner then sold Martinez-to-Benicia ferry to railroad company, which closed up the ferry service. Peyton Chemical Works built in 1900. California Transportation Company (river steamer line) built wharf and began regular service in 1909. Congregational church built in 1904. Alhambra water plant established in 1903, bottling water piped from Alhambra Springs, six miles out in Alhambra Valley.

Under bond issue in 1911 city acquired fifty-five acres of water-front land and built municipal wharf and city hall. Pacific Gas & Electric Company purchased Contra Costa Electric Light & Power Company in 1911 and entered local field. Great Western Power Company came in 1913. Contra Costa Gas Company began service in 1915. Corporate limits of town extended in 1909; second extension attempted in 1916 but failed. Alhambra high-school building erected in 1904, and grammar-school building in 1909. Bonds voted for new $51,000 grammar school.

New home sites opened for settlement in last few years, water mains extended, many miles of cement sidewalks laid, electric-lighting system extended, new homes built, street paving commenced.

The Martinez-Benicia ferry was established in 1913. The State highway is how building from Martinez to Berkeley. The county highway connects with tunnel road and Mount Diablo Boulevard and new bayshore highway to Bay Point, bringing Associated Oil Refinery within three miles of city.

CHAPTER XXVI. RICHMOND

To speak or write about Richmond in a historical way is exceedingly difficult, for as it is a record of achievement from beginning to end, and this achievement has been so truly marvelous, it must sound to the uninitiated more like romance than history. The old saying that "Truth is stranger than fiction" holds good with Richmond, for no fiction writer could possibly chronicle one continual chain of big achievements on the part of a small city as it grew to large dimensions and show a more startling array of fancies than are the true facts and figures concerning the growth and accomplishments of the city of Richmond.

The strategic location of Richmond upon San Francisco Bay, its deep-water harbors, its proximity to the metropolis of San Francisco, its being the terminal of the Santa Fe Railway and an important shipping-point for the Southern Pacific Company, two great transcontinental arteries of world-wide commerce, the early location here of the great Standard Oil Company with the refining and manufacturing plant now grown to be the second largest in the world, are facts enough of themselves to convince almost anyone who would make a study of the general causes which lead up to the location, establishment, and growth of important cities that all of the necessary ingredients are at hand in Richmond.

The fact that San Francisco, the cosmopolitan metropolis and money center of the Pacific Coast for the past half century, is situated upon a peninsula across the bay several miles from the mainland, and the further fact that Richmond is the only city on the mainland side of this greatest bay in America having main-line connections with the through railways, and land-locked deep-water harbors where the ships from the Orient and all over the world can dock and at once connect with these railroads, could bring but one logical conclusion to the student of city building who realized these facts and then took a glance into the probable future. This conclusion must be that as the Pacific Coast grew and expanded commercially and in population a great manufacturing and shipping port had in time to spring up and grow into importance, just as Richmond is now doing, and in part has already done.

Unquestionably the expert financiers and heads of departments of the Standard Oil Company had all these facts in view when its monster refinery was located at Richmond instead of at Oakland, San Francisco, or elsewhere, and many other immense manufacturing concerns, such as the Pullman car shops, which have located at Richmond since then, had these facts well in mind.

I had these facts in view when I purchased years ago a large tract of land along the southern water-front of Richmond, adjacent to its harbors, instead of acquiring land farther inland, where the first units of the city would quite likely grow up into commercial activity before the water-front sections. I built for the future, and am still so building, and have never had the slightest reason for believing that the logic mapped out in the first place was not correct. In fact recent great developments have proven this logic beyond all cavil or possibility of error. What all great maritime cities of the world are to their respective localities, Richmond is destined to be to the San Francisco Bay region, and its truly marvelous achievement up to this time, during its as yet very short period of existence, is absolute and positive proof of this.

So rapid has been this growth that it is not equaled by any other city in the West, and not surpassed by any in America. This has given Richmond the nicknames of

"The Wonder City" and "The Pittsburg of the West," and has already made it known all over this country and in many foreign lands.

Fifteen years ago there was no Richmond—nothing but a few grain and grass ranches inland and barren hills and marshlands along the water-fronts. Today, as this is written, Richmond boasts of a population approximating 23,000 inhabitants, a tonnage of manufacturing products shipping second in all California, and a commercial activity and prosperity of which it may well be exceedingly proud.

In the recording of history it is also permissible, to a small degree at least, to prophesy the future, basing it upon the facts of the history of the past, and that I shall here do briefly, in order that future historians may not only record facts but verify the prophecy.

My prophecy of the future greatness of Richmond as an important ocean and railroad shipping port is based upon substantial facts in the history of every other great maritime city, and is not guesswork in the slightest.

These historical facts made Broadway the great business thoroughfare of New York, the intersection of Market and Broad streets the business center of Philadelphia, and Market Street the big business avenue of San Francisco. The map of California and Nevada shows this San Francisco Bay region as the gateway of the vast central valleys drained by the Sacramento and San Joaquin rivers, each stream navigable for many miles through a rich, populous, rapidly developing territory beyond which lies the great mineral, timber, stock and other wealth of the Sierra Nevada Mountains, and beyond them the vast mineral and grazing wealth of the State of Nevada. The San Francisco Bay cities form the gateway, and the only gateway, of this vast and wonderfully productive area, connecting it with the commerce of the world.

This gateway was not made by man, but by nature, and man cannot change it.

A glance at the map shows a practically impassable range of mountains raising its great bulk as a barrier against transportation, and extending north to the Columbia River, the northern boundary of Oregon, compelling the commerce of northern California, Nevada, and even eastern Oregon to seek this San Francisco Bay region for an outlet, and the only outlet, to the outer world. To the south another portion of the same range of mountains reaches an arm around the greatest oil-fields in the world and the San Joaquin Valley, blocking the commerce of that vast and productive region from seeking any other gateway than this bay region also. This is proven by the fact that when the Standard Oil Company built its pipe-line from the great oil-fields to its refinery it was compelled by these barriers to come three hundred miles to Richmond for deep-water harbors, when Santa Barbara is but eighty miles from the oil-fields and San Pedro but one hundred and twenty miles.

Thus we see that Richmond, with its deep-water harbors and connection with the transcontinental railroads, is the logical and practically the only gateway for the largest and richest area on the Pacific Coast, on the only harbors worthy of mention between Astoria on the north and San Pedro on the south, a distance of approximately one thousand miles—and nature will not permit of a rival within this territory.

As one fact worthy of note, it may also be mentioned that already this San Francisco Bay region, with Richmond its only east-bay harbor city, already shows bank clearings exceeding those of all other Pacific Coast cities combined, including

Vancouver and Victoria in British Columbia, by fifty million dollars a week, and indicating clearly that this business field is worth just that much more than all the rest of the business fields put together, from Mexico to the Arctic Circle.

These are only a few of the reasons which have given to Richmond an investment in manufacturing enterprises of over fifty million dollars and have given to its workmen a pay-roll of nearly a million a month. There are many other good reasons which the space allotted to this article will not permit of enumeration.

Richmond, situated on the northeastern side of a low range of hills forming the headland of a broad peninsula projecting from the east (or mainland) shore of San Francisco Bay, divides the bay into two sections. The northern section, known as San Pablo Bay in its main portion, and Suisun Bay in its upper portion, is the connecting link between San Francisco Bay and the great interior waterways that teem with the commerce of all central California. Every bit of this commerce must pass Richmond's door before it can reach any other point on the bay or get to the outside world.

The United States Government chart of San Francisco Bay shows that the headland of the peninsula on which Richmond is located is six miles long, extending from Point San Pablo at the north to Point Potrero at the south. This headland faces a natural deep-water channel for its entire length. The channel varies in depth from ninety feet at the northern end to eighteen feet off the southern shore. The channel is directly against the northern shore of this headland and diverges slowly until at the extreme southern end the deep-water line is about a mile off shore. Thus while no wharfing out is required at Point San Pablo, a short wharf will reach deep water at any point in the whole six miles.

It was this six miles of deep water which induced the Santa Fe Railway to select Richmond as its western terminal in 1899-1900. The Standard Oil Company soon followed, locating its great refinery in 1902. This was quickly followed by other large manufacturing industries, and this record is still going on, one of the largest concerns of the kind in the country, the General Roofing Company, having just completed a very large factory here during the year 1916, and others are now negotiating so to do. Among the largest of the earlier locations was that of the California Wine Association's immense winery, one of the most extensive in the world, operated by one of California's largest corporations.

The first water shipping in Contra Costa County (or in Richmond) had its headquarters, back in the '50s, at the old Ellis Landing. Previous thereto it was the burial ground for ages untold of prehistoric man. Scientists from all over the world have known and studied the Ellis Shell Mound; their researches unearthed many relics of value before making way for modern improvements.

After the rush of 1849 Captain George Ellis began operating schooners between Ellis Landing and San Francisco. He delivered hay and grain from the rich fields of Contra Costa County to the new city of San Francisco. In those days the channel ran from San Francisco, past Ellis Landing, to San Pablo Bay, through the present site of the Standard Oil Refinery. The Potrero Hills formed an island, subject to government occupancy. Later on the channel was closed, which made this section part of the mainland.

In 1859 Captain George Ellis (after whom the landing was named) acquired the property. He operated two schooners, the "Sierra" and the "Mystery," carrying produce and freight between the landing and San Francisco. The late John Nystrom, one of Richmond's most respected public men, was the manager of the landing at that time. Upon the demise of Captain George Ellis, his children inherited the property. The old Ellis home, with ninety acres of harbor property, was purchased from George Ellis and his sister, Selena Ellis, by the present owners, the Ellis Landing & Dock Company, of which M. Emanuel is president.

A great inner harbor became imperative for the future growth of the bustling young city of Richmond, and this was the logical center. At tremendous expense, the Ellis Landing & Dock Company is improving this ground to make it worthy of the position it occupies as the front door of this great industrial city.

Nature's invaluable gift of deep water close to shore, together with the great transcontinental railroads, an ever-flowing supply of cheap fuel oil, and ample electric power, gives Richmond overwhelming trade advantages. Add to these the ship canal and inner harbor now under construction, an unsurpassable climate, and abundance of land along its shores for factory sites, and we have a locality so richly endowed that it has attracted and must continue to attract with irresistible force the industrial and commercial enterprise not only of this nation but of the world.

A history of Richmond to be anywhere near complete would require a larger volume than this history of Contra Costa County, of which Richmond is but a part, so necessarily only a few facts can be given and these hurriedly handled.

EARLY PIONEERS

A few of the old-time settlers who played an important part in the upbuilding of this city should be given brief mention, for they will not be here when the next history is written, but their memory and their good deeds will live on and on, to be related with veneration to generations now unborn. Among these is the Nicholl family, who came to what is now Richmond in 1857 from San Leandro, now a suburban town to Oakland, arriving there from New York in 1850. John Nicholl, Sr., was a stone mason and contractor in Scotland, and later in New Jersey, and was actuated in coming to the Far West and the Pacific Coast by a desire to acquire land and to partake of the possibilities of a new and growing country. John Nicholl, Jr., now known as "The Daddy of Richmond," was born at San Leandro, and was brought here when an infant, in 1853, where he obtained a common-school education in the little country school-house in the village of San Pablo, now a suburb of Richmond. As he facetiously remarks, the first map of Richmond was engraved not upon blue-prints, but upon the posterior of his overalls by the San Pablo schoolmaster. The father died in 1914, at the good old age of 83, leaving a large farm worth about two millions of dollars up against the city limits of Richmond. Half of it has been sold in city lots and is now an important portion of the city, a fast-building civic center, containing the city hall, business blocks, and many fine residences. The other half is still sown to waving grain, but by the time this book shall become circulated it also will become city lots, and its plows and harrows, reapers and binders will give way to the onward rush of civilization and commercial activity. The Nicholls bought much land among the west hills and along the water-front, and these also have turned into great riches and are all important portions of the city of Richmond. Nicholl is considerable of a philanthropist as well as a millionaire and gives liberally to public enterprises and civic upbuilding.

His latest pet plan is to get the proposed United States Naval Academy located at Point Potrero, now Point Nicholl, and at this writing the chances of this great governmental enterprise coming to Richmond seem bright.

George H. Barrett at one time owned four hundred and twenty acres in what is now the heart of the business district of Richmond. The old Barrett homestead was located at what is now Nevin Avenue and Ninth Street, where a few of the old fruit-trees still remain. Barrett Avenue, one of Richmond's finest thoroughfares, was named for him. He traded much of his land to Edson Adams for Oakland property, who in turn sold a lot of the Barrett property to A. S. Macdonald, for whom Richmond's main business thoroughfare—Macdonald Avenue—is named.

Macdonald later subdivided the land he bought into town lots and the same were sold to the public generally by the Richmond Land Company, of which George S. Wall is president. At first these lots on Macdonald Avenue sold at from $150 to $250 apiece, but today many of them would readily bring $10,000 to $20,000 each.

Another old-timer was Owen Griffins, who owned much land and lived in what is now the southern section of the city. His land was subsequently subdivided into town tots, in what is yet known as the Griffins & Watruss tract, while part of it was sold to John Nystrom, who in turn put out the Nystrom addition to Richmond. Owen Griffins died years ago, leaving a son, Ben Griffins, now a prominent attorney at law, bank director, wealthy realty owner, and long among the leading men of affairs.

Probably the oldest man in the valley in the early days was Benjamin Boorman, who came to what is now Richmond in 1859 from Kansas and is still a resident here at the ripe old age of eighty-five years, hale and hearty and able to do a good day's work. Toward the close of the year 1916 "Ben" Boorman, as he is affectionately known, went fishing along the wharves of the Richmond harbor and landed a large shark, and the local and San Francisco papers alluded to the feat as being accomplished by a young fellow of only eighty-five. Boorman was a young farmer of twenty-six when he came to this section and is still at it in some degree. He raised a family of six children here, and now lives at 2750 Cutting Boulevard, good for many more years yet, enjoying prosperity and the respect and veneration of many thousands of good friends.

Many of the old-timers moved away years ago, before the Richmond boom commenced, and have left little or no trail upon which to trace them now. Among these is George D. Reynolds, neighboring farmer in those olden days to the Nicholls and the Barretts; also Charles Mayhew, who moved to Oakland and died there years ago.

Peter Dooling was another of the pioneer settlers. He had a big farm in what is now the southern section of Richmond, part of which is still intact and belonging to his widow and three sons, James, John, and Peter, and two daughters, now married. Among the very valuable holdings of the Dooling family is twenty acres in the northern part of the city, purchased in later years by Mrs. Dooling. This is still being farmed, but beautiful home places, apartment-houses, and villas are springing up all around it, and it is fated to go the way of all near-by farmland, giving way to macadamized streets, trolley cars, and the rush and roar of a modern metropolis.

Away back in those pioneer days Doctor J. M. Tewksbury came to what is now the city of Oakland, and in the early '60s cast his lot among the hardy settlers in an uninhabited stretch of new country, whose velvet verdure was trodden down only by the moccasin of the more or less noble red man. The old Tewksbury home place still stands, much the worse for the wear of many years, in the northeast part of the city, near the little town of San Pablo. He at one time owned seven thousand acres in this vicinity, the same being a part of the old Spanish grant.

Later on this was divided, and Nicholl and others of the early settlers bought much of it. Doctor Tewksbury died in the early '70s, leaving a widow, a son, Lucio, and a daughter, Eugenia. The son died in 1889.

Eugenia married an army surgeon named Ware, who died at Panama. Later she married William Mintzer. The widow, Emily Tewksbury, and her daughter sold fifteen hundred acres of their land to Ben Schapiro, who subdivided it and put it on the market as lots and villa sites.

Schapiro is still one of the largest realty dealers of Richmond. They also sold off many acres to the Standard Oil Company, to the Santa Fe Railway Company, to John Nicholl, and to others. There is still a large tract of land in Richmond known as the Tewksbury estate, and another known as the Mintzer estate. Since the coming of the original owners in those early days fortunes have been made from that real estate, and more fortunes will be made in future.

Prominent among these pioneer trail-blazers were Juan B. Alvarado, now long since passed to his reward, and later on his son, Henry Alvarado, today one of Richmond's most prominent attorneys at law.

Juan Alvarado was governor of California from 1836 to 1842, under the olden Mexican regime, and ruled with credit and honor to himself, his country, and his constituency. In 1836 the inhabitants of California declared it to be a free and independent state, but the project fell through for lack of means and power of the sparse population to defend it sufficiently. The state capitol was then at Monterey, where Governor Alvarado lived during his official terms. During that time he acquired large and valuable real-estate holdings in San Francisco, in Oakland, and in the village of San Pablo, and after his retirement from office the family lived alternately at all these places. Three children were born to Governor and Mrs. Alvarado at Monterey, and subsequently they moved to Contra Costa County, which at that time included what is now Alameda County. This move was made in 1844, and at Oakland in 1857 Henry Alvarado was born. The father died at the San Pablo home in 1882, aged 73, but today he is ably represented by his son, than whom no man stands higher, in the legal profession, financially, socially, and in the hearts of the people.

The Castro family is another monument in memory of those early days. Of Spanish origin, they came early to this country, when it was under Mexican rule, and owned large holdings of land in this immediate section, and at various other sections in this part of California. Patricio Castro lives today near the village of San Pablo, now a part of Richmond, a prosperous farmer and land-owner, at the age of seventy years.

Before him his father, Victor Castro, owned the land and was among the earliest settlers. Victor Castro died in 1898, in the old family residence at what is now the county line—the line dividing Contra Costa County and Alameda County, but which in those days did not exist, for the reason that it was all Contra Costa County. This old family residence still stands amid a clump of tall cedars and cypress-trees, and it, together with other lands of the Castro estate, is now owned by a daughter of Victor Castro, Mrs. Julia B. Galpin, residing at Piedmont, a residential section lying between Berkeley and Richmond.

Another old-time pioneer resident who should be briefly mentioned in any history of Contra Costa County or Richmond is Fred Bouquet, early-day blacksmith—the village smithy at San Pablo, now Richmond.

He came to San Pablo in 1860, fifty-seven years ago, and was well known and highly honored by the settlers hereabouts in those olden days. His son, John Bouquet, resides here yet, and is among the wealthy property-owners of the city, being largely interested in several residential tracts that he and his associates have subdivided, improved, and sold to hundreds of happy and contented citizens.

One year later than the arrival of Fred Bouquet came the Matoiza family to San Pablo, and a large line of descendants and relatives now remain as residents in and adjacent to that suburban village. The Matoizas are well and favorably known all over this county and have held many places of high honor and trust.

There are, of course, many more deserving of mention, but space forbids, so only a few of the earliest settlers have been given mention in this article upon Richmond. They blazed the way that we of these later and more prosperous and modern days could enjoy the fruits not only of our own labor and endeavors but also of theirs.

A CITY OF CASH

Probably Richmond's greatest asset is its million-dollar-a-month payroll, which is disbursed to many thousands of busy toilers in the railroad shops and manufacturing establishments. This is all good clean money, coming from the outside world and expended, in the main, right at home in building up the city in a thousand different ways.

In nine cases out of ten it is the town or community with the big payroll that grows into the large and prosperous city, for such towns and communities are less affected by local conditions than any others.

The great Standard Oil Refinery here is employing three thousand men at top-notch wages and pays out in cash to them every two weeks over $125,000, or $250,000 monthly. The refined product of this immense industrial plant is shipped out on thousands of trains and hundreds of ships to all parts of America and the civilized world, so that the return in cash comes from China, Japan, England, Australia, Germany, France, Russia, and other foreign countries, and goes into immediate circulation, not only to the army of workmen, but also into constant enlargement of the plant, now being made into the largest oil refinery in the world.

The Santa Fe railroad shops have several hundred employees here, all of whom are paid first-class wages, and that money comes from the great system of railways grid-ironing the country from Chicago to the Pacific Coast—that cash rolls in from people all over America and is expended here in the building of homes and the upbuilding of the community.

The Pullman car-shops employ seven hundred men and women on both repair and construction work, and that millionaire corporation picks up the cash from the entire traveling public of the United States and spends $40,000 a month of it in Richmond to pay its employees, to say nothing of the $2,000,000 it has invested in the property and plant.

The grounds comprise approximately twenty-two acres. Construction was started in May, 1910, and shops started operations November 27, 1910. There are two three-story buildings and fourteen single-story buildings. Buildings are constructed of steel, brick, and concrete. The average number of employees is 525. The shops have a capacity of twenty-four stalls, and the output approximates sixty-five cars per month. The shop is equipped to handle all classes of work from the heaviest to the lightest required to maintain cars in first-class condition.

The Southern Pacific Company runs eighty-one trains daily to and from Richmond, employing hundreds of men and paying them good wages; many of them live and have property interests here and distribute their wages around among the local merchants.

The Western Pipe and Steel Works employs many men, ships its products all over the country from San Francisco to the Missouri River, from Puget Sound to the Gulf, and the cash is returned to Richmond, where it goes into the local markets and channels of trade.

The Porcelain Works makes fine porcelain ware, which is in great demand all over America. There are three factories in Richmond, the only ones on the Pacific Coast, and about two hundred men are employed.

The smoke rises from the tall chimneys of a dozen other manufacturing concerns, and the busy hum of industry goes on day and night.

Among these may be mentioned the Western Pipe and Steel Works, a very large manufacturing industry with a big pay-roll and employing upward of one hundred men on an average.

Richmond Pressed Brick Works furnishes a splendid product in its line for the building of Richmond and other towns and cities for hundreds of miles around.

Metropolitan Match Factory supplies the trade of this section of California and the west with a grade of matches that are well known all over the Pacific Coast.

The California Cap Works, turning out caps and cartridges day and night, furnishes work for a large number of men and women. At this writing this industry is especially busy on account of the unusual large demand for all kinds of munitions in the European war.

The latest addition to Richmond's manufacturing industries is the General Roofing Factory, which company has another large plant in New Jersey. It came to Richmond in 1916, and now has a plant covering several acres in the northern section of the city, with an investment of over a million dollars and employing about two hundred men.

All of the manufacturing industries of Contra Costa County may be said to be in a way tributary to Richmond, for the reason that Richmond is the metropolis and main shipping-port of the county. Among these are the following: California Paper Mills, Antioch; California Fruit Packers' Association, Oakley; Columbia Steel Company, Johnson-Laterni Shipyards, Redwood Manufacturing Company, Diamond Brick Company, American Fish & Oyster Company, Pittsburg; General Chemical Company, Nichols; C. A. Smith Lumber Company, Bay Point; Associated Oil Company, Avon; Mountain Copper Company, American-Oriental Oil Company, Shell Oil Company, Martinez; Port Costa Brewing Company, Brick Works, and Grain Company, Port Costa ; Selby Smelting & Lead Company, Selby; Union Oil

Company, Oleum; Cowell-Portland Cement Company, Cowell; Hercules Powder Works, Pinole; Giant Powder Works, at Giant.

Some sections have climate, others have industry, and still others have cash. Richmond is blessed in the possession of all three. With a climate unequaled anywhere in the world, an industry that has built up a town in fifteen years of nothing, beginning with a wheat-field and ending at this date in a city of 23,000 inhabitants, Richmond is doing a strictly cash business with countries far and near, attracting their money as a magnet does steel.

BANKS

There are three splendid banking institutions in Richmond—the First National Bank, the Bank of Richmond, and the Mechanics Bank, each of which has its savings department in connection with its main business. Every one of them is strong financially, backed by ample capital and having the confidence of the people.

PUBLIC UTILITIES

One of the things of which Richmond is proud, and deservedly so, is its street-car system. Starting with a single track between the Standard Oil plant and the Southern Pacific depot, the first car was operated in July, 1904. The car was an old one of an obsolete type, purchased by the infant company from the United Railroads of San Francisco, and has long since passed into oblivion, being succeeded by cars of modern design.

The men responsible for the promoting and building of the line first known as the East Shore & Suburban Railroad were W. S. Rheem, Clinton E. Worden, and W. S. Tevis, the late E. A. Gowe, and others. But to Colonel Rheem more than to any other belongs the credit for the successful promotion and operation of what has since become one of the best-patronized and best-paying semi-interurban lines in the State.

In January, 1905, the company began the extension of its line from the Southern Pacific depot in Richmond to the county line, the work being completed and the first car operated over it in May of the same year. The same year also saw the completion of the Ohio-Street line, which made connections with the main line at Ohio Street and the Santa Fe right of way, but which has since been merged with the A and Eighth Street line, which line was completed in 1907.

The original line between the Southern Pacific depot and the county line ran by way of Macdonald and San Pablo avenues, and the company in 1905 built a branch line to the town of Stege, connecting with the main line at a point which has since been known as Stege Junction.

In 1908 the company built a line from Macdonald Avenue, starting at Twenty-third Street and paralleling the Southern Pacific to Potrero Avenue, where it made connection with the Stege branch, opening up A new territory which has been a strong factor, as the Pullman Company has erected a mammoth plant, employing hundreds of men, most of whom ride back and forth on the cars of this line, which pass directly in front of the gates.

Since the completion of this extension the cars operating between Richmond and Oakland are routed that way, that portion of the original line from Twenty-third

Street to San Pablo Avenue being now a part of the San Pablo-East Richmond line, which runs from the town of San Pablo to East Richmond, or Grand Canon Park. The line from Macdonald Avenue to the town of San Pablo was built in 1905, and furnished means of transportation to an enterprising people who had been wont to hitch up and make the long drive into Oakland.

The extension from the junction of Macdonald Avenue to East Richmond, completed in 1910, serves a scattered community which is rapidly filling up with small homes, creating a consequent increase in traffic, and carries during the summer season thousands of persons to Grand Canon Park, a beautiful natural pleasure ground located right at the end of the car-line.

In February, 1911, the East Shore & Suburban Railroad was purchased by the United Properties Company, which also absorbed the Oakland Traction Company, the California Railways, and the Key Route lines, this system becoming known as the San Francisco-Oakland Terminal Railways.

In the spring of 1912, the United Properties Company, in pursuance of its progressive policy, began a series of improvements, chief of which was the double-tracking of San Pablo and Potrero avenues from the county line to Pullman, completed that year, the laying of track on Ashland Avenue and the improvement of that thoroughfare, the completion of which necessitated the removal of the original line, which was laid on the Santa Fe right of way. In 1914 the double-tracking and macadamizing of Macdonald Avenue in Richmond was completed.

Where a few years ago there was a twenty-minute service to Oakland, with a change of cars at the county line, requiring an hour and ten minutes to make the trip, there is now a ten-minute through service, which is accomplished in forty-five minutes.

T. S. Walker was the first superintendent, holding that position until March, 1006, being succeeded by C. H. Robinson, formerly of the United Railroads of San Francisco, who resigned January 1, 1912. His successor, C. F. Donnelly, also formerly connected with the United Railroads, is still in charge of the Richmond division, and his capable management and genial manner have been strong factors in cementing the friendly relations between the company and the people it serves.

From a small beginning the business of the Western States Gas & Electric Company in Richmond has increased wonderfully. At the present time it operates in the territory comprising Richmond, Stege, Pullman, San Pablo, and Rust, and has approximately one hundred miles of distributing lines, a modern plant, and all the latest improved machinery for supplying an up-to-date service to the city and its annexed and surrounding territory.

The Pacific Gas & Electric Company is another large corporation of the city of Richmond, supplying the community with gas for cooking and heating. The lines of this company also bring electric power to Richmond, where it is wholesaled to others.

The People's Water Company has been supplying Richmond and vicinity with an ample supply of water for domestic and municipal use for some years. At this writing the company is expending $2,000,000 in the construction of a concrete dam on San Pablo Creek back of Richmond, with a capacity of 20,000,000,000 gallons.

RICHMOND SCHOOLS

As soon as Richmond's little dot began to appear on the map of California an effort was made to provide ample school facilities. And as the city grew by leaps and bounds, the same effort to keep the school system apace with its growth continued. From the little ungraded school of but a few years ago, with one teacher, there is now a city school system with a corps of nearly half a hundred instructors, and a high school with a corps of nearly a score.

To provide buildings and equipment for such an institution within a period of fifteen years was in itself a stupendous task. However, the issue was met, and Richmond now has a high-school building costing $95,000, besides five grammar and elementary school buildings totaling in value over a quarter of a million dollars, with arrangements and appointments most modern in school construction and architecture. No city of its size in the West excels Richmond in the excellency of modern schools.

It has been the aim of those in charge of the school department of Richmond to make it one of the strongest features of the city—to make those who have selected Richmond for their future home feel that in doing so they have not deprived their children of educational advantages. They have endeavored to be progressive and to adopt such of the modern advances in education as experience has justified, and to avoid such fads and fancies as are always springing up in all lines of endeavor.

RICHMOND CHURCHES

Having broken all records of cities of its age and size in the way of building up a splendid public-school system, sparing neither time nor money in the accomplishment of great results, Richmond turned its attention to no small extent in building up and helping out its churches, its ministry, and its church workers, and the results show that the city heeds its spiritual welfare as well as the education of its children and the commercial success of its enterprises.

The city now has within its limits fourteen church organizations, as follows: Two Methodist, three Roman Catholic, two Baptist, one Christian, one Presbyterian, one Christian Science, one Episcopal, one German Lutheran, one Unitarian, and one Congregational.

All of the churches of Richmond are increasing in membership and influence, and all have flourishing Sunday-schools, young peoples' societies, men's Bible classes, and other auxiliary organizations, in which are enrolled a large number of the leading influential business men of the city. All have strong boards of trustees, and all have splendid working societies among the women of the church world.

The missionary organizations of the various churches are also good workers in the Lord's vineyard. The salaries and current expenses paid by the church organizations of Richmond amount to over two thousand dollars monthly.

Richmond is justly proud of her churches and her clergy. Where strangers are looking for homes where churches and schools are among the leading factors in the life of a city, Richmond bids them enter her open door.

In the past few years wonderful strides have been taken in the upbuilding of the churches and the church work, and the future is bright with promise of a continuation of this work so necessary to the life and the welfare of all mankind.

SOCIAL AND FRATERNAL ORGANIZATIONS

Of secret society organizations and civic and social clubs, Richmond has its full quota, there being no less than thirty of such institutions, all enjoying a good membership and financial prosperity. All the main secret societies are represented, and two of them—the Elks and Knights of Pythias—own their buildings. Both of these are imposing structures and modern in every way. The Elks building cost over eighty thousand dollars.

There are two leading women's club organizations—the Richmond Club and the West Side Women's Improvement Club. The former owns its own club building, a magnificent two-story structure, and the latter plans to build this year (1917). In addition to these are numerous civic improvement clubs and women's auxiliaries of the same, the Grand Army of the Republic, and the Women's Circle of the G. A. R.

This would not be complete without mention of the Native Sons and Daughters, both of which have strong organizations here.

EVOLUTION OF JOURNALISM IN RICHMOND

The editor is under obligations to Juan L. Kennon, an old-time printer and newspaper man of Richmond, for much of the data contained in this article. Kennon was connected with the early-day Record, and followed its career for many years, later establishing a job-printing plant of his own, which was purchased in 1916 by the writer and merged into the Daily News plant. Later Kennon was foreman of the News, but toward the end of 1916, owing to failing health, he was forced to retire from all active work and business.

The history of Richmond's newspapers is as interesting as the history of the city. Richmond's present greatness is, in a measure, due to the indefatigable efforts of those who came here in early days and started the first newspaper, together with those who have entered the field in later years.

It was on the 7th of July, 1900, that the Record, a weekly publication at that time, made its initial bow to the then sparse population of this municipality. Lyman Naugle, the pioneer newspaper man of Richmond, came to what was then only a small community of some 250 inhabitants and cast his lot with what his prophetic vision told him would someday become one of the principal industrial communities of the Pacific Coast.

He had a small printing outfit, which consisted of a few cases of type and an Army press; the press could have been conveniently carried under one's arm without much difficulty. He rented a small room near Wanske's saloon, on what is now Barrett Avenue. In those days the Record office faced on the county road.

The first issue of the paper was six columns in width and was set by hand, as were many other subsequent issues of the Record. Richmond had no post-office in those days and the first issue of the paper was mailed at Stege post-office. In the first issue Editor Naugle had this to say relative to the lack of post-office facilities: "We are looking every day for the establishment of our post-office. The demand for mail facilities is very pressing. It is to be hoped the department will not keep us waiting very long. This issue of the Record will have to be mailed at Stege, as well as all future issues until we get a post-office."

It may not be amiss to retrogress a little in order to explain that the original townsite in this vicinity was called Point Richmond and took in that district now bounded by the property of the Santa Fe Railway Company, Barrett Avenue east as far as Sixth Street, and the lands lying north between First and Sixth streets. This was the original town of Point Richmond. Subsequently the John Nicholl Company laid out what was then known as the First, Second, and Third additions to the town of Richmond. William Mintzer afterward subdivided what is now known as the Fourth addition to the city of Richmond. The John Nicholl and the Mintzer holdings were included in what is now known as the Point, or west side.

Naugle issued the Record regularly every week for several months in his location on Barrett Avenue, and the paper was mailed regularly at Stege. The department finally gave Richmond a post-office and Lyman Naugle was appointed as the first postmaster. He combined the duties of attending to the mail for the Government with the editing of his newspaper. As the Point began to show signs of growth, Naugle conceived the idea of moving over to the west side. He packed the post office up in a soap-box and with his small plant opened an office on Richmond Avenue, near the present location of the Bank of Richmond.

The next day after moving a United States post-office inspector arrived in town, and he gave Editor Naugle just thirty minutes to move the post-office back to its original location. It is needless to add that Naugle lost no time in complying with the demand of Uncle Sam's representative, and he had time to spare at the end of the job.

Although the post-office was moved, Naugle remained with the plant in his new location. Steps were immediately taken to induce the Government to establish a new post-office. After several months the Point people secured a post-office and it was named "Eastyard, California," in order that there would be no conflict in names.

We herewith reproduce the editor of the Record's salutatory from the first issue of this paper: "The Record is glad to look the people of Richmond and Contra Costa County in the face. It makes no pretense of greatness. It is very humble. Point Richmond is yet but a budding village, but its future is bright and the Record will keep pace with its progress. The mission of the Record will be to record the local news, to write a history in weekly installments of the growth and grandeur of this community. The Record is not in politics. More important and more material affairs claim its attention at the present time. It will throw its weight toward building up a little city here that will honor its neighbors on either side. It solicits the patronage of every resident of the valley and of everyone interested in building up Point Richmond. Everyone who lives here will take it, and it will be indispensable to those who own property here and live elsewhere. It will faithfully report the progress of the town and strive to be enterprising and truthful. The Record would love to visit the homes of San Pablo, Stege, and Schmidtville, our neighbors on either side, and to this end will have representatives at these places to furnish the local news. It is the only newspaper between Berkeley and Pinole. It lays claim to all that territory and will endeavor to merit support therein."

The daily edition of the Richmond Record was launched on February 8, 1902. Lyman Naugle continued as editor. Frank Hull, the present managing editor of The Record-Herald, was its first city editor. The writer laid out the first forms and made the first issue of the paper up for the press.

The Record was several years afterward moved to the east side. In 1910 J. L. Kennon established the Weekly Herald. Subsequently the Herald was merged with the Record, hence the hyphenated title, Record-Herald.

The Richmond Daily Leader was established by G. A. Milnes in Richmond in March, 1902. That paper's first editor and business manager was B. J. Baker, now a prominent official of Imperial County. In the fall of 1911 F. J. Hulaniski, the editor of this history, moved to Richmond from San Francisco, and took editorial and business management of the Daily Leader for Milnes, the owner, and, finding that the business did not warrant the publication of three daily newspapers in Richmond at that time, it was upon his advice that a consolidation was affected between the Daily Leader and the Daily Record-Herald in March, 1912, and he became editor of the consolidated publication, and so remained for three years, during which time he established the Contra Costan, a weekly publication which is still being issued from the office of the Record-Herald.

In August, 1914, the writer established the Thinkograph Magazine, a publication intended for national scope, the same being to a certain extent along similar lines of Elbert Hubbard's famous Philistine. The Thinkograph was published in San Francisco for two years, and in 1916 was moved to Richmond, at the same time this writer became editor and manager of the Richmond News, and is still being published at the News office. The Thinkograph has achieved a semi-national reputation, being handled by the news companies pretty generally throughout the United States.

About the time that the first issue of the Daily Record was issued from the press, a portly gentleman entered the Record office one evening and stated that he wanted a job. He was not particular about the work, he said, but was willing to do anything to make an honest living.

He had been a schoolteacher and had also practiced medicine. That man was Warren B. Brown. He was given a job soliciting subscribers for the new daily.

Later Brown established the Santa Fe Times in what is now the Santa Fe district. Subsequently Editor Brown moved his plant to the vicinity of Macdonald Avenue and published the Terminal, which paper is still doing business in Richmond. The Terminal, under Warren Brown's management, accomplished much good for the then growing town of Richmond. The present editor and manager of the Terminal, George Ryan, assumed charge of the paper in 1914, Doctor Brown retiring from the field after a successful and honorable career as editor of one of Richmond's newspapers. He died and passed to his reward in 1916.

The Richmond Daily Independent was established in Richmond in 1910 by I. N. Foss and M. J. Beaumont. The latter had managed the Leader for several years, having succeeded to that position after the retirement of W. H. Marsh. I. N. Foss, who was at that time editor of the Leader, joined with Beaumont, a stock company was formed, and the Independent became a reality in the newspaper field of this city. It is still one of the flourishing daily papers of Richmond, under the direction of John F. Galvin, a newspaper man well known in this section of California.

The newspaper graveyard in Richmond is still quite small. Of the papers suspended may be mentioned the Daily Leader, a small semiweekly called the Tribune, established in 1903 by a San Francisco journalist, and a weekly called the Messenger. The latter was printed in San Francisco and circulated in Richmond.

Neither the Tribune nor the Messenger lasted more than a few months before they finally rested in the journalistic cemetery.

The Daily News was established in January, 1914, by the Daily News Company, incorporated, which company was organized by the various labor organizations of Richmond, numbering twenty local bodies, with a membership of approximately two thousand. The News was a phenomenal success for the first year of its career, being backed by the labor element of the city, which is very large and strong, Richmond being pre-eminently a wage-earning and pay-roll community, with the bulk of its male population affiliated in the ranks of organized labor.

The News, however, in time began to strike upon the rocks and shoals always inevitable when a newspaper is controlled by any element or class of society lacking that experience in the business which is absolutely necessary for its success The board of directors of the new publishing company were skilled artisans in their various trades and callings, but knew next to nothing about the newspaper business and the many ins and outs mastered only after long experience and by the best abilities of men skilled in journalism, politics, and public policies, as well as in the mechanical intricacies of the printing trade. Political controversies brought about libel suits, damage suits, and bad blood, with the result that financial difficulties naturally followed. The venture as a daily newspaper lost a large sum of money for the stockholders, and in March, 1916, the paper was reduced to a weekly publication. Financial reverses continued to follow, and in April, 1916, this writer took over the whole combination and assumed the editorial and business management of the paper. In August of the same year he bought it outright from the company, organized the Richmond Printing & Publishing Company, and in January, 1917, resumed daily publication of the paper.

That same month it was made the official paper by the authorities of the city of Richmond, and the Daily News at this writing is again upon a sound financial and business basis.

It might not be amiss to tell of some of the early experiences of those who came to Richmond and entered into the newspaper game. At the time the Record was launched as a daily it became necessary to discard the hand-press and install a cylinder press. The editor secured an old plant at Nevada City and had it shipped to Richmond. The cylinder press, which had done duty at the former place for many years, was unpacked from the barley-sacks and assembled. At that time H. B. Kinney had installed a small electric-light plant in the city, but the concern did not operate in the daytime. It became necessary to rig up levers on the big press, and in this manner the paper was issued regularly until the town grew large enough to justify a day electric service.

At one time a pugilist came over from San Francisco to fight a local pug, and he was induced to do his three weeks' training in the Record office. He was a godsend for the Record force during the three weeks that he sweat and grunted grinding out the daily edition of the paper.

It may be needless to add that the pugilist who so kindly served the Record force was knocked out in the third round by his antagonist.

The tribulations of the Record force in the early days of the town were many. The failure of the "ghost to walk" was a trivial matter compared to the work of getting out the paper with two feet of water in the shop during rainy weather. The

Record had moved into its own building, now the Bank of Richmond, and the paper was published in the basement. The water was in the habit of coming in in torrents whenever it rained, and in those years it used to rain every day throughout the winter. The mechanical force was divided into shifts and the office was bailed out with buckets. The editor provided rubber boots for the printers, and the paper never missed an issue. The main trouble was in keeping the water down below the level of the bed of the press. Two lady compositors, who set the type by hand, were carried by the men on the force to their stools, where they perched above the water and waves beneath them. After a while the Record became more prosperous, and a gasoline engine was purchased. This proved to be less reliable than the pugilist who so faithfully ground out the few hundreds of copies of the paper. The engine used to have a habit of going on a strike occasionally, when the hand process of issuing the paper was again resorted to.

At the time Doctor Brown published the initial issue of his paper he had no press and secured the loan of the Record machinery. He had his forms made up in Santa Fe and hauled over to the Record shop at the Point. The man who undertook the contract of delivering the forms did not know what a delicate job he had on his hands and proceeded to handle the type pages as he would sacks of coal. The result was that the Times did not issue that week. The forms were "pied" in the street on Washington Avenue, and Doctor Brown secured some sieves and recovered his type from the fourteen inches of dust.

The journalistic history of Richmond is interesting and contains much of the strenuosity and characteristics of the upbuilding of the city in all other lines of endeavor. There are now three daily newspapers representing fairly well a little city of the size and capabilities of Richmond—the Record Herald and the Independent in the evening field, and the Daily News in the morning field, with the Terminal, a weekly publication, also in a state of more or less active journalistic eruption—and it is to the credit of the city of Richmond that this number of publications can obtain support sufficient to maintain them in a creditable amount of excellency.

MYSTERY OF THE SHELL MOUNDS

The many and extensive shell deposits, or "Indian mounds," existing all along the Gulf and Pacific Coast have greatly excited the curiosity of people newly arrived in the country, and especially those of an educational turn of mind. The reason for the existence of such mounds has been sought for without much satisfaction. The theory most generally accepted is that the Indian tribes spent their winters on the seashore, subsisting chiefly on fish and oysters, and the shell banks remain as monuments of age-long appetite for crustaceans.

Probably the greatest shell mound on the Pacific Coast is at Richmond, and it has attracted much attention and curiosity for many years.

Now it is to be entirely removed to make room for modern improvements along the bay shore, where great activity in the way of shipping interests is confidently expected before long.

Researches were made in this gigantic mound from 1906 to 1908 by direction of the University of California, and 146 skeletons were found and taken out. Professor Nelson of the university gave an opinion at the time that the big Richmond mound was the official burying-place of prehistoric men. He estimated that there were over

630 specimens of implements, weapons, and ornaments found in the mound by excavation, consisting of spear points, pottery, charm stones, shell jewelry, mortars and pestles, bowls, needles, and similar articles made of stone, bone, shell, and baked clay; also curious whistles were found, made of bird bones.

STANDARD OIL COMPANY'S REFINERY

A new town was virtually put on the map when the Standard Oil Company established its Richmond Refinery. When the company broke ground for its plant in 1901 Richmond was a little community of scarcely two hundred people. Today it is a thriving city of twenty-three thousand inhabitants.

The steady, normal development of a great manufacturing plant to the point where this refinery is today employing twenty-seven hundred people, with a monthly pay-roll of two hundred and sixty thousand dollars, could not but act as a great stimulus to any community. But the benefits and the influence of the Richmond Refinery are not to be measured by the development of any one town. Rather, might the plant and the industry it represents be designated as one of the important factors in the recent development of the entire Pacific Coast.

The establishment of the Richmond Refinery was one of the biggest single boosts to manufacturing and home industry in the history of California—possibly the biggest. And this because it provided what was so badly needed—a means whereby a larger percentage of the output of the California petroleum fields could be placed on the market at its full worth, as refined products instead of as crude oil. To the advantage of both consumer and producer, its benefits extend the length of the western coasts of two continents, from Nome to Cape Horn; also into Oriental countries. Wherever petroleum products are now marketed on the Pacific Coast, they are not Eastern products, but the output of our own California fields.

"But just what is an oil refinery?" some of our readers have asked us.

"How do you refine oil, and what do you manufacture at Richmond?"

Briefly, crude oil is a complex mineral compound, and it is the work of a refinery to break up this crude material into its constituent parts— clarify and treat them and manufacture them into finished products ready for the public's use. The plant at Richmond is one of the largest refineries in the world and manufactures practically all the main products obtainable from crude oil. The detailed, technical processes by which they are obtained can only be hinted at here.

If you are familiar with Civil War history, you will perhaps recall the story of the resourceful "Johnny Reb," prisoner of war. To vary the monotony of confinement and to cater to his appetite for spirituous liquor, he built a miniature still out of a coffee-pot. Having filled this with corn bread and water, he put it over a hot fire, and as the vapors came off caught them in an improvised condenser—an old can soldered to the top of the pot. Primitive and miniature as was this improvised still, it is illustrative of one of the main processes of oil refining—the process of distillation—which in essentials is the same whether carried on in a coffee-pot or in a great battery of thousand-barrel stills. Beyond this the refining process is complex and technical—suitable only for scientific discussion.

Despite this fact, an oil refinery is by no means an uninteresting place to the layman. From point of size alone, Richmond is somewhat impressive, covering as it does a territory of 788 acres, or 1.225 square miles.

The raw material, or crude oil, for this Refinery City is supplied from the "Tank Farm" at San Pablo, five miles distant. San Pablo is the terminus of the 330-mile pipe-line from the California oil-fields, and the oil which is stored here in great tanks—holding an aggregate of four and a half million barrels—is run down to Richmond by gravity as needed.

The selection of the correct crude oil for the particular product to be manufactured is an important consideration, for all Standard illuminating and lubricating oils and other products are made from selected crudes. If asphaltum for roofing or paving materials is to be made, a crude oil shown by test to be best suited for this purpose is selected. In the same way, by rigid tests, crude oils are chosen for the manufacture of Pearl oil, Red Crown gasoline, Zerolene, and other products. A stock especially suited for one product may almost entirely lack the essentials that go to make others, and the laboratory experts who determine these things, and who later, after exhaustive tests, give a refined product its clearance papers, conduct their work with the greatest possible care.

And this Refinery City, to which the crude oil comes, is not merely big—it is busy; busy night and day, week in and week out, Sundays and holidays, from January 1st to December 31st, distilling, treating, filtering, testing—with frequent shifts of men so that none of the work is slighted, no one overworked.

Directed by executives of long experience; manned by expert chemists, superintendents, and other men of scientific as well as practical training; provided with a physical equipment thoroughly modern and second to none in the world, Richmond Refinery is in a position to maintain with efficiency this intensive pace of manufacture. One hundred and forty-one big stills, with a total charging capacity of 60,000 barrels; adequate condensers and receiving houses; fifty-five agitators (which "look like giant truffles," as one visitor put it)l; four hundred and seventy-six storage tanks; an engine-house capable of developing twenty-four thousand horse-power; an acid plant manufacturing two hundred and sixty-five thousand pounds of sulphuric acid daily; a grease plant; an asphaltum plant; a can factory, with a capacity of 25,000 five-gallon cans a day; a cooperage or barrel works; a machine-shop; a tank-car repair-shop, and several pump-houses, are some of the main divisions of the refinery's equipment. And interconnecting the entire plant, making it a manufacturing plant, runs a maze of pipe lines—360 miles in all —through which are handled the crude and many of the refined oils, as well as the steam, air, fresh and salt water used in their manufacture and in the hospital.

In addition to its manufacturing facilities, Richmond is admirably equipped for the prompt and economical loading of its products for distribution to the consumer. Pipe-lines leading directly to the railroad yards are run along the "loading racks" beside the tracks, and from these refined oils, gasoline, and other products are run into the big railroad tank cars with which everyone is familiar. The extensive loading racks permit fifty cars to be filled at one time. All barrel and case goods are loaded into box cars direct from the warehouse platforms.

Of greater interest, perhaps, are the refinery's facilities for discharging its products by sea. A short distance from the refinery, extending almost a mile out into the bay, is the Richmond pier where Standard Oil Company tankers take on fluid cargoes for bulk distribution to its main distributing stations on the Pacific Coast, and to inland points reached by light-draft steamers that ply on the Sacramento and

San Joaquin rivers. At Point Orient, about five miles distant from the refinery, an ideal shipping point because of the deep water and protected location, the company has another pier, storage tanks, and docks. Products are pumped from the refinery to the storage tanks and then run by gravity down to the dock and into the tankers and other vessels for shipment to the Orient and Central and South American ports. During the present year shipments bound for New York have also cleared from this dock, for the superiority of California asphaltum has brought about a fast-increasing demand for this product in the East.

Such is the Richmond Refinery, the company's largest manufacturing plant. Its development from small beginnings to its present size has been healthy, logical, and in entire accord with the demands of the market for refined products, and with the development of the company's crude product and that of the producers from whom it purchases oils. The first stills were completed and fired at Richmond on July 2, 1902. At that time but eighty men were employed at the refinery, and during the first months they refined only 780 barrels of crude oil a day.

Since its beginning construction work at Richmond has never ceased, and today twenty-seven hundred men are required to operate the plant which is refining on an average 60,000 barrels of crude oil daily.

The refinery is still growing and will continue to grow, healthily and logically, as it has in the past. As the demand for its product increases, so will the capacity of the refinery be increased to meet that demand— just as El Segundo, and the company's newest refinery at Bakersfield, were built to supply the increasing southern trade of California and adjoining States. And always will every care be taken, every known means be employed, to make Standard products everything that their name implies— uniform products of the highest quality and reliability.

Stege is situated near the southern boundary of Contra Costa County, not far from the Alameda County boundary line, in direct communication with both Oakland and Richmond. This community is rapidly forging ahead. Located here are the California Cap Works, the United States Briquette Company, the Stauffer Chemical Works, and the Stege Lumber Manufacturing Company.

CHAPTER XXVII. ANTIOCH

Antioch is one of the oldest towns in California, having been originally founded in 1850, the year following the discovery of gold, and has a history in every way as interesting and romantic as any of the early settlements in the Golden State. In the brief space allotted me it will be impossible to more than scratch the surface of things historical, and it will be my purpose to refer only briefly to the more important and interesting items of the early history of our beautiful little city, which gives promise in the not distant future of becoming one of the leading interior cities in California.

During the past few years a considerable number of people have made inquiry at the Ledger office for information concerning the name "Antioch." "How did Antioch get its name?" is the question usually asked, though some have wanted to know the derivation of the word. For the purpose of supplying satisfactory answers to these questions I have been asked to prepare an article that will give such information as is available. I have found the subject intensely interesting, and am constrained to add such other data, historical and otherwise, as have come to my notice in the course of my investigations.

Most of my readers, I dare say, are aware that the name is often mentioned in the Bible, and some at least will recall that it was in the ancient city of Antioch the followers of the meek and lowly Nazarene were first called "Christians." Some may not know, however, that the ancient city of Antioch in Asia was named in honor of the tyrant king Antiochus, the arch-enemy of the Maccabean Jews. The following historical sketch will furnish such information as is now extant concerning our ancient namesake: "Antioch, the ancient capital of the Greek kings of Syria, and long the chief city of Asia, lies in a beautiful and fertile plain, on the left bank of the river Orontes, fourteen miles from the sea. In ancient times, by its navigable river and its harbor, Seleucia, it had communication with all the maritime cities of the west, while it became on the other hand an emporium for the merchandise of the east, for behind it lay the vast Syrian desert, across which traveled the caravans from Mesopotamia and Syria. The city was erected by Seleucus Nicator about 300 B. C and was the most splendid of sixteen cities built by him in honor of his father, Antiochus. In early times a part stood upon an island which has now disappeared. The rest was built partly on the plain and partly on the rugged ascent toward Mount Cassius, amid vineyards and fruit-trees. The ancients called it 'Antioch the Beautiful,' and 'The Crown of the East.' It was a favorite residence of the Seleucid princes and of the wealthy Romans, and was famed throughout the world for its splendid luxury. Its public edifices were magnificent. The city reached its greatest glory in the time of Antiochus the Great, and under the Roman emperors of the first three centuries. At that time it contained 500,000 inhabitants and vied in splendor with Rome itself. Nor did its glory fade immediately after the founding of Constantinople; for though it then ceased to.be the first city of the east, it rose into new dignity as a Christian city. It was one of the earliest strongholds of the new faith—indeed, it was here that the name "Christian" was first used.

During the apostolic act it was the center of missionary enterprise, and it became the seat of an£ of the four patriarchs. Ten councils were held here from 252 to 380 A. D. Churches sprang up exhibiting a new style of architecture which soon became prevalent; and even Constantine spent a considerable time here, adorning it, and strengthening its harbor, Seleucia. The downfall of the city dates from the fifth century. In 538 it was reduced to ashes by the Persian king Chosroes but was partly rebuilt by Justinian. The next important event in its history was its conquest by the Saracens in the seventh century. In the ninth century it was recovered by the Greeks under Nicephorus Phocas, but in 1084 it again fell into the hands of the Mohammedans. The Crusaders besieged and took it in 1098. At the close of the thirteenth century, the Sultan of Egypt seized it. At present it forms a portion of Syria, in the province of Aleppo, and has a population of 17,500, mostly Turks, employed in silk-culture, eel-fishing, and in the production of corn and oil.

It exhibits almost no traces of its former grandeur, except the ruins of the walls built by Justinian, and of the fortress erected by the Crusaders. It suffered from an earthquake in 1872.

"Another ancient city named Antioch is situated in Pisidia, founded also by Nicator. It was declared a free city by the Romans in the second century B. C, and made a colonia under Augustus, with the name Caesarea. It was often visited by St. Paul."

The thoughtful reader will notice several interesting points of resemblance in this description of the ancient Antioch and our own fair city. First, note that it lay on the left bank of the river, in a fertile and beautiful plain, fourteen miles from the sea. Next, note the reference to the rugged ascent toward the mount (substitute Diablo for Cassius, and you will note a topographical likeness) amid vineyards and fruit trees. A close scrutiny of a map of the locality in which the Asian city stands will reveal other striking points of resemblance. Also, a picture of the water-front of Antioch in Asia is remarkably like a corresponding view of Antioch, California, as seen from the river. The principal difference which will occur to you is in the matter of size, in which detail the ancient city compares better with San Francisco or Los Angeles. These resemblances, striking as they are, however, are purely coincidences, as there is not the slightest reason for believing that they occurred to the minds of the people who chose the name for this place, the name having been selected, as will be shown further on in this article, by a minister of the Christian denomination, for reasons which are obvious.

Antioch is one of twelve towns in the United States bearing this name. There were thirteen, but one of the post-offices—Antioch, Arkansas—was discontinued by the Government in 1916, its patrons now being served by a rural free delivery route from Beebe. Believing that you will be interested to learn something of these twelve namesakes, I have sent inquiries to them, and everyone has responded, some with very interesting letters. This much may be said now, however: Antioch, California, is the largest and most important of them all, many of the others being little more than country post-offices. Antioch, Illinois, is the next largest, and is the only other one in which there is a newspaper published.

Antioch was not the first name of this locality, it having been originally adjacent to a settlement known by the more pretentious title of "New York of the Pacific," which was designed to become the metropolis of the Pacific Coast. It was known in early times as Smith's Landing, from the Rev. W. W. Smith and his brother, Joseph H. Smith, who were among the original settlers. In the following paragraphs we give historical sketches written by the Rev. W. W. Smith and Captain George W. Kimball, which will be especially interesting to those who are disposed to hark back to the early days. Captain Kimball's article follows: "In 1848 I ran a packet between Maine and New York, and on my last trip I made up my mind to go to California and conceived and drew up a plan for building a ship to carry poor people like myself. It resulted in the following agreement: 'We, the undersigned, are desirous of engaging in an enterprise on the golden shores of California, the Paradise of America, where summer reigns perpetually; while the fertile soil is yielding its increase abundantly, fruits growing spontaneously, fishes sporting most plentifully, and where wild game is most prolific, on the shores of the Pacific. Our object is to settle a township or effect a permanent settlement on the coast of California, at some central point, in some capacious and commodious harbor, where the salubrity of the climate, the fertility of the soil, mill privileges, timber for ship-building, and other purposes, conveniences for fisheries, for coasting, and other natural advantages, shall warrant a healthy and rapid settlement. For the accomplishment of the above-mentioned object, we appoint George W. Kimball, of Frankfort, county of Waldo, State of Maine, as our lawful agent, to purchase or build, man and equip, a ship suitable to perform said voyage to California; said ship to be ready for sea by the 10th day of October, 1849. From two to three hundred of us will build and own a fine packet of six hundred tons, by paying $101 each; this packet will make one voyage per annum from Maine to California, taking out passengers, produce, etc., and returning with the exports of the Pacific. We will take our families, farming utensils, tools for the mechanic, and apparatus for a sawmill. On our arrival the first object will be to select a township; second, build a sawmill; erect a public depot for our families and baggage, until private dwellings can be built. When the packet sails, a school will commence for all on board, where the art of reading, writing, arithmetic, navigation, surveying, and such other branches of natural science will be taught as will be most needed in the new settlement.' "In pursuance of the above plan we went into the woods with a crew to get out timber for constructing a ship. Robert Douglass, a carpenter, commenced laying the ship's keel about the first of April, 1849.

Douglass was alone the first week; the second week two young men joined him. The company increased until sixty-five men were at work on their own ship. On the 14th of November the ship, partly rigged, sailed for Boston. As the enterprise was a novelty, we were freely advertised by the newspapers; merchants contributed freight and became interested in seeing the vessel supplied with all needed ship chandlery.

"March 4, 1850, we set sail for California, with two hundred persons on board, and arrived at San Francisco, all well, August 24th. The cholera was in San Francisco; many were sick, and some had died. I landed in good health the number that sailed from Boston, and three marines who swam aboard our ship in Rio Janeiro, and fourteen passengers who came aboard at Valparaiso, making 217 men, women and children. My company soon scattered, and many went to the mines. I sold the ship, paid my bills, and sat down to rest. About the 15th of September, Rev. W. W. Smith came on board our ship, and invited us to go to Antioch and settle. It was then called New York Township. My brother, S. P. Kimball, went to Antioch; several others went with him and built houses for their families east of where my house now stands.

A ship's galley was moved to a lot, near where the present brick schoolhouse now stands, and Martha Douglass taught the first school in our settlement. After that my daughter, Adelia, taught the school. My brother and I hired a man and cut hay on Kimball and Sherman islands.

I took it to San Francisco in my scow and sold it for sixty dollars per ton. Mr. Smith afterwards moved away from Antioch, so that I am the first permanent settler. I built two small wharves for receiving coal. I was the first postmaster, the first notary public, the first justice of the peace, and the first school trustee in Antioch.

"I supposed I owned the section I lived on until 1865, as I had bought all the titles I knew of. Garcia told me his New York ranch did not reach me, but they finally located it over my place, and covered my improvements, and the courts said it was all right. After the New York grant took my land I bought a few parcels of land to save some improvements, and then fled to the tule island opposite Pittsburg Landing with my stock. I spent part of two seasons there, dairying and raising hogs. I also bought the little island opposite Antioch; from this island my son, Edgar H. Kimball, supplies Antioch with milk."

Rev. W. W. Smith says: "We sailed from Boston harbor on the 11th of January, 1849, together with my brother, Joseph H. Smith, J. C. McMasters, and about fifty others. On the 6th day of July, 1849, we passed through the Golden Gate, amid the cheers of the passengers, and three or four hours later came the ship 'Edward Everett,' which we had not seen since leaving Boston harbor. As we gazed upon the shore from the ship, nothing but a city of tents could be seen. Before leaving the vessel, the captain called us on deck to have a friendly chat before bidding each other farewell and separating on our various ways. Arriving on shore, we found but five American families in the city, the balance being Mexicans and Indians. We remained in San Francisco five days, when we shipped on board the schooner 'Rialto' for the mouth of the San Joaquin River, where we arrived on the 11th of July, just six months from Boston Bay.

"Colonel J. D. Stevenson and Doctor William Parker had purchased a part of the Los Medanos grant, and had sent up the lumber, fixtures, etc., to commence the building of a city, to be called 'New York of the Pacific' W. W. Smith, being a practical architect and builder, was engaged at fourteen dollars per day to take charge of and superintend the building of a house for the two families, who, for the present, had only a tent for protection. Mr. Beener and Antonio Mesa and family lived two miles farther up the river. Mesa's house was built of redwood logs stood on end for the sides and was covered with tules in bundles for a roof, with a hole in the center to allow the smoke to escape and contained two rooms.

"New York of the Pacific was fast becoming an inland city, and the harbor was full of vessels with men and cargoes for the mines. At the first election, under the new constitution, in 1855, we found, on shore and on shipboard, that we had from five hundred to eight hundred voters when all were at home. Business continued to increase, and the New York House, conducted by the Smiths, became a popular temperance eating-house, while all the others sold liquor. When coin was scarce a pinch of gold dust paid for a drink.

"The proclamation of Governor Riley had been issued to have all needed officers elected. W. W. Smith was the first elected alcalde of New York of the Pacific and of this newly formed district. The alcalde had charge of all sanitary, civil, criminal, and judicial affairs in his district, with full power to appoint his officers, levy taxes, and collect fees.

The alcalde spent some two thousand dollars in time, money, and medicines, in caring for the sick and dead, none of which was ever reimbursed, and he found the position honorary and very expensive.

"In September, 1850, W. W. Smith, hearing oi the arrival of a shipload of settlers in San Francisco, hastened down and found a number of families who wished to obtain land and settle in California. Captain George W. Kimball and brother, Robert Douglass, four or five Hathaways, a Mr. Marshall and son, and a Mr. Dennison, came to Antioch, which at that time was called Smith's Landing. A street was laid out running east by compass, and each family that wished to settle upon land was presented with a lot to build on. The Pulsifer brothers then established a garden on the point, watering the same by a simple wooden pump, fixed in the slough between the point and the mainland. By the united work of all, a fence and ditch were completed from the tules on the west of town to the tules on the east, in the spring of 1851, to keep the wild animals from entering the town.

"On the Fourth of July, 1851, a basket picnic was held at the residence of W. W. Smith, then standing on the high ground near where the Antioch Ledger office now is. The all-absorbing topic of the day was 'What shall we name our town?' Between thirty and forty men, women, and children had gathered from far and near. Several names were proposed, among them 'Minton,' after a steamer that plied on the river, that she might be induced to stop at our town. Another proposed that the name be 'Paradise,' but Deacon Pulsifer remarked that there were many claimants to the lands in California, and they might lose their land, and then it would be 'Paradise Lost.' W. W. Smith proposed that, inasmuch as the first settlers were disciples of Christ, and one of them had died and was buried on the land, that it be given a Bible name in his honor, and suggested Antioch, and by united acclamation it was so christened."

The foregoing articles dispose quite thoroughly with the very early history of Antioch. Just at this juncture a few words of explanation might not come amiss. It must be remembered that the articles quoted above were written a good many years ago, and changes have occurred which make some of the statements not quite accurate today. For instance, Captain Kimball speaks of those who built houses "east of where my house now stands." Captain Kimball's house stood at that time near where Scout's Hall now stands. In fact, the Griswold home, next door to the hall, is the Captain's old house remodeled and added to, and is therefore the oldest house in Antioch, and is said to be the oldest residence building in Contra Costa. The other buildings have all disappeared, other more modern structures having replaced them. They were located east by compass from the Captain's house, the last one standing not far from where the water-tank is now located. Again, Captain Kimball speaks of a ship's galley being moved to a lot where "the present brick schoolhouse now stands." The brick schoolhouse is no longer standing, but Mrs. A. B. Schott, Captain Kimball's daughter, informs me that it stood just about where the present grammar-school building is now located. Edgar Kimball still lives in Antioch but is no longer the official milkman. With these exceptions, however, Captain Kimball's sketch corresponds quite closely to present-day conditions.

The residence referred to in Mr. Smith's article as standing on the present location of the Ledger office is the old frame building now standing just east of the Belshaw building and is not the present location of the Ledger. At the time Mr. Smith's article was written it stood on the present site of the Bank of Antioch building. The early settler mentioned in Mr. Smith's article who had died and was buried on the land was his brother, the Rev. Joseph H. Smith, and his earthly remains rested at that time in the old burying-ground, then located about where Mrs. Meyers now lives, on the corner of F and Tenth streets.

The Colonel J. D. Stevenson mentioned in Mr. Smith's sketch seems to have been a sort of early "Get-Rich-Quick Wallingford." He is described as a rather picturesque and romantic sort of grafter by Miss Pauline Jacobson in a series of articles dealing with the early history of San Francisco, published last year in the San Francisco Bulletin. With Miss Jacobson's kind permission, I give a brief extract from her article, dealing with the smooth Colonel. The reader will note that Miss Jacobson is rather unjust in her estimate of the geographical location of New York of the Pacific; but this is undoubtedly caused by lack of accurate information as to its correct location. Excerpts from her article follow: "The Colonel was now a 'land commissioner.' He was clad in closely buttoned frock coat and military fatigue cap, a fashion which clung to him till death. The Colonel could never quite live down his military past.

And according to the account of Massett (a young adventurer of argonaut days), no modern method had anything over the Colonel when it came to disposing of real estate in his 'New York of the Pacific,' which was somewhere in the region of the mosquito-infected, malarial-ridden marshes of Sacramento. The dodge was for the forfeiture of the lot if a house was not erected in thirty days. Lumber was hardly to be had, and the houses purported to be on the way by the Horn never came. The Colonel, upon finding that Massett had no definite object in coming to California, but was following his bent of drifting about, suggested that he come the next day to his office, in Montgomery Street, between Washington and Jackson.

"'You are just the young man for me,' said the Colonel. 'You, of course, understand drawing deeds, mortgages, etc.; in fact, the general routine of a lawyer's office. You've been in a good school, and I think we can get along very well together. I have just purchased a tract of land—am going to build a new city—a second New York, sir! I'll make you alcalde, sir! Notary public, sir! Mayor of the city, sir! Come and breakfast with me, sir, tomorrow.' "'At what time, Colonel?' asked Massett.

"'At six o'clock, sir—always rise with the lark,' replied the Colonel. 'There's nothing like getting up early, sir—business man, sir. Go to bed early—keep steady—don't drink, and your fortune's made in no time!' "The next day, bright and early, Massett went to his office. The walls were adorned with large maps, most gorgeously got up. . . . On the outside the people were informed that that was 'J. D. Stevenson's Land Office and Agency of Lots in New York of the Pacific.'"

Colonel Stevenson's dream of a second New York at this point has not yet been realized, though it is hardly too much to say that in a measure it may be yet, for Antioch and Pittsburg are now growing by leaps and bounds and will ere long be manufacturing and shipping centers of no mean proportions. It is quite evident that the Colonel's first thought was to make money out of real-estate speculation, and it is hardly likely that the future greatness of his city in reality gave him any serious concern. It is also evident, however, in the light of present conditions, that he chose better than he knew. It is certain that if he could live again and see the scene of his activities of those early days, he would observe many things that would cause him the utmost astonishment. It must be remembered that he never saw a telephone, a phonograph, an electric car or motor, or an automobile. In fact, the railroad trains of his day were few and far between, and, compared with the palatial systems with which we are all so familiar, were crude and clumsy affairs. The past sixty years have been years of tremendous progress, and the New York City of 1850 actually compared quite poorly in all save size with the Antioch and Pittsburg of 1917.

Of the original settlers of Antioch only two are living here today—Edgar H. Kimball and Mrs. Adelia B. Schott, son and daughter of Captain Kimball, who have many interesting reminiscences to relate of life in Antioch as it was in the days of the argonauts. Of the buildings which housed these original families, none are now standing intact, though one, the house now occupied by G. C. Griswold and family, next door to Scout's Hall, is composed for the most part of the material contained in the original residence of Captain Kimball, some of this material having been brought from Maine on the initial voyage of the Captain's good ship.

About the year 1859 coal was discovered in several places in the hills south of Antioch and formed the first substantial industry aside from farming and dairying of the inhabitants of this locality. This new industry resulted in the founding of the towns of Somersville, Nortonville, and Black Diamond (now Pittsburg), and added greatly to the importance and prosperity of Antioch. The Empire Coal Company was formed in 1876 by John C. Rouse and George Hawkhurst, and a railroad built, which passed out of Antioch toward the mines over what is now F (formerly Kimball) Street. The mine and railroad later passed into the hands of the Belshaw brothers. The mine has long since ceased operation and the railroad track has been taken up, though the building which served as the Antioch terminus of the road still stands on the corner of F and Fourth streets, and the grading, trestles, etc., still remain much as they were in these early days.

In 1863 a great excitement arose over the discovery of copper near Antioch. Smelting-works were erected at Antioch, and from fifteen dollars to twenty-five dollars per ton was paid for ore, according to its richness. The bubble eventually burst, to the discomfiture of all concerned.

Petroleum was first bored for near Antioch in 1865, but oil in paying quantities could not be obtained.

So much for the early days of the town. Antioch was ideally located and grew, developed and prospered much as many other communities of that period, and in due time churches, fraternal societies, and business enterprises were founded, many of which remain with us to the present. Mention of the principal ones will be made as we pass along.

The Antioch Ledger was first issued on March 10, 1870, and in all its forty-seven years never missed an issue. A copy of its first number has been framed and hangs over the desk of the present editor. It is five by eight inches in size, printed on one side only, and its sole news item is a report and editorial comment on a woman's suffrage meeting which had just been held in the town. This paper was founded by James W. E. Townsend and Harry Waite, and conducted by them jointly until August, 1870, when Townsend became the sole proprietor. Townsend was a prolific and versatile writer and had the reputation of having established more newspapers than any other man in California. He was a man of strong personality and captivating manner, and a raconteur of rare ability. So numerous and so wonderful were the anecdotes with which he used to regal his listeners, it is said that they earned for him the sobriquet of "Lying Jim" Townsend. Paradoxical though it may sound, in some of the works of Bret Harte he is referred to as "Truthful James." Whether this was satire or an indication of reformation on Townsend's part cannot be definitely stated now, but it is certain that many of the stories immortalized in the works of Bret Harte, Samuel Gemens (Mark Twain), and other Western writers of that period actually originated in the fertile brain of Townsend, for he was an intimate friend and associate of these writers.

In December, 1870, J. P. Abbott succeeded Townsend as editor and proprietor of the Ledger, and during the eleven years it was conducted by this able journalist it was an important factor in State and county politics. After some years Abbott sold the paper to Charles F. Montgomery, who changed its politics from Republican to Democratic. He was also an able and aggressive writer and took an active part in political matters. Upon his death the management of the Ledger was taken up by his son, Curtis F. Montgomery, who remained in charge until April 1, 1905, when the paper was purchased by C. G. McDaniel, the present owner, who changed its politics back to Republican.

In both its news and editorial columns the Ledger has always been progressive but conservative and has been an important factor in the development of Antioch and its vicinity, enjoying the friendship and respect of all, even of those who may not altogether agree with its political policies.

Antioch's pioneer church, the First Congregational, celebrated its fiftieth anniversary in September, 1915, with elaborate exercises, reported in detail in the Ledger of subsequent date. It seems that a church had been founded prior to 1865 by a young man named Morgan, but was short-lived, and it was revived at this time and absorbed by this Congregational church, which has had a continuous existence from 1865 to the present. A Sunday-school, founded by Miss Adelia Kimball (Mrs. A. B. Schott), was later conducted by the Misses Drusilla Boobar and Annie Morrison (Mrs. Joseph Galloway)! prior to the church organization. This school met in the town hall, which then stood about where the Kelley undertaking parlor is now located. The Congregational church, however, was the first permanent religious enterprise established in Antioch. Briefly, the details of its formation are as follows: On June 12, 1865, a meeting of those interested was held in the schoolhouse for the purpose of forming a church. Captain G. W. Kimball acted as chairman and the Rev. J. H. Warren as secretary. A constitution was adopted which, with slight changes and amendments, is still in force after more than a half century. As nearly as can be determined the charter membership consisted of the following persons: Mrs. R. H. Aldon, Mr. and Mrs. F. C. Barrett, Mrs. M. H. Boothby, G. W. Brown, G. C. Carmen, Miss Ida Fuller, Isaac Hardy, G. W. Kimball, Mrs. J. C. O'Brien, Almon Walton, and S. S. Woodruff. The first permanent board of trustees consisted of Joseph Galloway, David Woodruff, G. W. Brown, Captain G. W. Kimball, and William Utter. From this parent organization have sprung the other Protestant denominations—first, the Advent Christian, later the Methodist Episcopal, and, last of all, the Church of Christ, Scientist. The Congregational society owns the beautiful church and grounds on the corner of Sixth and F streets, also the parsonage next door.

The Catholic church has been one of the most important religious institutions of Antioch for the past forty-five years, and the circumstances regarding its institution and development are briefly as follows: In 1872 the Rev. Father Vincent Vinzes, of

Benicia, was called to the Empire Mine, then being operated about six miles south of Antioch, to attend one of the miners who had been seriously injured. Taking advantage of the occasion, Father Vinzes called the men of the Catholic faith together and celebrated mass in the home of John Mulhare, located a short distance southwest of Antioch, near where the high school now stands. Then for more than a year regular services were held at the Mulhare home. In 1873 the "old" church was built on the block between G and H streets, on Seventh, this land being donated by Captain George W. Kimball and a Spanish gentleman whose name could not be obtained by this writer. This building is still standing and is used as a hall for lodge-meetings and other secular purposes. In 1875 Father Patrick Calahan came to Antioch and became the first resident priest, and in 1880 the rectory was built for his residence. Father Calahan died in 1902, and was succeeded by Father Antone Riley, and it was during his ministry, in 1905, that the beautiful new church was erected, on the church property adjoining the old structure. This building is of white sandstone brick, Romanesque in architecture, and is one of the most beautiful church buildings in Contra Costa County. The cost was over $25,000. Altogether the church property is valued at about $40,000, and the location is one of the most attractive in Antioch.

Father Riley left Antioch, and was succeeded by Father J. G. Rourke, formerly of St. Dominic's Church, San Francisco, in 1912, and shortly afterward Father Rourke was joined by Father E. Lawrence, who came from Benicia to act as his assistant. These priests are still in charge, and are constantly improving the grounds and buildings, and under their able leadership the Holy Rosary Church of Antioch is growing and prospering.

The Advent Christian church was organized on September 25, 1877, by Mrs. M. J. Clark, an evangelist of that denomination, with a charter membership of more than thirty, most of whom were at the time members of the Congregational church. Prominent among these were John Schott, wife and daughter (Miss Louisa), T. N. Wills, H. F. Beede and wife, S. P. Joslin and wife, Isaac Hardy and wife, Dr. E. L. Wempler and wife. The evangelist, Mrs. Clark, remained for some time and served the church in the capacity of pastor. The Rev. W. R. Young was the first resident pastor, and remained with the church until about 1900, when he removed to Oakland, to assume the editorship of The Messiah's Advocate. The Adventist church owns its house of worship, located on the corner of Fourth and I streets.

The Methodist Episcopal church of Antioch was organized in September, 1899, the principal figures in the movement being Judge J. P. Abbott (now deceased) and Doctor W. S. George. The preliminary meeting, at which a temporary organization was effected was called by Wesley Dunnigan, L. S. Lafferty, Isaac Lafferty, and Doctor W. S. George in the old Hamburg Hall, which then stood near the present site of the Santa Fe station. These men secured the services of the Rev. James Blackledge, who held regular services and assisted in perfecting the organization of the new church. The State Conference sent the Rev. Dr. Brill late in the fall, and he completed the details of organization, and the men whose names appear earlier in this paragraph were appointed the first board of trustees. Doctor Brill at once began a vigorous campaign to raise funds for the purchase of a building-site and the erection thereon of a house of worship. His efforts were successful, and the building now occupied by the church, located on the corner of Sixth and G streets, was erected in 1890. The church also owns the parsonage property on Sixth Street, next door to the church.

Early in the year 1910 six Christian Scientists began to read the lesson sermon at the residence of one of their number, and through the work accomplished by this little company the number gradually increased until in the fall of 1910 it became necessary to secure larger quarters, and Union Hall was rented for midweek and Sunday meetings. In July, 1911, a society was organized with a charter membership of fifteen, and in 1912 a church building-lot was purchased on the corner of Fifth and D streets. On March 12, 1915, the temporary chapel now occupied was begun on the rear of this lot, leaving room for a main church building when such is needed. This chapel was completed and the first meeting held on April 4th following. The seating capacity is about one hundred. The continued growth both in regard to attendance and membership attests the permanence of Christian Science in Antioch and its vicinity.

FRATERNAL SOCIETIES

San Joaquin Lodge No. 151, of the Independent Order of Odd Fellows was organized in Antioch on January 9, 1869, by District Deputy Grand Master G. P. Loucks. William Girvan was elected Noble Grand, M. S. Levy, Vice Grand; George Thyarks, secretary; Russell Eddy, treasurer. Fred Wilkening was the only one of the five charter members who did not at once assume an official station. San Joaquin Lodge now has a membership of about 140, and jointly with the Masonic Lodge owns the lodge building on the corner of H and Second streets.

This lodge is one of the largest and most important in Contra Costa County. Antioch Encampment No. 114, I. O. O. F., consisting of members of San Joaquin and Byron lodges, was instituted October 9, 1908, with a charter membership of twenty-three. J. T. Belshaw was elected the first Chief Patriarch. This organization has grown and prospered and is now one of the leading fraternal societies in the town. Mizpah Rebekah Lodge, I. O. O. F., was instituted June 28, 1888, with a mere handful of members, but has grown very rapidly, until it now outnumbers the older San Joaquin Lodge of Odd Fellows. Many of Antioch's younger set are active members, and Mizpah Lodge is one of the prominent social as well as fraternal societies of the city.

General Winn Parlor No. 32, Native Sons of the Golden West, was instituted July 26, 1884, being one of the oldest parlors. Every year since its organization it has held a grand masque ball, which has become one of the principal social events of the year, and for the last eight years this parlor has given an annual amateur theatrical performance, the entire proceeds being donated to the Homeless Children Fund.

This parlor has the honor of having in its membership one of the Past Grand Presidents of the order, Hon. Chas. M. Belshaw, and many of the most prominent citizens of this section are included in its list of members.

Antioch Aerie No. 785, Fraternal Order of Eagles, was instituted September 1, 1904, with a charter membership of 105, and has enjoyed a remarkable growth, having at the present time more than 300 members—the largest of any order in the city. It is also said to have the strongest treasury of any organization of a fraternal or social nature in this section.

Antioch Lodge No. 1612, Loyal Order of Moose, was organized in February, 1915, with Doctor W. S. George as the first dictator. The lodge hold its meetings in the Foresters of America building, and maintains elegant club-rooms over the Bank of Antioch. The membership is large and growing.

Among the other fraternal societies that are well established and active in Antioch may be named the Foresters of America, the Improved Order of Red Men (Pocahontas Lodge), and the Young Men's Institute, a Catholic order; also, the U. P. E. G, U. P. P. E. C, L D. E. S., and S. P. R. S. I., the last four named all being Portuguese orders.

G. Azevedo, member of Antioch Council No. 51, U. P. E. C, has just finished a term of one year as Supreme President of the order.

Of clubs by far the most important is the Antioch Woman's Club. Besides being a popular social organization, this club has accomplished much for the material advancement of Antioch. It was through its efforts that the town has its modern automatic fire-alarm system, and also the beautiful public library building on the corner of Sixth and F streets. Other important improvements have received substantial aid from the Woman's Club.

Among the business enterprises of Antioch with a continuous existence from their first establishment to the present day, the Antioch Lumber Company is without doubt the oldest. This industry was established in the year 1864 by the late Joseph Galloway and E. C. Boobar, who at that time owned a considerable portion of the town-site, as well as the water-front. The office and yards were located on the block on which the Arlington Hotel, Wall Shoe Store, etc., now stand, while the main steamboat wharf at the foot of H Street was utilized by the company for loading and unloading schooners, this being before the day of railroad transportation facilities. Joseph W. Galloway, son of the founder, acted as manager of the business until the death of his father in 1877, when he sold the business to William R. Forman, John C. Rouse, and Henry F. Beede, the latter having been in Mr. Galloway's employ as a clerk for some years. After a few years Forman sold his interest to J. P. Abbott, and in 1887 Rouse sold half of his half interest to the Simpson Lumber Company. After operating several years as a co-partnership, Feb. 20, 1907, the Antioch Lumber Company was incorporated, and still exists as a corporate body. Upon the death of Captain Simpson, in 1914, the Simpson heirs disposed of their stock to H. F. Beede, Mrs. Abbott, and Collins Rouse, of Berkeley. Beede has been the efficient general manager of this concern for many years, and under his direction the business has prospered and grown far beyond the most sanguine expectations of its founders. Besides handling lumber and mill products on a very large scale, this firm deals in coal, oils, grain, feed, etc. Nor are its activities confined to this city or the immediate environs, but, particularly of late years, extensive contracts have been secured from distant points, all of which have been handled in a manner mutually profitable and satisfactory to all the parties concerned and have reflected great credit upon the local firm. The Antioch Lumber Company now has its planing mill, yards, offices, wharves, and storerooms near the foot of Second Street.

The paper-making industry, while not the oldest, is today the most important in Antioch. The mill was first established in 1889, by M. D. Keeney and operated by him and his three sons, E. M., W. C, and C. W. Keeney, on its present site, for about ten years. Straw, manila wrapping, and tissue papers comprised the principal part of the output, though some other varieties were made to special order. The capacity at that time was from three to five tons a day, according to the weight of the grade being made. In 1900 the Brown Brothers—Peter and James —bought the mill from the Keeneys and brought a number of their employees and some new machinery from Coralitos in Santa Cruz County, where they had been conducting a paper-mill, and in due time remodeled the buildings and enlarged and improved the plant, adding the manufacture of various varieties of cardboards and folding boxboards to their accomplishments. The industry was under this management until March, 1912, when the mills were acquired by the Paraffine Paint Co., of San Francisco, and incorporated as the California Paper & Board Mills. On November 13, 1912, the entire plant was destroyed by fire, but the work of rebuilding was begun at once on a much larger and more elaborate scale than before, and early in the summer of 1913 work was resumed. Besides all the varieties of papers and boards manufactured by their predecessors, the new company began the manufacture of "Amiwud," a wall board of unusual merit, which imitates grained hardwood with a fidelity which practically defies detection. This product has been extensively advertised and is sold all over the United States and in many foreign countries. The normal day's output of this mill is more than ninety tons of finished product, and it is the largest and finest paper-making establishment west of the Mississippi River.

On January 1, 1917, this factory changed from a twelve-hour to an eight-hour work-day, with no reduction in wages. It now employs in excess of 150 men, and the wages paid are the highest in the trade.

EARLY DAYS OF ANTIOCH

It was in 1849 that William Smith and his brother Joseph pre-empted the land where Antioch now stands. More than a year before this Captain Kimball had formed a company among his poor neighbors along the coast of Maine to build for itself a ship in which to go to California. This ship, the "California Packet," arrived in San Francisco August, 1850. Smith went on board this ship and induced twenty or thirty of the passengers to come and settle here, offering them building-lots along the river, while they would farm the land toward the hills. They built five or six small houses in a row, extending nearly to the tules east of the town. Kimball's house, at the western end of the row, was built in the fall of 1851. Smith's house was larger than the others and stood on the bluff overlooking the river.

Besides these dwelling-houses, was a very small ship's cabin, that occupied a position near the site of the present schoolhouse. This Captain Mitchell removed from his ship and gave to the town for a schoolhouse.

In this Miss Martha Douglas was installed as teacher. She soon resigned and Smith turned the school over to me. I was twelve years old. The house was small and dark, while out of doors was big and bright, and we had fine recesses. We still have in our midst two survivors of that most primitive school. They are Mrs. D. Parkison, of Oakland, and E. H. Kimball.

In the fall of 1851 the little settlement thought it time to know what to call itself, and a meeting was held to decide the matter. No one but Smith had any special choice, so he had little difficulty in persuading the people to adopt Antioch as the name, his reason for this choice being that "the disciples were called Christians first in Antioch."

Early in the settlement of the place there was an epidemic of cholera, resulting in several deaths, and chills and fever prevailed. Farming failed. There was plenty of hay, however, as the valley and foothills were covered with luxuriant wild oats, and the tule land produced an abundance of coarse grass. But this could not yield sufficient income for the year round. The discouraged little band scattered. Some took their houses with them. The others abandoned theirs, either entirely or temporarily, and in 1852 Antioch was literally a deserted village.

However, it did not remain long unoccupied. Smith and Kimball returned. McMaster came and built near the river front. Other families, at longer or shorter intervals, moved into the vicinity. There were no town limits, and the Hendersons, at the Arata place, the Thompsons, at Marsh Landing, Madam Fuller, at Oak Point, Wyatt and O'Brien, southwest of the paper-mill, Robert Fuller, at the ranch, Doctor Adams, at Oak Springs, and the Hustels, in the sand-hills, were our near neighbors. The arrival of each family made an epoch in our history, and we welcomed them gladly.

The leading industry was cattle-raising. Doctor Marsh had large herds of wild Spanish cattle, and those who wished could have the use of a limited number, and half the increase for breaking them. Had their milking qualities equaled the length of their horns and their athletic abilities, they would have been very valuable. However, what little milk they did give was very rich and they proved a fair investment to those who chose to avail themselves of Doctor Marsh's offer.

In those days the only public conveyance between Antioch and the outside world was the schooner "Enterprise," commanded by Captain Miller, with "Charley" as the crew, which made a weekly trip between here and San Francisco, carrying passengers and the mail and the various products of the farm and dairy, and bringing back from the city the numerous things needed by the community. My recollections of this craft are a mixture of gratitude and misery—gratitude for the means of transportation and for the invariable kindness of the captain and crew, and the misery of the trip—sometimes three days, and the inevitable seasickness. It gave me all the boat-riding I wanted for many years.

There were a number of children within walking distance, and we had several terms of school in one of the abandoned houses, at which I trust there was more work and less play than in the first school.

The social function was a monthly sewing-bee and lunch, which met "turn about" at the several neighbors, and sewed for the hostess, and exchanged news. Smith often conducted a service on Sunday, and there was occasionally a traveling preacher.

California in its early settlement was much hampered by the Spanish grants, which roamed around devouring every fertile spot, and giving the settlers no rest for the soles of their feet. Antioch had its full share in this kind of trouble. Being between the Marsh grant and Los Medanos the people were "warned off" first by one and then the other.

Finally, after years of harassment and wearing litigation, it was taken by Los Medanos, and Galloway and Boobar bought the town.

Antioch has always been a town with a great future. Its advantages as a manufacturing center were early recognized, and more or less feasible enterprises have marked its entire history. More than forty years ago McMaster started brick-kilns, and several houses were built from the product. Potteries have been tried many times, with sufficient success to prove it could be done if properly managed. Hope rose with the smelting works. A furnace and chimney seventy-five feet high were put up, and twenty or thirty more were to follow, if this was a success in reducing the copper ore brought from Copperopolis. The sequel is evident. There were no more chimneys, but the one stood many years— a monument to dead hope and a perennial subject for the inquisitive traveler.

The development of the coal mines in the hills south of town about 1860 was the occasion of Antioch's becoming a town in any real sense.

It was made a shipping-point, and many teams and men were needed to handle the coal. This made blacksmiths and other mechanics necessary.

Families came and stores followed. More children required better school facilities, and a wooden schoolhouse was built.

There were enough who wanted regular church services. A young man named Morgan preached very acceptably in the schoolhouse, and the Congregational church society was formed. So many people made sufficient travel and traffic for it to be worth the while of the Stockton boats to stop, and wharves were built. Meanwhile people had learned by slow degrees that the land in eastern Contra Costa was very productive, if properly worked. This kept Antioch still alive when the shipping of coal was diverted to other points.

These imperfect glimpses of the past show that, although our history has been marked all the way along by sufficient disappointment and failure to insure our keeping properly humble, yet the present condition of the town proves that while the growth has not been rapid, we have very noticeably advanced and are very comfortably expecting our great future.

There is no particular in which Antioch has changed more than in its facilities for travel. In a previous chapter allusion has been made to the difficulties of communication with the outside world. These were the inconveniences incident to the development of new countries. Public conveyances are not liable to exist where there is a very small public to accommodate.

The various plans to bridge over the lack of transportation were often amusing and sometimes disagreeable. Once, when the Stockton boat attempted to put a party ashore in a rowboat, they landed them by the high bank where the warehouses now are. The tide was so high that there was only a narrow strip of beach to stand on. Fortunately, there was a gentleman in the party, and by the help of his cane and the bushes growing on the bank he managed to reach the top. He went to the nearest house for help, and, finding no one at home, helped himself to their clothes-line, and lowering that to the others succeeded in hauling them to the top.

At another time a party of three started from San Francisco in a small sailboat quite early in the morning. For a wonder, the wind was low and they were still in sight of the city at sundown. By night the wind was rested and ready for action and made things almost too lively for the little craft, but it kept on till Bay Point was reached, where it was tied up to wait for a change in the tide, to come with the morning.

When morning came one of the party, seeing a wagon loaded with hay and headed east, begged the privilege of finishing the journey by land.

A strong norther was blowing; the ride was very tedious and not at all luxurious; but toward night the wagon reached New York Landing, where an old couple took the wanderer in for the night. In the morning the small boat was on hand, and the journey was finished according to the original plan.

Soon after the development of the coal mines and the increase of the population the commerce of the town warranted the building of a wharf, and then the Stockton boats would stop. Then, as now, that brought all the travel in the night. Antioch felt proud when the "Parthenius" started to make daily trips from Antioch to San Francisco. She left here at six in the morning and returned in the evening, giving people several hours in the city, and was a great convenience. But when the Southern Pacific was put through the steamboat was altogether too slow, and she soon ceased to make the trip. Now there are fifteen different ways of getting out of town every day, ten by railroad and five by boat, which is quite a contrast to once a week on a little schooner.

PIONEER SCHOOL OF ANTIOCH

The first attempt at a school in Antioch was held in a small cabin, which had been removed from an abandoned ship, belonging to Captain Mitchell, to a site near the present school building. The first permanent teacher was Adelia B. Kimball (now Mrs. A. B. Schott), a girl of 12 years, daughter of Captain G. W. Kimball. There were about half a dozen young children. She taught a few months at a time for several years.

The next building was a small one-room house, in the vicinity of E Street. Afterward Joseph Galloway gave the present grammar-school site, and a small wooden building was erected. Next was a two-story brick house, supplemented, as population increased, by wooden class rooms, one north and the other south of the brick building. These rooms becoming inadequate, and the brick building of doubtful safety, the present grammar-school edifice was put up in 1890.

The second teacher was James Cruickshank, who taught a few terms. He was followed by Mrs. Woodruff, an exceptionally fine teacher. Afterward the school had for principals J. P. Abbott, Warren Abbott, and Miss Carpenter, which brings it to comparatively modern times.

In the early days we had no California State Series school books, but such books as the various families brought from the East. The furniture was anything that came handy—chairs brought from home, boxes for desks, anything one could reasonably use as a seat.

STREET IMPROVEMENT

Until a few years ago Antioch had a deserved reputation for having about the poorest streets of any town in the State; now it is known far and wide for having the best thoroughfares of any place of equal size in California, and it is believed that its streets are not excelled by any city of its class in the United States. In fact, it was not until 1908 that any permanent street improvement was undertaken. Then the greater portions of L, G, Second, Fourth and Sixth streets were paved with the petrolithic process. These being the principal business and central residence streets, the improvement was of marked value; but the process of paving proved unsuited to this climate, and the pavements were soon worn out. It was about this time that compulsory laying of sidewalks was begun. The cost of the improvements at this period was slightly in excess of twenty-two thousand dollars, exclusive of sidewalks. In 1912 the matter of further street improvement was taken up under the provisions of the street improvement act of 1911, and about forty blocks on Third, Fourth, F, H, and I streets were paved with one-course oil macadam. These streets, which were completed in 1913, have proved very satisfactory, and give promise of great durability. The cost of paving these streets was, in round numbers, seventy-two thousand dollars. In 1915-16 the streets previously paved by the petrolithic process were repaved with four-inch and five-inch concrete base, with Topeka top dressing of one and a half inches. Also, the majority of the streets which had not been previously improved were paved, either through legal proceedings or by private contract, so that some fifty-one blocks of the town are now paved with concrete, which is conceded to be the very best and most substantial paving to be secured. Besides these improvements, many blocks of good sidewalks were laid. The cost of the street work, not including sidewalks, retaining walls, etc., was in excess of one hundred and eleven thousand dollars. Altogether Antioch has expended since 1908 for street betterment close to a quarter of a million of dollars.

WATER AND SEWERAGE SYSTEMS

Antioch was one of the first towns of this section to adopt municipal ownership of its water supply and has proven a splendid example of the practicability and desirability of publicly owned utilities. Prior to the year 1903 the water supply was furnished by a private company, of which the Hon. Charles M. Belshaw was the head. Owing to the rapid growth and development of the town, the securing of more adequate facilities was deemed desirable, and bond issues of twenty-two thousand dollars were voted for a water plant and eight thousand dollars for sewers. In 1904 installations were completed of a modern sewer and drainage system and an up-to-date water system electrically operated.

In due time the water system became inadequate to meet the demands of the growing population, and additions were found necessary. Accordingly, in 1913 another bond issue of twenty-five thousand dollars was voted, and in 1914 larger mains were installed, a high-pressure filtration plant and an Alberger fire underwriters' centrifugal pump put in commission, and in 1916 an efficient chlorination plant was added, so that now the water supply is equal to any demand likely to arise for many years, and the quality is such that it passes the most severe tests of the State Board of Health for purity and wholesomeness. The average daily consumption is five hundred thousand gallons, and the average rate (flat-rate plan) is $1.25 a month.

Antioch has a two-thousand-dollar Gamewell automatic fire alarm system and an excellent volunteer department, with splendid equipment, including an auto chemical truck. Insurance rates are accordingly lower than in many of the larger cities.

LIGHTING SYSTEM

Until comparatively recent years Antioch's residences had to depend upon oil or acetylene for lighting, and such street lights as were installed were coal-oil lamps, which were far from satisfactory. On July 14, 1902, H. F. Beede secured from the board of trustees a franchise for an electric-light system, which, however, without any profit whatsoever to himself he turned over to L. A. Reniff early in 1903, who installed a dynamo (driven by a gasoline engine) in a building near the planingmill. While this was some improvement over former conditions, the service was not perfect by any means, and before long the plant was closed down and current purchased from the Pacific Gas & Electric Company to supply the customers. In July, 1910, the franchise passed into the hands of the latter company, which now gives what is well-nigh perfect service and at a very reasonable rate. The streets are well lighted with lamps ranging in candle-power from 250 to 600. Current for operating motors is also supplied. In 1915 the Contra Costa Gas Company secured a franchise and extended its lines to this city, and now furnishes a very high grade of gas for both lighting and fuel purposes.

CELERY, ASPARAGUS, ETC.

Not least among Antioch's manifold industries and resources is the growing, packing, and shipping of celery, asparagus, and other fruits and vegetables. More asparagus is shipped from this place than from any other town in the world, and more celery than from any other point in the United States. About two-thirds of the potatoes grown in the State are raised on the islands in the Sacramento and San Joaquin rivers in the immediate vicinity of Antioch. The Santa Fe Refrigerator Dispatch operates steamers that ply the rivers and collect green fruits and vegetables, bringing them to Antioch, where they are placed in iced cars and sent to Eastern markets. So important is Antioch as a shipping point for this company that its Pacific Coast manager, S. M. Fulton, resides here. Exact figures were not obtainable in time for this article, but the approximate volume of shipments of a few of these commodities is annually as follows: Celery, 1200 to 1500 carloads; asparagus, 250 carloads; almonds, 7 carloads; grapes, 70 carloads; apricots, 10 carloads; peaches, 8 carloads; dried fruits (apricots and peaches), 2 carloads; hay (wheat, barley, and oats), 500 carloads; wheat, 10 carloads; barley, 8 carloads.

There are large pits of a fine quality of sand located just east of town, and hundreds of carloads and boatloads are shipped annually. Other miscellaneous products, such as potatoes, onions, beans, and various small fruits and berries, contribute many more carloads to the grand total. Altogether close to eight thousand carloads of varied products are shipped from Antioch every year.

Among other interesting items concerning Antioch are the following: It has the finest climate on earth; deep water-frontage where oceangoing vessels can and do come; the largest paper mill west of the Mississippi; one of the best equipped high schools in the State; a municipally owned water system with plenty of filtered water; the best streets of any town of its size in the country; numerous river transportation lines; two transcontinental railroads; two electric-power lines; two banks with combined resources of nearly a million dollars; many modern stores with complete stocks, where goods are sold at prices so moderate that there is no temptation to shop in the city; a beautiful public library, and many modern business and residence buildings. Antioch has a population upward of twenty-five hundred, and is fifty miles from San Francisco, at the junction of the Sacramento and San Joaquin rivers.

This town is entering upon an era of unusual growth and development, and the prospects are that within a very few years it will be one of the most important interior towns in California. Since the completion of the new street improvements, building has taken on fresh impetus, and within the past year or two many handsome residences and new business buildings have been erected. A fine large brick garage (the third one in town) has just been completed, and the new telephone building will be ready for occupancy in a few weeks. Antioch is truly the "Metropolis of eastern Contra Costa."

CHAPTER XXVIII. DANVILLE

Danville is eighteen miles south of Martinez and is in the very choicest portion of the famous San Ramon Valley, with the beautiful Los Tampos Range on the west, whose varying shadows change with every hour of the day's sunshine and are ever admired, while Mount Diablo rears its towering height of nearly four thousand feet on the east. These physical features account for the uniform climate of the place which renders it so desirable for homes.

The town had its inception sometime about 1859, when Andrew and Daniel Inman, then owners of what is now Kelly brothers' property, put up the first building to be used for a blacksmith shop. Not long afterward M. Cohen, of the firm of Wolf & Cohen, merchants, of Alamo, then a flourishing business center, saw the advantages of the location for a store and erected the building on the corner which, after defying the elements for nearly sixty years, was torn down only recently.

About the time the store was built came the question of a name for the town. Inmanville and a number of others was suggested, but all proved unsatisfactory, when Andrew Inman proposed they should leave the naming to his mother-in-law, "Aunt Sallie" Young, grandmother of A. J. Young. She asked that it be called Danville, after her native place in Kentucky.

A two-story hotel, afterward destroyed by fire, was built by a Mr. Harris. In this building the post-office found a home, in a windowless 7 by 9 room, in which Harris, as postmaster, often performed his clerical duties by the aid of a lantern. For many years the mail was carried from Walnut Creek on horseback. J. Madison Stowe, now mayor of Pacific Grove, was the mail-carrier at one time. The mail was due at Danville at 4 p. m. daily, and was always on time, unless "Jim" was challenged by some boy on the road to play a game of marbles for "keeps," at which time it was "unavoidably late." A second store was established by P. E. Peel. He was succeeded by John Conway, who for many years carried on a successful business. Thus by the addition of one enterprise after another the little town had a prosperous growth.

The Grangers' hall, the first public building of the place, came in 1872-73, and two years later the Presbyterian church was built, at that time the finest church edifice in the county. The first schoolhouse was an old building, built in 1865, and stood one mile south of town. In 1870 it was moved to town and occupied the identical spot where the grammar-school building now stands and which took its place in 1895.

In the summer of 1891 the Southern Pacific Railroad reached the town. Soon after John Hartz surveyed and offered his addition to the town of Danville, the lots being soon sold, and from that time progress has been rapid, and the result is the achievements of the present time.

The Oakland, Antioch & Eastern Railway made its advent in 1914, and by it the distance from San Francisco to Danville is reduced from fifty-six miles to thirty-two miles, and the schedule time is cut to half the former time required to make the trip.

Danville's future is promising. Many improvements are in contemplation, among them the erection of the high-school building at a cost of $15,000, which is to meet the requirements of the school organized five years ago, and a new grammar-school building will soon be needed.

Enterprises of various kinds are to be developed. The magnificent improvements at Diablo, with the expected influx of population as a result of the sale of many lots in that estate, together with the scenic highway to the summit, promises much. El Rio has done much and will do more for the future of Danville.

It is eminently proper here, in addition to those already mentioned, to name a few of the many pioneers who have been instrumental in the development of Danville and the adjoining region: Thomas Flournoy, J. J. Kerr, John P. Chrisman, J. E. Close, R. O. Baldwin, William Z. Stone, William Meese, D. N. Sherburne, Charles Wood, Dr. J. L. Labarce, A. J. Young, J. O. Stewart, and R. B. Love.

CHAPTER XXIX. PITTSBURG

Pittsburg, with about six thousand people, is the second largest city in Contra Costa County. Its location is a logical one for the building of a manufacturing and distributing city, being at the point where the Sacramento and San Joaquin rivers join with the deep waters of Suisun bay, and also on the principal railways that radiate from the bay cities to all parts of the State and Nation, thereby having access to both river and ocean traffic.

The natural advantages of the present site of Pittsburg first attracted attention as far back as 1847, when the United States Army and Naval Engineers investigated it as a possible military and naval base. Their report was in every way favorable, but the project was never carried out.

A townsite was surveyed and christened "New York of the Pacific." Upon the discovery of coal near Mount Diablo, about fifty years ago, the place became known as Black Diamond. It is believed that a large coal-field in that region still remains undeveloped. In 1909 the present name of Pittsburg was appropriately bestowed, the town having shown conclusively that it was to become a great manufacturing center.

It is interesting to note that in 1850 a strong effort was made to remove the State capitol, then at San Jose, to New York of the Pacific.

The proposition was submitted to a vote of the people but was defeated by a small margin. General Sherman, in his "Early Recollections of California," says: "I made a contract to survey for Colonel J. D. Stevenson his newly projected city of New York of the Pacific, situated at the mouth of the San Joaquin River. The contract also embraced the making of soundings and the marking out of a channel in Suisun Bay.

We hired in San Francisco a small metallic boat with a sail, laid in some stores, and proceeded to the United States ship 'Ohio.' At General Smith's request we surveyed and marked the line dividing the city of Benicia from the government reserve. We then sounded the bay, back and forth, and staked out the best channel up Suisun Bay. We then made the preliminary survey of the city of New York of the Pacific, which we duly plotted."

About ten years ago Pittsburg began its industrial growth, which will undoubtedly continue until it ranks as one of the larger cities of California. Its previous support had been that of the coal mines and the fishing industry. The present industrial growth is largely the result of the industry and foresight of the late C. A. Hooper, one of the State's most successful financiers, who some years ago became the owner of the Rancho los Medanos, an old Spanish grant on which the townsite is located. Mr. Hooper was a man of extraordinary vision as to the future, and believed firmly that Pittsburg was a city of destiny. In every way possible he fostered and promoted the town's upbuilding. At his death, in July, 1914, he was succeeded in the management of his enterprises and companies by W. E. Creed, his son-in-law, a well-known lawyer of San Francisco. Mr. Creed, since assuming the management of the estate, has demonstrated that he too is deeply interested in Pittsburg's welfare and development, and is devoting himself with earnestness and vigor to that end.

As a deep-water shipping point, Pittsburg possesses advantages unsurpassed by any other city on the Pacific Coast. Ocean-going vessels, loading and unloading cargoes, are a daily sight at her docks. Her shipping facilities will be further enhanced by the dredging operations in Suisun Bay from Martinez to Pittsburg, a survey having been reported upon favorably by the chief of the Army engineers in January, 1916.

With thousands of acres of level land stretching away from the waterfront, the town has every incentive for becoming a great manufacturing center.

Pittsburg has a pay-roll of more than two million dollars annually, with a list of industrial enterprises that have long since passed the experimental stage and are in fact among the largest and most important of their kind on the Western Coast.

The transportation facilities of Pittsburg are unexcelled by any other city on the bay. In addition to the splendid shipping advantages noted above, Pittsburg is served by two main-line railroads, the Southern Pacific and the Santa Fe, and the interurban electric line of the Oakland, Antioch & Eastern Railway. There are forty-two passenger trains daily. Several lines of river steamers also run to and from her docks, carrying freight and passengers.

Pittsburg takes great pride in her public schools. She has recently completed an eighty-five-thousand-dollar grammar school and employs the latest methods along every line for the mental, physical, and esthetic advancement and uplift of the children. The pupils receive instruction in music, athletics, folk-dancing, and military drill. Thus their growing characters are rounded out in a manner equal to the results attained in much larger cities. The physical welfare of the pupils is carefully watched by a trained nurse, who daily visits the various classes, whose average daily attendance is 850 pupils.

Turning to Pittsburg's various industries, we find that one of the earliest established plants was that of the Redwood Manufacturers Company, which has a capitalization of one million dollars and operates here one of the largest woodworking plants in the world, making into finished products redwood and pine lumber, which is brought in by coastwise vessels from the great forests of the northern coast. The company also carries large stocks of northern fir and other woods. The manufacturing facilities of the Redwood Manufacturers Company is second only to their immense stock, and its product finds a ready market in almost every civilized community in the world where wood products are used.

Residents of Pittsburg are justly proud of the modern plant of the Columbia Steel Company. Many improvements have been made since the establishment was founded, about seven years ago, the company having recently made extensions that will increase its capacity by fifty per cent. By its modern and efficient methods of manufacture, the Columbia Steel Company has secured the bulk of the steel-casting trade on the Pacific Coast, and by continually improving its plant and keeping up a high order of skill among its employees, of whom there are five hundred, there is no prospect of anything but progress and advancement.

A few years ago almost all steel castings were made in Eastern foundries and shipped out to the coast, thereby entailing much expense and delay to the customers. Now it is possible to obtain quick deliveries and excellent quality at lower prices than was ever before possible. As a consequence the whole Pacific Coast has been benefited, and the industries using this product have been greatly stimulated.

Again we use a superlative in describing another of Pittsburg's interests. The Bowers Rubber Works is the largest factory for the manufacture of rubber products west of Chicago. Fire hose, belting, packing, automobile tires, and several other products comprise the output of this concern. Its plant is equipped with up-to-date machinery, and the buildings and grounds cover a considerable acreage. The plant is a model of neatness and is located on the water-front, giving the plant access to both water and rail transportation. A ready market is found, not only in the principal cities of the United States, but in many foreign countries.

About 250 men are employed in the work. Bowers Rubber Works is a valuable asset to the county, and Pittsburg in turn is proud to be its home.

The only electro-chemical plant on the Pacific Coast is in operation at Pittsburg. There is no other plant of this kind west of Detroit. The Great Western Electro-Chemical Company is the name of the organization, which is capitalized at two and a half million dollars. Caustic soda and chloride of lime, commonly known as bleaching powder, will be manufactured at the plant. Caustic soda, or lye, enters largely in the manufacture of soap, and is also an important adjunct in the refining of oil and the preserving of fruit. There are many uses for chloride of lime, but the largest demand for it arises from the fact that it forms the base of a large number of fire extinguishers. Salt and burnt lime are important agencies in the manufacture of these chemical products, and as both are found in large quantities around the bay section, the selection of Pittsburg as a site for the plant was a fortunate one. As the name, electro-chemical, implies, electricity is used as an aid to the mechanical manufacture of the chemical products. Two hundred or more men are employed in this plant.

Pittsburg has as one of its water-front industries the plant of B. P. Lanteri, shipwright and dredger builder. His plant is situated on the south banks of what is known as New York Slough, about three-quarters of a mile east of the city of Pittsburg. The location is particularly well adapted to this plant, inasmuch as it is close to the delta country, where dredgers are extensively operated, and also on account of its shipping facilities, with spur tracks from two transcontinental main lines in the yard, with deep water so that steam schooners and sea-going vessels can discharge lumber and materials on the wharf, making a minimum cost for cartage and handling. Here have been built six of the largest clam-shell dredgers in the world, some of them swinging 230-foot booms, which until the present had never been attempted. Although this firm does considerable dredger building and repairing, it also does all kinds of boat and barge building and designing, having designed and built some of the best gasoline towboats in and about the bay regions, and having just completed and launched from its ways the ferryboat "City of Seattle," which is to operate between Martinez and Benicia.

On account of the rare facilities found here for distribution, Pittsburg is made the base of operations for the largest fish concerns on the coast and is the center of the fishing industry of the rivers of the State.

Fully a thousand men devote their entire time to the catching of fish, and to this class of labor half a million dollars is paid annually. The fish chiefly taken from the Sacramento and San Joaquin rivers are salmon, striped bass, shad, and catfish. In order to give some idea of the extent of this industry, it is only necessary to state that during the canning season three tons of shad-roe (fish eggs). are obtained daily by one firm from that one kind of fish. Shad-roe is a new by-product that is being extensively developed and for which there is a growing demand.

While the principal offices of some of our fish concerns are located in San Francisco, the business of packing and distributing the products is carried on at

Pittsburg because of the superior advantages found here for shipping. The fishing business is followed largely by Italians, whose large families have supplied much of the labor employed in other industrial lines. The business of fishing is carried on in such a quiet way that the casual observer has no conception of the magnitude of the industry, covering, as it does, shipments to all parts of the world.

Among the large operators of the fishing industry are the American Fish & Oyster Company, and the F. E. Booth Company, the latter employing from two to three hundred men several months in the year in their canning operations, in addition to their packing business.

The Los Medanos Rancho, a tract of land of approximately ten thousand acres, was originally granted by the Mexican Government in 1835 to Jose Antonio Mesa and Jose Miguel Garcia, or Mesa, and was finally patented October 8, 1872, by the United States Government to their successors, Jonathan D. Stevenson et al. In 1849 and 1850 the Mesas conveyed the ranch to Stevenson and others, who laid out upon it a site for a city, known for a long time as "New York of the Pacific."

From this circumstance it derived the name "New York Ranch," by which it is sometimes known. Its true name, "Los Medanos," is derived from the sand hills that sweep down to the river adjoining the eastern boundary of the ranch; the word "Medanos" means sand-drift, or sandhill, or what is commonly known as a "sand spit." Stevenson and his associates disposed of the property to one of the pioneer banking concerns of San Francisco, namely, Pioche, Bayerque & Co., who after a term of years in turn transferred it to L. L. Robinson, a California pioneer railroad builder and mining operator, and he at his death bequeathed the property to his sister, Mrs. Cutter, of San Francisco, from whom the title passed to the present owners, C. A. Hooper & Co.

The tract as a whole is a rich agricultural property, and during early years and up to the ownership of L. L. Robinson was devoted to grazing and stock-growing. Robinson during his lifetime divided the property into farming subdivisions containing from three hundred to six hundred acres and leased them to farmers, some of whom are still on the property, having found it both a pleasant and profitable place to live.

There has grown up on the rancho, on its water-front, two considerable towns—Antioch, on its eastern boundary, and Pittsburg, about midway. With the rancho's central location at the confluence of the San Joaquin and Sacramento rivers, and at a point where the traffic from the interior of the State and country passes to and fro from the cities around San Francisco Bay, very likely it will not be long until its acreage will pass from agriculture to an industrial manufacturing and distributing center and furnish homes for a large mercantile and industrial population.

Pittsburg has about twelve miles of paved and macadamized streets, well lighted, and every street in the improved area is sewered and macadamized. Contrary to the general rule of the newer towns of the Pacific Coast, Pittsburg is compactly built, although in no way congested, thus enabling it to have every street fully improved.

A hotel (The Los Medanos) has just been completed on Cumberland Street between Eighth and Ninth streets, which doubtless marks a new era in the development of the town. The building will probably cost $60,000. It is to be one of the best hotels on the Pacific Coast outside of the larger cities and will be modern in every respect. Every convenience necessary is to be had. Every room has hot and cold water, electric lights, telephone, steam heat, and rooms en suite with private baths. The hotel is to be luxuriously furnished throughout.

Within the last two years there have been erected in Pittsburg many brick business blocks, and there are now planned several more. Also within the year there will be under way the building of the new Catholic church, at a cost of from $25,000 to $30,000, the site having already been secured. The Congregational people have also planned a new building and intend to spend an equal if not greater amount in their improvement.

The Pittsburg Dispatch, of Pittsburg, California, was financed and launched by A. P. Betterworth, recently postmaster at Elk Grove, and H. C. Jackson, reporter of the Sacramento Union, the first issue being published January 3, 1917. For one week the experiment was tried of publishing a daily, but at the end of that time the owners decided that the field was hardly ready for such a publication, hence the sheet was placed on a semi-weekly basis. The plant of the Pittsburg Dispatch is well equipped, and as soon as the growing business of a growing town justifies the move the publication of the daily will be resumed.

CHAPTER XXX. BAY POINT

In connection with his great lumber interests in Oregon and California, C. A. Smith during the summer of 1907 began an investigation of the possible sites on San Francisco and adjacent bays for the establishing of a much-needed manufacturing and distributing plant for his product. Three essentials had to be considered— proximity to railroad lines for shipment of the forest product, deep water for his vessels that brought the raw product from the mills, and proper drying conditions for lumber. After much investigation, the Contra Costa County shore and Suisun Bay was decided upon as most attractive. The present site of Bay Point was then ranch land and tule bog. Smith, with a companion, went over the district afoot, and in crossing the fields now occupied by the town-site was held up at the point of a gun by one of the owners of the property as a trespasser and ordered off the premises. Naturally, he complied with such moral suasion.

However, the attractive site and suitable location for his purpose was settled in his mind, and shortly thereafter he became acquainted with the owners of the property he coveted. On November 26, 1907, a deal was made with the Cunningham heirs and those of A. H. Neeley, conveying to Smith's interests about fifteen hundred acres and a mile and a half of tide-water frontage, now Bay Point. This land, while originally a part of a Spanish grant, had been patented to the antecedents of the Cunninghams and Neeleys by General Grant when President of the United States.

On part of this tract was immediately established the Bay Point plant of the C. A. Smith Lumber Company, and a strip 2658 feet wide on tidewater, extending back to the foothills, was reserved for the town-site, officially designated on the filed plats as "The City of Bay Point." The transcontinental tracks of the Southern Pacific Company and the Atchison, Topeka & Santa Fe Railway Company divide the town-site into practically two equal parts. That portion between the railways and the bay was set aside for manufacturing sites, and the portion between the railroads and the foothills of Monte del Diablo was immediately platted as the town proper, the idea being to provide a site for the homes of the employees of the C. A. Smith Lumber Company.

At the time of the purchase the property that later became Bay Point consisted of a post-office, a grain warehouse, a ranch house, a saloon, and a general store. Before long it began to grow, and today it has a population of about one thousand people. The town has a ten-thousand-dollar graded school and a number of excellent stores handling groceries, meats, drugs, hardware, general merchandise, and in fact everything necessary in a community of this kind. There are two churches (Congregational and Catholic), with another (Lutheran) about to be built. Here in the shadow of Monte del Diablo, where rail and water meet, are the neat and happy homes of hundreds of contented citizens.

The Club House and office building of the C. A. Smith Lumber Company are notable for a city of the size. Streets, curbs, and sidewalks are established and a sewer system is completed.

The water supply is provided by four wells, each one hundred feet deep, located in the foothills one and a half miles from the town. The water is pumped from these wells to two large tanks upon the hill back of the town. The bases of the tanks are from seventy to ninety feet higher than the town, and the water is distributed by gravity at good pressure.

In disposing of the town property, the C. A. Smith Lumber Company put into the deeds a clause forever preventing the sale of liquor; so Bay Point until recently had no saloons. Owing to the activities of "bootleggers" and "blind pigs" the liquor question became a serious one to the citizens. After a conference, the company consented to put a saloon upon its land not included in the liquor restrictions and turn the whole business over to a club of the citizens of Bay Point as a municipal saloon as soon as it had paid for itself. This was done May 10, 1916.

This arrangement makes Bay Point unique in the family of cities and has brought her much note from political economists and sociologists the country over. The municipal liquor business is being watched with interest by many people. In the conveyance of the saloon to the club of citizens provision has been made that all profits from the business shall be used for the benefit of all the people of Bay Point; and further, that the sale of wines and liquors shall be conducted in such manner that the cause of temperance will be legitimately promoted. As a result, the traffic in liquor has been lessened, drunkenness done away with absolutely, and new sidewalks, streets, and improvements are planned and under way which will make the town a model village at no cost to the taxpayer.

Bay Point is admirable as a manufacturing site and will undoubtedly in the future be a strong rival of other San Francisco Bay cities in the manufacture of Pacific Coast products.

CHAPTER XXXI. CROCKETT

This town on the Straits of Carquinez, about six miles below Martinez, named in honor of ex-Judge J. B. Crockett, late of the California Supreme Bench, is pleasantly located, with a fine outlook over the San Pablo Bay to the Coast Range, from Mount Tamalpais to the mountains of Mendocino in one direction, and to the Sierra Nevada in another.

The location of Heald's extensive machine-shops and foundry at that point created the necessity for the considerable growth of the town.

Crockett is located on a part of what was known as the Edwards ranch. As originally planned, the town-site consisted of eighteen blocks, divided into lots fifty by one hundred feet, the streets running east and west.

The following item, taken from the Sacramento Record-Union of November 24, 1881, is the earliest mention of the town: "A town to be called Crocker [Crockett] has been laid out on the south shore of Carquinez Straits, seven miles below Martinez at Vallona Station. It is named in honor of Supreme Judge Crocker [Crockett]."

Thomas Edwards, the original owner of the town-site of Crockett, was born in North Wales, April 5, 1812. When fourteen years of age Edwards left his native country and began a seafaring life, which he followed for ten years. After quitting the sea, he obtained employment in the capacity of mate on the steamers engaged in the immense trade of the Mississippi. It was at this time that he formed the acquaintance of W. C. Ralston, then steamboat clerk, and also of J. B. Crockett, who had just commenced the practice of law. The friendship thus began lasted throughout life. On February 19, 1843, he married Mary Pugh, a native of North Wales, born July 20, 1819. In May 1849, he started for California. Spending the winter in Louisa County, Iowa, he went westward to Council Bluffs the following spring, where a company of about forty men and ten wagons was formed. Mrs. Edwards and a friend from St. Louis were the only ladies in the party. The final march was commenced early in May, 1850, via Fort Hall and Lassen's Cutoff. After traveling a few hundred miles together, Edwards and his family stopped for a day on the Platte River to rest the teams, thus allowing the remainder of the party to hurry on. The rest of the way across the plains was made alone. Journeying two thousand miles, California was reached in September, 1850, the first stopping-place being on Mormon Slough, near Stockton, where they remained three weeks.

After conducting affairs in Knight's Ferry and other localities, they moved to Carquinez Straits and engaged in farming and stock-raising.

The farm comprised 1800 acres. In 1881 an arrangement was entered into with Heald by which a foundry was established on the place and the town of Crockett laid out.

Joseph Bryant Crockett was born in Kentucky, 1809, of an old Scottish-American family. He was admitted to the practice of the law in Kentucky at the age of twenty-two, and soon after founded the St. Louis Intelligencer, a Whig paper, which he conducted with great ability for some time. Arriving in California in 1852, he again took up his law practice, his partners being Page, Whiting, Joseph Napthaly and Congressman Piper. In 1868 he was appointed Supreme Justice by Governor Haight, and in 1869 was elected to succeed himself for the long term (ten years), which he filled out. Judge Crockett called and presided over the first public meeting held for the purpose of establishing the public library of San Francisco.

CROCKETT A GREAT SUGAR CENTER

(From the Fifth Booster Edition of the Byron Times)

Crockett is one of the most substantial, busy, and energetic industrial cities of Contra Costa County, made famous because of the splendid achievements and enterprise of the California & Hawaiian Sugar Refining Company, whose annual production of manufactured sugar products is valued at about $30,350,000; its payroll is $625,000 a year, and nearly 700 employees are made happy.

The big plant and improvements at Crockett represent an investment of some $7,000,000, making this one of the most modern and complete sugar refineries in the world.

Crockett has many attractions and conveniences; has a fine waterfront, with a commodious harbor capable of receiving the largest of ocean-going steamships; has fine hotels, general merchandise stores, business establishments, and schools and churches, and provides everything necessary for the happiness of its inhabitants.

Public parks and playgrounds for children, with rest-rooms and many conveniences that aid health and create happiness, are special features provided by the founders of Crockett.

Every year a great May Day celebration is held in Crockett under the personal direction of the general manager of the California & Hawaiian Sugar Refining Company, which is participated in by officials of that big organization and by the hundreds of employees of the company, the citizens of Crockett, and thousands of invited guests from all parts of the county and State.

The big event in 1916 was unusually noticeable because it was combined with dedication exercises in honor of the new Y. M. C. A. Building, the new Carquinez Women's Clubhouse, and other grand improvements given to the city by the California & Hawaiian Sugar Refining Company for the pleasure and comfort of the citizens of Crockett.

A special feature was the May-pole dance, participated in by several hundred beautiful little children, daughters of the employees of the sugar refinery and business men and women of Crockett.

The 1916 celebration was made a royal holiday event. Invited guests from the cities and towns around were there through special invitation.

There was a great floral and decorated float parade. Automobiles gaily bedecked added to the grandeur of the occasion, while bands of music played, and everyone was made welcome and happy as the guests of the people of Crockett.

In the evening a grand carnival was held, followed by a masked ball, which was attended by many notable and prominent people of San Francisco, Crockett, and the country around.

It was a happy, joyous event, creating, as it did, a feeling of friendship and reciprocity among employers and employed, making them for the time being one big family of people interested in the present, future, and advancing interests of Crockett, as a home place for intelligent and contented workmen who appreciate the very best of treatment, such as is accorded by the California & Hawaiian Sugar Refining Company and its officers and heads of departments.

It is such interests as these May Day occasions and celebrations which have done much to cement the strong friendship existing between capital and labor at Crockett, and which go far toward making this an ideal industrial city.

In this connection, it is a pleasure and very timely to mention George M. Rolph, general manager of the California & Hawaiian Sugar Refining Company, who as the head of this big industry at Crockett has always taken much interest in the people and the development of the city.

He has taken that personal part in activities which proves his sincerity, and he enjoys the personal regard, respect, and esteem of every man, woman, and child in Crockett, not only among those employed by his big refinery, but among the people of every class.

George M. Rolph is really and truly a man who does things. His men rely upon him in time of need and are ever ready to work for and with him in time of emergencies. It is men of this character and heart who are recognized as leaders in action and who are usually found at the top directing great industrial enterprises.

Crockett also has a Citizens' Improvement Association, organized for exploitation, publicity, and the general advancement of the city. Meritorious enterprises are fostered, aided, and encouraged, entertainment features are provided for the town, and the idea is to create more interest in Crockett and its attractions. Like every other city in Contra Costa County, Crockett enjoyed unparalleled building activities in 191516, which still continue unabated. Nearly all of the new edifices are residences, modern in every respect. The residence section is rapidly extending on the hills overlooking the business section.

CALIFORNIA AND HAWAIIAN SUGAR REFINING CO.

The town of Crockett—Queen City of the Carquinez Straits—is to be congratulated on having within its boundaries one of the largest industries of the Pacific Coast—the California & Hawaiian Sugar Refining Company.

This refinery is in operation 300 days of the year and is the only sugar refinery in the world where the men work in shifts of eight hours each. The output of refined sugar is about 950 tons per day, or 280,000 tons per annum.

This sugar is shipped in packages of various styles and weights, not only to all the Pacific Coast States—some of it going as far north as Alaska and as far away as the Philippines—but its distribution extends as far east as Illinois.

The raw sugar from which this refined product is obtained comes principally from the Hawaiian Islands in the great freighters that ply between San Francisco and the Hawaiian ports. At times it has been even necessary to bring it from points as far away as Peru and Java.

Almost any day from December until the following October, steamers of immense carrying capacity may be seen discharging at the wharves of this company.

Mechanical contrivances of all sorts, such as slat and belt conveyors of every description, aid in unloading one of these 8000 to 13,000-ton steamers, discharging 2500 tons daily.

The raw sugar is then placed in one of the vast warehouses located on the company's land, which, by the way, has a deep water-frontage of 2400 feet. It is drawn on by the refinery later as needed in the process of manufacture.

A visit to this refinery would prove most interesting. Here one may see the large vacuum pans which boil fifty tons of sugar every two hours, the great boilers which require hundreds of barrels of oil per day to keep the machinery in motion, machines for weighing and sacking the granulated sugar, machines for putting sugar in cartons which automatically pack and seal thirty-two five-pound cartons every minute.

In turning out from 17,000 to 18,000 bags of sugar per day, each bag containing the finished product, 25,000 yards of cotton cloth are made up daily as inner-liners, which are fine, white bags, placed inside the coarser jute bags to keep the sugar immaculately clean.

While the refinery and extensive warehouses are a great part of this industry, the company has also given a substantial evidence of its interest in the town of Crockett and the welfare of its employees in the splendid hotel it owns, equipped with all modern conveniences, lobby, card rooms, and a pleasant dining-room, where the best food is served; the Y. M. C. A. Building, erected at a cost of about $50,000, with its splendid swimming pool, gymnasium, library, billiard room and numerous sleeping rooms; and that the feminine portion of Crockett and vicinity may not feel neglected, the management has built a beautiful building which is used as a women's club, where spare hours may be comfortably enjoyed.

In fact, no better example can be found in the West of an effort on the part of a corporation to maintain right relations between employer and employee than exists in the town of Crockett.

CHAPTER XXXII. OAKLEY AND SAND LANDS

In the fall of 1897 I bought a small acreage in the northwest quarter of section 25, township 2 north, range 2 east, in eastern Contra Costa County, and moved on it the following February. At that time there had been five surveys made by the Santa Fe Company, but no definite decision was reached as to its location. It was evident the railroad wanted to avoid the orchards as much as possible and at the same time enter Antioch by the water-front. Our nearest station was at Neroley, a flag station on the Southern Pacific Railroad, about three miles south from where Oakley now stands. Something of an effort had also been made prior to this time to get a post-office established there. It was a little premature, however, and the effort was abandoned.

A few days after I had moved in a surveying party came along near my cabin, carefully setting a line of stakes. They told me that was to be the Santa Fe line, and that my house would have to be moved. A short time after the agents came along, trying to buy the necessary rights-of-way. The company had figured upon having but one station between Antioch and the San Joaquin River, and there was quite a difference of opinion among its officers as to where it would be best to locate this station. G. W. Knight's place, three and a half miles east from this point, was finally chosen as being the nearest to the Southern Pacific line and would very likely draw most trade from that point. That station the company proposed to name Meganos. It had not, however, made a good guess on the loyalty of our leading sand-lappers, viz., James O'Hara, Andrew Walker, and B. F. Porter. These leaders said, "No, gentlemen; we will not sell you a right of way across the northwest quarter of section 25, but we will give you the land desired if you will sign an agreement to put down at least a half-mile of side-track, put up a small room for shelter while waiting for trains, and build us a station whenever the business will justify." That agreement was signed in due time, and the sand-lappers had scored their first home run.

Before grading was well under way an agitation was started for a post-office, without waiting for the advent of the trains, and I was selected as the one to represent our people before Uncle Sam. This was done successfully, and in due time I received the first letter that was ever addressed to Oakley, Cal. It was mailed by our Postmaster-General at Washington, D. C, September 9, 1898, certifying to my appointment as postmaster at Oakley, California. My commission was dated September 7, 1898. The usual amount of supplies was sent to the postmaster at Antioch for me. My instructions were to open the office whenever I was ready, run it to suit myself for two months, then report. The office was opened November 1, 1898, the instructions were followed, and the rest is detail work and public history. Our first eight months of mail service was conducted from here to Antioch and return six times a week, by cart, and was largely successful, through the loyalty of A. N. Norcross and Daniel Methven, with an occasional quarter from other loyal hearts to help buy horse-feed, and yours truly running a relief trip semi-occasionally to help out. At the end of eight months Uncle Sam took charge of the carrying service and sent us our mail from Brentwood via Oakley to Bethel, another new post-office back in the big bend of the San Joaquin River. The change relieved me from some of the responsibilities, as well as indicating permanency of establishment.

The Santa Fe Company had undertaken to build across the tule lands to get into Stockton, and consequently had a great deal of trouble from its tracks sinking. The road ran southeast from here until it reached the section-line, two miles south of Oakley, and from there into Stockton on the section-line. After what we thought were many long delays the company named July 1, 1900, as the time to put on its first passenger train. I was ready for it, receiving and dispatching mail by the first train—and the sand-lappers had scored their second home run.

Oakley had been located on section 25, township 2 north, range 2 east. This section was railroad-grant land and was put on the market in 1897 by James O'Hara at fifty dollars an acre, all being sold inside of two years. Much of it has been resold two and three times over, and always at an advance. This so-called orchard land is quite sandy, and in early days was a haven of rest for coyote and jack-rabbit, and those people that had courage to locate on it were sneeringly referred to as "sand-lappers." When fruit-trees were introduced the jacks became a bane to the fruit-grower. This section was known far and wide as the happy hunting-ground of the river men, where the tired hunter, after his evening feed of broiled jack-rabbit, would be serenaded to sleep and dreams of shining gold nuggets by the silver-toned coyotes. There are but few hiding-places left for Mr. Jack Rabbit. The almond is boss of the road now in these parts.

James O'Hara was the most extensive real-estate dealer in this part of the country and was generally reckoned as the pioneer and father of the Oakley fruit and almond industry. This is decidedly correct. He is also sometimes referred to as the "Father of Oakley." Strictly speaking, that was not correct. But by forcing the deal he made with the Santa Fe Company, he helped to make possible the Oakley of the future. It might have come later anyway, but not so soon. Being postmaster here then, I was naturally looking for a line on coming developments, and first bought a flat-iron corner of Porter & Walker that the Santa Fe had cut from off the southwest corner of section 24. I offered J. A. Jesse the best lot of the piece absolutely free of cost if he would build on it and put in a stock of groceries. He complied, and we traded.

While that was being done I moved the post-office building onto another part of the lot—and Oakley town was in embryo. Shortly after this I got a line on the Haven nineteen-acre lot across the road in section 25.

Associating N. A. Norcross with myself, we purchased that property, platted and recorded it—and Oakley was on the map. We next made substantial concessions to J. M. Augusto to get a blacksmith-shop started. To show that Augusto is satisfied, I quote his own words—that he has made a thousand dollars for every dollar that he invested in the lot.

Then two lots were sold to Brentwood parties for $125. They were resold inside of two weeks for $250. The boom was on.

In the early spring of 1905 our loony sand-lappers began to swell up to an alarming extent, thirsting for more notoriety. A public meeting was held, and Oakley was pledged to a Fourth of July celebration, with a jack-rabbit barbecue dinner. What a guffaw went up over the whole country. "What gall! What monumental cheek!" came from all points.

Our boldness gave other towns the shivers, and not one of them dared enter the field against us. We got a flag-pole from Washington, an orator from Stockton, a quartet from Antioch, and our neighborhood rhymsters being at their best, there was no lack of entertainment. As fifteen hundred gift fans were far short of the demand, two thousand guests was the estimate of the number present. Thirty gallons of ice-cream was licked up before one o'clock. One stand took in eighty-five dollars for soda-water alone—and Oakley scored another home run.

Great guns! it was a hot day—110 in the shade! While this town and the surrounding sand country have had no phenomenal growth or land boom, there has been at all times a steady, healthy increase in population as well as in improvements and over five hundred per cent increase in land values, with a certainty of further advance in the near future.

The Rickert lot of fifteen acres on the east was added to the townsite in 1909 by the late James O'Hara and has been largely settled upon already. Another addition of larger suburban lots was added by R. C. Marsh. We have one rural free delivery route eighteen and a half miles in length, serving a hundred and twenty families, and we are to get another in the near future. With two halls subject to our whims for social and club entertainments, with four churches to lead the people in the way they should go, with a three-room schoolhouse (now badly overcrowded) to teach the young idea how to shoot, and a gradual increase in population, it is only a question of time for us to reach corporation and judicial district size. I have said the next station east of us was named Meganos by the Santa Fe Company. It being located on Knight's farm, the people there wanted it called Knightsen, and beat the Santa Fe to it by asking Uncle Sam for a post-office, to be named Knightsen, with George W. Knight as postmaster. They won out, and Knightsen had scored a home run. Lyon Brothers, or what is now known as the Miller-Cummings Company, have an asparagus packing plant here, in which they pack and ship asparagus for the Eastern market, sending out from two to four cars a day during the shipping season, which lasts about seventy-five days.

We have a farmer's club of fifty members that keeps in touch with our State University, which sends us lectures on any subject whenever desired, free for the asking, and which is appreciated by all. There is also a live-wire Ladies' Oakley Improvement Club of about thirty members that helps us look after our dimes and quarters when it thinks there are any improvements needed. Its members are top-notchers, too, and grease the track for an occasional progressive whist party.

Why are there so many churches in Oakley? That question has been asked many times. The one word "jealousy" would give almost a complete answer. At the time I located here there was a small Methodist church in the country two and a half miles southwest of Oakley. A few of our people went to church there quite regularly for a time, several denominations being represented. Finally a get-together meeting was called, with the idea of moving the church to Oakley and all joining in one service. Five meetings, I believe, were held, two of them in my house, and the more we got together the farther we got apart, and finally the effort was abandoned. The Congregational Mission was first on the ground here, with preaching and Sunday-school under an oak tree, services being conducted by Rev. Paul Bandy. They soon had a church organization in sight, two lots donated, and the lumber on the ground for a Congregational church. That woke up the Methodist people, and soon after they moved their church into Oakley. Finally, in 1908, they removed the old church and built a larger edifice, presumably anticipating future needs. Soon after this the Catholics, who, by the way, had been preparing for several years to build a commodious church here, started to erect a building on their lot in the O'Hara addition. The Baptists shortly after followed suit, with a very creditable structure, the fourth church building for our village. Further efforts have been made for a more united religious service, but some ism or other is always in the way.

INTRODUCTION OF THE LOGANBERRY

The wonderful loganberry of commerce was introduced into the Oakley district in 1900 by the Rev. C. S. Scott, a well-known resident here.

Scott brought the plants from southern California and set out a measured acre of sediment land with rooted vines. They were irrigated from a well and carefully cultivated, so that a handsome growth was secured, and a wonderful crop of berries was produced the following year. This crop was peddled at good prices, the income from the berries alone being six hundred dollars. But the principal idea was to create a demand for cuttings. The canes were lopped down, weighted, mulched, and irrigated, with the result that the following January he sold two hundred rooted cuttings at twenty-five cents each, realizing an income of eleven hundred dollars from one acre the next year after planting.

CHAPTER XXXIII. KNIGHTSEN

When the Santa Fe Railway in the summer of 1898 made its preliminary survey through this part of Contra Costa County the town of Knightsen was founded. In the fall of the same year the road-bed was graded, and late in 1899 the company began to lay its track. In the spring of 1900 passenger and freight trains began to run. The first building erected in the new town was the company's section-house, and this was soon followed by the railroad station, with a pumping plant to supply the locomotives with water.

In the winter of 1899-1900 I received my commission as postmaster, and immediately proceeded to put up a building to be occupied by the new post-office and grocery, the first store in Knightsen. The post-office is still in the same building. I continued as postmaster for thirteen years.

The shipment of milk by the dairy farmers of this section is considerable. The daily average since the advent of the railroad is about twenty-five hundred gallons. Stone Brothers were the first to engage in this industry to any extent. At present there are five other dairies shipping through this station—those of Fox, Bridgford, Burrows, Emerson, and Hotchkiss—and it is likely that in the near future the milk output at this point will be greatly increased.

Knightsen being an inland town grows slowly, but new improvements are being added from time to time. In 1913 electric lights were installed, which gave a decided addition to the town's importance. New dwellings are being constructed. A general merchandise store, a blacksmith-shop, a garage, and a saloon comprise the business district.

It is said that the local Santa Fe station has shown a wonderful record in recent months, especially in December, 1916, its business at that time being larger than at any other period in the history of Knightsen. This is greatly due to the shipping of celery and general farm produce. This section has advanced rapidly in this line recently.

Knightsen is situated in a rich agricultural district, and doubtless will be an important shipping point in the future.

SERICULTURE

In the early days several extensive experiments in sericulture were made in this county. That the mulberry will grow here, and that the worm will do well, admit of no question. The trees made a wonderful growth, and the silk produced was of superior quality.

Many years ago Mr. Sellers, near Iron House Landing, planted a large field in mulberry-trees, which made a fine growth and produced a great quantity of leaves for feeding. A place was fitted up for a feeding-room for the worms, and the business was carried on quite successfully. At the county fair in 1878 Mrs. Sellers exhibited cocoons and silkworms that attracted much attention from visitors.

The silkworm is a very delicate animal, and it is subject in Europe to many diseases, most of them directly traceable to climatic influences from which this State is exempt. Climate is a matter of vast importance to the breeder of the silkworm, and nowhere is it more favorable than in Contra Costa County. The worms are exceedingly healthy and prolific, the cocoons large, the fiber strong and fine, the mulberry luxuriant in growth and hardy. The colds of forty-five degrees, the heats of one hundred degrees, the thunder-storms, and the summer rains, which frequently prove fatal in France and Italy, are almost unknown in our coast valleys. In Europe, even when there is no rain, there are many damp, cloudy days that prevent the evaporation of the dew, and if there is any moisture on the leaves the worms sicken and die. It is customary in Europe to feed three or four times a day, with leaves plucked oft separately; but in California they may be fed but twice, or even once, with sprouts, each cut having a number of leaves on it. They increase at the rate of a hundred-fold at each generation. The female generally lays from two hundred to three hundred eggs, and it may be assumed that two hundred worms will survive and make cocoons; and as the females are about half, the total number may be multiplied by one hundred, to represent the increase.

Two crops of cocoons are raised in the year, in May and July, a season during which the atmosphere of California is almost free from clouds, there being neither thunder-storms nor wet, cold spells, to check the progress of the cocoons or to injure the mulberry leaf, such vicissitudes being not only destructive of the health of the worms, but fatal to the quality of silk they produce.

Some years ago the State of California, with the view of establishing the business of silk-making as one of its fixed pursuits, offered a premium of two hundred and fifty dollars for every five thousand mulberry trees, to be paid when they were two years old, and a premium of three hundred dollars for every one hundred thousand cocoons. The business, for various reasons, has not proved profitable, largely for the want of energetic capital to engage in the manufacture.

CHAPTER XXXIV. RODEO

With the best of water-front facilities, and with factory sites held at a very reasonable figure, the outlook for Rodeo, situated on San Pablo Bay, is very promising.

The virile quality of Rodeo's citizenship shone forth brilliantly following a devastating fire of July, 1915. Although the main business district was completely wiped out, in less than six months the heap of ruins was replaced by handsome brick buildings. These building activities have afforded unusual opportunities for bricklayers, carpenters, and artisans of all kinds, who have prospects of being steadily employed for an indefinite time to come. Other fields of employment are the plant of the Union Oil Company, about two miles distant, the local plant of the Western Oil Company, the Union Oil Company at Oleum, adjoining the town-site of Rodeo, the powder factories of Giant and Hercules, and the near-by lubricating plant of the Shell Oil Company. Having no unemployed class, Rodeo may be considered to be well along on the road to prosperity.

Of historical interest is the fact that Rodeo derived its name from the "rodeos," or roundups, held by the cattle kings in the days of the old Spanish grandees.

Some time ago, a sanitary district was formed in Rodeo, and a bond issue was decided upon to supply the sum of $17,000 needed for the construction of a sewer system.

Rodeo is one of the smallest towns in the State to have its own sewer system. The undertaking has been a very large one, and the fact that it has been carried to success reflects considerable credit upon those who are leaders in the town's affairs.

The prospects for a brilliant future for Rodeo are very alluring. A splendid water-front is to be found there, and splendid factory sites can be secured at a very reasonable figure. The town is now situated near enough to several large industries to be assured of steady progress.

UNION OIL COMPANY OF CALIFORNIA

The Union Oil Company of California is the outgrowth of an amalgamation of a number of the smaller oil companies established in the early days of the California oil industry. It has always been independent of other and larger corporations, having no connections of any kind to enforce upon it a policy of subservience to special interests. Its present strong position is the result of twenty-five years of able management as the Union Oil Company of California, following several years of pioneering in the Ventura fields on the part of Lyman Stewart, now chairman of the board, and his associates. Mr. Stewart, having first satisfied himself as to the oil prospects of the surrounding territory, located at Santa Paula in Ventura County, and gathered about him a number of his former associates in the Pennsylvania fields. Amongst these were W. L. Hardison and John Irwin. In 1883 as the Hardison-Stewart Oil Company, with John Irwin as field superintendent, operations were begun in Pico Canon, near Newhall, on land leased from the Pacific Coast Oil Company, which had a small group of wells there and a small refinery in Alameda. That company and the Rowland & Lacy Company operating at Puente, near Whittier, alone occupied the field at that time.

Leases were also taken in Adams Canon, on the old Rancho ex-Mission de San Buenaventura, and in Santa Paula Canon.

Operations began with a field force of thirty-five oil men recruited from the East. Six wells were drilled and about $135,000 spent before striking a paying well. In these days of large expenditures in oil development this sum looks small, but, considering the times, and that these men were operating in a country several thousand miles away from the nearest commercially proven oil field, and in one where at the same time proper facilities and markets were yet to be developed, it will be appreciated that no little faith and courage were required. To add to their difficulties disputes arose over land titles, but eventually these obstacles as well as those of a physical character were overcome. Operations were extended and additional land acquired by purchase. More wells were drilled—one of these, No. 16, on the Rancho ex-Mission, was brought in with an initial production of one thousand barrels of oil a day. Other successes followed, and, encouraged by results obtained, two other companies were organized, in both of which Hardison and Stewart were interested—the Sespe Oil Company and the Torrey Canon Oil Company. In 1890 the three companies, together with the Los Angeles Oil Co., Rainbow Oil Company, Mission Transfer Company and others, were merged into one, as the Union Oil Company, with a capitalization of $5,000,000; later this was increased to $10,000,000 and then to $50,000,000, at which figure it stands with the opening of 1915.

At the beginning of 1915, somewhat over $31,000,000 of this had been issued. The operations of the company have now been enormously extended in all directions. Its landholdings comprise over 226,000 acres, not including those of companies controlled by it. Its oil lands, rights, and leases are conservatively valued at approximately $23,000,000, while its wells, of which more than three hundred are producing and forty-six drilling, represent $7,000,000 more. Pipe-lines and storage systems serve all the important fields, and its water-transportation facilities are represented by a fleet of twenty-six steamers and barges, of which but six are chartered, the whole fleet having a carrying capacity of 800,000 barrels. Investments in transportation and storage facilities now amount to nearly $7,000,000.

Early in its career the company undertook refining operations on a small scale at Santa Paula. This plant was destroyed by fire in 1896, but later was replaced. The success experienced demonstrated that more extensive facilities were required, and in 1895 a site was purchased at Oleum on San Pablo Bay near San Francisco, at which point its principal refinery is now located. In addition to these two refineries, three others are now operating at strategical points—Bakersfield, Stewart, near Los Angeles, and Avila, on the coast near San Luis Obispo. The company is also engaged in the extraction of gasoline from the large amount of natural gas produced on some of its leases. One of these plants is probably the largest yet installed anywhere. When the construction work now under way is completed the company will have invested over $3,000,000 in its refineries.

An extensive system of distributing and marketing stations has been developed all over the Pacific Coast, ranging from Alaska to South America. Unusually complete stations have been erected in all of the principal cities, with less elaborate ones in the smaller communities, at a cost of nearly $4,000,000. These are being continually increased in number.

The company now produces, transports, refines, and distributes all products derivable from California petroleum, having last year marketed over $20,000,000 worth of products. Its ships carry fuel oil to all the principal ports of the Pacific Coast in both American continents and reach westward to Hawaii. Its refined oils are delivered by the shipload not only to domestic ports but to Europe and Asia. Asphalt is shipped to Atlantic ports by steamer and sail, and by rail to the Middle West, and in normal times to Europe. In fact, the Union Oil Company now has practically the entire world for its market and competes successfully everywhere.

Fuel Oil.—First, in point of mere bulk, ranks fuel oil. On the face of it no particular interest would appear to attach to the fuel-oil business. It would seem that all that might be necessary would be to produce the oil from the ground and hand it over to the consumers to be burnt without special preparation. However, the actual facts are unfortunately somewhat more complicated and the users of oil fuel have manifold requirements; each particular industry using fuel has its own, and nearly every customer has special needs—either actual or fancied.

In any case all of these conditions must be met, and while many consumers are properly served with carefully selected and cleaned crude oil, a very large class requires specially prepared fuel to meet highly specialized conditions, with the result that no little care and skill are demanded in the manufacture of a suitable material having the desired characteristics. In metallurgical operations and the manufacture of gas, for example, requirements are different than for use on board ship.

The different navies, again, have different specifications; Diesel engines and semi-Diesel engines differ from each other in the kind of fuel needed, and so on in almost infinite variety. All of these manifold service conditions the Union Oil Company of California has provided for, and supplies for each instance the particular fuel best adapted to it, so that whether it be for the United States or foreign navies, for the manufacturers of ordinary illuminating gas or Pintsch gas, or to meet the specifications of marine classification societies, or for Diesel engines, household use, smudge oil for orchards, for steel works and smelters, for briquetting coal, or for hatching eggs, proper fuels have been prepared.

Each industry demands certain flash or burning points, specific gravity, viscosity, heat value, freedom from sulphur, and other technical characteristics of no particular interest to the layman, but involving proper selection of raw material and subsequent treatment to produce.

Asphalt.—In the refining of California oils the final or end product of the distillation process may be either a fuel oil, usually known as residuum, or asphalt, best known to the public in the form of asphalt pavements. The best refining oils, however, are not necessarily the best for the manufacture of asphalt, so the Union Oil Company of California does not manufacture asphalt as a by-product of the refinery, but selects for the specific purpose of making asphalt only such oils as have the proper physical and chemical characteristics; as a result of this procedure and the careful attention given every stage of the operation to control the quality of the product, the company believes that it has perfected the manufacture of asphalt to the highest degree yet attained. A special booklet has been prepared, copies of which may be had on request, covering the application of this material to paving. Many other uses are made of it, however, and special types are prepared for each service.

Refined Oil and Lubricants.—The products derived from petroleum and manufactured by the company cover the entire range from the lightest volatile substances which boil actively at the temperature of the hand to the heaviest of lubricants. The company has been perhaps fortunate in that as it is comparatively young it has not inherited an outworn assortment of refining conventions. It has not hesitated therefore to depart from methods established by tradition and has developed processes and apparatus of its own, peculiarly fitted to California conditions, and capable of manufacturing economically products of the highest quality. Continuous investigations are conducted to improve its facilities and the character and variety of its products. That this policy is effective is best evidenced by the fact that in the face of increased competition, backed by powerful financial interests, its sales of refined goods have uniformly increased in volume more rapidly than can be accounted for by the increase in the consuming population of its tributary territory, and this without any attempt being made to undersell competitors.

CHAPTER XXXV. WALNUT CREEK

Walnut Creek, "the Gateway to Contra Costa County," is an incorporated city of the sixth class and possesses a population of upward of 750. It possesses a climate that is not surpassed by any section of California, and its scenic features, encompassed as it is by the foothills that buttress Mount Diablo, are attractions of more than ordinary note. It is a trade-center of no small importance, as it is surrounded by a fertile area that during the year 1916 brought to the tillers of the acreage over three million dollars for their products of field, orchard, vineyard, nut groves, poultry yard, dairy, and stock pastures. Its two banks, the First National Bank and the San Ramon Valley Bank, hold the savings of the people of this section in an aggregate amounting to over six hundred thousand dollars, and present statements showing combined assets in excess of a million dollars. The varied business activities, housed in substantial and modern buildings that line both sides of Main Street, the chief thoroughfare of the community, are further testimony to the prosperity of the town and the tributary country. Among the leading structures to be listed are the First National Bank, the Silveira block, the James M. Stow building, the San Ramon Valley Bank, the W. S.

Burpee block, the Grimes & Nottingham building, and the new structure now building for Colonel William L. White. Walnut Creek is municipally well directed, with low taxation. It is provided with a modern sewerage system and is supplied with the finest water by a well-equipped plant of the latest design. It is served by both the Southern Pacific Company, being situated on the San Ramon Valley branch of that traffic system, and the Oakland, Antioch & Eastern Electric Railway, which extends from San Francisco and Oakland to the State capital at Sacramento. By this traffic route Walnut Creek is happily placed within cheap, frequent, and quick commuting distance of the populous Bay centers. Within the past three years hundreds of families have reared model homes, set within extended areas of garden and orchard, within the charming area about Walnut Creek.

Catholics, Methodists, Presbyterians, Christian Scientists, and Episcopalians maintain flourishing congregations and attending societies.

The Walnut Creek grammar school has an enrollment of nearly two hundred pupils, is conducted by four teachers, and is housed in a beautiful school building amid a most sightly area. The Merchants Association is a factor for progress and civic improvement. The Walnut Creek Women's Club is an organization that commands State fame for the activities of its members along those lines of achievement in which woman is particularly endowed.

Amongst its notable works is the establishing of the Carnegie Library in a model structure, where books are supplied the public without price.

Walnut Creek is within one mile of being in the exact center of the county and is but eight miles from the municipal boundaries of Oakland. It is six miles from Concord to where is located the model educational institution known as the Mount Diablo High School, to which the graduates of the Walnut Creek grammar school are accredited, and whose transportation in attendance is borne at public expense over the electric railway.

Mention is due the imposing Masonic temple at Walnut Creek, reared by Alamo Lodge, F. & A. M. It is one of the finest order structures in the interior of the State. Tenancy is shared by Almona Chapter, O. E. S. Walnut Creek has a newspaper, The

Contra Costa Courier, newsy, alert, and of extended circulation. It is owned by Colonel William L. White, with its management in the hands of Francis H. Robinson, aided in the news department by Lyman E. Stoddard. The Courier was established by George C. Crompton and went the way of the initiatives in newspaper flesh by the entrance of the sheriff. It was purchased under the hammer by O. H. King, now publisher of the Amador Ledger at Jackson. He sold the publication, together with the Danville Journal, to Colonel William L. White, of White-Hall Acres, Alamo. Under the ownership of the latter both the Courier and the Journal have prospered and take rank among the representative weekly papers of the State.

HISTORY

The Indian mounds unearthed while excavating for the First National Bank building reveal the existence here in bygone centuries of an aboriginal race of far superior endowment to the Digger tribes with whom history makes us more conversant. In excavating, skulls and bones were brought to light which are significant of a race of giants, while the stone utensils and trinketry and tokens of exchange are mute testimony of the mental status of the men and women who dwelt in these valleys before the advent of the Caucasian. Tradition has it, as handed down among the Spanish families, that Padre Juan Crespi and Pedro Fages, the ensign of the mighty monarch of the Escorial, first trod these lands on their way to discover the great harbor now known as San Francisco Bay. After the coming of the padres the Spanish adventurers that came in their entourage sought the lands about here as royal gifts. They afford rich pasturage and are abundantly watered, and at one time Walnut Creek and vicinity harbored many of the sons and daughters of Iberian blood, who housed themselves on sightly, well-chosen spots in adobe homes which in wreck and wrack are today in occasional evidence.

It was not, however, until late in the fifties that Walnut Creek, or "The Corners," as it was then known, found a place on the map. It derived its early importance from being the crossroads of two important traffic highways. One led from Oakland to Antioch on to the San Joaquin Valley, and the other from Livermore and its great grain-growing valleys to Pacheco, then a leading shipping-point, milling town, and cereal center. It came by its present-day name in recognition of it being the habitat, and the only one in the West, of the black walnut, which flourishes in all its glory along the banks of the waterway which meanders through the town and is fed by a thousand rills and brooks that reach torrential heights during the rainy season.

Walnut Creek began its evolution from a crossroads point to community semblance when Homer Shuey laid off a town-site on lands purchased from H. P. Penneman, who in turn had acquired the area from George Thorne. The latter derived ownership from William Slusher, who held under possessory title which held against the much-muddled Spanish grants. Homer Shuey was not amiss in laying out a townsite, for several of his allotments of land found purchasers and homebuilders, and during the years of the Rebellion there was such a gathering of population at Walnut Creek that Uncle Sam opened up postal connections. James M. Stow, then a lad, had the mail contract from Oakland to Clayton in part with his brother John Stow, and also the star route between Walnut Creek and Danville.

In 1860 James McDonald and Charles Whitmore established the first mercantile business in Walnut Creek. Their store was located on what is now Main Street, at the northeast corner of the Lafayette road. They afterward sold out to H. P. Penneman and W. H. Sears who latterly became Governor of Oregon. Milo J. Hough conducted the first hotel in 1860 on the site where J. C. Laurence now has his home. It was destroyed by fire. He had a blacksmith-shop opposite the hotel. About this time the Morris Brothers operated a stage-line between Oakland and Clayton via the old Fish Ranch road, which then came out of the hills about where the Claremont Hotel now stands.

In 1864-65 the business activities of Walnut Creek were further augmented by L. G. Peel, who established a store opposite to where St. Mary's Catholic Church is now located. He also purchased the Hank Sanford ranch that is now owned by Mrs. Botelho. The ranch he afterward sold to Antone S. Botelho and the store to Albert Sherburne.

W. C. Pratt purchased the Penneman & Sears store in 1869. Shuey Brothers, who had been conducting a general express and produce buying business, engaged in general merchandizing in 1871. They sold their business, then on the site of the present town hall, to C. W. Geary, who was burned out, inflicting a loss of $20,000. The lot was taken over by Mrs. X. R. Hill on a mortgage, and she generously deeded it to the community as the site for a town hall for all time.

In 1871-72 John Slitz added another store to the business community.

He dealt in groceries and hardware, and was also a notary public, and was further appointed postmaster. He had previously resided in the Moraga Valley. He latterly resigned the postmastership and was succeeded by James M. Stow, who was appointed by President Hayes. Stow purchased the store.

In 1872 the Methodist Episcopal church was built upon the site now occupied by the James M. Stow building. The land for the site was donated by H. S. Shuey. Captain R. S. Fales and William Rice each donated $500 toward the church construction fund, with the balance subscribed by W. S. Burpee, E. A. Thumway, John Larkey, James M. Stow, Milo J. Hough, H. S. and M. M. Shuey, John Baker, J. W. Jones, Frank Webb, and Arthur S. Williams.

Since those days and until the coming of the electric line the growth of the community was steady but slow. The opening of the Tunnel Highway, which was effected through the efforts of James M. Stow, made possible through the contributions of Oakland's generous merchants, Theo. Gier, Wilbur Walker, A. Jones, M. J. Keller, and H. F. Sohst, who as members of the Merchants Exchange raised a subscription of $12,000 to aid Contra Costa County in meeting its share of the opening in the hills. This engineering feat opened the way for traffic into the valleys of southern Contra Costa. It was an achievement that was the forerunner and inspiration to the construction of the electric line, and today this same Tunnel Highway, boulevarded, ranks among the notable roads of the State. It is a veritable extension of Broadway, Oakland into the hills and valleys of Contra Costa.

THE CONCORD FIRE

A disastrous fire, which wiped out an entire block in the business section of Concord, causing damage estimated at $200,000, occurred here early in the morning of April 25, 1917. The fire was discovered by a cook in the Concord Inn, at two o'clock. It spread rapidly until the post office, the Bank of Concord, the apartments over the bank, the Concord Mercantile Company, the store of B. Neustader, the offices of Doctor Louts Martin and Doctor Edward Johnson, and the hardware store of M. Q. Meehan were completely destroyed.

The twenty-five guests at the Concord Inn escaped from the blazing hotel in their night clothing. Two waitresses, Miss Nettie Dean and Miss Beatrice Arthur, were trapped in a room under the roof and overcome by smoke. They were rescued by a squad of firemen, led by Guy Berger, clerk of the hotel, and carried out in an unconscious condition.

D. H. Chambers, manager of Concord Inn, and his wife returned to their rooms to rescue their pet bulldog, which had been overlooked in the excitement, and lost their valuables in saving the animal. The guests lost practically everything they had.

Finding themselves unable to cope with the blaze, the Concord fire department sent calls for assistance to Oakland, Martinez, Bay Point, Antioch, and Walnut Creek. Chief Elliott Whitehead of the Oakland fire department and Captain Charles Bock and Corporal Herman O. Rumetsch of the police department responded to the call and gave assistance in rescuing and directing the fire-fighters. Company One of the Oakland fire department also responded to the call, but when they reached Walnut Creek it was met by Chief Whitehead and sent back home, as the fire was then under control. Postmaster C. H. Guy saved the records and safe in the Federal building.

The loss to the Bank of Concord is estimated at $35,000, that of the post-office building from $1000 to $5000, the apartments over the bank at $3000, the doctors' offices at $5000, and the other buildings at various amounts, bringing the total up to $200,000, partially covered by insurance.

MOUNT DIABLO ESTATE

Mount Diablo Estate, comprising ten thousand acres on the slopes of the mountains and in the near-by valleys, is a holding to which few others anywhere are comparable. It includes the Mount Diablo Park Club and Mount Diablo Park, where resident members have their homes.

The club, with its extensive grounds, golf course, private lake, clubhouse, club inn, and chalet apartments, is open only to members and their guests.

Forty years ago what is now Mount Diablo Estate was famous as the Oakwood Park Stock Farm of Seth Cook, who had made a fortune in mines and settled down to being a horseman. Many were the notable entertainments he had there, with celebrities for guests. He had a racecourse of his own, with a row of eucalyptus about it; this is now the forty-acre community farm of the country club.

One phase of his career came to light recently during the construction of the scenic boulevard up Mount Diablo. Two old gold mines were rediscovered, just as they had been left when Mrs. Cook compelled him to abandon their development, for fear the gold fever would return to make him unhappy.

The Estate today is a place of beautiful homes, with gardens being developed by a score of skilled men, with orchards of its own, and with the country club as a center of social life that draws members and guests from long distances.

Diablo, terminus of the Oakland, Antioch & Eastern Railway branch from Saranap, is the business center of the community. Building activity in Mount Diablo Park has been such that in the spring of 1917, with building material shipments of a hundred cars in one month, the station became the busiest in freight traffic of any on the railroad, except for industrial points. There is no other club and home community in California to rank with that at Diablo.

THE MOUNT DIABLO SCENIC BOULEVARD

In Mount Diablo, Contra Costa County has one of the most remarkable peaks in the world—one declared by such noted men as the late Professor J. D. Whitney, after whom the highest peak in the United States was named, to have a broader view from the top than any other mountain. The view from the summit of Mount Diablo has been made accessible by the Mount Diablo Scenic Boulevard, and, with its fame spreading, it is doing much to draw the attention of tourists to this region and central California.

Under favorable atmospheric conditions, from the top of Mount Diablo thirty-five of California's fifty-eight counties can be seen without a glass. The entire heart of the State lies outstretched like a giant relief map, and even such distant points as Mount Shasta, two hundred and fifty miles north, and the six-hundred-mile snow-line of the Sierras.

The boulevard, winding through Mount Diablo Estate, was built in 1916 by R. N. Burgess and his associates. In two branches, it has a total mileage of nearly twenty-three miles. Though the climb rises to 3849 feet, the average grade is seven per cent and the maximum eight, except for a final climb up a pinnacle at the summit. One branch leads from Diablo and the Mount Diablo Park Club, the other from above Walnut Creek.

A feature of the drive is the Garden of the Jungle Gods, a mile-long collection of giant freak rocks, and the Devil's Slide. For eight miles the road was lined with wild-flower seed this year.

LAFAYETTE

Lafayette lays claim to be the first community founded in southern Contra Costa County. Its first settler was Elam Brown, who upon his coming in 1846 reared his home, the first to be built within the present Lafayette section. The name of the settlement was bestowed in 1852 by Benjamin Shreve, who opened the first school at Lafayette in that year.

Elam Brown engaged in farming, which rewarded him in bounteous harvests of grain, but difficulty was encountered in getting his product to the mill, which at that time was located in faraway San Jose. The grain had to be hauled by ox-teams to that remote town, and the round trip usually consumed a week. It was this condition of affairs that impelled Elam Brown in 1853 to erect his own mill, which he conducted at a profit for many years. About this time the small community erected the first church building in the county for interdenominational use. A cemetery was also laid out close to town. In 1853 Milo J. Hough settled in Lafayette and built a hotel, which he conducted for two years, when he removed to Walnut Creek.

The Contra Costa County Agricultural, Horticultural and Mechanical Society was organized temporarily January 15, 1859, at Lafayette, with L. I. Fish as president. The first regular officers were elected May 14, 1859, as follows: President, Hon. T. A. Brown; vice-presidents, W. Bradford, D. Small, E. H. Cox, W. T. Hendricks, J. O'Brien, John A. Hamilton, D. Goodale, W. J. Caldwell, D. Carrick, and Jose

Martinez; treasurer, Elam Brown; recording secretary, H. H. Fassett; corresponding secretary, N. Jones. At this meeting Lafayette was selected as the place for holding the fair, which was to take place on October 11, 1859. At a later date the place of holding the fair was changed to Pacheco. The society was very successful, holding annual fairs, which did much to stimulate farmers and mechanics to a more thorough knowledge of their various vocations. The society owned six acres of land, about half a mile from Concord and one mile from Pacheco, in the Mount Diablo Grant, and all the improvements thereon, the whole valued at $1,500. They also leased fifty-four acres adjoining for a racetrack. Fairs are held every year about the last week in September. For 1877 the receipts were $2,269.25. From this was paid for premiums, $546; for purses, $585; and for incidentals, $1,125.05. The officers for 1878 were as follows: President, W. Renwick; vice-presidents, R. O. Baldwin and S. J. Tennant; directors, Wm. Calvin and J. E. Durham; treasurer, S. W. Johnson; secretary, E. W. Hiller.

In 1860 the Lafayette Library Association was formed, which signalized the first effort made in the county to bring to the homes of the public the advantages of reading.

The country about Lafayette is prodigal in the products of its soil. Adjacent to the town is the noted Happy Valley, where climatic conditions insure the earliest vegetables. With the completion of the tunnel on the highway to Oakland a new era opened up to this section, and with the advent of the O. A. & E. electric line Lafayette at once came to the front as a suburban community, attracting many to build their homes about on its hills and in the adjacent valleys.

The town supports well-stocked stores, a garage, and other activities and, being on the fine drive, the Tunnel Boulevard, it has become an object of increasing interest to thousands of autoists.

The Lafayette Auditorium is the most imposing structure in the community. It was built through its public-spirited citizenry.

CHAPTER XXXVI. PINOLE

The town of Pinole, situated on San Pablo Bay, twenty-three miles from San Francisco, has a population of fifteen hundred, and is one of the thriving manufacturing towns of western Contra Costa County, being adjacent to the Hercules powder plant, the largest explosives concern west of the Rockies. The town has excellent shipping facilities by rail, both the Santa Fe and Southern Pacific roads passing directly through it.

Pinole is one of the oldest towns in the county, the first settlers locating in the year 1839, when the Mexican Government held sway over California. A great many old Spanish families resided in the beautiful fertile valley a short distance to the southeast of the town's present location. Here were built many adobe mansions by Spanish grandees, whose landholdings were very extensive.

Just before the "Gringo" came Pinole and its valley were the hunting and recreation grounds for the Spanish soldiers stationed at the Presidio in San Francisco. Deer and other wild game abounded in the valley, and it was during these expeditions in quest of game that the settlement received its name. The hunters carried little sacks of ground parched corn, in the early days considered a delicacy in the food line. The corn in its prepared state was called pinole, and no traveling equipment was complete without it. While going through the thick underbrush in the hills and valley many of these sacks were torn and a large quantity of pinole was lost. This circumstance occurred so frequently that the hunters, when referring to an expedition, invariably used the word pinole in designating their favorite hunting locality. Hence the present name, Pinole.

With the advent of the California Powder Works the town grew in size. In 1896 Pinole was incorporated, and it now has a fine sewer system, macadamized streets, cement sidewalks, a fire company, and excellent lighting and water facilities.

The Bank of Pinole, established in 1905, is one of the staunchest banking institutions in the county. A fine new banking building was erected in 1915, and this structure, and the Downer, Ruff, and Pinole Theatre buildings in the center of the business district, are some of the latest valuable improvements to the town. Pinole also has a large department store, numerous smaller stores, an opera-house, a union public school, and two churches. St. Joseph's Catholic Church was erected in 1889 and remodeled in 1915. The Methodist Episcopal Church was constructed in 1886 and has since been extensively improved.

The Pinole-Hercules school building is one of the largest in the county and was erected on an imposing site in 1907. Several new rooms and an assembly hall have recently been added to the building. A corps of nine teachers is now employed.

Those principally identified with the early history and advancement of the town were the late Bernardo Fernandez, who settled in Pinole in 1849, and conducted a general merchandise store and a large hay and grain business; E. M. Downer, the present mayor of the town and president of the Bank of Pinole, and J. Bermingham, Jr., superintendent of the old California Powder Works.

There are many beautiful residences in Pinole, among which are the Downer, Fernandez, Poinsett, and Ellerhorst homes.

The Pinole Times was established in 1894 by E. M. Downer and Doctor M. L. Fernandez and was issued in pamphlet form from the press of a job-printing office at Martinez. About six months later the paper was enlarged to a six-column folio, and printed in Pinole, Downer assuming full control. A few years later John Bermingham, Jr., superintendent of the California Powder Works, took over the management of The Times and issued the paper for a period of two years. In 1901 the present editor and manager, E. C. Ebsen, took charge and is now issuing the paper. The Times is the pioneer newspaper of Western Contra Costa, and, with the exception of the Antioch Ledger and the Contra Costa Weekly Gazette of Martinez, is the oldest newspaper of continuous issue in the county. As regards political affiliation, the Times is, and always has been. Republican.

CHAPTER XXXVII. PORT COSTA

Port Costa first came into prominence along in 1879, when the late G. W. McNear, Sr., purchased a large strip of frontage along the shore and built the immense grain warehouses that have had a prominent place in Port Costa's commercial history. Out of his large holdings he laid out the town of Port Costa and founded the Port Costa Water Company, which supplies the principal towns along the northeastern shore. Since his death the interests that he founded have been ably conducted by his son, G. W. McNear, Jr.

Port Costa has always been a great grain port, shipping wheat and barley from interior California points to all parts of the world. Of late years the volume of grain has fallen off to some extent, due to the fact that the soil has been utilized for other purposes; but this has resulted in no commercial loss to Port Costa, for her warehouses have been constantly filled with other products.

The Southern Pacific operates the largest ferry boats in the world, the "Solano" and the "Contra Costa," between Port Costa and Benicia, across the Straits of Carquinez.

Several large brick factories play a prominent part in Port Costa's commercial activities.

An institute for seamen, located at Port Costa, branch of the San Francisco Mission to Seamen, watches after the welfare of sailors on the Carquinez Straits and does much good, affording means of wholesome recreation and amusement for crews of visiting ships.

CHAPTER XXXVIII. AVON

THE ASSOCIATED OIL COMPANY'S PLANT

The Associated Oil Company was incorporated October 5, 1901, with a capitalization of forty million dollars, and consisted of some thirty-five oil companies, controlling about three-fourths of the Kern River and McKittrick oil-fields.

The company's policy of expansion soon after brought it into control of the Amalgamated and the West Coast oil companies and many other valuable holdings in the various fields. In 1905 the company purchased the property of the National Oil Transportation Company, and thereby secured pipe-line facilities from the Coalinga field to tidewater at Monterey, and from the Santa Maria field to its refinery at Gaviota, Santa Barbara County. In 1906 the Associated Oil Company completed its first eight-inch pipe-line from the San Joaquin field to Port Costa, and shortly thereafter, this line being inadequate, another eight-inch line was built, giving a total capacity of about fifty thousand barrels a day. In 1906 the company constructed an eight-inch pipe-line from the Santa Maria field to its refinery at Gaviota, a distance of about thirty-five miles.

In 1911 the Associated Oil Company decided to erect a refinery on San Francisco Bay, and for this purpose purchased a six-hundred-and-twenty-acre site at Avon, Contra Costa County. This refinery, although not as large as some other refineries in the United States, is of the latest design. It was completed and put in operation in August, 1913, at that time having a capacity of about ten thousand barrels of crude oil a day. The high quality of its products was immediately recognized by the trade, and as a result almost continuous additions have been made, until at the present time this plant is capable of handling twenty-five thousand barrels of crude oil a day. This refinery has been pronounced by experts as one of the most modern and complete in the United States. The location of Avon refinery is ideal, having deep-water shipping facilities and being traversed by both the Southern Pacific and Santa Fe railroads. The company's two eight-inch pipe-lines from the valley oil-fields serve as a source of supply.

The Associated Oil Company has established some thirty-five distributing stations and about twenty-five service stations in the principal cities of California, as well as stations in Oregon, Washington, and Nevada. It has a fleet of eight oil-tankers, having a combined capacity of about three hundred thousand barrels; also, necessary tugs, barges, and tank-cars.

It is estimated that the company has invested over two and a half million dollars in Contra Costa County and furnishes employment to several hundred men. During the year 1916 the company expended over half a million dollars in improvements at its Avon refinery alone.

The refinery capacities of the Associated refineries at Los Angeles and Gaviota have also been increased in order to take care of market demands. This company is pursuing a policy of increasing its landholdings, and during the last year made heavy investments in oil-lands and developments.

CHAPTER XXXIX. BYRON

In the extreme eastern section of Contra Costa County, surrounded by fertile and productive farms and orchards, is the thriving and attractive town of Byron. It had its beginning in the fall of 1878, when the Southern Pacific Company began to run its trains through this section. Byron is located about five miles northwest of Brentwood and a like distance from the county line and is situated in the midst of one of the best agricultural districts in Contra Costa County. Two and a half miles from the town is located the famous Byron Hot Springs.

The first house erected in Byron was used as a hotel by F. Wilkening in 1878. Fish & Blum erected a large warehouse about this time.

Eden Plains and Point of Timber derived their names—the first from the wonderful fertility of its soil, the other from the peculiar form in which the belt of timber grew that then covered that section. It was V-shaped, the point coming to the vicinity of the site of the store kept by James A. Salts at that place. The Point of Timber landing was burned in the winter of 1881-82 by tule fires. Although it was the property of the neighboring farmers, it never proved of any great utility or monetary advantage to them. Point of Timber had an A. O. U. W. lodge, instituted on April 12.

1870. Excelsior Lodge No. 349, I. O. G. T., was organized on March 7, 1869. Point of Timber Grange No. 14, Patrons of Husbandry, was organized May 21, 1873, and was the outgrowth of the Point of Timber Farmers' Protective Club.

After the advent of the railroad through this section Byron commenced to expand and several houses and stores were erected. The town now numbers about five hundred residents.

While grain was the main harvest for many years, latterly it was found that the soil was adapted for other products. Almonds and walnuts have shown surprising crops, and hundreds of acres have been put out to alfalfa. Almost every product of the soil thrives. There are a number of dairies in the community that are operated under the most sanitary conditions, much milk and cream being shipped.

For years the farmers depended upon the natural rainfall for their crops, but during 1915-16 the Byron-Bethany irrigation project was got under way. This great enterprise will furnish water for fourteen thousand acres of choice land, at an approximate cost of ten dollars an acre.

The company was organized with a capital stock of one hundred thousand dollars. It commenced to run water through its ditches in May, 1917, from the Brentwood line to the Western Pacific tracks west of Tracy.

There are four thriving fraternal societies in Byron—the Native Sons, the Odd Fellows, the Woodmen of the World, and the Native Daughters.

There are four churches—the Methodist Episcopal, the Congregational, the Seventh-Day Adventist, and the Catholic. The latter is to be dedicated in June, 1917, and cost five thousand dollars. Bishop Hanna will have charge of the dedication, assisted by Father E. S. McNamara, the first priest in charge. The church is of concrete and will seat two hundred and fifty people.

The Byron school is a modern building, costing about four thousand dollars. The first teacher was Miss Ella McCabe. Miss W. H. Diffin is the present principal, assisted by Miss Anna L. Polak.

Permanent concrete and rock roads radiate from Byron in all directions. The town is on the route of transcontinental motor travel via the Borden Delta Highway from Stockton and the Mount Diablo Boulevard.

The history of Byron would not be complete without a mention of Mrs. William R. Wilder, who on October 10, 1916, had been a resident of this section half a century. Her husband came to what is now Byron in 1865, and after erecting a small house, brought his family here from Sacramento. Mrs. Wilder is a daughter of the late Captain George Donner of the famous Donner party, most of whom perished crossing the Sierra Nevada range in the early days.

In order to get the station on the railroad in the proper spot, the people were forced to purchase and donate the land for its present site to the Southern Pacific Company.

Herewith we give the names of some of the early settlers in the Byron section: 1860-61—A. Plumley, H. C. Gallagher, and T. Hoffman; 1865-67—J. E. Carey, J. F. Carey, A. Richardson, W. R. Wilder, D. Perkins, J. S. Netherton, D. K. Berry, M. Berlinger, C. J. Preston, Thomas McCabe, J. P. McCabe, H. C. McCabe; 1868-69—George Cople, A. T. Taylor, J. Christensen, R. N. McEntire, and W. J. Cotes.

There are many beautiful hom.es in Byron. Harry Hammond, editor of the Byron Times, has a modern bungalow of eight rooms and about two acres of land. Electricity is installed throughout the dwelling for heating and cooking, and an automatic electric pumping plant is a feature of the yard. He has about one hundred varieties of trees and shrubs. His one-acre orchard demonstration farm is intended to show visitors to this section what can be accomplished here. He has fifty-seven varieties of fruit trees, and seventeen varieties of vegetables are grown.

The Byron Times, was started in 1906 by Harry Hammond, the present owner and editor. Mr. Hammond has built up his paper to one of influence and power. He is well known to newspaper men throughout the State. The Byron limes is the first paper in the State to use red ink, and the initials in red are a feature of each issue. These initials read a word or words. The paper covers twenty-one points in the three counties of Contra Costa, San Joaquin, and Alameda.

PART II BIOGRAPHICAL

CLARK L. ABBOTT, M. D.—Among the best-known physicians of the Bay counties is Doctor Clark L. Abbott, an active, capable, and much respected citizen of Richmond, Contra Costa County. He was born in Seneca County, Ohio, October 5, 1874. His father, Abraham Lorenzo Abbott, is a native of Ohio, and is a man of high general standing in his community, a man of genial and cordial manners, and above all he is a man of noble aims. He has many friends and has the confidence and respect of all in his community, where he has followed agricultural pursuits all his life.

Doctor Abbott's mother, Calena (Titus) Abbott, is also a native of Ohio, and to her were born three sons and three daughters. Of these the only surviving ones are Clark L. and one sister, Elvira, who resides on the home place in Ohio. The Abbott family was one of the first to be founded in America, and Doctor Abbott's great grandfather was one of the sturdy pioneers who assisted in settling that region now Ohio after the war of 1812.

The family genealogy dates back to Revolutionary ancestry, and there were many in his family that took part in the Revolutionary War, the War of 1812, the Civil War, and the Spanish-American War, and a goodly number of the Abbott family in Ohio have enlisted in the present conflict. Many in the family are members of the Sons and Daughters of the American Revolution. The Doctor's great-grandfather was among the men who assisted this Government in taking the Seneca Indians to Iowa. Doctor Abbott was reared on the home farm. He attended the public schools. He is a self-educated man and has always been a careful student and close observer. Intent upon the successful study of medicine, in 1891 he entered Heidelberg University, at Tiffin, Ohio, from which he graduated in 1806 with the degrees of B. S. and M. S. He then entered Rush Medical College in Chicago, graduating from that institution in ,1000. He served as intern in the leading Chicago hospitals for some time, when he decided to cast his lot with the Golden State and located in San Francisco, where he served as lecturing physician in the College of Physicians and Surgeons. At the same time Doctor Abbott had opened an office in San Pablo, where he practiced his profession.

He removed to Point Richmond, where he opened an office and began the general practice of medicine and acted as physician and surgeon for the Santa Fe railroad for this district. Doctor Clark L. Abbott was married in Ohio in 1901 to Miss Nellie Rule, a native of that State and a daughter of one of the representative farmers in his locality. Mr. Rule was a man who took an active part in local politics, and his death, which occurred in 1901, was mourned by a wide circle of friends. His wife passed away in 1915. In his political affiliations Doctor Abbott is a Republican, and has taken an active part along party lines for the past twelve years. During the early days in Richmond, the Doctor was one of a committee who had charge of the incorporation of the town and was a member of the freeholders who drew up the first charter. During his residence in Ohio he was made a Mason, becoming a member of Greensprings Lodge. He served as Exalted Ruler of Richmond Lodge, B. P. O. E., for three terms, and for some time past has been president of the board of directors of that lodge. He is also a member of the I. O. O. F. lodge. Doctor Abbott is a member of the county and State medical associations, a Fellow of the American College of Surgery, and is chairman of the Auxiliary Committee of Medical

Defense of Contra Costa County. Personally, he is a genial and companionable man, and those who come in the circle of his friendship find him broad-minded and liberal, a supporter of public movements, and one whose success has been well deserved. He was elected coroner in 1906, which office he now holds.

CHARLES M. BELSHAW is numbered among the distinguished citizens of California because of the prominence he has attained in promoting the permanent interests of Contra Costa County along all lines, and also by reason of the extent and importance of his business connections. Mr. Belshaw is associated with industrial, commercial, and financial enterprises. He was born at Fiddletown, Amador County, California, March 11, 1861, and was reared principally in San Francisco, where he attended the City College and University Mound College. In 1879 he took a college preparatory course under Professor George Bates, of San Francisco, and then matriculated in Harvard University, Cambridge, Massachusetts, from which he graduated in 1883. Returning to California, he became timekeeper, paymaster, and wharf clerk to the Empire Coal Mines, and later superintendent of the mines. At the time of his father's death Charles M. Belshaw succeeded to his mining interests. In politics he is affiliated with the Republican party. In 1894 he was elected to the Assembly on that ticket. Evidence of his faithful service is given in his re-election to this office, in which he has served three full terms and the extra session of 1899. In 1900 he was elected to represent the district in the State Senate. Mr. Belshaw was twice married; the first union was to Miriam E., daughter of Tyler K. and Marietta (Warren) Waite, a native of De Kalb County, Illinois, who died January 20, 1914. The second marriage was to Maud E. Spencer. He is a member of the B. P. O. E. and Native Sons of the Golden West. He assisted in organizing the parlor at Antioch and is a past grand president of that order.

MORTIMER W. BELSHAW, deceased, was born in Herkimer County, New York, April 20, 1830, son of William and Mary (Rhodes) Belshaw.

Without assistance from anyone he acquired an education superior to most of his associates. At sixteen years of age he began to teach school during the winter months; with the money thus earned he took a course of study in Oxford Academy, Chenango County, New York. About the same time he learned the trade of watchmaker and jeweler. Later he entered Geneva (now Hobart) College, from which he was graduated in 1850. For two years subsequent to graduation Mr. Belshaw acted as collector for the Erie Canal locks at Little Falls. Meanwhile he had heard reports about California and its possibilities—attracted by these reports he decided to seek a livelihood on the Coast. In 1852 he came via the Isthmus of Panama to San Francisco, thence proceeding to Mokelumne Hill, Calaveras County, where he worked as carpenter for a time. His next business venture was the opening of a jewelry store at Fiddletown, Amador County, where he also held the position as agent for the Wells Fargo Express Company. About 1864 he removed to San Francisco, where he became connected with the Pacific Refinery. Possessing mechanical genius, he invented a number of useful devices, among them the Belshaw water-gate, still used in many mining districts. In 1868 he went to Inyo County and opened the Cerro Gordo Mines. While there he successfully solved the problem of smelting the rebellious galena ore and invented the water-jacket furnace now used in all smelters. An important enterprise in connection with the mines was the establishment of a freight route that utilized about fifteen hundred mules and horses for the conveyance of the bullion over the mountains and desert. On severing his connection with the mines as manager he retained a large financial interest. Mr. Belshaw came to Antioch in 1877, and in company with Judson and Rouse opened the Empire Coal Mines in the foothills of Mount Diablo. They built a railroad and dockage. As a stockholder and director, he was interested in the Kennedy Mining & Milling Company, near Jackson, Amador County. He was president of the Gwin Mine Development Company of Calaveras County. He was the Republican candidate for assemblyman from Amador County in 1856. Many of his articles bearing upon the silver question were published in papers throughout California as well as in other parts of the country. The failure of his health led to his retirement from personal control of his various interests. After an illness of six months he died at the home of his son, in Antioch, April 28, 1808. Mr. Belshaw was united in marriage in 1858 to Miss Jane E. Oxner, a native of Herkimer County, New York; she died in 1000, at the age of sixty-four years. Their older son, William Conrad, was born June 5, 1859, and died July 5, 1864.

ELAM BROWN BARBER is a son of Mathew Root Barber, one of the respected pioneers of Contra Costa County, and who was born in Delaware County, Ohio, August 7, 1815. When two years of age he was taken to Bond County, Illinois, where his father engaged in farming. His father died when Mathew R. was young, and he made his home with the family of the Honorable Elam Brown. Here Mr. Barber's father attended school and resided until he was twenty-one years of age. In 1837 he took in a partner and followed farming and wagon-making. On March 15, 1849, he joined a party and crossed the plains, making the journey in six months. The first place at which he stopped in California was Hangtown, now Placerville. This was in September. Mr. Barber mined for a time, and then engaged in lumbering near San Antonio, then in Contra Costa County. While working in the redwoods he wrote tickets for the first election of officers in this and Alameda County.

He erected many of the first houses in Martinez, and on February 14, 1851, he sailed from San Francisco via Panama and New Orleans and went to Illinois. Remaining one year, he, with his wife and family, drove a band of stock across the plains to California, arriving at Martinez, August 22, 1852.

In the fall of 1852 he purchased a beautiful tract of land consisting of four hundred and forty-three acres. Mr. Barber was elected to the office of Public Administrator for four successive terms. He was married in Pike County, Illinois, November 14, 1837, to Orpha Bean. The subject of this sketch was born June 13, 1846, near Jacksonville, Illinois, and crossed the plains with his parents when five years of age. He was educated in the public schools of Martinez and Heald's College, San Francisco. Finishing his education, Mr. Barber returned to the home ranch and has remained here since. There were six children in the parents' family, and our subject is the only one living. Mr. Barber is a Republican, but never aspired to public office.

JAMES E. RODGERS, one of the prominent attorneys of Contra Costa County, is a man to whom success has come as a result of unfaltering determination, untiring industry, energy, and enterprise, for he has worked his way upward to the success which he now enjoys. Mr. Rodgers is a native of California, his birth having occurred at Sonora, Tuolumne County, May 2, 1865. His father, P. F. Rodgers, was a native of Ireland, and came to America in 1849. He came to California via Cape Horn, and settled in Sonora County, where he became interested in mining until 1868, when he removed to Pleasant Hill, Contra Costa County. Here he took up ranching until his death, which occurred in 1891. Mr. Rodgers' mother, Mary (Holland) Rodgers, was also a native of Ireland. His parents were married in Sonora County, and four children were born of this union. John F., of Oakland, California; Rose M., wife of John G. Duane, of Martinez; Sadie J., wife of T. S. Duane, of Martinez; and the subject of this sketch. In 1897 Mr. Rodgers was admitted to the bar, and the same year was elected county clerk, which office he held for ten years. He resigned in 1908 to take up the practice of law in Martinez, where he has since resided. Mr. Rodgers was united in marriage April 29, 1890, to Miss Alice Buckley, a daughter of William H. and Mary Buckley. To this union have been born James E., Jr., and Alice, who is at present attending the Berkeley School of Art. Mr. Rodgers is affiliated with the Republican party. Fraternally he is a member of the I. O. O. F., W. O. W., B. P. O. E., and Native Sons. He is an able lawyer, and his professional attainments put him in the front rank of the legal fraternity of the Bay counties.

ALFRED S. ORMSBY is one of the prominent attorneys of Contra Costa County, California, and occupies a place today among the leading jurists of the State. He was born in Petaluma, December 23, 1871, and is the son of Alfred Walter and Lucy G. (Price) Ormsby. His father was a native of New York State, and his mother was born in London, England. Mr. Ormsby's father died in Oakland on December 11, 1877. His mother makes her residence in Walnut Creek. The subject of this sketch acquired his education in the public and high schools of California. He studied law and passed his examinations with high honors, winning his admission to the bar in 1897. He practiced in Oakland for a period of ten years, and then removed to Contra Costa County. Was justice of the peace at Walnut Creek and resigned and was appointed chief deputy to the Honorable A. B. McKenzie, then district attorney for Contra Costa County. He is now chief deputy under Thomas D. Johnston, present district attorney. Mr. Ormsby is affiliated with the Republican party. Fraternally he is a member of the Masonic lodge and Eastern Star chapter. He also is a member of the B. P. O. E. of Richmond, the I. O. O. F., and is an active member of the Native Sons. He was united in marriage to Miss Alice A. Waite, of Walnut Creek, November 30, 1893. Their children are Walter A., born June 29, 1898, a high school student, and Alice Marian, born August 1, 1906.

RUDOLPH A. WILSON was born near Scottsboro, Jackson County, Alabama, November 5, 1882, being the eldest son of William Yancey and Emma (Ulrich) Wilson, both natives of Alabama. At the age of ten years he moved with his parents to Arkansas, and a few years later to Texas. He attended the public school until he had attained the age of fourteen years, when he accompanied his father, who had become an evangelist, on a tour of the Southern States. Possessing a good voice and some musical ability, he conducted the musical part of revival meetings with his father for some years. In 1808 the family removed to Hopkinsville, Kentucky, and it was here young Wilson began to learn the printing business, and by close application mastered the details of the trade and became a competent mechanic. In 1902, with his family, he came to Southern California, and in January, 1903, came to Oakland, to take a position on the staff of the Messiah's Advocate, in which position he did both mechanical and literary work. On May 19, 1905, he was married to Miss Lena

Evans, of Sherman, Texas, a young lady whom he had met some years previously while with his father in evangelistic work.

To this union there have been born three daughters: Vida, born July 10, 1007; Ruth, born May 27, 1909; Margaret, born July 12, 1916. In 1905 he established a job-printing business in Oakland, which he conducted about a year, after which he was engaged by various printing establishments in San Francisco until July, 1908, when he became editor and proprietor of the Spreckels Courier, in Monterey County, later disposing of his interest in this paper and establishing the Spreckels Enterprise, which he conducted successfully for some years. He also organized the Tri-County Publishing Company, Inc., and became its president and manager. This company published a monthly agricultural journal. Mr. Wilson was one of the founders of the Spreckels Improvement Association and its first secretary, being also a member of the State Association of Commercial Organization Secretaries. In August, 1913, having disposed of his Monterey County interests, Mr. Wilson came to Antioch and became associated with the Antioch Ledger, which position he still holds. He has displayed at all times a keen interest in the collection of historical data and publicity work generally. Fraternally, Mr. Wilson is a member of the Antioch Lodge of Free Masons, a past grand and a past chief patriarch (of the Encampment branch) of the Independent Order of Odd Fellows, and a member of the Rebekah Lodge. He is a member of the official board of the First Congregational Church of Antioch; also a member of the executive board of the Contra Costa County Christian Endeavor Union; and is vice-president of the Martinez Typographical Union. He has the reputation of standing for that which is cleanest and best in community affairs.

JOEL D. WIGHTMAN, deceased, was born in Council Bluffs, Iowa, April 1, 1853. His parents came to California in 1854 and settled in Santa Clara Valley for a short period, after which they moved to Dutch Flat, Placer County, where Mr. Wightman's father engaged in farming. From here the family went to Solano County, where the father died. The family removed to Carson City, Nevada, where Mr. Wightman acquired his education. The family removed to Santa Cruz, and later to Vacaville, at which place Mr. Wightman learned the wheelwright trade. He came to Antioch and learned the contracting business. He purchased the first land sold in the vicinity of Oakley and was successful in conducting an orchard. While in the contracting business Mr. Wightman was practically the first choice of both Democrats and Republicans for the office of supervisor for his district and was elected twice by large majorities. He has always taken a deep interest in county affairs and was largely instrumental in securing the new courthouse. Mr. Wightman was united in marriage in Antioch to Sarah Osborn, of Carson City, Nevada, March 5, 1874. To this union were born Carleton E., Charles B., Percy S. (of Byron), Ray S., and Misses Bessie and Minerva (of Antioch). Mr. Wightman was one of the highly respected and representative men of the county. His death was due to injuries received nearly twelve years ago. At the time of the accident, June 29, 1905, Mr. Wightman was superintending the raising of a large flag-pole at the Live Oak School near Oakley, when the staff slipped and pinned him to the ground, badly fracturing his spine. From that time until his death he was compelled to use a wheel chair. Mr. Wightman was a man of sound business judgment, and was eminently fitted to hold the responsible positions with which he was honored.

He served the people of Antioch district for two terms as justice of the peace with honor to himself and credit to his constituents. He served in this office nearly six years. Fraternally, Mr. Wightman was a member of the Masonic lodge of Antioch. His death occurred March 5, 1917. He was a man of many sterling qualities, and he won the respect and confidence of all who came in contact with him. In official and social relations he held steadily to high ideals.

GEORGE H. FIELD is one of the successful and prominent contractors of eastern Contra Costa County. His birth occurred in Kent County, Canada, May 12, 1864, a son of Benjamin and Mary A. (Mitten) Field, both parents being natives of Canada. Mr. Field's mother passed away when he was but eight years of age. His parents removed to Reed City, Michigan, when George was young. Here he acquired a common school education. Early in life Mr. Field assisted his father and learned the carpenter trade. This vocation he has always followed with gratifying results. At the age of sixteen Mr. Field came to the Pacific Coast, where he readily found employment at his trade in Tacoma and Seattle, Washington. He removed to Stockton, where he resided for twenty years. Many fine business buildings and residences in Stockton, Pittsburg, Antioch, and surrounding communities testify to his skill and ability. For eight years he was identified with the Santa Fe Railroad, and had charge of bridges and buildings. Twelve years ago he severed his connection with the railroad, and has since followed contracting and building. Politically, Mr. Field is a Democrat. He takes a keen interest in local affairs but has never aspired to office. He was united in marriage to Mary A. Sexton, of Stockton, California, on May 29, 1888. To this union have been born five children: Ruth, born December 29, 1890; Genevieve, born October 28, 1892; Percy, born January 10, 1897; Cyril, born January 24, 1895; Wesley, born February 21, 1900. Fraternally, Mr. Field is a member of Charity Lodge No. 6, I. O. O. F., of Stockton. He is held in high regard by his business associates by reason of his enterprise and integrity.

ALDEN NATHAN NORCROSS is one of the highly respected and representative citizens of eastern Contra Costa County. Energy, ability, and well-directed ambition, controlled by sound judgment, have constituted the foundation upon which Mr. Norcross built his success. He was born in Woodbury, Vermont, November 27, 1828, a son of Captain James R. Norcross and Eleanor (Blanchard) Norcross, who were from among the representative families of their section. Mr. Norcross's parents were both born in Vermont. His father was a farmer, and Alden assisted on the home place and attended school. At the age of twenty-one Mr. Norcross started out in life for himself. He went to Boston, where he engaged in the dray business, and has the distinction of building the first low dray in the United States, as far as he can ascertain. In 1861 he enlisted for three years and was assigned to light horse artillery in Captain Nim's battery. Mr. Norcross served in the army three years, and during this time his brother Joseph carried on the business in Boston. In 1864 Mr. Norcross received an honorable discharge and returned to Boston, and there was actively engaged in his business for twenty years. Mr. Norcross has always been a lover of good horses and always owned the best, and it may be related here that while in the army he was selected on several occasions by his General and sent on one occasion to New Orleans, where he selected and took one hundred and seventy mules and one hundred horses back to camp. The General told Mr. Norcross's captain that when he wanted horses to have Mr. Norcross get them; that he knew good horses and could get back in half the time required by the commissioned officers. Mr. Norcross spent some years in Texas, where he did farming and freighting. In 1890 he removed to California, and settled in the sandland section, which is now Oakley, where with Mr. Marsh he purchased twenty acres of land and platted the town-site. Soon after laying out the town Mr. Norcross and Mr. Marsh severed their business relation, and Mr. Norcross gave a half block for school and playgrounds and presented two lots as a site for the Methodist church. In March, 1861, Mr. Norcross was married to Julia Langmaid, of Pittsfield, New Hampshire. To this union were born six children, of whom two are living, Bert Leland and Florence, the latter making her home in Antioch. Mrs. Norcross, wife of our subject, died in Pittsfield, N. H., in the early '70s. Politically Mr. Norcross is a Republican. While he has taken a keen interest in national affairs, he has never aspired to local office.

BERT LELAND NORCROSS, son of Alden N., was born at Summerville, Massachusetts, a suburb of Boston, January 4, 1872. Mr. Norcross acquired a common-school education, coming to California with his father in 1890. After reaching San Francisco and remaining overnight, Bert started out alone over the mountains and landed in Brentwood, where he found employment with Henry McCabe at ranching. He worked out for five years and then purchased ten acres; to this soon after he added twenty-one acres, and has been constantly purchasing land, until now he owns one hundred and fifteen acres, all in almonds and walnuts of the choicest varieties. In 1915 Mr. Norcross shipped sixteen tons of nuts. Politically, he is a progressive. He has taken a keen interest in educational work, and assisted in building the first school in Oakley, and serves as a trustee. Mr. Norcross has taken an active part in the temperance movement in this county. He was twice married, the first union being to Phyllis Trembath, of Antioch; her death occurred in San - Francisco. The second marriage was to Sophia Hamma, of San Francisco, October 30, 1915. Mr. and Mrs. Norcross are members of the Methodist Church. Mr. Norcross is one of the successful members of the county, and to him belongs the title of self-made man. Through his energy he has risen to be one of the leading men of the eastern part of Contra Costa County.

JAMES M. STOW.—Ceaseless industry, supplemented by sound judgment, has rendered possible the success gained by James M. Stow. He is a man of progressive and enterprising ideas and methods and is one of Contra Costa County's leading and influential citizens. Mr. Stow was born in Illinois in 1847, a son of Josephus Stow, a native of Massachusetts, who was united to Susan Dodd in marriage and made a journey to Illinois. Mr. Stow's father took up Government land and was one of the leading farmers in his locality. During the gold rush to California Mr. Stow's father left his ranch in competent hands and joined the rush, coming overland by ox-team. He engaged in mining and was fairly successful, and in 1856 he sent for his wife and three children to join him. They came via the Panama route, and lived in Nevada County until 1859, when the family came to San Francisco, owing to the health of the father. His death occurred in 1860. Afterward Mrs. Stow settled in Danville, where she married John Perham, and the family removed to Walnut Creek. Her death occurred in 1884. She was born in South Carolina in 1818. From his twelfth year Mr. Stow was reared in Contra Costa County, and has ever since resided here, with the exception of a few years, when he removed to Pacific Grove, where he erected one of the palatial homes of that city. He served as city councilman and mayor of Pacific Grove and resigned the office as mayor in order to return to Walnut Creek to look after his many interests there. Mr. Stow acquired his education in the public schools of Oakland. His early business training was gained in a general store in Walnut Creek, and he later clerked for Shuey Bros. In 1875 he opened a general store in Walnut Creek, where he continued in business until he was elected to the office of assessor on the Republican ticket in 1880.

This office he filled to the entire satisfaction of the people of this county for a period of seven years. In 1887 he disposed of the store interests, when he engaged in the real estate and insurance business. He is, and has been, one of the county's best promoters. Mr. Stow has made an acceptable and faithful postmaster and competent Wells Fargo agent; has been notary public and was one of the chief promoters and organizers of the first telephone company in this county. For a time he was the owner of the Martinez Gazette.

He is a stockholder in the Bank of Martinez, the Bank of Walnut Creek, and the Bank of Pacific Grove. When a tunnel was projected through the mountains, making a direct outlet to Oakland from Contra Costa County, a distance of 1026 feet, there were several bids from contractors to build the part belonging to this county, but the county voted to have the construction work done by the supervisors. Mr. Stow stepped in and built the necessary road, and in so doing saved the county over $17,000 over the amount of the lowest bidder. Fraternally, he is a Mason and for a number of years he served as secretary of the Walnut Creek lodge. At one time he was active in the ranks of the Ancient Order of United Workmen. Mr. Stow has been a member of the Methodist church for many years, and has served as trustee of the Pacific Grove church. He purchased the pleasantly situated estate of Captain Fale near Walnut Creek some years ago. He has continually added to the improvement of this property, making it one of the comfortable and attractive places near the town. All told, he owns about five thousand acres of valuable land. Mr. Stow was twice married, the first union being to Alice Glass, a daughter of Joseph Glass, one of Contra Costa's respected pioneers, on April 22, 1873, and her death occurred in July, 1912. The children of this union have been Dr. Eleanor M. Bancroft, born June 2, 1874; Hattie, born March 20, 1876 (died in 1877); Carrie, wife of R. L. Palmer, of Walnut Creek, born June 8, 1878; Garfield, engaged in the real-estate business in Oakland, born April 30, 1880; Rufus, in the employ of the Government, born August 29, 1882; Pearl, wife of Joseph Lawrence, born July 29, 1884; Orville, at present constable at Walnut Creek, born August 3, 1886; Harry, identified with the Burgess Company, born August 7, 1888; Armond, born August 17, 1890; Russell, born December 17, 1893; Forrest Chadbourne, born July 19, 1896.

The second union of Mr. Stow occurred March 20, 1912. To this union was born Berring, June 25, 1914. During Mr. Stow's last term of office as supervisor he was an important factor in the building of the new courthouse at Martinez. He is a Republican and a "standpatter." He has always taken a keen interest in political matters, and he is widely known and esteemed by all.

COL. J. R. COATES, deceased, was born in Charlotte, Maine, March 26, 1826. At the age of twenty-three, together with his brother-in-law, John Beckford, he left home in the brig "Sirocco," December 6, 1849. In addition to paying fifty dollars for his passage, he worked before the mast, and arriving in San Francisco he was employed in lightering work on the docks.

He went to Sacramento with Captain Crocker on the schooner "Elizabeth," of Barnstable. Leaving Sacramento he went to Boone's Bar on the Feather River, where he soon made a small fortune. Learning there was a great demand for pork in the Hawaiian Islands, he and a companion decided to buy a shipload of hogs and take them to the islands. However, when about halfway to their destination the hogs were taken ill and all died with cholera.

The young men had invested all their money in the cargo, and, being penniless, signed as able seamen and continued their voyage. They visited the South Sea Islands, and during a trip to Tahiti the queen of that domain fell in love with young Coates. She proposed marriage to him and agreed to make him king. He did not care to accept, and through the strategy of his friends he was smuggled aboard the ship at night while the queen was looking for him. He then followed a roving life and visited many of the countries of Central and South America. He afterward returned to California and took up mining. He was again successful, and later returned to his native city, where he purchased a farm and engaged in the lumber business and ship building. On March 3, 1852, Colonel Coates was united in marriage to Miss Juliet M. Fisher, also a native of Charlotte, Maine, the bride belonging to one of the well-known and highly respected colonial families. To this union there were two children, Mrs. Juliette C. Harding, of Antioch, California, and Margaret Reynolds Coates, who died at the age of seven. When the call for troops was made at the beginning of the Civil War, Colonel Coates organized Company A, Fifteenth Regiment, Maine Volunteer Infantry, being selected as sergeant. He had a fine military record, being promoted rapidly for bravery until the end of the conflict, when he returned with the rank of colonel. He was wounded many times, one ball shattering his left hand, another ploughing a furrow through his scalp, and a third shattering his ankle. The latter wound was received during Banks' Red River campaign, the wound being received at the battle of Mansfield, Louisiana, following which he was captured. He saw service with General Butler when he captured New Orleans, and also was present with Grant's troops during the siege of Richmond. Being mustered out on parole, he soon afterward joined his regiment in the Shenandoah Valley, and served until the end of the war, being finally mustered out at Charleston, South Carolina. After getting back to Maine, Colonel Coates decided to return to California. He arrived here in 1867, with his family. He went to the mines but found he had lost all right to his claims. He finally located in Contra Costa County and bought a tract of land upon which is now located Bixler Station on the Santa Fe Railroad. His original holding was the one-hundred-and-sixty-acre soldier's grant, but he soon bought more land until he owned six hundred and forty acres. In 1874 Mrs. Coates and her daughter returned East for her health, and she died in 1878. In 1880 Colonel Coates was united in marriage to Elizabeth Blanche Madigan, of Baltimore. Directly after the death of his wife, in 1878, he left the Bixler tract and made his home on what is known as the Hill Ranch, south of Antioch, where one of the most improved dairy ranches in the State is operated. Colonel Coates first engaged in the cattle business and gradually changed to farming. At one time he engaged in a general merchandise business with Henry Brewer. When oil was first discovered south of Antioch, Colonel Coates purchased eight hundred and three acres in Oil Canon. About thirty-one years ago he purchased property in Brentwood, and erected Coates' Hall in that place. He was affiliated with the Masonic order for many years. Colonel Coates' death occurred in Antioch on July 27, 1015. In all the relations of life he proved himself a useful, conscientious citizen of sound ideas and principles, and one who considered an untarnished name of greater value than the mere acquirement of wealth. He was a man of excellent judgment, fair in his views, and highly honorable in all his relations with his fellow-man. Two grandchildren survive him, John Coates Harding, born in San Francisco, July 8, 1882, and Stacy L. Harding, a graduate of the University of California, born in Waltham, Massachusetts, September 20, 1892. The latter is now employed in the Commercial Bank of Santa Barbara and will eventually look after the property and business interests of his father.

JOSEPH A. VON BUREN, one of the prominent ranchers of eastern Contra Costa County, was born in Switzerland, March 21, 1858, a son of Henry and Anna (Nederberger) Von Buren. In the parents' family were two girls and five sons. Joseph is the only one who came to Contra Costa County. He received his education in the public schools and attended college at Luzern, Switzerland, for three and a half years. He studied for a teacher, but before he had finished he was called home, where he assisted on the farm. His father died in 1886, and his mother passed away in 1866. At the age of eighteen Joseph went to Germany and worked on a farm at Essen for five years. He then returned home for a year and then spent two years in France. In the spring of 1882 he left Havre, France, and sailed for America. He went to St Louis, where he found work at dairying, and milked thirty-six cows, for which he received twenty-five dollars a month. He remained here for two years, and in 1884 came to California, finding employment in Oakland at the dairy business for one year. He then removed to Marin County, where he worked at butter-making for seven years. In 1898 he went to the Paris Exposition, and while home, he married Theresa Gwerder, a native of Switzerland. To this union were born six children. Mr. and Mrs. Von Buren returned to Marin County where they remained one year, and then rented one hundred and sixty acres near Oakley for three years. In 1898 he bought one hundred and sixty acres known as the Winters Ranch, in 1902 purchased three hundred and twenty acres of the Harkinson family, and in 1906 bought one hundred and sixty acres known as the Crocker Ranch. The children born to Mr. and Mrs. Von Buren are Lillie, born May 10, 1898; Violet, born November 11, 1900; Orville, born October 24, 1901; Werner, born August 24, 1904; Edward and Daniel, twins, born September 15, 1906. Mr. Von Buren is a Republican, and the family are members of the Catholic church.

ARCHIE V. McFAUL.—Characterized by the same energetic activity, mental vigor, and business foresight that distinguished his father, James Reid McFaul, the subject of this review holds a high position among the leading business and fraternal men of Contra Costa County. He was born in Hampshire, Illinois, the son of James Reid and Francis M. (Davis) McFaul, both natives of Ontario, Canada. The parents of Mr. McFaul were married in Kingston, Ontario. Sometime after their marriage they moved to Illinois.

The father became identified with the C. B. & Q. R. R. at McCook, Nebraska, a division point. The family removed to California in 1894, and the father engaged in business in Watsonville. In 1905 he came to Contra Costa County, and in 1908 located in Pittsburg, where he engaged in the furniture, hardware, and plumbing business under the firm name of J. R. McFaul & Son, which continued until the death of James R. McFaul, which occurred March 6, 1912, when Archie, his son and the subject of this sketch, took the management. James McFaul was buried by Pittsburg Lodge No. 429, F. &. A. M.

He was honored and esteemed by all who knew him, and his death was mourned by a wide circle of friends. Archie V. McFaul acquired his education in the public schools of California. For eight years he worked at millwork and then associated himself with his father. His political affiliations are with the Republican party, and he has served on the River View school board for some time. He is a member of the Pittsburg board of health. Mr.

McFaul was united in marriage September 18, 1910, to Miss Lillian A. Rouner, of Grass Valley. To this union Janice R. was born in Pittsburg, October 15, 1915. Mr. McFaul is past master of Pittsburg and Antioch lodge, and has always taken a keen interest in Masonic affairs. He is now serving as secretary of Pittsburg lodge. Both Mr. and Mrs. McFaul are members of the Eastern Star. He has one sister, Vera, wife of James S. Hornsby, who is salesman and bookkeeper for the firm. Mrs. McFaul before her marriage was identified with the Redwood Lumber Company as stenographer, for a period of three years, and in the Contra Costa County Bank in the same capacity for two years. Mr. McFaul's father was a thirty-second-degree Mason.

WILBUR S. PIERCE, one of the leading and successful attorneys of Richmond, engaged in the general practice of law, was born in Yolo County, California, March 12, 1889, a son of Charles E. and Virginia Pierce. His father is a native of Missouri, and his mother a native of California. Wilbur S. attended the graded and high schools in the acquirement of an education.

Following his graduation from the high school, in 1910, he entered the Hastings Law College, graduating in 1912, and was admitted to the bar at Sacramento in 1913, beginning the practice of his profession in the district attorney's office at Woodland, California. He later removed to Richmond, where he has remained up to the present time, having built up an extensive and lucrative clientage as a practitioner of law. On November 15, 1914, Mr. Pierce was united in marriage to Miss Gertrude Eakle, daughter of J. B. and Lillian Eakle. Her parents were among the pioneers of Richmond. Mrs. Pierce's father died in 1906 and was numbered among the well-known and highly respected business men of the Bay counties. He was identified with the lumber interests of Richmond, was well known for his upright character, and was held in high esteem by all who knew him. Mrs. Pierce's mother makes her home in Portland, Oregon. Mr. Pierce has served as assistant district attorney of Richmond for one year. Politically, he is a Republican, and has taken considerable interest along party lines. Fraternally, he is identified with the Richmond lodge of Masons and belongs to the chapter. He is also a member of the Elks of Richmond. He is the legal adviser of the Merchants Association, the Tilden Lumber Company, and other interests in Richmond. His professional knowledge is unexhaustive, and in his practice he is tactful, his ability winning him a greater degree of success than usually falls to the lot of an attorney of his age and experience. Mrs. Pierce's grandmother deeded the land where Woodland is located and gave the town its name. She is still living in her eighty-ninth year. Her grandfather was numbered among the most respected citizens of Yolo County, and at one time was a candidate for governor of California.

AUTY O. DUGGAN, by his own energy, ambition and enterprise, and guided by sound practical judgment, has worked his way upward to a place among the representative real-estate men of Richmond. He was born in Texas, March 17, 1886. He acquired his education in the public and high schools of his native State. Early in life he went to Clifton, Arizona, and worked in the copper mines. In 1905 he removed to Richmond, California, and became identified with the East Shore Suburban Railroad, remaining for a period of seven years. In 1912 he became identified with D. W. McLaughlin in the real-estate business as salesman for two years. Previous to Mr. McLaughlin's death he had charge of the office, and since his death Mr. Duggan has been associated with the East Richmond Heights Land Company as manager. This corporation is made up of the following well-known men: E. M. Downer, president; Chas. Lehmkuhl, secretary; A. Greenfield, treasurer; L. E. Hart, auditor; A. O. Duggan, manager. Mr. Duggan has advanced along lines which have brought success, and he has been actuated by a spirit that recognizes the fact that efficiency and capability are the only qualities which really entitle one to advancement. He was united in marriage to Miss Florence Duncan, of Richmond, July 15, 1914. To this union one son, Auty Wilson Duggan, was born April 27, 1915. Fraternally, Mr. Duggan is affiliated with the B. P. O. E. No. 1251, of Richmond. Mr. and Mrs. Duggan have a wide circle of friends in and around the Bay counties.

WALTER A. LA SELLE is an active factor in the commercial circles of Richmond and is regarded as one of the enterprising and progressive young business men of his city. He was born in Nortonville, California, April 2, 1886. His parents are Erastus P. and Hattie B. La Selle. His father is a native of New York State and his mother was born in Montana. Mr. La Selle's parents came to Contra Costa County in 1887, locating in Crockett, where his father became actively engaged in business, remaining in Crockett about eighteen years. He removed to Oakland, where he was engaged in business for two years. In 1904 he came to Richmond, and at once established a furniture store, the firm then being known as La Selle & Smallwood. This firm continued for about two years, when Mr. Smallwood disposed of his interest to his partner. The subject of this review received his education in the public schools of Oakland, graduating from the Polytechnic High School. He took a course in the medical department of the University but did not finish.

He decided to take an interest in his father's furniture store in Richmond, where he has since remained. Politically, Mr. La Selle is affiliated with the Democratic party, and has served on the Democratic county central committee. Fraternally, he is a member of the B. P. O. E. of Richmond. On October 10, 1914, he was united in marriage to Miss Hester Rickabaugh, a native of Lake County, California, and a member of the Native Daughters of the Golden West. Mr. La Selle concentrates his energies upon his business affairs. He is a young man, and the progress that he has made already indicates the success which will come to him in the future. He has the confidence and esteem of those with whom he has been associated in business, and of all who are in any way connected with him.

GUSTAV W. PENNING.—Through the successive stages of progression, Gustav W. Penning has advanced to his present position of responsibility and importance as manager of the Santa Fe Foundry Company, of Richmond. He was born in Honolulu, September 3, 1883. He is the son of Henry and Charlotte Penning, both natives of Germany. His parents removed to California and located in Berkeley, where the mother still resides. Our subject received his education in the public schools, and at the age of seventeen he started to learn the molder's trade, which vocation he has followed all his life. He started with the Enterprise Foundry Company, of San Francisco, and remained with this firm until July 27, 1912, when he removed to Richmond and erected for the Enterprise Company the present commodious foundry. It has since been incorporated under the name of the Santa Fe Foundry Company of California, with the following officers: President, J. W. Mason; vice-president, J. C. Owens; secretary and manager, Gustav W. Penning. The firm manufactures iron and brass castings and does a general foundry and machine business. In politics Mr. Penning is a Republican. Fraternally, he is a member of Hermann's Sons of Berkeley. He was united in marriage to Miss Emma Klemm on June 6, 1907, and they have one son, Henry, born March 16, 1909.

HON. JAMES C. OWENS is numbered among the distinguished men of California because of the prominence he has attained in promoting the permanent interests of the State along all lines. Senator Owens was born in Maysville, Kentucky, November 22, 1871, and acquired his education in the public schools of his native State. He is the son of J. S. Owens, who was one of the representative farmers and stockmen of his locality. In 1893 Senator Owens came to California and was identified with the San Francisco Street Railroad Company. He later engaged in the tobacco business. At the outbreak of the Spanish-American War he enlisted and went to the Philippines, where he saw active service for eighteen months. After the war he served as chief sales clerk in the United States Depot Quartermaster's Department at Manila, and later as secretary-treasurer for the Provincial Government under Governor Taft. Upon his return to the United States, Senator Owens came to Richmond and took the management of a brick-manufacturing plant for a period of two years, after which he was identified with the hotel business at Richmond for several years, and in 1911 he engaged in the real-estate business. He is interested in several properties, the most important of which is the Owens Addition to the city of Richmond. Previous to his election as State senator the honors of the mayoralty of Richmond were conferred upon him, and he served during 1911 and 1912, resigning to take the office of State senator. While mayor he carefully studied every situation that bore upon the welfare of Richmond. The knowledge he gained in this office had much to do with shaping the policy of State matters. During his office as mayor bonds amounting to $1,170,000 were voted by the city to improve the water-front. Senator Owens is the first democratic senator to be elected from his district in forty years. He was elected in 1912 by a plurality of fifteen hundred votes over the Republican candidate. He was very active and particularly successful in getting legislation for the benefit of his district Among the bills that he introduced and passed were a bill providing that all the tide-lands along the Richmond water-front be granted by the State to the municipality, so that it might improve these lands as it saw fit, a bill providing that saloons be closed between the hours of two and six a. m., and a number of bills simplifying the street and other municipal improvement acts, which he found cumbersome during his term of office as mayor of Richmond. During Senator Owens' administration as mayor Richmond expended three million dollars on street and other improvements. On May 22, 1907, he was united in marriage to Miss Edith Berryman, a native of California. To this union one child, Mildred B., was born on August 29, 1909.

Senator Owens is prominently identified in the fraternal and commercial circles of Richmond. He was the organizer of the Richmond Industrial Commission and has served as president of the Sequoia Commercial Club. In 1913 he was the official representative of the city of Richmond, heading the delegation which went to Washington to lay their project before the Engineering Board for the approval of the district engineer's plan to improve the Richmond water-front and harbor three miles in length. Fraternally, Senator Owens is a member of the B. P. O. E. and I. O. O. F. of Richmond, and a member of the Spanish-American War Veterans. He is a man of progressive views and staunch honesty of purpose and rose to a high place among the representative citizens of California. His name adds to the list of those whose labors have been so far-reaching and beneficial in effect that they have influenced many phases of community development.

ERNEST WILLIAM REHNERT.—One of the strong, forceful, and resourceful men, active and energetic among the early pioneers of Contra Costa County during the early days, was Ernest William Rehnert. He was born in Prussia on September 24, 1824, and in his youthful days he learned the trade of blacksmithing. About the age of twenty-one he started out in life for himself and traveled extensively. In 1847 he sailed for Galveston, Texas.

He there worked at his trade for one year, after which he was identified with the United States army as blacksmith and veterinary. In September, 1851, he started overland through Mexico to Mazatlan, with horse-teams part of the journey and the balance of the way on pack-animals. He was accompanied by his wife and seven companions, who later sailed from Mazatlan on the schooner "Cornelius," arriving in San Francisco on December 16, 1851. In October, 1859, he removed to Contra Costa County and located on the San Pablo road, about two and a half miles from Pinole. Mr. Rehnert was united in marriage in San Antonio, Texas, June 13, 1851, to Barbara Miller, a native of Germany. To this union have been born five children: Charles W., Louise K., Annie Wilhelmina, whose death occurred on May 21, 1892. The other two children were twins and died in infancy. Mr. Rehnert originally had about one hundred and twenty-five acres of land. This land was in litigation for forty years, the suit being finally decided against him and others in this locality, and he was forced to lose about one hundred and twenty acres. He held the homestead, of about five acres, and in order to have more land was obliged to pay one hundred and thirty dollars an acre. There are now about seventeen acres in the old home place. Mr. Rehnert's death occurred on September 6, 1892, and on July 28, 1898, his widow passed on. Charles W., the only son, was educated in the public schools and college. Finishing his schooling, he followed various vocations. He has been assistant superintendent in the Giant Powder Works and was identified with the United States Powder Company at the time of the explosion. He married Hattie Ward, of San Pablo, on May 13, 1893, and their three children are Ernest V., who died at the age of nine years; Cecil Ward, born April 5, 1898; Thelma E., born May 8, 1906. The names of Ernest William Rehnert and his wife have long been held in the highest esteem in Contra Costa County, and their deaths were mourned by a large circle of friends.

JAMES P. ARNOLD.—One of the widely known and enterprising men of Richmond, California, and one who has the confidence and esteem of all who know him, is James P. Arnold, former chief of police of Richmond. Mr. Arnold is a native son, and was born in Merced, April 26, 1875, a son of James W. and Mary Jane (Hargrave) Arnold. His father was a native of Iowa, and his mother was born in Illinois. His parents crossed the plains in 1853 and settled in Nevada County. Mr. Arnold's father was a cattleman, and later moved to Merced County, where he became one of the prominent citizens of that locality and was largely interested in the cattle business. He removed to Santa Clara County and died in San Jose in February, 1907. The mother of Mr. Arnold makes her home in San Jose. The subject of this review acquired his education in the public schools of Santa Clara County. He took up farming and rented four hundred acres south of San Jose. In 1901 he came to Richmond and was identified with the Santa Fe Railroad, where he remained for several months. He engaged in business and continued for nearly two years. He worked for the Standard Oil Company, and in 1909 was appointed chief of police of Richmond. Resigning in July, 1914, he became a candidate for sheriff of Contra Costa County. He is now the manager of the B. P. O. E. Club of Richmond. He was married on October 19, 1899, to Miss Edith Johnson, of San Jose. Mrs. Arnold is a native of Boulder, Colorado, a daughter of Daniel Johnson, a retired orchardist of Santa Clara County. There were four children born to Mr. and Mrs. Arnold—Ila Lucile, Wesley James, Howard Stanley, and Ogden Mills. Politically, Mr. Arnold is a Republican and takes an active part in the ranks. He is a man of excellent judgment, fair in his views, and highly honorable in all his relations with his fellow-men. Fraternally, he is a worthy member of the B. P. O. E., W. O. W., and F. O. E. Mrs. Arnold holds membership in the Rebekah lodge, and takes an active part in all social affairs of Richmond.

WILLIAM E. DE LAND is numbered among the representative business men of Richmond. His activities have been a force in progress and his citizenship a valuable municipal asset. Mr. De Land resides in North Richmond, San Pablo District. He is one of the leaders in the promotion of construction and progress in the community's advancement. He was born in Connersville, Indiana, on September 23, 1872. His parents were Lyman W. and Anna (Thompson) De Land. His father was a native of Broome County, New York, and for many years he was identified with Wannamaker & Brown, of Philadelphia, as traveling salesman. His death occurred in 1901.

The mother of Mr. De Land was a native of Pennsylvania, and her death occurred on October 5, 1000. The subject of this sketch acquired his education in the public schools, graduating from the high school of New Haven, Connecticut. He attended Yale College and took up the engineering and millwright course. After leaving college he became identified with the well-known contracting firm of John Metcalf Company, of Chicago. For many years his advancement was steady, and, owing to his ability, he was promoted to many important positions. Mr. De Land came to California in 1912, locating in Bakersfield for some months, where he followed contracting.

Later, in 1912, he removed to Richmond, and bought large holdings of land in North Richmond, which he has subdivided. Mr. De Land erected a large hotel and business place in this locality. He also has business interests in Richmond. He operates a moving-picture theater, has a transfer business, and has the contract for the sprinkling of the streets in Richmond. Whatever he undertakes he carries forward to successful completion. This reputation has made him a person on whom his associates can always depend, and he is known for his upright character and his straightforward dealings in business circles. Since taking up his residence in Richmond, he has been particularly active in the good roads improvement and has done much to stimulate interest along those lines. On December 9, 1891, Mr. De Land was united in marriage to Miss Linna M. Perkins, a native of Pennsylvania, daughter of Albert A. and Melvina Perkins. Her father was one of the prominent oilmen in his locality. The great-grandfather of Mr. De Land came to America with Lafayette and fought in the Revolutionary War. Mr. DeLand's father during the Civil War enlisted in the thirty-fourth New York Infantry, and was discharged owing to disability. He served under Captain Baldwin and received seven gun-shot wounds, which incapacitated him for further service. Politically, Mr. De Land is affiliated with the Republican party, but he has never aspired to office. There have been two children born to Mr. and Mrs. De Land, namely, Bernice, born in Chicago, November 20, 1892, and William A., born in Cape Girardeau, Missouri, May 7, 1895. Mrs. De Land is a member of the Womans' Relief Corps of the G. A. R. and holds membership in the Baptist church of Richmond. Mr. De Land concentrates his attention upon his business affairs, in which he has been very successful, and much credit is due him for the position he has attained among the substantial men of Contra Costa County. William A. De Land is identified with his father in his various business interests in and around Richmond.

EDWARD J. RANDALL, one of the successful and prominent business men of Martinez, whose interests extend to many fields, was born in Napa County, California, on October 6, 1863. His father, Edmund Randall, was a native of England, and came to America in 1850. He resided in Illinois for a time, when he came to the Golden State via the Isthmus route. Remaining in San Francisco for a brief period, he afterward located in Napa. Later he had large interests in Stanislaus County, where the town of Newman is now located. In 1879 Mr. Randall's father removed to Contra Costa County and settled in Ignacio Valley, where he was identified along agricultural pursuits. He farmed seven hundred acres, provided his place with substantial barns and outbuildings, and engaged largely in the live-stock business. He passed away in 1901. Mr. Randall's mother's maiden name was Mary Tormey, a native of Ireland. She was the mother of seven children, only four of whom are now living. The subject of this sketch was educated in the public schools of Contra Costa County, and at St. Mary's College in San Francisco.

His further education has been that acquired in the school of experience. He has never feared to venture where favoring opportunity has led the way, and his ability and energy have brought him into prominent relations with the financial affairs of his chosen county. After his schooling he farmed for five years. He then engaged in mercantile business in Concord with his brother Samuel, under the firm name of Randall Brothers. Here he continued until 1909, when he sold his interests. Some years ago he assumed the management of the L. Anderson lumber business, which was started in 1859 and incorporated in 1899. This business has grown under his leadership, and today is one of the best-equipped plants in the country. His initial step toward the banking business was when he and four others subscribed and started the First National Bank of Martinez. He has been one of the bank's directors ever since, and has held the position of cashier since 1910. In politics, Mr. Randall is affiliated with the Democratic party. He has been supervisor for eight years, and is now acting as trustee for the town of Concord. Fraternally, he is a member of the B. P. O. E. of Richmond, Woodmen of the World, Redmen, and Native Sons. He was united in marriage to Miss Nora Anderson on October 30, 1888, and she died December 6, 1000. Mr. Randall's second marriage was to Marguerite Anderson, a sister of his first wife, on October 29, 1904. There were five children born of the first union and one to the second.

HERSHEY ANNIN STIVER, freight and passenger agent for the Southern Pacific Company at Richmond, California, is a railroad man of experience who has won his position entirely on his own merits. His birth occurred in Benton, Indiana, on March 20, 1878. He acquired his education in the public schools of Goshen, Indiana, afterward attending the Michael University, at Logansport, Indiana, and the Davis Business College, at Toledo, Ohio. In 1897 he became identified with railroad work on the Wabash, and filled positions as telegraph operator at Millersburg, Indiana, and Adrian and Detroit, Michigan, remaining with the Wabash Railroad nearly four years.

Mr. Stiver has held various positions of importance and trust and has traveled all over the country for the various roads he has represented. In 1903 he became associated with the Southern Pacific Company, acting as relief agent, and traveled largely over the Coast Division, being appointed in 1906 as assistant freight agent at San Jose. He came to Richmond early in 1908, being promoted to freight and passenger agent, which position he now holds to the eminent satisfaction of his company. Fraternally, he is a Mason, and has the distinction of serving as the first master of Alpha Lodge No. 431, F. & A. M., of Richmond. He is also a Royal Arch Mason, a member of the Council, the Commandery, Order of the Eastern Star, Aahmes Temple, Order of the Mystic Shrine, and the B. P. O. E. No. 1251, of Richmond. In July, 1906. Mr. Stiver was united in marriage to Miss Myrtle Alice Estle, a native of Kansas. To this union have been born two children—Laura Elizabeth, born May 9, 1907, and Martha Frances, born June 11, 1911. Mrs. Stiver takes an active part in the social and church circles of Richmond, being the worthy matron of Acantha Chapter No. 249, of the Eastern Star, for the year 1915, also president of the Mendelssohn Club during 1915, vice-president of the Richmond Club, and a member of the Methodist Episcopal Church.

EARL L. SCOFIELD holds an important position with the Standard Oil Company of California, as assistant superintendent of the white oil and filtering plant. He also held the position of superintendent of the asphalt department for some time. There is great credit due him for having obtained his present position, as he enjoys in full measure the confidence and respect of his fellow-men. Mr. Scofield was born in Alameda, California, August 5, 1800. He is a son of D. G. Scofield, formerly identified with the Standard Oil Company of California as president. Earl Scofield acquired his education in the schools of Alameda. Completing his education he became associated with the' Standard Oil Company. Fraternally, he is a member of the B. P. O. E.

On March 2, 1911, Mr. Scofield was united in marriage to Miss Marian Troy, a native of Louisville, Kentucky. Mr. and Mrs. Scofield are popular in social circles in the Bay cities. They have one daughter, Helen Frances, born August 11, 1912.

MANUEL LAWRENCE FERNANDEZ, M. D., who is actively engaged in the practice of medicine and surgery at Pinole, is recognized as an able representative of the profession, whoever keeps in touch with the most advanced methods and discoveries. His birth occurred July 13, 1876, his parents being Bernando and Carlota (Cuadra) Fernandez. Bernando Fernandez, one of Pinole's most prominent citizens, a capitalist and real-estate owner, was born in Portugal, November 15, 1828. He was reared in his native land, but at thirteen years of age he went to Brazil and remained in that country for some time, coming to New York in 1850. In 1853 he came to California, landing in San Francisco. He mined for some months, after which he sailed on the bay for some time. Subsequently he became owner of a schooner and carried provisions and freight from Pinole to San Francisco. He sold his boat and bought another, which he operated until 1856. Later he engaged in the mercantile business in Pinole until 1804. He also engaged in the hay and grain business on a very large scale and erected several large warehouses.

As his financial ability increased he invested in real estate in Pinole, San Francisco, Oakland, and Martinez; in the latter town the Martinez Hotel was a part of his possessions. In 1894 he erected his handsome residence in Pinole. Mr. Fernandez was united in marriage to Carlota Cuadra, and they became the parents of six children. Fraternally, Mr. Fernandez was a Mason, a member of the Martinez lodge, and a Royal Arch Mason. He died on May 12, 1912. Doctor Manuel Lawrence Fernandez was educated in the public schools and in Berkeley Gymnasium, graduating in 1895. He then entered the University of California, where he took up medicine and graduated from that department in 1000, receiving the degree of M. D. Subsequently he removed to New York, where he entered the Willard Parker Hospital, and from 1901 to 1903 he studied in Berlin and Vienna. Returning to San Francisco, he became identified as a practicing physician, remaining here until the fire in 1006, when he removed to Pinole, where he has since resided and practiced his profession. Doctor Fernandez has served as health officer for the town of Pinole for some time and is a member of the State Lunacy Commission from Contra Costa County. He is a member of the County and State Medical Society, and also a member of the Society for Prevention of Tuberculosis. Fraternally, he is affiliated with the B. P. O. E. Politically, he is a Republican. Doctor Fernandez holds the position as physician and surgeon for the Hercules Powder Company, and also for the Union Oil Company. He holds to high ideals, not only in professional service, but in citizenship and in social relations, and his sterling manhood has gained for him the warm and enduring regard of all with whom he has come in contact.

HARRY DAY CHAPMAN, city engineer of Richmond, California, is numbered among the most reliable and worthy representatives in his chosen profession on the Pacific Coast. He has risen to a position of trust and responsibility with various great corporations in the West and has a detailed knowledge of every branch of this business. This reputation has made him a man on whom his associates can always depend. Mr. Chapman was born in St. Louis, Missouri, on October 20, 1868. His education was acquired in the public schools and the Washington University of St. Louis, where he studied civil engineering. After finishing his schooling he entered the railway survey work for some years, and then was identified with the city engineer's office at Sioux City, Iowa, for a period of five years. Removing to Seattle, he became identified with the city engineer's office under R. H. Thompson, for a period of two years. He was then connected with the power-house construction on one of the Stone-Webster properties on the Puyallup River. Then, in 1905, he was placed in charge by the Abbott Kinney Company in building "Venice of America," at Venice, California. He afterward removed to St Croix, Wisconsin, and took charge of the engineering work for Stone & Webster and had charge of the construction. He then went to Ocean Park, California, and for two years acted as city engineer, after which he built the pumping plant of Redondo Beach, California. He was appointed city engineer of Richmond in 1910, which position he now holds, and he is widely recognized as one of the foremost engineers of the coast. Politically, he is a Democrat. Fraternally, he is affiliated with the Masonic lodge, being a Royal Arch Mason and a member of the chapter. He is an associate member of the American Society of Civil Engineers. On January 23, 1906, Mr. Chapman was united in marriage to Miss Edith De Luna, a native of New York State.

EDWIN A. MAJORS, all his life a resident of Contra Costa County, is known as one of the community representatives and honored citizens, and today holds the important position of president in the First National Bank of Martinez. Mr. Majors was born in San Ramon, April 19, 1869, a son of David F. and Sarah (Dorman) Majors. His father was a native of Kentucky, and his mother of Ohio. His father was one of the prominent agriculturists in his locality, locating here in 1852, and was considered a man of broad and liberal mind. The parents of Mr. Majors have both passed away some years ago. Edwin A. Majors acquired his early schooling in the public schools of Contra Costa County, after which he attended the Oakland High School.

For a time he followed ranching on the home place, and later became identified with the mercantile interests in Concord. Here he continued for three years, and in 1907 was one of the organizers of the First National Bank of Martinez, and has acted as president of the bank since it started, and in this position his excellent business and executive ability has been called forth.

The fact that the bank has had a remarkable growth, the development of the institution is largely due to him. The bank has steadily prospered, being today one of the strong, safe and conservative institutions of Contra Costa County. Politically, Mr. Majors is affiliated with the Republican party. His father was supervisor at the time of his death, and Edwin A. was appointed to fill out the unexpired term. He was then elected and served some years. He was elected a member of the board of town trustees on April 10, 1916.

Mr. Majors was united in marriage to Miss Alice Brawand, also a native of Contra Costa County, and a daughter of one of the county's respected pioneer citizens. To this union was born a daughter, Margaret.

JOHN NICHOLL.—The death of John Nicholl occurred on July 28, 1914, and he was buried from his home, 1721 Fourth Avenue, Oakland. The many floral pieces and flowers sent as tributes of love and respect by individuals and societies served as a slight indication of the place he held in the estimation of the people of the Bay counties, of the State, and of the United States.

His demise brought to a close a long, useful, and honorable life, the influence of which was felt as a factor in the pioneer development of Contra Costa County. He was numbered among the most representative men of California, and among the men who played an important part in the history of the State. Mr. Nicholl passed away at the age of ninety-two years, after a life of ceaseless activity, philanthropy, and enterprise. He was one of the few keen-minded men among the early pioneers who discerned the possibilities of the land. At the time when prospectors were digging for gold he was developing farms, building schools, and laying the foundation for a fortune. John Nicholl was born on November 19, 1822, in the north of Ireland, and was of Scotch ancestry. He emigrated to New York in 1849, and there married Agnes Booth (Hodge), a playmate of his childhood, who came to this country a year after her fiancé. The two started to California for a wedding trip across the Isthmus of Panama with a party of thirteen, when the railroad ran only halfway. The bride rode a mule and the groom walked. When they arrived in San Francisco Mr. Nicholl paid one dollar to cross the Bay to San Antonio, now Oakland. He went from there to San Leandro, where for a time he worked a grain ranch on shares. So successful was this venture that in four years he was able to extend his holdings and acquire two hundred acres of the San Pablo Rancho, now Richmond. At that period a stagecoach ran out to the rancho. Prophesying that a town would someday cover the territory, he purchased more land. Here he made his home and started the first school, hauling the lumber in his own wagons. He became the chief owner of San Pablo Rancho, which for thirty-five years was involved in litigation, and in 1900, when the title was cleared, he started the town of Point Richmond, now known as Richmond. Mr. Nicholl became a close friend of Claus Spreckels and together the two pioneers engaged in great and successful business enterprises. He extended his holdings over other parts of the State, securing a vast tract from a Spanish grant in Ventura County, and introduced the culture of lima beans, an industry which has grown to great agricultural importance in Ventura. Business was not the vital interest of Mr. Nicholl's life. He was devoted to his home, an ardent churchman, and a ceaseless worker in the cause of education. He desired the advancement of the community of civic enthusiasm and welfare. He was one of the founders of the First Presbyterian Church, erected in Oakland, and an elder in the branch church of San Pablo for forty years. He erected the first brick structure on Washington Street in Oakland. His charitable work was extensive, though never mentioned by himself, but many testified to his kindness and fine character. After the death of his wife, which occurred May 13, 1895, Mr. Nicholl made his home with his daughters in Oakland. There were nine in the family: Mrs. J. C. Weir, of Vacaville, John H. Nicholl, Miss Mary E. Nicholl, Miss Hester H. Nicholl, and Mrs. Lulu G. Wilson, of Oakland, Mrs. Agnes B. Clark, William B. Nicholl, of Ventura, Joseph L. Nicholl, of Richmond, and Mrs. Ruth A. Wells, of Ventura, deceased.

EDWARD J. BURG.—The name of Edward J. Burg has come to be regarded as synonymous with development and progress in Richmond, California.

Being a native of Sweden, where he was born on January 12, 1868, he acquired the foundation of his early education in the public schools of that country. At the age of twelve he came to America, locating in Illinois, where he resided for a year. In 1881 he moved to San Francisco, remaining there a short time and later located in Contra Costa County, where he secured employment on a farm and continued his studies in the public schools. He attended the California Military Academy in Oakland, graduating with the class of '87. Mr. Burg later identified himself with the newspapers on the Pacific Coast in various capacities. He traveled extensively, and was in Chile, South America, during the revolution between President Balmaceda and the navy. For a considerable time he resided in Central America. In 1899 he went to Seattle, joining in the gold rush to Alaska in that year. In 1900 he moved to Berkeley, California. In 1901 the Burg brothers (Edward J. and Carl H., who came to California in 1888) began operations in Richmond. Five years later the Bay Cities Land Company was organized and incorporated in 1912, the firm of Burg Brothers being incorporated in 1910. Throughout the various stages of the growth and development of the company the energy and broad business policies of Edward J. Burg are apparent. It was due largely to his untiring efforts that the pastures of Richmond were converted into city lots, covered with homes and business structures, which increased in value to such a remarkable degree in the short space of fifteen years. To give some idea of the success attending his efforts it is only necessary to state that the real-estate corporations, of which he is the secretary and manager, are the third largest taxpayers in the city of Richmond, paying more in taxes than the Santa Fe Railroad Company or the Pullman Palace Car Company. In addition, Mr. Burg is largely interested in the Bay Cities Land Company and Burg Brothers Lumber & Building Company. He is one of America's typical self-made men, having planned and successfully developed the many enterprises with which he has been identified entirely through his own efforts and resource. The firm of Burg Brothers presented to the city of Richmond thirty-four city lots located in the Nicholl Macdonald Avenue Civic Center tract, valued at seventy-five thousand dollars. This property, consisting of two half blocks and a sum of twenty-five thousand dollars in cash, was accepted by the citizens of Richmond at a special election held October 15, 1915, for the purpose of selecting and locating a permanent civic center. The Richmond city hall, now completed, is the first building to grace the Civic Center, while other municipal buildings will soon follow as they are required. This splendid property and munificent gift by the Burg Brothers to the city of Richmond will remain a lasting monument to their enterprise and generous public-spiritedness. On November 30, 1893, Edward J. Burg was united in marriage to Miss Beatrice M. Ramus, of San Diego, California. Of this union have been born nine children, five sons and four daughters. Mr. Burg is prominent in fraternal circles, being a member in high standing of the Masonic Lodge, a Knight Templar and Shriner. He is also a member of the Woodmen of the World and the Benevolent and Protective Order of Elks. He is one of the founders of the Richmond Industrial Commission and is affiliated with a number of other civic organizations.

CARL HENRY BURG was born in Sweden, January 19, 1866, and to him belongs the title of "self-made man." He is the son of John August and Augusta Burg, and was left an orphan at the age of fourteen, his mother having passed away in 1873 and his father in 1880. His early education was secured in the public schools of his native land. Starting out in life without experience or resources, he has through his own energy risen to be one of the leading real-estate men of the Bay counties and is classed among the "pioneer builders" of Richmond. Emigrating to America in 1881, he located in Kansas, where he remained for a period of nine years, during the first two of which he engaged in farming and later in business along mercantile lines.

In 1888 he moved to San Francisco, where he accepted a position as clerk in a dry-goods house, which he held for three years, at the same time continuing his studies at a business college. In 1892, going to Central America, he turned his attention to the development of a coffee plantation, securing nearly five hundred acres of land for this purpose. Disposing of his holdings he returned to the United States, settling in San Francisco, where he became actively engaged in the real-estate business. He was identified with the first subdivision in Richmond during its early days and has since continued to be one of the leading operators in this section. The firm of Burg Brothers, consisting of Carl H. and Edward J. Burg, is among the largest and most important around the bay section, Burg Brothers having the distinction of being the largest real-estate operators in Richmond. In May, 1910, they placed upon the market the Central Richmond and Pullman Town Site tracts, and by January, 1911, 1150 lots had been sold. The following March the Spaulding Richmond Pullman Town-site was placed upon the market, and by March 1, 1912, contracts for the sale of 1475 lots (practically the entire tract) had been issued, being the highest real-estate record ever made in Richmond. In 1912 they also developed and sold the Grand View Terrace tract, and in November of the same year purchased and put on the market the Nicholl Macdonald Avenue Civic Center tract, consisting of one hundred and ten acres, paying $725,000 for this property or nearly seven thousand dollars an acre. This is the highest price ever paid in the United States for a piece of undeveloped property of its size for subdivision purposes. Burg Brothers sold one fifty-foot corner in this tract for fifteen thousand dollars; fifteen years previously this land was offered for sale at seventy dollars per acre, while the fifty-foot corner is now valued at $23,000. Mr. Burg was among those who first recognized Richmond's wonderful opportunities, and, taking advantage of the same, made rapid progress in a business way, and his enterprising spirit brought him into important relations. He was one of the charter members of the Richmond Industrial Commission and is a member of the Richmond Chamber of Commerce. He was twice married, the first marriage being to Emily Brugge, and there was born of this union one daughter, Thelma A. Burg, April 4, 1900. The second marriage was to Mrs. Clara B. Gardner, July 14, 1913. Fraternally, Mr. Burg is a Mason, being a Knight Templar of California Commandery No. I and a Shriner. He is a member of the Woodmen of the World and the National Union. He is also a member of the Union League and Masonic clubs of San Francisco.

BERNARD SCHAPIRO.—This history presents the record of no other citizen more thoroughly infused with the spirit of public progress than the subject of this review, Bernard Schapiro, and Contra Costa County numbers him among its representative citizens. Mr. Schapiro's life record may well serve to inspire and encourage others, showing what may be accomplished when determination and energy lead the way. Starting out in life with no capital, he has gradually advanced until now he is numbered among the largest real-estate operators in the Bay counties. Mr. Schapiro was born in Prussia, January 11, 1865, and is a son of Elias and Hannah Schapiro. He attended the public schools of his native land, and at the age of twenty-one he crossed the Atlantic to the New World, settling first at Philadelphia, where he found employment in a clock factory. He became identified with other pursuits and traveled throughout the Eastern States, after which he decided to cast his lot with the Golden West, and in 1892 he settled in San Francisco.

For a time he was engaged in running an optical store, and in 1901 he worked for McEwen Brothers' real-estate firm, as salesman for one year. Mr. Schapiro then embarked in the real-estate business for himself, and one of his first ventures along this line was to act as selling agent for some of the officials of the Standard Oil Company in selling a tract of land they had placed on the market. He was one of the first operators in Richmond, and since 1901 Mr. Schapiro has subdivided and sold over two thousand acres in and around Richmond; besides this he has subdivided five thousand acres in the Sacramento Valley and five thousand in the San Joaquin Valley. These different colonies are in a very prosperous condition. He is connected fraternally with the Elks and the Knights of Pythias. Politically, Mr. Schapiro has always been a Republican. He was nominated from the fifth district of San Francisco as alternate to the Republican national convention held at Chicago in June, 1916. Mr. Schapiro was united in marriage November 3, 1895, to Miss Birdie Stern, a native of New York State. To this union have been born— Esmond, born October 19, 1896; Zara, born May 25, 1900; Dorothea, born October 4, 1905. All three children were born in San Francisco, California. Mr. Schapiro is identified as a stockholder in the bank at Pinole, the First National Bank of Richmond, the Merchants Bank of Richmond, and the California Trust Company of San Francisco. He is a life member of the Press Club of San Francisco, and holds membership in the Commonwealth Club of San Francisco, and is a charter member of the Pioneer Club of Richmond, California. Mr. Schapiro deserves great credit for what he has accomplished in life, for he started out in the business world a poor boy, and by his energy, enterprise, and ambition has steadily worked his way upward to success.

Mr. Schapiro is a resident of San Francisco and maintains spacious offices in the Phelan Building. He has proved himself trustworthy and faithful in business, progressive in citizenship, and loyal to the claims of friendship, and he has thus commanded and kept the esteem and high regard of all who are associated with him.

JOSEPH FRANKLIN BROOKS, a highly respected and representative citizen of Richmond, ably discharges the duties devolving upon him in the capacity of assistant superintendent of the Standard Oil Company of California. Mr. Brooks was born at New Bedford, Mass., March 18, 1872. He acquired his education in the public schools of Oakland, where his parents removed when he was ten years of age. He graduated from the high school, after which he became identified with the Arctic Oil Works of San Francisco. He continued with this corporation for ten years, as assistant superintendent, and when it was taken over by the Standard Oil Company he removed to Richmond. This was in 1902. Mr. Brooks has filled many positions of responsibility and trust with his company. That he was capable and reliable is indicated by his rapid promotion, until he now holds the office of assistant superintendent. Politically, he is affiliated with the Republican party. He is a member of the board of trustees of the Richmond Public Library, member of the board of education, and an ex-member of the board of health. Fraternally, he is a member of the B. P. O. E., and a valued member of the Woodmen of the World. He is the president and one of the organizers of the Pioneer Club. Mr. Brooks was united in marriage July 14, 1897, to Miss Catherine S. Hambright. Their one son, Franklin, was born March 14, 1900. Mr. Brooks is a stockholder in the First National Bank of Richmond, and a stockholder in the B. Schapiro Real Estate Company. He is also one of the organizers of the Richmond Building & Loan Association. The parents of

Mr. Brooks were Joseph Franklin and Elizabeth (Baxter) Brooks. His father was a sea-captain and followed this vocation for many years. He died and was buried in Alaska. Both parents were natives of Massachusetts and come from French ancestry. The subject of this sketch is a man of broad culture, progressive, has high ideals, and is well and favorably known in the business and social life of the Bay cities.

ERNEST NAVELLIER, a man of genial personality and keen business ability, is numbered among the representative and enterprising business men of Contra Costa County. His birth occurred February 1, 1864, and he is a native of France. He acquired his education in the schools of his native land, graduating at the age of fifteen. His first work after completing his education, at the age of sixteen, was to teach school. He continued teaching for two years, when he came to America, and located in San Francisco. Here he engaged in the laundry business, in which he continued for ten years. Later he removed to Seattle, where he became identified with the laundry business for three years. In 1892 he removed to Stege, where he operated the first laundry established in Richmond. About this time Mr. Navellier purchased five acres on the hillside near Stege, where he erected an imposing home. He disposed of his interests in the laundry and became identified with the California Cap Company for nine years, in the capacity of shipping clerk and foreman. He purchased land on San Pablo Avenue, and was the founder of Lafayette Park, which is considered one of the finest picnic grounds on the bay. He has contributed in no small degree to the growth and success of Richmond as a manufacturing center. His most recent success has been in the establishing of a factory for the manufacture of rustic furniture and art ware, which products have been sold in large lots all over the United States. Politically, Mr. Navellier is affiliated with the Republican party, but has never aspired to public office further than to act on the local school board for three years, and on the sanitary commission. He has been instrumental in establishing two schools in the Stege district. Fraternally, he is a member of the Eagles lodge and Foresters of America. On December 28, 1889, he was united in marriage to Josephine Pontacq, a native of France. To this union have been born five children—Victor, at present shipping clerk for the California Cap Company; Lucy, now postmistress at Stege; Louis and Ida, residing at home; and Mary, who died at the age of six years.

EDWARD C. HOFFMAN holds the important position of superintendent of the Metropolitan Match Factory, at Stege, Contra Costa County. A spirit of enterprise and progress has actuated him in all that he has done through life, and success has attended his well-directed efforts. Mr. Hoffman was born at Badelster, kingdom of Saxony, Germany, on February 5, 1865. Here he received his early education, and in 1888 he came to America, locating in San Francisco. He was employed as a machinist at the Union Iron Works and had the distinction of working on the battle-ship "Charleston," in 1889, remaining here for two years. He then became identified with the Metropolitan Match Company, San Francisco, in 1891, where he has since remained.

Mr. Hoffman has, owing to his executive ability, been promoted until now he holds the position as superintendent of the Stege-factory. He is a member of the high-school trustees and has served on the Stege board of education. He is a member of Hermann's Sons. On April 25, 1891, Mr. Hoffman was united in marriage to Miss Emilie Wacker, a native of Germany.

To this union have been born three children—Alma Emilie, wife of Roy Dubbers, an engineer in the employ of the United Railroads of San Francisco; Edward Adolph, a student at the University of California; Walter, a student attending high school. The family are members of the Presbyterian church of Stege.

JOSEPH T. BRENEMAN, M. D.—The history of Contra Costa County would be incomplete and unsatisfactory were there failure to make prominent reference to Doctor Joseph T. Breneman, who has been actively engaged in practice as a physician and surgeon in Contra Costa County since the early '90s, and he is an able and representative member of the medical profession. Doctor Breneman was born in Hancock County, Ohio, January 23, 1849. He acquired his education in the public schools, the academy at New Middletown, Ohio, and the University of Iowa, graduating from the medical department in 1879. He began practice in Audubon, Iowa, where he remained for some years. Removing to Wellington, Kansas, he practiced until 1890, when he removed to California, located in Oakland, and practiced two years. He then went to Walnut Creek, where he acted as county health officer. He then took up his profession in Martinez, where he remained for fifteen years. While a resident of the county seat he acted as surgeon for the Mountain Copper Company for five years. He owned and operated a private hospital in Martinez. The Doctor has always enjoyed a large practice, which is proof of his skill and ability in the line of his chosen vocation. In 1911 he removed to Stege, where he has since resided. Doctor Breneman was one of the founders of the County Medical Society and acted as its first president.

For years he was identified with the California State and American medical associations. He has filled all chairs in the I. O. O. F. Politically, he is a Democrat. On May 14. 1883, he was united in marriage to Miss Fannie I. Humphry. To this union have been born Fay, a teacher in the Fairmont School at Stege, and a graduate of the Lowell High School and the University of California; Hazel, a graduate of the Alhambra High School at Martinez and the State Normal school at San Jose, at present a teacher in the Stege public school; George, a graduate of the Martinez High School, at present in business in Martinez; Eullaia, wife of W. M. Staley, residing in Oregon; Flint and Frances, residing at home. Joseph Clayton, son of John R. Breneman, now deceased, also made his home with the Doctor. Doctor Breneman was reared on a farm, and his record is that of a self-made man.

He has won distinction as an inventor, and patented the first hay elevator, under United States Patent No. 6,100,044. He has also invented many surgical instruments, and has a patent pending for a combined harvester.

JULES TOUSSAINT, one of the men of Contra Costa County who may be termed progressive, is the subject of this sketch. He is regarded reliable and foresighted, and he is a self-made man. He was born in Belgium, August 8, 1874. He received some schooling in his native land, and at the age of ten years he came with his parents to America and located in Texas. His father was a farmer, and after attending school for a time in Texas, Jules assisted on the farm for a period of three years. His parents removed to San Francisco, and Jules, determined to gain a better education, attended the San Francisco schools. He then learned the painting trade and followed this vocation for a period of six years, after which he became engaged in a candy factory, where he remained for ten years. After the big fire he became associated with the Ramona Candy Company, of West Berkeley, where he remained for two years. His ambition and enterprise led him to Stege Junction, where he engaged in the grocery business, where he has since resided and carried on a profitable business. Politically, Mr. Toussaint is a Republican. Fraternally, he is affiliated with the Eagles lodge of Richmond. He was united in marriage on October 15, 1899, to Miss Juliet Alphonse, a native of Oregon. Three children have blessed this union—Jules, born July 21, 1900: Lucile, born September, 1902; Ruth, born March 6, 1910. Mrs. Toussaint has shown a great deal of business progressiveness, and much of her husband's business success has been due to her energy.

SIMON DEASEY, creditably filling the position as manager of the Pacific Porcelain Ware Company at Richmond, was born in Trenton, New Jersey, on November 26, 1864. Following the completion of a public-school education, he entered the pottery business in his native town, and has been connected with that kind of work since he was seventeen years of age. Mr. Deasey devotes all of his time and attention to the conduct of this concern, and, thoroughly understanding the business principles and detail, has met with gratifying success in his new field at Richmond. He was identified with the largest concerns in Trenton until he came to California, with the exception of eighteen months that he resided in Canada. In April, 1911, he took charge of the Pacific Porcelain Ware Company's plant, and has since filled this important position with gratifying success. Mr. Deasey is a member of the Moose lodge of Richmond. He was united in marriage to Miss Clarinda Bailey, a native of Staffordshire, England, October 14, 1885. To this union one son, Harold, was born in Trenton, New Jersey, on April 15, 1891. Mr. Deasey holds office in and is a director of the Building & Loan Association of Richmond.

ARCHIBALD H. CAMPBELL, a highly respected and representative citizen of Contra Costa County, ably discharges the duties devolving upon him in the capacity of superintendent of the California Cap Company, at Stege.

His birth occurred in Oakland, California, on November 20, 1882. He acquired his education in the Oakland public schools, after which he attended the California School of Mechanical Arts, graduating from the chemical department. He became identified with the sugar factory at Oxnard for a time, and later removed to Stege, where he became associated with the present concern, which he is representing as superintendent and chemist. His next promotion was to take charge of the plant as superintendent. In this connection he has proven a valuable and efficient representative of the corporation. On July 7, 1906, Mr. Campbell was joined in wedlock to Miss Mae Watrous, daughter of C. L. and Betsy Watrous. To this union have been born two children—Archibald H., Jr., born August 11, 1907, and Cheryl Beth, born August 15, 1911. Fraternally, Mr. Campbell is identified with the Masons, being connected with the organization as a member of McKinley lodge of Richmond and the Royal Arch degrees. He also belongs to the Eastern Star and is active in the ranks of the B. P. O. E. Politically, he is a member of the Republican party.

FRED HARTWICK, a successful and enterprising citizen of Richmond, acts as manager for the Enterprise Brewing Company. His birth occurred in San Francisco on January 16, 1885. He was educated in the public schools, and at an early age he became identified with the Enterprise Brewing Company, in the shipping department. Mr. Hartwick is a man of many sterling traits of character, reliable in business and progressive in citizenship. His company transferred him to Richmond on February 19, 1912, where he was placed in charge, and he still assumes the management of the Richmond business. Mr. Hartwick is a member of the Masons, Elks, Eagles, and the Hermann's Sons. He was united in marriage to Miss Bertha Seibert, of San Francisco, and their one son, Frederick, was born in San Francisco, March 26, 1912. Mr. and Mrs. Hartwick have gained the good-will and esteem of all who have been in any way associated with them, either in a business or social way.

JOHN KOCH.—One of the men who have acquired success and is numbered among the representative men of Stege is John Koch. He was born in southern Germany, on December 25, 1862. He acquired his education in his native land and served two years in the army. He had a desire to see the New World, and came to America via Honolulu, locating in San Francisco.

He went to work for the Stauffer Chemical Company and the Judson Dynamite & Powder Company, where he remained for seven years. He then became identified with the Pacific Guano & Fertilizer Company and owing to his ability has been promoted from foreman to superintendent of the plant at Richmond. He is a member of Hermann's Sons. On September 12, 1885, he was united in marriage to Anna Erdel, a native of Germany. To this union have been born six children—Adam, Lena, Anna, Emma, William, and George. Mr. Koch is interested in a company that owns about five thousand acres of land in Siskiyou County. At a future date they contemplate putting down wells and engaging in the stock business.

JOHN M. BEST.—Numbered among the successful and enterprising business men of Richmond is John M. Best, now the manager, secretary, and treasurer of the Home Laundry Company. His laundry experience extends over many years. The institution with which he is associated is one of the best in the Bay cities. Mr. Best was born on January 22, 1874, in Shasta County, California, where he acquired his early education. He is the son of John C. Best, a native of Missouri, who came west and located in Carson City, Nevada. Here he operated a store and hotel for many years during the pioneer days. He then removed to Shasta County. The subject of this sketch removed to Seattle, where he engaged in the laundry business, and continued in that calling for eighteen years. Here he mastered the laundry business in principle and detail, and his knowledge, combined with the spirit of enterprise which actuates him in all that he does, has brought him success. Mr. Best came to Richmond in August, 1911, and immediately started the Home Laundry Company, and was one of the prime movers in this organization.

Politically, Mr. Best is affiliated with the Republican party, but has never aspired to office. Fraternally, he is a member of the B. P. O. E. and the Woodmen of the World. He was united in marriage to Miss Ethel A. Nellie, of Seattle, Washington, October 16, 1897. To this union have been born Myrtle, Mildred, Jack, and Roy.

JAMES DEMINGS, who enjoys recognition as one of the leading and enterprising business men of Richmond, has won merited success as one of the proprietors of the Richmond Feed & Grain Company, the largest concern of its kind in Contra Costa County. His birth occurred in San Francisco, January 15, 1874. He was the son of Peter and Barbara (Melville) Demings. His father was of English descent and his mother came from Scotland. Mr. Demings' father came to America and settled in San Francisco in 1865 and controlled a line of boats around the Bay district. The subject of this sketch acquired his education in the public and high schools of San Francisco, after which he took a business course. Following his schooling he became associated with Eppinger & Company, where he learned the milling business, continuing with this firm for a period of fourteen years at Crockett, California. In June, 1911, Mr. Demings, with George Prytz, erected the present commodious and up-to-date flouring and feed mill at Richmond, which has a capacity of one hundred tons a day. The warehouse, which is located directly aside of the Santa Fe tracks, gives them the best of transportation facilities. Here they conduct a wholesale and retail business. Mr. Demings is affiliated with the B. P. O. E., of Richmond, and is a member of the Native Sons, of Crockett. He was united in marriage on November 17, 1896, to Miss Mary Hunter, of Crockett, a Native Daughter. To this union have been born two children, James, born in 1898, and Richard, born in 1900.

EDWARD E. GROW.—Occupying a position of distinction among the representative men of Contra Costa County is Edward E. Grow. He has been a resident of Richmond since 1907 and followed surveying as a vocation. During the long period of his residence here he has taken an active interest in all community affairs. Mr. Grow was born in Iowa, on December 18, 1871. He acquired his education in the public schools. At an early age he removed with his parents to California. Here he continued his higher studies by attending Stanford University, graduating from the English department in 1898. In 1900 he removed to Pinole, and in 1907 took up his residence in Richmond, where he has since remained. Politically, Mr. Grow is affiliated with the Republican party. While a resident of Pinole he served on the local school board of Pinole and Hercules, as president of the board. Mr. Grow is a Spanish War veteran. He was a member of the First California Infantry, and was sent to the Philippines, where he served his country in a creditable manner. He received an honorable discharge in Manila in September, 1899.

On April 8, 1901, he was united in marriage to Miss Caroline E. Zehringer, of Philadelphia. To this union have been born two children—Blanch Anna, born in 1902, and Edward E., born in 1007. Mr. Grow had charge of all construction work for the Du Pont Powder Company while a resident of Pinole. He is active in politics at the proper time, but concentrates his attention upon his chosen profession, of which he is today a leader in this field.

PAUL GLASER, deceased, was one of the men who was prominently known as a building contractor in Richmond. He was successfully engaged in business in this city since 1903. He was a native of Indiana, and was born on July 4, 1874, and died February 12, 1915. He was the son of George and Mary F. (Coon) Glaser, both natives of Germany, who came to America in 1865, and settled in Indiana. Mr. Glaser's father is still a resident of his chosen State, while the mother died in 1896. There were nine children born in the parents' family, six of whom are still living. The subject of this sketch was reared on a farm and received his education in the public schools of Indiana.

He came to California in April, 1898 and started to learn the carpenter's trade in Crockett. Remaining here some time, he finally removed to Richmond in 1003, and at once started contracting and erected many of the finest homes and business places in the town. He met with gratifying success as a general contractor. That his ability was widely recognized is attested by the fact that many important contracts have been awarded him. Among some of the most substantial buildings he has erected are the Nystrom School and No. 2 Fire Department Building. Mr. Glaser was a

Republican. On October 28, 1895, he was united in marriage to Miss Celina Leloy, a native of Sacramento. Their son, George Leloy, was born February 19, 1910.

JOHN BALRA, one of the representative ranchers and respected citizens of Contra Costa County, resides near Rust. His birth occurred on March 23, 1869, and he is a native of Portugal. Mr. Balra acquired his education in the old country. At the age of seventeen he left his native land and came to America. He came to Contra Costa County, where he found employment at ranching, which he followed seven years. He then rented a place and started a dairy in Alameda County. Later he took on more land and continued to operate the dairy and two ranches for eight years. Mr. Balra came to this country thoroughly qualified by training and understood his work. His father, Joseph Balra, was a farmer and stockman in the old country. After continuing successfully for eight years in his business, Mr. Balra bought twenty-five acres in the Stege district. Later he acquired more land, until he now has fifty-two acres of the choicest dairy land in Contra Costa County, adjoining the city of Berkeley. In connection with the operation of his own ranches, he rents two ranches on San Pablo Creek and one in the Moraga Valley. Besides the dairy business he carries on general farming. In politics Mr. Balra is Republican, but he has never aspired to office. He is recognized as one of the foremost men in the community. As a stockman, he has reached a creditable place in the business world. He is a stockholder in the Jersey Milk & Butter Company of Oakland, in the West Berkeley Bank, in the Portuguese & American Bank, and holds stock in various other concerns. Fraternally, he is a member of the B. P. O. E. and the Eagle Lodge of Berkeley. He is also a member of the Druids, U. P. E. C., and I. D. E. S. He has made a success in business circles that places him in the front rank of progressive and able business men.

JAMES F. ARMO.—One of the popular citizens of Stege who has merited success along his chosen field is James F. Armo, superintendent of the plant of Wheeler, Reynolds & Stauffer. He was born in New York City on February 1, 1876. He received his education in the public schools of New York. He laid aside his books and joined the gold-seekers who went to Alaska, where he remained three years. At the age of twenty-four he located in San Francisco, where he was employed in bridge-construction work. In 1903 he removed to Contra Costa County and became identified with the Stauffer Chemical Company, and later took the position as superintendent of the Wheeler, Reynolds & Stauffer plant. Mr. Armo is broad-minded, liberal in thought, and honorable in purpose. He has attained success and gained results to the company with which he has identified himself. In politics Mr. Armo is a Republican. On May 4, 1903, he was united in happy wedlock to Miss Mae E. Park, a Native Daughter. Three children have blessed this union: James F., Jr., Charles S., and Mary Elizabeth. Mr. and Mrs. Armo have a host of friends and are held in the highest esteem by all who know them.

HARRY FREMONT SPENCER is one of the public-spirited and progressive business men of Contra Costa County, his activities extending to many fields. He was born in York County, Maine, on June 13, 1856. He was educated in New Hampshire, where his parents removed when he was young.

His father, William M. Spencer, was a native of New Hampshire, born in the White Mountains, and died at Salmon Falls in 1861. He was largely identified with the manufacturing interests of his native State. Mr. Spencer's mother was also a native of New Hampshire and died in 1908. The subject of this sketch, after receiving his education, entered the cotton mills at Lawrence, Massachusetts, with which he was identified until he came to California, in 1877. Locating at Bryant Station in Contra Costa County, he took up ranching, and became connected with Major Bryant, of San Francisco, remaining here for one year. He then removed to Livermore, California, where he was united in marriage to Miss May Smith, on November 29, 1883. To this union the children are Raymond, born December 7, 1887, and Guy Fremont, born April 7, 1806. Mrs. Spencer's father was one of the representative men of Alameda County and took a great interest in everything that was for the betterment of the country. He was active in moving the county seat to San Leandro, and later to Oakland. Mr. Spencer resided in Pacheco for a period of six years and was identified with the California & Hawaiian Sugar Refining Company as superintendent. In 1910 he removed to Walnut Creek, and in 1911 he started a lumber-yard and erected warehouses for hay and grain.

Later S. L. Ayer became associated with him. In March, 1915, he took over the interests of Mr. Ayer, and the firm's name now is Spencer & Ayer, Inc.

Mr. Spencer was elected president of the Business Men's Association of Walnut Creek in May, 1913, and re-elected in May, 1914, and when the town was incorporated, on May 18, 1914, he was elected mayor for a four-year term.

Mr. Spencer only follows the fairest methods. He has discharged all obligations laid upon him by the people of his locality and has fulfilled expectations which the people had in him when they entrusted their interests to his care. Mr. Spencer is affiliated with the Masonic fraternity, being a member and a past master of Alamo Lodge No. 122. He is a past worthy patron of Alamo Chapter, order of Eastern Star. His son Raymond is a thirty-second-degree Mason, and a graduate of Cornell University, and has been identified with the Government as superintendent of the Government building at Santa Barbara, California.

CHARLES B. DESMOND has shown himself able and faithful in the discharge of his duties with the Standard Oil Company of Richmond and has won the confidence and esteem of his employers and fellow-men. Mr. Desmond was born on March 27, 1868, in Syracuse, New York, where he was reared and educated in the public schools of that city. Laying aside his books, he started out in life and, like many young men, followed various occupations. He has been largely identified with the live-stock business throughout the East. He became associated with the Standard Oil Company at Whiting, Indiana, where he had charge of the company's horses. In 1901 he was transferred to the Richmond plant, where he has since resided. Mr. Desmond has charge of the road construction on the Standard's vast grounds, and personally has charge of all the teams. He has made many friends in Richmond and takes an active interest in the Knights of Pythias lodge, of which he is a member in Richmond.

FRANK A. MARSHALL, residing in Walnut Creek, and filling the position of assistant cashier of the San Ramon Bank, was born April 13, 1892. He is the son of Joseph D. and Rosie (Duarte) Marshall. His father is a native of Portugal, while his mother is a native of California. The subject of this review received his education in the public schools of Contra Costa County, and the business college of Oakland, graduating with high honors from the latter in 1907. After completing his education he entered the grocery store of J. L. Silveria & Co., where he was identified as clerk for a period of three years.

He then took up his course of studies in the business college, after which he entered a branch bank of the San Ramon Bank, of Walnut Creek, in 1907, as bookkeeper. This position of trust he held to the satisfaction of the bank. He was then transferred to the main bank at Walnut Creek for a period of six months as assistant, when he was again returned to the branch bank and promoted to assistant cashier and manager. By this time Mr. Marshall had mastered the details of banking. His knowledge, combined with the spirit of enterprise which actuates him in all that he does, has brought him a great degree of success and a high place in the business circles of his locality. Mr. Marshall only remained here for a time and was given the position as assistant cashier in the Walnut Creek Bank. Fraternally, he is a member of the I. D. E. S., and U. P. E. C, and the Independent Order of Foresters. He was united in marriage to Miss Leonora Fereira, a native of San Ramon, June 8, 1913. To this union has been born Ella Mae, March 30, 1914.

JOSEPH MUNDAY, a worthy native son, is among the younger men prominent in the welfare and upbuilding of Richmond. He is deeply interested in all that pertains to the welfare of the city, and his support can ever be enlisted in any good cause. Mr. Munday was born in Oakland on December, 22, 1876. He is a son of Frank Munday, who has the distinction of making the first dynamite caps on the Pacific Coast and has been associated with the various powder companies in California for many years. He is now in his eighty-sixth year. The subject of this sketch was educated in the public schools of Berkeley. He associated himself with the Standard Oil Company and had charge of the barrel-filling department for five years. During this time he was active in various movements of interest to Richmond. He has served in the police department, and his ability has always been recognized.

Mr. Munday was united in marriage to Miss Katie Bennett, a native of Georgetown, El Dorado County, California. To this union have been born two children, Cly and Louis. Mr. Munday has served as foreman for the California & Hawaiian Sugar Refining Company and for the Spreckels Sugar Refinery. Both positions he has held with unfaltering energy and has given satisfaction. He is a member of the Native Sons.

HENRY F. ELLERHORST.—After an eventful period of close identification with mining interests in the various Western States and Alaska, Henry F. Ellerhorst came to Contra Costa County and located in Pinole, where he is now retired and living with his brother Christopher, one of the representative and highly respected citizens of his locality. Mr. Ellerhorst was born near Bremen, Germany, in 1838. Here he received his education, and in 1853 he came to this country and located in Charleston, South Carolina, where he engaged with his brother, who was in the mercantile business, and operated a grist mill, remaining three years. He then removed to San Francisco, where another brother resided, and operated a grocery store. He was employed until 1858, when he went to Washoe, Nevada, then the county seat of Washoe County, and where all the business was transacted for the Comstock mines. He worked in the mines in Virginia City and operated a store for four years. He then went to Montana and worked at mining until 1872, when he removed to San Francisco. Later he went to Alaska and did placer mining for two years. He sold out and returned to San Francisco for a time, and later went to Dakota and Idaho, where he remained for about forty-three years. In 1912 he came to Pinole. Politically, Mr. Ellerhorst is a Democrat.

EUGENE A. MARSHALL, prominently connected with the business interests of Richmond, has been a resident of California all his life. He was born at Vacaville on July 9, 1862. His father, Robert C. Marshall, was born in Ohio, and in 1852 came to California. His wife was Sarah McCartney, native of Indiana. The parents of Mr. Marshall came to the coast in the pioneer days, locating in Solano County, where the father followed the army of gold seekers, after which he took up ranching and later read law. He passed away in 1893, and his wife died in 1873. The subject of this sketch acquired his education in the public schools, after which he learned the painter's trade. This vocation he followed all his life. In 1002 he removed to Richmond, where he has since resided. During the long period of his residence in this city he has attained a wide reputation as a broad-minded, liberal, and public-spirited citizen, and his strict integrity has built up a lucrative business. In politics, Mr. Marshall is a Republican, but has never aspired to office. Fraternally, he is a member of the Modern Woodmen of the World and of the Royal Neighbors. He was united in marriage to Miss Mabel Mayfield, a native of Colusa, California, April 22, 1887. Their one son, Carroll, was born in Willows, California, February 5, 1891. Mr. and Mrs. Marshall are numbered among the highly esteemed citizens of Richmond.

ALFRED L. BOVO.—The success which marks the career of Alfred L. Bovo has been the result of his own unaided efforts, the concentration of his energies and ability in the one time that meant for him a competence for the future. He is well known in banking circles in eastern Contra Costa County and has been identified with the Bank of Byron since its organization, which was in May, 1911. Mr. Bovo was born in San Francisco, December 23, 1886, son of Gabriel and Marie (Silveria) Bovo. His father died in 1902. Alfred acquired his education in private schools and at St. Ignatius College, San Francisco, after which he studied abroad and took a course in the College of Languages and Commerce at Turin. He remained in the old country nearly three years, becoming an accomplished linguist, speaking no less than five different languages. Returning to San Francisco, he became identified with the Central Trust Company, now the Anglo-California Trust Company. He remained with this institution for over six years. Mr. Bovo started with this bank as messenger, and by his ability he rose to the position of receiving teller. He then associated himself with the Nevada County Bank, of Nevada City, California, where he remained as acting cashier for nearly three years and served as interpreter in the Superior Court of Nevada County. He removed to Tracy on April 1, 1911 and accepted a position as acting cashier of the Bank of Tracy for a brief time. When the new bank building at Byron was completed Mr. Bovo was made cashier of that institution, later becoming manager, and has filled this position to the satisfaction of all concerned. His political affiliations are with the Republican party, but he has never aspired to public office. He has served three years as a member and clerk of the Byron school board. On April 6, 1906, Mr. Bovo was united in marriage to Miss Grace L. Marron, a native of San Rafael, and a daughter of Frank M. Marron, one of the best-known and respected financial men of the Bay section. Mr. Marron's death occurred in 1914. Mr. and Mrs. Bovo have one daughter, Pauline, born in Berkeley, July 25, 1907. Mrs. Bovo is past president of Donner Parlor, Native Daughters, of Byron, while her husband is secretary and treasurer of the Byron Improvement Club. Mr. Bovo also organized the Byron Chamber of Commerce, which has its rooms in connection with the Byron bank. He is recognized as one of Byron's substantial, esteemed, and respected citizens.

HENRY JOHNSTON.—Energy, ability, and well-directed ambition, guided and controlled by sound judgment, have constituted the foundation upon which Henry Johnston of Giant has built his success. These qualities have brought him success. He was born in Brant County, Ontario, December 27, 1835. He came west and located in San Francisco in October, 1872. Here he remained for some time. In 1873 ne purchased from Treadwell & Co. two hundred and thirty-five acres of land in Contra Costa County. He was at this time a traveling man for various concerns on the coast. While holding his position he was far-sighted enough to buy this ranch and have something for a rainy day. Two railroads cut through Mr. Johnston's farm, so that he only has one hundred and eighty-five acres left. He was married in 1860 to Galetsa F. Page, a native of Canada. To this union nine children have been born, five of whom are now living. In politics Mr. Johnston is a Republican. He has acted as road-master for a number of years. He has rented his ranch and is now retired. Mr. Johnston is a public-spirited man and gives his support to any movement that will promote the best interests of Contra Costa County.

CHAUNCEY M. BREWER, serving in a creditable manner as manager for the Western States Gas & Electric Company, has demonstrated his ability in public service along this line. His record entitles him pre-eminently to the distinctive title of one of the "builders" of Richmond. Mr. Brewer was born at Marshall, Michigan, August 5, 1882. He received his education in the public schools of his native town, after which he attended the law department of the University of Michigan, at Ann Arbor. He then entered the employ of the Commonwealth Power Company, at Jackson, Michigan, where he remained one year. Removing to Grand Rapids, Michigan, he became associated with the Grand Rapids & Muskegon Power Company. Later he occupied a better position with the H. M. Byllesby Company, of Chicago, and was sent to Muskogee, Oklahoma, where he assumed the business management of his company. Recognizing Mr. Brewer's substantial qualities, his company then transferred him to Minnesota, where he had the business management, and later he was again transferred to Everett, Washington, and Sandpoint, Idaho, where he filled positions of importance. In 1912 Mr. Brewer removed to Richmond. Fraternally, he is identified with the B. P. O. E. lodge, and in politics he is a Republican, and stands at all times for advancement in every relation of life and is a man well liked and esteemed.

FREDERICK E. BECK, prominently connected with the Pullman works at Richmond as general manager, was born in Wilmington, Delaware, May 29, 1875. He acquired his education in the public schools. Completing his studies, he entered the employ of the Pullman Company at Wilmington as office boy.

He later entered the mechanical department, and was soon transferred to Chicago, where he was identified as mechanical inspector. He was transferred to Wilmington again as assistant manager of mill-shops for one year, when he was again sent by his company to Denver in 1902, where he filled the position of assistant manager for five months and was there made manager of the Denver shops in 1903. Mr. Beck remained in Denver until 1910, when he was transferred to Richmond, where he took the management of the Pullman plant. He has achieved remarkable success in the various positions he has taken with his company. He is well known in Masonic circles, being a member of the blue lodge, Shrine, and is a Knight Templar. He was united in marriage to Miss Elizabeth H. Day, a native of Pennsylvania, in September, 1903.

MICHAEL J. CURTAIN.—One of the most prominent, able, and representative agriculturists in Contra Costa County is Michael J. Curtain. He was born on July 1, 1866, in Ireland, where he received his schooling. In June, 1887, he came to America, and in October, 1904, located in Contra Costa County. Here he turned his attention to the dairy business and has always followed this occupation. He is an expert stockman, and during his early days in the county he had as high as two hundred head of cattle. On August 1, 1914, he disposed of his dairy interests and retired. Mr. Curtain has gained the friendly regard and good-will of all with whom he has been associated through life, either in business or social relations, and he is well entitled to a foremost place among the respected men of the county. Politically, he is a Democrat. In 1906 Mr. Curtain was united in marriage to Elizabeth Elkson.

JAMES T. NARBETT.—Among the men whose enterprise and ability have been active factors in promoting the remarkable growth and prosperity of the city of Richmond is numbered James T. Narbett. He is a native of that far-off country, India, he being born aboard a ship at Rangoon, British Burma, August 31, 1874. He is the son of William and Eleanor Narbett. At the age of two years he was brought to America, his parents locating in Washington. His father conducted a summer resort at Fort Canby, remaining there for some time. He later removed to San Francisco, and then to Oakland, where he followed contracting. In 1879 the parents went to Benicia. In 1880 they removed to near Crockett, this being the year before the laying out of the town. Here in the public schools James T. Narbett received his preliminary education, afterward attending the Vander Naillen School of Engineering. In 1896 Mr. Narbett took up contracting. In 1898 he spent one year in Alaska. Returning to Crockett, he entered school again, and graduated in 1900. In 1904 he removed to Chico, Butte County, and was awarded the contract for the addition to the State Normal School. He erected the Colonial Hotel at Biggs, and the Shotover Inn at Hamilton City, in Glenn County.

Mr. Narbett also had many large contracts in various parts of the State. On January 1, 1907, he discontinued contracting and took up special studies from eminent architects. He shortly passed the State examination, becoming a licensed architect. He designed the Masonic temple at Oroville and Chico and many other large buildings in Chico, Orland, Willows, Dunsmuir, Sacramento, and other parts of California. In 1910 he opened offices in Sacramento in connection with his Chico office. In 1911 he removed to Richmond, where he established offices in the La Selle Building, which was one of the first designed by Mr. Narbett after locating in this city. He designed the Elks' temple, which cost seventy thousand dollars, the new city hall, the fire houses, and many other handsome buildings in Richmond. In politics Mr. Narbett is a Progressive, and previous to 1913 he cast his lot with the Republican party. He is prominently identified with various fraternal and social organizations, being a member of Masonic blue lodge. Royal Arch chapter, Commandery. Aahmes Temple of the Mystic Shrine of Oakland, and the Eastern Star. He is a member of the B. P. O. E. of Richmond, I. O. O. F. of Crockett, and the Eagles' lodge of

Richmond. He was united in marriage to Miss Gussie McDowell, of Alturas, California, February 2, 1902. Their one son, Keith Oliver, was born November 5, 1905. Mrs. Narbett is a progressive member of the Richmond Improvement Club, Eastern Star, and at one time held the office of State Secretary of the Christian Endeavor Society.

RICHARD F. PAASCH, well known in Contra Costa County, who is now serving as captain of the Point Richmond fire department, was born in Germany on August 1, 1874. He acquired his education in Berkeley, where his parents settled on their arrival from their native land. Mr. Paasch's father, Theodore Paasch, is a tailor by trade, having learned his business in the old country, where he followed this vocation for many years. On his arrival in Berkeley he engaged in business and continued for some years before retiring from active life. He is now in his eighty-eighth year. Mr. Paasch's mother died in March, 1912. There were ten children in the parents' family. After finishing his schooling, Richard F. Paasch learned the blacksmithing trade, and continued in this line faithfully for fifteen years. He served in this capacity with the Standard Oil Company for some time, and on May 1, 1912, he was appointed by the city council as chief of the volunteer fire department.

He served in this capacity in a most able manner for eight years, and when the paid department was inaugurated he was appointed captain, which office he still holds. Politically, Mr. Paasch is a Republican. Fraternally, he is a charter member of the Knights of Pythias of Richmond, and a member of the military rank. He is also a member of the I. O. O. F. of Richmond. On September 5, 1900, he was united in marriage to Elizabeth Burcher, of Berkeley, a native daughter. To this union there have been three children—Walter T., born February 23, 1002; Richard Albert, born February 20, 1904; Robert W., born May 19, 1905. The family attend the Methodist church.

CHARLES G. BACON.—One of the commanding figures of the business life of Contra Costa County is Charles G. Bacon, who is at the head of the Richmond Abstract & Title Company. His career is one of distinct usefulness and a benefit to the community in which he lives. He has many important interests that under his leadership have grown and expanded. He was born at Columbia, Tuolumne County, California, March 25, 1868, son of Pyam Bartlett and Marion Helen (Bowne) Bacon. Mr. Bacon's father was a native of Ohio, and his mother was from Michigan. In 1853 they came to California and settled in Tuolumne County, where they always resided. The mother passed away in 1899. The father is living a retired life at the old homestead, one of the most influential and representative citizens of his locality. He has -always taken a keen interest in political matters, serving his county in the State Assembly, and for many years was postmaster in Columbia. He had the distinction of installing the first hydraulic mining machinery in that county. The subject of this review acquired his education in the public schools of his county. Laying aside his books, he became identified with ranching and the wood business, and this he followed for five years. For the past twenty years he has been engaged in searching records. In 1007 he removed to Martinez, where he opened an abstract office. Here he soon had an extensive business. In this connection he became familiar with conditions and the need of a similar business in Richmond, and in 1914 the Richmond Abstract & Title Company erected its present commodious brick building on Twenty-second Avenue, where he is now located. Mr. Bacon has displayed extraordinary executive ability and has succeeded in building up one of the most successful systems in the State for handling his work. In this connection the Richmond company has installed the only photographic plant in California. Careful of his own interests in Martinez, he has always considered those of others who are identified with him in the company. The Richmond Abstract & Title Company is composed of the leading real-estate men, bankers, and attorneys. Politically, Mr. Bacon is registered as a Republican, and has served four years as city trustee of Martinez. Fraternally, he is a member of the B. P. O. E. of Richmond and the I. O. O. F. of Sonora. On June 22, 1008, he was united in marriage to Miss Irene Hall, a daughter of Josiah and Sarah Hall, of Sonora, Tuolumne County. Her father was engaged in the mercantile business, and at one time owned many of the valuable mines in Tuolumne County. Mrs. Bacon is actively engaged in the club and social circles and is a member of the Women's Improvement Club of Martinez. She is also an active member of the Episcopal church.

CHARLES JOHNSON.—Prominent among the representative men of Richmond, and one whose ability is recognized as a contractor, is Charles Johnson. He is a native of Sweden and was born March 28, 1875. He received his education in his native land. Laying aside his books, he started to learn the carpenter's trade, which he followed for some time. He saw the possibilities of the New World, and came to this country in 1896, at the age of twenty-one, locating in Chicago. There for one year he followed his trade, and then removed to Cadillac, Michigan. Later he heard the call to the West, and went to Washington, locating in Spokane County, where for four years he was connected with the Great Northern Railroad in its car department. In March, 1902, he removed to Richmond, where he readily found employment with the Santa Fe Railroad, remaining with that company eight years. In the spring of 1911 he began contracting with gratifying success. Politically, Mr. Johnson is a Progressive. He was united in marriage to Miss Nanei C. Westman, a native of Michigan, December 2, 1903. Their one child, Axel Fairchild, was born September 18, 1907. Fraternally, Mr. Johnson is affiliated with the Independent Order of Odd Fellows, and his wife is an active member in the sister lodge, the Rebekahs. Mr. and Mrs. Johnson have made many friends in Richmond and are popular in lodge work.

INTHUS EMLEN MARSHALL, the present tax-collector and assessor of Richmond, is one of the well-known, popular, and representative men of this community. He was born in Guernsey County, Ohio, July 5, 1848. His father came to California in 1852, during the gold excitement, and settled in El Dorado County. Here he followed gold mining, and in 1855 the mother and her two children, Florence (now deceased) and our subject, made the trip across the continent. In 1858 the family located in Solano County, where the father became interested in agricultural pursuits until his death, which occurred in 1894, the mother having died in 1874. In 1880 the subject of this sketch removed to Contra Costa County and settled in Martinez, where he filled the office of deputy assessor in an efficient manner for eight years. In 1901 he moved to Richmond, where he became a prominent contractor, and in 1909 he was appointed tax-collector and assessor, which office he has since capably filled. Mr. Marshall was united in marriage in 1884 to Mary Bent, of Martinez. Fraternally, he is affiliated with the Masonic lodge, being a member of the blue lodge and chapter. He is also a member of the Red Men and the W. O. W. Mr. Marshall has proved himself eminently well qualified to fill the office which he holds. His record is above reproach, and the long period of his residence in the county has been fruitful and of great good to the community in which he resides.

HENRY L. PENRY has been actively and successfully identified with the business interests of Contra Costa County as a contractor, and he is today one of the leaders in his chosen field. Mr. Penry is a native son, and was born in Santa Barbara, November 15, 1872. He is a son of Henry Thomas Penry and Annie (Davis) Penry. His father was a native of Cleveland, Ohio, while his mother came from Pennsylvania. Mr. Penry's father was a brick contractor, and after Henry L. finished his education he took up this vocation under his father and thoroughly mastered the trade and has followed it all his life. From 1898 to 1901 Mr. Penry resided in Washington and British Columbia, where he followed his chosen trade. In 1903 he came to Richmond, and in 1004 he removed his family to this city, where he has since resided.

He is public-spirited and readily endorses any public measure for the betterment of Richmond and public generally. Politically, Mr. Penry is a Republican. He was elected city councilman in May, 1911 and is serving his fourth year in this capacity. Fraternally, he is a Mason and a member of McKinley lodge. He is also a member of the Modern Woodmen. He was united in marriage to Miss Emily A. Blanchard, of Madera County, California, in December, 1901. To this union there have been five children—Harry Roswell, born September 26, 1902; Erwin L., born April 8, 1904; Muriel Elizabeth, born November 13, 1905; Kathleen Avis, born May 12, 1909; Ruth Emily, born January 6, 1913. The family are members of the Christian church of Richmond.

OTTO A. POULSEN.—Among the men who by reason of their personal integrity, ability, and business enterprise have come to be regarded as representative citizens and leading business men of Contra Costa County is numbered Otto A. Poulsen, who has been engaged in Richmond since 1906, in the retail jewelry business. He was born in San Francisco on December 5, 1876.

son of Hans C. and Johanna Poulsen. His father, a cabinetmaker, came to America in 1868. He located in various places in the East and removed to California in the early '70s. He died in 1899. The mother still survives and makes her home with Otto A. There were six children in the parents' family.

The subject of this sketch acquired his education in the public schools. Laying aside his books, he took up the trade of jeweler and silversmith, at which he became very proficient. He followed his trade for seven years, and then enlisted in the First Battalion, California Heavy Artillery. He was attached to Battery A, and was sent to the Philippines, where he served sixteen months. He was discharged in San Francisco in September, 1899. Following his army career, he became identified with a wholesale and retail jewelry house in San Francisco, where he remained for seven years. In 1906 he removed to Richmond and established a retail jewelry store at 703 Macdonald Avenue, and in 1911 he removed to his present commodious store. Success has steadily attended his well-directed labors since that time, and his business has expanded yearly, the entire credit for its rapid growth being directly due to Mr. Poulsen's enterprise and progressive spirit. Fraternally, he is a member of the Masonic lodge of Richmond, the Royal Arch chapter, and Scottish Rite of Oakland.

He is also a member of the B. P. O. E., the Red Men, the Native Sons, the Moose, and is an active member of the Shellmound Rifle Club. In politics Mr. Poulsen is a Republican. In May, 1910, he was elected on the Richmond school board, taking office July 1, 1910, and serving until July 1, 1914. He was married to Miss Ottoline M. Williams, a native of San Leandro, July 14, 1907. To this union there have been four children—Alexander W., born May 17, 1908; Esther F., born March 14, 1910; Stanley A., born December 30, 1911; Clarence R., born June 28, 1914. Mrs. Poulsen is a member of the Ladies Auxiliary of the Spanish-American War Veterans and of the Eastern Star.

CHARLES F. DONNELLY is superintendent of the street-car system at Richmond, and is a railroad man of experience, who has won this position entirely on his own merits. He was born in Cairo, Illinois, July 15, 1874. He is a son of Leonidas and Mary Donnelly, both natives of Ohio. His father served in the Civil War from Ohio, was made prisoner and confined in Libby Prison, and died from its effects in 1876. His mother died in 1895. Mr. Donnelly acquired his education in the public schools in the middle part of Ohio.

After his school days he followed various occupations. In 1892 he came west and located in San Francisco, where he became identified with the Market Street Railway, as gripman on the Valencia-Street line. He is a thoroughly able man and knows all details of railroading from the ground up. His executive force was soon recognized, and his managerial ability was largely the cause of his rapid advancement. He served as inspector in San Francisco for the United Railroads. He came to Richmond in the capacity of dispatcher, and was promoted to superintendent on January 1, 1912, which office he now holds. In the estimation of his superiors he stands high and is popular with his associates and men who work under him. Mr. Donnelly was united in marriage in April, 1894, to Miss May H. Cain, a native of Maine. To this union was born Harold C. Mr. and Mrs. Donnelly enjoy an extensive acquaintance in Richmond and the Bay cities. Mrs. Donnelly is a member of the Pythian Sisters and the Richmond Club. Fraternally, Mr. Donnelly is a member of the B. P. O. E. of Richmond. On April 8, 1915, he was elected dictator of the Richmond lodge of the Loyal Order of Moose.

JOHN RICHARD NYSTROM.—The late John Richard Nystrom, who died on December 24, 1913, was for many years numbered among the prominent and valued citizens of Richmond, where he was regarded as a pioneer settler, his residence there dating from the year 1871. From that time on he was active in the real-estate business as a developer of several subdivisions and tracts, and took a leading part in public affairs, lending the weight of his influence to all projects for the advancement and growth of the community. He was a native of Finland, his birth having occurred on August 24, 1848. His parents, John and Johanna (Kallis) Nystrom, died in their native country.

In their family were eight children, of whom the subject of this review was the eldest. John Richard Nystrom acquired his very early education under the instruction of his mother, and later entirely by his own efforts in private study. When he was twenty-three years of age he emigrated to America, making a permanent location in California. Previous to this, however, he traveled over a large portion of the world, visiting the Land of the Midnight Sun, and then journeying far enough south to see the Southern Cross. Having heard a great deal of the wonderful resources and matchless climate of California, he finally decided to locate in this State, and after his arrival was first employed in boating on the bay. He had been a sailor before the mast, and in his new work took charge of the vessel of his former captain, for whom he carried on a freighting business for nine years. In the meantime he had purchased seventy acres of land in what is now Richmond. After retiring from boating he farmed this tract until 1903, when he subdivided the property and sold it for building lots, retaining a piece for his own home.

All of the land is within the corporate limits of Richmond. It is now fully developed, and on it many houses are built. In addition to this, Mr. Nystrom had an interest in seven other subdivisions in Richmond and did some important work in the line of land development. He was a member of the Richmond Industrial Commission and a director of the Mechanics Bank of Richmond. In 1881 he was married to Miss Mary Griffins, a daughter of Owen and Kate (Evans) Griffins, both of whom have passed away. Mr. and Mrs. Nystrom became the parents of twelve children—Alfred, John, Edwin, Mary E., Mabel, Alice, William, Louise, Hazel, Edna, Raymond, and Richard. The last-named has passed away. Mr. Nystrom was a member of the Masonic fraternity, having become a Royal Arch Mason at Berkeley, and a Knight Templar at Oakland. He was a trustee in the Presbyterian church of Richmond. He gave his political allegiance to the Republican party, having served for fifteen years as school director, and for a long period as a member of the city council.

ROY LEMOIN.—One of the most able, progressive, and enterprising young men in public life in Contra Costa County is Roy Lemoin, of Richmond, now creditably serving as chief of the Richmond fire department. He was born in Grand Rapids, Michigan, July 30, 1876. He came from a family of fire-fighters. His father, Henry W. Lemoin, was a prominent factor in the Grand Rapids fire department and has served as chief for thirty-seven years.

He is still living in Grand Rapids, is an active member of the department, retaining his position of chief, and has the distinction of being one of the oldest volunteer members in the State. The subject of this sketch since his appointment as chief has discharged his important duties to the entire satisfaction of the people of Richmond. He received his education in the public schools of his native town. At an early age he learned the plumbing trade and later became identified with telephone work, having charge of cable construction work for some years. He then entered the fire-alarm service in Grand Rapids, Michigan, where he remained for nearly three years. In October, 1905, he removed to Oakland, where he followed his trade as plumber for two years. He then became identified with the city of Oakland, in the city fire bureau, for nearly three years. Mr. Lemoin then accepted a position with the Gorham Engineering & Fire Apparatus Company, as salesman and demonstrator of motor fire apparatus. He resigned this position later to accept a better one with the Gamewell Fire Alarm Telegraph Company, the pioneer fire-alarm telegraph company of the world. During his stay with the latter company he acted as salesman and superintendent of construction, and on August 11, 1013, sold to the city of Richmond its present fire-alarm system, for $28,500. Chief Lemoin took charge of the construction work, and had the system installed July 1, 1914. Mr. Lemoin's record is that of a self-made man who has won recognition and success entirely by his own efforts and wisely directed energy. He was united in marriage to Miss Ethel H. Wells, of Grand Rapids, Michigan, June 28, 1898. Their children are Howard, born January, 1901; Wells, born October 20, 1904; Jack, born January 26, 1908.

Fraternally, Chief Lemoin is a member of the B. P. O. E. and K. of P. of Richmond. Both Mr. and Mrs. Lemoin have an extensive acquaintance in the Bay cities. Mrs. Lemoin is a soloist of ability and leads the choir at the Christian church at Berkeley.

SAMUEL F. JENKINS, a highly respected and representative citizen of Richmond, ably discharges the duties devolving upon him in the capacity of postmaster of Richmond, having been appointed to that office on April 10, 1910. His birth occurred February 4, 1873, at Elmira, New York. He acquired his education in the public and private schools of New Mexico and Kansas.

He read law in Albuquerque, New Mexico, with R. W. D. Bryan, and was admitted to the bar in 1894. He removed to Larned, Kansas, where he practiced his profession for two years, and in 1000 he located in Richmond, where he became prominently identified and followed contracting. In April, 1910, he was appointed postmaster. In July, 1912, the Point Richmond post office was consolidated with the Richmond office, and both offices are now under the supervision of Mr. Jenkins. Politically, he is affiliated with the Republican party. Fraternally, he belongs to the B. P. O. E. and the Modern Woodmen of America. Mr. Jenkins was united in marriage to Miss Daisie McCrea, of Ogden, Utah, September 12, 1894. To this union have been born two children, Merle and Stanley. Mr. Jenkins is a man of exemplary habits, strict integrity, and strong personality, and is held in high esteem by all who know him.

IRA RAYMOND VAUGHN was made city treasurer of Richmond on April 1, 1913, and this important position he has held ever since, discharging his duties in a prompt, capable, and reliable manner. Previous to taking this office he held a position of trust and responsibility for four years with the Standard Oil Company, in the auditing department. Mr. Vaughn was born in Eagleville, Modoc County, California, April 16, 1885. He acquired his education in the public schools, and attended high school in Santa Rosa, later taking a business course in Oakland. He then became identified with the Santa Fe Railroad at Richmond, and later went with the Standard Oil Company. On July 1, 1910, he was appointed city clerk, which office he filled to the credit of Richmond until April 1, 1913, when he was made city treasurer.

Politically, Mr. Vaughn is affiliated with the Democratic party. Fraternally, he is a member of the B. P. O. E. of Richmond, the Moose, and the Modern Woodmen of the World. He was united in marriage to Miss Mattie Eleanor Mitchell, of Tulare County, California, June 24, 1906. Mr. Vaughn has many friends in Richmond, by all of whom he is respected and highly esteemed.

He stands for progress at all times and seeks his own success and the city's advancement along lines of activity which will bear the closest investigation and scrutiny.

BETHOLD SCHMIDT, engaged in the merchant tailoring business in Richmond, is a native of Germany, and since his residence in Richmond, dating from May, 1914, he has gained wide prominence in his chosen field.

He was born at Weimar, Germany, March 26, 1876. He acquired his education in the old country, and at an early age he learned the ladies' and gentlemen's tailoring business. Mr. Schmidt has held responsible positions in the various tailoring establishments in France. He came to America in 1911 and located in Merced, California, where he remained for a time, and then returned to Germany, where he remained for three years. Again he came to this country and located in Richmond, where his establishment has advanced from an humble beginning to its present large proportions. Mr. Schmidt was married in Germany in 1905, to Miss Helen Legue, a native of Holland. To this union there have been three children—Anna, born August 8, 1906; Wolfgang, born August 5, 1908; Lucy, born August 1, 1911. Mr. Schmidt served for a period of two years in the German army. Since his residence in Richmond he has won a place among the substantial citizens of his community.

ARTHUR C. FARIS.—Among the men who, by reason of their personal integrity, ability, and business enterprise, have come to be regarded as representative citizens is Arthur C. Faris, the present city clerk of Richmond.

He is a native of Aurora, Nebraska, born August 29, 1878. His parents moved from Nebraska to southern Oregon in 1888. His father died when Arthur C. was a lad of thirteen years of age. His father was numbered among the highly esteemed men of Medford, Oregon, and held the office of city recorder for some years. The subject of this sketch at an early age entered the grocery store of Davis-Pottenger Company and acted as bookkeeper and clerk for two years. He then attended business college and removed to Fresno in 1897, entering the grocery store of John C. Nourse as clerk. Later he went with the Hughes Laundry, of Fresno, and there he became connected with the Fresno fire department. He removed to Richmond in August, 1901 and was employed by the Santa Fe Railroad as brakeman. He was afterward promoted to freight conductor, and in 1908 again promoted to passenger conductor. In October he was injured by a piece of steel entering his eye, which impaired his sight. He was appointed city clerk on April 1, 1913, which position he has since held. Politically, Mr. Faris is a Republican. Fraternally, he is affiliated with the B. P. O. E. and the Moose lodge of Richmond. He was united in marriage to Miss Bessie Carpenter, formerly a teacher in the Fresno High School, September 26, 1906. To this union was born one daughter, Elizabeth Maradean, December 22, 1913. Mr. and Mrs. Faris manifest at all times a public-spirited devotion to the general good of Richmond.

JAMES A. McVITTIE, a man well known in Contra Costa County for his public spirit, his broad views, and his excellent business ability, is now acting in an efficient manner as city auditor of Richmond. He was born in Parkersburg, West Virginia, February 5, 1885. He acquired his education in Hamilton, Ontario, in the public schools and business college of that city, graduating from the latter in 1903. He removed to Richmond and became associated with the Standard Oil Company as clerk and filled the position in a most efficient manner for seven years. On July 1, 1910, Mr. McVittie was appointed city auditor of Richmond, which office he has since filled. Fraternally, he is affiliated with McKinley Lodge No. 374, F. & A. M., Twilight Lodge No. 119, I. O. O. F. of Richmond, Contra Costa Encampment No. 09, I. O. O. F., and Richmond Lodge No. 1251, B. P. O. E. Politically, he is a standard-bearer of the Republican party. Mr. McVittie's father, George McVittie, has been identified with the Standard Oil Company for many years, starting in Parkersburg, West Virginia, and has filled positions of trust and responsibility all over the United States. The mother of our subject was Florence McVittie, a native of West Virginia. She passed away in Parkersburg in 1888.

CHARLES R. BLAKE, M. D., in the practice of his profession, having specialized to a great extent on the eye, ear, nose, and throat, is acknowledged today as one of the most skillful and successful practitioners in the Bay cities. At the present time he is acting as health commissioner of Richmond, having been appointed by the city council in 1907. He was born in Visalia, California, September 9, 1869. He acquired his education in the public schools and colleges of California. He attended the medical department of the University of California, graduating with his class in 1891. Upon completing his course he immediately started to practice his profession, and in 1903 he removed to Richmond, California, where he has since resided. The Doctor is progressive in thought, as well as active, and believes in keeping abreast with the latest ideas and discoveries in his profession. Fraternally, he is affiliated with the Masonic lodge and has taken the Royal Arch degrees. He is also a member of the I. O. O. F., the B. P. O. E., and the Woodmen of the World.

Socially, he is a member of the University of California Club. Politically, he believes in the doctrines of the Republican party. Doctor Blake was united in marriage to Miss Lillian M. Hoogs, of Oakland, California, in 1898. Their one son, Herbert, was born December 30, 1900. Doctor Blake has made many friends since coming to Richmond, and all admire him for his steadfastness of purpose, his determination, his industry, and his business and professional ability.

ALFEUS ODELL.—In all the Bay cities no man is more conspicuous for progress and fair dealing, nor no man has done more for the development of the educational, religious, and commercial interests of Richmond, than has the subject of this sketch. Mr. Odell is a native of Thorntown, Indiana, where his birth occurred on February 7, 1836. He was educated in the Thorntown Academy and Asbury University. After the completion of his education, he took up teaching with gratifying success, and followed this vocation most of his life. He came to San Pablo in 1898. In 1900 he removed to what is now Richmond and established a residence in 1901. He has the distinction of teaching the first school in Richmond, which position he filled in a most satisfactory manner. He saw the possibilities of Richmond and engaged in the real-estate business with his son. Mr. Odell was the first agitator in reference to incorporating the town, and wrote and circulated the first petition, and led the fight before the Supervisors. He also wrote the petition for annexation, and fixed the boundaries of the city, which continued until the last annexation was made, in 1913. He was very active, and one of the first to advocate the tunnel through the mountain for a municipal wharf. He gave a great deal of time and attention and called the first meeting to institute a Masonic lodge and was one of the prime movers for the erection of the Methodist church, serving as its first Sunday-school superintendent. Fraternally, Mr. Odell is a Mason, and a charter member of the Eastern Star. He was united in marriage to Miss M. Julia Archer, of Spencer, Indiana, November 29, 1862. To this union have been born six children— Clarence A., an attorney of Richmond; Lola, wife of C. Mackay, of Richmond (deceased); J. Winifred Stidhman, of Richmond; Stella W. Logan, of Salinas, California; and two who died in infancy. Mr. Odell is a man of energy, resource, and capacity, and whether in business or social relations holds the good-will and confidence of all who are associated with him.

VIRGIL AUGUSTUS PHILLIPS, inspector of the bureau of identification of Contra Costa County, residing in Richmond, is a man well qualified for the important position which he holds. When Mr. Phillips assumed his duties he took hold of the office with the firm resolution of keeping the detective bureau up to a high standard of efficiency. During his administration many important and intricate cases have come under his supervision. He is a native of Boone County, Missouri, and was born on December 10, 1877. He acquired his education in the public schools of his native State. At an early age he became associated for some years with the Kansas City Southern and the Missouri Pacific railroads out of Kansas City. He removed to Richmond in 1906, where he became associated with the Standard Oil Company for a period of five years. In October, 1911, he was appointed on the Richmond police force, and on July 1, 1914, was promoted to inspector of the bureau of identification, which office he now holds. Mr. Phillips was united in marriage to Miss Lena La Force, a native of Missouri, March 8, 1907. She is of French ancestry and a descendant of one of the oldest families of Missouri. Their one son, Donald, was born January 31, 1910. Mr. Phillips is a member of McKinley Lodge, F. & A. M., of Richmond. His great-great-grandfather was one of the representative men of Missouri and was one of the founders of the Missouri State University.

JOHN H. GREGORY, of Richmond, was elected constable in 1910, and his labors in this connection have since been of incalculable benefit in the work of moral uplift in his locality. He was born in Nashville, Lee County, Iowa, May 9, 1850. He came to California with his parents overland with an ox team, taking six months to make the journey. The family landed in Ione, California, September 15, 1853. His father died in Ione in 1883, and his mother still resides on the old homestead, and has reached the age of eighty-eight years. The subject of this sketch acquired his education in the common schools of Amador County. He followed harness work for one year, then took up carpenter work, which he followed for nine years, and then worked four years at blacksmithing. He was identified with the Ione Coal & Iron Company for fourteen years, and during that time had charge of twenty-two thousand sheep for his company. In 1902 he removed to Richmond and associated himself with the Standard Oil Company from June, 1902, until June, 1906, at which time he was elected city marshal. He served in this office two years and was re-elected and served one year up to the time the charter was established, when he was elected constable, which office he has held in a most gratifying manner. Mr. Gregory has achieved success in his official positions. Under him lawlessness in Richmond has been kept down. Politically, he is a Republican, but of late he is a nonpartisan. Fraternally he is affiliated with the Masonic lodge of Richmond, the Eastern Star, the Knights of Pythias, the Pythian Sisters, the Maccabees, Palm and Shell, the Eagles, the Odd Fellows, and the Knights of the Acerian Cross. Mr. Gregory has been identified with the Masons for forty years, and with the Odd Fellows for thirty-five years, and has held various offices in the different lodges of which he is a member. On June 10, 1874, he was united in marriage to Miss Mary Eleanor Kirby, a native daughter, of Ione, California, who died November 10, 1914. Four children have been born to this union.

ROBERT L. FERNALD, a highly respected and representative citizen of Richmond, ably discharges the duties devolving upon him in the capacity of city councilman, having been elected to that office in April, 1913, for a six-year term. He was born near Lafayette, Indiana, January 11, 1859, and was educated in Topeka, Kansas, where his parents removed in 1866. He graduated from the Topeka High

School in 1875. Mr. Femald learned the carpenter trade with his father, and later took up the marble-cutting trade. He engaged with his brothers, W. H. and C. H., in the marble business in Topeka, where he remained two years. He sold his interest and removed to New Mexico, where he remained one year. He then returned to Topeka and engaged in the marble business for himself for two years, and removed to Dodge City, Kansas, and engaged with the Santa Fe Railroad. He then went to Los Angeles for a time, but returned to Topeka, where he operated a grocery store for five years. This he sold and returned to Los Angeles and engaged in the grocery business there. Three years later Mr. Femald was again employed by the Santa Fe Railroad, and was transferred to various places. In July, 1900, he came to Richmond as car foreman. He later went to Oakland in the planing-mill business for one year. Returning to Richmond, he was interested for five years with Tilden & Eakle. Owing to his health, he disposed of his interest and went to Los Angeles. Returning to Richmond, he has since been engaged in contracting. He served one year as street superintendent, and in April, 1913, was elected councilman. Mr. Fernald is a member of Richmond Lodge No. 13, K. of P., and has served as master of finance since the lodge started, eleven years ago. He is president of the Richmond K. of P. Hall Association, and a member of the Brotherhood of American Yeomen. He was married to Miss Eva Estella Wild, a native of New York State, March 14, 1883. Their two children are Grace, wife of B. C. Dailey, of Berkeley, born June 9, 1884, and Roy C., born November 19, 1889, at present deputy assessor and tax-collector of Richmond, also worthy patron of the Eastern Star and holds membership and office in McKinley Lodge, F. & A. M., of Richmond.

JOHN ROTH, the efficient justice of the peace of Richmond, is popularly and widely known in Contra Costa County. The width of the continent separates him from his birthplace, for he is a native of Pennsylvania, born December 17, 1846. He attended the public schools of his native place, and when a mere boy became identified with the Western Union Telegraph Company, filling positions at various points in Pennsylvania and Ohio. He came west in 1865 and located near Cache Creek, Yolo County, California, where he became interested in agricultural pursuits. In 1901 he removed to Richmond, where he filled various positions of trust. He represented Tulare, Kern, and Inyo counties in the State legislature for one term. In 1906 he was elected justice of the peace, which office he has held ever since. In political matters Judge Roth is a staunch Democrat, and he has a well-earned reputation for unfailing good-nature, thus enjoying wide popularity.

He is, moreover, regarded as one of the most substantial citizens of Contra Costa County, his record at all times being an honor and a credit to the people of Richmond that honored him with his present office. Judge Roth was united in marriage on January 1, 1887, to Johanna A. Henry, a native of New York State. To this union has been born five children, all living— George, who resides in Los Angeles, California; Ruby, wife of John Galbraith, of Richmond, California; Elizabeth, wife of William Sutherland, residing at Brea, California; Barbara, who has been identified with the Mechanics Bank of Richmond for over eight years; Walter, an electrician, of Richmond. Judge Roth is affiliated with the Masonic and the I. O. O. F. lodges of Richmond.

WILLIAM LINDSEY.—Among the men whose enterprise and ability have been active factors in promoting the remarkable growth of Richmond is numbered

William Lindsey. He was born in England, April 22, 1839. His father, Edward Lacklin Lindsey, was the owner and captain of the ship "Palmyra," and he had the distinction of carrying the first prisoners from England to Botany Bay, Australia. Mr. Lindsey's father came to America from England in his own ship, and located in San Francisco, where he engaged in the lumber and brick business. He was a well-known and representative business men of that city for many years and died in 1852. The mother of Mr. Lindsey (Virginia) died in 1000. The subject of this sketch is the last of seven children. He was educated in San Francisco. In 1865 he entered the real-estate business in San Francisco, following this vocation for many years. Owing to poor health, he removed to Belmont, San Mateo County, where he remained for two years, and in 1899 engaged in the real-estate business in Richmond for a time. Later he was elected justice of the peace on an independent ticket, and was afterward appointed police judge, which office he has had for three terms. Politically, he is affiliated with the Republican party, and in matters of citizenship he manifests a progressive and public-spirited interest. Mr. Lindsey was united in marriage to Augusta Anna Batchelor in 1867, and they became the parents of seven children, five of whom are now living. His wife died on September 6, 1913.

WILLIAM F. RUST.—The life record of William F. Rust entitles him preeminently to the distinctive title of one of the "builders" of the town which bears his name, and he has contributed a notable share to the material progress of Contra Costa County. He has been a resident of the county since 1883, has been a substantial influence for the upbuilding of Rust, and possesses the respect and esteem of his fellow-men. Mr. Rust was born in Germany, November 27, 1854. He acquired his schooling in the old country, and at a comparatively young age learned the blacksmithing trade in his native land. He followed this for some time, and in 1880 he migrated to America and located in Chicago, where he readily found employment at his trade. He remained in Chicago for one year. He then went to Wyoming for the United States Government, in the quartermaster's department. He remained in Wyoming for some time, and was transferred to Arizona, where he worked at his trade for the Government, remaining there one year. He then removed to California and located in San Francisco, following his trade for three years. His good business judgment prompted him to locate in Contra Costa County in 1883, where the town of Rust is now located. Here in 1889 he established a blacksmith-shop, which he continued until 1901. He then disposed of his shop and erected the most imposing block in Rust, engaging in the hardware business. A post-office was established here and Mr. Rust was appointed the first post-master. He continued to operate the hardware store until January 1, 1914, when he disposed of his interest and retired.

Politically, Mr. Rust is a Republican, but has never aspired to public office. Fraternally, he has been affiliated with the Independent Order of United Workmen for twenty-six years. He is also a member of Hermann's Sons, and has been honored with the highest office in that order, grand president. In 1886 Mr. Rust was united in marriage to Lina Wagner, a native of Germany, and two children have blessed this union, William G., a plumber, and Herman, an electrician. Mrs. Rust passed away on June 13, 1914, in her fifty-sixth year. She was sincerely mourned by a large circle of friends won in the course of a long and useful life. Her funeral was largely attended, and among the many floral tributes laid upon the casket were some from those in humble positions who had found in her a true and loving friend. She had always been active in the social and church work of the German faith. She was for many years a member of the sister lodge of Hermann's Sons.

JAMES HOEY, one of the highly esteemed and respected citizens of Contra Costa County, engaged in the grocery business in Martinez for thirty-seven years. To him belongs the title of self-made man, for, starting out in life without experience or resources, he has through his own energies risen to be one of the leading business men of Martinez. He was born on March 2, 1856, in Ireland. He received a limited education in the old country, and when a young man he came to America alone and went directly to Martinez, where his uncle, John Colman, was engaged in business. Here he remained in the employ of his uncle for five years. He then engaged in the grocery business and has remained in this business, with the exception of four years, when he went to San Francisco and took a position in the United States Mint under President Cleveland's administration. Politically, Mr. Hoey is a Democrat. He has always taken a deep interest in political affairs in county, State, and national matters. For years he has loyally upheld his party and has taken up many arduous duties in its support. He has served as secretary of the county committee for twenty years and has been a delegate and attended every county convention and many State conventions since he was old enough to vote but has never aspired to political office. He is a member of the K. of C. and the Y. M. I. He was united in marriage on November 9, 1881, to Mary Tormey. To this union have been born five children, two of whom died in infancy. Those living are Mary Agnes, a teacher in the Concord public school; Hilda Genevieve, a high-school teacher at Gustine, Merced County; and Villani Rosemond, an employee of the abstract office in Martinez. The family are members of the Catholic church.

MICHAEL HENRY HURLEY, a representative and esteemed citizen of Martinez, has held the office of county recorder since 1006, and has made a most creditable record in that connection. He was born in Lowell, Massachusetts, September 29, 1868, son of Michael and Margaret Hurley. His father died in 1886, and his mother died in 1902. There were eleven children born of this union, only three of whom are now living—John, of Martinez; Rose, wife of F. A. Milliff, of Kern County; and Michael Henry, the subject of this sketch. He acquired his education in the public schools of Martinez, where his parents removed in 1878. Mr. Hurley, after finishing his education, learned the printer's trade. Later he became identified with various business firms of Martinez and Oakland, where he occupied positions of trust. He was elected to the office of public administrator in 1902, serving one term, discharging his duties in such a satisfactory and commendable manner that he was elected to fill the office of county recorder in 1006, which position he now holds. He also filled the office of town clerk from 1892 to 1907. He was united in marriage to Miss Flora Irene Morford, a native of California, December 25, 1912. Fraternally he is affiliated with the B. P. O. E. of Vallejo and various other orders.

REX LADELL BOYER, who is successfully engaged in the practice of law in Martinez, is a man of clear, logical mind. He was born in Walla Walla, Washington, August 5, 1889, and was educated in the public schools of Concord, California. He later took a business course in Oakland and studied law under J. E. Rodgers. On May 1, 1912, he graduated from Kent Law School in San Francisco, and on the day of his graduation he was admitted to the bar. His father, Joel Jerome Boyer, is a native of

Pennsylvania, and his mother was born in Washington. When Mr. Boyer was but five years of age his parents removed to Lafayette, where his father followed agricultural pursuits and engaged extensively in the chicken business. Mr. Boyer is affiliated with the Republican party. He was appointed deputy sheriff under Sheriff R. R. Veale, and while in this office he started and is still connected with the criminal identification known as the "Bertillon System," which is being successfully used throughout the country. He had made a study of this system in the Oakland police department. In May, 1913, he opened law offices in the Gazette building, in Martinez, where he has since engaged in general practice. In all social, official, and professional relations he has held steadily to high ideals and has the confidence and regard of all who know him. Mr. Boyer, during the extra sessions of the Superior Court, acts as official stenographer. Fraternally, he is a member of the Masonic lodge of Martinez, also of the K. of P., and has served as chancellor of the Martinez lodge of this order. He is also a member of the Woodmen of the World.

JOHN J. HAUSER has been connected with the business interests of Martinez since January, 1907. He is one of the best-known undertakers in the Bay cities and conducts one of the best-appointed establishments in Contra Costa County. He was born in Napa County, September 27, 1881, and is a son of John and Mary Hauser. His father is a native of Germany; his mother came from Switzerland. His parents came to America in 1875, locating in Napa County, where his father died when John J. was but one and a half years of age, and his mother passed away when he was fifteen. Early in life he started for himself and decided to learn the undertaking business. In this connection he became identified with many of the leading establishments in California. He has won a well-merited measure of prosperity and has gained recognition among the substantial men in Contra Costa County. Mr. Hauser worked three years in San Francisco for leading establishments, and subsequently filled positions in San Jose, Fresno, Alameda, and other places. He has passed the rigid examinations that qualify one for this work. On January 1, 1907, he removed to Martinez and became chief deputy coroner under Doctor C. L. Abbott. This position he has since held. He is a member of the State Funeral Directors' Association and the San Joaquin Funeral Association, which embraces Contra Costa, San Joaquin, and Stanislaus counties.

In both associations Mr. Hauser has held and is now holding important offices. Politically, he is a Republican, and takes an active part in the affairs of that party. Fraternally, he is a member of the Odd Fellows, and holds the office of noble grand in Martinez lodge. He is treasurer of Martinez Aerie, F. O. E., a member of the Mt. Diablo Parlor, N. S. G. W., the Rebekah lodge of Alhambra, Martinez Council, I. D. E. S., the Moose of Martinez, Laurel Camp of Woodmen of the World, and Alameda Tent K. O. T. M. Mr. Hauser was united in marriage to Miss Mary Adeline Pope, a native of Vallejo, October 12, 1904. To this union has been born one son, Paul Herbert, who died at the age of two years. Mrs. Hauser is also active in club and social work, being a member and past president of Ramona Parlor, N. D. G. W. She also holds office in the Women's Improvement Club and is a trustee of the Ladies' Institute.

JASPER HENRY WELLS.—One of the most valued and representative citizens of Martinez is Jasper Henry Wells, well known in official circles in Contra Costa County from his many years in continuous service as county clerk. He was born in

Santa Rosa, Sonoma County, January 27, 1871. He is the son of Philip and Margaret Wells. His father was a native of Kentucky, and his mother was from Illinois. There were six children born of this union —Eva, wife pf C. A. Tarwater, of Concord; Lillie, of Concord; Myrtle, wife of John Sutton, of Berkeley; Ernest, who resides in Portland, Oregon; Samuel, of Martinez, who is deputy county clerk; and Jasper H., the subject of this sketch. He received his education in the public schools, after which he attended the San Francisco Business College, graduating from the latter in 1898. After the death of Mr. Wells' father, which occurred in 1890, Jasper managed the ranch in a capable manner for the next eight years. He then completed his business course and entered the county clerk's office in the capacity of deputy under J. E. Rodgers, serving until November 21, 1908, when he was appointed to fill the office of county clerk, owing to the resignation of Mr. Rodgers, who had taken up the law business as a profession. Mr. Wells has held the office continuously, and has made a conscientious and capable official, holding the confidence and good-will of all who are in any way associated with him. In politics Mr. Wells is affiliated with the Republican party. Fraternally, he is a member of Pacheco Lodge No. 117, I. O. O. F., of Concord; Mount Diablo Parlor No. 101. Native Sons of the Golden West; Richmond Lodge No. 1251, B. P. O. E.; and Rebekah lodge of Concord. Mr. Wells was united in marriage to Miss Anna Ardelia Webb, a daughter of Frank and Phoebe Webb, of Walnut Creek, January 8, 1902. To this union was born Melvin Thomas Wells, July 4, 1903. Mrs. Wells has won a wide circle of friends in Contra Costa County and throughout the State, as she is an active worker in the Congregational church and the Rebekah lodge of Concord. She is a graduate of the San Jose Normal School and taught in Concord nearly seven years. Mr. Wells' mother was from one of the sturdy pioneer families who crossed the plains in an ox-team when she was but two years of age. Her parents settled in Contra Costa County, on what is known as the Government Ranch, which they later found was grant property; they then proceeded to Sonoma County.

HON. R. H. LATIMER.—Among the prominent and representative men of Contra Costa County, none stands higher nor possesses a wider circle of friends than the Honorable R. H. Latimer, superior judge of Contra Costa County, a self-made man who, by his natural leadership, initiative and unswerving principles of honor, has risen from humble station through the several positions he has held from drug clerk to the office of superior judge of his adopted county. Judge Latimer is broad and liberal-minded, absolutely fair and impartial in his judicial actions, and ever ready to mete out justice to the poor and needy. His record on the bench is one that any man might well feel proud to possess. His rulings have never been reversed. Judge Latimer was born near Miami, Missouri, January 28, 1854. He is the son of Randolph Latimer, a pioneer farmer and surveyor, and a native of Virginia, born in 1800, and died August, 1861. He was a self-made man, beloved by all who knew him. He removed to Missouri, took up farming, and was numbered among the prominent men of that State. He served two terms in the State legislature of Kentucky, and the year of his death was nominated in Missouri to run on the legislative ticket but owing to ill health he was obliged to decline. Judge Latimer's mother, Nancy Latimer, was a native of Virginia and reared in Kentucky. The parents of Judge Latimer were married in Kentucky, and had fourteen children, only two of whom are now living, the subject of this review and a brother, Robert K., a prosperous real-estate man residing in Seattle, Washington. The parents of Judge Latimer have traced their ancestry back for many generations in England. His great-great-grandfather came from England and located in Maryland about the time Lord Baltimore died. On Mr. Latimer's mother's side the family tree can be traced back to Revolutionary times. Judge Latimer was educated in the private and public schools of Missouri, graduating from the Mt. Pleasant College, of Huntsville, in the class of 1877. Two years later he came to California, locating in Concord, in this county. He afterward removed to Walnut Creek, where he was employed in a drug-store. It was about this time that he decided to adopt law as a profession. He began reading law while working in the drug-store and was admitted to the bar in August, 1884. He later opened an office in Walnut Creek, where he practiced his profession for two years, after which he removed to the county seat. In the larger place his legal talent soon won recognition, and he became prominent in many big actions, gaining a prestige that endeared him to the hearts of all with whom he came in contact. Judge Latimer soon rose in his chosen profession and became one of the leading attorneys in California. In 1908 he was urged by his friends to become a candidate for superior judge of Contra Costa County.

He was elected by a nattering majority and has been repeatedly honored by being returned to the bench. For thirty years he has been a factor in the profession, and his advice and council is often sought by other lawyers and jurists. During his service on the bench, Judge Latimer has been called to preside over the courts of other counties and has decided many notable and celebrated cases. As a leading man of affairs, a trained lawyer, and a judge of the superior court, he has established a name that the people of Contra Costa County and of California are proud of. He has a brilliant past and a future that is most inviting. In 1889 he was united in marriage to Miss Madora Garner, of Los Gatos, California. Fraternally, he is a member of the Masonic lodge of Martinez, and has filled all the chairs in his lodge, except that of master. He is an active member of the I. O. O. F. of Martinez and has held every office in that order. Judge Latimer served two years as justice of the peace in Concord and was district attorney for three years. He also held office in the California State Iroquois Club. His wife is a member of the Eastern Star and Women's Improvement Club of Martinez and takes an active part in all club and social events and is a lady of education and refinement.

EVERETT B. TAYLOR, a practicing attorney of Martinez, has won success, and is numbered among the able representatives of his profession. Mr. Taylor is a native son and was born at Byron, Contra Costa County, California, August 1, 1879. He is the son of Volney and Agnes E. Taylor. His father is a native of Canada, while his mother is a native of Illinois. Mr. Taylor's father is widely recognized as one of the county's most esteemed citizens, and has always followed agricultural pursuits. He is still a resident of Byron. The subject of this review received his education in the public schools of Contra Costa and Alameda counties, and the University of California.

Later he studied law and was admitted to the bar in 1904. Subsequently he started to practice his profession in Alameda County, and afterward removed to Contra Costa County, locating in Martinez, where he has since resided. Mr. Taylor gives his political allegiance to the Republican party.

Fraternally, he is identified with the Woodmen of the World. On December 11, 1901, he was united in marriage to Miss Carrie F. Bohmen, of Sacramento, a native daughter. To this union has been born a daughter, Beatrice V., born May 6, 1906. Although a young man, Mr. Taylor has won a prominent place in the ranks of the legal fraternity in this part of the State. His father is an extensive farmer and owns eight hundred acres near Byron. He is affiliated with the Masonic lodge, also a member of the Odd Fellows. He has taken a prominent part in the temperance work throughout the State and county. He enjoys in a full measure the confidence and respect of all who know him.

EARL B. FITZPATRICK, M. D.—Among the many brilliant and able men who have gained prominence and distinction among the medical profession of the Bay cities is Doctor Earl Fitzpatrick, practicing in Martinez. He is numbered among the foremost representatives of his profession. He was born in Redding, California, March 23, 1887. He is a son of John W. and Mary Louise Fitzpatrick, both of whom are dead. His father was a native of California and his mother a native of Washington. At the time of his death, his father was associated with the Southern Pacific Company, as land agent in Nevada. Doctor Fitzpatrick was educated in the public schools of Redding and graduated from the Oakland High School. Later he attended the Oakland Medical College and graduated in 1910. He served as intern in the Alameda County Hospital for a period of ten months. In March, 1911, he removed to Martinez, where he has since carried on a general practice. Politically, Doctor Fitzpatrick is affiliated with the Republican party. He acts in the capacity of assistant county physician and is now serving as secretary of Contra Costa County Medical Society and is a member of the American Medical Association. Fraternally, Doctor Fitzpatrick is affiliated with the Masonic lodge of Martinez, holding membership in No. 41. He is also a member of the B. P. O. E. of Richmond, No. 1251, the Woodmen of the World, the Eagles, the Moose lodge of Martinez, the Red Men, the order of the Eastern Star, and is a member of the Native Sons. While a resident of Martinez Doctor Fitzpatrick has built up a large and representative patronage, accorded to him in recognition of his unusual proficiency in his chosen field of labor. Doctor Fitzpatrick is medical examiner for the following insurance companies: Metropolitan Life and Mutual Life (of New York), Western States Life, West Coast Life, Mutual Life (of Des Moines, Iowa), Aetna Life, and Travelers', and also serves in this capacity for many fraternal organizations. He has a sister, Mabel, wife of Clarence F. Murdig, who resides in San Diego.

EDWIN MERRITHEW, M. D., has been successfully engaged in the practice of medicine at Martinez for the past eight years, and is widely recognized as one of the able and representative members of the profession. He was born at Gold Run, Placer County, California, November 23, 1880, son of Moses W., born July 4, 1837, and Annie Elizabeth Merrithew, born in 1854. His father is a native of Maine, and his mother was born in San Francisco. The parents still reside in Placer County. The subject of this sketch was educated in the public schools of Placer County. He also attended the Stockton Normal School. He then entered the Cooper Medical College and graduated in 1905, becoming intern at the Lane Hospital in San Francisco. He practiced his profession in Sonoma County, and in June, 1907, he removed to Martinez, where he enjoys the full confidence of the people of his locality.

In March, 1911, Doctor Merrithew was appointed county physician, which office he has since held. He has served as health officer of the city of Martinez since January 1, 1914. He is local surgeon for the Santa Fe Railroad.

Fraternally, Doctor Merrithew holds membership in the Odd Fellows, the Knights of Pythias, the Woodmen of the World, and the Elks. He has held the chairs in the Odd Fellows and the Knights of Pythias, and now serves as camp physician of the Woodmen of the World. He is especially interested in and a member of the Native Sons. He is a member of the Contra Costa Medical Society, the California State Medical Association, and the American Medical Association. He has served as vice-president of the County Medical Society. In politics the Doctor is a Republican. He was married to Miss Emma Kriner, of California, October 29, 1910. To this union one son, Wallace Kriner, was born on July 29, 1913. Mrs. Merrithew is a member of the Women of Woodcraft and is active in all matters pertaining to promote the general welfare and growth and expansion of the community.

REUBEN H. CURRY.—An enterprising and prosperous representative of business interests in Richmond is Reuben H. Curry. His birth occurred in Contra Costa County, at Clayton, August 10, 1864. He acquired his education in the public schools of this county. He is a son of Edward Curry, a native of Missouri, who came to California via Cape Horn in 1849. He located in Clayton, and after a time he returned to his native State and in 1855 was united in marriage to Annie Goodwin, a native of Indiana. They then crossed the plains with an ox-team, which took six months, and again located at Clayton. The father was an experienced stockman and followed this business all his life. He died in 1865. While crossing the plains the parents of Mr. Curry had many narrow escapes from the Indians, and on one occasion rescued a lady who had been scalped by the Indians while en route. Mr. Curry's mother is still living and makes her home in Alameda. Four children were born in the parents' family—Martha, wife of Augustus Houston, deceased; Edward, a mining man; Josephine, wife of John Breen; and the subject of this sketch, who embarked early in life for himself, and has been engaged in various places in the hotel and soda business. He operated the Geyser Hotel in Sonoma County for ten years and run a hotel at Angels Camp for six years. In 1901 he removed to Richmond and established the first manufacturing business in the city, called the Richmond Soda Works. He continued in this about three years, then sold out and left Richmond for ten years, when he returned and repurchased the business which he had originally started, and since his return has met with gratifying success. Mr. Curry was united in marriage to Georgia B. Dingley, a native of San Francisco, April 5, 1883. To this union were born Grace D. and George Franklin. Mr. Curry is a Republican. He has been honored by being elected on the water commission, and took office in April, 1913, which he now holds. He is a member of the I. O. O. F., the Rebekahs, the Moose, the Eagles, and is a Native Son.

WILLIAM J. JOHNSON, one of the representative men of Martinez, has won a place among the leading and progressive business men of his locality. He is genial and pleasant in manner and has made many friends in the business world. He was born in that far-off land, Poland, on July 17, 1868. He was reared and educated in the old country, attending the public schools and a technical institute. At the age of eighteen he came to America and located in Boston, where he remained for seven years and followed his trade as machinist. May 15, 1895, he came to Contra Costa

County and located in Martinez, where he first engaged in the bicycle business. Later he manufactured medical machinery and dental appliances. The importance of this line of work gained him prominence all over the United States. Of recent years he has given his attention to expert automobile work and has the agency of several high-class cars. Politically, Mr. Johnson is a strong Progressive, and in his co-operation in political matters he has been a strong Roosevelt man.

Fraternally, he is a member of various organizations. On February 2, 1907, he was married to Miss Mary Kobylanski, of Chicago. To this union have been born two children, Kazimir and Louisa. The family are members of the Catholic church. Mrs. Johnson takes an active part in all church work and is a valued member of the Improvement Club of Martinez.

JOHN H. NICHOLL.—Among the men who, by reason of their personal integrity, ability, and business enterprise, have come to be regarded as representative citizens and leading business men of Contra Costa County, California, is John H. Nicholl. He has been active in promoting the best interests of the community along many lines, and throughout his entire life he has directed his efforts where mature judgment and keen discrimination have led the way. Mr. Nicholl was born in San Leandro, Alameda County, in 1855, and is the son of John and Agnes Booth (Hodge) Nicholl, natives of the north of Ireland and both of Scotch ancestry. His father died on July 28, 1914. The subject of this review acquired his early education in the San Pablo public schools and later attended the California Military Academy of Oakland, and the Pacific Business College of San Francisco. Following the completion of his studies, he operated the Nicholl Hotel in Oakland for four years, after which he engaged in mining on Wood River, Idaho. He moved to Salt Lake City, and in 1809 returned to Oakland, organizing in the same year the John Nicholl Company, a closed corporation, of which he has since been secretary and manager. He maintains offices in Richmond and Oakland, through which passes daily an immense amount of business. The John Nicholl Company controls valuable real-estate holdings in Ventura, Contra Costa, and Alameda counties, and also valuable tracts of land around Richmond. Land belonging to the company was sold in 1806 for the right of way for the Santa Fe Railroad. The company made the first sale in Richmond to Claus Spreckels for the use of the San Francisco & San Joaquin Valley Railroad. The consideration was $80,000, and the land was located in the best part of Point Richmond. Mr. Nicholl recently sold for $525,000 one hundred and eleven acres in the heart of Richmond, land which had been acquired by him in the early days for thirty dollars an acre. This was the largest sale of undivided and unimproved property ever made in the United States. Mr. Nicholl is now the owner of some of the most valuable ranches in Ventura County, Spanish grants acquired in 1867, and has one thousand acres in that locality planted in lima beans and English walnuts. He still has large property holdings in and around Richmond and other sections in California. Although he is a man of power and prominence in real estate circles, his interests have not by any means been confined to this field, as is evident from the fact that he was the founder in 1901 of the Bank of Richmond, which, starting with a capital of $30,000, has under his administration as president increased this to $100,000. Mr. Nicholl is also known as the organizer of the first water company of Richmond. His knowledge of present-day business conditions is comprehensive and exact. To the solution of many difficult problems which have confronted him in the course of years he has brought keen discrimination and penetrating sagacity. Mr. Nicholl is an ex-member of the Richmond Industrial Commission, and in the summers of 1913 and 1914 made trips to Washington as a delegate to secure an appropriation from the United States Government for harbor improvements in Richmond. He can always be counted upon in the furtherance of any plan for the advancement of the city, where he has gained prominence as a man of marked ability and substantial achievements. His unbending integrity of character, his marked business ability, and his public spirit make him a citizen whose worth is widely acknowledged.

HARRY W. WERNSE, one of the foremost men in Contra Costa County, is worthy being styled a self-made man, for, starting out in life without resources, he has through his own energy and initiative risen to be one of the leading real-estate operators and promoters in the Bay region. Mr. Wernse was born February 11, 1878, in St. Louis, Missouri, his parents being William F. and Minna (Hintze) Wernse. His father came to America from Hanover, Germany. His mother is a native of Missouri. The subject of this sketch acquired his education in the public and high schools of St. Louis. After graduation he went to Texas, where he rode the range for two years. He then took up mining in Arizona and Colorado. This vocation he followed for five years. In 1902 he came to California, locating in San Francisco, where he engaged in the real-estate business and operated largely in Richmond. He has been associated with H. C. Cutting in the development of the Point Richmond Canal & Land Company of Richmond since 1904 and has served as secretary and treasurer of that company ever since. Mr. Wernse was united in marriage to Miss Helen J. Owens of St. Louis, Missouri, June 14, 1899. To this union in 1902 was born one daughter, Helen Mildred, who ranks high among her associates as one who enjoys and takes part in many children's operas. In politics Mr. Wernse is affiliated with the Republican party. Fraternally, he is a member of the Masonic order and the Elks. He has been prominently identified with Richmond's harbor project. He was elected as a committee of one to appear before the Rivers and Harbors Committee of the House of Representatives in support of the bill for the improvement of Richmond's harbor. He has been secretary of the Richmond Industrial Commission for the past four years and is ever working in the interest of the city of Richmond's great industrial and commercial progress.

CHARLES LUTHER TRABERT is a man of marked ability and judgment, a resident of Berkeley, California, and prominently identified with the industrial interests of California. He is connected with the C. A. Smith Lumber Company as secretary. Mr. Trabert was born at Ephrata, Pennsylvania, April 30, 1871, son of the Rev. George H. Trabert, pastor of an English Lutheran church. Mr. Trabert has devoted his entire life to the lumber business and has been associated with the C. A. Smith companies longer than any of his business associates. He has made a scientific study of forestry and has accomplished a great deal of important work along this line. His father, in his seventy-second year, is still active in the ministry as pastor of the Salem English Lutheran Church in Minneapolis, Minnesota. He was the only English Lutheran minister for years in the Northwest, and he established churches in Duluth and Red Wing, Minnesota; Fargo, North Dakota; La Crosse, Wisconsin; and many other cities. His wife who was in her maidenhood Miss Mary Elizabeth Minnigh, is of mixed Pennsylvania Dutch and English stock, an ancestor of the family having come from Munich in 1622.

Charles L. Trabert received his education in Lebanon, Pennsylvania, and Minneapolis, where he attended high school for three years. He was a member of the first manual training class in that city, and was for three years a student in Gustavus Adolphus College, at St. Peter, Minnesota. During his last year in college he became identified with the C. A. Smith Lumber Company in the office, drawing maps and plans. In this way he became interested in the lumber business and gained a knowledge of standing timber.

Mr. Trabert spent some time in the Pine River district and accompanied the driving crews, thus becoming familiar with the details of practical lumber. At this time Mr. Trabert decided to take his final year in college, and attended Newberry College, North Carolina, graduating in 1894, and receiving the degree of B. A. He returned to Minneapolis and permanently entered the employ of C. A. Smith & Company, then a partnership of C. A. Smith and ex-Governor John S. Pillsbury. Mr. Trabert became connected with the timber end of the business, and in one year became private secretary to Mr. Smith, which position he held for seventeen years. January 1, 1904, the C. A. Smith Timber Company was organized with a capital stock of one million dollars; this company took over all the timber holdings of the former concern, and in May, 1912, removed their offices to Oakland, California. The C. A. Smith Timber Company acquired interests in the West, and their business grew rapidly, and subsidiary corporations were formed, and Mr. Trabert was made secretary of the various holdings. As the Smith timber was cut off in Minnesota and the various interests on the Pacific Coast grew, Mr. Smith, in looking for a western location, decided upon Oakland for the reason that the five timber districts controlled by the Smith interests—two fir tracts and one spruce in Oregon, with one redwood and one sugar-pine and yellow-pine tract in California—were tributary to tide-water. He therefore moved all of his interests to Oakland, and established yards, planning mills, and a box-factory at Bay Point, California. Mr. Trabert is a member of the National Foresters Association, the National Geographical Association, the Archaeological Association of America, a kindred body. He also belongs to the Oregon Conservation Association. He has frequently lectured before the University of California and the Forestry Club on the subjects of forestry. On June 25, 1894, Mr. Trabert was united in marriage to Miss Harriett Abney Wells, of Newberry, South Carolina, a daughter of Osborne Wells, one of the most prominent men of that city and an officer in the Civil War. To this union a daughter, Dorothy, was born in 1895. Mr. Trabert was well known in social circles of Minneapolis. He held membership in the University Club, the Interlochen Minneapolis Choral Club, the Philharmonic Club, of which he was president, and the Federation of Men's Clubs.

He was a member of the Minneapolis bar, having received his degree in law from the University of Minnesota in 1899. In Oakland he holds membership in the Athenian and Commercial clubs and is a member of the University Club of San Francisco, and the Faculty Club of the University of California.

During his entire life Mr. Trabert has been active in the affairs of the Lutheran church, assisting in the organization of the St. Michael's Lutheran Church of Berkeley, which was incorporated September 29, 1913, and is vestryman and choirmaster. He is a director in the Berkeley Ontario Society, and a member of the Sons of the Revolution, while Mrs. Trabert is treasurer of the John Rutledge Chapter, D. A. R. She is in addition a member of Joseph Le Conte Chapter, Daughters of the

Confederacy. She is also a member of the Wednesday Morning Musical Club and the Ebell Society of Oakland.

CHARLES BERNDT JOHNSON.—Throughout the years of an active business career Charles Berndt Johnson, of Bay Point, has given all or most of his time and attention to the lumber business, and is today one of the most trusted and valued lumbermen in California. He has risen through the various departments to be general superintendent of the C. A. Smith Lumber Company, of Bay Point, California. This position he is now filling with credit and distinction. He was born in Sweden, May 2, 1871, and is a son of Johnnas Anderson. In his country the son takes the first name of his father. His mother, Assarina (Anderson) Johnson, was also a native of Sweden.

Our subject received a limited education in the old country and at an early age worked on his father's farm. At the age of twenty he came to America and located in Minnesota, where he found employment in a lumber-yard as a common laborer. He progressed and was promoted to shipping clerk for the Shelvin-Calpenter Lumber Company. Here he remained for fifteen years.

He then removed to Freece, Minnesota, and there followed the same work for three years. In 1911 he came to Bay Point and became identified with the C. A. Smith Lumber Company, as shipping clerk and general foreman, after which he was promoted to the office of general superintendent, which position he now holds. He is watchful of all indications concerning trade conditions, is energetic, and has achieved a measure of success, which is the direct reward of persistent earnest effort. Mr. Johnson is a Republican. He has repeatedly been elected on the Bay Point school board. Fraternally, he is affiliated with the Masonic lodge and the I. O. U. W. Mr. Johnson was twice married; the first union was to Hannah Larson, a native of Sweden. This marriage occurred in 1892. His first wife died in 1903. To this union were born two sons and two daughters—Myrtle, wife of H. L. Taylor; Edna, who resides at home; Berndt, of Bay Point; and Henry, deceased. The second marriage was to Helena Elmgrem, also a native of Sweden, in October, 1905. To this union two children have been born, Bernice and Leslie. Mr. Johnson has many friends in the Bay cities, and he is popular among those with whom he is connected.

SIMON W. CUNNINGHAM.—The life record of Simon W. Cunningham is interwoven with the history of Contra Costa County. His parents, indeed, are of the true pioneers of the country; his father was one of the first men to locate in this part of the State. Simon W. was born at Bay Point, April 30, 1868, a son of Daniel and Fannie (Hickey) Cunningham, both natives of Ireland. His parents were united in marriage in Albany, N. Y., and came west in 1850, locating in Sonoma County. His father worked at ranching for a time for Colonel Swift, and later became identified with Mr. Hood in buying large numbers of sheep. Mr. Cunningham's father brought the sheep to Contra Costa County and made all the arrangements to locate in this county on government lands. He took up six hundred and forty acres of land at Bay Point, afterward adding to his holdings. When the C. A. Smith Lumber Company located at Bay Point in the spring of 1908, Simon W. and his brothers disposed of one thousand acres to this concern. Mr. Cunningham's father died in 1901, and his mother passed away in 1914. There were eight sons and one daughter born into the parents' family. The subject of this sketch acquired his education in the public schools of Bay Point, after which he looked after the ranch interests and became interested in business at Bay Point for ten years. In 1910 he engaged in the dry-goods and gentlemen's furnishing-goods business and is recognized as a far-sighted and resourceful business man. In politics Mr. Cunningham is a Democrat. Fraternally, he is affiliated with the Modern Woodmen of America, I. D. E. S., and the U. P. E. C.

He was united in marriage to Miss Louisa Williams of Concord. To this union there have been two children—Warren, born April 19, 1905, and Mervin, born July 2, 1914. Mrs. Cunningham's father, Joseph Williams, Sr., is one of the respected ranchers in his locality, and has been a resident of Contra Costa County for many years.

VOLNEY TAYLOR.—Among the men who assisted materially in the development of eastern Contra Costa County prominent mention should be made of Volney Taylor, a man of enterprising ideas and methods. He was born in the Province of Quebec, Canada, June 20, 1851, and came with his parents to California when he was fifteen years of age. His father, Alexander T. Taylor, was born in the township of Bolton, Province of Quebec, Canada, September 15, 1821, and at the age of twenty he started in life for himself.

In 1844 he rented a farm in Canada, and later purchased the land, which he operated for eleven years. Disposing of his landholdings he returned to the place of his birth, where he remained until his removal to the Pacific Coast.

Accompanied by his family he sailed from New York on November 6, 1866, to the Isthmus of Panama, and from there to San Francisco, arriving December 6th of that year. He located near Vallejo, Solano County, where he rented a farm for two years. In September, 1868, he removed to Contra Costa County, locating in the Point of Timber district, where he purchased three hundred and twenty acres of land. From the first he was successful, and large crops of grain made his land a valuable investment. The marriage of Alexander T. Taylor occurred on June 17, 1845, to Miss Louisa Bruce, a native of Vermont. To this union were the following children: Valeria M., born July 14, 1846, wife of C. A. Foster (passed away in 1908); Avyette, born October 27, 1848, wife of A. Richardson (passed away in 1907); Alexander V., born April 11,1853; and Volney, the subject of this review. The Taylor family originated in England, and established themselves near Quebec, Canada, during the early history of America. Alexander T. Taylor died in 1912 and was numbered among the most prominent and representative men of eastern Contra Costa County. He came empty-handed to the State and won his way to a position of prominence, and his death was mourned by a wide circle of friends. Volney Taylor acquired his education in the public schools of Vallejo, and in 1872 he graduated from the Pacific Business College in San Francisco, after which he returned to the home place and took up farming. He purchased the home farm from his father, and in addition to this he bought two other ranches. He now owns about eight hundred acres of the finest land in the eastern part of the county, being especially adapted to grain and alfalfa, and Mr. Taylor now has about one hundred and fifty acres of the finest alfalfa raised in this county. From 1896 to 1905 Mr. Taylor made his home in Oakland. He was united in marriage to Miss Agnes E. Andrews, a native of Illinois, and to this union was born one son, Everett B., now a prominent attorney residing in Martinez. On December 11, 1901, he was united in marriage to Miss Carrie F. Bohmen, of Sacramento, and their one daughter, Beatrice B., was born in 1905. Volney Taylor has gained a place of influence in Contra Costa County, and has won for himself a fine reputation for his business ability. He is president of the Byron-Bethany Irrigation Company.

Fraternally, he is a Royal Arch Mason and a member of the Eastern Star. He also holds membership in the Independent Order of Odd Fellows and in the Independent Order of Good Templars.

JAMES SIMEON HOOK.—An early pioneer of Contra Costa County and a prominent member of its agricultural community, James S. Hook is widely and favorably known throughout the Bay section as an upright man of honest integrity and sterling worth. Mr. Hook is a son of William Hook, one of the first settlers in Contra Costa County, who died July 24, 1882. William and Elijah were twin brothers, born in Salem, Virginia, February 4, 1805.

Their father died when the boys were fourteen. They moved with the family to Howard County, Missouri, where they engaged in building houses. In 1827, they purchased a quantity of dry goods and joined an expedition for Santa Fe. The night previous to their arrival at Santa Fe they met some Mexicans who informed them the following day there was to be a massacre, which took place and many were killed. William Hook hired mules and packed the goods over the mountains into Sonora, where Elijah joined him.

They visited the principal towns in Sonora, sold what goods they could, and returned to Santa Fe. Learning that the Indians were troublesome on the way home, they went to Matamoras, where the brothers parted, Elijah taking passage to Philadelphia. He had fifty thousand dollars with him, which he put in the safe, no one but the captain knowing that he had the money.

After being at sea for some days, a man tossed Elijah overboard. Just as he was sinking for the last time, he caught a rope and was pulled aboard. When William and Elijah parted William purchased a drove of mules and started for Missouri, through Texas. On the way he was taken sick and was cared for by a family in northern Texas. He recovered and finally reached the mouth of Red River, where he sold the mules, and after three months he reached his destination. The brothers then engaged in the merchandise business for several years. They also took up the steamboat business and made a trip to New Orleans. Cholera broke out and the crew died except the Hook brothers. On the second trip to New Orleans, Elijah died of yellow fever, in August, 1835. The same year William married Miss Miranda Brown.

In 1850 he and his wife crossed the plains, arriving in Placerville on September 1, 1850, just before California was declared a State. Their daughter Emma was the first white child born in Placerville. The following spring they removed to Sacramento. In 1853 they came to Martinez. Here Mr. Hook engaged in business. In 1854 he purchased land in Contra Costa County, and in 1855 and 1856 he bought more land and owned nearly three thousand acres.

James S. Hook was born January 27, 1853. At the age of six years his parents moved onto land near Pacheco. He was educated in the public schools, Braden College, a private school in Oakland, and the University of California, graduating from the department of agriculture in 1874. He returned to the home place, where he has always been active in agricultural pursuits. He has been enterprising in fruit culture and has about nine thousand trees and ships annually nearly four hundred tons of pears. He was united in marriage on October 24, 1883, to Miss Louise Gambs, a daughter of John and Helen Gambs. Her father was one of the pioneer merchants of Pacheco, and one of the first to engage in the manufacture of wine in this county. He died in June, 1907. Her mother is still living and is now nearly seventy-five years old. Mrs. Hook was born July 30, 1864. To this union there are three sons, Theodore Harold, born August 14, 1885; Cyril Randolph, born March 1, 1888; James Stanley, born July 29, 1897. James S. Hook is a member of the Masonic lodge of Walnut Creek, and the Woodmen of the World. Both Mr. and Mrs. Hook are members of the Eastern Star and Artisans. In politics Mr. Hook is a Republican. Theodore Harold married Josephine Russi, of Pacheco, in June, 1913, and their daughter, Lucille Marie, was born October 20, 1916. Cyril Randolph married Flora Dewing, of Walnut Creek, in March, 1913, and their one child, Flora Jane, was born July 26, 1915. In fraternal circles Theodore H. and Cyril R. are members of the Masonic lodge of Danville and hold membership in the Royal Arch. At the age of twenty-five Theodore H. held the office of worshipful master of the Masonic lodge at Walnut Creek for two terms. Vincent Hook, a son of William Hook, graduated in civil engineering from the University of California in 1876, and follows general farming. He was married on September 26, 1885, to Adele Raap, a native of Contra Costa County. He is a Republican, and was elected supervisor in 1906, and has since held this office. He is a Royal Arch Mason, a member of the Native Sons, the I. O. O. F., the W. O. W., and the Eastern Star. The Hook family is accordingly respected and esteemed by a wide circle of friends in the Bay region.

LUKE BULGER has been actively identified with business interests of Contra Costa County as a contractor and builder for the past thirty-nine years. He was born in Canada, near Montreal, June 6, 1852, a son of James and Margaret Bulger, both natives of Ireland. Mr. Bulger acquired his education in the public schools of Chicago, Illinois. He took up the carpenter trade when a young man and has since been identified with contracting and building. Thirty-nine years ago he came to Martinez, where he embarked in business as a building contractor on his own account. He first erected cottages and did carpenter work and gradually branched out into larger construction. He has erected and been identified with many important structures. He was superintendent of the Contra Costa County courthouse and town hall, and also had charge of the Byron Hot Springs Hotel. He has erected many of the finest homes in Martinez. Politically, Mr. Bulger is a Democrat. He has served as school trustee for twenty-four years. He was united in marriage thirty-five years ago to Margaret Hurley; her death occurred seventeen years ago. There were eight children born to this union. Mr. Bulger is a member of the Woodmen of the World.

HERMAN H. BRUNS, a representative pioneer settler of Contra Costa County and a true type of the brave, hardy, and energetic men of nearly fifty years ago who, coming to this country in manhood's prime, contributed largely toward its growth and advancement. He was a man of excellent ability, sound judgment, and good principles. Being a native of Germany, he was reared and educated in his native land. In the early '70s he purchased one hundred and sixty acres of land in the Antioch section, where he successfully carried on general ranching. Mr. Bruns married Catherine Bruggamann, also a native of Germany, and to this union there are two children-John, born June 12, 1888, and Herman H., Jr., born December 31, 1885. Both boys received their education in the public schools of Byron and Brentwood, after which they assisted on the home place. John H. was united in marriage to Esther L. Davidson, a native of Antioch, July 31, 1915, and to this union was born John Donald, December 6, 1916. Fraternally, John H. Bruns and his brother are members of the I. O. O. F. of Byron and the Masonic lodge of Brentwood. Politically, they both are affiliated with the Republican party, and they adhere to the principles which are advocated in the platform of their party in national affairs, but locally reserve the right to cast their ballots for the man whom they consider best qualified for public office. In Brentwood Bruns Brothers erected a concrete and modern garage, 75 by 120 feet, which would be a credit to a larger city. They have erected a modern and substantial garage in Antioch, 50 by 100 feet, on the corner of Third and F streets. The firm of Bruns Brothers have the agency for the Buick and Ford automobiles. They are held in the highest esteem both in business and social relations in their community.

GEORGE W. SMITH.—Among the most beautiful as well as the most productive ranches in eastern Contra Costa County is that of George W. Smith, residing near Brentwood. It is located beautifully and commands a sweeping view of Mount Diablo. Of this property, consisting of fifty-six and a half acres, fifty-four acres is given over to the production of the finest varieties of walnuts and almonds. The care and attention which have been exercised in the management of this ranch place it at once among the most valuable properties in this section. Born in Illinois on August 4, 1858, George W.

Smith was one of a family of four children. His parents were Oscar and Sarah Jane Smith. His father came to California in 1863 and located in Lodi.

where he farmed for about one year. He then moved to Napa and remained for two years. Afterward he made his home in Davis for a period of three years. Seeing the possibilities of eastern Contra Costa County, he purchased one hundred and sixty acres and engaged in general farming. His death occurred in 1910. His wife died in 1865, while they resided in Napa. The subject of this sketch received his education in the public schools of Brentwood. At the age of twenty-one he rented a place on the Marsh grant, where he remained for sixteen years. Nineteen years ago he returned to the home place and took the management of his father's interests, which he has successfully conducted up to the time of his father's death. Mr. Smith was united in marriage to Miss Mattie Walton, a native of Texas, in 1884. To this union have been born two children. Alma, the first daughter, on July 21, 1903, married Joseph W. Pfaff, and resides on the home place. Their three children are Evelyn, George, and Violette. Mr. Smith's second daughter, Eunice, was united in marriage to William Meuser, of San Francisco, on September 5, 1009. Politically, Mr. Smith is a Democrat, and has always sought to advance the principles which he indorses. He gives his aid toward good government as well as the general welfare of his locality. Fraternally, he is a member of the Masonic lodge of Brentwood and holds membership in the Eastern Star.

He is also a member of the Independent Order of Foresters. The other children in Mr. Smith's parents' family are Henry C, residing in Santa Cruz; Mattie, wife of William Douglass, residing in Marin County; and Charles, who died at the age of twenty-five.

ROBERT WALLACE, JR.—Prominently identified with the active and enterprising business men and agriculturists of Brentwood is Robert Wallace, Jr. He is a man of ability and is numbered among the substantial men of his community. He is successfully engaged in the insurance business, and the high reputation which he enjoys is greatly to his credit, for it stamps him as a man who follows only the fairest methods. For fourteen years he has served as justice of the peace, and he has fulfilled the expectations which the people had in him when they entrusted their affairs to his care. Mr. Wallace was born in San Francisco on September 28, 1859, being a son of Robert and Ann (Shepard) Wallace. Both parents were natives of North Shields, England. His father learned the trade of ship-caulker and came to San Francisco in 1857, where he readily found employment. In 1870 he purchased one hundred and sixty acres of land south of Brentwood, and upon this place Robert, Jr., began his manual labors. After finishing his education, Robert assumed charge of his father's place. After a time he rented the ranch, and soon purchased one hundred and sixty acres adjoining his father's property.

Mr. Wallace was united in marriage to Miss Alice J. Murphy, daughter of John Murphy, of Concord. To this union have been born four children—Robert, Jr., Ray, Elaine, and Richard. In his fraternal relations Mr. Wallace is affiliated with Brentwood Lodge No. 345, F. & A. M., in which he served as master for a period of five years. He also occupied the various chairs in the order. He is a member of the Eastern Star and has served as patron of the latter. He also holds membership in the I. O. O. F. lodge of Byron. He is a member and director of the Point of Timber Cemetery Association and the Contra Costa Agricultural Association. He has taken a keen interest in good horses, and was a member of the Concord Driving Club of Contra Costa County. Mr. Wallace is a Democrat in politics, and in casting his vote he exercises the same caution and judgment which characterize his business enterprises. His mother passed away in 1892, and her death was mourned by a wide circle of friends.

GEORGE W. KNIGHT.—No one man has done more to advance the agricultural, horticultural, and commercial interests of eastern Contra Costa County than George W. Knight, of Knightsen. Enterprising, energetic, and progressive, he has developed one of the best paying ranches in that section.

Mr. Knight was born in Chelsea, Maine, January 20, 1843, and is a son of John and Adeline (Tibbetts) Knight. At the age of twenty-three he became dependent upon his own resources, and went to Massachusetts, where he followed the occupation of landscape gardening. He saved considerable money, and in 1874 he determined to cast his lot with the Golden West and sailed for California via the Panama route. He went to Santa Barbara, where he found employment on a ranch. His desire was to own a fine ranch.

Through the result of close economy, after working out in San Francisco, Marin County, Livermore Valley, and Antioch, he obtained a sufficient sum to enable him to rent a ranch in connection with G. Dunbar and N. B. Hewitt. Later Mr. Knight engaged in the hay-pressing business. He followed this and other work until 1883, when he purchased one hundred and ten acres, a part of the Barkley ranch, and began to improve it. He devoted the land to the cultivation of grain and hay and met with financial success. He then purchased eighty acres, and again ten acres adjoining. Mr. Knight set out several acres of almonds. He raised all of his own trees and did considerable nursery work. He propagated the "Klondike" almond and made exhibits at the St. Louis Exposition in 1904. Foreseeing the need of a shipping station and post-office at that point on the Santa Fe Railroad, in 1900 he had surveyed seven and a half acres of land, erected a store and post-office, and on May 15 was appointed postmaster. Mr. Knight was united in marriage on March 2, 1885, to Christina Christensen, a native of Denmark, the daughter of Johan and Anna (Hansen)

Christensen, and it was the combination of the two names which gave the name to the town of Knightsen. To this union have been born Amy Marie, wife of Harvey Nelson Rook, of Williamsport, Pa., married September 5, 1902, and engaged in the grocery business in Los Angeles. They have four children—Virginia Margaret Amy, born January 31, 1904; Harvey Nelson, born January 23, 1906; Robert McClellan, born January 14, 1909; and Ellen Marie, born October 1, 1912. Addie Flora Knight was married to Phillip Cohen Mecum, of Chico, California, July 17, 1911. Their one child, Vernon Claire, was born July 27, 1914. Essie Wilmena Knight was united in marriage to Lewis Ervin Lehmer, of Harrisburg, Pa., June 2, 1912.

Their one son, Lewis Erwin, Jr., was born April 24, 1913. Mr. Lehmer is connected with the Southern Pacific Company as station agent at Raisin City, Fresno County, California. George W. Knight has been a lifelong Republican. He has served on the Knightsen school board for a period of fourteen years and served as clerk of the board most of the time. He has never aspired to public office. Mr. Knight raised 2065 sacks of barley on sixty-five acres in 1915, and he has twenty-five acres set out to almonds, and ships annually on an average about eight tons of the finest almonds grown in California.

EDSON H. FOX, president and manager of the ranch of the Central Creamery Company, with offices at corner of Twelfth and Jefferson streets, Oakland, is a man of much energy and activity. He is held in high esteem by his large circle of friends and acquaintances. He was born in Aurora, Illinois, April 6, 1871. His father, Daniel Fox, was a soap manufacturer during his residence in Illinois. His mother, Jennie (Baker) Fox, was a native of Illinois. The family came to the Pacific Coast in 1883, and settled in Oakland, where Edson H. received his education. Laying aside his books, Mr.

Fox worked at the baking business for a time, and later worked for the Fairmont dairy for six years. The Central Creamery Company now owns three hundred acres of choice land near Oakley and has a herd of three hundred and thirty selected cows. The buildings are of the most advanced type, and the sanitary regulations in this dairy are the most modern and up to date.

Politically, Mr. Fox is a Republican, but he has never aspired to office. He was united in marriage to Miss Louisa Ransom, a native of Nevada County, California. To this union one son, Ransom Fox, was born in 1899. The stockholders in the Central Creamery Company are J. M. Carr, J. J. O'Neil (manager and secretary), Mrs. Jayne, George Hickman, and E. H. Fox. The subject of this review is a public-spirited man and ever ready to lend his best efforts toward the promotion of any movement calculated to advance the interests of eastern Contra Costa County.

HENRY W. HEIDORN is an active representative of business interests in eastern Contra Costa County. He is engaged in the general mercantile business at Knightsen and was born July 16, 1876. He is a son of Christopher Heidorn, a representative rancher, who came to this county in 1868. Entirely through his own efforts he acquired a position of importance in the county, and by his constant and undivided attention and by exercising economy he became the owner of a two-hundred-and-forty-acre ranch. Mr. Heidorn's father was a native of Germany and came to America when a young man and settled on the Alfred ranch near Knightsen. Three years later he purchased two hundred and forty acres and engaged in general farming operations, raising grain and hay, and had considerable land set out to fruits, nuts, and vineyard. His death occurred on November 21, 1906. Henry W. Heidorn, the subject of this review, acquired his education in the public schools of Brentwood and Antioch, after which he attended college in San Francisco. After finishing his education he became identified with general merchandise stores in San Francisco, Crockett, and Antioch, and in January, 1904, he opened a store in Knightsen. In his parents' family there were three children—Emma, wife of Thomas White, residing on the home place; Edna, a teacher in the public school of Knightsen; and our subject. Mr. Heidorn is affiliated with the Republican party and has served on the local school board for a period of ten years. He has served six years as deputy county assessor for the fifth district and has acted as a delegate on the county central committee for six years. He has been postmaster at Knightsen and takes a keen interest in the upbuilding and modern activities of the eastern part of the county. Fraternally, Mr. Heidorn is a Mason and a member of No. 345, F. & A. M., a Royal Arch Mason, and is past patron of the Eastern Star, besides being a member of the I. O. O. F. of Byron and the Independent Order of Foresters of Brentwood. He was married September 27, 1905, to Miss Helen Southerland Johnston, a native of San Francisco and a daughter of James and Helen C. Johnston. Mrs. Heidorn's father was a prominent contractor in San Francisco and died in 1910. Her mother is still living. Mr. Heidorn's father came to this country via Panama accompanied by his brother. His father first settled in Dixon. He later went to Pacheco and worked for Mr. Loucks, and at a later time worked for the Antioch distillery. He returned to Germany, where he remained for one year, when he again made the trip to this country, where he remained and became one of the leading ranchers in eastern Contra Costa County.

DAVID FRANKEL—The history of David Frankel, of Pittsburg, California, is that of a representative business man of the West, alert and energetic. He has certainly won a place among the leading and progressive business men of Contra Costa County. Mr. Frankel was born in Germany, October 10, 1874. He acquired his education in the old country, and after coming to America he pursued his studies in the public schools of San Francisco. Early in life he learned the painting and decorating trade in his native land. He followed this business for about fourteen years. In 1904 he removed to Contra Costa County. Previous to coming here he operated a store in Mariposa County, which he conducted with gratifying success. On taking up his residence in Pittsburg he engaged in business to a successful degree. Politically Mr. Frankel is affiliated with the Republican party. He was elected April 10, 1916, as one of Pittsburg's city trustees for the four-year term. Fraternally, he is a member of the Knights of Pythias Lodge No. 18, of Pittsburg. He is also a member of the Foresters of America, Golden West Court No. 20, of San Francisco. Mr. Frankel was united in marriage to Miss Nellie Olander, a daughter of Isaac and Minnie Olander, January 12, 1902. To this union have been two children—Minnie, born in San Francisco, January 22, 1003 and Bessie, born in Pittsburg, California, November 13, 1906. Mrs. Frankel is also known in club circles and holds membership in the Pythian Sisters.

Mr. Frankel has been an active member of the Knights of Pythias, and has held the office of inside guard, at present acting as outside guard. He has shown himself able and faithful in the discharge of public duties and has gained the indorsement of the people of his locality, both in a business and political way. Both daughters of Mr. and Mrs. Frankel are popular and are musicians of considerable ability.

JOSEPH PAZZI is one of the prominent and well-known business men of Bay Point. His record is that of a self-made man who has won success in the business world entirely by his own efforts. He was born in Italy on January 1, 1881. He received a limited education in the old country. He came to America on April 17, 1906. At the age of fifteen he went to England and remained in that country until he was twenty-five years of age. He was identified with the confectionery business in England, and coming to the United States, he located at Jerome, Arizona, where he remained for a few months.

He removed to Contra Costa County and operated a meat market at Point Richmond, and then entered the same business in Bay Point. He then went into the general merchandise business at Bay Point. He has many friends in the county and among the business men and is trusted by all because of his high principles. Mr. Pazzi was united in marriage to Ernestine Miller, a native of France. To this union have been born three children—Marguerite, Florence, and Ernestine. Mr. Pazzi is public-spirited and interested in all matters that are to the interest and for the welfare of the community in which he lives.

CAPTAIN JOHN B. TURNER was one of the oldest residents of Antioch. In early days—the '50s—he was captain of a steamboat called the "Antioch" which plied between Antioch and Collinsville. It was his delight to relate incidents of early California history in which he took part and tell anecdotes of the prominent men of that time, with most of whom he had a personal acquaintance. The bell in the belfry of the Antioch Methodist church was once on the old schoolhouse, then opposite the present school, and was at one time his property away back in the '50s when the bell was used on steamboats instead of a whistle. He left a large family that was his particular pride. He taught his family one principle that is frequently overlooked. They have the true family affection and love for each other. They are as closely knit by the bonds of love and affection, due to the family tie, as any family we have known. His father, Thomas Turner, was a pioneer of the great West, and built the first fort in Missouri, during the Black Hawk War. The decedent, John B. Turner, came to California in 1849, and settled on the San Joaquin, where, with his two brothers, he was connected with the cattle business. In 1863 he moved to Antioch and engaged in the steamboat business in company with his brother, Captain Abe Turner. His wife, who was Miss Maria Fleming, was born in Dunsmore, Galway County, Ireland, in 1847, and sailed for San Francisco with friends in 1869. A short time afterward she came to Antioch, where she met Captain J. B. Turner, of the ferry steamer "Antioch," and following a short courtship was married to the prominent river man. Never was there a more devoted mother, whose every thought was for her children, while the latter always considered her comfort. They left a large family to mourn them—eight boys and three girls: Thomas, John B., George A., James T., Lillie E., William G., Frank M., Bert, Ruth, Ben, and Sadie.

ALVA SHERMAN SHERLOCK, a practicing attorney of Concord, has won success at the bar and is numbered among the able representatives of the legal fraternity in Contra Costa County. His birth occurred in Zanesville, Ohio, September 26, 1869; his parents being Abraham and Adeline (Sandel) Sherlock. Alva S. attended grammar school in Poneshiek County, Iowa, where his parents removed in 1875. His father was a farmer and died in 1882. The mother is now residing in Chicago. There were seven children born in the parents' family, and all are living. Hugh, a rancher, at Madrone; Lewis F., a rancher, residing near San Jose; and Roy W., a resident of San Francisco, identified with the S. P. R. R., are the only ones residing in California. The subject of this review studied law under H. A. Haines, of Chicago, and was admitted to the bar in Chicago and admitted to practice before the Supreme Court of Illinois in 1897. He was united in marriage to Miss May B. Kent McLeod in Chicago, September 26, 1901. Mr. Sherlock practiced his profession in Chicago for a period of nine years. In 1906 he removed to Newport, Washington, and represented many large mining interests of that State. He was admitted to practice in that State on motion or license from Illinois. He served in the Spanish-American War and was a member of Troop F. of the First Illinois Cavalry. He served from April 26, 1898, to October 11, 1898. He went to Chickamauga Park, Georgia, a training camp, and was honorably discharged at Fort Sheridan October 11, 1898. He served as city attorney at Newport, Washington, from January, 1908, to January, 1910. He also served as city attorney at Deer Park, Washington, from February 5, 1910, to February 7, 1911. He incorporated the town of Ione, Washington, and rendered legal services to many towns and corporations during his stay in Washington. Mr. Sherlock gives his political allegiance to the Democratic party. He was a candidate for the House of Representatives from the sixtieth district, Washington, in 1912. He removed to Spokane in June, 1913, and remained in that city until May, 1915, when he came to California. Mr. Sherlock was admitted to the bar of this State on June 11, 1915, and admitted on motion August 1, 1915. He opened an office in Concord, in the Bank of Concord building, where he has done a general law business with gratifying success, and on April 10th he was appointed city attorney.

Fraternally, Mr. Sherlock is affiliated with the Royal Arcanum No. 1622, of San Francisco. Mr. and Mrs. Sherlock have one daughter, May Ruth, born in Chicago, August IS, 1902. Mrs. Sherlock's father, Frederick Kent, was a native of New York State and died there. Her mother was Jennie (McLeod) Kent-Tresham, a native of Ohio, who died in 1913. Both parents of Mrs. Sherlock were well-known theatrical people of the early days and made a success all over the United States. They had the respect and esteem of all who knew them, and they used to tell of their many reminiscences of the early days.

EUGENE BLYTHE ANDERSON has for a number of years been connected with educational work in Contra Costa County. He was born on January 25, 1857, at Petaluma, California. His parents were William L. and Emma R. (Ferguson) Anderson, the former a native of Tennessee, and the latter of Kentucky. After pursuing his studies in the public schools Mr. Anderson attended and graduated from Christian's College of Santa Rosa. At an early age he began to teach school and followed this vocation for over seventeen years in Sacramento, Contra Costa, and Lake counties. He became one of the eminent educational authorities in this county, and for many years served on the county educational board. In 1898 Mr. Anderson engaged in fruit-growing extensively and owns ninety acres of fruit adjoining the town of Walnut Creek, which he has brought up to a high state of cultivation. He specializes in prunes and pears and handles five hundred tons of dried fruits annually. He has two drying plants and uses ten thousand drying trays in order to dry his fruit. He is a large realty dealer in Richmond, having $50,000 invested in real estate. He is proprietor of the Anderson Hotel, located at Point Richmond, and is recognized in business circles as a resourceful and discriminating man, whose integrity is beyond question.

Politically, Mr. Anderson is a Democrat, but he has never been active along party lines, and has never aspired to any political office. He represented Contra Costa County for fifteen years on the California Development Board, which was an honorary position. On June 14, 1888, he was united in marriage to Lena C. Jones, a native of Contra Costa County, and daughter of John M. Jones of Alamo. Their one adopted daughter, Rosalie, was born in 1900. Mrs. Anderson, previous to her marriage, was connected with educational work in this county. She taught school in Walnut Creek district for twenty years; she served on the board of education for some years after her resignation. Mr. Anderson is identified fraternally with the Masonic fraternity, being a member of Alamo Lodge No. 122. Mrs. Anderson is a member of the Eastern Star and has held the office of worthy matron of her lodge. Mr. and Mrs. Anderson are held in high esteem in the community by all who know them.

CHARLES DUNN is an active and enterprising representative of business interests of Concord, being identified with the wholesale and retail butcher business. His birth occurred in Lafayette, Contra Costa County, California, October 14, 1867, his parents being Lemuel J. and Asenith (Millard) Dunn.

Mr. Dunn's father crossed the plains during the pioneer days of California, and his mother, accompanied by her father, came to this State via the Isthmus route. His parents were married in Contra Costa County and had five children; his brother, Davis, died in 1906. The subject of this review acquired his education in the public schools of Contra Costa County, after which he took a business course at Heald's Business College. Laying aside his books, Mr. Dunn became identified with agricultural pursuits. This he followed up to 1000, when he removed to Concord and worked for Randall Brothers for a period of ten years in the warehouse. He held the position as bookkeeper in Randall Brothers' general merchandise store for two years, and then became identified with Foskett, Elworthy & Keller, in the meat business. Mr. Dunn, with H. P. Brubeck and Joseph Levada, bought out this firm in May, 1911, and they have since continued in the wholesale and retail meat business. Mr. Dunn is progressive and he has succeeded in life for the reason that he has always ceaselessly applied himself to his business. The firm follows the most honorable methods, and its members are well worthy of the confidence and respect which they enjoy in their community. The father of Mr. Dunn died in 1870; his mother is still living; she was twice married, the second union being to Austin Dorman, of Concord.

The subject of our review was united in wedlock to Laura E. Jaquith, of Concord, in 1895, and her death occurred in 1900. Mr. Dunn's second marriage was to Victoria M. Railsback, a native of Indiana. To the first union there were two children—Lemuel, born in March, 1897, and Laura E., born September, 1898. By the second marriage there were four children—Ruth E., Ellen G., Esther B., and Mildred Pearl. Mr. Dunn gives his political allegiance to the Democratic party. He is now serving as town trustee, being elected to that office in April, 1914, for the four-year term. Fraternally, he is a member of the Red Men, the Native Sons, and the Woodmen of the World.

The grandfather of Mr. Dunn came to California and located in Sacramento in 1852, where he died of cholera. His wife and two sons removed to San Jose. All the worldly possessions they had consisted of two yoke of oxen.

With no money or food, the boys started out and found employment at freighting. Mr. Dunn's father was one of these boys. By his determination to win, he saved up some money and removed to Lafayette, where he eventually bought land. He was a man of culture and progressive views and was recognized as one of tried integrity and worth.

FRED J. WEBER is an active representative of business interests in Contra Costa County, being located at San Pablo. His father, Frank Weber, was a native of Germany, and died in 1896. Mr. Weber's mother was Julia (Willem) Weber, also a native of Germany. In 1856 Mr. Weber's father came to America and located in San Francisco. The parents were married in San Francisco, and six children were born to this union. A brother, Frank J. Weber, is associated with our subject in the meat business. Fred J. Weber was educated in the public schools, after which he assisted on the home ranch until 1902, when he and his brother Frank engaged in the meat business, and by straightforward and honorable business methods have now a place among the prominent and well-to-do business men of the county. They have a well-equipped market and operate their plant for handling and killing stock. There are four sisters—Reca, Julia (wife of Frank Schrick, of San Francisco), Lillie (wife of James Murphy, of Sacramento), and Louisa. Mr.

Weber's father owned one hundred acres of general farming land, which has since been brought up to a high state of cultivation. Fred J. Weber is affiliated with the Democratic party but has never aspired to any political office. He has served on the local school board and is interested in matters for the betterment of local conditions. He is a member of the Foresters, the Odd Fellows, and the Native Sons. His brother, Frank J. Weber, is also a member of the Foresters and the Native Sons.

WALTER A. ROGERS.—Among the men who by reason of their ability and business enterprise have come to be regarded as representative citizens and leading business men of Contra Costa County is numbered Walter A. Rogers, who for many years has been engaged in the hotel business at Walnut Creek. He is a son of William B. Rogers, who was born in Ripley County, Indiana, June 26, 1827. When fifteen years old William B. Rogers, the father of Walter A. Rogers, went to Burlington, Iowa, where he attended school during the winter months and farmed in the summer. In 1846 he proceeded to Van Buren County and learned the cooper's trade. The same year he was united in marriage to Elizabeth Shaffer. In 1852 he crossed the plains, arriving in Drytown, Amador County, California, October 20, 1852. He at once opened a laundry. In the fall of 1852 he erected the Iowa Hotel at Empire City, and a year later he removed to San Ramon Valley. In 1856 he commenced farming, which he followed until 1867. Mr. Rogers then removed to Walnut Creek In 1861 he went to San Francisco and engaged in the draying business from 1870 to 1878. He served on the San Francisco police force, where he was widely known as an energetic and efficient officer. In 1880 he again removed to Walnut Creek and erected the Rogers Hotel. In 1870 Mr. Rogers was married to his second wife, Elizabeth Anderson. To the first union were born five children, two of whom died in infancy, Mary, who died at the age of sixteen, and William. William served as sheriff of Contra Costa County for three terms and was succeeded by R. R. Veale. He was afterwards constable of

Martinez, and later he became identified with the Southern Pacific Company, when his health failed and he died in 1913. Walter A. Rogers received his education in the public schools of San Francisco and Contra Costa County. After acquiring his education he followed various vocations. In 1881 he returned to Walnut Creek and bought his brother's interest in the hotel, and, associated with his father, continued to operate the hotel until 1892, when he bought the interest of his father, who retired. The hotel is one of the leading hotels around the Bay district and popular with automobile parties. The hotel contains forty rooms and has always been kept up to the highest standard. Walter A. Rogers was united in marriage to Anna Buck, a native of Kansas, in 1902. To this union one son, Walter A., Jr., was born on November 9, 1909. Mr. Rogers gives his political allegiance to the Republican party. He served as deputy constable under his brother for some years. He has always co-operated with any movements that tend to the upbuilding and substantial improvements of his city, and manifests at all times a public-spirited devotion to the general good of the county. Mr. Rogers is the only survivor of his family.

ORVILLE E. HAYWARD began his independent career at an early age and his record furnishes a splendid example of the value of energy, perseverance, and resolution in the attainment of success. He was born in Macoupin County, Illinois, in 1852, a son of Ansel and Rebecca (Silsby) Hayward. His father was a native of Massachusetts, and his mother was a native of Illinois.

Mr. Hayward's father died in 1862, and his mother passed away in 1863. The subject of this review acquired his education in the Blackburn University of Illinois and on coming to California he took a course in a business college of San Francisco. His health failed and he removed to Sonora County, where he remained until 1881. The same year he purchased ten acres of land two miles from Martinez. He undertook farming in principle and detail, and his experience and practical methods brought him gratifying results. He now owns thirty acres of the most valuable land in the Alhambra Valley, and is considered one of the leading horticulturists in the county. Mr. Hayward was united in marriage to Miss Mary E. Bagge, of Oakland, March 28, 1883.

To this union were born two children. Mrs. Hayward's father was one of the foremost men of Oakland. He was a large realty holder both in city and country lands. He served as land agent for the San Francisco Savings Union for a period of twenty-five years. He owned much of the land where Elmhurst is now located. He died on May 17, 1901, and Mrs. Hayward's mother died in 1907. Mr. Hayward is especially prominent and active in the affairs of the Masonic fraternity, which he joined in 1896. He is now serving as secretary of Martinez Lodge No. 41, the oldest lodge in Contra Costa County. Mrs. Hayward also takes an active interest in Masonic affairs and has the honor of being secretary of the order of Eastern Star of Martinez and is a past matron of Los Ceritos Chapter No. 234.

CHARLES H. GUY, a representative and esteemed citizen of Concord, and who is now holding the office as postmaster of that town, has made a most creditable record in that connection. Under his management the post-office has had a substantial growth. Mr. Guy was born in Nortonville, Contra Costa County, December 22, 1879. He is a son of John W. and Lavinia T. (McCain) Guy. His father was a native of Alabama and a Civil War veteran. He died in 1910. Mr. Guy's mother was a native of Tennessee. The parents removed to Contra Costa County in 1870.

The father of Mr. Guy was a carpenter and contractor and was identified with the coal mines of this county and was timber boss for many years. He later served as county coroner and conducted an undertaking business. The subject of this sketch received his education in the public schools of Concord; finishing his education, he became associated with the United Railroads and the gas company of San Francisco for a period of four years. In 1908 he returned to Contra Costa County and learned the undertaking business with his father. At the time of his father's death Mr. Guy took in two partners, and the firm name became Guy, Palmer & Ford. Mr. Guy was appointed postmaster by President Wilson on July 8, 1914 and took office on September 1 of that year. He served as town clerk for two years and resigned, owing to the duties connected with his office as postmaster. Fraternally, Mr. Guy is a member of Richmond Lodge No. 1251, B. P. O. E., a member of Concord Parlor No. 245, Native Sons, the Odd Fellows, the Woodmen of the World, the I. D. E. S., and the U. P. E. C. He was united in marriage on April 19, 1910, to Miss Amelia Galindo, of Concord. Mrs. Guy holds membership in the Women of Woodcraft.

Mr. Guy is a useful and valued citizen, and his appointment to the position of postmaster of Concord was met with the ready approval of all the residents of his town. Those who know him personally find him a genial and courteous gentleman and value his friendship most highly.

EDWARD P. JACKSON is a man of culture, progressive views, and high ideals, and is well and favorably known in the community around the Bay cities. He now occupies a formal position in the business world. He has one of the most modern and best-equipped furniture stores in Contra Costa County. Much credit is due Mr. Jackson for the success he has made in the business world, for he started out in life without funds and in a strange country. He has always been an obliging and courteous man and ever ready to render a service to those in need, and to extend a helping hand. Mr. Jackson was born in Cincinnati, Ohio, January 12, 1873. His parents were Charles J. and Mary E. (Parris) Jackson, and both parents were natives of Ohio. The parents removed to Newton, Kansas, when Edward P. was a mere lad of ten years. He acquired his early schooling at Newton, Kansas. He entered the employ of the Wells Fargo Express Company at an early age as messenger on the road and in office work. In January, 1895, he came to Concord and opened an upholstery shop, which he followed for one year. He then removed to San Francisco and followed the same vocation for a time. He returned again to Concord and was acting constable for three years; resigning in 1902, he established his present furniture business, which was in February, 1007. Shortly after he was married he went to Livermore, where he engaged in the purchasing-agent business, which he continued for five years. After the San Francisco fire he returned to Concord, where he has since resided.

He was appointed justice of the peace in 1911, and in 1914 he was elected to the same office for a four-year term. He served as town clerk up to the time of his election as justice of the peace. He is an ardent Republican and takes a keen interest in the welfare of his party. Mr. Jackson was united in marriage August 4, 1902, to Jettie Jaquith, a native of Canada. To this union there is one son, Loyde E., born January 10, 1905. Fraternally, Mr. Jackson is affiliated with the Red Men, the B. P. O. E. of Richmond, and the I. O. O. F., the I. D. E. S., U. P. E. C., and the Rebekah lodge. He has served as treasurer of the Red Men lodge of Concord for six years. He also served for many years as secretary of the I. O. O. F. lodge of Concord. Mrs.

Jackson is a member of the Rebekah lodge, and both have the respect and esteem of a large circle of friends.

HENRY COLMAN CUTTING can indeed be numbered among the builders and promoters of California's growth and greatness. His efforts have found tangible result in the development of Richmond, and he is now president and practical owner of the Point Richmond Canal & Land Company. Previously he was the real builder of Tonopah, Nevada. He seems to possess almost an intuitive perception in recognizing opportunities that others pass heedlessly by, and in utilizing such opportunities he has advanced to a prominent position among the citizens of central California. He was born in Iowa on April 3, 1870 and is a son of George and Jean McGown Cutting. The family moved to Nevada in 1873, and the son, making his own living since he was twelve years old, pursued his education in the public schools of Reno and in the Nevada State University, being a member of the first class graduated from that institution, in June, 1891, on which occasion he won the Bachelor of Arts degree. In addition to classical studies he had completed a course in mining engineering. Later he took up the profession of teaching, which he followed for three years in Candelaria, Nevada, and for four months at Wadsworth, where he was principal. In 1804, while teaching there, he was elected State Superintendent of Public Instruction, which position he filled for four years, during which period he studied law and was admitted to the bar. During this period he wrote what is the basis of the mining laws of Nevada, after which he gave to the State its first compilation of mining laws, and these the legislature adopted. In 1899 the legislature named him as compiler of the statutes of the State, which had not been compiled previously for fifteen years. He accomplished the work in a most satisfactory and efficient manner within the next year, after which he turned his attention to prospecting, in order to regain his health, and was one of the first men in Tonopah, Nevada. In fact, it was Mr. Cutting that advertised that place to the world. He was not only associated with the development of the mineral resources of that section but was active in almost every line of endeavor leading to the organization, upbuilding, and development of a new community. He built the first telephone line, opened the Wells Fargo Express offices in Tonopah, Goldfield, and Manhattan, and has a record for having handled more money with a smaller percentage of loss than any other frontier agent. He established several large mercantile stores and operated big freight teams, besides carrying on extensive mining operations. Besides doing all the legal business of the community, he preached the first two burial sermons in Tonopah, and on the occasion of the second acted also as undertaker and leader of the choir, following which he administered the estate.

He was also the first notary public in Tonopah and granted a couple a divorce, being probably the only notary public who has ever performed such a service. On leaving Nevada Mr. Cutting came to San Francisco for the purpose of advertising Tonopah to the world. When the San Francisco Mining Exchange refused to list the Tonopah stocks he immediately gave his attention to establishing a mining exchange where the Tonopah stocks would be handled, and in less than two weeks organized the San Francisco & Tonopah Mining Exchange, of which he was president for the first two years, when the two exchanges merged. One feature of his success is the thoroughness with which he masters every phase of a business with which he is connected, not only in its direct, but also in its subsidiary interests. He learns what may be gained by reading, and adds to this thorough practical experience and investigation, and, with thorough understanding of the situation, he is often able to utilize and improve opportunities which others have passed heedlessly by. In 1904 he became interested in the development of the town of Richmond, California, and is now president and practical owner of the Point Richmond Canal & Land Company. He originally conceived the idea of the inner harbor at Richmond, advocating the project, and has been so successful in his efforts to bring it before the public notice that the city of Richmond has voted $1,170,000 for carrying out the project, and the longest and widest street in Richmond, Cutting Boulevard, is named after him.

He is known as the father of Richmond's inner harbor project. He has his offices in the Monadnock Building in San Francisco, and he has been a stalwart champion of the interests of that city, ardently advocating the cause of Greater San Francisco, having been a vice-president of the Greater San Francisco Association since its organization. Mr. Cutting was at one time an officer in the Nevada State militia. He is prominent in Masonry, belonging to Occidental Lodge No. 22, F. & A. M., California Chapter No. 5, R. A. M., Golden Gate Commandery No. 16, K. T., and Islam Temple. He belongs also to the Union League Club and the Bohemian Club of San Francisco and is a life member of the Elk Lodge No. 597, Reno, Nevada. Pleasantly situated in his home relations, he was married April 19, 1903, to Minetta Chesson, a daughter of James and Elizabeth Chesson, of Benicia. The children of this marriage are Helen E., George C., Jean, Clara, and Daisy. Such in brief is the history of Henry Colman Cutting, but it tells comparatively little, except to those who read between the lines, of the intense energy, the strong purpose, and the indefatigable perseverance of the man. He has always been a student, but nothing of the dreamer. He has had visions, but is not visionary, for he has proceeded to put into execution the plans and theories which have arisen before his mind, seeking out practical methods to materialize these and make them forces in the country's progress and development as well as sources of individual gain. Mr. Cutting's latest accomplishment is the writing and publication of a book entitled "Financial Independence and How to Attain It," which gives a solution of our financial troubles and incidentally our tax problems as well as an uplift to our business morals and integrity. The avowed purpose of the book is to give to the country a new and better financial system. The courage to attempt such an enormous task calls for universal admiration. It is well known that he accomplishes what he undertakes, that he is a broad-minded, enterprising man, and one whose efforts have been of great value in shaping the history of the West. His latest effort is of nation-wide importance. A later history will have to record the measure of its success.

RALPH R. ARNOLD—On the roster of county officials of Contra Costa County is numbered Ralph R. Arnold, who is serving with credit and ability as county surveyor. He is a native of Pennsylvania and was born in Clearfield County on March 26, 1874. In 1877 his parents removed to Kansas, where he received his public-school education. Mr. Arnold began his independent career in Colorado, where he followed engineering and surveying.

Since engaging in this vocation he has worked in California, Utah, Wyoming, and Nevada. During this time he established a record for honesty, reliability, and efficiency. In April, 1913, he came to Martinez, Contra Costa County, where he has met with gratifying success. He was chosen by the people of his county as county surveyor in the fall of 1914, and the voters of the county can rest assured that Mr. Arnold will conduct his office along the most approved and businesslike lines. He is affiliated with the Republican party. He was united in marriage to Miss Winifred Stuart on October 3, 1007. To this union have been born Mary and Ralph James. Mr. and Mrs. Arnold are popular among a host of friends in Contra Costa County.

SAMUEL HOFFMAN has been engaged in the manufacturing and retail cigar business in Martinez for the past seventeen years. and the many years he has been identified in business have brought him increased patronage and the absolute confidence of his customers. He has been a valued factor in business progress in the community in which he has made his home so many years. He was born in Hungary, December 12, 1872. He received his education in the public schools of his native land. In 1889 he came to this country and located in New York City, where he worked at the manufacturing jewelry trade. On May 1, 1899, he removed to San Francisco, where he remained for three years. He was united in marriage to Miss Celia Lichtensten, a native of New York State, August 19, 1894. To this union have been born five children—Harry, Morris, Joseph, Henry, and one son who died in infancy.

Mr. Hoffman is registered as a Republican, but he can always be counted upon to support the best man, irrespective of party lines. He has served on the Republican County Central Committee and has been a delegate to various parties of the county. Fraternally, he is affiliated with the I. O. O. F., the K. of P., the Red Men, the Eagles, the Woodmen of the World, the Moose, and the Royal Arch. Mr. Hoffman engaged in his present business seventeen years ago in Martinez and has been in his present location since 1906. He placed on the market his famous brand of cigars, "Hoffman's Blue Buds," seventeen years ago, and he also makes the Flor de Martinez. These high-grade cigars have stood the test for many years. Mr. Hoffman's life has been fruitful of good results, not only in the attainment of success, but in his support of progressive public measures which are of benefit to the community.

COLONEL ERNEST A. PREBLE is one of the most prominent men of Richmond and has contributed a notable share to the material progress of this substantial city. He was born in Lincoln County, Maine, July 27, 1864, a son of Lieut. A. H. Preble, a Civil War veteran, and Eglantine (Turner) Preble, both of English descent. The Turner family were among the first and most prominent settlers in Maine. Colonel Preble acquired his education in the schools of his native State, after which he attended the Maine Wesleyan Seminary, at Redfield, Maine. At an early age he came to this coast and located in Tacoma, where he became identified with the commercial activities of that city. In 1913 he established the Preble Grocery Company at Monterey, and continued until 1907, and while a resident of Monterey Colonel Preble was one of the organizers of the First National Bank.

In 1907 he removed to San Francisco and engaged in the wholesale cigar business until 1912; he then came to Richmond and engaged in the lumber and building business. He erected the modern plant at the corner of Tenth and Ohio streets, and, owing to his health, he disposed of the plant, engaging in the land business. While residing in Monterey Colonel Preble was appointed a member of ex-Governor Gillett's military staff. On January 1, 1915, he again engaged in the lumber and mill business, and merged his interests with Burg Bros., and the new firm was known as the Burg Bros.

Lumber & Building Company, of which Colonel Preble was vice-president and manager. Politically, Colonel Preble is affiliated with the Republican party. Particularly on account of protective tariff, he has always declined any public office. He was united in marriage to Emma H. Bowers, of Alameda, in 1910. Colonel Preble has always taken a keen interest in matters pertaining to Richmond and has been a valued factor in its development, having sold several of the largest tracts for subdivision around the Bay section, among which was the north half of the million-dollar Nicholl ranch, to Burg Bros. This tract of land is most ideally situated in Richmond, and the deal was written up in one of the New York financial papers; it was said that this land brought the highest price ever paid in the United States for a piece of unimproved land of that size. There were over one hundred and eleven acres, and the purchase price was fully five thousand dollars an acre. Colonel Preble is at present identified with many financial men on the coast in promoting a railroad and breakwater, known as the Monterey & Fresno Railroad. He has been connected with many large and important projects, and his energy and ambition entitle him to credit which he has achieved. He has won his way upward to success and is known among his associates as the man who always calls a spade a spade and knows which is which.

CHARLES LUDDEN is one of the foremost, and in point of residence one of the oldest, contractors and builders in Contra Costa County. He was born in Beverly, Massachusetts, on September 16, 1853, and is a son of Benjamin and Elizabeth (Woodbury) Ludden. His father was of Welsh descent, and located in the State of Maine, and died July 4, 1897. His mother was of English birth and died in 1907. Mr. Ludden's grandfather was one of the pioneers of Beverly, Massachusetts, and a butcher by trade. During the gold excitement in California he came to the coast during the rush in 1849, but finally located in San Francisco and conducted a butcher-shop in Stockton Street from 1850 to 1852. The subject of this review received a limited education in the public schools of his native State, and at the age of fifteen he started to learn the carpenter's trade with an uncle. He has followed this vocation for forty-eight years continuously. He left home August 14, 1876, in company with two friends, and continued westward until he reached Oakland. Here he remained for a few months and then removed to Martinez in 1877, where he has since resided, and has been active in his occupation. He has erected many fine buildings in Martinez which have added considerably to the beautification of the city. Among these structures are the Curry building, the Library, Gazette building, and the National Bank, besides many of the finest houses and store buildings in the county seat. On September 16, 1879, Mr. Ludden was united in marriage to Miss Eudora Smith, daughter of Captain John R. L. Smith, of New Bedford, Massachusetts, formerly a whaling captain, who followed the seas for many years and was one of the respected citizens of his community. To this union were born three sons, and one daughter—Everett, who is identified with the United States Mint at San Francisco; Harris, a carpenter residing in Oakland; Raymond, a chemist, with the Mountain Copper Company of Martinez; and Elizabeth, wife of James F. Hocy, deputy tax collector, a resident of Martinez. Mr. Ludden is a Republican, and he has served as town trustee for eight years. Fraternally, he is a member of the I. O. O. F., having joined this order in Massachusetts in 1876, and in July, 1882, was one of the charter members of Martinez Lodge No. 297. He is also a member of the Knights of Pythias and the Woodmen of the World. He has gained for himself a position of prominence in the building line and his influence is always given in support of whatever he feels will promote the best interests of the community.

JANCE J. ANDERSON, a native son and popular business man of Martinez, devoted his attention to the duties devolving upon him as owner and manager of the warehouse and wood and coal business. He was born in Contra Costa County on March 5, 1870. His father came to the coast via the Isthmus route on the steamer "Oregon," and settled in this county. He operated boats on the bay and river for many years. He was a native of Denmark and died in 1910. Mr. Anderson's mother was a native of Ireland and makes her home with her daughter in Pacheco. Jance J. acquired his education in the public schools and St. Mary's College of San Francisco. He afterward assisted his father in the lumber business at Pacheco and Martinez. The Pacheco yard was one of the first lumber yards to start in Contra Costa County. In 1909 the subject of this review engaged in the warehouse and wood and coal business in Martinez. He is also identified with the interests on the bay. Politically, Mr. Anderson is a Democrat. He has served as town trustee for a period of four years. Fraternally, he is a member of the W. O. W. He was united in marriage October 5, 1895, to Minnie Loring, of Concord, a daughter of one of the representative business men of Concord. To this union have been born three sons—Jepson D., Cecil A., and Loring L. Mrs. Anderson holds membership in the Women of Woodcraft and is a member of the grand board of directors of the Young Ladies' Institute of California and has served as president of the Women's Improvement Club of Martinez. Mr. Anderson is a man of enterprise and ambition and is numbered among the representative business men of Martinez. He received the appointment as postmaster of Martinez from President Wilson and took office in the fall of 1916.

FRANK R. JONES, one of the representative young men of Martinez, is a native son, his birth having occurred at Martinez, California, June 19, 1886, a son of Rees and Margaret Jones. His father was born in Wisconsin on April 15, 1860, and when quite young came to California with his parents to settle in Stewartsville, Contra Costa County, where he grew to manhood. In the year 1885 he was united in marriage to Miss Margaret Hughes, and since his marriage has resided in Martinez. To this union there are three children —Frank, the subject of this review; Raymond, born February 13, 1892; and Mildred, born April 27, 1902. During his residence in Martinez Mr. Jones filled the responsible positions of constable and town marshal and deputy sheriff, and during his incumbency in these offices was noted for his fearlessness and determination in the pursuit of criminals. For many years he was identified with Henry Curry in the livery business and was a partner in the Bay View Pavilion property. Politically, he was a strong Republican and took an active interest along political lines. He was a member of the I. O. O. F. for many years. Rees Jones was a public-spirited and patriotic citizen and was well liked by all who knew him, and he was a courteous and painstaking official. His death occurred October 12, 1908. Frank R. Jones, the subject of our sketch, was educated in the public schools of Martinez and the business college of San Francisco. Laying aside his books, he engaged with the Bank of Martinez, the oldest banking institution of Contra Costa County. He entered the employ of the bank at the age of eighteen, and has, through his energy and persistent purpose, been promoted until he now fills the important position of assistant cashier. He was united in marriage to Miss Hattie M. Osborne, a native of Illinois, February 12, 1914. To this union there is one son, Frank R., Jr., born November 26, 1915. Frank R. Jones was elected a member of the town trustees on April 10, 1916, for the four-year term. He is a member of the Native Sons, Woodmen of the World, and Knights of Pythias. He has the good-will and confidence of all who are associated with him.

WARREN H. McBRYDE.—Ambition, energy, and progressive spirit have brought Warren H. McBryde to a position of prominence and distinction among the representative men of Contra Costa County. He was born in Mobile, Alabama, January 20, 1876, a son of Thomas C. and Julia (Horton) McBryde. Both parents were natives of Alabama. Warren H. McBryde received his education in the public schools of his native State, after which he spent four years in the State Polytechnic Institute at Auburn, Alabama, where he graduated from the electric and mechanical engineering department in 1897 with the degree of Bachelor of Science. He at once began his active career with the Electric Lighting Company of Mobile, Alabama, where he remained for one year. He then became connected with the Government in the Engineering Department and had charge of the submarine mines at Fort Morgan, at Mobile Bay, during the Spanish-American War in the summer of 1898. He then became identified as chief electrician with the United States transport "Sheridan" for a period of one year and made the first trip through the Suez Canal to Manila from New York and on via Japan to San Francisco. In 1809 he served as assistant resident engineer for the Colgate Hydro-Electric Power Plant, which was the first of its kind in the State, and which was erected for the Yuba Power Company, now the Pacific Gas & Electric Company. He was assistant superintendent for the Peyton Chemical Company, of Martinez, for the first two years of its existence. He then went to San Francisco and engaged in the engineering department for the Pacific Gas & Electric Company. In 1903 Mr. McBryde went East and located in New Jersey and had charge of the construction work for eighteen months for the Dupont Powder Company. He left the East and returned to Contra Costa County, where he became resident engineer for the Hercules Powder Company, having charge of all engineering and construction work for two years. In 1909 he was promoted to the position of assistant superintendent, which position he now holds in a most efficient manner. Politically, Mr. McBryde is affiliated with the Progressive party. He was chairman of the county committee when Governor Hiram Johnson was elected. No progressive public movement and no project instituted for the benefit or welfare of the county lacks his co-operation and hearty support. He was president of the first good roads organization in the county and has always been an enthusiast for better roads. He served in a capable manner as county supervisor during 1913 and 1914. Fraternally, he is affiliated with the B. P. O. E. of Richmond. He served on a committee which went to Washington, D. C., in the interests of securing the inner harbor appropriation for Richmond, and delivered a speech showing the advantage to the outlying districts of Richmond and the county. He is a director in the First National Bank of Richmond and the Richmond Savings Bank. Mr. McBryde was united in marriage to Miss Abbie Ford White, of Philadelphia, February 15, 1905. To this union there are three children—Lucile, born January 29, 1906; Warren, Jr., born July 16, 1914; and Janet, born November 6, 1915. For ten years Mr. McBryde has been and is still a member of the executive committee of the Hercules Club. He organized and has been president of the Hercules-Pinole Hospital Association for the past eight years. He is a trustee and clerk of the Pinole-Hercules school board and is president of the board of trustees of Hercules, where he resides.

WILLIAM G. TURNER is prominently connected with the business interests of Antioch and is regarded as one of the most progressive and enterprising young men of Contra Costa County. He was born on January 12, 1877 and is a son of John B. and Maria Turner. William G. Turner was educated in the public schools, after which he learned the barber trade, which vocation he followed in Antioch for over ten years. He then became identified with Fred Dahnken in the amusement business. Politically, Mr. Turner is affiliated with the Republican party, and successfully held the office of chairman of the town trustees of Black Diamond for one term. He was identified with the business interests of Black Diamond for some time, and in 1908 he removed to Antioch. In 1008 he engaged in the wholesale business and took over the Arlington Hotel and personally looked after the management of both interests. Mr. Turner is a member of the Native Sons, Eagles, Moose, and the U. P. E. C. On October 17, 1895, he was united in marriage to Ella Calvin, a daughter of Charles Calvin, who is connected with the Navy Yard at Vallejo. To this union there are two children—Harold C., born March 27, 1897, and Hene E., born June 26, 1898. The family are members of the Catholic church. Mr. Turner is regarded as a reliable and progressive business man.

WILLIAM J. BUCHANAN is one of the representative business men of Contra Costa County and is at the head of one of Pittsburg's business houses that dates its origin from a time when Pittsburg was a mere country village twenty years ago. The general store of William J. Buchanan since its foundation has been in the hands of a progressive, far-sighted, and able man, under whose direction it has advanced to its present large proportions. The store was founded in 1896. Mr. Buchanan was born at New York Landing, now Pittsburg, on September 11, 1867, a son of William and Katherine Buchanan. His father was a native of Scotland, and came to America in the '50s, locating in Placer County, where he followed mining. He removed to Contra Costa County in 1866, locating in Antioch, where he remained for two years. In 1867 he removed to the country near Pittsburg, where he took up farming, which vocation he always followed. He died in 1904. Mr. Buchanan's mother was a native of Scotland. His folks married in Rochester, New York, and came west. His mother died on January 14, 1910. There were two children in the parents' family, the subject of this sketch and Jennie, born July 16, 1863, the wife of James Syme, a native of Scotland, and who resides on the home ranch. William J. Buchanan received his education in the public schools and the Stockton business college. Finishing his education, he returned to the home farm, where he was actively engaged until 1896, when he entered the mercantile business. In 1905 he erected his present commodious building. Mr. Buchanan is affiliated with the Republican party. He has served as supervisor for twelve years. Fraternally, he is a member of the Masonic order of Pittsburg, the I. O. O. F. of Antioch, and holds membership in Diamond Parlor of the Native Sons, the Knights of Pythias, and the Eagles lodge of Pittsburg. Mr. Buchanan was united in marriage to Nora Carroll, a native of Portland, Oregon, January 4, 1893, a daughter of William and Mary (Keefe) Carroll. To this union there are two children—Warren G., born May 11, 1898, and Norine, born October 28,

1900. Mr. Buchanan is a stockholder and vice-president of the Contra Costa Bank of Pittsburg. Mrs. Buchanan for fourteen years was postmistress of the Black Diamond post office, and she obtained the highest reputation for ability and faithfulness during her long term in office. Mr. Buchanan served as Wells Fargo agent here for sixteen years, thus showing the interest he took in his company who entrusted its affairs to him.

LEE D. WINDREM, a man of forceful personality and effective ability, is numbered today among the most able lawyers of the Bay counties. He has been active in various movements and projects designed to promote the permanent interests of the community where he resides. He was born in Lancaster County, Nebraska, December 25, 1870, the son of Samuel and Nettie E. (Cooper) Windrem. His father was a pioneer settler in Nebraska and was active in political and financial matters in his State. He died in 1003. Mr. Windrem's mother was a native of Iowa, and now makes her home in Richmond. There were eight children in the parents' family, only three of whom are now living—Nettie, a teacher in the Richmond public schools for nine years; Guy Windrem, a traveling salesman, and formerly manager for Nolan Bros. Shoe Company, with headquarters in Madera, California; and our subject, Lee D. Windrem, who acquired his education in the public schools of Nebraska. At the age of twelve he became identified with the merchandise business, which he followed for fifteen years. He studied law under Miles Wallace, of Madera, was admitted to the bar in August, 1895, and practiced in Madera one year He removed to San Francisco, where he practiced his profession seven years, and in 1902 he came to Richmond, where he has since resided. Mr. Windrem is counsel for the Santa Fe Railroad, transacts much work for the Standard Oil Company, and is legal adviser of some of the banks in Richmond. He is a stockholder in the First National Bank and the Richmond Savings Bank, and being one of the incorporators of both banks.

While residing in Madera he served as chairman in the County Democratic Committee during the first campaign of W. J. Bryan. In 1903 he served as chairman of the Democratic County Committee of Contra Costa County and was appointed chairman of the Contra Costa County Democratic conventions three times. His activities in Democratic politics were recognized by his appointment as a member of the executive committee of the Democratic State Central Committee. During the three years he served as city attorney in Richmond, he handled the legal proceedings for the bonds for the Tunnel & Harbor Improvement, amounting to $1,170,000. While he has always taken a keen interest in politics, he has refused to accept any political office. He has been repeatedly asked to run for State Representative in Congress, district attorney, and superior judge. He has always declined the nomination owing to his large practice. Fraternally, Mr. Windrem is identified with the I. O. O. F. and the B. P. O. E. of Richmond. He was united in marriage to Miss Marjorie D. Rickabaugh, a native of Lake County, California, July 23, 1903. To this union have been born two children—Marion Lee and Philip Douglas. Mr. Windrem has the distinction of being one of the seven appointed by the League of Pacific Municipalities at its meeting in 1910, held at San Diego, to draft the "Improvement Act of 1911," which act was passed the same year, and under which all of the street work of California is being done at the present time. While a resident of Richmond Mr. Windrem enjoyed a trip around the world in 1905, visiting the principal cities of Europe and the Orient.

BERT CURRY needs no introduction to the people of Contra Costa County. He has become widely and favorably known as a man whose high integrity and excellent business ability constitute him a prominent factor in community advancements and progress. He is a native of Contra Costa County and is a representative of one of the time-honored families of this county.

Mr. Curry was born June 1, 1882 and is a son of James R. and Ellen Curry, who settled in Clayton, Contra Costa County, during the early days. His father engaged in teaming and the livery business, and also established and conducted stage-lines from Oakland to various parts of his home county, continuing his various enterprises until 1903, when he sold out and removed to Martinez. Bert Curry received his education in the public schools of this county, after which he took a business course. He learned the undertaking business with his brother, Henry J. Curry, at Martinez, and remained with him for a period of seven years, when he removed to Point Richmond, where he became identified in the same business in 1008. Mr. Curry has served as deputy coroner for five years. Fraternally, he is connected with the B. P. O. E. of Richmond, I. O. O. F., Eagles, Rebekah lodge, and Yeomen. In politics Mr. Curry is affiliated with the Democratic party and is an active worker. His attention, however, is concentrated upon his business affairs, in which he has met with well-deserved success.

AARON E. DUNKEL is one of the most progressive and capable men in Contra Costa County. He was born in Angels Camp, Calaveras County, California, October 20, 1862. He acquired his education in the public schools of San Francisco. He followed various occupations and vocations during his early career, and in January, 1878, removed to Contra Costa County. In 1885 he accepted a position in the county recorder's office and filled the office of deputy for a period of nine years. He was elected recorder, and in this office he did efficient work for twelve years. He always discharged all of his duties in a thorough and businesslike manner. While county recorder, Mr. Dunkel was interested in the Contra Costa Abstract Office. The Contra Costa Abstract Office was established in 1887, this being the oldest abstract office in the county. Politically, Mr. Dunkel is a Republican; he voluntarily retired from public office to put all of his time and attention into the abstract office, owing to the increasing business, and he has realized his ambition of making the Contra Costa Abstract Office one of the best in the State. Mr. Dunkel was united in marriage to Eva Hathaway, a native of Contra Costa County, June 10, 1891. To this union was born one son, who is identified with the Shell Oil Company of Martinez. Mrs. Dunkel's father, R. B. Hathaway, was one of the respected and time-honored citizens of this county. He served as county treasurer for eight years. Fraternally, Mr. Dunkel is a member of the B. P. O. E. of Richmond, the I. O. O. F., and is a member of Mount Diablo Parlor of the Native Sons of Martinez. He is one of the best-known men around the Bay cities, and his substantial traits in business have gained for him the warm regard from all with whom he has been associated. He is also vice-president of the Bank of Martinez, the oldest and largest bank in Contra Costa County.

JUDSON EDMUND COLTON.—One of the commanding figures of the business life of Martinez is Judson Edmund Colton. He has made steady progress toward prominence and is today largely connected with the manufacturing interests of the Bay counties of California. He has important financial interests and has been and is today in a large measure instrumental in making Martinez what it is—one of the most flourishing cities on the Pacific Coast. Mr. Colton is a native son, being born in Sacramento County, April 7, 1863, a son of Louis Colton, a native of New York State.

His mother was a native of Erie County, Pennsylvania. The parents removed to Illinois, where they resided for a period of five years. In 1852 Mr. Colton's parents came overland to California, taking six months to make the trip, and settled in Sacramento County. The father was a millwright by trade and erected many of the quartz-mills in the mountain counties. He operated mills himself, and later took up ranching, which he followed for twenty years. There were six children in the parents' family. The subject of this sketch acquired his education in the public schools of Sacramento.

At the age of twenty-three Mr. Colton came to Contra Costa County and located in the Alhambra Valley, where he engaged in the growing of grapes and the manufacture of wine. He has been identified with Martinez for the past twenty years. In 1008 he erected his present establishment. In his winery he produces one hundred and fifty thousand gallons of the finest dry wines that can be produced in any country, and his goods find a ready sale.

He owns and operates a fine fifty-acre vineyard, one-half being devoted to table and the balance to wine grapes. The Colton winery is the largest independent winery operating in Contra Costa County. Politically, Mr. Colton is affiliated with the Republican party, and has always taken a keen interest in matters pertaining to the beautifying of the county seat. He is desirous of seeing a city park along the waterfront and is especially interested in a children's playground and municipal bath-house. It is but natural that he was elected a member of the town trustees on April 10, 1916, for a two-year term, and on April 12, 1916, at the regular board meeting, he was chosen mayor. Mr. Colton was united in marriage to Miss Sadie L. Jones, a native of New York State, October 16, 1888. To this union there are two children— Hattie, wife of Fabian Joost, of San Francisco, born September 29, 1889, and Judson Edmund, Jr., born June 13, 1008. Mr. Colton is a stockholder in the Bank of Martinez, in the Contra Costa Gas Company, and in the Martinez & Benicia Ferry Company. In the advancement of his individual success he has contributed also to the commercial advancement of Martinez, where he makes his home, and where he is held in high regard by his business associates by reason of his enterprise, integrity, and sterling personal worth.

JOHN DUANE needs no introduction to the people of Contra Costa County, for during his years of residence in Martinez he has become widely and favorably known as a man of excellent business ability. He was born in Canada on May 23, 1859. His parents removed to Batavia, New York, when he was but three years of age. His parents, Patrick and Margaret, were the parents of six boys. John Duane, the subject of this sketch, came to Contra Costa County in October, 1886. He received a limited education as he started out in life at the age of twelve years and went to work at the nursery business at Batavia, New York, for Bogue Brothers. He remained here four years. He then worked two years for M. Dailey of Batavia, who was in the furniture and undertaking business. He then returned to the home place and remained several years, and at the age of twenty-seven he came to Martinez, where he has since resided. He, with his brother, engaged in the nursery business. They planted many of the first elms in Martinez.

In politics Mr. Duane is registered as a Republican. He served as town trustee for four years. He was married to Rose Mary Rogers, a native of California, January 11, 1893. To this union are seven children—Agnes Mary, born August 27, 1896, a graduate of the Martinez High School; Rometa Margaret, born February 28, 1897; John Lawrence, born March 16, 1898; Rose Helena, born February 2, 1900; Clarence Haven, born November 7, 1903; James Aloysius, born February 10, 1905; Frances Rogers, born April 2, 1909. Mr. Duane is a member of the W. O. W. The father of Mrs. Duane came to the coast during the gold excitement in 1849 from Philadelphia via the Isthmus route. Mr. Duane owns nineteen acres just outside the city of Martinez, and has it planted to trees and vineyard.

JOHN MARCHI is a man who has, by his own energy, ambition, and enterprise, guided by sound and practical judgment, worked his way upward to a place among the representative men of Martinez. He is prominently connected with the city government as trustee. He was born on May 7, 1881, in Switzerland. Mr. Marchi acquired his education in the public schools and later attended college for two years in his native land. In November, 1897, he came to America, locating in New York City for a period of three years. While a resident of the metropolis he was connected with some of the large dairy firms in New York and Brooklyn. In 1890 he came to San Francisco and engaged in the restaurant business for six years. He then came to Martinez, where he has resided since. For nearly eleven years he was identified with the business interests of Martinez. In July, 1915, he disposed of his interests and engaged in the real-estate business and is now associated with Schapiro & Company. Mr. Marchi has always used his power and influence toward promoting the good of Martinez. He was elected on April 10, 1916, as city trustee for the four-year term. He was married in Martinez, California, to Clara Righetti, a native of Switzerland, January, 1905. To this union there are three sons—Alfred, born January 29, 1906; Leo, born December 21, 1906; Ernest, born May 21, 1910. Mr. Marchi is affiliated with the following lodges: The Moose, the Eagles, the U. P. E. C., and the I. D. E. S., all of Martinez. The family attends the Catholic church. He has many friends in these organizations and among the business men of the city and is trusted by all because of his high principles.

CHARLES H. WALKER, present chief of police of Richmond, is a highly trained, well-informed officer, who is eminently fitted for the important position which he holds. He was born in Kentucky on April 18, 1880 and acquired his education in the colleges and public schools of his native State.

He joined the army and served in the Philippines, holding the position of acting sergeant. He served three years and received an honorable discharge on April 1, 1904. Mr. Walker remained in San Francisco for a time and removed to Richmond in July, 1905, where he filled various positions of trust and importance. He became connected with the East Shore & Suburban Street Railway, remaining until November, 1907, and on April 1, 1908, he assumed the duties of police officer of Richmond. He was appointed deputy sheriff under Sheriff R. R. Veale in July, 1905, was made sergeant in July, 1912, and on July 1, 1914, was appointed chief of police, to succeed J. P. Arnold, which office he now holds. Mr. Walker has shown himself adapted to this work and ably handles all cases entrusted to him. He was united in marriage to Miss Ruby Bullock, of Oakland, March 5, 1914, a daughter of John C. Bullock, one of Oakland's representative business men. In politics Chief Walker is a

Republican and takes exceptional interest along party lines. He is affiliated with Eclipse Lodge No. 403, I. O. O. F. Both Mr. and Mrs. Walker take active interest and give their ready support to movements which have for their purpose the advancement of the community.

HARVEY ABBOTT SELLERS.—The majority of men are content to remain in positions where circumstance or environment has placed them, lacking the ambition and the determination which would enable them to advance and become active in control of business enterprises or important interests. Contrary to the general rule, and therefore standing as a central figure among his fellows, is Harvey Abbott Sellers. Mr. Sellers is a native of Contra Costa County and was born at Black Diamond (now Pittsburg) in 1890. His father, Stephen Abbott Sellers, is a native of Brentwood, this county, and his mother, Mary Louise (Wight) Sellers, is a native of Contra Costa County. Mr. Sellers' father followed agricultural lines for many years and is now retired and resides in Berkeley. He still owns two ranches, consisting of four hundred and eighty acres. In the parents' family there were three sons—the subject of this sketch, Eugene, an employee of the Alhambra Mineral Water Company, of San Francisco, and Martin, who is attending school. Harvey A. Sellers was educated in the public schools of Pittsburg; graduating from high school he took up the automobile business and became connected with the Mount Diablo Garage in 1910. Here he remained for three years. He then engaged in the garage business for himself in Kingsburg, California, where he remained for one year. In January, 1915, he located in Richmond, this county, and became connected with the business interests of this city, engaging in the automobile business. He has had a rapid rise and is considered among the substantial and representative business men of the county. He has the agency of the well-known Dodge and Hudson automobiles, besides having a well-equipped and modern garage in connection. Fraternally, Mr. Sellers is affiliated with Richmond Lodge No. 1251, B. P. O. E. On May 29, 1914, he was united in marriage to Miss Rose Ginnelli, of Richmond. Mr. Sellers' grandfather, Randolph H. Wight, crossed the plains in 1849 with an ox-team, taking six months to make the journey. He mined in and around Placerville. Returning to the East, he married Orpha Durfee, and the couple made the trip to the coast via Cape Horn. The grandfather is still living and is now residing in Berkeley. The subject of this sketch is prominent in business and equally proficient in civic and social affairs.

HENRY A. JOHNSTON is a man of enterprise and discrimination, and in the course of a long and successful business career has been connected with a number of important interests on the Pacific Coast. For a number of years he has been identified with the real-estate business of Richmond and controls a large representative patronage. Mr. Johnston was born in Canada on December 5, 1862. His parents, Noble and Letitia Johnston, removed to California in 1869 and located in Marin County. The father passed away in 1914, and the mother in 1871. The subject of this sketch acquired his education in the public schools of Sonoma County. Much credit is due him for the success he has made in life. He left home when a mere boy of eleven years, working for his board for some time, and later employed by S. W. Martin, near Petaluma, on a ranch. At the age of seventeen he rented Mr. Martin's ranch and owing to his executive ability he made a success of the venture.

After giving up the ranch he removed to San Diego, California, where he remained for two years. While a resident here he was identified with and handled the coke output of the San Diego Gas Company. He attended night school and graduated from the San Diego Business College. From San Diego he removed to Rio Vista, where he engaged in the mercantile business for eight years, and in November, 1001, he disposed of his store interests and removed to Richmond, California. Here he engaged in the real-estate business as agent, and later subdivided the Richmond Park Tract. He has developed a large business in real estate and is one of the owners of the Richmond Traffic Center Tract. On December 16, 1912, he formed a copartnership with Mr. Baine, and engaged in the fuel, feed, grain, and warehouse business. Mr. Johnston has risen steadily, and by merit only, and there is great credit due him for what he has achieved in the business world.

During the pioneer days of Richmond, Mr. Johnston erected the first brick building on Macdonald Avenue. He is a director and stockholder in the Merchants' Bank. Fraternally, he is a member of the McKinley Lodge, F. & A. M., of Richmond. He was united in marriage to Miss Margaret Christie, a native of San Francisco, June 6, 1906. Their children are George Henry, born September 6, 1008, and Helen C., born October 11, 1910. Mr. Johnston has been actively concerned in municipal affairs of Richmond, and he is actuated at all times by the spirit of modern progress.

CHARLES H. LIND, head of the De Luxe Studio in Richmond, is one of the well-known and representative young business men of the county. He was born in St. Cloud, Minnesota, February 8, 1890, and is a son of Thomas H. and Matilda Lind. The subject of this sketch acquired his education in the public schools of California. After his schooling he took up the study of photography and has been identified with many leading men in his chosen field. Mr. Lind removed to Richmond in October, 1912. He has one of the finest-equipped studios in the county, and he keeps in touch with the most advanced ideas in his chosen profession. He makes his business duties his first interest and is one of the most enthusiastic and capable photographers in the Bay counties. Mr. Lind is affiliated with the Republican party and holds membership in the Moose Lodge of Richmond.

EDWARD HOWE HARLOW holds an important position with the Atchison, Topeka & Santa Fe Railway as master mechanic, with headquarters at Richmond, California. There is great credit due Mr. Harlow for having attained this position, as he succeeded entirely through his own efforts, rising from a humble position as water-boy to one of foremost importance. Mr. Harlow was born in Janesville, Wisconsin, September 1, 1856. He acquired his education in the public schools of Janesville and the Episcopal parish school. Early in life he went with the Chicago & Northwestern Railroad as water-boy. He then entered the shops in March, 1871, to learn the mechanic's trade, remaining until the summer of 1873, when he was laid off on account of panic. He then went to Fairbury, Illinois, and secured a position as hotel clerk. In January, 1874, he returned to West Chicago, at that time called Cicero, and entered the shops, later completing his trade as machinist. His next rise was to the position of gang foreman, and later was promoted to assistant roundhouse foreman, when he was transferred to Harvard, Illinois, where he remained until 1888. He resigned his position with the Chicago & Northwestern to accept a position with George Hackney, then superintendent of motor power for the Santa Fe at Chicago. Mr. Harlow was assigned a position at the Topeka shops as floor machinist and gang foreman; here he remained until September, 1888, when he was promoted to division foreman at Wallace, New Mexico. In 1890 Wallace was disbanded as a division point and all trains were run to Albuquerque, New Mexico, and Mr. Harlow was made general foreman of shops at Raton, New Mexico. Here he remained until April, 1891, when he was transferred to the Topeka shops, later resigning and accepting a position under George A. Hancock at Albuquerque, July 31st, with the Atlantic & Pacific Railroad, serving as gang and general foreman until 1893, and in March of that year he was transferred to Gallup, New Mexico, as division foreman, where he remained until August, 1900. Mr. Harlow was then made master mechanic of the Valley Division of the Santa Fe, with headquarters at Stockton, California. On January 26, 1901, he removed to Richmond, resuming the duties of master mechanic.

On February 1, 1907, he was transferred to Albuquerque, New Mexico, in the same capacity, remaining at this point until September, 1908, when he returned to Richmond as master mechanic. In politics Mr. Harlow is a Republican. He has served on the high school board of Richmond for three terms. Fraternally, he is a member of the F. & A. M., chapter, commandery, and shrine, serving as master of his lodge for four years while a resident of Gallup, New Mexico, and for three years he served as grand lecturer in New Mexico. Mr. Harlow was married to Miss Anna Cummings, a native of Janesville, Wisconsin, July, 1891. Five children were born to this union: Philip L., Edward George, Archibald Page, and two who passed away in infancy. Mrs. Harlow takes an active part in Episcopal church and social matters of Richmond.

WALTER B. TRULL began his independent career at an early age and his record since that time furnishes many splendid examples of the value of energy, perseverance, and resolution in the attainment of success. Mr. Trull was born in Brenham, Texas, September 26, 1862. His parents removed from the State of Illinois to Texas previous to the Civil War. His father began railroading and was the agent at Harrisburg, Texas, for the G. H. & H. R. R., and was superintendent for the C. & N. W. Ry. for many years. He died in 1914. After the war the parents of Mr. Trull returned to Illinois, and made their home in West Chicago, where Walter B. Trull acquired his education in the public schools. Laying aside his books, he became associated with the Chicago & Northwestern Railroad for a time. He then went with the Santa Fe system, and was sent to Deming, New Mexico, where he was identified with the operating department. Here he remained three years and was then transferred to San Bernardino, California. Like most successful railroad employees, he occupied various positions of importance and trust along different divisions of the road, and in 1901 he was transferred to Richmond, Contra Costa County, where he holds the important position as agent. Mr. Trull has charge of this terminal on this side of the Bay, handling all the freight and passenger business. He has held this important position since 1901. His long and varied experience makes him valuable to his road, and he is recognized as one of the most expert men in transportation matters on the coast. On June 16, 1890, Mr. Trull was united in marriage to Miss Carrie McDonald, of San Bernardino, California. To this union there have been two children—Muriel, born May 11, 1891, the wife of Chas. W. Claudius, of Oakland, California, and Laura, born May 11, 1895, wife of A. F. Rice, who is identified with the traffic department of the Santa Fe Railway at San Francisco.

RALPH DOBSON, deceased, was numbered among the representative agriculturists of Contra Costa County. He was born March 16, 1862 and was a native of this county. His death occurred on December 8, 1915. He acquired his education in the public schools at San Ramon. His father, Edward Dobson, was a native of Scotland. At the age of seventeen Ralph Dobson laid aside his school books and began ranching. He assisted on the home place for some years and then worked out for a time. At the age of thirty he returned home, where he always remained. He was united in marriage to Emma Horan, daughter of J. D. and Annie (Norris) Horan. Her father was a native of Missouri, and crossed the plains with his parents, taking six months to make the journey. Mrs. Dobson's mother crossed the plains with her parents, and they settled near Mission San Jose during the early days, when elk and other wild animals were plentiful. Mrs. Dobson's father died in June, 1903, and her mother passed away in November, 1915. Mr. and Mrs. Ralph Dobson after their marriage rented various ranches and in 1909 purchased twenty acres that was part of the home place. The subject of this review was affiliated with the Democratic party and served as roadmaster for eight years. Fraternally, he was a member of the I. O. O. F., the Foresters, and the Native Sons. Mr. Dobson gained many friends during the period of his residence in the county. He was held in the highest regard by all who knew him, and his death was mourned by a large circle of friends.

John B. Horan, a brother of Mrs. Ralph Dobson, died August 16, 1916. There was one son, Edwin, born to Mr. and Mrs. Dobson on February 24, 1895, and he died April 23, 1916. He was educated in the public and high schools of San Ramon and Danville. He accepted a position after graduation as bookkeeper in the San Ramon Bank, which he held until his death. His demise caused sincere sorrow to his many friends, all of whom esteemed him for his good qualities of character. He was courteous and obliging, and his genial manner won him the friendship of many in this county.

ROBERT GARWOOD DEAN is a representative pioneer of California and a prominent and highly esteemed resident of Brentwood. Mr. Dean came early to the State, arriving in San Francisco on January 21, 1850, on the topsail schooner "Francisco," direct from New York, from which port they sailed on July 4, 1849, passing out through the Narrows as the guns of Fort Hamilton were firing a national salute. The little vessel carried four passengers beside himself, and, being a fine seaboat, brought them safely to their destination. Off Cape Frio, on the coast of Brazil, a terrific storm was encountered that sprung the foremast and compelled them to seek refuge in the port of Santa Cathrini, about three hundred miles below Rio, where they lay about six weeks refitting. Their journey through the Straits of Magellan to California was without further incident. Mr. Dean went to Stockton and thence to the southern mines, digging his first gold on the Agua Frio. In the winter of 1850 he went to Bear Valley, built a log house, laid in a stock of provisions, and waited for rain to enable them to work the gulches. It did not come, but the Indians did, and flipped their arrows at them, and stole their mules and horses until the miners wearied of their sport and started out on the war-path, joining a company under Major Birney. They followed the Indians to the headwaters of the Fresno and defeated them in a hard fight, when Lieutenant Skeen was killed and several of the company wounded.

Continuing their search for the redskins, the company went as far south as the Four Creeks, where they buried a number of immigrants slain by the Indians. One of them, who had taken refuge in a log hut, was found hanging to the rafters and divested of his skin. For his services in the Mariposa war Mr. Dean received a land-warrant from Uncle Sam and four dollars a day from the State. Returning to Stockton in the fall of 1851, at the solicitation of his uncle, Seneca Dean, who had a store on the north side of the slough, and who was also a justice of the peace and subsequently a member of the legislature from Stanislaus County, he assisted in the store for a short time.

But store-keeping was too humdrum an occupation for the subject of our sketch, and on invitation of R. M. Harmer, one of General Fremont's dependable adherents, who owned a ranch on the river, he went out on the Joaquin "just for a hunt." Finding himself among congenial spirits and fond of the wild life, where grizzly bear, elk, and antelope were plentiful, and a chase after mustangs on the back of a fleet-footed horse was a pastime, he remained until the spring of 1853, when he came into Contra Costa County. In the summer of 1854 Mr. Dean, after being chewed up by a grizzly, returned to the mines, working on the Merced and Tuolumne rivers. In 1857 he followed the "rush" to British Columbia and paddled a canoe from Whatcom to Fort Yale on the Frazer River. Victoria was then little more than a hamlet, and Douglas was still the chief factor of the Hudson Bay Company. Not finding the mines as rich as reported, nor the climate on the Upper Frazer congenial to his tastes, he returned to the Sound and spent the summer in hunting deer for the Victoria market. Tiring of this and longing for the summer skies of his beloved State, Mr. Dean returned to renew his search for gold.

Fortune smiled on him, and he might have ended his career as a miner had he not received a letter from his Uncle Seneca, who had then become a stock-raiser on the San Joaquin, as a partner of Harmer, asking him to join him in a stock-raising venture. He suggested the plan of taking a hundred head of horses from the West Side, driving them to Salt Lake and exchanging them for the foot-sore and worn-out cattle of the emigrants. It was an appealing scheme to a fellow whose hands were calloused with the pick and shovel, and therefore gleefully accepted. Mr. Dean arrived in Carson Valley with his horses late in the summer of 1859, too late to drive through to Salt Lake, and made preparations to winter them. "Stock fed and flourished on the wild sage and bunch-grass of the valley," they told him, but hay was plentiful at five dollars a ton, loose. A storm in December covered the valley deep in snow, and this was followed by a thaw and a freeze that continued for two months. The mountains were closed and the grip of the Ice King was terrible. The Carson River was frozen solid, and a dense bank of fog, excluding the sun, hung over the valley. It was like living in a refrigerator.

The carcasses of three hundred head of American cattle on their way to California that had stopped there for the winter lay strewn along the river. The horses survived by browsing on the willows, but they fell away to skeletons. Then came the report of the discovery of the great silver mines and a wild stampede from California. Everything went booming. Hay ran to two hundred and three hundred dollars a ton, flour a dollar a pound; everything was turned topsy turvy by the inrush. The trip to Salt Lake was abandoned.

The opening of a wagon-road via the South Fork of the American River and the Old Johnson Cut-off, along which line the Overland Railroad it was supposed would follow, gave Dean his opportunity to go up into Lake Valley and locate a station. Mounted on a pair of Norwegian skis, with a pack on his back, he climbed the East Range of the Sierras and camped on fifteen feet of compact snow. The next day he was down in the valley, where there was only two or three feet of snow. Here he rolled the pine saplings together and made his location, later hewing the logs and whip-sawing the lumber for a two-story hotel building, which was completed and sold to William Mack, of Sacramento. This was afterward known as the Sierra House. William W. Lapham had made a location on the lake shore for a summer resort. He sold a two-thirds interest to Van Wagner and Seneca Dean. Lapham sold his interest to his partners, and later the property was purchased by R. G. Dean and J. H. Martin. The construction of the Central Pacific Railroad via Auburn and north of the lake transferred the splendid run of custom for the roadside and the resorts until they were obliged to abandon them for want of support. After the expenditure of thousands of dollars and the unrequited labor of years they went away, leaving their well-constructed and commodious hotels standing untenanted and empty— monumental of the unpardonable opposition of the toll-road owners of the Placerville route, who refused to enter into a satisfactory agreement with the railroad company to build over that route, thus driving it via Henness Pass and the Truckee— suicidal for themselves and disastrous to all the others. On leaving Lake Valley, Mr. Dean and wife went back to Carson Valley. Genoa once the county seat of Carson County, but now of Douglas County, had grown to a lively village, with a pretentious courthouse, stores, hotels, and school buildings. Mr. Dean was on his uppers, but far from discouraged and open for any suitable job that was obtainable. "Take our school," said the trustees, and he did at $125 a month. It was new business, but his wife had the experience, and midnight oil did the rest. The mixed school of sixty pupils, from seven years old to twenty-two, had no terror for the new teacher; on the contrary, he rose to the occasion and the school was a success. The second year his wages were raised to $140 and for the third year an offer of $150 was turned down. Teaching was abandoned to accept the position of manager of a grocery store established by Henry Van Sickle. This was in 1867, and Mr. Dean continued in this occupation until 1870, when his former partner in their original location on Marsh Creek died and turned his possessory right over to him. This inducement, coupled with the poor health of Mrs. Dean in that changeable climate, brought him back to Contra Costa County. Our subject entered into the spirit of his new vocation of farming with characteristic enthusiasm. He remembered the motto of Poor Richard, that "He who by the plow would thrive, himself must either hold or drive," and, notwithstanding the dry years and discouragements, Mr. Dean succeeded as a farmer. But he could not be tied down; he aspired to larger activities, and as an agent for G. W. McNear he began buying grain and shipping to tide-water. In 1880, in connection with others, he built the warehouses at Brentwood and Byron, disposing of his interest in the same to Fish & Blum. They in turn sold to Balfour, Guthrie & Co., who employed Mr. Dean as their agent, and when they purchased the Marsh Ranch they gave Mr. Dean the added responsibility of manager and superintendent. Continuing in this position, Mr. Dean retired from farming and removed to Brentwood in 1883, residing there continuously since. In 1912 he resigned from his agency, made an extended trip East, cured of his wanderlust, weary with the years of his occupation, yet still in the vigor of manhood, though wearing the fingermarks of the octogenarian. Mr. Dean and his wife now reside in quiet content in their cozy Brentwood cottage, an ideal couple. Mr. Dean is of Quaker parentage, dating back to the first settlers of New England. His mother was Helen Barker Dean, daughter of General Barker, of the New York State militia, and assigned to the staff of General Lafayette. He was born at Pleasant Valley, near Poughkeepsie, September 8, 1831. His parents moved to Michigan City in 1836, where his mother passed away, and he returned with his father to New York in 1840.

Six years later he was orphaned by the demise of his father, and at sixteen was thrown upon his own resources. He found occupation as clerk in a country store at the munificent salary of five dollars a month and board; that in two years was increased to twenty dollars, and he was engaged in that business when he caught the California gold fever that carried him off to the Pacific at the age of eighteen. In 1864—January 5th—Mr. Dean was united in marriage with Jerusha H. Martin, daughter of Reuben Martin and Bethia Gowey-Martin, of East Poultney, Vt., at the then new Geary-street church in San Francisco, by the Rev. Thomas Starr King. Mrs. Dean came to California via the Isthmus in 1860 and soon after accepted a position as teacher in the public schools of San Francisco, where she was engaged up to the date of her marriage. In 1865 they moved from the Lake House to Genoa, Nevada, where with his varied occupations, including two years' service as county superintendent of schools, teaching, and store-keeping, besides shying his castor into the political ring for State senator (that he only lacked five votes of getting), Mr. Dean left the battle-born State for sunny California and Contra Costa County, wherein his activities and his record are so far completed—by his election as president of the Bank of Brentwood, a position that he still retains.

HENRY BRUNS is numbered among the substantial and progressive ranchers in eastern Contra Costa County. He was born in Germany on August 28, 1853, the son of John and Geshe Bruns. The parents had eight children, two girls and six boys. Henry, the subject of this review, was educated in the old country. After school he worked out for a time. In 1875 he came to America and located in New York City, where he found work for two years.

In 1877 he came to San Francisco and worked at various vocations. In 1880 he went to the San Joaquin Valley and rented one hundred acres, following general farming for over two years. He removed to the Bethany district and farmed for two years. He then ranched near Haywards for a time. Later he located in the Mountain House section for three years. In the fall of 1891 he removed to eastern Contra Costa County and rented six hundred and forty acres from the McLaughlin estate, operating this place for two years.

He then bought his present farm of one hundred and sixty acres four miles from Byron. Mr. Bruns was married on November 12, 1886, to Ida Helena Lindeman, a native of Germany. She came to America in 1882. Two sons and two daughters were born to them. The elder daughter, Bertha is the wife of John Hensen, of Patterson, California. William married Lottie A. Petterson, and they have one daughter. Henry married Martha Mehrtens, and they have one daughter. Helena, the younger daughter of Mr. Bruns' family, resides at home.

CHARLES A. FRENCH serves in a creditable and able manner as postmaster of Brentwood. He was born in Tennessee on October 29, 1875, the son of Peter and Malinda French, both natives of Tennessee. His father died in 1902, and his mother passed away in 1909. The grandfather of Mr. French was one of the highly respected pioneers of Knox County, Tennessee. The subject of this review acquired his education in the public schools of his native State, after which he attended college.

In May, 1903, he came west and settled in Brentwood, California. He found employment on a ranch with Mr. Grigsby for a time, after which he bought a lease on the Marsh grant. He continued farming for two years. In the fall of 1005 he removed to Antioch, where he farmed for one year. He then took up his abode in Knightsen, where he farmed, and later removed to Brentwood again, where he followed agricultural pursuits for three years. He entered the mercantile business, and owing to his ability he managed the general store for R. E. LaMoine & Co. for two years. He has been associated with the East Contra Costa Mercantile Company since its incorporation. Mr. French was appointed postmaster in 1915. He was united in marriage to Miss Bertha Anna LaMoine on October 18, 1905. There have been two children to this union— Bertha Anna, born May 15, 1909, and Floy Elsa, born August 21, 1912. Mr. French gives his political allegiance to the Republican party. He enjoys a reputation as a reliable business man and has served on the high-school board for a period of four years, and on the grammar-school board for two years. Fraternally, he is a member of the Independent Order of Foresters, and locally he can be depended upon to co-operate in all movements that tend to the upbuilding and substantial improvement of his town.

FREDERICK MELBOURNE HOLWAY is recognized as one of the staunch and enterprising pioneers of Contra Costa County. He was born in Somersetshire, England, May 12, 1856, the son of John and Anna Holway. He received a limited education in the old country and came to America in 1872, locating in Chicago. He acquired his start in life in the hotel business in Chicago, and while a resident there determined to have a better education and attended the public schools for a time. In 1874 Mr. Holway determined to cast his lot with the West and started for Colorado, where he remained about one year. In July, 1875, he landed in San Francisco, where he learned the barber trade, and in connection followed the restaurant and hotel business. In 1878 he came to Contra Costa County, locating at Point of Timber for a time, removing to Byron in the spring of 1878. In 1878 Mr. Holway established the Hotel Byron, the leading hotel in that section until it was burned in 1884. The same year he erected the present hotel, disposing of it in 1891. In 1883 he established his present business, which he has since continued. On May 12, 1883, he was married to Emma Luhrsen, a native of San Francisco, of German parentage. To this union were born ten children— Eva (wife of Lee Acrey of Byron), Percy M. (of Oakland), Raymond F. (of Oakland), Herman (of Byron), Viola, Irene, Geraldine, Martha, and Alvira.

Aurora died at the age of eighteen months. Mr. Holway is a Republican and has always taken a keen interest in his party. He is now serving on the Byron school board as trustee. Fraternally, he is a member of the Odd Fellows lodge of Byron and has the distinction of filling all the chairs in his order. He has served as a delegate to the grand lodge that convened at San Diego in May, 1916. Mr. Holway's loving wife passed away on April 3, 1912. She was of a kind and genial nature and had hosts of staunch friends, and her death was mourned sincerely. Mr. Holway came to this section previous to the starting of the town and tells of shooting geese where Byron is now located. He therefore is the oldest living male resident of Byron. He has at all times shown a spirit of progressiveness and has aided in every way and done his share in the upbuilding of this section.

FRANK CABRAL.—The substantial and well-to-do citizens of Byron, California, have no better representative than Frank Cabral, who occupies a noteworthy position among the thriving and progressive men of this section. He has been actively engaged in the sheep business for years. He has likewise been occupied in agricultural pursuits and owns one of the finest farms in Contra Costa County. He was born in San Maria, Azores Islands, a Portuguese possession, where he received his education. Mr. Cabral came to America and direct to Contra Costa County thirty-seven years ago. For five years he worked out, after which he purchased fifty acres, and the care and attention he exercised in the management of his place place it among the most valuable in his vicinity. He has run as high as eight thousand sheep and has engaged in the cattle business on a large scale. Fraternally, Mr. Cabral is affiliated with the I. D. E. S. and the U. P. E. C. societies. He was married on May 18, 1893, to Mary Rodgers of Alameda County. To this union have been born four children. Stanley, the elder son, was united in wedlock to Miss Bessie Sanders, of Brentwood; Mae is the wife of F. Lewis, in mercantile business in Byron; Frank, Jr., and Rose are attending school. Mr. Cabral has richly deserved whatever success has come to him, for he now holds a prominent position in the financial world. Mr. and Mrs. Cabral have a host of friends in eastern Contra Costa County.

CHARLES B. WIGHTMAN.—Thoroughly identified with the growth and industrial prosperity of Byron is Charles B. Wightman, who takes an abiding interest in all that concerns the town's welfare and progress. He was born in Antioch November 7, 1882. He acquired his education in the public schools of Antioch and Oakley. His father, Joel D. Wightman, was one of the highly esteemed citizens of Contra Costa County. The parents of Joel D. Wightman were among the pioneers who crossed the plains during the gold rush, and he was born on a "prairie schooner" en route. Joel D. Wightman was active in politics, serving on the board of supervisors, being chairman of the board when the new courthouse was erected in Martinez. In the parents' family there were nine children. Charles B. Wightman, the subject of this sketch, learned the carpenter trade and followed this vocation for a period of twelve years. In 1909 he and his brother Percy engaged in the garage business in Byron, having one of the most modern establishments of its kind in Contra Costa County. Mr. Wightman was united in marriage to Miss Beatrice Wisdom on August 9, 1906. To this union were born two children, Sadie and Erma. Politically, he is a Democrat, but he has never aspired to office. Fraternally, he is a member of the Woodmen of the World and holds membership in the Native Sons. Percy Wightman was born in Antioch May 18, 1890 and received his education in the public schools of that place. Laying aside his books, he found employment on the river for a time, and later learned the machinist's trade, which he followed until he came to Antioch to engage in the garage and automobile business. He was married to Miss Mabel Campbell, a native of Byron, on February 16, 1916.

JOHN H. TRYTHALL.—Among the representative men of Contra Costa County, and among the most honored and public-spirited citizens of the eastern part of the county, the name of John H. Trythall occupies the position of pre-eminence. He has been conspicuously identified with the good roads movement since his election to office as supervisor in 1914 and has the distinction of building the first piece of concrete road in Contra Costa County. He is regarded as a citizen of more than ordinary importance, for he thoroughly interests himself in questions concerning the welfare of the county and has brought about results and great benefits in behalf of the people of the entire section. Mr. Trythall's birth occurred in Cornwall, England, July 26, 1852. He acquired his education in the schools of his native land, and at the age of eighteen he came to America, settling in New Jersey for a time. He took up the vocation of mining in Pennsylvania, Illinois, Iowa, Missouri, Michigan, Wyoming, and Nevada. In 1876 he came to Contra Costa County and found employment at the Judson Mines, where he remained for a time. He then went to British Columbia and Alaska. In 1879 he returned to this State and worked in the Knoxville quicksilver mines at Napa for one year. Following this he worked in the Belshaw coal mines, and then removed to Arizona. In June, 1884, he returned to Contra Costa County and acted as foreman and superintendent of the Pittsburg Coal Mine. This position he held for twelve years. Mr. Trythall then purchased twenty acres of land near Antioch and set out an orchard, which has been brought up to a high state of cultivation. He was twice married, the first union being to Priscilla Jones, deceased, a native of New York State. To this union were Raymond Henry, born June 2, 1884, and Helen Johannah, born April 16, 1889. The second marriage was to Ida Von Baum, a native of Napa, California. To this union a daughter, Hilda, was born September 16, 1004. Fraternally, Mr. Trythall is a Mason, being past master of Contra Costa Lodge, F. & A. M., and of Antioch Chapter No. 65, R. A. M. He was identified with the Odd Fellows of Somersville until the lodge was disbanded, having passed all the chairs. He also holds membership in the Eagle lodge of Antioch. His political affiliations are with the Republican party. He was elected by the people of Contra Costa County to represent them as their supervisor in 1004, and he has held that office continuously since. He has always taken an active part in educational matters and has served as trustee for many years in the Antioch district. While a resident of Somersville he served in the same capacity for nine years.

HENRY VAN TIENEN JANSSE, one of the successful and prominent business men of eastern Contra Costa County, was born in Holland on September 4, 1878. His parents died in the old country when Henry was young. At the age of seventeen he began his independent career and came to America. He at once came to California and located in Santa Cruz, where his brother Arie was already living, but later removed to San Jose, where he is now engaged in the real-estate business. His brother Dirk is identified with Sloan & Co. of San Francisco; Peter, another brother, is in Santa Cruz County; and his brother John is a traveling salesman. The subject of this review received a limited education in the public schools, after which he attended business college in Santa Cruz. He understood farming in principle and detail and he readily found employment. Later he became associated with Silva & Omeara, of Oakley, in the grocery business, and after two years he purchased the interest of Mr. Silva. In June, 1914, Mr. Jansse and his partner purchased the general store of R. E. La Moine & Co., of Brentwood, and incorporated both stores under the name of East Contra Costa Mercantile Company. Politically, Mr. Jansse is a Republican. Fraternally, he is a member of the Masonic lodge of Brentwood, and he is also a member of the Foresters. He was united in marriage to Johanna Agneta Rost Van Tonningen, a native of Holland, December 12, 1901. To this union there are three children—Helen, born January 22, 1906; Leonard, born October 10, 1909; Bernard, born February 14, 1911. The family are members of the Dutch Reformed Church of San Francisco. Mr. Jansse in his business has followed the policy of absolute integrity; his company has always lived up to the letter of all agreements, and this policy has won for it increased customers in both stores. Consequently, the company's standing is of the best, and its members are considered among the representative business men of eastern Contra Costa County.

GEORGE H. SHAFER is one of the representative business men of eastern Contra Costa County. He was born in Rio Vista, California, February 26, 1866. His parents were William and Elizabeth (Pierce) Shafer. His father was a native of Bedford County, Pennsylvania, who came west via Cape Horn about 1855. Mr. Shafer's mother crossed the plains in 1852 with her parents. In the parents' family there were five children, all living—Adrian H., a rancher, residing in Brentwood; Mabel, wife of George Geddes, of Byron; Winifred, wife of M. Preston, of Byron; Hannah, and the subject of this sketch. Mr. Shafer's father died on April 10, 1915. He was one of the early river men on the Sacramento. He later became identified with the stock business and ranched on a large scale, owning five hundred and eighty acres. He was one of the agriculturalists of this county who brought about personal success by application and industry, giving thought, time, and attention to the cultivation of his land. Mr. Shafer was active in politics, but never aspired to public office. He was on many occasions a delegate to the county conventions. He was a great temperance worker and did much to further the cause. George H. Shafer acquired his education in the Eden Plain School District, near Brentwood. He attended the Stockton Normal and Business College. Finishing his education he returned to Brentwood and engaged in the livery business. He was elected constable in 1888 and held this office to the satisfaction of the people continuously, with the exception of four years, when he did not run for the office, owing to other matters that occupied his time. He was appointed by W. C. Rogers in 1888 as deputy sheriff. He gives his political support to the Republican party. In 1905 Mr. Shafer engaged in the undertaking business and served as deputy coroner under Doctor C. L. Abbott, of Richmond. Fraternally, he is a member of the Masonic lodge of Brentwood, the Foresters, the Odd Fellows of Byron, and the I. D. E. S. of Oakley. Mr. Shafer was united in marriage to Martha C. Bainbridge, of Stockton, August 20, 1888. She was a daughter of Doctor J. A. Bainbridge, whose death occurred in 1914. Mr. and Mrs. Shafer have one son, Earl B., born May 19, 1800, who is now in the employ of the People's Water Company as surveyor. Mrs. Shafer is an active member of the Eastern Star and also holds membership in Companion Court Sister Lodge of Foresters. Mr. and Mrs. Shafer have gained an extensive circle of friends and acquaintances in eastern Contra Costa County.

CHARLES THOMAS SHELLENBERGER, a rancher for many years in eastern Contra Costa County, is a man who occupies a prominent place among the representative and highly esteemed men of that locality. He was born in Illinois on January 29, 1868, and is a son of John Shellenberger, who was numbered among the prominent men of Mackinaw, Illinois, and who served for many years as justice of the peace in his locality. In 1889 Charles T. Shellenberger removed to California. He worked out for a time, and later bought forty acres in Deer Valley. He afterward purchased the adjoining two hundred acres, part of which was known as the Woodhall Smith place. He has always carried on general farming. He is a man of industry and activity, and by wise judgment and forethought has accumulated a competency. Mr. Shellenberger was united in marriage to Miss Louisa Heidorn on

October 17, 1894, and to this union there have been four children—Emma Charlotte, born November 17, 1897; Frank Rattan, born March 20, 1899; Charles Thomas, Jr., born June 3, 1902; Henry Heidorn, born July 6, 1910. Politically, Mr. Shellenberger is a Progressive, He has served on the Deer Valley school board for many years. Fraternally, he is affiliated with the Masonic lodge and the Foresters of Brentwood. His mother, Elizabeth (Sargent) Shellenberger, was born March 19, 1834, and died August 21, 1876. His parents were married March 3, 1853 and had ten children. His father was born January 14, 1824 and died January 30, 1905. Charles T. Shellenberger made his home in Deer Valley until 1908, when he removed to the Lone Tree section, where he occupies the home formerly known as the Darby place.

LEE DURHAM is a man who has by his own energy, ambition, and enterprise worked his way upward to a place among the representative men of eastern Contra Costa County. Mr. Durham was born near Concord, Contra Costa County, April 15, 1873. He acquired his education in the public schools of Concord, after which he took a business course. He became identified with the Bank of Antioch, where he remained for a period of ten years as assistant cashier. He then went to Martinez and was connected with the Bank of Martinez as assistant cashier for ten years. A spirit of progress has actuated him in all he has done, and success along banking lines has attended his well-directed labors, so that he stands today one of the practical men of eastern Contra Costa County. When the Bank of Brentwood was organized, Mr. Durham was chosen as cashier and secretary, and has done much in making this bank a success. He was united in marriage on June 29, 1904, to Miss Alice L. Joslin, a daughter of S. B. and Mary Joslin. Mrs. Durham's father was one of the pioneer settlers in Antioch, dying there in 1902. Fraternally, Mr. Durham is affiliated with the Masonic lodge of Antioch, and both he and his wife hold a membership in the Eastern Star. Mr. Durham is a member of Mount Diablo Parlor of the Native Sons of Antioch. Politically, he is registered as a Progressive. In all official and social relations Mr. Durham adheres to high ideals and has the confidence and regard of the entire community, and his circle of friends is constantly increasing.

JAMES O'HARA.—Numbered among the representative and well-known fruitmen of eastern Contra Costa County was James O'Hara, deceased. He established a reputation as one of the substantial and progressive men of the county. He was a native of Bangor, Maine, and was born on November 8, 1840, the son of Henry and Ann O'Hara, both natives of Ireland. His parents came to America in the early days, locating in Bangor, where his father followed farming. James received his education in the public schools of Bangor. He worked on his father's farm until he reached the age of eighteen, when he left home and traveled through the Southern States. In 1860 he came to California and settled in Contra Costa County, where he found employment at farming and dairying. In 1887 he bought one hundred and sixty acres and later purchased six hundred and forty acres near Oakley at five dollars an acre. When he located here it was covered with chaparral, and thousands of rabbits were on his land. He cleared five sections of land, and established an almond orchard of eighty acres, afterward adding to this to the extent of one hundred and sixty acres of fruit and nuts, at the home place. Mr. O'Hara spent many happy and profitable years up to the time of his death, which occurred on September 9, 1912, his able and enterprising sons succeeding to the management of the ranch. Mr. O'Hara sold the land where Oakley is located, afterward buying back eighteen acres, which he subdivided and put on the O'Hara addition to Oakley. In politics he was a Democrat, and did much along party lines, although he never aspired to public office. Mr. O'Hara possessed great energy and did more for Oakley and surrounding country than any other man, and at the time of his death he owned seven hundred acres. On April 15, 1885, Mr. O'Hara was united in marriage to Miss Mary Hickey, a native of Massachusetts, who lived in the Berkshire Hills. Her parents were James and Catherine Hickey. Mr. and Mrs. O'Hara were the parents of four children—William J., born March 21, 1886; Anna C, born December 6, 1888; Elwin L., born February 15, 1890; Charles E., born September 23. 1893. Charles E. graduated from the University of California in May, 1916. He is now at Manila, Philippine Islands, and identified with Calamba Sugar Estate. The family are members of the Catholic church of Oakley.

WILLIAM C. WILLIAMSON.—Prominent among the more active, enterprising, and influential citizens of eastern Contra Costa County may be mentioned William C. Williamson, who has been identified with the agricultural pursuits of this county for many years. He was born in Taney County, Missouri, October 27, 1858, the son of Jesse and Ann (Stallcup) Williamson, who were the parents of seven children. At the age of twenty, Mr. Williamson went to Mendocino County and found employment with the Caspar Lumber Company for nearly two years. Returning to Missouri, he spent over six years farming, and in 1888 he returned to California and rented the Shannon ranch in eastern Contra Costa County. Mr. Williamson was united in marriage to Miss Elizabeth Shannon, who died in 1907. To this union were born seven children—Nellie (wife of Joseph Lynch, of San Francisco), William, John C., Aubry, Mabel, Frances, and Leslie. Aubry has the distinction of being one of twenty-four boys in California to receive a prize from the State Agricultural College at Davis for the best acre of corn grown. Aubry raised on one acre of his father's ranch ninety-eight and a half bushels of corn, winning a trip throughout the United States, with all expenses paid by the Davis Agricultural School. Mr. Williamson has five hundred and forty acres in one ranch, and twenty-four in another.

After an arduous effort, he has brought his ranch land into condition for profitable crops. He carries on general farming. Politically, Mr. Williamson is a Democrat. He has served on the local school board for twenty-six years. He is also a director of the First National Bank of Antioch. Fraternally, he is a member of the Masonic lodge of Brentwood, the I. O. O. F. of Antioch for the past twenty-five years, and the Maccabees lodge. He is always ready and can be relied upon to promote public-spirited plans and projects, and it has been his aim to promote the good-roads movement in the county.

JOSEPH G. PREWETT.—A man of progressive and enterprising ideas and methods, Joseph G. Prewett has made a success of his chosen occupation since coming to Contra Costa County. He is a prominent member of the agricultural community and has brought about his success by application and industry. He was born in Illinois on August 7, 1861. His parents removed to Missouri when he was quite young, and he received his education in the district schools of that State. Laying aside his books, he worked out for a time at farming, after which he found employment in the mines at Joplin, Missouri, for two years. In 1884, he came to California, landing here on June 22nd. He rented land in 1885, which he improved and cultivated for some years, and the first place he purchased was a large portion of the P. O'Brien homestead, consisting of two hundred and seventy acres. He has constantly added to his holdings until he now owns fifteen hundred and seventy acres. His attention is devoted to general farming and stock-raising.

Mr. Prewett was united in marriage to Miss Ellen O'Brien on November 13, 1899. Their children are three—Edward, born March 16, 1891; Raymond, born May 19, 1897; Harold, born June 13, 1904. Politically, Mr. Prewett is affiliated with the Democratic party. He has served for some years on the high-school board at Brentwood and is a member of the Lone Tree school board. He is vice-president of the First National Bank of Antioch and a director. He is president of the Antioch Warehouse Association, and president of the Oakley Horse Breeders' Association and the Brentwood Horse Breeders' Association. He also serves as president of the Lone Tree Telephone Company. a new line among the agriculturists in eastern Contra Costa County. Mr. Prewett has recently erected one of the most imposing residences in the county. He has taken a prominent place among the good-roads advocates of the county and has done much to further that interest by giving his excellent views. He has done much in the promotion of every worthy cause that will be of a material benefit to eastern Contra Costa County.

FRANK W. FOSKETT.—One of the most able, progressive and enterprising business men in public life in Contra Costa County is Frank W. Foskett, president of the First National Bank of Concord. It has often been said that the banks of a community are a fair index of its commercial, industrial, and financial prosperity. Especially is this true of the First National Bank of Concord, which dates its origin from March, 1911. The institution was founded on a policy of progressiveness and conservatism, and this has been adhered to steadily, the result being seen in the excellent condition of the bank, which is today one of the leading financial enterprises in the county.

Frank W. Foskett was born in Franklin County, Massachusetts, November 21, 1859. He is a son of John and Nancy (Stone) Foskett. His father was a native of Massachusetts, while his mother was born in New Hampshire. Mr. Foskett was educated in the public schools of Massachusetts. At an early age he came to Pittsburg, California, where he engaged in the butcher business with Mr. Elworthy. In 1885 the firm removed to Concord, and in September of that year purchased the store of William Hawes, and operated stores in Pittsburg and Concord, and in 1911 the firm purchased the store of Arthur Williams, of Walnut Creek, making a chain of three stores which was successfully operated by the firm. Also the firm held large land interests, and in 1911 they disposed of four thousand acres to the R. N. Burgess Company, at that time selling the wholesale and retail meat business. The firm of Foskett & Elworthy displayed sound judgment in the management of their business interests, and through their persistence of purpose won gratifying success in the business and financial world. The firm erected the finest business block and bank building in Concord, which would be a credit to the larger cities of the Bay region. Mr. Foskett has served as trustee on the grammar-school and high-school boards and gives his political support to the Republican party. He has served as treasurer of the town since it started. He was united in marriage to Alice L. Duncalf, a native of Canada, September 16, 1885. To this union have been born four children—Clifford John, Ethel Mae, Walter William, and Raymond Albert. Mr. Foskett is regarded as a reliable, far-sighted, and progressive business man. He has been a leading factor in the development and upbuilding of the town of Concord.

He has one of the most imposing residences in the county, which is an evidence of the excellent results which he has achieved in a financial way.

HENRY A. NELSON.—Among the Native Sons of California, prominent mention should be made of Henry A. Nelson, postmaster at Oakley. He was born in Stockton December 13, 1874, the son of Henry A. and Ellen (Crane) Nelson. His father was a native of New Hampshire, while his mother was born in Vermont. His father passed away in 1898, and his mother died in October, 1914. When Henry A. Nelson was but five years of age his parents removed to and located in Berkeley, where Henry A. received his education in the public and high schools of that place. Finishing his education, he entered the employ of the Southern Pacific Company, and was identified with the train service for a period of seven years. In 1902 he went to Mexico, where he followed mining engineering for over four years. He located in Oakley in 1907 and followed ranching for four years. During President Taft's administration he was appointed postmaster at Oakley, and again received the same office under Wilson's administration. The leading factor in the success of Mr. Nelson's holding office is faithfulness, integrity, and strict attention to details and he has won for himself a reputation for business ability. Mr. Nelson was united in marriage to Miss Lucy E. Holden, a native of San Francisco, March 29, 1896. To this union there have been three children—Jessie Viola, died at the age of four, in Mexico; Roland P., born February 19, 1906; Marion E., born March 3, 1909. Mrs. Nelson passed away on May 26, 1916. Her death was mourned by a wide circle of friends. Fraternally, Mr. Nelson is associated with the Masonic lodge of Brentwood and holds membership in the I. D. E. S. He has six and a half acres of land adjoining the town of Oakley.

ANDREW WALKER, deceased, was numbered throughout the eastern part of Contra Costa County as a pioneer of staunch and enterprising spirit, and one who gave no little of a useful life to the upbuilding of the best interests of his adopted locality. He was born in Scotland, December 29, 1832, the second son, and at an early age went to sea, which vocation he followed some years and made several trips around the world. He was comparatively young when he decided to cast his lot with the Golden State and located in San Francisco. He worked for Moore & Folger, wholesale merchants, for some time, after which he engaged with the Russian Consul in the wholesale and retail grocery business. Previous to this time Mr. Walker opened a hay and grain business for a time. While engaged in the grocery trade Mr. Walker made two trips to St. Petersburg. He sailed from San Francisco, stopped at the Sandwich Islands, went to Japan, crossed the Ural Mountains, and thence via Siberia into St. Petersburg. In 1868 Mr. Walker disposed of his business in San Francisco. Previous to selling out his business in San Francisco he purchased a ranch four miles from Berkeley, known as the San Pablo Creek ranch, and in 1873 he purchased four hundred acres in the swamp where Oakley is located. This place was very difficult to clear, as it was all chaparral. He was successful beyond the expectations of all his friends and cleared the land and raised large crops of grain, alfalfa, and hay. He increased his holdings, and in 1887 he purchased the Babbe ranch of two hundred acres. In January, 1893, he disposed of the latter place. He purchased the Foreman place of seven hundred acres, and in 1887 sold to B. F. Porter, of San

Francisco. Mr. Walker continued to run the four-hundred-acre ranch until November, 1905, when he disposed of his holdings to the California Canners' Association. Mr. Walker was married to Rhobe Anna Andrews, a native of Clinton, Louisiana, a daughter of Judge Thomas L. Andrews. To this union were born four children—Harriet M., wife of Henry Farnum (deceased), whose son, Lancelot, is station agent at Fellows, California; Robert Richmond Walker, who died in 1864; Arthur Merrill Walker, who was born in Edinburgh, Scotland, and died in 1869; Andrew Lathrop Walker, an orchardist of Oakley. Andrew Walker gave his political support to the Republican party. His death occurred on January 15, 1906.

CLAUDE R. LEECH, M. D—Noteworthy among the able and skillful physicians of Contra Costa County is Doctor Claude R. Leech, who during his twenty years of residence in Walnut Creek has built up an excellent practice. He was born in Pennsylvania, September 8, 1868, his parents being Thomas and Margaret (Reznor) Leech. Doctor Leech's father was one of the representative agriculturists in his locality, and his death occurred in 1884. His mother died in 1906. There were seven children born in the parents' family. At the age of seventeen, Dr. Leech came to California. He acquired his education in the public and high schools of Oakland, after which he attended the University of California and the Cooper Medical Institute, graduating from the medical class of the latter in 1894. In 1895 he began the practice of his profession in Oakland with gratifying success. In 1897 he removed to Walnut Creek, where he has since remained. Doctor Leech is a stalwart Republican. He has served on the Walnut Creek school board for a number of years. He is health officer in Walnut Creek, holding this office for some years. His study and research work has been a decided help to humanity in the prevention of disease in this locality. He is a member of the county and State medical societies. On February 9, 1896, Doctor Leech was united in marriage to Miss Eva Berry, a native of Minnesota. Fraternally, Doctor Leech is a member of the Masonic lodge of Walnut Creek and is loyal to its teachings, which he exemplifies in his life. In matters of citizenship he manifests a progressive and public-spirited interest. His professional duties are constantly growing in volume and importance. Mrs. Leech is an active member of the Eastern Star.

BRUCE W. STONE is a well-known and successful agriculturist of Contra Costa County. He was born in Kalamazoo, Michigan, December 14, 1840. He is a son of John and Matilda Stone. Both are natives of New England. His father was a successful contractor and builder, after which he followed farming and resided at Portage, Michigan. Mr. Stone's father came to California in 1865 and located in Green Valley with his son-in-law, William Z. Stone. Mr. Stone's father died in Green Valley in 1866 and was buried in the Alhambra Cemetery. Mr. Stone's mother died in 1870 and was buried in the same cemetery. Bruce W. Stone acquired his education in Michigan.

At the age of twenty he came to California and followed mining until 1869, when he bought two hundred and nineteen acres of land in Green Valley, Contra Costa County. He has since been identified with the farming and stock interests of the county. Mr. Stone was one of the first to go to Alaska and has the distinction of raising the first American flag at Sitka, where he was identified with the quartermaster's department. Mr. Stone was in the Government service and was sent to Alaska to take possession of Alaska, which was transferred by Russia. Sitka was the capital at that time, and Mr. Stone spent two years in that country. Previous to going to Alaska he went to Central America and followed mining. He was shipwrecked on the Alaskan Coast, at Cook's Inlet, and was compelled to live with the Indians for a period of three months, and during this time never saw a white man.

Mr. Stone was married on September 20, 1875, to Lydia M. Lattimore, a native of Ohio. He then removed to Illinois and Michigan, and later came to California. Mr. and Mrs. Stone have two adopted sons, Ben W., a resident of Niles, and Arthur F., who resides at Richmond. Mr. Stone has cast his vote in Contra Costa County since 1860. He is a member of the I. O. O. F. and the Grange. Mr. and Mrs. Stone are affiliated with the Rebekah lodge.

Mr. Stone was the instigator and worked hard for the Danville Fraternal and Social Hall Association and has served as president since its organization. The building cost ten thousand dollars, and the Odd Fellows and the Grange are equal owners in this modern building. Mr. Stone disposed of his ranch holdings in 1912 and has since retired. Mr. and Mrs. Stone are held in highest regard in Contra Costa County, and they have won the trust and good-will of all by reason of their pleasant personalities.

FRANK STEVENS COOK, M. D., who has been actively engaged in practice as physician and surgeon at Brentwood, Contra Costa County, for the past eleven years, is an able and representative member of the medical profession. He was born in Walla Walla, Washington, July 22, 1865. He was educated in the public schools of that place and received his high-school work in Prescott, Arizona, where his parents removed in 1876. He graduated from the medical department of the University of California with the class of 1887, following which he spent one year in the City and County Hospital of San Francisco as house physician and surgeon. Locating in San Francisco, he followed his profession until the summer of 1898, when he removed to Crockett, this county, where he spent two years, when he accepted an appointment with a large mining and smelting company in Durango, Mexico, spending four years in that country. During an epidemic of bubonic plague the Mexican Government called upon him for his services, the work being so strenuous that his health failed, compelling his return to California, where he spent some time in the mountains of Madera County recuperating, after which he returned to San Francisco and resumed practice in 1905.

He passed through the earthquake and conflagration of that city in 1906, where with one other doctor (Armisted) he had charge of the refugee camp at the foot of Third Street. His work in the hygienizing of the camp of five thousand received commendable mention from Colonel Toner of the United States Army. He is a member of the Contra Costa County Medical Society, and also of the Medical Society of the State of California. He is a member of several fraternal orders, Masonic, I. O. O. F., K. of P., W. O. W., and F. O. E. In politics he is a Republican and takes an active interest in the party.

ROBERT HARKINSON— Among the strong financial institutions of Contra Costa County is the Bank of Antioch, and among the bankers of prominence in that city is Robert Harkinson, who as cashier has done much toward securing for his institution the foremost position in banking circles that it now occupies. His banking experiences extend over many years, and he has since 1891 been connected with that institution. Mr. Harkinson was born in Pittsburg, Pennsylvania, the son of Charles and Katherine (Schmale) Harkinson. He received his education in the public schools of Philadelphia. In 1874 he came to California and at the age of nineteen became identified with the Bank of Dixon, California. He remained with this bank until 1883, when he went to San Luis Obispo, where he served with the Bank of San Luis Obispo until 1891, when he accepted a position as cashier of the Bank of Antioch, and still holds this position. He is careful, painstaking, and systematic, and, as a student of human nature and conditions, seldom has made an error in extending credit or making investments.

The institution of which he is cashier has greatly prospered through his efforts, and he is readily conceded to be among the able and well-informed men in his line of work in the county. Mr. Harkinson was united in marriage to Alice E. Brinkerhoff, a native of California. To this union was born Maud Bernice, wife of D. M. Roberts, of Berkeley, California. Mr. Harkinson is held in high regard by his business associates, by reason of his enterprise, integrity, and sterling personal worth.

HON. WILLIAM R. SHARKEY.—One of the most highly esteemed and deservedly respected citizens of Contra Costa County is William R. Sharkey, State senator from the ninth district, comprising Contra Costa and Marin counties. Senator Sharkey was born in Sierra County, June 6, 1876, the son of Richard and Mary Sharkey. He acquired his education in the public schools, after which he took up the printing trade and became identified with the Sierra County Tribune for a time. He then removed to Sierraville and for over a year was connected with the Mountain Mirror, discharging his duties in a manner that commended him to his employer and to those working with him. He then removed to Lassen County and worked on the Amadee Geyser for a time, when he returned to Sierraville and accepted a position on the Sierra Valley Leader, remaining there for a year.

He resigned, owing to his health, and rode the range. In 1896 Mr. Sharkey resumed his newspaper work and became associated with the Sierra County Enterprise at Downieville, and in 1899 he purchased the Sierra Valley Record, which he operated until 1902, when he disposed of his paper and accepted a position as coast manager for the Calkins Newspaper Syndicate.

In 1003 Senator Sharkey was made city editor of the Morning Miner, at Nevada City, and in the fall of 1905 he removed to Reno, Nevada, where he opened an office for the Calkins Newspaper Syndicate and represented the Orchard and Farm and the Pacific Miner, both Calkins publications. On April 1, 1906, he became manager of the Contra Costa Standard, and under his direction the paper rapidly increased in circulation and influence. In 1911 he established the Martinez Daily Standard, now one of the brightest and most influential papers published in the county. Senator Sharkey gives his political support to the Republican party and takes an active interest in public affairs. In 1915 he served for one term as a member of the State legislature from the eighteenth district. He was elected State senator from the ninth district, representing Contra Costa and Marin counties in 1916. Senator Sharkey was united in marriage to Miss Nannie Elizabeth Gott, a native of Plumas County, California, September 6, 1900. To this union have been born Muriel and William R., Jr. Fraternally, Senator Sharkey is a member and past master of Martinez Lodge No. 41, F. & A. M.; Mountain Vale Lodge No. 140, I. O. O. F., of Sierraville; Laurel Camp No. 145, W. O. W.; past president and secretary Mt. Diablo Parlor No. 101, N. S. G.

W.; California Camp No. 7079, Modern Woodmen of the World; Richmond Lodge No. 1251, B. P. O. E.; Los Ceritos Chapter No. 350, O. E. S.; and Alhambra Lodge No. 292, Rebekah. Senator Sharkey is chairman of the Rivers and Harbors Commission of California, to which position he was appointed by Governor Hiram W. Johnson. The Senator's personal characteristics have gained for him the warm regard and friendship of many. He is a public-spirited man and a valuable citizen, and he interests himself in all public measures that will better local conditions.

HERBERT HENRY ELWORTHY.—In the course of a long and successful business career Mr. Elworthy has been identified with the meat business.

He is now creditably filling the office of vice-president of the First National Bank of Concord. He was born in England, March 12, 1863. His parents removed to Canada, where Mr. Elworthy acquired his education. In 1881 he came to Contra Costa County and became identified with Mr. Frank W. Foskett, the firm of Foskett & Elworthy engaging in the meat business in Pittsburg, Walnut Creek, and Concord. Politically, Mr. Elworthy is a Republican. He has served as chairman of the board of trustees of Concord for some years. Fraternally, he is a member of the I. O. O. F. He was united in marriage on March 19, 1893, to Annie Brawand, a native of Contra Costa County. To this union have been born four children—Herbert, Paul, Mark, and Keith. Mr. Elworthy has resided in this county for a period of thirty-five years. In all business relations he has held steadily to high ideals, and he has the confidence and regard of all who in any way are associated with him.

BRADFORD HERVEY UPHAM, deceased, was numbered among the most progressive, able, and successful men in Contra Costa County. He was born in Windham, Vermont, March 25, 1843, and was the son of Zenas Upham. Mr. Upham engaged in the wine business in Chicago in the early days. He came west and located in San Francisco, where he engaged in the same business in 1871. He was also identified with Cunningham, Curtiss & Welch, of San Francisco, for many years. He enlisted in the Civil War, and for three and a half years served as Government telegraph operator at Mobile, Alabama. He operated the cable which crossed the river at that point.

The splice which Mr. Upham took out of the cable is on exhibition at the Smithsonian Institution at Washington, D. C. He enlisted from Vermont, in the Eighth Vermont Infantry. Mr. Upham came to Contra Costa County in November, 1889, and engaged in the wine business, and had four hundred acres of the best land in the Alhambra Valley. He was engaged in business in 1890 and continued until his death, which occurred July 29, 1898. He was married to Gertrude Ryer, a native of New York City. To this union were born Fred H., George P., and Elsa Louise, wife of J. C. Arnold, a civil engineer and surveyor, whose death occurred April 20, 1913. There were born to Mr. and Mrs. Arnold three daughters—Gertrude S., Elsa L., and Marion.

Fred Upham, the eldest son of Bradford Hervey Upham, was educated in the public schools and later attended business college in San Francisco. Finishing his education, he returned to the home place and managed the ranch until 1902. He then followed the carpenter trade for seven years, and in 1909 he returned to the ranch and erected the present large and modern cider-mill and packing-house, which is located in the heart of the best apple section of the county. Fred Upham is a member of the Native Sons and holds membership in Mount Diablo Parlor No. 101. He is a

Republican and has served as school trustee on the Alhambra school board. On September 5, 1915, Fred Upham was united in marriage to Frances H. Wardle, a native of Nevada, a daughter of Philip Wardle, one of the pioneer miners and business men of Virginia City. George P. Upham was born July 15, 1881. He received his education in the grammar schools of Contra Costa County and in a business college of San Francisco. He has the management of the ranch and the business. George was united in marriage to Lulu Pieratt, a native of Napa County, June 17, 1908. To this union have been born five children, two of whom died in infancy. Those living are Georgeane Holley, Oliver Putman, and Genevieve. George P. Upham is a progressive man in his political views and is now serving as school trustee. He is a member of Mount Diablo Parlor, Native Sons, and the Past Presidents' Association of Oakland. Upham Brothers' Cider Mill is an incorporation and owns lands and plants and has operated since 1905, with the following officers: Geo. P. Upham, president and manager; Fred H. Upham, vice-president and treasurer; Elsa L. Arnold, secretary. The firm is incorporated for $25,000. The firm makes a specialty of cider and vinegar, and nothing but the pure juice of the apple enters into their products. The average annual output of vinegar is twenty-six thousand gallons, and four thousand gallons of pure cider is shipped annually.

JACOB BUTTNER.—To one of the representative and successful ranchers of Contra Costa County, Jacob Buttner, belongs the title of self-made man, for starting out in life without experience or resources he has through his own energy risen to be one of the leading men in his locality. Mr. Buttner was born on August 14, 1856, in San Francisco, a son of George and Elizabeth Buttner, both natives of Germany. In the parents' family eleven children were born, seven of whom are living. Mr. Buttner's father died in 1911, and his mother passed away in 1905. Jacob acquired his education in Alameda County, where his parents removed when Jacob was very young. He attended the public schools in Sunol and Pleasanton. Laying aside his books, he assisted on the home ranch, and in 1872 started to learn blacksmithing in San Francisco, finishing his trade in Pleasanton. For four years he remained with the man from whom he learned his trade, then for another year he was connected with a shop at Mission San Jose, after which, in May, 1881, he embarked in business for himself at San Ramon, where he bought a blacksmith-shop including the property. Here he remained over nine years. In 1891 Mr. Buttner purchased fifty-five acres of the Boss estate, and for eleven years, up to 1907, he rented the land, when he moved on his place, and here he has remained continuously since, improving his land and bringing it up to a high state of cultivation. His record since he has been on the place speaks for itself. He now has one hundred and thirteen acres. He makes a specialty of grapes and fruit. Mr. Buttner was twice married, the first union being to Miss Eugenie Souc, October 2, 1881, and her death occurred on May 20, 1896. The second marriage occurred on October 31, 1906, to Elizabeth Atherton, of San Francisco. Four children blessed the first union, two of whom died when young; those living are Emily, wife of James O'Neil, of San Jose, and John J., of San Francisco. Politically, Mr. Buttner is a Democrat. He served one term on the Concord high-school board and is a member of the Woodmen of the World.

CLERMONT L. RICHARDSON—The eighty-acre farm belonging to Clermont L. Richardson is located near Byron and is devoted to orchard and general farming. Mr. Richardson purchased this place in 1893, and he was one of the many farmers of this locality who have brought about their personal success by application and industry, giving thought, time, and attention to the cultivation of the land upon which he was engaged in agricultural pursuits. Ford Richardson was born in Westfield, Ohio, March 24, 1883. His parents, Clermont and Annie Richardson, were natives of Ohio.

In the parents' family there were born four sons. The father came west in 1872, and later returned to his native State. In 1893 he returned and located in the Byron section, where he purchased eighty acres and carried on general farming. Ford received his education in the public schools of Byron, after which he assumed the management of the home place for a time. Four years ago he engaged in the meat business with gratifying success. In June, 1916, Ford Richardson took over the management of the Hotel Byron. He has made many changes in the interior of the hotel and caters to the general public. It is a typical American hotel of the best class. He was united in marriage in Antioch, to Miss Myrtle Boyd, a native of Canada, June 1, 1908. To this union there are two daughters—Wanta, born November 22, 1909, and Myrtle, born March 1, 1914. Mr. Richardson is a Republican and serves on the Byron school board.

LOUIS E. HART.—Among the bankers of Contra Costa County none is more progressive than the subject of this review. The banking institution of which he is cashier and manager, the Crockett branch of the Bank of Pinole, is one of the strong financial concerns in Contra Costa County. A native of San Francisco, Mr. Hart was born June 20, 1872, son of Jesse B. and Sallie (Coleman) Hart. His father was a native of Ohio, while his mother came from Louisiana. Mr. Hart's father died in 1888, and his mother passed away in 1892. They were the parents of three children. Louis E. Hart acquired his education in the public and high schools of San Francisco, after which he became identified with a stock-brokerage company, where he remained for ten years. He later accepted a clerical position with the California Powder Works for several years. While with this company his ability became recognized, and when the Bank of Pinole was organized Mr. Hart was a leading factor in its organization and did much of the detail work in connection with the new institution at Pinole. When the branch bank at Crockett was started, he was made cashier and manager, and by his careful and painstaking manner in business the bank has greatly prospered. He is one of the best-informed men in his line of work in the county. Politically, he is a nonpartisan. He has served as city clerk at Hercules. He is a stockholder in the East Richmond Land Company and holds membership in the B. P. O. E. of Richmond. Mr. Hart was twice married, the first union being to Augusta Ayres, of Petaluma, in 1808, and her death occurred in June, 1913. The second marriage occurred September 5, 1915, to Minnie De Kay, a native of San Francisco. Mr. and Mrs. Hart have many friends in the Bay section.

LOUIS ARATA.—Prominently connected with the business interests of Crockett is Louis Arata. He was born in Italy, December 14, 1850. He acquired a limited education in the public schools of his native land, and at the age of sixteen he came to America. Remaining in New York City for a time, he then removed to Philadelphia, where he worked at his trade of pastemaker for a period of three years. In 1871 he came to California and remained in San Francisco for about three months, when he removed to Somersville and found employment in the mines. He followed this vocation for a few months, and then engaged in the vegetable business until 1885.

Later in the same year he purchased eight hundred acres of land and engaged in general farming until 1891, when he disposed of his farm holdings and removed to San Francisco, where he resided four years. In 1809 he came to Crockett. Mr. Arata was united in marriage to Kate Treaso, a native of Italy, in 1883. To this union have been born four children. One daughter, Linda Del Monte, was drowned in the straits near Crockett. The other children are Silva, wife of Edward Prytz, of Crockett; Atilio, who is managing the business in Crockett; and Louis, who is attending Santa Clara College. In politics Mr. Arata is affiliated with the Republican party. He has served as a delegate to various county conventions, and at one time served on the election board. Fraternally, he is a member of the Antioch Lodge. I. O. O. F. The family attend the Catholic church. Mr. Arata is numbered among the pioneers of Contra Costa County and is well known in Crockett and vicinity.

RANDOLPH C. MARSH.—A distinguishing feature in the career of Randolph C. Marsh, an esteemed and honored resident of Oakley, where he has made his home since 1897, has been an unswerving integrity and uprightness, which have won for him the confidence of all who have had business dealings with him. He is the "Father of Oakley," and has made a success financially, being possessed of much business ability. He is a man of sound judgment and conservative methods, and he has done much to promote the general welfare and develop the resources of eastern Contra Costa County.

A native of Union County, Ohio, Mr. Marsh was born May 24, 1838, the son of Samuel and Mary (Ryan) Marsh. His father died at the age of eighty-eight, and his mother passed away in her sixty-fifth year. Randolph C Marsh received his education in the district school of Marysville, Ohio.

Laying aside his books, he found employment at farming until the Civil War broke out, when he was one of the first to answer the call to arms, which was in April, 1861. He served three months and re-enlisted twice for three years' service and was mustered out in July, 1865. Returning home, he again took up farming and continued to reside in Ohio until 1866, when he removed to Kansas and followed agricultural pursuits for six years. In 1875 he came to California and remained three years in Petaluma. He took up land in Lake County and remained there thirteen years, being identified with general farming and stock-raising. In 1897 he removed to Contra Costa County and purchased twelve acres, establishing and naming the town of Oakley. He gave the first business lot in the town gratis to Joe Jesse for a grocery-store, and upon completion of the building presented him with a deed. Mr. Marsh and A. N. Norcross purchased twenty acres and put on a town-site. After two years Mr. Norcross disposed of his interest to Mr. Marsh and he continued in the real-estate business. Mr. Marsh is the leading spirit of Oakley, regarding the establishment of schools, churches, etc. He has one daughter by his first marriage, Anna, wife of J. J. Every (deceased), of Lakeport, Lake County, California. Mr. Marsh's second marriage was to Eunice Coffin, a native of North Carolina, and to this union have been born two children—Kattie C, wife of E. E. Noyes, of Lake County, and Byron R., a resident of Los Angeles, at present business manager for Anita Baldwin.

Mr. Marsh's second wife died in January, 1913. Fraternally, he is affiliated with the Masonic lodge of Middletown, Lake County. He has served as postmaster of

Oakley for fourteen years, receiving his appointment from President McKinley. Mr. Marsh serves on the Oakley school board and is a member of the town board. He has aided in many ways in the upbuilding of Oakley and the surrounding country. His judgment is often sought on account of his fairness and absence of personal interest. Mr. Marsh has been an advanced thinker and something of a politician for a good many years— not seeking political office for himself but striving to mold more independence of thought on political lines, and of bringing our Government back nearer to the people. He is very fond of music and local home entertainments, and often writes little poems by request for such benefits.

PATRICK O'BRIEN—Among the citizens of eastern Contra Costa County none was more highly esteemed than Patrick O'Brien. He was educated in the Lone Tree public schools. His parents came to this section when Patrick was ten years old. His father bought three hundred and twenty acres of land, which is still in possession of the family. After leaving school Patrick assisted on the home place, where he always remained, and always was identified with agricultural pursuits. The family put out ten acres of almonds and eight acres of wine grapes. Patrick O'Brien married Ella Devery, a native of Ireland, November 23, 1893. Mrs. O'Brien was a daughter of Thomas and Ella Devery. Her father passed away in 1910, and her mother in 1914.

The children of Mr. and Mrs. O'Brien are Emmett, born October 2, 1895, and Carroll, born September 1, 1897, who resides at home and is now superintending the ranch. Mr. O'Brien was a staunch Republican. He served for many years as clerk of the Lone Tree School District. The family are members of the Catholic church of Oakley. His death was mourned by a host of friends, and the community at large lost a valuable citizen.

HENRY G. KRUMLAND is numbered among the highly esteemed citizens of eastern Contra Costa County. He was born in Byron on February 9, 1880, and is the son of George Krumland, a native of Germany, who came to America in 1848, and to California in 1850 via Cape Horn. The father engaged in mining for about ten years. He removed to Contra Costa County, where he found employment at ranching. Later he leased land and engaged in farming and stock-raising. He died in July, 1904. The mother of Henry G. Krumland was a native of Maryland. She was the mother of ten children, three of whom are dead. Henry G. received his education in the public school in Byron, after which he took a business course. Finishing his education, he returned to Byron and became identified with L. G. Plumley in the general mercantile business, and practically for twelve years has been associated with this establishment. In politics Mr. Krumland is a Democrat. In 1910 he was elected justice of the peace and was re-elected in 1914. Fraternally, he is affiliated with the I. O. O. F. of Byron and is a member of the Native Sons.

Mr. Krumland displays marked energy and determination in his business affairs, and has succeeded in life because of persistent, energetic, and honorable effort. He is well known and popular in all social and fraternal circles.

WILLIAM HENRY MURPHY.—Prominent among the men who were conspicuous and influential in developing and advancing the agricultural resources of eastern Contra Costa County was the late William Henry Murphy, a son of Thomas Murphy, an honored and esteemed citizen of this county, who came to California in 1856. Thomas Murphy, the father of William H., was born in County Cavan, Ireland, March 24, 1830. At the age of five years his parents left him in the old country with an uncle and came to America, residing in New York for five years. Thomas joined them at the age of seven. His parents removed to Connecticut. Thomas received a common-school education and in June, 1856, he started for California via the Isthmus route. He intended to return to New York State in one year, but, liking the climate and resources of California, he remained and sent for his family. On joining them he went to Napa Valley and followed farming until 1867, when he removed to the eastern part of this county and purchased four hundred and eighty acres where Knightsen is located. In 1873 he purchased eleven hundred acres in Round Valley. At a later time he purchased more land in Round Valley, and had at the time of his death, which occurred in August, 1005, sixteen hundred acres. Thomas Murphy was married in Mystic, Connecticut, to Miss Alice Ross. To this union have been born five children, William H., the subject of this sketch, James B., Annie L, Alice, and Hattie. William Henry Murphy was born in Napa, California, and died June 9, 1910. He received his education in the Iron House and Eden Plain schools, after which he attended the University of the Pacific, at San Jose. Finishing his education, he returned to the home place, where he was identified with general farming and stock-raising until his death. He was a systematic and thoroughgoing farmer, and after his father's death, by his enterprise, rendered both ranches the most attractive in this section. He was held in the highest esteem by his fellow-men. William Henry Murphy was united in marriage to Miss Christiana Braun, a native of San Jose, and a daughter of C. W. and Florentine Braun. Mr. and Mrs. Murphy were blessed with five children—Arthur Ray, born near Antioch, March 9, 1889; Katie, born near Antioch, July 24, 1890; William Henry, Jr., born in Round Valley, April 2, 1892; Esther, born in Round Valley, June 24, 1895; James Campbell, born at Brentwood, November 3, 1906.

ALEXANDER BURNESS.—Although of foreign birth, no American-born citizen takes a keener interest in the affairs of his country than Alexander Burness, superintendent of Balfour, Guthrie & Company's interests in the beautiful town of Brentwood, Contra Costa County. He has been a resident of California for twenty-eight years. He has not only won a material success through his energy and industry, but he is esteemed as a citizen of sterling worth, and one upon whom the honor of any community may safely rest.

Born in Dundee, Scotland, January 16, 1861, he received his education in the old country. He learned the machinist's trade and in western England was identified with the Singer Sewing Machine Company, in its clerical department, for a period of eight years, finally being made local agent. Upon coming to America, he located in Merced County, where he was associated with the Chowchilla Ranch, this corporation being originally known as the California Pastoral & Agricultural Company of Edinburgh, Scotland. He then went to Bakersfield in the capacity of superintendent of Balfour, Guthrie & Company's interests, where he remained for a period of thirteen years. In June, 1910, he was transferred by his company to Brentwood, Contra Costa County, as general superintendent of their vast holdings. Mr. Burness' political affiliations are with the Democratic party. Fraternally, he is a member of Brentwood Lodge No. 345, F. & A. M., and is now serving as senior deacon of that order. Mrs. Burness is an unusually capable and popular woman and has held the office of matron of the Eastern Star, but now fills the office of district deputy grand matron. Mr. Burness also holds membership in the Eastern Star and is past patron of the order. Their daughter is organist. Mr. Burness was united in marriage to Miss Bertha M. E. Johnson, a native of England, November 11, 1892, and to this union there are five children—Christine M., born August 29, 1894; Muriel H., born August 9, 1808; Alexander H., born November 2, 1900; Ernest H., born May 19, 1906. One child, a daughter, died in infancy. Mr. Burness is a stockholder and director in the Bank of Brentwood, in which he holds the office of vice-president.

Scotland was the original home of the Burness family, and the inheritance of Scottish descendants who through successive generations have displayed vigor of intellect and sagacity of judgment. The father of Mr. Burness was identified for over twenty years with the Denburn power-loom linen manufacture in Brechin, Scotland, as manager, but came to San Francisco, where he afterward died. He married Mary Forbes, a native of Scotland, and to this union were born ten children, of whom eight are now living, viz., Alexander, the subject of this sketch; Margaret, a resident of Oakland; William M., retired, and a resident of San Francisco; John E., formerly chief engineer of the Fairmont and Palace hotels; Robert D., a professor of music in San Francisco; Hector, who has been for many years superintendent for Balfour, Guthrie & Company at Fresno, California; Elizabeth, residing in Philadelphia; and Thomas N., a professor of music, who still resides in the old country, and has been for over thirty years organist in the Dalziel parish church in Motherwell, Scotland. The Burness family are respected for their industrious and well-directed lives, their integrity, and their devotion to their families and friends. The family history has been traced back to Robert Burns, the poet, whose family name was originally Burness. Mr. Burness has the original drawing of the Burness coat of arms in his possession, which he values very highly; the drawing was made April 26, 1869.

WILLIAM A. FOTHERINGHAM, who resides in eastern Contra Costa County, has attained a prominent place among the agriculturists of his neighborhood. He was born in Buffalo, New York, August 13, 1857, son of Alexander D. and Mary (McDonnell) Fotheringham, both deceased. His parents removed to Canada, where William was reared to manhood. His father was a native of England, while his mother was born in Canada; she died when William was but four years of age. He made his home with his grandmother and acquired his education in the public schools. He followed farming, and in 1877 he came to California and located near Byron, where he found employment and acted as foreman for a large land corporation for a period of seven years. He then purchased the Byron ranch near Byron, consisting of two hundred acres, which he has always devoted to general farming and stock-raising. On August 2, 1882, Mr. Fotheringham was united in marriage to Miss Mary B. Alexander, a native of East Kilbride, near Glasgow, Scotlanddaughter of Captain John Alexander, who lost his life at sea. To this union have been born six children—John Alexander, who resides in San Francisco; Jean, wife of William Redman of Stockton; Mabel Elizabeth, wife of John Bankson, identified with the Redwood Manufacturing Company of Pittsburg, California; Lillian A. and Ellen A., both residing at home; William Byron, who assists on the home place. Politically, Mr. Fotheringham is an adherent of the principles advanced in the platform of the Republican party. He has served as school trustee for many years in his section. He is connected fraternally with the I. O. O. F. of Byron and the Woodmen of the World. He makes his home on the William Gilchrist ranch. Mrs. Fotheringham's mother was twice married. The second union was to William Gilchrist, a native of

Scotland, who settled in Contra Costa County in 1851, and purchased three hundred and twenty acres of land, carrying on general farming and stock-raising and set out a thirty-acre orchard, principally of almonds.

He retired and made his home in Pacific Grove up to the time of his death, which occurred in 1915. His wife still resides in Pacific Grove.

JAMES ROST VAN TONNINGEN.—Although but a few years have passed since locating in this county. James R. Van Tonningen successfully established himself as one of the representative men and has made many friends in a business way who esteem him for his business ability and personal characteristics. He is a native of Holland, and was born December 29, 1880, the son of Marinus and Helena Van Tonningen, both natives of Holland. His father was manager of a Dutch syndicate having timber and agricultural lands near Riga, Russia. In his infancy his family removed to Russia, where James partially acquired his education. When he was ten years old, his parents returned to their native land, and here James received a year's schooling. In 1806 the family came to America and located in Santa Cruz County, at Aptos, where the father purchased twenty-five acres, which is devoted to horticulture. Marinus Van Tonningen is considered one of the best authorities in his section on fruit-growing, as he has made it a study for years. In the parents' family there are three children—Johanna, wife of Henry Jansse, of Brentwood; Agnes, wife of Cornelius Van Kaathoven, of Oakley; and James, subject of this review. James R. Van Tonningen completed his education in the public schools of Santa Cruz. After finishing his education he assisted on his father's place until 1907, when he engaged with the California Fruit Canners' Association, which is now the California Packing Corporation. For six years he did all sorts of manual labor, and three years ago was given the management of 1060 acres at Oakley. His success and recognized familiarity with the asparagus industry led to his promotion. He was married to Miss Muriel Bligh, January 22, 1914. She was a native of England.

ARNOLD VAN KAATHOVEN, a well-known and prosperous merchant of Oakley, Contra Costa County, was born in Holland, November 16, 1872. He acquired his education in the public schools of his native land. He is a son of Cornelius Van Kaathoven, deceased, at one time among the prominent physicians in his locality in the old country. His mother, Adriana Van Kaathoven, is now residing at Seabright, near Santa Cruz. Arnold Van Kaathoven, the subject of this review, came to America in 1889 and located in San Jose, where he was favorably known. While a resident of San Jose he was identified with the fruit interests of that locality for fifteen years. In 1909 he removed to Oakley and purchased the general store of J. S. O'Meara. Mr. Van Kaathoven has greatly enlarged his store, and his brother Cornelius is identified with the concern. It is now known as the East Contra Costa Mercantile Company. Arnold Van Kaathoven was united in marriage with Gertrude Keet, a native of Canada, July 20, 1910.

Since starting out in life Mr. Van Kaathoven has worked his way upward by hard work and persistent effort, and whatever success he has achieved is the direct reward of his labors. He is well known in business circles and is considered one of the leading business men of his locality.

ELISHA W. ROBBINS.—Among the well-known residents of eastern Contra Costa County none is better and more favorably known than Elisha W. Robbins. He is a native of Watertown, Massachusetts, and his birth occurred on December 30,

1858. He is a son of James and Anne (Winter) Robbins, the parents of eleven children. Mr. Robbins' parents removed to Wisconsin, where Elisha acquired a common-school education. His father was a miller by trade, owning and operating a mill at Madison, Wisconsin, for many years. The subject of this review came to California twice before making his home here. He farmed in Colorado before coming to this county and he now owns and operates twenty-one acres, which is all set out to almonds, apricots, and peaches. Mr. Robbins' sister Lois also makes her home here and has many friends in this locality. Politically, Mr. Robbins is independent. He has brought his place up to a high state of cultivation and is numbered as one of the representative men in eastern Contra Costa County.

ORLANDO C. PREWETT.—The name which heads this review is one of the well-known men of eastern Contra Costa County. He is an enterprising, progressive, and up-to-date farmer, a public-spirited citizen, and a prominent factor in the development of this section. He was born in Marion County, Illinois, September 7, 1864, the son of Grafton and Emma Prewett.

Orlando at the age of five years removed with his parents to Missouri, where his father farmed. In 1891 the family came to California and located near Brentwood. Orlando rented the Emerson place for sixteen years, and then bought his present farm of two hundred and forty acres. He also owns three hundred and six acres of range land and has always been identified with stock-raising. Mr. Prewett was married to Rebecca Williamson, a native of Missouri, November 22, 1891. Mrs. Prewett's father died February 12, 1870, and her mother passed away January 13, 1917, in Missouri. She was born in 1837. Mr. Prewett's father died on February 12, 1002, and his mother passed away November 11, 1912. Orlando C. Prewett gives his political allegiance to the Democratic party. Fraternally, he is affiliated with the Masonic lodge of Brentwood. He also holds membership with the I. O. O. F. lodge of Antioch. He has served on the school board in the Iron House district for some years and shows deep interest in educational matters. He is in every way a representative citizen of his section.

REUBEN LE MOIN is one of the energetic and representative men of Contra Costa County. He has by hard work and good judgment made a financial success. He was born in De Kalb County, Illinois, April 1, 1858, a son of L. E. and Anna (Flick) Le Moin. His mother was of German birth.

Mr. Le Moin's parents have the distinction of coming to California on the first train that crossed the continent. The parents came west owing to the father's health. His death occurred in his forty-eighth year, and the mother passed away in Brentwood. Reuben Le Moin acquired his schooling in the Eden Plain school. Early in life he began ranching and worked out. Twenty-one years ago he bought eight acres and set it out to almonds. Later he purchased one hundred and sixty-six acres and engaged in general farming and dairy business. At the present time he has ten acres of walnuts. Mr. Le Moin was married to Abba Chilson in 1888. Their three children are Bertha, wife of C. H. French, of Brentwood; Irene Floy, wife of Ralph Olsen, of Oakland; and Everett, who is identified with the Jackson Iron Works of Oakland. In politics Mr. Le Moin is a Republican. He has served on the school board of Brentwood for some years past. His experience and ability have made him well known and greatly respected. Mr. Le Moin also owns valuable business property in Brentwood.

JACOB JACOBSEN, one of the well-known and respected ranchers of eastern Contra Costa County, was born in Germany, November 19, 1862. He came to America in 1884 and located in Elgin, Illinois. Here he found employment at dairying and remained nearly two years. He came to the Pacific Coast and remained in San Francisco a short time. He then found work at ranching in San Mateo and remained here several months; then he came to this county in 1886 and ranched. Mr. Jacobsen now rents five hundred acres of what is known as the Sanford Ranch. Here he carries on general farming. Mr. Jacobsen was twice married. At the age of twenty-nine he married Miss Maggie Gibson, and to this union was born one daughter, who died in infancy. The second marriage was to Mabel Olsen, October 30, 1900, and to this union were born Burnett, Gladys, Howard, and Donald.

Mr. Jacobsen is a member of the Maccabees. The family is well known in their locality and have a host of warm friends. Mr. Jacobsen has always followed ranching and he has the ability to operate large tracts of land. He is honorable, upright, and public-spirited, and does much to benefit the community in which he lives.

PETER OLSEN, one of the well-known and representative men of eastern Contra Costa County, was born July 8, 1849, in Sonderburg, Denmark. He received his education in the old country and learned the brickmaking trade, which he followed for seven years in his native land. At the age of twenty-one he came to America and settled in Nebraska, where he found employment, and in 1871 he removed to Carbon County, Wyoming, where he followed mining. He then went to Utah, where he worked in the silver mines for a period of two years, when he returned to Wyoming and followed mining, and later assisted in the construction of a large stone building and barns for the Wyoming Coal Company. He then went on a cattle ranch for two years. At this time the Indians were hostile in his section, and Mr. Olsen relates many narrow escapes from the red men where he was working. In 1874 he came to California and located in Antioch, where he became identified with the coal mines. In 1879 he purchased two hundred and forty acres in the Black Hills, where he engaged in the cattle and wood business for seven years. In 1885 he removed to Marsh Creek and rented a half-section and followed general farming. Later he purchased a lease and operated two hundred and ninety acres for twelve years. In 1912 he settled in Brentwood. Mr. Olsen was married on July 28, 1878, to Mary E. Nathan, a daughter of Daniel Nathan, who came to California via Cape Horn, and settled in Antioch, where he died thirty-five years ago. To Mr. and Mrs. Olsen have been born four children—Mabel Elizabeth, wife of Jacob Jacobsen, of Brentwood; Edward James, engaged in the grocery business in Oakland; Ralph, who is bookkeeper for R. W. Kinney, of Oakland; and Cecil, who died at the age of four years. Mr. Olson is a Republican. Fraternally, he is a member of the I. O. O. F. and Rebekah lodges of Byron.

IRVING R. BAILEY, D. D. S.—Prominent among the representatives of the dental profession in Contra Costa County is Doctor Irving R. Bailey, of Brentwood. He was born April 3, 1881, and is the son of Angelo A. Bailey, a former superintendent of schools of Contra Costa County, who died July 6, 1907. Angelo A. Bailey was born on June 25, 1844, in Walworth County, Wisconsin. At the age of twenty-one he left home. He found employment in the forests of his native State. Later he came west and located in Denver. He engaged in the sheep business for a time, and then came to Santa Cruz County, California. Here he taught school, and in

1877 he removed to this county and was made principal of the Antioch schools for a period of three years. He was made county superintendent of schools in 1879. He was married in Richmond, Illinois, March 23, 1871, to Lottie Tibbetts, a native of that State. He served in the customs service and was located in San Francisco and Port Costa. Leaving the Government employ, he became principal of the Martinez schools. He was elected county clerk of Contra Costa County and served two years. He served as principal of the Concord schools for several years. Irving R. Bailey, the subject of this review acquired his education in the public schools of Martinez and the University of California, graduating in dentistry in 1903. He began practice in Pinole, where he remained until the fall of 1912, and owing to his health the Doctor gave up his profession and purchased a twenty-acre walnut orchard at Oakley. He has recently resumed his practice at Brentwood, where he enjoys a broad acquaintance. Doctor Bailey was united in marriage to Miss Lottie Lois Sherman, June 16, 1906. To this union there have been three children—Angelo Grosvenor, born June 26, 1907; Emily Edith, born April 24, 1910; and Robert Sherman, born August 7, 1916. The parents of Doctor Bailey had seven children—Mabel R., born May 10, 1873, died 1901; Effie L., residing in Berkeley; Mark G. Bailey, D. D. S., of Stockton; Edith, a school-teacher of Berkeley; Lloyd E., an agriculturist; Percy S., died in infancy; Angele H., residing in Berkeley; and the subject of this sketch. Doctor Bailey has reached a creditable place along his chosen profession, and both he and his wife have won an extensive circle of warm friends in eastern Contra Costa County.

HERCULES LOGAN.—Among the foremost contractors and builders of Contra Costa County is to be numbered Hercules Logan. He is a native of Scotland, and was born April 26, 1875, son of John and Christina (Watt) Logan. The subject of this review received his education in the old country. In 1903 he came to America and located in New York State for a short time. He then came to California and went to Eureka, Humboldt County, where his brother Adolph has resided for twenty-five years, and has always followed the merchant-tailoring business. Hercules learned the carpenter and building trade in the old country and readily found employment in Eureka; he assisted on the city hall. He then removed to San Francisco and worked on the German hospital and later on Government work on Angel Island and was identified with other large projects. In 1906, immediately after the fire, he erected the new building for Heald's Business College, at McAllister and Polk streets. In 1912 he removed to Brentwood and acted as superintendent on the Hotel Brentwood, the Bank of Brentwood, and the palatial home of the superintendent of Balfour, Guthrie & Company. He has been superintendent during construction for many of the best homes in this section. Fraternally, Mr. Logan is a member of the Masonic lodge of Brentwood. He was married to Ethel Jane Brangwin, a native of England, July 10, 1900. To this union there have been five children—John, born in Manchester, England, May 17, 1901; Hercules, born in Glasgow, Scotland, November 10, 1903; Adolphus, born in Dunoon, Scotland, March 8, 1904; Ethel, born in San Francisco, May 30, 1911; and Mabel, born in San Francisco, June 8, 1912. The parents of Mr. Logan reside in Alameda with his two sisters, Christina and Mary. The latter specializes in stage dancing. Since residing in Brentwood Mr. and Mrs. Logan have made a host of friends and have won the respect and good-will of all who know them.

PAUL F. BUCHOLTZ.—Among the most prominent and progressive business men of Brentwood is numbered Paul F. Bucholtz. He is a native of Contra Costa County, and was born in Byron, September 30, 1886, son of Rudolph F, who was born in Berlin, Germany, and died in 1895. When a mere lad Mr. Bucholtz's father came to this country with his father and settled on a place between Byron and Bethany, where his father worked for a time. He married, and then leased land which he operated for some years. He contemplated purchasing the land he rented at the time of his death, which occurred August 22, 1905. The mother of Paul F., Martha (Shafer) Bucholtz, was born in Germany. She came to this country with her parents and located in Stockton. In the parents' family there were three sons and one daughter. William, who is connected with Paul F. in the meat market at Brentwood, married Elva Pamberton, of Brentwood. They have one daughter, Helen. Paul F., the second son and subject of this sketch, received his education in the public schools of Byron. At the age of fourteen, he started the butcher business with A. Alexson. He worked for Mr. Alexson for six years and then removed to Mantel, San Joaquin County, where he followed his trade for four years. At the age of twenty-four he removed to Brentwood, where he engaged in business with his brother Rudolph.

Since engaging in business they have made steady progress, and today they have one of the most modern meat markets in Contra Costa County. Rudolph F., a partner in the meat business, was born February 7, 1882, and married Miss Maud Elizabeth Duncan, of Manteca, in 1909. They have two children, Violet and Frank R., Jr. The sister, Annie, is now the wife of Robert Duncan, and was married in 1910. Their daughter is Annie. Paul F. and Rudolph F. are both members of the I. O. O. F. of Byron and the Masonic lodge of Brentwood, the Eastern Star, and the Woodmen of the World. The mother passed away April 1, 1916, at the age of sixty-one years. The firm of Bucholtz Brothers has achieved success and it has been gained by honorable methods and upright business dealings.

GEORGE SELLERS.—Conspicuous among the extensive and successful fruit-growers of eastern Contra Costa County is George Sellers, the owner of one of the finest orchards and one of the most attractive homes to be found in the county. A man of keen intelligence and superior business attainments, he has been actively identified with the horticultural interests of this part of the county for years. Mr. Sellers was born in Fruitvale, March 1, 1854. He is a son of Samuel and Sarah (Abbott) Sellers. His father was a native of Pennsylvania and his mother was born in New York State. The grandfather of Mr. Sellers was one of the pioneers of the Bay section and named the town of Fruitvale. Both parents of Mr. Sellers came to California via Cape Horn. His father followed mining in Mariposa and other counties. In 1860 he removed to eastern Contra Costa County and purchased one hundred and sixty acres of the choicest land in that locality, which he successfully operated until the time of his death, which occurred in 1900.

Mrs. Sellers passed away about twenty years ago. George Sellers, the subject of this sketch, received his education in the public schools of Oakland, after which he returned to the home place, where he has always remained.

He was united in marriage to Adaline Buckley, of Alameda County, April 8, 1872. To this union have been born three children—Henry Abbott, Edwin Buckley, and Edith, wife of H. L. French, who is identified with the Salinas high schools as a teacher. Henry A. is associated with the Hotchkiss dairy of eastern Contra Costa

County, as superintendent. Edwin Buckley has the management of the home ranch adjoining his father's place. George Sellers is a stanch Republican and has been active along party lines. He has served for five years as deputy sheriff under Sheriff Veale. He has also served on the local school board. Mr. Sellers' magnificent orchard is devoted to the raising of walnuts, apricots, and general fruit-growing. He has also been actively engaged in the real estate business as well as general farming. He is identified with the good-roads movement. Mr. Sellers is highly respected by all in his locality.

LEWIS RISDON MEAD.—Among the many brilliant, able, and resourceful men who gained positions of distinction in the Bay cities was Lewis Risdon Mead, now deceased. The record of his career is the record of worthy and upright living, of strict adherence to a high personal standard, of talents and powers well used for worthy ends. These things need not be repeated to the readers of a history of this section of California, for Mr. Mead was one of Contra Costa County's most progressive and successful business men, and his name had been known and honored here for many years. Lewis Risdon Mead was born on September 7, 1847, at Saline, Michigan. His parents were Silas and Harriett Risdon Mead. In the parents' family there were two children—William, an agriculturist, who resides on the home place at Saline, Michigan, and the subject of this review. Lewis and William, when young men, went to New Orleans, and in 1863 Lewis came to California via the Isthmus route to be with his uncle, John Risdon, who originally started the iron works then known as Risdon & Coffey. The concern remained as such for some years when it became the property of Mr. Risdon and was familiarly known as the Risdon Iron Works. The Risdon Iron Works continued until 1914, when it was sold. Mr. Mead was identified with the concern for many years and held the important position of secretary and auditor until 1007, when he severed his connection with the concern, and took up his residence in Byron Hot Springs, located at the northern end of the San Joaquin Valley. In 1865 Orange Risdon and Lewis Risdon Mead took up two hundred acres from the United States Government, now known as the Byron Hot Springs. The land was patented and patent papers were received later in that year. The springs on this historic spot have been famous ever since the aboriginal days. The Indians came here; the wild animals knew it, and well they used the healing waters of the bubbling springs. Mr. Mead bought out Mr. Risdon's interests and took the active management of the springs and ran it up to the time of his death. The first building was erected in 1865. A fill of ten to twelve feet was necessary in order to make a garden and plant shrubbery and trees, owing to the fact that the land where the hotel and cottages are located was a vast lava bed. The first large hotel, costing $50,000, was destroyed by fire in 1901; in 1002 a new hotel of Moorish design was erected by Reid Brothers, of San Francisco, at a cost of $150,000. This magnificent structure was destroyed by fire in 1012. Mr. Mead had a difficult time with the insurance companies, but won the fight, which was in litigation for some time, and in 1914 he gave a contract to Reid Brothers again to erect a strictly fire-proof building on the site of the other hotel, at a cost of $100,000. Lewis Risdon Mead was a broad-minded man, liberal in thought and honorable in purpose. His life was fruitful of good results, not only in the attainment of success, but in his support of progressive public measures which are of benefit to the community. He served as a regent of the University of California. He was the founder of Brooklyn Lodge No. 225, F. & A. M., of Oakland. He was a member of Islam Temple and the Mystic Shrine. He was president of the Mechanics' Institute of San Francisco for many years. Mr. Mead was twice married. The first union was in 1873, to Blanche Durant, who died in 1005. There was one son, Louis Durant Mead, born March 31, 1875; he married Miss Charlotte Lanneau, of New York City, in 1905. They have one daughter, Blanche, born June 22, 1910, in San Francisco, California. The second marriage of Lewis Risdon Mead occurred on June 19, 1907, to Miss Mae Sadler, daughter of Charles M. Sadler, one of the representative business men of San Francisco, and senior member of the firm of Sadler & Co. At the time of the San Francisco fire Miss Sadler was in Europe completing her studies and returned to her home in San Francisco; the following year she was united in marriage. The present hotel at Byron Hot Springs was planned by Mr. and Mrs. Mead, and is truly a monument to Mr. Mead. After the second fire, wells were sunk at the river, two miles away, and connected with water pipes all over the grounds and in the hotel and cottages for fire protection. Mr. Mead's political belief was with the Republican party, and he was one of the most conscientious type of public men, ever holding to his ideals and principles without swerving. He served on the grand jury and was called upon at various times to serve on the Republican county and other committees. Hs was not only a very patriotic American, but an ultra-loyal Californian. Mr. Mead passed away on June 13, 1916, and his death was sincerely mourned by a wide circle of friends all over California and in the East. Mrs. Mead will erect a memorial over the original hot salt springs in memory of her husband, who will always be remembered among the most honored and eminent residents of Contra Costa County.

GUIDO TODARO.—Among the strong financial institutions of this county is the Contra Costa County Bank, of Pittsburg, and among the bankers of prominence in the county is Guido Todaro, who, as cashier, has done much toward the upbuilding of this financial institution. His banking experience extends over many years and he has traveled extensively. He is a native of Venice and received his education in his native land. After finishing his schooling he went to Calcutta, India, where he remained three years, and became identified with the large banking firm of Credit Lyonnais, of Calcutta, where his ability was recognized. In 1897 he came to San Francisco via the Orient. Mr. Todaro associated himself with the Justinian Caire Company of San Francisco for a period of two years. He was then employed with the Italian American Bank of San Francisco for five years, after which he accepted a call to this county, where he is connected with the Contra Costa County Bank. Mr. Todaro is a careful and painstaking banker, and he is readily conceded to be one of the most able and best-informed men in the county along banking lines. He holds the important position of cashier and manager of his bank. Mr. Todaro was united in marriage to Miss Rose Williams, a native of Sonoma County, California, August 20, 1904. To this union there have been two children—Guido, born May 18, 1007, and Marie, born October 24, 1910. The family are members of the Catholic church. Politically, Mr. Todaro is affiliated with the Republican party, but he has never aspired to office. Fraternally, he is a member of the Knights of Pythias and the Eagles of Pittsburg. While his duties largely confine him to his bank, Mr. Todaro is ever ready to join in public movements for the extension of trade or betterment of conditions. He enjoys the esteem and respect of his colleagues and the general public, and by his personality he has done much toward upholding the prestige which his bank enjoys. Mr. Todaro is a stockholder in his bank, as well as in the Contra Costa County Gas Company.

DAVID ISRAEL.—One of the most able, progressive, and enterprising business men of Contra Costa County is David Israel, of Pittsburg. He was born in New York City on November 29, 1874, a son of Meyer and Henrietta Israel. His parents were both natives of Alsace-Lorraine. The subject of this review received his education in the Antioch and San Francisco public schools. Early in life he worked for L. Meyer & Company, of Antioch, for a period of ten years. He was also identified with other business houses in different parts of this State. These various positions called forth his executive ability and his keen grasp of business details, and in matters under his charge he has clearly demonstrated his possession of these qualities, which have made his concern one of the favorably known business houses of Contra Costa County. In 1902, Mr. Israel started business in Pittsburg with B. Senderman, and he purchased the latter's interest in 1913. Politically, Mr. Israel is a Republican, but he has never aspired to public office. Fraternally, he is affiliated with the Masonic order of Pittsburg; he also holds membership in the Foresters, Eagles, and other orders. He was united in marriage to Miss Amelie Senderman, a sister of his former partner, and a native of Contra Costa County, November 3, 1907. To this union have been born two children—Robert Senderman, born May 30, 1909, and Royce Wexford, born July 16, 1911. Mr. Israel stands today a forceful factor in the improvement of business conditions of Pittsburg.

DIXON H. MacQUIDDY has been actively and successfully identified with the business interests of California as a contractor and builder since boyhood and is recognized today as one of the foremost contractors and builders of the Bay cities. He was born in Traver, Kings County, California, March 19, 1887, a son of John T. MacQuiddy, a native of Missouri, and Pauline S. MacQuiddy, a native of Tennessee. Dixon H. MacQuiddy was educated in the public and high schools of Hanford and Stockton. Finishing his schooling he went to Sonoma County, where he was identified with his father and where he learned his trade. In 1906 Mr. MacQuiddy moved to Concord, where he followed his trade, and erected many of the substantial buildings of that town. He erected the First Presbyterian Church, the Bacon block, and other fine buildings, as well as many of the finest homes in Concord. In November, 1914, he removed to Pittsburg, where he maintained an office as well as a branch office in Davis, California. Mr. MacQuiddy confines his operations largely to Solano and Contra Costa counties. In he is a Democrat. Fraternally, he is a member of the I. O. O. F. of Pacheco, and also of the Moose and Eagles. His children are Dixon Leroy, born in 1908, and Everett Merle, born in 1912. Mr. MacQuiddy has a partner, Mr. C. C. Bean, who has in charge the Davis office. Owing to their constantly increasing business, the firm has prospered with gratifying success, and has recently opened the M. & B. Paint & Building Material Company in Pittsburg. Many of the most attractive buildings in Contra Costa and Solano counties testify to the ability and skill of Mr. MacQuiddy and his partner, and they are well entitled to a foremost place among the builders of Contra Costa County, for they are representative men and respected citizens.

JOSEPH LUCAS.—Scarcely a habitable section of California but has its toilers recruited from the sea — strong, weather-beaten men who have stepped from slippery decks after years before the mast and have thereafter made homes and established industries in either town or country. The most interesting of this class are the old whalers, who still seem to carry around with them a breath of the sea—seasoned mariners, who at one time strained their eyes across the great expanse of waters for the sight of a spouting leviathan of the deep, and who dared all manner of danger that their ship might return to port heavily laden with oil. Joseph Lucas, who resides near Richmond, has many a tale to relate regarding his extensive whaling experience, and because he had the traits to make a successful sailor and whaler may account for his energy and wise management. Mr. Lucas was eighteen years of age when he first shipped before the mast of a whaler, setting sail from the Azores Islands, where he was born on January 18, 1826. He sailed during three or four seasons in the Arctic and Japan seas, and in 1846 put into San Francisco harbor on the whaling ship "Magnet," together with other whaling vessels. This was during the Mexican War, and all were afraid to venture beyond the Golden Gate, as a Mexican war vessel was lying in wait for them. For a time he made his home in New Bedford, Massachusetts. In 1850 he came around the Horn to San Francisco and was engaged on various pilot boats of this Bay. He served as quartermaster on the steamers "Winfield Scott," "Yankee Blade," "Sonora," and "Golden Gate." Later he spent a few years in the mines on the American River. In 1862-63 he worked as a stevedore in San Francisco, and in the fall of 1863 he located on forty acres now a part of the city of Richmond. Mr. Lucas purchased the farm in 1860. The property was involved in a disputed title, being a portion of the San Pablo grant, and for twenty-one years he was engaged in litigation. The ranch has since been cut up into town lots. In 1862 Mr. Lucas was united in marriage to Mary Prairo, who was born on the island of Nantucket, Massachusetts, and whose father, John Prairo, was a sailor by occupation. Taking a trip in 1849 to California, he mined along the American River. Successful beyond the average, his ambition proved larger that his opportunity, for he lost practically all he had in the world while promoting a scheme to dam the Sacramento River. Locating in San Francisco, Mr. Lucas engaged as a stevedore, and in 1862 came to the San Pablo grant, locating near Mr. Prairo. The similarity between the lives of Mr. Lucas and Mr. Prairo seemed quite remarkable, especially as both came from the same island, and chanced upon the same land occupations. Mr. Prairo died here the possessor of large landed estates, being survived a short time by his wife, Eunice (Colman) Prairo, who was a native of Nantucket, Massachusetts. Five children have been born to Mr. and Mrs. Lucas—Joseph, Mary (the wife of M. J. Keegan), John, Frank, and Henry. Mr. Lucas is a devout member of the Catholic church, and in politics is a Republican.

R. R. VEALE.—On the roster of county officials of Contra Costa County appears the name of R. R. Veale, who, following a period of efficient and capable service as sheriff, was elected to this important position in 1894, and has held this office since. He is a native of California and was born in Sonoma County on March 27, 1864. His father was one of the well-known figures in early days in California. He came to this State via the Isthmus route in 1855 and engaged in stock-raising and agricultural pursuits on a small scale. In 1867 he removed to Contra Costa County and became prominently identified with the development of this locality. R. R. Veale acquired his early education in the public schools, after which he took up the vocation of farming on an extensive scale. He had the distinction of being the first farmer in the county to use modern and up-to-date methods, such as steam plows and harvesters. He became identified in local and State politics, attended many State conventions, and served on the State Republican County Committee. In 1804 he was chosen by the people of Contra Costa County as sheriff, and he has since served in this office, discharging his duties in his usual efficient manner. As sheriff of the county, Mr. Veale has been connected with many prominent cases. He captured the criminal, Moore, who killed Kilroy at Nevada City. He also captured the criminal who stole over $300,000 of gold bullion from the Selby Smelting Company and hid it in the bay. He also captured the murderer, McFarland, who killed Garcia on Mount Diablo in 1908. Sheriff Veale originated the idea of the rock-pile for hoboes, which has been adopted by the sheriffs in many of the counties. He was one of the chief factors in gaining the State highway along the bay, which he obtained by inducing various corporations to build the road through their own property or contribute largely to the building fund. Mr. Veale went to Washington, D. C., as a representative of the county to boost the Richmond harbor project. Fraternally, he is a member of the Knights Templars, the Royal Arch Chapter, the Eastern Star, the Elks, the Odd Fellows, the Eagles, the Native Sons, the Woodmen, the Moose, the Red Men, U. P. E. C., the Knights of Pythias, the Rebekahs, and the Women of Woodcraft. He has served twenty years as secretary of the Sheriff's Association of California, an organization, including the sheriffs of the various counties of the State, which meets annually to discuss matters of interest to the different sections, and to compare records and exchange ideas and to add generally to the efficiency of the sheriff's office. Sheriff Veale's continual re-election to office is the best proof of his acceptability to the people. His tireless efforts and conscientious work in behalf of progress and general improvement, particularly in regard to the betterment of the roads and highways, has gained for him a reputation for well-directed activity in the county. Sheriff Veale was elected as a delegate to the Republican National Convention held at Chicago in June, 1016. He was also chosen commissioner from Contra Costa County to the Panama-Pacific Exposition held in San Francisco. Mr. Veale was united in marriage to Mary E. Martin, of East Oakland, November 11, 1883. To this union there are six children—Robert Howard, born May 18, 1885; William Minor, born September 10, 1887; Leila E., born January 13, 1800; Mortimer Belshaw, born November 18, 1893; Miriam Estelle, born April 21, 1897; Leola Rains, born March 22, 1809.

JOHN M. AUGUSTO.—A worthy representative of the type of citizen that has made California a great State is John M. Augusto, whose strong and earnest manhood, forceful character, business sagacity, and executive ability have been given in the past few years toward the development of Oakley. His birth occurred in the Madeira Islands on September 29, 1872, the son of Lawrence and Mary Augusto. His father passed away in 1885, and his mother makes her home in San Leandro. John M. Augusto acquired his schooling in the St. Louis College of Honolulu, after which he learned the blacksmith trade with the Hawaiian Carriage Manufacturing Company.

Here he remained for three years, and then became identified with the Oahu Railway Company of Hawaii, following his trade for two years. He then removed to San Francisco and followed the same vocation for a year. He afterward resided in Oakland and was foreman for the California Jute Mills for some time, after which he spent five years in San Leandro, where he worked for John F. Hopper. On April 1, 1900, the town of Oakley was on the map and Mr. Augusto saw the possibilities in this new section, and he removed to this town and purchased the first business lot in the place. He immediately erected a blacksmith-shop and has succeeded in building up a profitable business. Owing to the fertility of the soil, he purchased two ranches of ten acres each, and has all his land out to fruit and nuts, besides owning five valuable city lots. All through the changing years that have since elapsed since he came to Oakley he has had no desire to change his abiding-place. Today his orchards compare with the best in his locality. By his marriage to Ermina Fernandez Gonsalves on June 10, 1899, there are five children. Mrs. Augusto is a native of Honolulu, and a daughter of one of the highly respected families of the islands. The children of Mr. and Mrs. Augusto are George M., now in high school; Hazel, died in infancy; Martha G., Edward Lawrence, and Archibald, who died June 13, 1912. Hazel and Edward were the first two children born in Oakley. Mr. Augusto is a member of the Masonic fraternity; he is also affiliated with the I. O. O. F. He has produced results by hard work from a financial point of view. Starting in a small way, his business has increased until he now has over $8000 invested in machinery. Mr. Augusto is agent for the John Deere line of wagons, buggies, and farm machinery. He has the honor of being the oldest business man in Oakley. In his political views he is a Republican. He is an advocate and loyal booster for good roads and is interested in any movement for the betterment of conditions in Oakley and surrounding country.

HARRY ELLS, one of the progressive and representative citizens of Contra Costa County, was born in Canning, Nova Scotia, November 9, 1854, and is the fourth of the six sons and two daughters of William and Sarah (Newcomb) Ells, farmers in Nova Scotia. As a boy Mr. Ells found the Nova Scotia farm altogether too small to supply the needs of the large family, and accordingly he located on a farm near Winchester, Massachusetts, in 1871, this slight progression opening up yet broader fields of activity, and placing him in touch with the Far West, to which he came during the summer of 1874. Locating in Dutch Flat, he engaged in mining for himself and others, and after the incorporation of the Cedar Creek Mining Company, he became foreman under Colonel Ludman. Coming to Stege as assistant superintendent of the California Cap Company, he was advanced to the position of superintendent in 1889, which position he held for several years.

Mr. Ells branched out in various activities in the county. He became interested in the real estate and insurance business and is a director of the Bank of Richmond. An active and influential Republican, he has been postmaster at Stege for several years, and served for some years as president of the board of school directors of the Stege District. In 1902 he was elected to the State Assembly by a large majority from the twenty-second district, serving on the committee of roads and highways, fish and game, and as chairman of the committees on manufacturing and internal improvements. He was unanimously chosen as a candidate to succeed himself for the term of 1904, and his Democratic opponent, seeing nothing but defeat before him, withdrew from the contest, and Mr. Ells' election was assured. Mr. Ells was twice married, the first union being to Katie Seltzer in 1880. He was married in Sacramento, and his wife died at Dutch Flat one year after. The second marriage occurred on December 23, 1912, to Maybelle Perry Seavey, of Richmond. Mr. Ells is a member of McKinley Lodge No. 347, F. & A. M., of which he is past master. He is also a member of Siloam Chapter No. 37, R. A. M., the Commandery of Oakland, and the Eastern Star.

LOUIS BRACKMAN—The history of Contra Costa County would be incomplete were there failure to mention Louis Brackman, who resides near Martinez. He was born in Pinole on February 11, 1863, a son of William and Anne Brackman. Both parents were natives of Germany. The father of our subject was one of the pioneers of California, crossing the plains in 1849, starting from St. Louis, and taking six months to make the trip. After reaching San Francisco he engaged in the cattle business. Later he took up farming in Moraga Valley. He afterward moved to Pinole, where he followed ranching and stock-raising. The father died on March 7, 1898, when Louis was eighteen years of age, and his mother died on January 4, 1882. In the parents' family eight children were born. Frederick K., who died in February, 1915, was a rancher and lived near Muir Station. William resides near Concord. These are the only brothers of Louis Brackman who resided in this county of late years. Louis Brackman was educated in the public schools, after which he returned to the home ranch, where he remained until he was eighteen years of age. He then left home and found employment at ranching for a period of seven years, when he purchased his father's place in the Pinole Valley. Here he continued for a period of about sixteen years. He then bought a fruit-ranch near Muir Station, consisting of twelve acres. This he sold and removed to his present location, situated most ideally, and consisting of one hundred and thirty-eight acres. In politics Mr. Brackman is a Republican. He has served on the educational board in the various places he has lived with credit. He was married on August 20, 1895, to Miss Nellie Carpenter, a daughter of Daniel and Sarah Carpenter. To this union there are three children—Velda Lorain, born October 17, 1900; Louis Clarence, born July 15, 1908; Alice Ruth, born August 1, 1910. The family attend the Congregational church. Mr. and Mrs. Brackman have an extensive acquaintance and a host of friends, and they have the esteem and confidence of all who know them.

FRANCIS FELIX NEFF, M. D., who has been successfully engaged in the practice of medicine in Concord since 1890, was born in Williamsburg, Pennsylvania, February 9, 1862, son of Captain William Lewis Neff, an officer in the Civil War, and one of the seventh generation of Neffs who resided in Pennsylvania. The mother of Doctor Neff was Arabella (Van Devander) Neff, and she passed away in 1873. The subject of this review acquired his education in the public schools, after which he attended the academy at Hollidaysburg, Pennsylvania, and the Jefferson Medical College, of Philadelphia, graduating from the latter in 1887. He began the practice of his profession at Groton, South Dakota, where he remained about one year. Coming to California, he located in Lathrop, and in 1890 removed to Concord, where he has since resided. Fraternally, Doctor Neff holds membership in the Masonic lodge of Concord and the Royal Arch chapter in Martinez. On October 6, 1897, he was united in marriage to Anna Williams, of Concord, daughter of Joseph Williams, one of the prominent and highly respected citizens of his locality. Previous to her marriage Mrs. Neff taught school for several years in Concord. Doctor and Mrs. Neff are esteemed by a wide circle of friends in Concord and vicinity. The children of Doctor Neff are Dorothy, Philip Van Devander, Francis William, John K., and Benjamin Henry.

GEORGE A. PUTNAM holds a prominent place among the representative agriculturists in Contra Costa County. He was born in Fruitvale, Alameda County,

California, June 3, 1860, and is the son of John H. and Elizabeth S. Putnam, who had eight children, five boys and three girls, all living. John H. Putnam died in 1907, and his wife passed away the same year. George A. Putnam received his education in the Pleasant Hill school near Walnut Creek, and in the San Ramon school. He entered the mercantile store of his father and uncle for a time, and in 1879 he removed to Washington, where he followed farming until 1882, when he returned to this county and entered the store of his uncle, where he remained for three years. Returning to Washington, he married Miss Grace Bracket, a granddaughter of William Hook, February 15, 1887. To this union have been born five children—George Blalock (who married Miss Francis Vessing, a native of New York State), Grace Bell (who is attending high school), Marion Bernice, John Van Alstien, and Dorothy Hazel. Politically, Mr. Putnam is affiliated with the Republican party. He has served on the Concord high-school board for two terms. He is an extensive landowner and operates one of the most modern dairies in the county. He supplies milk and cream to the county hospital in Martinez. His dairy is a model along sanitary lines, and every modern condition exists for the handling of milk. Mrs. Amanda (Hook) Bracket makes her home at present with Mr. Putnam. She is one of Contra Costa County's most respected women. She was born in 1842 and crossed the plains with her parents in 1850. She was educated in Martinez and graduated from the Young Ladies' Seminary at Benicia. She was married to Rufus Bracket in January, 1861. He was a pioneer merchant and rancher and died in August, 1889. Mr. Putnam has been identified largely with real-estate interests. He has enlarged his buildings and increased his stock, and today caters to a large and remunerative custom won by his progressive business methods and by the sterling qualities which distinguish his personal character.

GEORGE FREDERICK GEARY, one of the representative ranchers and fruit-growers of Contra Costa County, was born in the Ygnacio Valley. He is a son of Lawrence Geary, one of the pioneers of California. His father was born in Baden, Germany, December 5, 1827. In March, 1848, he came to the United States. He landed in New York and went to Philadelphia, where he found employment on a farm. Remaining there six months, he went to St. Louis, and thence south to New Orleans, where he worked on a sugar plantation. In April, 1849, he went to Fort Leavenworth and resided two years.

In 1852 he, in company with three others, started across the plains for California, and arrived at Hangtown on August 26, 1852. He followed mining for a short time, and in the fall of 1852 he came to Contra Costa County and engaged in farming. In the fall of 1878 he purchased four hundred acres of land and engaged in general farming, in Pleasant Hill district. Mr. Geary was married on November 25, 1858, to Miss Jane Wallace, a native of Missouri. George Frederick Geary, the subject of this sketch, has fifty-five acres set out to walnuts, fruit, and vineyard. In politics Mr. Geary is a Republican.

He has served as clerk and trustee of the Pleasant Hill school district for some time. Mr. Geary was married on September n, 1889, to Emma Reeves, a native of Maine. To this union have been born two children—Mabel E., a teacher in the schools of San Leandro, and Gladys E., at home and attending school. The family attend the Methodist church.

HENRY A. FORSBURG.—Through the successive stages of orderly progression Henry A. Forsburg has advanced to his present position of responsibility and importance as general superintendent of the San Joaquin Valley trunk pipe-lines of the Standard Oil Company of California, with offices at San Pablo. He was born in Kane, McKean County, Pennsylvania, May 2, 1874. He acquired his education in the public schools. At an early age he became identified with the Southern Pipe-Line Company of eastern Pennsylvania as pipe-line inspector. He later was made foreman of the pumping station. He then removed to New Jersey and had charge of loading oil-carrying vessels. In 1903 he removed to Chicago and was made assistant superintendent on the Indiana pipe-line. In 1904 he was transferred to California as assistant superintendent of pipe-lines, and on March 1, 1905, he was promoted to superintendent of the Southern Division. In 1907 Mr. Forsburg had charge of building the pipe-lines to the Midway fields from Bakersfield.

Later, in 1907, he was transferred to the Northern Division, and in 1910 he was made general superintendent. He is a member of the American Society of Mechanical Engineers. Mr. Forsburg was united in marriage May 12, 1896, to Miss Cresence Eisenman, of Clarion County, Pennsylvania. To this union there are two sons— Joseph A., born November 2, 1897, and Frank E., born December 25, 1000. Both sons are in the high school. Mr. Forsburg is popular in both business and social circles and has won an extensive circle of warm friends in and around the Bay cities.

HENRY FULLER BEEDE.—The life record of Henry Fuller Beede entitles him pre-eminently to the distinctive title of one of the builders of Antioch, and as such he has contributed a notable share to the material progress of Contra Costa County. Nearly all of his life has been spent in California. He is still wielding a substantial influence for the upbuilding of his locality and possesses the respect and esteem of his fellow-men. He was vice-president and general manager of the Antioch Lumber Company, and is one of the oldest residents of Antioch, having located here in 1869. Mr. Beede was born in Farmington, Franklin County, Maine, November 16, 1850, son of Thomas and Lucia Sarah (Merrill) Beede. His father was a native of New Hampshire, and his mother was born in Maine. His father came by boat via the Isthmus route to California and remained in this State during the years of 1851 to 1853. He followed the livery business. He returned to his native State and took his family to Illinois when Henry was but five years of age.

At the age of eighteen the subject of this sketch came to Antioch, where he has since resided. He first worked for his brother George, who was identified with the mercantile interests of Antioch. He then, at the age of 21, worked for Galloway & Boobar, who were in the lumber business, and the originators of the present firm, of which Mr. Beede is now manager. He worked for them until 1877, when Mr. Galloway retired, and the business was run under the firm name of Rouse, Ferman & Beede. This firm continued until Mr. Rouse sold his interest to Captain Simpson, of San Francisco, and the firm is now known as The Antioch Lumber Company, Mr. Beede, being the only original stockholder left. This concern is capitalized at one hundred thousand dollars. They do a general retail and jobbing business and conduct a planing-mill and lumber-yard in connection. Mr. Beede has witnessed and helped in the growth of Antioch. He was united in marriage to Margaret Ellen McNulty, a daughter of J. J. McNulty, April 13, 1872. To this union there have been eleven children—Harry McNulty, born April 13, 1873, married to Leonora Scott, a native of California; Charles Frank Tyler, born October 15, 1874, married to Edith Little, a native of England, and their three children are Nancy Bell, Charles Austin, and Frank McNulty; Mary Lucia, born April 17, 1877, married to E. P. Rapp, whose death occurred July 10, 1916; Ralph Merrill, born January 14, 1879, married to Anna Katherine Menchen, a native of Colorado, and their children are Ruth May, Henry Fuller, and Katherine; Olive Beede, born November 1, 1883, married to R. V. Davis, a native of Missouri, and their two children are Margaret Olive and William King; Le Roy Wemple, born January 21, 1883, married to Winifred Bassett, a native of California, and their two children are Carroll and Winifred; Arthur Chamberlain, born September 13, 1885, died September 2, 1891; Nellie Geraldine, born August 6, 1888, married to W. J. Kelley, and they have one child, Patricia; Ramona Bell, born February 2, 1891, married to J. Ewell Cortner, a native of California; Margaret Alice, born August 14, 1893, died June 24, 1895; Frank Rattan, born April 30, 1897, is attending the University of California. Mr. Henry Beede has always taken an active part in community affairs. He served on the town board for many years and was a member of the Republican County Central Committee. He served as president of the Eastern Contra Costa County Promotion Club. He, in connection with the Hon. J. P. Abbott, is largely responsible for the entrance of the Santa Fe Railroad into Antioch. They were the owners of the water-front and deeded over their rights and warehouses to the railroad company at a very liberal figure. Mr. Beede is a director and stockholder in the Bank of Antioch and is a stockholder in the Robert Dollar Steamship Company of San Francisco. Fraternally, Mr. Beede is a Mason and past master of Antioch Lodge No. 175, F. & A. M., and is a member of the Royal Arch chapter and Eastern Star.

EDWARD P. RAPP.—The name of the late Edward Rapp will long be cherished by the residents of Antioch and eastern Contra Costa County. He was a man of industry, activity, and enterprise. He held a high position among the respected citizens of his community, and for many years was intimately associated with the business progress of Antioch. Mr. Rapp was a native of Jordanville, New York. Here he acquired his early schooling, and at the age of sixteen he came to California and located in Antioch, where he always remained. He was employed in the Belshaw store for a period of twenty-five years, where he held positions of importance and trust. In 1913 he left the Belshaw firm and engaged" in business, being associated with W. H. Weeks under the firm name of Rapp & Weeks. Mr. Rapp was united in marriage to Miss Mary Lucia Beede on February 15, 1899. There are left, besides the widow, three sisters and one brother. The sisters are Mrs. Margaret Belshaw, of Antioch, Mrs. Sadie DeWitt, of San Anselmo, Mrs. Teresa Griffith, of New Haven, Connecticut, and the brother is Carl Anthony Rapp, of Richfield Springs, New York. Fraternally, Mr. Rapp was a member of the Masonic lodge of Antioch. The name of Edward P. Rapp will be forever held in loving remembrance by the business men and community in which he lived. He was a broad-minded, public-spirited man and citizen. Mr. Rapp's death occurred July 10, 1916.

GEORGE COPLE.—Nearly sixty years have come and gone since George Cople became associated with the frontier State of California. When he crossed the plains he was a young man, full of ambition, courage, and perseverance. He has been a dominant factor in the development of eastern Contra Costa County. Mr. Cople was born in Switzerland in 1837. He came to America in 1854, landing in New York

City. He removed to Ohio, and later took up his residence in Chicago, where he remained until 1857. He had heard much about California, and it was about this time that he decided to cast his lot with the Golden West. He came here a young man, poor in pocket, but rich in ambition. In 1857, he drove teams from Leavenworth, Kansas, in connection with soldiers going to Utah, and in 1858 he was ordered on to Benicia. For several years he found work in various parts of the State, largely following farming, and in 1867 he purchased three hundred and eighty-five acres near Byron. Mr. Cople was united in marriage to Margaret Eachus on April 17, 1870, and her death occurred in 1908, in her sixty-ninth year. To this union there were three children. Charles, the eldest of the family, was born on February 17, 1871. He was educated in the Excelsior school, after which he took a course in the San Jose Business College. Laying aside his books, he returned to the home place, and has always devoted himself to agricultural pursuits and for many years has had the management of the farm. On December 27, 1809, Charles Cople was married to Miss Elsie Johnston, daughter of John and Mary Johnston, of San Mateo County. Mrs. Cople's parents were among the highly respected families and pioneers of their locality. Her father died in 1893 and her mother passed away in 1911. Mr. and Mrs. Charles Cople have one son, Kenneth D., born August 2, 1901, who is attending school. Mary Eva, the second child of George Cople, died at the age of sixteen years. Ralph G., the youngest child, was born July 15, 1882. He is identified with the stock business and resides in Livermore, California. He married Miss Georgia Tozer, a native daughter. Both George and Charles Cople give their political support to the Republican party. The latter is a member of the Native Sons and a member of Byron Parlor. Charles is a valuable assistant and manager of the home ranch. He is broadminded and public-spirited and is one of the foremost in promoting the welfare of eastern Contra Costa County and takes an active part in the prohibition movement.

PERCY J. MOODY.—Among the representative men of eastern Contra Costa County who have been successfully engaged in ranching and horticulture prominent mention should be made of Percy J. Moody. He is well known and progressive and is constantly keeping in touch with the most advanced methods along his chosen field. He was born in Maine, on December 4, 1859, a son of Gilman and Ellen Moody (deceased), both natives of Kennebec, Maine. In Mr. Moody's parents' family there were nine children, eight of whom are still living. One brother, however, of Mr. Moody came to the Pacific Coast. He makes his home in Fresno County. Percy J. Moody, the subject of this review, acquired his education in the public schools of his native State, and in 1879, at the age of nineteen, he came to California and located in Walnut Creek, where he learned the blacksmith trade with his uncle, J. S. Huntington, who was among the early pioneers of that locality. Mr. Moody remained in the employ of his uncle for three years, when he took over the shop and operated it for one year. He disposed of his interests and removed to Brentwood, where he engaged in business for nearly two years. He then engaged again in the blacksmith business at Brentwood and operated his shop from 1884 to 1892. While a resident of Brentwood, Mr. Moody was united in marriage to Mattie E. Pierce on August 6, 1885. Mr. Moody had eighty acres of choice land and set out twenty acres to orchard. He disposed of twenty acres to Frank Ayer and ten acres to Alfred Carlson. Mr. Moody has served as roadmaster for a period of twelve years, and his recent appointment in the same capacity will extend for another four years. To Mr. and Mrs.

Moody have been born three children. Nellie May, wife of Charles Ellsworth, of Knightsen, was born August 6, 1886. Rollin H. Moody was born in September, 1888, and married Miss Jean White, a native of California, on December 1, 1907, and their one daughter, Violet Martha, was born in 1908. John Moody was born December 16, 1901. At present he is connected with the Bridgeford Dairy Company. Politically, Mr. Moody is affiliated with the Republican party, and has attended the county convention for many years. He has served in the past as trustee on the local school board. Fraternally, he is a member of the Foresters Lodge of Brentwood and the I. O. O. F. of Byron. Mrs. Moody's father, John T. Pierce, was a native of Ohio, and her mother was Sarah (White) Pierce. Her parents were united in marriage in the East, and they had five children. Mr. and Mrs. Pierce crossed the plains in the early '50s and settled in Sonoma County. Later they removed to Sacramento County, and in 1867 they came to eastern Contra Costa County. Mrs. Moody's father died on January 14, 1898, and her mother passed away on September 25, 1897.

JOHN GEDDES.—Numbered among the representative and well-to-do agriculturists of eastern Contra Costa County is John Geddes. He is in every sense of the word a self-made man. By his energy and wise management he has earned a large and pleasantly located farm in eastern Contra Costa County. He is a native of Colchester County, Nova Scotia. He was born June 23, 1836, a son of William and Mary Elizabeth Geddes. There were eight children born in the parents' family. George, a brother of the subject of this review, came to California in 1800, and died in 1900. In 1868 John Geddes came to California, via the Isthmus route, and landed in San Francisco. He went to San Joaquin County where he found employment at ranching for a period of fourteen years. In 1883 he removed to eastern Contra Costa County and purchased three hundred and twenty acres near Byron, which he improved and brought up to a high state of cultivation. Mr. Geddes returned to Nova Scotia and was married to Miss Jessie Carroll, November 9, 1875, a daughter of Jerry Carroll. Mr. Geddes and his bride returned to Contra Costa County and began general farming. He has fifty acres of alfalfa. Each year he improved his place until now he has one of the best in the county.

There were four sons and three daughters born to this union. They were Emma, wife of Robert Clark, a contractor of Knightsen; Elizabeth Mae, residing at home; George, residing on the Shafer ranch near Knightsen, was united in marriage to Mabel Shafer; Herbert, at home; Benjamin Harrison, at home, was united in marriage to Ruth Ellsworth; Lloyd, a rancher, was married to Miss Edith Chadwick; Margaret, attending college, preparing for a teacher. Mr. Geddes is active in matters pertaining to the advancement of eastern Contra Costa County, and especially in the good roads movement.

Politically, he is a Republican. He has served for many years as trustee of the grammar and high school boards. Mr. Geddes has not only won the esteem of his neighbors but has a host of friends throughout his section. He is regarded as one of the main stays of his community.

COLBURN JOHNSON PRESTON.—Conspicuous among the most capable and successful ranchers of Contra Costa County is Colburn Johnson Preston. He is a man of enterprise and keen foresight. He is among the early settlers worthy of representation in the history of his chosen county and has been actively identified with the development of the eastern part of the county for many years. Mr. Preston was born in Bradford County, Pennsylvania, on July 16, 1837. He received his education in the public school of his native State and was reared on a farm. In 1864 he came west via the Isthmus of Panama and found employment at ranching in Nevada. On election day, 1864, he came to California, and in 1865 he located in eastern Contra Costa County. When he located on his present farm there were no houses between his place and Antioch. Mr. Preston was united in marriage to Melissa Woodard, a native of Pennsylvania, in October, 1859, and her death occurred on February 1, 1917. To this union there were seven children —Francis M., born January 23, 1861, married Ida Buress of Bay Point, and their two children are Marion and Lloyd; Eva Sarah, born October 23, 1869, was united in marriage to Frank M. May, and their children are Marjorie and Evelyn; Rosa May, born February 13, 1872, and married George Daunt of Petaluma, and they have one daughter, Dorothea; Ida, wife of W. H. Engle, of Oakland, was born November 20, 1873; Jennie, born November 10, 1875, and died September 8, 1902; Bertha Anna, born March 8, 1879, and married Leslie V. Richardson on August 27, 1902, and has two children, Reginald and Gwendolyn; Mott C., born July 16, 1882, and married Winifred Shafer on October 12, 1904. Mr. Preston has always been energetic and ambitious, and is a typical representative of a self-made man, and has always had the respect and esteem of his fellow-men. In 1904 Mr. Preston retired, and has spent some years in Berkeley, Antioch, Stockton, and now makes his home in Brentwood. He was one of the first ranchers to put in alfalfa in his locality. He set out every tree on his ranch, and in 1867 reaped all the grain on the west side from Bay Point to Visalia. In politics he is a Republican, and for many years served as a school trustee in the Excelsior district. He also served on the high-school board of Brentwood.

MORITZ GUNAUER.—Energy, executive ability, and well-directed ambition, guided and controlled by sound and practical judgment, have constituted the foundation upon which Moritz Gunauer has built his success, and these qualities have brought him prosperity in business. He was born in Germany on January 3, 1862. He acquired his education in his native land.

His parents passed away twelve years ago. In the parents' family there were four children. Johanna, wife of H. Chain of Tracy, is the only sister of Mr. Gunauer in America. After attending school, Moritz came to America and to San Joaquin County, where he had a second cousin who was identified with the mercantile business at Ellis, near Tracy. In this store, Moritz acquired his business training. He advanced naturally because he was ambitious, energetic, and quick to recognize opportunity. He remained in his cousin's store for twelve years. In 1881 he removed to Byron, where he engaged in the mercantile business. He made an excellent record in his cousin's store, and ever since he established the Byron store he has been known as a conscientious and painstaking merchant. He holds to high ideals in business relations, and his sterling manhood has gained for him the warm and enduring regard of all with whom he has ever come in contact. In 1882 Mr. Gunauer erected the first warehouse in Byron. This was destroyed by fire on June 19, 1916. He at once erected a modern, corrugated iron warehouse, 50 by 100 feet, which was completed October 1, 1916. He also owns four hundred and eighty acres of land, which he has leased. Fraternally, he is a member of the I. O. O. F. of Byron. He has served on the Byron school board for a number of years. Mr. Gunauer was united in marriage on December 6, 1888, to Miss R. Frank, a native of San Francisco, a daughter of Edward

Frank, a prosperous merchant of that city. To Mr. and Mrs. Gunauer has been born Jeanette Byron, wife of Roy A. Badt of San Francisco. He is a consulting engineer and a member of the firm of Fisher & Badt.

CHARLES A. SWEENEY.—Among the men who by reason of their personal integrity, ability, and personal enterprise have come to be regarded as representative citizens and leading business men of Contra Costa County, is numbered Charles A. Sweeney. He is a native of San Francisco, born on August 14, 1857, son of William B. and Nora (Hartnett) Sweeney, both natives of Ireland. Mr. Sweeney's father came to California in 1849 and his mother came in 1850. The father came in a sailing-ship via Cape Horn and was one of the first men to take up the vocation of teaming in San Francisco, which he followed for many years. His death occurred in 1909 in Antioch. His wife passed away in 1906. The subject of this sketch received his education in the public schools of San Francisco, and at an early age he learned the butcher business, which he followed for many years in San Francisco. In June, 1880, he removed to Contra Costa County. His first work in his new field was that of foreman for a firm which dealt extensively in hogs. The hogs were shipped from various points in the valleys to Antioch, and Mr. Sweeney would fatten them and put them in condition for the market. He was soon firmly established in Antioch, and was made constable, which office he held in a most satisfactory manner for over twenty years. He has also been identified with the business interests of Antioch for many years. He was appointed city marshal by the board of trustees of Antioch in February, 1914, which office he has held continuously since. In politics Mr. Sweeney is a Democrat and has taken a keen interest in matters pertaining to the upbuilding of his town and county. He served as deputy sheriff under James Rankin during his incumbency. In 1879 Mr. Sweeney was united in marriage to Mary J. Curtis, a native of San Francisco. To this union have been born three children—Charles D., of San Francisco; Estella J., wife of William J. Beasley, of San Francisco; and Edward S., a traveling salesman.

Mr. Sweeney is a member of the Native Sons, the Eagles, the Foresters of America, and the Young Men's Institute. The family are members of the Catholic church. Mr. Sweeney has served as secretary of the Eagles' Lodge No. 785 of Antioch for over ten years. He interests himself deeply in matters of public import, and his labors have been of distinct advantage to Contra Costa County.

PATRICK ROYCE.—The subject of this narrative was a native of County Wexford, Ireland. He came to this country in 1849 in the British ship "Atlantic." He served as first officer under Captain James Quinn. He followed mining in California and Idaho for a time. He again followed the seas for some years, and in 1873 he settled in Contra Costa County. He was identified to quite an extent in stock-raising on New York Island for some years, after which he engaged in the hotel business in Pittsburg. He was lighthouse tender for a time and for a number of years, and up to the time of his death, was mail carrier in Pittsburg. Mr. Royce was married to Mary Carty, a native of County Wexford, Ireland. To this union was born three children, one of whom, John Royce, was born in Pittsburg and received his education in the public schools of that town. He followed various vocations early in life, and in 1907 he went to Alaska, where he engaged in the fish business.

Returning to Pittsburg, he engaged in the electrical business and later opened a garage in connection with his other line. Fraternally, he is a member of the B. P. O.

E. of Richmond. His sister Margaret was appointed postmistress in December, 1911, and held that office until her death, which occurred on February 8, 1915. She discharged her official duties in a prompt, capable, and efficient manner. Her demise was regretted by all who knew her. Mary, John's other sister, was born in San Francisco on July 18, 1879, and was assistant in the post-office. At the time of her sister's death she was made postmistress, and still holds that office.

ROBERT F. ROBERTSON is numbered among the representative ranchers of eastern Contra Costa County, and the success he has achieved is the result of his own efforts. He was born in Scotland on September 6, 1884, son of John and Jessie Robertson, both deceased. Mr. Robertson acquired his education in the public schools of his native land. Early in life he assisted on his father's farm, and afterward worked out. In 1903 he came to America, and located at once in Contra Costa County, renting a quarter-section of land on Kellogg Creek, belonging to J. H. Brown. On March 11, 1909, he was united in marriage to Anna Isert, a native of San Francisco, daughter of John and Minnie Isert. A daughter, Edith, was born on December 7, 1910.

Fraternally, Mr. Robertson is a member of the I. O. O. F. of Byron. He has always been identified with farming pursuits, and during the summer months finds it profitable to operate a hay-pressing machine. He has also done much work for Balfour, Guthrie & Co. Mrs. Robertson's parents are now located at Lathrop, California. They were among the early ranchers at Knightsen and Antioch, having spent thirty years in each place doing general farming. Mr. and Mrs. Robertson have many friends in their locality. By good management they have brought their ranch to a high state of cultivation.

JOSEPH M. McAVOY is an active and enterprising representative of business interests in Pittsburg, as purchasing agent and manager for the David Israel General Store, which important position he has held since the fall of 1904. His birth occurred in Empire, a mining town near Pittsburg, Contra Costa County, October 4, 1878. He is the son of John and Maria McAvoy. His father was a native of Ireland, and his mother was from Pennsylvania.

The parents of Mr. McAvoy married in Pennsylvania and came to the Coast in 1853, settling first in Placer County, where his father became identified with mining interests. The mother, with their nine children, made her home in Somersville while her husband was working in Placer County. He passed away in the mining camp, and his body was brought to Downieville. Joseph M. McAvoy, the subject of this sketch, acquired his education in the public schools of Somersville. He was united in marriage to Miss Amy V. Harris on September 25, 1901, after which they moved to San Francisco and Mr. McAvoy worked at the coppersmith trade for a period of three years. In the fall of 1904 they returned to Black Diamond (now Pittsburg), and Mr. McAvoy became identified with the store. Their one son, Joseph Ernest, was born on June 9, 1902. The parents of Mrs. McAvoy were David D. Harris, a native of Wales, and her mother, Levina Harris, was also a native of the same country. They were married in San Francisco and were the parents of three children—Amy V., Daniel, and William. Mr. McAvoy is a Republican. He has served as town trustee for six years and has been on the school board for four years. He is a member of Diamond Parlor No. 246, N. S. G. W., the Fraternal Order of Eagles, and the Knights of Pythias, all of Pittsburg. Mrs. McAvoy served as postmistress in Summerville for two years after she finished her education in San Francisco. The grandmother of Mrs. McAvoy, Mrs. Mary Humphrey, came to California via the Isthmus route about 1850. She is still living and is now in her eighty-fifth year. Mrs. McAvoy is a member of Sterling Parlor No. 146, N. D. G. W., of Pittsburg, and takes an active part in its work. She was elected grand outside sentinel in 1910, which office she held one year. She then filled the office of inside sentinel for one year. She has served as grand inside sentinel and grand marshal. She served on the board of grand trustees for three years. She was clerk one year and chairman of board two years. Mrs. McAvoy established Sterling Parlor with twenty-two members, and now the membership has reached eighty-two. Mr. McAvoy instituted Diamond Parlor with twenty-two members, and it has increased to one hundred members. Mr. and Mrs. McAvoy are well-known and highly esteemed citizens, and their substantial qualities have gained for them many friends in the Bay counties, in fact all over California.

FRANK R. GREEN, one of the most prominent and progressive citizens of eastern Contra Costa County, and one whose labors have been effective forces in the development of the county, was born near Minneapolis, Minnesota, December 18, 1858, son of George W. (a native of New York State) and Mary E. (Roberts) Green, who was born in Massachusetts. The parents of Mr. Green were married in the early '50s. His father was one of the prominent attorneys in his locality and served as district judge in Beaver Dam, Wisconsin, for twelve years. He served as State Representative in 1857. The subject of this sketch received a common-school education, after which he attended the University in Minneapolis. In June, 1881, he came to California and located in Fresno County. Here he found employment at ranching, and for two years he milked a string of thirty cows. He taught school at Hills Valley for a period of six years and at River Dale for three years. He then taught in various other localities for a number of years. He ranched in Fresno County, having had three ranches of forty acres each. He disposed of his land holdings and removed to Merced County, where he was made principal of the Los Banos city school for a period of seven years and served as president of the board of education during this time. He also served as head of the Menlo Park schools in 1903. Mr. Green engaged in fruit-raising and owned two orchards in Monterey County which he traded for Oakland property. In 1910 he removed to eastern Contra Costa County and purchased the Heck place of forty acres, which is all in almonds and walnuts.

He is also engaged in the hog business to quite an extent and makes a specialty of registered Berkshire stock. Mr. Green has brought his place up to a high state of cultivation and has one of the most modern homes in the eastern part of the county. He is also engaged in the real-estate business, and at all times manifests a public-spirited devotion to the general good of his community. He was united in marriage to Miss Amy I. Malsbary on January 30, 1887. To this union have been born four children—Ivy (who died in childhood), Watros Earl, Henrietta Mae, and Grace Genevieve. In politics Mr. Green is an ardent supporter of the Republican party. He is a member of the Fraternal Brotherhood. His father died in 1897 at the age of seventy-seven years; his mother resides in Los Banos. Mr. Green concentrates his energies upon his business interests, which are of growing importance. He has met with success in the real-estate line, and the efforts of his wife along this line are of untold value. Mr. Green has an individual way in his advertising. He has erected a large sign in front of his handsome place which causes much laughter to the passing automobiles. It reads, "Slow down if you read this, Real Estate in all its branches."

IRA E. CARPER, a successful business man of Pittsburg, California, was born in Cass County, Nebraska, March 18, 1869. He is a son of Harvey and Agnes Carper, both honored citizens of Virginia. The parents of Mr. Carper had thirteen children—seven sons and six daughters—two of whom died when young. In all his relations of life the father has proved himself a valued and useful citizen, ever ready to give his support to those measures that were right. The subject of this review was raised on a farm and received a common-school education. Leaving the farm, he learned the barber trade.

He followed this trade with success and worked in many of the large cities in the West. In 1897 he came to California and drove cattle from Billings, Montana, to Idaho. He worked four years at Fort Bidwell in the cattle business. He then located in Sonora, Tuolumne County, California, and became identified with the Sierra Railway in the capacity of freight agent for one year, which was in 1901. He then removed to Watsonville and worked on a farm for two years. He also followed his trade for two years in Watsonville. He came to San Francisco and later to Oakland. In 1905 he removed to Black Diamond, now Pittsburg, following his trade from 1005 to 1908, and in September he removed to Antioch, where he operated a barber-shop. On September 27, 1911, he returned to Pittsburg and engaged in business. Politically, Mr. Carper is affiliated with the Democratic party. He was elected town trustee in the spring of 1908. He served until he removed to Antioch.

On May 10, 1916, he was elected town trustee for the four-year term. Fraternally, Mr. Carper is a member of I. O. O. F. of Fort Bidwell, the Eagles, the Ancient Order of Foresters, and the I. D. E. S. of Pittsburg. Mr. Carper was united in marriage to Katherine Ole, a native of Indiana, May 1, 1911.

Mr. Carper is a supporter of public movements for the betterment of his locality, and his success in life has been well deserved.

FRANK X. SMITH.—Prominent among the representative men of eastern Contra Costa County is Frank X. Smith. He was born in San Francisco on December 3, 1868, son of Andrew and Catherine (Kelly) Smith. Mr. Smith's father was a native of County Cavan, Ireland, where he was reared, and at the age of seventeen he came to America and located in Illinois. Later he went to Utah and then to California. He found employment in Los Angeles at different vocations for a time, and later worked in the mines at Knoxville.

He remained here for a time and then decided to engage in ranching. In 1868, he bought a settler's right to one hundred and sixty acres of land, which he improved and put out an orchard and vineyard. Ten years later he bought another quarter-section of land; a little later he purchased another quarter-section, and again one hundred and seventy acres, until he owned at the time of his death, which occurred in 1906, about eight hundred acres. For twenty years he rented and farmed five hundred acres of land on the Marsh ranch. The parents of Frank X. Smith were united in marriage in San Francisco, and to this union were born three children—Frank X., the subject of this review; Andrew J., identified with the home ranch; and John W., physician and surgeon, who died in 1908. Dr. John W. Smith was a graduate of the Cooper Medical College of San Francisco and was one of the prominent physicians of San Francisco. He assisted and did much professional work during the big fire in San Francisco. Andrew J., was born in 1870, educated in the public schools of Contra Costa County, and later attended the Stockton Business College. He has always been identified with agricultural pursuits. Frank X. acquired his education in the public schools after which he took a business course. Frank X. Smith was united in marriage to Mary A. Lynch, a native of San Francisco, daughter of Philip and Ellen Lynch, May 22, 1900. Their two children are Mary Alberta, attending high school in Brentwood, and Clarence F., attending school. Fraternally, Mr. Smith is a member of the Eagles lodge of Antioch and the Young Men's Institute. The family are members of the Catholic church of Antioch.

LORENZO GRANT PLUMLEY—Among the citizens of Byron and eastern Contra Costa County none is more highly esteemed or remembered with greater affection than Alonzo Plumley, the father of the subject of this biography. Alonzo Plumley was an early pioneer of Contra Costa County.

He was born in St. Lawrence County, New York, August 12, 1830, and died May 29, 1916. When but a small boy his father died and his mother married again, the family moving to Canada. At the age of seventeen Alonzo left home and went to Cook County, Illinois, where he remained until March 21, 1853. On that date, with his young wife, they started across the plains with horse-teams. They came direct to Contra Costa County, and settled in the Ygnacio Valley, and in the fall of 1864 he purchased the present farm of one hundred and sixty acres near Byron, where he successfully engaged in stock-raising and farming. Alonzo Plumley married Miss Julia E. Chilson, March 1, 1853. Of this union twelve children were born—Levina Elizabeth, Sarah Eleanor, Charles Eugene, Olive A., Ida E. (wife of A. F. Byer, of Byron, died December 20, 1897), Alonzo Monroe, Lorenzo Grant, Willard Olney, Emma Lydia, Edith Orela, Lillie Julia, and Lulu Maud. Alonzo Plumley was active in laying out and grading roads in the Byron section, and did much towards beautifying the town. Lorenzo Grant was born January 7, 1866. He was educated in the public school in the Point of Timber district.

He moved to Mendocino County, and took up one hundred and sixty acres of redwood timber, and after spending one year in that country he returned and ranched on the Marsh grant. Here he remained for five years. In 1809 he engaged in the mercantile business in Byron, which he has since continued. In politics he is a Republican but has never aspired to office. Fraternally, he is a member of the I. O. O. F. of Byron. Lorenzo Plumley was united in marriage to Mary Jane Gann of Brentwood, born December 1, 1879. To this union there have been three children—Rodney S., born October 1, 1902; Blanche Marietta, born May 16, 1908; Lorenzo Grant, Jr., born July 30, 1911. His wife is a member of Donner Parlor, N. D. G. W., of Byron.

Alonzo Monroe Plumley was born December 19, 1863. He was educated in the public school in Excelsior District, after which he returned to the home place and purchased twenty acres, later buying eighty acres more. In 1914, he sold the eighty acres, and is now identified with the fruit business and general farming. He was married to Elizabeth H. Livingstone on December 6, 1894. Their one son, Henry Alonzo, is in the automobile business in Berkeley. Charles Eugene Plumley was born January 9, 1859. After his schooling, he remained on the home place, with the exception of a few years he spent in Mendocino and Santa Clara counties. In the latter place he followed contracting and building. Willard O. Plumley was born April

20, 1868, and was educated in Santa Clara and Mendocino counties, where he followed millwork. Twenty years ago he returned to the home ranch, with which he has since been identified. He takes an active part in the prohibition movement and is a member of the Methodist church.

HENRY C. McCABE, one of the progressive and representative ranchers of eastern Contra Costa County, was born on October 5, 1844, in Illinois. He is a son of Thomas McCabe, who was numbered among the pioneers of this section, his activities being a force in progress and his citizenship a valuable asset to the eastern section. Thomas McCabe was born in Guernsey County, Ohio, May 28, 1810. He acquired his early education in the local schools of his locality. At the age of eighteen he engaged in boating on the Ohio River, and later on the Wabash River in Indiana, which was in 1830. Later he removed to Illinois, where he followed farming for four years. The balance of the time until 1850 he farmed in various counties in Illinois. On May 8. 1850, he with a company of others crossed the plains to the new mining camps. Mr. McCabe was chosen captain of the party. They arrived in Placerville, August 3, 1850. Mr. McCabe engaged in mining at once, and followed this vocation for two years, when he returned to his home in Illinois. In the spring of 1853 he returned with his family to this coast and located at Snow Point, Nevada County, where he again engaged in mining pursuits until 1857. He then took up farming in Solano County for three years. The next five years he spent on a ranch in Napa County. In the fall of 1867 Mr. McCabe moved to Contra Costa County and purchased one hundred and sixty acres of railroad land, and his son, Henry C, purchased one hundred and sixty acres adjoining. Thomas McCabe was united in marriage to Miss Maria Peacock, a native of Ohio, January 12, 1831. To this union have been born nine children. The subject of this review, Henry McCabe, became identified with ranching. This vocation he followed until he disposed of his holdings and retired three years ago. Henry C. purchased the one hundred and sixty acres belonging to his father after the latter's death, which occurred on December 3, 1888. and continued to operate both places until he retired. He disposed of fifteen acres to the Standard Oil Company, where they now have a pumping station named McCabe. The remainder of the ranch, consisting of three hundred acres, was sold to Doctor Fredericks, of San Francisco. Henry C. was united in marriage to Sarah A. Powell on March 23, 1870. To this union there have been four children. Henry Herbert was born January 3, 1891, and died December 1, 1916. Clara E. and Thomas Clifford (twins) were born on June 13, 1880. Clara E. died at the age of twelve.

Clifford has resided for the past three years in Fresno County, where he has managed his father's ranch. He married Miss Lena Grennenger, of Contra Costa County, and their three daughters are Genevieve, Helen, and Grace.

Pearl E. McCabe was born April 3, 1872, and was united in marriage to George E. Martin, of Watsonville, California. To this union have been born Henry A., Kenneth, and Maria N. Thomas McCabe was a broad-minded man, liberal in thought and honorable in purpose, and his life was fruitful of good results. His son, Henry C., whose name heads this review, is an intensely loyal and public-spirited citizen of Contra Costa County.

JOHN HENRY ADAMS, M. D., who is successfully engaged in the practice of medicine in Crockett, California, is well known as a representative of that class of progressive professional men who utilize the most advanced methods of medical science, his broad reading and earnest study keeping him in touch with the advancement that is being continually made by the profession. Doctor Adams is a native son, and was born in Lodi, San Joaquin County, March 7, 1888. He acquired his education in the public schools, after which he entered the College of Physicians and Surgeons of San Francisco, graduating with the class of 1911. He served as house physician in the Trinity Hospital one year. He was appointed to the chair of Visceral Anatomy in the College of Physicians and Surgeons. Doctor Adams practiced in San Francisco from September, 1912, to December, 1913, when he removed to Crockett. Fraternally, he is a member of the Native Sons, B. P. O. E., I. O. O. F., Red Men, Eagles, Moose, W. O. W., I. D. E. S., and the Y. M. C. A.

Doctor Adams was united in marriage to Miss Pauline Burgess on April 27, 1912. To this union there is one son, John Henry, Jr., born January 22, 1916. Doctor Adams is a member of the Alpha Kappa Kappa, a medical fraternity. He is a member of the American Medical Association and the Contra Costa Medical Society. He is the physician for the California Sugar Refinery. Doctor Adams' father was a representative rancher and citizen of Lodi. He died on May 27, 1909, and his mother passed away September 7, 1893. Doctor Adams is regarded as a reliable, far-sighted, and progressive professional man. He has secured a large and representative patronage.

WILLIAM W. MORGANS, who enjoys recognition as one of the leading and enterprising business men of Brentwood, has won merited success. He is engaged in the general mercantile business and was born in Nortonville, Contra Costa County, January 3, 1869. His father, Watkin P. Morgans, is a native of Wales, and was born in 1842. He came to America with his parents when a mere child, and they located in Pennsylvania. Watkin P. came to the Coast in January, 1864, via the Panama route. He followed mining for some years, and married in Sutter Creek to Elizabeth Davis, and her death occurred in 1892. In 1868 he removed to Nortonville, where he was identified with the mines for a number of years as assistant superintendent. William W. Morgans, the only son, received his education in the public schools of Nortonville, after which he attended a military college in Sonoma County. He then took a business course, and at the age of seventeen years he entered the general store of W. A. Davis, of Brentwood. He was soon made manager of the store. This position he filled in a capable manner, and under his management the business expanded. Later the business was made a stock company. In 1906 Mr. Morgans bought out the other stockholders and has since run the business in such a manner as to cause its growth and expansion until today it is one of the largest and best mercantile stores in eastern Contra Costa County. Mr. Morgans gives his political support to the Republican party. He served as school trustee for many years and during his office he was instrumental in freeing the school debt. Fraternally, he is a member of the Masonic lodge of Brentwood, and the chapter of Antioch. In November, 1890, Mr. Morgans was united in marriage to Ida L. Wills, daughter of Thomas N. Wills, one of the old and respected citizens who came to this county in the early days and bought much land where Antioch is now located. There were two children born to Mr. and Mrs. Morgans. One child died in infancy, and William J., born in 1891, is assisting in the store. Mr. Morgans is regarded as a reliable and progressive business man and takes a keen interest in matters pertaining to the development and upbuilding of Brentwood and surrounding country.

EDWARD M. DOWNER.—The name of Edward M. Downer has come to be regarded as synonymous with banking and business interests in Contra Costa County. He has been guided and controlled by a spirit of enterprise and progress. He is a man of varied interests, and for many years the influence of his ability and personality has been a constructive element in the advancement of the county. He was born in Yuba County, California, April 28, 1869, the son of James Edward Downer. His father was a native of New York State. Mr. Downer's father crossed the plains during the pioneer days and engaged in mining until his death, which occurred at the age of seventy-five. The subject of this review acquired his education in the public schools of Nevada City, after which he studied telegraphy and filled various positions of importance and trust with the Southern Pacific Company. On February 1, 1891, he was made station agent and operator at Pinole. He served as postmaster at this place for several years. In 1894 he established the Pinole Times, the first and only paper ever published in that town. Mr. Downer has been active in banking and real-estate matters in this county. He is president of the Bank of Pinole, of the Bank of Crockett, and of the Mechanics Bank of Richmond. Under his wise and able management all three banks have grown to their present proportions and importance. More extended mention of the history of these banks will be found in the banking chapter. It is largely due to Mr. Downer and to his progressive policies that the banks in Richmond, Pinole, and Crockett have become what they are today in the commercial and financial life of the three places. Mr. Downer was united in marriage to Miss Lizzie Bouquet, a native of Contra Costa County, and a daughter of the late Frederick Bouquet. To this union have been born two children—Hazel I., born April 15, 1898, attending Mills College, and Edward M., Jr., born August 13, 1905, now attending school. Mr. Downer is a Royal Arch Mason and has filled the various chairs in his chapter. He is regarded as one of the substantial and reliable upbuilders of Contra Costa County.

CHARLES AXEL SMITH.—High in the list of those who by their greatness of achievement in industry and commerce have added luster to the brilliant star of American enterprise is Charles Axel Smith, of the C. A. Smith Lumber Company, of the C. A. Smith Lumber & Manufacturing Company of Marshfield, Oregon, of the C. A. Smith Timber Company, and of the Coos Bay Lumber Company, holding probably twenty billion feet of standing timber in Oregon and California. He was born in the province of Ostergotland, Sweden, December 11, 1852. At the age of fourteen, with his father and sister, he came from his native land to the United States and settled, as has been largely the case with immigrants from his native country, in Minnesota. He attended the public schools of Minneapolis from 1869 to 1871, and from 1872 to 1873 he was a student of the University of Minnesota. While attending school he lived with John S. Pillsbury, who had served several years as Governor of Minnesota, working during his spare time in the winter and being employed in the Governor's hardware store in Minneapolis during his summer vacations. Because of his ill-health, he reluctantly abandoned his ambition for a complete university education and became a regular employee in Governor Pillsbury's hardware store until 1878. At that time, with the help of Governor Pillsbury, he went to Herman, Minnesota, then a new town on the line of the Great Northern Railway. He here built an elevator and opened an implement store and lumber business, conducting the enterprise for six years under the name of C. A. Smith & Co., with Governor

Pillsbury as an equal partner. In addition to this enterprise, retail lumber yards were opened by Mr. Smith at Evansville, Bandon, and Ashby, Minnesota. During these six years, Mr. Smith was successful, clearing in the Herman business for his firm $50,000, and in his other ventures $40,000, an equal half of this sum being his individual profits. In 1884 Governor Pillsbury, who had loaned a considerable sum of money to loggers who were unable to pay their debts, asked Mr. Smith to buy their logs and manufacture them into lumber. To this Mr. Smith agreed, and organized the lumber manufacturing firm of C. A. Smith & Co. The first purchases of logs, as well as all handled by the firm until 1891, were sawed at custom mills at Minneapolis. Then they bought a mill, which, however, burned down six weeks later. Another mill was shortly thereafter purchased. In 1893, when the business was incorporated as the C. A. Smith Lumber Company (Minnesota), it began its corporate career by building the largest, most expensive and complete mill up to that time erected in the Northwest, a mill which, in a few years later, broke all records in turning out in eleven hours with three band-saws and a gang approximately six hundred thousand feet of lumber, seventy-one and one-half thousand feet of lath, and one hundred thirty thousand shingles. It also made a weekly average of one million ten thousand feet a day of twenty hours.

With his business in Minneapolis firmly established, Mr. Smith was not blind to the fact that the future must be looked after if lumbermen would survive the day when the now almost depleted forests in Minnesota would be shorn of their standing timber. He then began investment on the Pacific Coast, first by the purchase of a redwood tract in Humboldt County, California, later by the accumulation of a huge acreage in southwestern Oregon and then by the buying of a large stand of sugar and Western yellow pine in El Dorado County, California. While the California properties have been allowed to stand for future needs, Mr. Smith early in 1907 began the erection of a model lumber-manufacturing plant at Marshfield, on Coos Bay, Oregon. As Mr. Smith's timber was all tributary to tidewater, and as he well appreciated the economy of ocean freights, he looked about for the establishing of a distributing plant that could handle the product of his timber holdings as the manufacturing plants were gradually installed. After investigating thoroughly, in the spring of 1008 he purchased a tract of land on Suisun Bay, forty miles from San Francisco, and established what is known as the Bay Point plant and the prosperous village of Bay Point at that place.

At Bay Point Mr. Smith has probably one of the most complete and model lumber, milling, and warehousing plants in the United States. The Marshfield sawmill and the Bay Point planing-mill plants are equipped with every modern device known to the industry. Mr. Smith has been a forerunner amongst the lumbermen for labor-saving devices in the manufacturing and handling of his product. Naturally the question of transporting the manufactured material from Marshfield to Bay Point necessitated the building of steamers. Of such, Mr. Smith has two in his service, the "Nann Smith" and the "Adeline Smith," named for his daughters. These vessels were constructed on Mr. Smith's own plans, and every stick of lumber is handled by electric cranes at the Marshfield end in packages, each package averaging fifteen hundred to two thousand feet, such packages being stowed on shipboard intact, and at Bay Point being removed by electric cranes in the same manner.

By this device, which has brought Mr. Smith much renown, he is able to load, transport, and discharge a vessel's cargo of a million and three-quarter to two million feet of lumber every five days, the distance traversed in that time being about eight hundred and fifty miles. As a lumberman, Mr. Smith has always been prominent, and has been signally honored in the highest councils of the industry, having served as vice-president of the National Lumber Manufacturers' Association, a member of its board of governors, and as adviser and director of the Mississippi Valley Lumbermen's Association. Despite his vast private interests, Mr. Smith has found time to be a patron of the arts, a spirited public citizen, a philanthropist, a church supporter, and an active participator in public affairs. In 1896, he was presidential elector from Minneapolis, destined to carry to the national capital that State's vote for McKinley and Hobart. He also was a delegate to the Republican National Convention which nominated McKinley and Roosevelt.

He has been an officer in the General Council of the Lutheran Church in America. He has served many years as a regent of the University of Minnesota, one of the highest offices in the gift of the governor of a State. Mr. Smith, while an American of undivided allegiance, is greatly interested in the welfare of the Scandinavian people in this country and the fatherland.

He took a prominent part in the relief of famine sufferers in Norland and has made substantial gifts to Scandinavian schools and churches in this country. In recognition of the services he has rendered the sons of Sweden in the United States and elsewhere, he has been signally honored by the King of Sweden, having been created Knight Commander of the Second Degree of the order of Vasa. For several years Mr. Smith occupied the post of Swedish consul in Minneapolis. On February 14, 1878, Mr. Smith married Miss Johanna Anderson. Of this marriage have been born three sons (Oscar, the eldest, accidentally killed when seventeen years of age, and Vernon A. and Carroll W., holding responsible position with the C. A. Smith corporations) and three daughters (Nann, now Mrs. Frederick A. Warner, Adeline, and Myrtle, now Mrs. Philip Rodgers, of Honolulu). The family home is located in Berkeley, California.

JOHN JOSEPH SULLENGER was born on January 8, 1868, at Oakville, Napa County, California, on the ranch of George Yount. He attended the public school at Rutherford, and afterward, in 1882, graduated from Heald's Business College in San Francisco. He then worked at surveying in different parts of the State, and at one time helped the noted engineer, A. W. Von Schmidt, lay out the Marsh grant. He was next employed for some time by T. N. Wills, of Antioch. Eventually, in 1888, he bought the ranch in Lone Tree Valley, where he now resides. In 1897 he was married to Annie Elizabeth Love, and of this union there are three sons and one daughter— John Dugald, born September 14, 1899, graduating 1917 from Liberty Union High School, Brentwood; Archibald McKinnon, born March 27, 1901, second year in high school 1917; Robert Love, born September 4, 1902, attending grammar school; Annie Elise, born May 26, 1905, attending Deer Valley grammar school. Mr. Sullenger still does odd jobs of surveying for his neighbors and is considered an excellent mathematician.

ROBERT LOVE, one of the pioneer settlers of Lone Tree Valley, eastern Contra Costa County, was born in Kilburnie, Scotland, on September 10, 1828. He was the recipient of a limited education, as his parents died when he was young and he was brought up by his wife's people in the Highlands of Scotland. At the age of seventeen he decided to cast his lot in the New World, and came to America, settling in Kentucky and Pennsylvania, and readily found employment in the coal mines, where he remained for some time. He came to California in 1852 and worked at quartz-mining in Placer County and was interested with partners in a large quartz-mill near Michigan Bluff and Forest Hill. He owned a farm in Napa County, near Suscol, known as the Stanley Ranch. He paid a visit to Scotland, and later, on his return to California, he sent for his intended bride, and was married to Elizabeth McKinnon, on March 21, 1861, in San Francisco. They made their home in Napa County, and conducted a dairy while interested in the mines. Eventually, he sold his farm, gave up mining, and moved to Contra Costa County.

In 1867 he pre-empted one hundred and sixty acres of Government land in Lone Tree Valley, which he farmed, and also worked at different times in the mines at Somersville, Stewartville, and Judsonville. Mr. Love died in 1900, and his wife passed away in November, 1904. The family consisted of four sons and four daughters—Janet Montgomerie, born at Napa January 9, 1862, died November 16, 1874; Archibald, born February 8, 1863; Annie Elizabeth, born April 21, 1865; Robert, born November 21, 1866, in Napa, died May 1, 1893; John, born August 9, 1869; Lizzie, born October 4, 1871, died in December, 1894; Flora, born 1873; Dugald, born March 30, 1875, died in October, 1886. Archibald and John are still on the home place and are numbered among the representative ranchers in their locality.

TURNER & DAHNKEN—At this point in their business career, through their remarkable powers of foresight and business faculties, they made the real step to their business future by entering the film supply business about one year after the great San Francisco fire and earthquake. Their new location was in a small storeroom at Ellis and Fillmore streets. At this time there were few producers in America, which necessitated the importing of their films from Europe, which was then the center of the industry. The next few years brought immense developments in the motion-picture business on this coast and throughout the world. The Film Exchange grew and grew, and outgrew its quarters on Ellis Street; so then they moved to a large and more spacious store on Eddy Street near Mason, where business is now conducted by the General Film Company. The General Film Company of America, commonly known as "The Trust," saw the great possibilities of this coast and purchased the business of the firm of Turner & Dahnken at the enormous price of $200,000 for contracts and leases for films held on this coast. "The Trust" people found that the name of Turner & Dahnken stood so big with the public as moving-picture exhibitors that they desired to retain that name as the title of the Film Exchange maintained in San Francisco. Mr. Turner refused, and this almost broke off negotiations, but the coast men retained the right to use their own name. They had other plans for the trademark which they had established by years of honest treatment and a progressive policy. They had decided to enter the theatrical ownership field themselves, and their first real substantial investment in the exhibition of moving pictures was in two small theaters on Market Street, which turned out to be another big advance in the march of progress that had marked the success of Turner & Dahnken's career. They sold their lease to a Market Street location on which these two theatres were conducted to Alexander Pantages, who built the present Pantages Theater on this site. Turner & Dahnken received the amount of $28,000 for this transfer of lease. This sale, however, did not interfere with their future plans, and immediately upon the execution and close of this sale, they still proceeded to advance in the amusement business, with the policy clearly set in their minds to exhibit pictures of the most intense interest, pictures of sound morals clearly portrayed and cleverly executed, and by a rigid enforcement of these policies they have become the greatest entertainers with motion pictures to the West Coast public. They now have theaters located in every important city of the West Coast, not theaters of the ordinary store-room type, but beautiful, commodious, elaborately furnished theaters, with uniformed attendants to wait upon the pleasures of the theater-going public. The headquarters of this vast circuit is located at 942 Market Street, San Francisco, and it occupies one entire floor of the Garfield Building, where the photographic, sign-writing, card-writing, supply department for all necessities to maintain their circuit, clerical work, official work, directing, etc., is carried on. Such theaters as the famous Tivoli Opera House, seating two thousand people, known all over the world as the home of Tettrazini, Caruso, and other famous opera singers, has become one of their large places of entertainment. One of the largest theaters in America was constructed for the vast interests of the Turner & Dahnken firm, located at Eleventh and Broadway streets, Oakland, California. This theater has many innovations for the accommodation of the lovers of the silent drama—handsome upholstered seats, a maid in attendance for the comforts of the ladies, large and spacious waiting-rooms with telephones at their command, a tearoom for ladies to rest, and between sips of their tea to pass their opinions upon the wonderfully pleasant entertainment they have received from the hands of the Turner & Dahnken Circuit. This elaborate place of amusement seats about 3500 people, and patrons are able to reach the gallery without the assistance of steps, a gradual incline from the main entrance being provided for their convenience, something entirely new to the theatrical public of the West Coast. The decorative scheme of this magnificent theater is of the latest and most up-to-date design, so arranged that when worked in conjunction with the lighting scheme, the house can be immediately converted into the environments of the subject being exhibited upon the curtain. The house can be made into twilight, dawn, the surroundings of a volcano, or become part of a fire scene. A wonderful master pipe-organ is installed to give all the necessary effects lending realism to the silent drama, such as the gradual approach of cavalry, or of the distant rumble of cannon, the singing of birds, or the eruption of a volcano, the echo of distant noises. In fact, space will not permit the naming of the wonderful advancement these two exponents of the silent drama, as pioneers in the theatrical game, have developed in the moving-picture theater. Their theaters are the last word of improvement, and they have traced the exhibition of the motion picture to the zenith of its glory from a humble inception through phenomenal evolution to an inspiring development. James T. Turner was born in Antioch on July 25, 1873. Educated at Antioch grammar school until the age of thirteen, then sought employment as farmer. Then became associated with his present partner, Mr. Dahnken, as manager in the Arlington Hotel, Antioch.

In the fall of 1809 he left for San Francisco and made his first real business venture, which proved very successful, and which afterward turned out to be the coming together of the firm of Turner & Dahnken in the spring of 1001. In the summer of 1904, Mr. Turner opened up the beginning of the amusement business in Fresno, and after three months of success, their attention was drawn to the Lewis & Clark Exposition. They immediately moved their shows to the city of Portland, and after a successful season were unable to renew their lease, which necessitated their storing the shows.

Mr. Turner then returned to Fresno, and Mr. Dahnken resumed the hotel business at Antioch. Immediately after the great San Francisco earthquake and fire Mr. Dahnken came to San Francisco to seek a possible location for their shows and sent for Mr. Turner and wired Portland to ship their shows to San Francisco at once. In the meantime they prepared their location to receive their automatic vaudeville shows, located on Fillmore Street, San Francisco. Business was very profitable for about one year. Mr. Turner has a way of remaining patient and calm under the most trying circumstances—just aggressive enough to be forceful, and just amiable enough to be loved. He has a way of saying "Thank you" that makes you feel good all over. He makes people like to do things for him.

FRED DAHNKEN is a son of Fred and Bridget Dahnken, one of the prominent and representative families of the Bay region. His father was a native of Germany, and his mother came from Ireland. At the age of fifteen Mr. Dahnken's father left his native country and came to America. He remained in New York for a few years and later decided to cast his lot in the Golden West. He came to San Francisco via Panama route and engaged in business for some years. Later he moved to Sherman Island, where he followed farming, and in 1865 he located in Antioch. He followed the draying business, and for thirty-five years, owing to his absolute integrity, he filled the office of wharfinger, and while in this office he was identified with the hotel interests of Antioch. He was especially active in politics and was a loyal supporter of the Democratic party; he served in a creditable manner on the school board and was city trustee for some years. His death occurred in 1913. He was a broad-minded man, liberal in thought and honorable in purpose, and always supported any progressive measure that was for the benefit of his locality. His death was mourned by a wide circle of friends. The mother of our subject passed away in 1915. In the parents' family four children were born, two of whom died in infancy. Henry, a brother of our subject, died in 1911. He had been identified for many years with his father in Antioch. Fred Dahnken was born in Antioch on February 17, 1868. He attended the Antioch Grammar School until of a sufficient age to act as clerk in L. Meyers' grocery-store, Antioch. After two years he became associated in business with his father as wharfinger, and a few years later he ventured in the hotel business, which he still retains. In 1896 he started for British Columbia to make a further venture in the hotel business, which did not prove successful and necessitated his return to Antioch. However, not satisfied, he followed the big gold rush to Alaska in the year 1900, but after looking the situation over he did not believe there were possibilities there for substantial investment or of making a business venture with a future, and he returned again to Antioch. At this time the firm of Turner & Dahnken laid its cornerstone. Mr. Dahnken has the courage of his convictions, but his convictions very seldom require much courage to support them. He is gifted with an incredible measure of business instinct and a wonderful power of perception. His inventive and creative mind has been responsible for most of the popular improvements in the theatrical business. On February 11, 1903, he was united in marriage to Margaret Kearney, a native of San Francisco, and daughter of Patrick Kearney, who erected the Palace Hotel of Antioch, and a granddaughter of Mrs. Tregalles, of Antioch. To this union there were two children—Carsten, born December, 1903, and Margaret, born in 1905. In politics Mr. Dahnken is affiliated with the Democratic party, but he never aspired to office. Fraternally, he is a member of the Fraternal Order of Eagles of Antioch, the Press Club, and Indoor Yacht Club of San Francisco.

CHARLES FISH (deceased).—The name of Charles Fish is remembered throughout Contra Costa County as that of one of the men who gave his best efforts toward the cultivation of the broad farming lands of the county.

Before his death, which occurred on February 28, 1911, he, with his brother, Lafayette I. Fish, became the owner of large tracts of land. In the death of Charles Fish Contra Costa County and the whole bay region lost one of its largest and most successful ranchers, and one of the most energetic, capable, and public-spirited pioneers. Mr. Fish was born in Batavia, New York, October 24, 1818, son of Libeus and Polly (Holcomb) Fish, descendants of Colonial settlers of New England, and the former was a son of Lieutenant Josiah Fish, who served during the Revolutionary War as a lieutenant under Captain Win. Hutchins. Mr. Fish acquired a common-school education, and in October, 1834, he secured a position as clerk in the store of Foote & Beebe, at Batavia. After six months he was transferred to a store at Careyville, owned by the same firm. In April, 1837, he went to Gallatin, Mississippi, as clerk for his brother, Josiah Fish, who paid him fifty dollars for a time, and later raised his salary to eighty dollars a month. In the fall of 1838 he removed to Monticello to take charge of a branch store. With one thousand dollars he had accumulated, he engaged in business with W. D. Larkin, whose interest he purchased in 1843. After conducting the business alone for about ten years, in January, 1853, he sold out and took passage from New Orleans on the whaler "Independence," which was wrecked off the lower coast of California. He arrived in San Francisco on the last day of March, 1853. He at once found work in a store operated by Jerry Ford, and June, 1854, found Mr. Fish located in Martinez. After taking charge of a warehouse at Pacheco for a few months, he acquired an interest in the concern in connection with his brother, Lafayette I. Fish, and for eleven years he continued in this partnership, after which he sold his interest in the concern, and, with his brother, acquired large tracts of land, which were operated by tenants. Mr. Fish assisted in the organization of the Martinez Bank and became one of the directors. From 1880 to 1882 he was a member of the firm of Fish & Blum, and at other periods he maintained an interest in the grain business. Mr. Fish and his brother at one time purchased about three thousand acres in Fresno, San Joaquin, and Kings counties. In 1906 Charles Fish retired from active business, and after his retirement his advice was often sought in matters of importance. Mr. Fish was united in marriage to Mary Elizabeth Grimes, who was born in Bethany, Genesee County, New York, and reared in Erie County, her parents being William and Elizabeth (McCullough) Grimes. To Mr. and Mrs. Fish were born four children—Charles Stanley (who married May Howland, a native of St. Louis, Missouri; he received the appointment from the Board of Supervisors in March, 1904, as commissioner in charge of the Contra Costa County exhibit at the Louisiana Purchase Exposition at St. Louis), Grace Emily and Blanche Ellen (who reside at home), and Eli, who died in 1886. For many years the family occupied an attractive residence erected by Mr. Fish on an eminence overlooking the city of Martinez, the surrounding valley, and the bay in the distance, the whole forming a charming scenic environment for the comfortable home. He was always a liberal contributor in the advancement of educational and religious work.

Charles Fish and Mrs. Lafayette I. Fish donated the ground upon which the Martinez high-school building was erected. Martinez, the adopted town of Charles Fish, owes much to his progressive spirit and broad-minded citizenship, and in the annals of the place his name will always be remembered and cherished.

HENRY MYERS BUCKLEY is numbered among the representative men and substantial farmers of Contra Costa County and has followed this occupation successfully all his life. He is a son of William Heywood and Jane Ann (Myers) Buckley. The father of Henry M. Buckley was numbered among the pioneers of California, where since very early times his activities have been a force in progress, and his citizenship a valuable municipal asset. He first came to California in 1849, from Ulster County, New York, via Mexico, and was among the early gold-seekers to reach the California mines. Later he was identified with Government work at Benicia for a time. Again he went to Placer and El Dorado counties, where he mined. Returning to the Empire State, he married Miss Jane Ann Myers, a native of Dutchess County, New York, a descendant of the Knickerbocker and other prominent families of Revolutionary ancestry. Mr. Buckley with his wife made the trip together to California this time via the Isthmus route, locating in San Francisco for two years. He then took up holdings of land where Fruitvale is now located, and in 1857 he removed to Contra Costa County, where he took up five hundred and twenty acres and engaged in general farming and stock business. Here he remained until his death, which occurred May 18, 1912, in his eighty-ninth year. Since pioneer times Mr. Buckley's father has taken an active interest in public affairs. He was a staunch Republican for many years, and later joined the People's party.

He watched the community develop along all lines. He was considered authority on everything pertaining to the early settlement and the later development of the county. His wife died June 14, 1914, at the age of ninety-one years. Although she has ceased from her labors, and no longer her smile brings gladness to the many who knew her, yet her memory is green, and her name is spoken in eulogy throughout Contra Costa County. The subject of this sketch acquired his education in the public schools of Contra Costa County. Laying aside his books, he became actively engaged on the home place, where he has always remained. He has recently rented the ranch, but up to 1914 he was largely identified with the stock and dairying interests of the county. There were six children in the parents' family— Adeline, wife of George Sellers, of Oakley; Frances W., died October 5, 1916; Joseph H., a resident of Pinole, married Miss Zitella Higgins; Annie E. and Jennie L., both residing at home; and Henry, the subject of this sketch.

HARCOURT GALTON BIGGS is the son of the Rev. G. Hesketh Biggs, who was justice of the peace of Worcestershire County, England. His death occurred at Stratford-on-Avon in 1903. Mr. Biggs is an active and enterprising representative of the business interests of Contra Costa County.

He is superintendent of the manufacturing department of Blake Brothers Company. His birth occurred in England in 1863, and he acquired his education in the same town where Shakespeare lived, Stratford-on-Avon. In 1881 he came to America and settled in Texas, where he rode the range for a period of five years. He next went to Wyoming, where he followed the range for four years. Mr. Biggs came to California and located in San Francisco in 1890, and became identified with Warren & Company, a wholesale machinery firm, for two years. He then took a position with the Minturn ranch in Fresno County, where he acted as foreman for two years.

Throughout his career Mr. Biggs has been successful in every business he has undertaken and was especially successful in handling horses. He conducted a business for three years in San Francisco, corner of Van Ness and Golden Gate avenues, where he bought and sold horses, after which he became associated in his present position. Politically, Mr. Biggs is affiliated with the Republican party. He held a position as foreman of the jute-mill at San Quentin for nearly two years, and acted as deputy sheriff in Fremont County, Wyoming. While he was acting in this capacity the sheriff was killed while hunting horse-thieves, and Mr. Biggs served three months as sheriff to fill the unexpired term. He was then appointed deputy sheriff under the new administration. Fraternally, Mr. Biggs is affiliated with the B. P. O. E. lodge of Richmond, and he has the recognition of having held the office of exalted ruler. He was elected to this office April 1, 1914, and his term expired April 6, 1915. At the expiration of his office, Mr. Biggs was presented with a handsome gold watch. He was united in marriage to Gertrude Lindsay, daughter of Judge Lindsay, August 29, 1894. Their two children are Adele, born September 19, 1895, and Reginald, born May 5, 1900. Mr. and Mrs. Biggs are esteemed by all who know them.

NORMAN H. BENNETT.—Numbered among the esteemed and popular residents of Walnut Creek, Contra Costa County, is Norman H. Bennett, cashier of the San Ramon Valley Bank, who is filling the position with marked ability. He is a man of entrusted integrity, possessing good judgment and tact. He is performing the duties devolving upon him to the entire satisfaction of the public. Mr. Bennett was born in Iowa, June 12, 1883, a son of Rudolphus and Mariette (Peck) Bennett, who were the parents of nine children, of whom six sons and two daughters are living. The father was a native of Vermont and was prominently identified with his community as a newspaper publisher. In 1887 he came to California, and located in San Diego, where he published a newspaper. He is now retired, in his ninety-second year. Mr. Bennett's mother was a native of Clinton, Iowa, and her father was identified with the early history of that State and was a large landowner. The subject of this review has one brother, Ira E. Bennett, editor of the Washington Post, in Washington, D. C. He is one of the remarkable newspaper men and authors who have gone to the East from the San Francisco Chronicle. On December 9, 1916, he was elected president of the Gridiron Club, the famous organization of the Washington newspaper correspondents. This most coveted honor in the newspaper world has come to Mr. Bennett after a long and distinguished service both in the East and in the West. Norman H. Bennett acquired his education in the public schools of San Diego. He afterward became connected with the Trans-Pacific Steamship Line, after coming to San Francisco. He later went with the Bank of California, where he worked for many years, filling various positions of importance and trust. In 1912 he organized the Farmers and Merchants National Bank of Merced, California, with a capital stock of one hundred thousand dollars. Remaining with this institution for some time, he then accepted a position with the San Ramon Valley Bank. Mr. Bennett was united in marriage to Miss Harriet L. Blackburn, a native of Paso Robles, California, June 1, 1905. Their one daughter, Peggy, was born November 8, 1907. Mrs. Bennett's father was one of the representative pioneers of that locality, and founded the town of Paso Robles. He erected the magnificent hotel in that place, which is connected with the baths known all over the country for their curative properties. He was an extensive landowner, and was largely connected with the stock business. He run at one time over twenty-two thousand sheep. Mrs. Bennett takes an active part in the social life of Walnut Creek, while her husband exercises a marked influence toward the advancement of the best interests of his town. Politically, he is affiliated with the Republican party.

M. EMANUEL.—Richmond is indebted to M. Emanuel, the founder and the president of the Ellis Landing & Dock Company, for the development of Ellis Landing and the Ellis Canal, which adjoin the great inner harbor.

It was from that point the produce and freight of Contra Costa County were shipped in pioneer days by Captain George Ellis, who operated the schooners "Sierra" and "Mystery" until the Santa Fe Railroad established its terminal at Richmond. Mr. Emanuel is one of San Francisco's most esteemed business men. His past success and unquestionable integrity are a matter of record. He was prominently associated with the wholesale and importing business of California for twenty-five years. This practical experience combined with his personal knowledge of the principal American and European harbors caused Mr. Emanuel to appreciate the commercial advantages of the geographical location of Ellis Landing and to foresee the great values there when Richmond's destiny as a shipping and manufacturing center is fulfilled. Mr. Emanuel is a native of California; born in San Francisco in December, 1866; educated in London, England, Göttingen, Germany, and other European schools. His father came to California from Bavaria in 1850; his mother was born in Brooklyn, New York. Mr. Emanuel is married and has one daughter, Josephine E. Emanuel.

NUMA S. BOONE.—No one perhaps has done more to advance the agricultural and banking interests in Contra Costa County than the subject of this review. Mr. Boone is a man of marked ability, of enterprise and progression, and he is numbered among the Native Sons of Contra Costa County. His birth occurred in Danville, May 14, 1867, a son of James O. Boone, a native of Kentucky, who crossed the plains in 1852, in company with his wife, two children, and his brother Wellington. It took the party six months to make the trip with ox-teams. James O. Boone was a representative pioneer of California, and a true type of the brave, hardy, and energetic men who contributed largely toward California's advancement.

Instead of going to the mines, like the majority of men who came to California at that period, Mr. Boone saw the advantages and necessity of engaging in the freighting business. He hauled supplies from Sacramento to Dutch Flat with a pair of oxen, receiving twenty dollars a day for his services. It required a week to make this trip. His brother Wellington was associated with him in his business venture. They freighted the first lumber into Dutch Flat, assisted in erecting the first shanty at that place, and took an active part in the development of that mining camp. Numa S. Boone acquired his education in the public schools of Danville, after which he attended high school in Oakland. His father, after residing at Winters, California, removed to Contra Costa County, and was one of the first settlers to locate near Danville. Here Mr. Boone purchased a ranch, and with characteristic energy began to improve his place. After finishing his education, Numa S. Boone returned to the home place, and assisted his father. At the age of twenty-one he rented the Love estate, where Danville is now situated. The first year Mr. Boone planted wheat, and his first business venture was a success. He cleared about nine hundred dollars that season. He was happily married to Miss Minnie T. Thorne, a native of Santa Clara County, on August 31, 1899. Their two children are Travis M., born August 10, 1901, and Eleanor Sims, born August 17, 1905. Mrs. Boone's father was Captain Charles Thorne, a native of New York State, and her mother was Mary J. (Travis) Thorne. Her parents were married in New York State in 1841. Her father followed the seas from the age of eighteen until a few years previous to his death, which occurred January 16, 1897. He served as port warden at San Francisco for two terms. Captain Thorne came to California via the Panama route in the spring of 1850. Previous to this he operated on the Atlantic Coast. He opened the steamboat route between San Francisco and Alviso, and the fare at that time was eighteen dollars. Captain Thorne's wife came to California in 1852 with their three children via the Panama route. They were the parents of eight children— seven sons and one daughter. Those living are Mrs. Numa S. Boone, John P., of Alameda, and Frank B., of Portland. Mrs. Boone's mother passed away October 27, 1909, at Forest Home, the residence of Mr. and Mrs. Boone. Fraternally, Numa S. Boone is a member of the Woodmen of the World. He is also a member of San Ramon Parlor, N. S. G. W., and takes an active part and is a member of the Danville Grange. Politically, he casts his ballot with the Democratic party. While he is active locally he has never aspired to office. With the exception of one year, Mr. Boone has served on the Democratic Central Committee since he cast his first vote. For many years he has served on the San Ramon school board. Besides being an extensive landowner, to the extent of owning two hundred and fifty acres, he works about seven hundred acres. He is president of the San Ramon Valley Bank, which also operates a branch bank at Danville. He is a man of unusual business ability, has a large circle of friends, and is respected and esteemed wherever known. He is a stockholder in the California Investment Company, and the R. N. Burgess Company, who have large realty holdings in Contra Costa County, and have recently promoted Mount Diablo Park, one of the most beautiful residence property sections in the Bay region.

RALPH H. WIGHT is numbered among the representative attorneys of Contra Costa County. He was born on November 29, 1887, on a ranch four miles from Pittsburg. His father was one of the large landowners of this section. Ralph H. Wight acquired his education in the Ambrose public school, after which he graduated from the Mount Diablo high school. He entered the University of California and graduated with the class of 1909, receiving the degree of B. L. He completed his law course and received the degree of Juris Doctor in 1911. He at once returned to Martinez, where he engaged in the general practice of law with gratifying success. Mr. Wight was united in marriage to Miss Marguerite F. Haskins on May 14, 1913. Politically, he is a Republican and served as city attorney in Concord for a period of four years. Mr. Wight has been further honored by being chosen president of the Martinez Chamber of Commerce in 1917. He was a member of the county and State Republican conventions in 1910. In 1914 he served as a member of the Republican State Convention, representing the senatorial district of Contra Costa and Marin counties. Mr. Wight is a man of unusual professional ability and has a wide circle of friends.

CHARLES N. WIGHT (deecased).—The opportunities that California offered to men of enterprise and sterling worth are nowhere better exemplified than in the successful career of Charles N. Wight, a pioneer of Contra Costa County. He was a native of Johnsonburg, Wyoming County, New York, and his birth occurred on August 5, 1833. He acquired a common-school education and at the age of thirteen he went with his brother Randolph H. to Delaware County, Iowa. In 1849 he returned to his birthplace, and after attending school for a short period he gave his attention to farming and dairying for eight months. In January, 1852, Charles N. and Randolph came to the Pacific Coast via Panama, arriving in San Francisco on February 26, of the same year. Mr. Wight at once took up mining on the Trinity River, remaining there for a short time. He then went to El Dorado County, where he followed the same vocation until the spring of 1853, when he removed to Contra Costa County, where he took up seven hundred acres of Government land four miles from New York Landing (now Pittsburg). He was united in marriage to Miss Sarah E. Huntington. a native of Maine, January 13, 1870. To this union there have been six children—Nellie, wife of Frank H. Turner, of Sierra County, and their one daughter, Sarah Gilberta, was born December 19, 1906; Martha Louisa, residing at home, was born April 19, 1875; Charles Huntington, born November 13, 1874, was united in marriage to May Violet Thomas, and their two daughters are Minnie E. and Carol Marjorie; Walter Wallace, born February 6, 1879, and was married to Arline L. Brooks, and their children are Theron Brooks, Charles Randolph, and Walter Wallace; Albert R. was born July 26, 1881, and was married to Maud E. Pettitt; their children are Verna Louise and Albert Charles; Ralph H., born November 29, 1887. Charles N. Wight, the subject of this review, died on April 17, 1913. His name will always be held in loving remembrance by all who knew him.

The present generation can learn much from the lives of such men as Charles N. and Randolph Wight. In politics Charles N. Wight was affiliated with the Republican party. He served as trustee of the Ambrose (then Bay Point) school for many years. He also served as roadmaster for a long period. He was a practical stockman and engaged in general farming. Randolph H. Wight was born August 18, 1827. Early in life he worked at farming. In 1847 he joined a train and came to this coast, locating in Oregon, taking eight months to make the trip. Randolph located in Corvallis, Oregon. In February, 1848, he started for San Francisco, and finally located at Sutter's Fort, two miles from Sacramento. The latter place was then called Embarcadero. Mr. Wight was one of the first to go to the mines after the discovery of gold was announced. He proceeded to Hangtown (Placerville), where he remained for nine months. New Year's Day, 1849, he went to San Francisco, where he took passage for home. He remained in the East until 1852, when the two brothers started for the Golden West. The Wight brothers' ranch originally consisted of six hundred and ninety acres. Randolph married Miss Orfa Durfee, of New York, January 28, 1858. To this union were born, Sarah E. (deceased), wife of L. M. La Selle, and Mary L., wife of S. A. Sellers. Randolph Wight is now living with his daughter, Mrs. Sellers, at their Berkeley home.

ABSALOM FRANCIS BRAY.—One of the most able, progressive, and enterprising young attorneys of Contra Costa County is Absalom Francis Bray. He was born January 21, 1889, in Butte, Montana. His education was acquired in the public schools of that city. He afterward entered the Military Academy at San Rafael, graduating with the class of 1906. He entered the law department at the University of California, graduating from that department in 1910. He began the practice of law in San Francisco and remained in that city until 1912, when he removed to Martinez. Politically, Mr. Bray is a Republican and stands high in the councils of his party. He is president of the Martinez Republican Club, secretary of the Contra Costa County Republican Club, and a member of the County Republican Central Committee. On March 1, 1917, he was appointed city attorney of Martinez.

Mr. Bray has always used his power and influence toward promoting the good of the city of Martinez and Contra Costa County. He was united in marriage on September 17, 1913, to Miss Leila Elizabeth Veale, a daughter of Sheriff R. R. Veale, one of Contra Costa's most prominent and distinguished citizens. Fraternally, he is affiliated with the Masonic lodge of Martinez. He is a member of the Sigma Chi, the Phi Delta Phi, and the Theta Nu Epsilon fraternities of the University of California. Mr. Bray's father, Absalom Francis, was a native of England. He came to America, settling first in Texas and later in Montana, where he was identified with the mercantile and wholesale interests of both States. He died in 1006. Mr. Bray's mother, Nelia (Copenharve) Bray, was a native of Indiana. The subject of this sketch deserves great credit for what he has accomplished along professional lines, and through his own energy and perseverance has worked his way upward to success and is now numbered among the representative men of the legal profession of the Bay counties.

GEORGE S. WALL.—This history presents the record of no other citizen more thoroughly imbued with the spirit of public progress than George S. Wall. He has ever been a man of fair judgment, broad-minded and sagacious, and is constantly working for the public welfare of Richmond and Contra Costa County. The Bay cities number him among their most representative, useful, and worthy citizens, to whose initiative spirit the city of Richmond owes much. He established the first permanent city hall in Richmond and many of the important industries. Several of the finest subdivisions placed on the market in Richmond are due to Mr. Wall's resolute energy and public spirit. He was born in Sonoma County, California, and is a son of Henry C. Wall, a native of North Carolina, and Julia (Sallec) Wall, the latter being a native of Wisconsin. Mr. Wall's father was a California pioneer, coming to the coast in 1849. He drove an ox-team overland, taking six months to make the journey, and settled in Sonoma County, where he acquired large holdings in land, and for a time was identified with mining.

The substantial progress and success made by Mr. Wall's father show what may be accomplished when determination and energy lead the way. He was largely identified with the stock-raising business of this State in the early days, and several land deeds that George S. Wall has in his possession bear the signature of President Grant. In the parents' family there were three children—Henry, who died in 1898 at the age of twenty-six years; Ella, wife of Ira Krotser, a contractor and builder of Santa Rosa, California; and the subject of this review. George S. Wall acquired his education in the public schools of Santa Rosa, after which he attended private school. He took up mechanical engineering, which he followed until 1902.

He has been associated with many large projects throughout the State, and his work and qualities have been widely recognized and have made him popular wherever he has gone. Mr. Wall's success in Richmond is only the natural result of earnest, persistent, and well-directed labor. He first served as manager of the

Richmond Land Company, one of the first subdivisions, consisting of four thousand seven hundred lots in the center of what is now Richmond. In 1909, he embarked in the real-estate business for himself, and organized the New Richmond Land Company, a million-dollar corporation. He has been one of the chief factors in making Richmond a manufacturing center. He was also largely instrumental in getting the Pullman Company to locate here. Other manufacturing concerns were induced to locate in Richmond through the efforts of Mr. Wall, among the most prominent of which are the General Roofing Manufacturing Company and the Pacific Sanitary Manufacturing Company. Mr. Wall distinguished himself with the people of Richmond when he presented to the city its first permanent city hall, the building and land being valued at sixty thousand dollars. Politically, Mr. Wall is affiliated with the Republican party, but he has never aspired to office. He has served as president of the Richmond Industrial Commission for five terms. Fraternally, Mr. Wall holds membership in the Masonic lodge. In 1898 he was united in marriage to Lena Blanche Slack, daughter of Darwin D. and Sarah E. Slack. She passed away on December 3, 1916. To this union there were two children— Thelma Gertrude, born January 26, 1904, died September 26, 1916, and Harold Chelsley, born February 17,1905. Mr. Wall belongs to the Transportation Club of San Francisco, and Mrs. Wall was an active member of the Eastern Star.

Mr. Wall has placed on the market several valuable tracts of land in Richmond and owing to their favorable position has had phenomenal success in disposing of his holdings. He promoted the City of Richmond tract, Wall's Addition to Richmond, Wall's Center Tract, and Wall's Second Addition to Richmond. In all the above tracts nine thousand lots have been put on the market. All his properties are superbly located, and so situated that they cannot but increase in value to a remarkable extent. Mr. Wall is a man of sterling traits of character, progressive in citizenship, and has gained the confidence, good-will, and esteem of all who have been in any way associated with him.

WILLIAM LINCOLN WHITE, of Alamo, one of the notable factors in the recent development of southern Contra Costa County, was born at East Aurora, New York, close to where Elbert Hubbard reared his famous Roycroft community. He took up the profession of chemistry and is today the sole owner of one of the largest drug stores in Michigan. Being an enthusiast in the National Guard of that State, Colonel White was commissioned a regimental commander, and during the Spanish-American War held that rank in command of Michigan volunteers. He is also prominent in life-insurance circles and was vice-president of the Federal Life Insurance Company of Chicago and director in the Niagara Life Insurance Company of Buffalo. It was in the furtherance of his insurance interests that Colonel White visited California, and while touring the State passed through the San Ramon Valley. He was so impressed with its attractions that four years ago he decided to make it his permanent home. He purchased the Benson ranch at Alamo, consisting of eight hundred and twelve acres, which is now known and famed as White-Hall Acres, one of the most hospitable homes in Contra Costa, over which Colonel White's charming wife reigns as chatelaine. The subject of this sketch is vice-president of the First National Bank at Walnut Creek, president of the Tassajara Land & Live-Stock Company, a corporation that farms seven thousand two hundred acres in Contra Costa County. He is a director in the Berkeley Thousand Oaks Realty Company, a commissioner of the famed Mount Diablo Park Club, one of the notable organizations of its character in the United States.

Colonel White is the owner of the Contra Costa Courier at Walnut Creek and the Danville Journal at Danville. Despite his multifarious business and professional interests, he always finds time to devote his energies to the promotion of Contra Costa County's interests.

H. W. BESSAC is the editor of the Brentwood News. The News was founded in 1914 by J. B. Dixon, who issued it for a period of one year. He was followed by J. J. McCulloch, who ran the paper eight months. McCulloch sold the News to Mr. Bessac on September 1, 1915. It is an eight page five column paper, and independent in politics. Mr. Bessac has been identified with country papers on this coast since 1883. He was the first foreman on the Tacoma News, and he was also the first foreman on the Tacoma Ledger when it became a daily. He is public-spirited, and his paper gives its indorsement to every movement inaugurated that will advance the interests of eastern Contra Costa County and Brentwood.

SEELEY JAMES BENNETT (deceased).—One of the representative and pioneer citizens of Contra Costa County that is worthy of recognition in this work is Seeley James Bennett. He was born in Delaware County, Ohio, October 9, 1833, son of Stephen R. and Susan (Gregory) Bennett. Mr. Bennett received a common-school education and assisted on his father's ranch until 1854. He then removed to Iowa and found employment with the Western Stage Company. Here he remained until February, 1859, when he decided to go to California. He went to New Orleans and sailed via the Gulf route, arriving in San Francisco the last day of March, 1859. He came directly to Contra Costa County. Here he found employment at different things until March, 1860, when he engaged in the livery business in Pacheco, and there remained until 1862, when he removed to Martinez. In 1861 Mr. Bennett started and operated the first stage line from Pacheco to the Mount Diablo coal mines. Later he sold this line and established a stage line from Martinez to the summit of Mount Diablo. Mr. Bennett was united in marriage to Miss Jane E. Hough, a native of Ohio. To this union there has been one son, Stephen E., born July 13, 1864. He died in 1906. Seeley J. Bennett's death occurred on May 14, 1905.

LAFAYETTE IRVING FISH—To a certain extent a record of the life of the late Lafayette Irving Fish is a history of the county of Contra Costa.

From the time he made his first investment in land here, during the fall of 1852, until his career ended, October 9, 1000, he was inseparably associated with many of the leading interests of the locality. After enduring the hardships attendant upon both an ocean voyage and an overland journey to California, after having shared with the gold-seekers their scanty fare, their hard beds in the lap of Mother Earth, and their life of toil, and after having experienced the vicissitudes of pioneer farming, it was his good fortune to reap the reward of his labors and to enjoy in the twilight of his useful existence all the comforts his industry and executive ability had rendered possible. During the colonial history of New England the Fish family bore an honorable part in commercial and military affairs, and Josiah Fish served during the Revolutionary War as a lieutenant under Captain William Hutchins. Lafayette Irving Fish was a grandson of this Revolutionary officer, and a son of Libbeus and Polly (Holcomb) Fish. He was born in Batavia, New York, October 7, 1824, and received a common-school education in his native town, later becoming a student in a seminary for boys at Jackson, Michigan, where his parents had settled. After two years in the seminary, he earned his livelihood as a clerk in a mercantile store owned by C. W. Penny. For two and a half years he remained with Mr. Penny, resigning in order to accept a similar position with his brother Charles in Monticello, Mississippi. However, not liking the South, his sojourn there was short, and he returned to his former employer. When news reached him of the discovery of gold in California, Mr. Fish determined to seek his fortune in the West. With this purpose he left home and friends on August 8, 1849, and proceeded to Mississippi, where he visited his brother.

From there he traveled via the Isthmus and the Pacific Ocean to San Francisco, where he arrived on January 8, 1850. In February he proceeded to Marysville and the mines. To engage in mining, a company was formed consisting of E. S. Rockwell, J. W. Fish, J. G. Scott, Albertus Scott, G. W. Brown, B. T. Graves, and L. I. Fish. With an ox-team, provisions, and other supplies, they left Marysville on June 25th, bound for Slate Creek. Before they had arrived at their destination they found that camp had been deserted for a new one on the Feather River. Leaving Josiah Fish to follow with the goods, the others joined the rush and located claims on Nelson Creek, a tributary of the South Fork of the Feather River. In addition to mining, the company opened a store, building a log cabin, which they were often forced to use as a hotel for the accommodation of passing miners.

Their guests were glad to pay for the privilege of sleeping on the bare earth (for the floor of the cabin was of dirt). While much is written and said concerning the high civilization of the present century, Mr. Fish often remarked that he never lived in any community where all men seemed as brothers, where each respected the other's rights, where robbery was unknown, and where all were governed by so high a code of honor as was displayed in this camp. Men were accustomed to leave their sacks of gold dust in their cabins, and no one ever molested them. Mr. Fish and Mr. Lathrop soon purchased the interests of their partners, afterwards buying an interest in the mercantile business of William and Jerry Ford at Marysville. In the fall of 1852 the two purchased a part of the Welch Rancho in Contra Costa County. Soon after this they formed a company to go East and buy sheep for the California market. In 1853 Mr. Fish and others went East and spent a year buying sheep and preparing a wagon-train for crossing the plains. The sheep were wintered at Vermont, Cooper County, Missouri. The journey was begun on May 2, 1853, with five thousand sheep, about eight ox-teams, a herd of cattle, and several saddle horses and mules.

They arrived in the Sacramento Valley, crossing the river about twenty miles below Shasta, in the latter part of October, 1854. At that time they had three thousand sheep, one hundred and forty cattle, twelve horses and mules, etc. The sheep had cost a dollar and a half apiece in the East and brought from seven to ten dollars each in California, so that the profits were large, notwithstanding the losses en route. In 1855 Mr. Fish and his partner divided their holdings, and the former then entered into partnership with his brother Charles, who had arrived here while he was in the East. In addition to engaging in farm pursuits, Mr. Fish engaged in warehousing, bought and sold grain, and had many other business interests. He was one of the first successful farmers of California and was one of the first to practice summer-fallowing, so common now. Desiring modern equipments with which to conduct his work, he sent East for improved farm machinery, and kept himself and his foreman busy in harvesting his own grain and that of others. In early days his principal product was wheat, and one year's crop sold for fifty-two thousand dollars. He raised and shipped the first wheat ever sent from San Francisco to New York as a business venture. While at times he met with reverses, such as will come to all, he was almost uniformly successful, his business sagacity enabling him to conduct his various interests in a profitable manner. Having considerable money to invest, and seeing an opening for a bank at Martinez, in 1873 Lafayette I. Fish, with the support of leading men of the county, established a financial institution, of which he was the first president, with William Hale as cashier and Henry Hale as teller. The directors of the bank were L. I. Fish, W. W. Cameron, William Hale, Henry Hale, and Simon Blum. With a capital of fifty thousand dollars, the bank embarked in business, but soon the capital stock was doubled, such was its success under the administration of Mr. Fish, who continued its executive head until his retirement, in July, 1890. At that time the holders valued their stock at two hundred per cent, and none was for sale even at that premium. The grain business was another industry that engaged the attention of Mr. Fish, who, in July of 1878, with Messrs. Baldwin and Simon Blum, began to buy and sell grain and established warehouses at various towns; from this business he retired in June, 1884. In 1858 Mr. Fish and his brothers fitted up a house and sent for their sisters, Caroline and Cornelia. The latter died in 1861, but Caroline and the elder brother, Josiah, remained in the family circle until their death in 1893. On March 31, 1881, Mr. Fish was married to Miss Frances Lillian Webster, a teacher in the State Normal School at San Jose, and daughter of Samuel Warren and Mary (Nichols) Webster, representatives of Colonial New England families. Two children were born of their union, one of whom was Irving Webster Fish, who was united in marriage in Honolulu to Miss Clare Bristol, of Berkeley, California, February 16, 1910; they reside in Mendocino County, where Mr. Fish has large landholdings, and is identified with the stock business in that county. The other child, Anne Holcomb Webster Fish, was married in Berkeley, July 20, 1909, to Robert Noble Burgess; they have two children, Robert Noble Burgess, Jr.. born May 13, 1910, and Frances Webster Burgess, born June 22, 1914.

JOHN C. ROUSE (deceased) was one of the pioneer and representative business men of eastern Contra Costa County. He was an important factor in the upbuilding of various enterprises in Antioch and the surrounding country. He was a man of energy and great executive ability. His birth occurred in Watertown, New York, June 20, 1828. He acquired a common school education, and early in life he was identified with the drug business.

On January 3, 1853, he started, via the Panama route, to cast his lot in the Golden State. He arrived in San Francisco on February 3, 1852. He engaged in mining in Calaveras County for a brief period, after which he mined in Tuolumne County for eight years. In April, 1861, Mr. Rouse came to Contra Costa County, where he became foreman of the Pittsburg Coal Mine at Somersville for about three years. His next venture was to engage in the hotel business at Somersville. He operated the Pittsburg Hotel for three years, when he again gave his attention to coal mining and worked the Central Mine for five years. In 1876, Mr. Rouse, in partnership with G. W. Hawxhurst, opened the Empire Mine, located at Judsonville. In 1877 Judson and Belshaw took an interest in the Empire Mine, and the company built and equipped a railroad from Antioch to the mine. In 1881 Mr. Rouse purchased the Central Mine and extended their railroad to the same, and Mr. Rouse became resident manager of the company, of the name of Belshaw & Co. He also was senior member of the firm of Rouse, Forman & Co., an extensive lumbering firm of Antioch. On February 21, 1872, Mr. Rouse was united in marriage to Miss Alice Nichols, a native of Watertown, New York State. To this union have been born two children—Charles Rouse, deceased, and Collins Nichol Rouse, a graduate of the University of California with the class of 1910. No man has given greater efforts or accomplished greater results for the business prestige of Antioch. His death occurred in Berkeley on November 16, 1907, and his wife passed away on May 27, 1012. At the time of Mr. Rouse's death he was president of the Bank of Antioch; he was also associated with the lumber and hardware business of Antioch. In 1005 Mr. Rouse moved to Berkeley, and for a number of years he had retired from active business.

JIERGEN CHRISTENSON (deceased).—In reviewing the lives of the settlers of Contra Costa County due mention should be made of the name of Jiergen Christenson, one of the most prominent and enterprising ranchers of the eastern section. He was a native of Denmark, born December 10, 1834. At the age of eighteen he came to America, arriving in New Orleans in January, 1853. A short time afterward he went to St. Louis, where he remained until 1858. Then he crossed the plains with ox-teams and came to San Francisco. Here he first found employment in a coffee and spice house with Charles Bernard, and by close application to business was made manager and conducted the business for sixteen years. About 1865 he settled on two hundred and fifty acres, and at one time he leased over seven hundred acres, in Marsh grant. While a resident of Utah, Mr. Christenson was united in marriage to Hanna Wallace on April 6, 1850, and she died on January 20, 1917. To this union there were twelve children, five of whom are now living. Thomas W. Christenson, a resident of Oakland, was born October 26, 1861. Hanna Wallace Christenson, wife of Joseph Sloan (deceased), was born January 12, 1863. Mr. and Mrs. Sloan had three children, Joseph, Jr., born November 6, 1885, and his children are Margery, born October 25, 1911, and Violet, born January 7, 1913; Violet Sloan, born June 8, 1894; Rosetta Sloan died at the age of two years. Charles Bernard Christenson was born April 3, 1869, and is now a resident of Taft, California; his children are Jiergen, born August 4, 1901, and Wallace, born September 8, 1902. James Henry Christenson was born January 3, 1888, and is engaged in the grocery business at Capitola, California; his son, Henry M., was born July 15, 1902. Florence A. Christenson was born January 27, 1881. Thomas W. Christenson, the eldest son, was united in marriage to Emma Brown, of San Francisco, in 1891; to this union was born Blanche, wife of A. Hudson, and Chrissie, who died at the age of fifteen years. Jiergen Christenson was a Republican in his political views. Fraternally, he was a member of the Independent Order of Odd Fellows. The land he bought Mr. Christenson improved in many ways. He erected a large and commodious residence, besides barns and other buildings, which were above the average in his locality. He was a man greatly beloved by all, and his death, which occurred on June 4, 1910, was deeply mourned, and his useful deeds perpetuated his memory.

ADRIAN H. SHAFER is distinguished not only for his able assistance in developing the horticultural resources of eastern Contra Costa County, but as a representative of one of the most prominent and honored pioneer families of this section of the county. Adrian H. Shafer is a man of energy, well-educated and well informed. He carries on fruit-growing in a systematic and scientific manner. Mr.

Shafer was born at Rio Vista, Solano County, June 3, 1862, and is a son of William and Elizabeth Shafer. His father was born in Everett, Bedford County, Pennsylvania, and was reared and educated in his native State. In 1851, at the age of twenty-one, he came to California via the Isthmus of Panama and located in Sacramento, where he engaged in freighting on the Sacramento River. Later he engaged in stock-raising on Andrews Island, making his home at Rio Vista. In 1867 he disposed of his land on the island and came to Contra Costa County and engaged in farming. He acquired much land in this section and set out a large part of it to almonds.

William Shafer, father of our subject, married Elizabeth Pierce, of Indiana. To this union were born five children—Adrian H., Hannah J., George H., Mabel, and Minnie. Adrian received his education in the Eden Plains school and business college. He followed bookkeeping in San Francisco for five years and in Los Angeles two years. He returned to the farm for a time and later removed to Oakland, where he became associated with the Paraffine Paint Company for five years. The past six years he has spent on the ranch, where he owns one hundred acres largely set out to almonds. He also rents a one-hundred-acre almond orchard from the Shafer estate. In politics Mr. Shafer gives his support to the Republican party. He has served on the Brentwood school board for six years and takes an active interest in educational matters. Adrian H. Shafer was twice married, the first union being to Julia Carroll, of New Jersey, in 1888, and her death occurred in 1903. To the first union were born Raymond A., a student in the manual training school of Wisconsin, and Helen, a high-school student in Brentwood. The second marriage occurred on November 1, 1905, to Abbie W. Call, a native of California. Fraternally, Mr. Shafer belongs to the I. O. O. F. lodge of Byron.

EDWARD T. MARTIN.—A man of great energy, intensity of purpose, and strong convictions, Edward T. Martin has taken an active interest in the county, although a resident of Contra Costa County for only a few years. He was born in Oakland, California, September 17, 1889, a son of James and Mary (Guckian) Martin. Both parents are natives of Ireland and came to this country with their parents when young. The parents of Mr. Martin were married in San Francisco. His father is one of Oakland's respected citizens and is engaged in the plumbing business. In the parents' family there were four children—James, Jr., Leo, Joseph, and the subject of this review, Edward T. Martin, who acquired his education in the public schools of Oakland, afterward attending St. Mary's College, graduating with the degree Bachelor of Arts. Mr. Martin did his duty at home, assisting his father by taking an active part in the business, and performing his work with efficiency. Later he took up the study of medicine and followed the drug business for some time, and in 1911 he became associated with the R. N. Burgess Company as bookkeeper in the San Francisco office. In 1913 he took the management of the Homestead Nursery for R. N. Burgess, with excellent results. Through his energetic and capable management this nursery has become one of the finest in California. Mr. Martin has acquired a wide reputation for skill in this line of work, having devoted a great deal of time to the study of foreign and domestic plants. Mr. Martin occupies a comfortable home on what was formerly the Rice ranch. The nursery occupies about six hundred acres, and here friends and the public receive a hospitable welcome.

Mr. Martin was united in marriage to Miss Mercedes G. Mendezabal, a native of Alameda County, April 22, 1914. To this union one child, Eleanor M., was born on

July 24, 1915. In politics Mr. Martin is a Republican. While he has never aspired to office, he has always taken a keen interest in all matters for the betterment of the county. He is a member of the Knights of Columbus, Oakland Council, and holds the rank of lieutenant in the League of the Cross Cadets. The family are members of the Catholic church.

NATHAN I. BALDWIN.—The opportunities offered by California to men of enterprise and sterling worth are nowhere better exemplified than in the successful career of Nathan I. Baldwin. He was born in Ogdensburg, New York, March 15, 1861, son of Frank B. and Elizabeth (Tallman) Baldwin. In the parents' family there were born four children. Nathan, the subject of this review, acquired a grammar-school education. In early life he started out for himself and followed various vocations, filling positions of importance and trust. In 1888 he decided to cast his lot with the Golden West and located in Fresno. He took the management of the fair grounds at Fresno and held this position for three years. He then became identified with the California & Hawaiian Sugar Company as farm superintendent. Here he remained for eight years. Coming to Contra Costa County, he became associated with the Cowell Portland Cement Company as lessee of the commissary department, which he has held for eleven years. Mr. Baldwin was twice married. The first marriage occurred in Morristown, New York, to Ada Bolton, in 1883. To this union was born one daughter, Helen, now the wife of W. E. McMullen, of Canton, New York. The second marriage occurred on July 23, 1909, to Ida Hudson, of Oakland, California. Two children have blessed this union—Margaret, born April 4, 1911, and Barbara, born January 8, 1913. In politics Mr. Baldwin supports the Republican party. Fraternally, he is a Mason, holding membership in Vallejo Naval Commandery. He is also a member of the B. P. O. E. of Vallejo. Mr. Baldwin is a member of the Cowell school board. He has one of the palatial homes of central Contra Costa County and has about eleven acres devoted to the finest varieties of walnuts, almonds, and grapes.

ROBERT HARROWER (deceased).—One of the representative pioneers of Contra Costa County, and one of the highly esteemed citizens of the county, was Robert Harrower, whose death occurred on December 12, 1916, at his home in Antioch. He was born in Dufferline, Scotland, in 1838. Here he received his education and grew to manhood. He worked in the mines, later becoming a seafaring man, and for seven years he visited many ports. Hearing about America in his travels, he came to San Francisco on July 4, 1868.

This ended his life as a sailor. He found employment in the quarries near San Francisco and Santa Cruz. In September following his arrival in San Francisco he was married to Christina Athie, a native of Scotland. He came to Black Diamond (now Pittsburg), where he found work in the mines. In 1871 he purchased what is known as the Harrower ranch south of Antioch and owned four hundred and eighty acres of land. Into the family there were born three children—Robert, Jr., Lizzie (married to Charles Richey, of Antioch, and to this union were born May, Stella, and John), Maggie (married to William Leishman, of San Francisco, and has three children, Hazel, Grace, and Elizabeth). Robert Harrower, Jr., was born on May 25, 1871 and resides on the home place and carries on general farming. He was educated in the Deer Valley and Empire schools, after which he attended business college in Stockton. Returning home he took an active part in the ranch management. He is a member of General Winn Parlor, N. S. G. W., the Masonic lodge of Brentwood, and the I. O. O. F. lodge of Antioch. In politics Mr. Harrower, like his father, has always been identified with the Republican party.

CHARLES H. HAYDEN, one of the men of Contra Costa County who, by reason of his personal integrity and ability, is recognized as one of the leading men of Martinez, was born in Calhoun County, Iowa, June 29, 1870. In 1896 he located in Martinez, where he became identified with E. Morgan in the hardware and plumbing store for a period of eight years. On July 10, 1905, he was appointed justice of the peace to fill out the unexpired term of David S. Carpenter, and Mr. Hayden has held the office since. In the last two terms he has had no opposition at the polls. Politically, he is a Republican, and he has done much toward increasing Republican prestige in the county and enjoys in full measure the confidence and respect of his fellowmen. Fraternally, Mr. Hayden is a member of the Knights of Pythias and the Woodmen of the World. He was united in marriage to Miss Lettie M. Cottrell, a native of Texas, December 28, 1808. To this union there have been three children—Hoyt H., born August 31, 1903; Hilda H., born May 25, 1907; and Ruth M., died in infancy. Mrs. Hayden is a member of the Pythian Sisters and the Women of Woodcraft and takes an active part in the social circles of Martinez.

FRED ALMOND.—The ability that Fred Almond has manifested in his agricultural operations in Contra Costa County has placed him among the representative farmers in his locality. Mr. Almond is a native of England and was born on July 26, 1869. He is a son of James and Hannah (Busfield) Almond, both natives of England. At the age of eight years Mr. Almond came to this country with his parents and located in Allegan, Michigan, where his father took up farming. Fred acquired his education in Allegan and assisted on the home place until he was nearly of age, when he went to Kalamazoo, Michigan, and worked in a hospital for nearly three years. In 1892 he came to San Francisco, where he worked for the City Railway Company for a period of seventeen years, and up to the time of the last strike, in 1907, at which time Mr. Almond left his employment with the road and never went back to take up his old position. In 1009 he removed to Contra Costa County and purchased, with his brother John, the Los Lomas ranch, which has been highly improved and set out largely to fruit and grapes. Mr. Almond was united in marriage to Lillie Westerberg, a native of San Francisco, June 10, 1896. To this union there have been six children—Irving W., born May 2, 1897; Lloyd J., born August 27, 1808; Frederick V., born May 24, 1908; Vernon W., born September 4, 1910; Ellis B., born June 30, 1912, and Hester Virginia, born February 21, 1914. Mrs. Almond's parents, Amanda and Frederick Westerberg, were among the early settlers in San Francisco. Her father owned and operated the schooner "Ringleader." Mr. and Mrs. Almond have recently erected a new home on a conspicuous spot having a fine view of the surrounding country.

URSA S. ABBOTT, M. D.—Among the prominent physicians of the Bay counties is Doctor Ursa S. Abbott, who for many years has practiced in Richmond with ever-increasing success. He is a native of Ohio, being born at Clearport on June 3, 1873. He is the son of Lafayette and Mary E. (Lysinger) Abbott. His father was a native of Vermont, and his mother a native of Pennsylvania. His father was a successful merchant and was numbered among the representative men of his locality. His death occurred in 1895, and Doctor Abbott's mother died in 1897. In the parents' family there were ten children, of whom seven are still living. Doctor Abbott, the seventh in order of birth, received his education in the public schools in Clearport, Ohio. He attended Heidelberg University at Tiffin, Ohio, for two years. He then entered the University of Michigan, at Ann Arbor, but owing to ill-health in his senior year was obliged to discontinue his studies there. In 1898 he entered the Ohio Medical University at Columbus, where he remained one year, spending the following year in Chicago, where he entered the College of Physicians and Surgeons. On account of failing health he was obliged to seek a different climate, and went to Denver, Colorado, where he entered the Gross Medical College. Later Doctor Abbott came to California and graduated from the College of Physicians and Surgeons in San Francisco in 1902. He received a position as physician on a German steamship, and sailed in December, 1902, for Hamburg, Germany. The trip covered seventeen thousand miles, calling at various ports in Central and South America, Cape Verde and Canary Islands, France, England, and Germany. Returning to New York, Doctor Abbott took a postgraduate course at the postgraduate school and hospital and was appointed as physician on the New York City Board of Health in 1903. Here he continued until the following fall, when he removed to Colorado, locating at Grand Junction, where he remained for a period of five years. In 1908 he returned to Richmond and began practicing his profession, forming a copartnership with Doctor C. L. Abbott in 1909. Doctors C. L. and U. S. Abbott are constantly in touch with the most advanced medical thoughts of their profession, and their personal characteristics have gained them the warm regard and friendships of many, while in professional lines they have attained that eminence which comes only in recognition of merit and ability. On September 7, 1904, Doctor U. S. Abbott was united in marriage to Miss Rose Carolyn Keller, of Lancaster, Ohio, daughter of John B. and Elizabeth (Hartman) Keller, both natives of Germany. In his political views Doctor U. S. Abbott is an ardent Republican.

He holds membership in the Knights of Pythias, Woodmen of the World, the Elks, and is a Royal Arch Mason. He is medical examiner for the Woodmen of the World, the New York Life Insurance Company, and various other insurance companies. He served as president of the Contra Costa Medical Society in 1914-15. He is a member of the Phi Chi Fraternity of Ann Arbor, Michigan, and the Union League Club of San Francisco. Doctors C. L. Abbott and U. S. Abbott are local surgeons for the Santa Fe Railroad, the Pullman shops, the Atlas & Giant Powder Company, and are also on the medical staff of surgeons for the Standard Oil Company. They have just completed and moved into the Abbott Building, 912 Macdonald Avenue, Richmond, one of the most modern buildings in the city. Mrs. U. S. Abbott is prominently identified with the social affairs of Richmond and has served on the Woman's Board of the Panama-Pacific Exposition. She is now actively engaged in the work of the Red Cross.

LOUIS N. BUTTNER (deceased).—Although several years have elapsed since Louis N. Buttner passed from the scenes of his activities, his memory is still green in the hearts of his family and friends. Mr. Buttner was born in Sunol, Alameda County, January 20, 1867. He was the son of George and Elizabeth Buttner, who were among the pioneer settlers in Alameda County.

Louis N. Buttner acquired his education in the public schools of Alameda County. Early in life he became associated with the Southern Pacific Company at Port Costa. He remained with this company for a period of fifteen years. He was then appointed to fill out the unexpired term as county treasurer of George Wiley, and at the following general election he was elected to that office. He continued in office seven years, still holding at the time of his death, which occurred June 27, 1913. Mr. Buttner gave his political support to the Republican party. He served on the education board of the Crockett high school, and on the Port Costa grammar-school board. Fraternally, Mr. Buttner held membership in the Masonic lodge of Martinez, and for two terms he served as master of his lodge. He is also a Knight Templar. On August 2, 1887, he married Miss Mary Hendry, of San Francisco, daughter of William and Margaret Hendry. Mrs. Buttner's father was a native of Scotland and came direct to California in 1851 via the Isthmus route and settled in San Francisco. Her mother came to this State in 1854 and located in San Francisco. Mr. and Mrs. Buttner have had three children—Harold, born at Port Costa on November 3, 1894, graduate of the University of California, taking an electrical engineering course; Edgar, born in San Francisco on August 17, 1899; Ethel, died in infancy.

JAMES N. LONG.—One of the most progressive and enterprising men of Richmond is James N. Long. He is recognized as a far-sighted and resourceful man in his locality. He was born in San Francisco on May 7, 1883.

His parents are Frank W. and Katherine Long. His father is a native of Sonoma County, California, and his grandfather came from Missouri to California in the early days. The father of James N. Long was for many years one of the leading contractors in the Napa Valley. He is now retired. His mother is still living. The parents of Mr. Long had three children—Doretta, wife of J. L Hohn, of Napa; Edna, residing with her parents, and the subject of this review. James N. acquired his education in the public schools of Vallejo, after which he learned the plaster trade. This vocation he has followed all his life. He is trustworthy and always to be relied upon to fulfill any contract to the letter; therefore, he enjoys a high reputation, which has secured him many important contracts. On December 16, 1906, Mr. Long was united in marriage to Miss Della A. Johnson, daughter of M. A. Johnson, of Sonoma, one of the respected pioneers of his locality. Politically, Mr. Long is a Republican, and has been active along party lines. He served as a member of the Richmond educational board for a number of years. He is interested in the growth and prosperity of Richmond and the whole county and is ever ready to bear his share in promoting advancement and development. Mr. Long is prominent in the Masonic order, holding membership in the Richmond lodge and chapter. He is a member of the I. O. O. F., Modern Woodmen, Eastern Star, and other orders. About eight years ago Mr. Long removed to Richmond. In matters of citizenship he is intensely loyal and public-spirited and gives his indorsement to every movement that will advance the municipality or promote the welfare of the community along the various lines of human activity.

ZEB. KNOTT, one of the representative business men of Richmond, was born in Knoxville, Tennessee, October 9, 1878. He acquired his education in the schools of Knoxville, after which he learned the painting and decorating trade. He has always been identified with this business and has worked in many important cities. He came to Richmond, Contra Costa County, in 1910.

He has had many important contracts, among which was the contract for the Pullman shops from R. & S. Solitt Company. In 1013 Mr. Knott established his present store, and carries a complete line of wall-paper, paints, etc. He was married to Amanda Fellwock, a native of Illinois, in 1007. Mr. Knott was chosen by the people of Contra Costa County to represent them as supervisor in 1914 for the four-year term. He is a progressive and enterprising business man and gives his support to any movement for the betterment of conditions in Richmond and Contra Costa County.

MANUEL J. PIMENTEL, one of the representative men of eastern Contra Costa County, was born in Portugal on March 17, 1868. He acquired his education in the schools of his native land, and at the age of sixteen he came to America. He located in Fresno, where he readily found employment. Later he removed to Madera, where he engaged with a sheepman for a period of one year. He then bought sheep and has always been engaged in this business. He was identified with this business in Contra Costa County, while he was a resident of Madera for some years. Mr. Pimentel was married to Mary Lawrence, and her death occurred in 1904. His second marriage was to Anna Ramos, of Santa Rosa, California. To this union was born one daughter, Josephine E. Mr. Pimentel gives his political support to the Republican party. Fraternally, he is a member of the I. D. E. S. and the U. P. E. C. He deals extensively in sheep and is one of the prominent men of Byron.

WILLIAM A. HALE.—A native-born citizen of Contra Costa County, and a son of a pioneer of prominence, William A. Hale, cashier of the Bank of Martinez, has taken a great interest in the welfare of the county in which he was born, and especially in Martinez. He has been actively identified with the promotion of its industrial and business growth, and as a man of ability and energy he is highly esteemed. Mr. Hale was born in Pacheco in this county. His father, William Morrell Hale, was a native of Ohio, and came to California and located in Placerville, later removing to Pacheco, where he and his brother Henry engaged in mercantile business for many years. William A. Hale, the subject of this review, was born on December 31, 1864. He received his education in the public schools of this county, after which, in 1883, he became associated with the Bank of Martinez. In 1899 Mr. Hale was made cashier, which office he has filled continuously since. He gives his political support to the Republican party. He has served as trustee of Martinez for some twelve years and was chairman of the board. Mr. Hale was married to Miss Jennie Ipswitch, a native of San Francisco, October 12, 1887. They have two children—William Morrell, born June 27, 1893, and Ida May, born October 27, 1891, the wife of E. C. Livingston, of Los Angeles.

Fraternally, Mr. Hale is very prominent in the Masonic fraternity and has done much to promote the good of the order. He is a member of Martinez Lodge, F. & A. M., Martinez Chapter, R. A. M., a Knight Templar, and a member of the Eastern Star. Mr. Hale is popular with his business associates and has the good-will of all who know him.

WILLIAM MORRELL HALE (deceased).—Among the influential men of Contra Costa County who occupied a position of prominence was William Morrell Hale. He was born on September 20, 1831, at Milford, Union County, Ohio. His father was a farmer and settled in that locality in the very early days and assisted in settling the country. William M. Hale was reared on a farm, receiving a common-school education, after which he attended an academy for boys. Finishing his schooling, he worked at the mercantile business in Columbus, Ohio, and in 1853 he came to California and located in Placerville, where he was prominently identified with the business interests of that flourishing town during the boom days. Mr. Hale and N. C. Fasset operated a mercantile store for some time, when they removed to Pacheco in 1858 and opened a store here under the firm name of Hale & Fasset. Later Mr. Fasset resigned from the business and Henry M. Hale, a brother of William M., came on from Ohio, secured an interest in the business, and the firm then became Hale Brothers. They were potent factors in the upbuilding and promotion of Pacheco. Hale Brothers started a bank at Pacheco, which was operated in connection with the general mercantile store for a long time. Eventually they disposed of their holdings and removed to Martinez, and in connection with Lafayette I. and Charles Fish and others, started the Bank of Martinez, William M. Hale becoming cashier. Mr. Hale was married to Mary Lyon, a native of Detroit, Michigan, in 1863. She was reared in Illinois. There were four children to this union, two of whom died in infancy.

Ida May died at the age of nineteen, and William A. succeeded his father in the bank as cashier. In politics William M. Hale was a Republican, but never aspired to public office. He served as chairman of the Republican Central Committee at different times and was a school trustee many years in Martinez. His death occurred on August 20, 1883, and his brother Henry died on January 6, 1809. Hale Brothers were men of unswerving integrity and of high general standing in Contra Costa County, and their noble aims in life secured the confidence and respect of all who knew them.

CHARLES G. YONCE, identified with the business interests of Richmond, California, is a native of eastern Tennessee. He was born on October 16, 1879, son of Calvin and Mary M. (Jackson) Yonce. Mr. Yonce's mother is a great-granddaughter of General Jackson of the Confederate Army. Three children have been born in Mr. Yonce parents' family—Nora, Eugenia, and Charles G. The subject of this review acquired his schooling in Kings College, Bristol, Tennessee, while his sisters received their education at Sullins College in the same town. Completing his education, Charles G. Yonce enlisted in the Spanish-American War and went to Cuba, where he remained one year. He was with the Fourth Tennessee regulars and served on detached duty. He received his discharge at Savannah, Georgia, in 1800. He then removed to Richmond, Virginia, where he became identified with the gentlemen's furnishing business. He went to Pittsburg, Pennsylvania, Houston, Texas, and Washington, D. C. In the latter city he remained eight years and was associated with the same business. Mr. Yonce came to Oakland, California, where he spent nearly two years, when he then settled in Richmond, Contra Costa County. He purchased the clothing and gentlemen's furnishing goods store of Linville Brothers, near Sixth Street, in 1012. He moved into his present commodious store on May 22, 1013. Fraternally, Mr. Yonce is a member of the B. P. O. E., the Moose, the Knights of Pythias, the Modern Woodmen, the Yeomen, and the Red Men. He is also a member of the Spanish-American War Veterans. On November 8, 1009, he was united in marriage to Miss Elizabeth Gertrude Culp, of Washington, D. C. Mrs. Yonce is a daughter of John and Catherine Culp. Her father for many years had charge of the gun-carriage shop at the Washington Navy Yard. His death occurred in April, 1914. Her mother resides in Washington. Mrs. Yonce takes an active part in the social duties of Richmond.

MADISON RALPH JONES.—Characterized by the same energetic activity, mental vigor, and business foresight that distinguished his father, Madison Ralph Jones, holds a high position among the leading attorneys of San Francisco and the Bay counties. He was born in Martinez, California, December 15, 1872, the son of Hon. Joseph P. Jones, who was a native of Owen County, Indiana, and was born on January 27, 1844. When he was nine years of age his parents removed to Marion County, Oregon, where he attended the public schools and afterwards entered the Willamette University at Salem, graduating in 1864. In 1865 he returned to his native State and attended the State University at Bloomington, where he graduated from the law department in 1867. Returning to Oregon, he remained for a time, and then located in the mining section of northern California, where he resided until December, 1869. In that year he came to Martinez and entered upon the practice of his profession and achieved success. He was appointed deputy district attorney under H. Mills, and continued in this office until the fall of 1875, when he was nominated and elected on the Republican ticket to the office of district attorney, which office he held until March, 1878. In the fall of 1880 he was elected to the Assembly and served at the general and extra sessions of the legislature, being a member of the judiciary committee, as well as chairman of the committee on federal relations. Mr. Jones practiced his profession in Martinez with H. Mills under the firm name of Mills & Jones for a long period. Mr. Jones was elected by the people of Contra Costa County to represent them as superior judge, and he served in this capacity for thirteen years. His death occurred in January, 1900. Madison Ralph Jones, the subject of this review, acquired his education in the public and high schools, after which he attended the University of California, graduating in 1895, receiving the degree of A. B. He graduated from the Columbian Law School, Washington, D. C., with the degree of B. L. L. in 1897. In 1900 he returned to Martinez and practiced law until he removed to San Francisco, when he entered the law firm of Titus, Creed, Jones & Dall. Mr. Jones served as a member of the State legislature in 1911. He was married to Carolyn L. Oliver, of Oakland, February 12, 1908. To this union have been born Madison Ralph, Jr., Oliver Randolph, and Carleton Letts. Politically, Mr. Jones adheres to the principles advocated in the platform of the Republican party.

HON. WARREN BROWN (deceased) was born in Morgan County, Illinois, June 19, 1826. His parents removed to Platte County, Missouri, where he received his education. Mr. Brown, with his father, the Hon. Elam Brown, started from Missouri for California in the latter part of April, 1846. Elam Brown was appointed captain of the train, and all went well en route until the north fork of the Platte River was reached, when typhoid fever broke out and Warren Brown was stricken. He was taken to Fort Bridger, where he was compelled to remain, while the train proceeded. Mr. Brown's recovery was slow, but his health was restored, and he took his departure from the fort on October 12th and arrived in Portland on December 9, 1846. Here Mr. Brown engaged in the cooperage business until September of the following year, when he joined his father in the San Antonio redwoods, where he remained until June, 1848. On the discovery of gold Mr. Brown was one of the first to go to the mines. After mining successfully on the American River, he returned to Contra Costa County and, with his brother, the Hon. T. A. Brown, and N. B. Smith, opened a general merchandise store in Martinez. In 1850 Warren Brown was elected county surveyor. He resigned in 1853, and in 1854 he was elected to the State

Assembly. In 1869 he was elected sheriff and served until 1871. For four years he farmed near Martinez, and then purchased five hundred and fifty acres adjoining his father's place at Lafayette. The Hon. Warren Brown was married to Laura A. Hastings, a native of Ohio, October 16, 1854, and her death occurred April 9, 1914. Warren Brown's death occurred on May 14, 1889.

HENRY TOLER BROWN.—One of the representative and highly respected citizens of Lafayette is Henry T. Brown. His birth occurred on July 3, 1859, in Los Angeles, California. He acquired his education in the public schools of Contra Costa County, after which he graduated from the Pacific Business College in San Francisco. Early in life Mr. Brown learned the printer's trade and followed this vocation for about three years. He then returned to Lafayette, where he took up ranching. After remaining in Lafayette for some time, he removed to Berkeley, where he resided for two years, while his son attended the university. Aside from the brief stay in Berkeley, Mr. Brown has always been identified with agricultural pursuits. He has one of the prettiest home places in Lafayette and has about five hundred acres of choice land. Mr. Brown was united in marriage on December 18, 1879, to Miss Annie Willebrands, of Oakland, a daughter of J. H. and Margaret Willebrands. Four children have blessed this union—Laura Estella, born September 3, 1880, wife of J. H. Mulliken; Lloyd Lansford, born July 29, 1886, died July 19, 1914; Chester Warren, born September 28, 1889, died October 17, 1900; and Sybil Erminia, born May 4, 1893. During his long term of residence in Contra Costa County Mr. Brown has witnessed the growth and development of his section with pride, and in many ways he has assisted in advancing the interests of his immediate locality. In his political convictions Mr. Brown is a staunch Republican. For several years he has served as school trustee, always taking a deep interest in educational affairs.

ALBERT LITTLE BANCROFT.—When our country was still in the colonial period of its existence the Bancroft family became identified with its history and bore an honorable part. During the Revolutionary period Mr. Bancroft's ancestor on his mother's side was a Colonial governor. Albert L. Bancroft was born in Granville, Ohio, May 15, 1841, son of A. A. and Lucy (Howe) Bancroft. Mr. Bancroft's father was identified with the Government as Indian agent in Washington for some years. After attending the schools of Ohio, at the age of eighteen, Albert L. Bancroft decided to cast his lot with the Golden State and came to California via the Isthmus route.

At an early age he engaged in the book-publishing business with his brother, H. H. Bancroft, and for many years operated the largest book-store and publishing concern on the Pacific Coast. On the retirement of H. H. Bancroft, Albert L. Bancroft continued in the business, under the firm name of A. L. Bancroft & Company, and while he maintained his office in the city, and also gave his personal attention to that business, he purchased one hundred and eighty-three acres of the choicest land in the Ygnacio Valley, and Mrs. Bancroft took charge of all agricultural and horticultural developments. Mr. and Mrs. Bancroft added to their holdings in the valley until they had six hundred acres. With a wise judgment that would have done credit to an experienced man, Mrs. Bancroft took the management of the ranch, superintended its cultivation, gathered in its harvest, and carefully looked after all details. The A. L. Bancroft place was the second commercial orchard in the Ygnacio Valley. It has been set out to the choicest varieties of pears, peaches, apricots, French prunes, and almonds. The value of the property is enhanced by substantial buildings, and through the energetic and capable management of Mrs. Bancroft this orchard became one of the best in Contra Costa County. Mrs. Bancroft has acquired a wide reputation for her skill along horticultural lines. When Mr. and Mrs. Bancroft took up their residence here they had the land cleared of a great many handsome oak trees, although about two hundred have been left for shade.

While Albert L. Bancroft led a busy life, he never neglected his duty as a citizen, but was always ready to assist in the promotion of worthy projects. When the Bohemian Club was formed he was one of its first members and was also a member of and at one time president of the Olympic Club. He was a life member of the Institute of Art and a member of many organizations. He did much good and contributed freely toward charitable works and educated many boys and girls so they secured profitable positions in life. On January 11, 1866, Albert L. Bancroft was married to Miss Fannie A. Watts, a native of Indiana, and a daughter of John S. and Elizabeth Ann (Howe) Watts. To Mr. and Mrs. Bancroft have been born five children— Bert H., Frank W., Alberta (wife of J. S. Reid, deceased), Sarah (wife of Donald H. Fry, residing in southern California), and John S., now in the East. Bert H. Bancroft was manager of Aloha Farm for many years. He planned and carried through successfully the first irrigating system used in this part of the county. Mrs. Bancroft has been a member of the Daughters of the American Revolution for many years and served as regent of Sequoia Chapter and later filled the chair in the California Chapter. She is a member of the Century Club of San Francisco and was elected an honorary member of the State Board of Trade. She served as honorary vice-president to represent Contra Costa County at the Panama-Pacific Exposition. She has traveled extensively, making her home in Europe three years. She crossed the Atlantic eight times and during the winter of 1016 visited in Honolulu.

Mrs. Bancroft's son, Frank W. Bancroft, was identified with the faculty of the Rockefeller Institute of New York City, and resigned to take charge of his mother's interests. "Aloha Farm," as Mrs. Bancroft's estate is known, is ideally located and is unexcelled for fruit-growing. Twenty-two thousand boxes of fruit was shipped during the season of 1916, and a dam has been built that will irrigate about five hundred acres of land, with a capacity of 653.445 cubic feet. Bancroft Station is situated on the property, and a modern packing-house was erected during 1917. Albert L. Bancroft passed away October 14, 1914. He was an upright and generous man, contributing to worthy causes, and his death was mourned by all who knew him.

ELY I. HUTCHINSON, a pioneer rancher and orchardist, holds a prominent place among the most representative citizens of Contra Costa County. He was born in Kenosha, Wisconsin, August 22, 1847, son of Champion I. and Catherine L. (Hatch) Hutchinson. His father was a native of Connecticut, and his mother was from Virginia. Mr. Hutchinson acquired his earliest education in the public schools of Sacramento, after which he attended the old College of California, in Oakland, the predecessor of the University of California. Afterward he attended Yale College, graduating with the class of 1869. He was admitted to the bar of California in 1873, and began the practice of law in San Francisco, in which he continued for ten years. Mr. Hutchinson before coming to Contra Costa County resided in Sacramento, in Yolo County, near where Davis now stands, and in San Francisco. He gave up the practice of law and moved to Ygnacio Valley, where he purchased six hundred acres of the Munson Gregory ranch. This property is now one of the most valuable in Contra Costa County and is set out largely to apricots and walnuts. Mr. Hutchinson might fairly be termed the pioneer in walnut-growing extensively, by grafting foreign varieties on the California black walnut trees. He was united in marriage in 1885 to Helen J. Woodward, a daughter of Robert B. Woodward, a well-known pioneer, and the founder of the once celebrated Woodward's Gardens of San Francisco. To Mr. and Mrs. Hutchinson have been born three daughters—Ruth, now the wife of Martin W. Joost, of Martinez; and Catherine and Mary, residing at home. Fraternally, Mr. Hutchinson is a Mason, being a member of lodge, chapter, and commandery of San Francisco. He is past master of Oriental Lodge, F. & A. M., and also an honorary member of the I. D. E. S. and the U. P. E. C., Portuguese societies. Mr. Hutchinson's father was several times mayor of Sacramento, president of the State Agricultural Society in the fifties, and a leading organizer of the first company to make beet sugar in California.

DANIEL W. McLAUGHLIN (deceased) was one of the representative business men of Contra Costa County. He was one of the foremost in Richmond's activities along real-estate lines. He was both forceful and resourceful, recognized possibilities and utilized them, and he planned big things and accomplished them. He was born in Dubuque County, Iowa, June 27, 1867. He acquired his education in the public schools of his native State. He attended college and taught school in Dakota during the territorial days. He rode the plains and lived among the Indians. In 1888 he removed to California and located in Berkeley, where he was identified with the planning mill business for a period of eight years. He then became actively engaged in the life-insurance business and traveled extensively for six years. Mr. McLaughlin's wide acquaintance and experience among all classes of people gave him exceptional opportunities. He embarked in the real-estate business in Berkeley for a time. In 1907 he saw the possibilities of Richmond and removed there, confining his interests to this locality largely. He became one of the most progressive men of that city, controlling large and important interests. He was vice-president and manager of the East Richmond Heights Land Company, which controls five hundred acres in five tracts. He was also identified with the Richmond Boiler & Machine Works. Politically, he was affiliated with the Republican party. He served on the Berkeley library board for several years. Fraternally, Mr. McLaughlin was a member of the B. P. O. E. of Berkeley, and the I. O. O. F. He was united in marriage to Miss Katherine Maloney on December 28, 1893. To this union were born four children—Margaret, Nell, Daniel, and Linwood. Mr. McLaughlin was ever enlisting his powers and abilities in the support of any movements that made for the betterment of conditions in Richmond.

THOMAS B. SWIFT.—No greater evidence of popularity or eminent fitness for the important responsibility is required of Thomas B. Swift than the fact that he is successfully filling the position of superintendent of the Mountain Copper Company at Martinez. He was born on April 29, 1872, at St. Louis, Missouri, son of Benjamin S. and Carrie A. Swift, both parents being natives of Maine. Thomas B. Swift received his education in the New York public schools, the College of the City of New York, and graduated from the chemical department of the New York City night school. He became identified with the chemical and metallurgical laboratories of New York City for three years. He then became connected with the Mountain Copper Company, of Elizabeth, New Jersey, for a period of ten years. In 1906 Mr. Swift came to Martinez, where he holds the position as superintendent of his concern. He was married on February 1, 1896, to Miss Nellie B. Smith, of New York City, and their three children are Thomas Brewster, Margaret B., and Eleanor C. Mr. Swift has served as clerk of the Martinez grammar-school board for a period of four years, and he has also served on the grand jury in Contra Costa County during 1916-17. Fraternally, he is affiliated with the Masonic lodge of Martinez and is master of his lodge. He is a broad-minded and public-spirited man and has won success and is liked by his fellow-man.

EDWARD B. SMALLWOOD—The name which heads this review is one of Richmond's representative business men and is well known throughout Contra Costa County. He was born in Missouri on December 20, 1856, and acquired his education in the University of Missouri, at Columbia. In 1876 Mr. Smallwood came west, locating in Santa Rosa, and there learned the undertaking trade. He remained in that town five years, and then removed to Oakdale, California, where he engaged in the undertaking business until 1891, when he went to Los Banos, where he was identified with the business for ten years. In 1004 Mr. Smallwood located in Richmond, engaging in the furniture and undertaking business. Afterward he disposed of the furniture business to L. H. Schrader and continued in the undertaking business exclusively. In politics Mr. Smallwood is a Republican. Fraternally, he is a member of the Masons, the B. P. O. E., the Red Men, the Moose, the Druids, and the I. O. O. F. Mr. Smallwood was married to Nellie Ingalls, of Iowa, and to this union was born one son, Walter.

ALVARADO J. SOTO (deceased) is remembered throughout Contra Costa County as a representative of the best type of citizenship. His name is widely known and carries with it an influence and power toward the betterment of the community in which he lived. Alvarado J. Soto was a son of the late Silverio I. C. Soto. The pioneer history of California is replete with interesting experiences of many of her first citizens. Prominent among them was the Soto family, well known throughout the State. The grandfather of A. J. Soto served as secretary to Governor Arguello under the Spanish regime.

His grandmother was a Pacheco. Mr. Soto's father, Silverio I. C. Soto, was born in Santa Clara County in 1831, and came to this county in 1855. The subject of this review was born near Concord on April 10, 1858, and he was prominently identified with the development of this section. Mr. Soto served as deputy county auditor in 1880 and 1882, and was elected to that office in 1882, and afterward re-elected many times. He served as district attorney for some years and served as special inheritance-tax appraiser for three years. Mr. Soto was married to Miss Minnie O'Neil, a native of Solano County, and to this union have been born Hazel, wife of William Dockstadter, of Martinez; Adele, wife of William R. Selby, of Richmond; and Earl Soto. Fraternally, Mr. Soto was a member of the Native Sons, the B. P. O. E. and the W. O. W. Before the funeral the Bar Association of Contra Costa County met and adopted resolutions of respect to the memory of Mr. Soto. The resolutions are as follows: Resolved, That in the death of A. J. Soto we have lost a beloved friend and brother, endeared to us not only by his simple, frank and pacific temperament, his consideration for others, his genial humor, his sweet voice, so often heard in song on occasions festive as well as sad, his generosity and manliness of character, his freedom from narrow and sordid views, but also by his simple manner; by his stern sense of right; his high standard of honor; lofty citizenship; his clear intellect; his appreciation of the good, the noble and true, his love for the hills, the trees, the flowers, and the beautiful in nature, his enlarged and liberal views; his love of family, fondness for home, fidelity to friends and loyalty to and love of country.

Resolved, That as a lawyer our deceased brother was eminent in the high standard of integrity he always maintained; his devotion to his clients' cause, his clear and logical perception coupled with a nice sense of professional honor.

Resolved, That we deeply deplore his loss, and shall long cherish his memory as that of a beloved friend and brother to whom we are bound by no ordinary ties of affectionate respect, Resolved, That the President of the Bar Association of Contra Costa County, request that a copy of these resolutions be spread upon the minutes of this Court and that a copy thereof be suitably engrossed and delivered to the family of the deceased with an assurance of our sincere sympathy in their great bereavement, and that this Court be requested to now adjourn in deep respect to his memory. Committee: J. E. Rodgers, R. L. Bover, Ralph H. Wight.

GABRIEL MEYER.—To Gabriel Meyer belongs the title of self-made man, for, starting in life without experience and resources, he has through his own energy and initiative risen to be one of the leading merchants and business men of Antioch. He was born in France on March 16, 1859. His parents died when he was very young, and he received a very limited education. When old enough he entered his uncle's store in his native town in France. At an early age he came to this country and worked for a relative in Ulster County, New York. He came to Contra Costa County in 1879 and started to work for his brother Leopold, who died in 1913. In 1882 the brothers formed a copartnership, and the management of the store was given to Gabriel Meyer.

Mr. Meyer served the town of Antioch as treasurer for many years, his term expiring in 1904. Fraternally he is affiliated with the I. O. O. F. of Antioch and holds membership in the Encampment. Mr. Meyer was united in marriage on March 10, 1898, to Miss Mildred A. Wolf, a native of San Francisco, and a daughter of S. Wolf. Their daughter, Annette, was born on April 24, 1899. Mr. Meyer erected one of the first general merchandise stores in Antioch. He deserves great credit for what he has accomplished in a business way, for he started out in life empty-handed, and through his own energy and perseverance has worked his way upward to success. He is a stockholder in the Bank of Antioch and in the Delta Dredging Company.

HON. THOMAS D. JOHNSTON.—Standing high among the keen, enterprising, and progressive attorneys of Contra Costa County and the Bay region is Thomas D. Johnston, the present district attorney of this county.

He possesses rare ability and holds a high rank among the professional men of this section. He was born in Kirksville, Missouri, November 7, 1877, son of John W. and Laura (Bell) Johnston. In the parents' family there were three children. Thomas D., the subject of this review, acquired a grammar school education in his native State. He received a teacher's certificate and taught school for a period of five years in Mendocino County, where his parents moved in May, 1895. Mr. Johnston's father afterward removed to Sacramento and practiced law, and was associated with Grove L. Johnson, the father of ex-Governor Hiram Johnson, the law firm being Johnson & Johnston. His father still resides in Sacramento and is a man of ability, standing high among the attorneys in the Capital City. Thomas D. Johnston while teaching school studied law and was admitted to the bar of California in December 1901. He began practice in Fort Bragg, Mendocino County, and served as city attorney of that town for a period of four years. In 1906 Mr. Johnston removed to San Francisco, where he remained for a time, and on June 10, 1907, he located in Richmond, Contra Costa County, and began to practice his profession. On April 21, 1908, he was appointed police judge of Richmond, and during his term, in the fall of 1908, he was elected to the State legislature. In December, 1908, he resigned the office of police judge to take up his duties in Sacramento. During 1909-10 he was in the State legislature, and in 1911 he served as chief deputy under Hon. A. B. McKenzie, then district attorney. After serving in this capacity for one year, Mr. Johnston resigned and engaged in practicing law. In the fall of 1912 he was a candidate for the legislature, and was elected, serving during the sessions of 1913-14. In the fall of 1914 Mr. Johnston was elected by the people of Contra Costa County to the office of district attorney for a period of four years and took office on January 1, 1915. This office he has filled with marked ability and judgment. Mr. Johnston was married on June 7, 1903, to Adah Elizabeth Wilson, a native of Mendocino County, and a daughter of William and Mary (Reardon) Wilson. Their children are Thomas Donald, born April 14, 1904; William Reardon, born November 8, 1007; and Richard Curtis, born May 10, 1914. Fraternally, Mr. Johnston is a member and past officer in the I. O. O. F. and Encampment. He holds membership in the Eagles lodge of Richmond, the B. P. O. E. of Richmond, the Moose of Martinez, and was past sachem of the Improved Order of Red Men—Santana Tribe No. 60, of Fort Bragg. Mr. Johnston has been especially active in the good-roads movement in this county, is a broad-minded, public-spirited citizen, and is one of the representative men of Contra Costa County.

GEORGE E. NETHERTON (deceased) was one of the representative ranchers who resided near Martinez. He was a son of John S. Netherton, one of the respected pioneers of eastern Contra Costa County, who now resides at Santa Cruz, California. George E. Netherton attended the Excelsior School, near Byron, and afterward went through business college. He assisted on the home place, and was married on July 31, 1895, to Clara Hoffman, a daughter of William Hoffman, who died in 1891. Mr. Hoffman for many years operated a tannery on his farm near Martinez, this being the only tannery in Contra Costa County. Mr. Hoffman started a tannery in Alameda County in 1853. From there he went to Sacramento and worked at his trade until the spring of 1856, when he came to this county. He had eighty acres and did general farming, besides having about three thousand vines of choice grapes and many varieties of fruit. Mr. Hoffman was born in Prussia in 1821. He came to America in 1845, and to California in 1851. He made the trip to California via Cape Horn, and after a voyage of nine months landed in San Francisco on February 1, 1851. He then went to the mines, remaining there one year. Mr. Hoffman was married to Elisa A. Myers, a native of Prussia, in 1858, and their children were Hermann, who died in 1804; Ferdinand, who died in 1892; and Clara, who married George E. Netherton, the subject of this sketch, and his death occurred on January 31, 1916. To Mr. and Mrs. Netherton were born two children—Hertha and Clarence P. Mr. Netherton for some years operated a dairy. After his death his wife disposed of the stock and rented the ranch.

JOHN B. ROOT (deceased) was one of the highly respected agriculturists of Contra Costa County, and was among the representative men in his locality. His birth occurred on September 28, 1859, and he died on December 10, 1910. He was a son of John Foster Root, whose birth was on February 29, 1836. The father followed mining for some time, and settled in Monterey County, where he took up farming in 1866. His parents crossed the plains to California with ox-teams, taking six months to make the journey. John Foster Root is now residing in Lafayette, where he has made his home for some years. John B. Root, the subject of this review, was united in marriage to Evelyn Esther Hain, a native of Michigan, and to this union have been born five children—Edna E., Effie Maud, Robert Raymond, Helen Uldene, and Mildred Mabel. Edna E. Root married Lloyd L. Brown, now deceased, and to this union have been born two children—Kenneth, born February IS, 1907, and Warren, born January 12, 1914. Erne Maud Root married George F. Stahle, residing in San Francisco, and their one daughter is Muriel Evelyn. Robert Raymond Root married Hazel Irene Ward, of Oakland, and they reside in Happy Valley on the home place; their one daughter is Dorothy Ward Root. Helen Illdene and Mildred Mabel Root reside with their mother and sister, Mrs. Edna E. Brown, in Berkeley. The subject of this sketch was one of the most capable and progressive ranchers in the county and his death was mourned by a wide circle of friends.

EDWARD WILLIAM O'BRIEN, D. D. S.—Numbered among the representative professional men of the Bay counties is Edward William O'Brien, D. D. S., of Richmond, California. He was born in San Francisco on October 12, 1877, son of James W. and Sarah T. (Woodward) O'Brien, now residing in Nevada. In the parents' family there were six children—Edward W., the subject of this review; Josephine, who resides in Portland, Oregon; Albert M., a surveyor; Alice W., Edwina J., and Harold. Doctor O'Brien's father has been a resident of Nevada for many years, always taking an interest along educational lines. He served on the school board at Wadsworth for twenty years, also as a member of the school board at Sparks, Nevada. Edward W. O'Brien acquired his education in the public schools of Nevada. He attended the university of that State for a period of three years and took a special course in chemistry. He graduated from the dental department of the University of California with the class of 1901, and he at once commenced to practice his profession in Nevada, where he remained six years.

In 1908 Doctor O'Brien removed to Richmond, where he is now located, and occupies spacious offices in the Abbott Building. He was married in August, 1909, to Alice E. Henderson, of Eureka, Nevada, a daughter of George S. Henderson, one of the respected pioneers of that State. Fraternally, Doctor O'Brien holds membership in and is a charter member of the B. P. O. E. lodge of Richmond and served as one of the first trustees of that order.

www.ingramcontent.com/pod-product-compliance
Lightning Source LLC
Chambersburg PA
CBHW050059170426
43198CB00014B/2391